PRACTICAL PROBLEM SOLVER

READER'S DIGEST

PRACTICAL PROBLEM SOLVER

*SUBSTITUTES, SHORTCUTS,
AND INGENIOUS SOLUTIONS
FOR MAKING LIFE EASIER*

The Reader's Digest Association, Inc.
Pleasantville, New York / Montreal

STAFF

Project Editors
Jim Dwyer
Sally French

Art Editors
Evelyn Bauer
Perri DeFino

Senior Editor
Suzanne E. Weiss

Senior Research Editor
Laurel Gilbride

Associate Editors
Fred DuBose
Diana Marsh
Thomas A. Ranieri

Art Associate
Susan Desser

Assistant Editor
Jennifer Moses

Editorial Assistant
Jean Ryan

Editorial Intern
Melanie Williams

CONTRIBUTORS

Editors
Lee Fowler
Mary Lyn Maiscott

Art Production Associate
Bruce R. McKillip

Writers
Marty Anderson
Ann Arnott
Pauline M. J. Bradshaw
Therese Hoehlein Cerbie
Rita G. Christopher
Thomas Christopher
Sarah Clayton
Donna Dannen
Kent Dannen
Gene Hamilton
Katie Hamilton
Signe Hammer
Lorna B. Harris
Sherwood Harris
Merle Henkenius
Penny Hinkle
John H. Ingersoll
Peter H. Johnson
Frank B. Latham
George deLucenay Leon
Margaret Moore
Boyd Norton
Cinda Siler
Elizabeth Tener
Joseph Truini
Frank X. Wamsley
Jeff Yablonka

Illustrators
Stephen Gardner
John Gist
Linda Gist
Ed Lipinski
Marianne E. Markey
Ray Skibinski
Mario Stasolla
Victoria Vebell
Mary Wilshire

Copy Editor
Virginia Croft

Researchers
Sandra Streepey Burgheim
Mary Hart

Art Assistant
Eleanor Kostyk

Editorial Assistant
Marjorie V. Thomas

Recipe Testing and Development
Therese Hoehlein Cerbie
Ben T. Etheridge
Sandra Gluck
Ann L. Rafferty

Indexer
Sydney Wolfe Cohen

READER'S DIGEST GENERAL BOOKS

Editor in Chief
John A. Pope, Jr.

Managing Editor
Jane Polley

Executive Editor
Susan J. Wernert

Art Director
David Trooper

Group Editors
Will Bradbury
Norman B. Mack
Kaari Ward

Group Art Editors
Evelyn Bauer
Joel Musler

Chief of Research
Monica Borrowman

Copy Chief
Edward W. Atkinson

Picture Editor
Robert J. Woodward

Rights and Permissions
Pat Colomban

Head Librarian
Jo Manning

The acknowledgments that appear on page 448 are hereby made a part of this copyright page.

Copyright © 1991 The Reader's Digest Association, Inc.

Copyright © 1991 The Reader's Digest Association (Canada) Ltd.

Copyright © 1991 Reader's Digest Association Far East Ltd.

Philippine Copyright 1991 Reader's Digest Association Far East Ltd.

Library of Congress Cataloging in Publication Data

Reader's Digest practical problem solver.
     p. cm.
     ISBN 0-89577-346-5
     1. Home economics — Miscellanea. I. Reader's Digest.
II Title: Practical problem solver.
TX158.R38 1991
640 — dc20   89-27729
                                 CIP

CONTENTS

ABOUT THIS BOOK

Here is a remarkable reference tool to help you conquer the everyday difficulties that confront us all. This craftily structured book approaches those commonplace (and some not so commonplace) problems in five ingenious ways.

Problem Solver's Dictionary offers effective and imaginative solutions to more than 1,000 knotty problems, from dripping faucets (page 67) to telephone sales calls (page 206), from locating lost friends (page 129) to coping with cracking walls (page 58).

Look up your problem as you would look up a word in a dictionary. If you don't find it right away, turn to the comprehensive index at the back of the book; the answer may be given under another subject heading. In addition, the numerous cross-references scattered throughout the book will help you find related information.

> ❯ This red arrow is an emergency symbol. When you see it next to a particular heading, you'll know that you're dealing with a problem that could be a life-or-death situation.

Charts & Checklists presents solid information in concise packages, touching on everything from getting organized to getting married to getting your money's worth. This diverse collection of lists, charts, and quizzes provides essential advice (*Protecting your home,* page 270), money-saving tips (*Paying for your house,* page 274), illuminating self-evaluations (*Are you in love?* page 262), and more.

Common Things With Uncommon Uses reveals how familiar household items can be used in creative ways to solve hundreds of commonplace problems. Arranged from A to Z, the list includes aluminum foil, berry baskets, carpet scraps, fabric softener, garden hoses, jar lids, mirrors, neckties, oven mitts, pipe cleaners, quilts, rubber bands, socks, tennis balls, umbrellas, wastebaskets, and zucchini.

Recycling & Renewing tells you how to prevent waste and save money by converting potential discards into attractive furnishings. In addition, illustrated step-by-step instructions show you how to use such special techniques as marbleizing and stenciling to give your furnishings a refreshing face-lift.

Formulas & Recipes gives you the secrets for making your own health and grooming aids, household cleaners, and culinary delights—while saving money in the process. Here you'll learn how to make cough drops, after-shave lotion, graham crackers, lip balm, porcelain cleaner, puddings, soups, and a whole lot more. And you'll also

find a great selection of delectable gifts you can easily make yourself, including chutney, mustard, and fruit liqueurs. Each of the 230 easy-to-make formulas and recipes has been tested and retested; they're all-natural and as good as or superior to store-bought items.

Even if you don't have a problem at the moment, you know that sooner or later you will. That's when you'll turn to PRACTICAL PROBLEM SOLVER. In the meantime, have some fun browsing through these fascinating pages. You're almost certain to find at least one item to attract your attention on every page. On page 110, for example, you'll discover how to make horseradish, prepare for a hospital stay, find inexpensive hotel accommodations, make a substitute hot-water bottle, and deal with house guests. On page 333, you'll learn how to turn a wading pool into a cooler, wallpaper into a jigsaw puzzle, a washer into a fishing sinker, wax paper into a buffer, weatherstripping into cleats, and a window screen into a sieve.

Clever substitutes, unexpected shortcuts, and original solutions to everyday problems—you'll find them all in these pages. PRACTICAL PROBLEM SOLVER is packed with helpful, easy-to-understand information. It's a book to turn to again and again for helpful ideas, trustworthy advice, and enjoyable reading.

1. PROBLEM SOLVER'S DICTIONARY

YOU MAY NOT FIND A CURE FOR ALL THE WORLD'S WOES IN THESE PAGES, BUT YOU'LL FIND PLENTY OF INVENTIVE AND COMMONSENSICAL WAYS TO DEAL WITH THE SORTS OF PROBLEMS THAT BEDEVIL DAY-TO-DAY LIFE. SOME EXAMPLES: WHAT TO USE WHEN YOU DON'T HAVE THE RIGHT TOOL, HOW TO COPE WITH EMERGENCIES, INGENIOUS SHORTCUTS TO MAKE YOUR CHORES LESS TEDIOUS.

Abdominal flab

1. Proper posture can do wonders for the way your stomach looks. Stand up straight, put your shoulders back, and tuck in your abdomen and buttocks.

2. Breathe correctly: deeply, from the diaphragm.

3. Pull in your abdominal muscles and hold for several seconds. Make the exercise part of your routine; do it while you're brushing your teeth or sitting at your desk, or whenever you're stuck in traffic or waiting for a bus or train.

4. If you don't have a bicycle, try this bicycle exercise. Lie on your back, arms stretched out for support and both knees drawn up to your chest. Extend one leg straight out; as you draw it back, extend the other. Repeat 10 to 20 times.

5. Do a set of bent-leg curl-ups. Lie on your back, as shown below, and slowly curl your head and shoulders upward, sliding your hands up your thighs toward your knees. When you've gone as far as is comfortable, inhale, then slowly curl down to a resting position, keeping your head raised. Exhale. Repeat 10 times.

6. While doing any exercise, contract your abdominal muscles to keep yourself in alignment. During an abdomen-toning supine exercise, keep the small of your back on the floor; otherwise your hip flexors will take on the abdomen's work.

7. For a bit more fun while exercising, take belly dancing lessons.

Bent-leg curl-up: This exercise fights flab by strengthening the abdomen and back.

Abrasive paper

1. Fresh out of sandpaper? Look under your kitchen sink for abrasive nylon pads, with or without sponge backing. Or try steel wool; back it with a piece of canvas or a sponge to protect your hands.

2. A pumice stone—the kind used to smooth calluses from hands and feet—is good for smoothing wood and plastics.

3. An emery board is handy for tight, hard-to-reach areas. And because it's flexible, it's great for contours and curved surfaces.

4. Save old sanding belts and discs; cut them up for hand sanding.

5. For rough sanding, use a brick or a piece of concrete block—both are surprisingly effective. The weight helps provide the necessary pressure. Try them on wood, plastic, and masonry surfaces. (You'll end up with many scratches that will need additional smoothing.)

6. Smooth large areas, such as a tabletop, by first spreading out a good amount of fine sand or ground pumice. Then wrap a sanding block in canvas or other tough cloth and rub with it in the direction of the wood grain; tap it clean frequently.

Adult children at home

1. Set a clear time limit on how long an adult son or daughter may live at home.

2. To reduce the intergenerational friction, write out a contract outlining the rules for sharing facilities, food, expenses, and chores. All wage earners living at home should pay their own way as well as share the household duties.

3. Adult children should get and pay for their own telephone lines.

4. Coordinate social plans by setting up a family calendar or bulletin board. (A parents' night at the symphony might be a good time for an adult son or daughter to have a dinner party at home, for example.)

5. To accommodate excess books, baggage, furniture, and off-season clothing, rent a self-service storage unit. These range from closet to garage size and are usually accessible 24 hours a day.

Aggressive pets

1. Does your bird peck at you when you're filling its water dish? Use a baster or a long-stemmed watering can. And keep your fingers out of the cage!

2. If your cat tries to attack your bird, suspend the cage from the ceiling or place it on a pedestal.

Spray an aggressive cat with a plant mister. Or smack the floor next to the animal with a rolled-up newspaper. Follow up with positive reinforcement.

3. Dogfight? Don't yell; make a loud noise—honk your car horn, ring a bell, or beat on a frying pan. If this fails, douse the combatants with a hose or with buckets of water.

An aggressive dog is always potentially dangerous. But if your dog misbehaves in a nonthreatening manner around a new baby, the mailman, or anyone else, you may be able to modify its behavior with positive reinforcement. Try showering it with attention and treats when the disliked person is present. The dog may gradually begin to enjoy the person's presence.

Airline delays

1. Avoid delays by checking up on the airline and on the flight you're considering. Newspapers often publish the track records of various airlines, and you can call the airline itself to find out the on-time record of a specific flight.

2. Carry a portable phone so that you can notify people who are waiting for you that you'll be late.

3. Find out why your flight is being delayed. If it's something that affects only your flight, such as a mechanical problem, you can ask the airline to reschedule you on another flight or airline.

4. Be assertive and persistent. If you don't get satisfaction from a ticket agent, ask for a supervisor.

Airline tickets

If possible, pay for your ticket with a credit card. That way the ticket number will be on the receipt and flight insurance will probably be included in the price.

Read your ticket immediately to see if there are restrictions and to make certain that all information is correct. Policies on exchanges and refunds vary among airlines.

Make a photocopy of your ticket or write down the number. Keep this record in a safe place; it will help you get reimbursed if the ticket is lost or stolen.

In that eventuality, file a lost-ticket application immediately. On most domestic flights, you will be asked to buy the replacement at the full fare even if you held a discounted ticket; you may, however, plead your case with the airline's supervisor. Many international flights will issue replacement tickets, provided you agree to reimburse the airline if the lost ticket is recovered or used.

Airsickness

1. If you're subject to this problem, reserve a seat over a wing. Fly well rested and wear loose clothes. Eat light, easily digestible food before and during the flight; avoid alcohol and cigarette smoke. As soon as you're seated, direct the air from the vent above you toward your face.

2. If your child is susceptible to airsickness, bring his favorite games, toys, and puzzles for distraction.

3. Instead of motion sickness medications, try powdered-ginger capsules (available at drug or health food stores); take two 15 minutes before you leave and another anytime during your trip.

4. As soon as you begin to feel dizzy or nauseated, recline your seat and close your eyes or stare at a fixed point. Breathe deeply through your mouth. Alternately tense and relax your body.

Air travel

1. You can fly at greatly reduced rates by delivering a package for an air courier. Some companies advertise for freelance couriers in newspapers or magazines. You can also check the Yellow Pages under "Air courier," although some listed companies don't use freelancers.

2. If you're a senior citizen, use an airline that offers reduced rates.

3. Even if you don't fly regularly, consider joining a frequent flyer program. Many have no time restrictions. And don't forget that children also qualify.

4. Avoid traveling by air if you have a cold, flu, or sinus blockage (see *Ear popping*, p.69).

Alarm clock

1. An electronic timer can serve as a backup alarm clock for home or travel. You can get one that times up to 10 hours and, with three separate channels, can even work as a "snooze alarm."

2. Ask a friend or relative to give you a morning wake-up call—and offer to return the favor.

3. Check with your local telephone company; for a price, many of them will provide a wake-up service for their customers.

4. Set an automatic timer to turn on all the lights, the radio, and the TV in your bedroom for the time you want to get up.

5. You're in luck if you live in an area where you can have breakfast delivered. On the night before you have to get up at a special time, call for a wake-up order of juice, coffee, and muffins.

Alcohol

If your alcoholic drink is too strong and there's no room in the glass for any more mixer, you can float a thin slice of cucumber on the surface; it will absorb much of the harsh taste. Floating long slivers of cucumber in a punch bowl will mellow punch in the same way. (See also *Tips on Tippling*, p.261.)

Allen wrench

Lacking an Allen wrench, you can still tighten or remove an Allen-head screw; just try different sizes of plain screwdrivers until you find one that fits the opening.

Or, if the Allen screw protrudes above the work surface, use a hacksaw to cut a slot in the top; then use a standard screwdriver to tighten or remove it. Or grip the head of the screw with a pair of locking-grip pliers to loosen.

❯ Allergies

Honeybee venom is a potent allergen to some people.

Many people have physical reactions to such allergens as pollen, dust, foods, feathers, insect venom, animal dander, and medications.

HAY FEVER

This is the most common allergy. Its familiar symptoms: sneezing and a stuffy, runny nose. It's usually a fairly mild reaction to pollen and can be treated with over-the-counter or prescription antihistamines.

Removal of the irritant is the best cure. If that isn't possible—in pollen season, for example—stay indoors with the windows closed and run the air conditioner, without cooling if necessary.

ANAPHYLACTIC SHOCK

This is the most severe form of allergic reaction. It can develop in minutes or even seconds after contact with an allergen, or it may appear half an hour or more later or even progress suddenly from an apparently mild allergic reaction.

The face, chest, and back become flushed, itchy, and burning; hives may appear. The face, tongue, and lips may swell and the lips turn bluish. Breathing is labored and wheezing. The pulse becomes weak. Pale skin, dizziness, nausea, and headache may follow. Finally, the person may faint and lapse into a coma.

The victim needs an immediate injection of epinephrine. There is no substitute. If he has a treatment kit with a syringe of epinephrine, help administer a dose; follow the instructions on the kit, injecting into a muscle or under the skin—not into a vein. Take him to an emergency room or call an emergency medical service. (See also *Asthma*, p.13.)

Altitude adjustment

Planning a vacation in the mountains? To avoid altitude problems, take it easy during your first day. Don't work out or do aerobic exercise. Drink plenty of water but no alcohol. If you begin to feel sick (headache, dizziness, or nausea), go to bed and rest.

Serious mountain climbers need to take further precautions to help prevent acute mountain sickness (AMS). If you have a heart or lung condition, consult your doctor before you go. Even if you're in good health, ask about prescription drugs (most contain acetazolamide) that prevent the symptoms of AMS.

If your destination is higher than 8,000 feet, spend the first day at an intermediate level. Then proceed upward at a daily rate of 500 to 1,000 feet, resting often and drinking at least 2 quarts of water a day. If you're already used to living at a high elevation, you can probably ascend or descend as much as 5,000 feet with few problems.

Breathing pure oxygen will ease discomfort, as will descending to a lower level to rest. If you develop a headache or a nosebleed or feel dizzy or nauseated, immediately descend 2,000 to 3,000 feet; get medical attention promptly.

Anchor

Going canoeing or rowing? Take along an old basketball net, a net shopping bag, or even a sturdy burlap bag. When you arrive at your anchorage, fill it with rocks and close the ends with cord, wire, or a mountain climber's snap-link carabiner. (For salt water, use a brass snap shackle.) Attach a rope, lower the net to the bottom, and you have a handy, disposable anchor.

❯ Antiseptics

1. Soap and warm water are your first line of defense against germs; wash minor scrapes, burns, cuts, and blisters thoroughly.
2. An alternative to a store-bought antiseptic: the juice from the pulpy center of a fresh aloe leaf applied directly to the skin.
3. Crushed raw, fresh garlic, or the freshly extracted juice of garlic, can be applied to gauze (not directly to the skin); garlic contains allicin, a powerful germ killer.
4. Hydrogen peroxide is inexpensive and can be used full strength. (Rubbing alcohol may irritate the skin and is too strong to be used on open wounds.)
5. Nonprescription topical antibiotic ointments are good for cuts and have the added advantage of preventing the dressing from sticking to the wound. Use them with caution, however; antibiotics can produce an allergic rash and may sensitize you to oral antibiotics as well. They may also cause antibiotic-resistant bacteria. (If the wound isn't healing after a couple of days, see a doctor.)

Ants

Ants enter houses in search of food, warmth, and shelter. When they find food, they establish a trail that leads back to their nest outside. Follow the trail to the point of entry into the house and seal it off, if possible, with caulk.

Destroy and wipe up every ant you find. Locate nests and destroy them by pouring several gallons of boiling water into the entrances. Then stir up the soil and repeat the process. Or, using a small hand duster, blow some boric acid powder (available as roach powder) into

nest entrances and into any cracks, crevices, and wall voids where ants are seen.

Some organic ant repellents may also be effective; scatter talcum powder, cream of tartar, borax, powdered sulfur, or oil of cloves at entry points, or plant mint around the house foundations. (See also *Carpenter ants*, p.38.)

Apartment & house plants

The key to success in indoor gardening is finding the appropriate plants for the available light. Consult a reliable houseplant guide or the people from whom you buy your plants to find out a particular plant's needs.

Professionals use a light meter to match the plant to the location; you

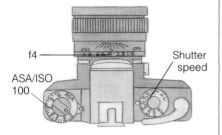

f4 — ASA/ISO 100 — Shutter speed

can substitute a 35mm camera with a built-in light meter and adjustable f-stops and shutter speeds.

Set the camera's ASA/ISO dial to 100 and the aperture ring to f4. Focus on a white mat card at least 1 foot square, in the spot where you plan to keep the plant. Move closer, taking care not to block the light, until the card fills the viewfinder. Then adjust the shutter speed until

the correct exposure is indicated. The reading on the shutter equals the intensity of the light: strong light, 125 to 500; medium light, 60 to 125; low light, 30 to 60.

Aphids

1. Wash aphids off houseplants under a gentle flow of tap water. Spray a large infestation with a solution of mild detergent in water. Or dab the leaves with a cotton ball dipped in rubbing alcohol. (Don't use alcohol on such delicate plants as African violets, however.)
2. Outdoors, use an aluminum foil mulch; the reflection confuses the insects and drives them away.
3. Interplant vegetables with aphid-repellent plants, such as onions, garlic, and chives.

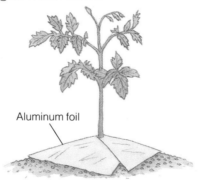

Aluminum foil

Appetite control

1. Avoid crash or fad diets. A sensible goal for a diet is a weight loss of 1 to 2 pounds a week.
2. Eat foods low in fat and high in complex carbohydrates (fruits, vegetables, grains, and legumes). Animal fat readily turns to human fat.
3. Don't skip a meal; eat five or six small meals a day instead of three big ones—you won't feel as hungry, and your body will use more energy in digestion.
4. Eat slowly, savoring each bite. It takes about 20 minutes for the feeling of fullness to register; wait that long before eating more.
5. When you feel hungry between meals, have a sugarless cup of tea; caffeine inhibits the appetite.
6. Exercise regularly; not only does it burn up calories, but it can also make you feel temporarily less hungry.
7. After about 3 weeks of dieting, you may stop losing weight altogether until your body accepts its new norm. The trick is to get past this 3-week mark without gaining back what you've lost. When you finally reach your ideal weight, maintain it for at least 3 weeks to establish a new norm.

LOOK BEFORE YOU LEAP

Common diet myths

☐ The only way to lose weight is to eat less. Not necessarily. A dieter may lose weight in the short term but may regain much of it. Exercisers, however, tend to keep it off—as long as they keep at it.

☐ A calorie is a calorie is a calorie. Not so. All calories are not created equal. About 25 percent of the calories from starches such as pasta, whole-grain bread, or potatoes are burned up for energy. Not so with fat. If you switch from a high-fat diet to a diet rich in complex carbohydrates, you should lose weight in time.

☐ Margarine is less fattening than butter. False. Margarine and butter both have about 35 calories per pat. The difference is that butter contains saturated fat, which is high in cholesterol, whereas soft margarines (especially the kinds made from such polyunsaturated vegetable oils as corn and soybean) may actually help lower the blood cholesterol level.

☐ Starches are fattening. Also false. The only thing that makes starches fattening is the butter, sour cream, and rich sauces that people like to put on them.

Appetite loss

IN CHILDREN

If a toddler seems to have lost his appetite, he may just be growing more slowly than before. Don't force him to eat. Give him as much as he wants at meals; cut down on snacks so that he'll be hungry at mealtime.

IN TEENAGERS AND ADULTS

1. Check that you're getting the recommended dietary allowances of the B vitamins and zinc, which stimulate the appetite.
2. Eliminate all caffeine (in coffee, tea, chocolate, colas), an appetite suppressant.
3. Try eating faster; you may be able to beat the brain signal that, 20 minutes after you start eating, says you're full.
4. See a physician; loss of appetite may be caused by illness.
5. A prolonged appetite loss in an adolescent girl could be anorexia nervosa, a serious disorder that requires the care of a specialist.

IN OLDER PEOPLE

1. At about age 65, many people lose some sense of taste and smell, and the appetite suffers. Try stimulating it with a variety of strongly flavored or spicy foods, such as curry or chili; older people often find such foods more palatable than youngsters do.
2. Vary the texture, color, and temperature of your food; this may compensate for the lack of strong flavor.
3. Savor each bite. Chewing slowly and moving the food around in the mouth before swallowing increases contact with the taste buds and, via the back of the mouth, with odor receptors in the nose.

› Appliance fires

1. If flames are shooting out of an appliance, or if you see smoke or smell burning odors coming from one, immediately pull out the plug or shut off the main power (p. 162). If the appliance continues to burn, zap it with an ABC fire extinguisher (p.81). Do *not* use water. If it's still burning after 2 minutes, call the fire department at once and get out of the house.
2. If smoke comes from your oven, check to see if you left any food inside. If not, try cleaning the oven. (A continuous-cleaning oven normally smokes a little.)
3. If broiling creates smoke, food may be too close to the heat. Or fat may not be draining properly; if you use foil or a disposable broiler pan, cut slashes in it to allow fat to drip into the pan below.
4. If smoke comes out of the microwave, interrupt the cycle, eliminate the problem, and restart the cycle.

To be on the safe side, never leave an appliance operating when you are away from home.

Appointments

There is no such thing as being fashionably late for an appointment. If you are habitually late, you are guilty of wasting others' time and will certainly lose respect. Here are some habits that will help you become a more punctual person:

1. Give yourself extra time—just in case you're delayed by weather, traffic, or other circumstances.
2. Keep only one date book; carry it between home and workplace.
3. Use a watch, a calculator, or an electronic "secretary" with a beeper to remind you when to leave.
4. If possible, take scheduled transportation, such as a train, so that you'll have to depart at a set time.

LATENESS IN OTHERS

1. Ask a chronically late person to call you just before he leaves.
2. Avoid meeting him for scheduled events, such as movies. If you must do so, plan to meet early, perhaps for a meal.
3. If your doctor or dentist is known to overbook patients, call first to see if she's running late.

Aspirin

1. Acetaminophen, the active ingredient in most aspirin substitutes, doesn't irritate the stomach, and so it's safe for people with ulcers. Asthmatics should also take it.

Although acetaminophen reduces fever and pain, it does not reduce inflammation. What's more, it can't help prevent heart attacks as an aspirin every other day may.
2. Aspirin substitutes with ibupro-

IN TIMES GONE BY

The history of the first wonder drug

Before there was aspirin, there was willow bark. About 400 B.C., Hippocrates, the "father of medicine," advised chewing it to ease the pain of childbirth. For centuries people all over the world knew of, but did not understand, its power to treat headache, fever, and inflammation.

Enter chemistry. In Germany in the 1820's, the magic chemical was isolated and named salicin. Later in the century, acetylsalicylic acid was developed, but no one knew what to do with it. Meanwhile, people still took a crude form of the drug that, they said, burned in their stomachs like fire ants.

Then a young chemist at Bayer and Company tried acetylsalicylic acid on his arthritic father. Aspirin was born.

Why it was named aspirin is a subject of debate. One theory holds that the word was derived from *Spiraea*, the plant from which salicin was actually isolated. Aspirin tablets first appeared in stores at the turn of the century. Except for coatings and buffers, they have hardly changed since.

fen can reduce inflammation and may be somewhat effective against heart attacks, but they also may irritate the stomach (although somewhat less than aspirin). To reduce inflammation, ulcer sufferers should take aspirin that is specially coated to dissolve in the small intestine rather than in the stomach. **Caution:** Children and teenagers should not take aspirin when they have a virus because of the danger of Reye's syndrome, a rare but often fatal disease linked to viral infections and aspirin. Acetaminophen and ibuprofen are safe alternatives.

›Asthma

1. If someone is having an asthma attack, he will cough, wheeze, and have difficulty breathing; reassure him and try to keep him calm.
2. To ease breathing, have him sit up and lean slightly forward, resting on his elbows. Or turn on the hot water in the bathroom and have him sit and breathe the moist air.
3. Give him his prescribed medication along with liquids to prevent dehydration.
4. If the medication doesn't bring immediate relief, take him—quickly but calmly—to the nearest hospital emergency room.

EXERCISE AS TREATMENT

Although exercise is usually recommended for asthmatics, if it is too strenuous it can trigger an attack—especially outdoors during cold weather or allergy season.

Indoor swimming is best for most asthmatics. Aerobic exercise is also good; a physically fit person gets more oxygen into his body—important during an asthma attack.

An asthmatic should begin his exercises with a slow 15-minute warm-up and finish with an equally slow cool-down. (See *Warm-up & cool-down exercises,* p.224.)

To help keep his airways open, he should exercise in 1- to 2-minute spurts, breathing through his nose to filter the air somewhat.

Atomizer

1. If your atomizer gets clogged, unscrew it from the bottle, raise it, and let the perfume drain out of the stem. Immerse the atomizer in water. Pump a few times, take it out of the water, and pump until no more water sprays out.
2. Any small spray bottle, available in dime stores, can be a short-term substitute for a perfume atomizer. But don't leave perfume in a plastic container; the plastic will interact with its ingredients.

Attics

1. Think hard—what's stored in your attic? If you can't remember, it's time to take inventory. Make a list and post it near the entrance. From then on, whenever you store or remove items from the attic, note the changes.
2. If your attic is unfinished, create a floor by nailing down two or more plywood panels. To support walking and storage safely, the panels should be at least ⅝ inch thick (¾ inch is better) and span at least three ceiling joists.
3. No electrical wiring in the attic? Battery-powered lights, found in most hardware stores, provide an easy means of illumination.
4. Short on closet space? Install a wooden rod or a metal conduit between rafters, for hanging out-of-season clothing. Drill through the rod and secure it with lag bolts. Or use pipe straps or pipe clamps to hold it against the rafters.

Attic ventilation

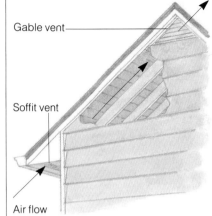

Gable vent

Soffit vent

Air flow

An unventilated attic can cause serious moisture problems in the walls and ceilings of the entire house. To increase airflow, use an electric fan at least 20 inches across. Set it at the entrance so that it draws air up from the house. If the opening is a ceiling cutout, lay the fan across it.

LONG-TERM IMPROVEMENTS

You can buy soffit vents, or you can make your own from screening. With a saber saw, cut a round hole in the soffit between rafter and joist. Cut a piece of window screen about ½ inch larger on all sides than the opening and staple it over the hole. For a neat appearance, frame it with wood.

A cupola on the roof ridge should be more than an attractive detail; it can help exhaust hot, stale air. Cut an opening in the ridge (but not the ridge board) beneath it. To further improve airflow, install an electric ventilating unit in the cupola.

Keep all vents clean and free of debris. Gable vents are a favorite place for birds and wasps to build nests; staple a piece of window screen over the exterior of these vents to keep them clear.

Avocados

1. You can keep a bowl of mashed avocado or guacamole from darkening by burying the pit in it until time to serve. Or press a piece of plastic wrap flat on the surface and smooth out any air bubbles.

2. To keep sliced or cubed avocado from discoloring, sprinkle with lemon or lime juice. Coat larger pieces with softened butter, margarine, or mayonnaise before refrigerating; they should keep for 3 to 4 days.

3. Avocados ripen almost twice as fast if sealed in a brown paper bag and stored in a warm (not hot) place. For even faster results, put an apple in the bag, too. Even a cut avocado will ripen this way, but first coat its cut surfaces as described above.

Awnings

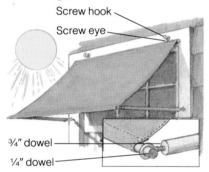

Screw hook
Screw eye
¾″ dowel
¼″ dowel

Instead of an old-fashioned, pulley-operated awning, install a single piece of canvas attached to a wood pole at top and bottom. Secure the top above your window with hooks and attach the lower pole to the wall, as shown. Or you can create a natural awning by constructing a trellis above your window and growing a flowering vine or ivy on it.

Babies' names

The name you choose for your child must last a lifetime, so it had better be pleasing—to him and to you.

1. Make sure that the initials don't spell something strange. (Ulysses S. Grant changed his name from Hiram Ulysses at West Point because he was tired of being called HUG.)

2. Think of the possible nicknames.

3. Imagine calling the name at the top of your voice to summon the child home.

4. If you'd like a namesake but you don't want to be known as Big Mary or Big Bill, give the child a variation of your name, perhaps a foreign version.

5. Choose a name that can grow with the child and continue to give pleasure at every stage of the name-bearer's life.

6. Vary the number of syllables to create a pleasant rhythm.

7. If you select a poetic or unusual name, give the child a choice: a commonplace middle name.

Baby fitness

As infants develop basic coordination and reflexes in their first few months, parents can provide soothing and stimulating activities to help them. Try not to push your baby; her own movements will let you know what's good for her.

Even in your baby's first days, her eye-head and eye-hand coordination can be helped by brightly colored mobiles and toys to look at, as well as friendly people to interact with. After the first month, you can foster body awareness and confidence simply by holding your baby in different positions. Carefully support your child in the bath so that she will enjoy the water and start to become aware of the feeling of her muscles.

You can massage your baby. Use no more pressure than your hand's weight with the palm open. Stroke smoothly outward in slightly circular motions; this relaxes tension, soothes cramps, and lets your baby develop a sense of her body.

To stretch and strengthen your baby's arms and legs, place her on her back; raise one arm smoothly above her head while bringing the other down by her side, then reverse. Always make sure your baby's head is well supported.

Keeping her legs straight, gently bend one knee toward her stomach, then straighten the leg again. Alternate legs—and let her participate as much as she wants to.

Backaches

PREVENTION

1. Avoid any sudden strain; exercise regularly to limber the back and strengthen its supporting abdominal muscles.

2. If you sit for long periods, make sure your back is properly supported. Place a small roll in the arch of your lower spine (at belt height) to maintain its normal S-curve. (Stuff the inside of a paper towel roll with rags and strengthen it with masking tape.)

3. When lifting, never bend down from the waist—lower and raise yourself at the knees. Keep your back straight and hold the object close to your body.

4. Balance items you carry evenly on both sides of your body and hold them close—or use a backpack.

5. Sleep on your back if possible, with knees raised on a pillow. If you sleep on your side, a pillow between the knees is a big help.

6. For a firm bed, place a bedboard between the mattress and the box spring. (Cut a sheet of ¾-inch plywood 1 inch smaller all around than your mattress and sand its edges.)

TREATMENT

1. Limit activity or stay in bed for 48 hours.

2. Depending on which works better for you, apply either heat or a cold pack for 15 minutes at a time every couple of hours over a period of 2 days. (Keep an athlete's soft cold pack in the freezer or use a bag of frozen peas; both will mold easily to your back.)

3. Aspirin or ibuprofen will help combat both pain and inflammation; acetaminophen, only pain.

4. To minimize chronic minor back pain, tip your pelvis back, then forward, until you find the position of least pain; maintain it.

Back exercises

Strengthening and stretching the muscles of your lower back will help prevent lower back strain. The following exercises progress from gentle to strenuous. Do only what's comfortable for you; stop exercising the moment you feel pain. If you've had back problems, consult your doctor before starting.

PELVIC TILT

Lie on your back with both of your knees bent. Keeping your spine against the floor, squeeze your buttock muscles as hard as you can, pull your stomach muscles in, flatten the small of your back to the floor, and hold for 5 seconds. Your pelvis will tilt slightly upward of its own accord; don't try to raise it. Repeat 10 times.

CAT STRETCH

Kneel on your hands and knees. Then arch your upper back upward, contract your stomach muscles, and let your head drop. Hold for 5 seconds. Follow this by raising your head and reversing the action, until you return to the kneeling position. Avoid pushing your pelvis forward to create a swayback. Repeat 5 to 10 times.

HIP ROLL

Lie on your back, both arms out for support. Raise your knees toward your chest and then roll them gently from side to side, keeping your shoulders on the floor if you can. Roll 10 to 20 times.

BACKWARD LEG RAISES

Lie flat on your stomach, resting your head on folded arms. Keeping your pelvis on the floor, slowly raise one leg from the hip until your foot is 6 inches above the floor. Repeat 5 to 10 times with each leg.

SINGLE LEG RAISES

Lie on your back, knees bent, arms crossed under your head, and both elbows touching the floor. Straighten one leg, then slowly raise it as high as you can. Hold it 5 seconds, then lower it slowly to the floor. Repeat 5 to 10 times with each leg.

DIAGONAL REACH

Start on your hands and knees. Slowly reach your right arm out in front of you; at the same time, reach your left leg straight out behind you. Stretch and hold for 5 seconds; then return to your original position. Then stretch your left arm and right leg. Repeat 10 times.

Cat stretch: Arch your upper back upward while contracting your stomach and letting your head drop. Hold for 5 seconds.

Then raise your head and reverse the action until you return to the kneeling position. Avoid pushing your pelvis forward.

Backpacks

To make a temporary backpack for carrying your lunch on a short hike, bringing home trailside treasures, or transporting other light objects, just close the waist of a long-sleeved sweatshirt or jacket with pins or string. Knot the sleeve ends together to form a strap. Stuff your cargo inside, slip the strap over your shoulders, and you're on your way.

IN TIMES GONE BY

Victorian backaches

Consider the Victorian corset. Made of heavy canvas, with vertical stays of whalebone or steel, it encased a woman in a rigid cage from hip to bust. Many little girls got their first one at age 3 or 4; by adolescence they were wearing adult versions, tightly laced up the back to achieve something close to Scarlett O'Hara's triumph of a 17-inch waist.

Ladies of the time were thought to be so delicate that their muscles couldn't hold them upright without assistance. The corset made this myth a reality. By the time girls were ready for adult corsets, their back and abdominal muscles had atrophied so badly that many couldn't sit or stand without one.

Backseat drivers

To deal with one of these pests:

1. Use humor ("Hey, do you want to *cause* an accident?") or distraction ("Please add up the miles to the turnoff").

2. Turn up the volume on the radio or tape deck, without saying it's to drown out unwanted advice.

3. Sing while you drive. You may even inspire your passenger to sing along with you.

4. Take the other passengers aside before setting out and ask them to keep up an active conversation.

Bad breath

1. Brush your teeth with a paste of baking soda and water to keep your breath fresh. Baking soda neutralizes the acids in which the bacteria that cause bad breath and tooth decay thrive. (A mouthwash of hydrogen peroxide and water is also antibacterial.)

2. Chew fresh parsley after eating. It contains an antiseptic that kills bacteria in the mouth. It's effective against garlic and onions too, as are mint leaves and cloves. (Suck, don't chew, the latter.)

3. Floss daily to dislodge decaying food particles. If your gums are red, swollen, and sore, see your dentist.

Bait & switch

You see a bargain price advertised for a specific product, and so you go into the store to purchase it. There you discover that the advertised item is out of stock, but the store just happens to have a slightly more expensive version.

That's called bait and switch, and it's illegal unless the ad specifies that only a limited supply is available. Look for such a disclaimer before rushing to the store to buy. If the ad doesn't include one and you encounter a bait-and-switch technique, call your local Better Business Bureau.

Bait and switch also rears its head in home improvements. You get an amazingly low estimate, only to find at the last minute that important and costly details have been left out. Never commit yourself until you have a written estimate from several contractors detailing the work to be done, listing the materials to be used and supplied by the contractor, and setting a limit on how much the cost may exceed the estimate.

Ask each contractor for the names of people in nearby areas for whom he has done similar work; then call and check out the references.

Baking ingredients

Margarine or vegetable shortening works as well as butter in most cakes and quick breads, although the finished product may look and taste somewhat different.

If you're out of cake flour, replace each cup called for with 1 cup minus 2 tablespoons of sifted all-purpose flour. For 1 cup of self-rising flour, substitute 1 cup all-purpose flour plus 1½ teaspoons baking powder and ½ teaspoon salt.

Here are some other substitutes:

For 1 ounce of baking chocolate: mix 3 tablespoons unsweetened cocoa powder with 1 tablespoon softened butter, margarine, or vegetable oil.

For 1 cup of whole milk: ½ cup evaporated milk plus ½ cup water.

For a whole egg: 2 yolks mixed with 1 tablespoon water.

For 1 teaspoon of double-acting baking powder: ¼ teaspoon baking soda and ½ teaspoon cream of tartar. Or use ¼ teaspoon baking soda plus ½ cup buttermilk or sour cream (omit ½ cup of another liquid from the recipe).

For 1 cup of granulated sugar: 1 cup honey or corn syrup (omit ¼ cup of the liquid that is called for in the recipe).

For ½ cup of brown sugar: ½ cup white sugar plus 2 tablespoons molasses. Keep in mind, however, that both this and the granulated sugar substitute will make your baked goods heavier. (See also *Buttermilk*, p.29.)

Ballpoint pen

Has your ballpoint pen clogged up? Get the ink flowing by holding a lighted match under the point. Keep rotating the pen so that the plastic doesn't melt.

Bamboo furniture

To clean dust from the crevices of bamboo furniture, use the brush attachment of a vacuum cleaner.

Sponge dirty bamboo with a solution of warm water and mild detergent or ammonia; rinse and wipe dry. Apply liquid wax occasionally.

To prevent drying out and splitting, take bamboo furniture outside once a year and wet it down with a fine spray from the garden hose. Or give it a quick shower in the bathroom. Let dry slowly, out of the sun. If any bindings come loose, rewrap them and tack in place.

❯Bandages

1. Improvise an adhesive bandage by moistening a cotton puff with antiseptic and holding it in place with adhesive tape, masking tape, or clear plastic tape.

2. If you need an emergency dressing for a serious wound, use the cleanest material available: a sanitary napkin, a clean handkerchief, a sock, a shirt, a T-shirt, a folded sheet or towel, or a washcloth. Fold the material to make a pad that covers the entire wound.

Hold the dressing in place with wide strips torn from a shirt or a sheet, or with a tie or folded scarf.
3. For a deep cut, make a butterfly strip from adhesive (not plastic) tape. Singe the folded part quickly with a match to sterilize it. (See also *Cuts & abrasions*, p.60.)

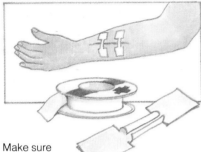

Make sure the edges of the cut align before applying the bandage.

Baseball jargon

Here's a guide to what the television announcers are saying:

Balk. An illegal movement by the pitcher (definitions vary from time to time); runners advance a base.

Bases loaded. When runners are on first, second, and third bases.

Beanball. A pitch intended to hit the batter.

Boot. To commit an error.

Breaking ball. Any pitch that changes direction in flight.

Brushback. A pitch thrown close enough to the batter to make him move back from home plate.

Bullpen. An area where relief pitchers warm up.

Bunt. A lightly tapped ball, generally meant to advance a base runner. If the batter himself reaches base, he has "beat out" the bunt.

Called strike. A pitch in the strike zone at which the batter doesn't swing.

Curveball. A sharply breaking ball.

Cutoff man. An infielder who relays a throw.

Fan. To strike the batter out; to be struck out.

Fielder's choice. When a batter reaches base only because a fielder chooses to put out another base runner; not counted as a hit.

Find the handle. To field and control a batted ball.

Forkball. A breaking pitch, thrown with the index and middle fingers spread wide apart, that curves sharply downward.

Grand slam. A home run hit with the bases loaded.

Hanging pitch. A pitch that should break but doesn't.

Hit-and-run. A play in which a base runner starts to run as the ball is pitched, causing an infielder to forsake his fielding position in order to prevent a stolen base, and the batter hits the ball into the spot from which the fielder moved.

Jam. To pitch a ball close to the hitter, but not so close as a brushback.

Load the ball. To put saliva, petroleum jelly, or another forbidden substance on a ball before pitching it.

Pick off. To put a runner out by catching him off base.

Screwball (scroogie). A pitch that appears to go straight but unexpectedly swerves right or left.

Slider. A fast breaking ball that curves less sharply than a curveball.

Slurve. A breaking ball that curves less sharply than a curveball and more than a slider.

Smoke. Very fast, hard pitching.

Squeeze. A play in which the batter bunts and the runner on third base tries to reach home plate. In a safety squeeze he waits to see that the bunt is good; in a suicide squeeze he runs no matter what.

Strike zone. The area over home plate that ranges roughly between a batter's knees and armpits, through which a pitch must pass in order to be called a strike.

Baseball mitt

To break in a stiff new mitt, rub the center with few drops of cooking oil or a dab of shaving cream. Place a ball in the glove and fold the sides of the mitt around it; secure with rubber bands. Tuck the mitt under a mattress and leave it there overnight. If you have a *genuine* leather glove, you can beat it up without hurting it; you might even try wrapping the mitt securely in an old towel and running over it once or twice with a car.

For pickup games, when there may not be enough gloves to go around, you can improvise. Secure a piece of corrugated cardboard over your palm with a piece of masking tape. Or take a thick oven mitt and stuff it, for extra padding, with paper towels. Heavy gardening gloves with paper towels stuffed into the palms will also protect hands from fast balls.

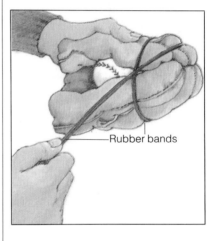

Rubber bands

Basketball jargon

Here's a guide to what the television announcers are saying:

Air ball. A shot that misses both basket and rim.

Backcourt. The half-court that is being defended; the defense's backcourt is the offense's forecourt.

Draw a foul. To provoke a foul.

Dribble. To bounce the ball on the floor; a player who stops dribbling and starts again has committed a double dribble.

Double-team. To guard an offensive player with two defenders.

Dunk. To put the ball into the basket with your hands above the rim.

Foul out. To commit more than the allotted number of fouls (six in the pros, five in college ball) and therefore have to leave the game.

Free throw. The reward for being fouled: an undefended shot at the basket, worth one point if made.

Full-court press. A defense in which the entire court is guarded.

Goaltending. Interfering with the ball as it arcs downward over the rim of the basket.

Hook. A shot delivered while lifting the arm over the head.

Lay-up. A shot delivered by jumping up and tossing the ball lightly off the backboard or over the rim.

Loose-ball foul. A personal foul committed while trying to gain control of the ball.

Pick. An offensive maneuver in which a player, by standing still, blocks a defender.

Point guard. A guard who directs his team's offense, usually from behind the offensive foul line.

Rebound. To gain possession of a ball after a missed shot.

Shot clock. The device used to time the 24 seconds during which a professional team with possession of the ball must attempt a shot.

Slam dunk. A dunk that is jammed hard into the basket.

Swish. A shot that goes into the basket without touching the rim.

Three-point play. The result when a player is fouled while making a basket and therefore gains the right to a free throw.

Trap. A defensive maneuver in which the ball handler is quickly double-teamed in order to steal the ball or force a passing error.

Traveling. Taking two or more steps without dribbling the ball.

Basting

1. Spare yourself the nuisance of picking out stitches; baste with water-soluble thread, which disappears under a steam iron.

2. For seams, use a glue stick; apply dabs at 1- to 2-inch intervals to join the seam allowances.

3. For trims, zippers, and pockets, lay dissolvable basting tape tacky side down along a seam; lift off the paper covering and position the other fabric on top. (Don't worry; both glue and tape wash out.)

Bathing on camping trips

Take along a waterproof vinyl bag for heating water by solar energy. Fill it in the morning, set it in the sun, and you'll have warm water for a sponge bath by evening. The plastic bladder from a boxed wine dispenser works well, and it comes complete with faucet.

Bathtub rings

To avoid bathtub rings, don't use oily bath preparations; use a water softener if you live in a hard-water area; rinse the tub immediately after bathing.

If a ring does form, wipe it off with undiluted ammonia (wear rubber gloves) or a wet sponge generously sprinkled with baking soda; rinse clean and wipe dry. For a more stubborn stain, scour with automatic dishwashing detergent or rub with a cloth dipped in vinegar.

Batteries

1. To avoid batteries that have been on the store shelf too long, buy from an outlet that has a high turnover—a toy store, for example. Pick from the center of the stack.

2. Shop for the best price; there are few real differences among brands.

3. Choose zinc carbon batteries for clocks, flashlights, and pocket calculators. Use heavy-duty zinc carbons for small radios and penlights; save alkaline batteries for high-draw items such as tape recorders, photo flashes, and toys.

4. Store batteries away from hot spots in the house or car and keep them out of the sun. Best of all, store them in the refrigerator, wrapped in a plastic bag to keep moisture out. Let them warm to room temperature before using.

5. Remove batteries from items that you seldom use. Bundle them together with a rubber band and store in a plastic sandwich bag. Don't allow them to touch metal objects during storage or they may lose power.

6. When using battery-operated equipment in freezing weather, keep the batteries warm in your pocket until you need them.

7. If you can avoid it, don't mix old batteries with new. New ones can put stress on old ones, causing them to leak acid.

Bears

PROTECTING YOURSELF

In bear country, wear bells to avoid surprising bruins. Don't approach a bear, but don't run away from one either. Movement may incite a charge, and a bear can outrun you.

If a bear approaches you, talk to it calmly in a low, firm voice. Slowly

To protect food from bears, hang it at least 10' from ground.

back away until the bear is out of sight. If you climb a tree, get at least 12 feet up.

If a bear senses that its food may be stolen or that its cub is in danger, it may charge. If this happens, drop to the ground and assume a fetal position, protecting your head with your arms, and play dead. Keep your pack on; it may serve as armor.

PROTECTING FOOD

Store food in the trunk of your car. If backpacking, hoist food out of a bear's reach, well away from your sleeping area. Use two lines; a bear may be able to release one.

Bedding plants

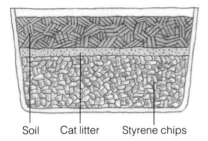

Soil   Cat litter   Styrene chips

Instead of consigning all bedding plants to a fixed place in the garden, make them portable so that they can do double duty or more. Let them brighten a party on your patio one night and adorn your front steps the next morning.

1. To save strain, choose containers that are strong but light, such as fiberglass pots or ones with wheels; even a large redwood tub is easy to move if it's set on casters. Or you can use an old wooden wheelbarrow; its big wheels make it both portable and decorative.

2. To lighten the load of a large container, fill it to within 10 inches of the top with styrene chips or a similar foam-based packing material; sprinkle this with a 2-inch layer of cat litter for drainage, and top with potting soil.

3. To save still more pounds, blend 3 parts of a soilless potting mixture with 1 part potting soil and 1 part peat moss.

Beds

Company coming and you don't have enough beds in the house? If the couch alone won't solve the problem, consider sleeping bags, air mattresses, or pads of thick foam rubber. All are easy to store when not in use.

A futon—a cotton-filled, pliable mattress—is another alternative, although more expensive. You may consider it worth the cost because it can be shaped into a low couch for extra seating when it is not being used as a bed.

To make a double bed, place two air mattresses or futons side by side and hold them together with a fitted double sheet. (Foam rubber is not rigid enough for this.)

For more comfort and to prevent sliding during the night, place temporary beds on a thick rug.

For infants, a playpen will do. Or take a drawer from a chest of drawers and pad it, checking to see that there are no splinters in the wood. A third choice is a plastic laundry basket, also padded.

Bedsores

1. An air mattress—or even a thick sheepskin pad over a standard mattress—relieves pressure and prevents bedsores on heels, buttocks, elbows, head, and shoulders. Pads or pillows at these points help too.

2. Change a bedridden person's position every 2 hours.

3. Moisturizer and 100 milligrams of vitamin C every day help sustain skin tone.

4. Three 3-ounce servings of protein a day help maintain muscle tissue and aid healing if bedsores begin to develop.

5. Bedsores are easier to prevent than to treat. If you notice any red spots on the skin, keep pressure off the area and call a physician.

Bedtime rituals

Most children love bedtime rituals. They ease the transition from play to sleep and provide a reassuring pattern. But what happens when the pattern must be broken?

1. If both parents will be absent, the person left in charge should

---

IN TIMES GONE BY

The evolution of the bed

For most of us, a bed is not only the place where our lives begin and end, but also the place where we spend about one-third of the time between those milestones.

Early beds were probably little more than pits lined with leaves, reeds, or other natural cushions. Later, to keep out crawling insects and animals, latticed thongs were attached to an elevated wooden frame and topped with skins. The Egyptians went much further; their beds were topped with a mat, linen sheets, and woven blankets. A footboard even prevented sleepers from sliding down their beds, which were tilted upward at the head. A separate hard headrest protected the coiffure.

It was not until about 3500 B.C., in the royal palaces at Sumer in Babylonia, that the bed got its own room. Such luxury, however, was reserved for the master of the house. He occupied the bedroom; his wife, children, servants, and guests slept elsewhere—on couches or the floor.

The Greeks were the first to use headboards, against which the wealthy laid embroidered silk pillows. The Romans, who were good farmers, invented the first true mattress: a sack stuffed with straw, wool, or feathers. Water beds, developed in the early 19th century for hospital patients with bone fractures or bedsores, made a big splash in the 1960's and are still popular, along with bunk beds, loft beds, and other variations.

know the routine. List bedtime activities on a big chart and instruct the child to help the adult check them off.

2. Before leaving, tape-record a special good night. A simple "We love you, sweet dreams, see you soon" in the parents' own voices can be very reassuring.

3. When special guests visit, find ways to include them in the ritual. A guest might pour the milk, turn down the covers, tell a little story.

4. If you're caught away from home without a beloved teddy bear, improvise a floppy animal from a pillow, or stuff knotted socks or a soft turtleneck shirt to make a substitute cuddle object.

Bedtime stories

Instead of reading from a storybook, try improvisation. One parent begins a story and after a few minutes turns the narrative over to the other, who, after a few more turns in the plot, lets the kids pick it up.

Most children's favorite themes are familiar people or animals, who may live in other worlds but are actually their family, friends, and pets and, *coincidentally,* even have their names.

A parent who's away from home can participate in the story hour by telephone or, prior to leaving, can tape-record several segments for the stay-at-homes to complete.

An alternative: Prepare a picture story about your trip or your dinner out. Make your own drawings or cut out illustrations from magazines and write a simple text to tell what Mommy or Daddy is doing.

Bedwetting

1. Don't scold or punish your child for a wet bed; it will only make him feel guilty. Be patient; praise him for his dry nights and encourage him to keep a record of them.

2. Restrict fluids before bedtime, but only within reason.

3. Awaken the child for a trip to the bathroom before you go to bed. Or

try setting an alarm clock to remind him to get up himself.

4. A shower curtain makes a good mattress cover.

5. If bedwetting persists past the age of 6, consult a pediatrician.

Beetles

1. Bark beetles may come into the house on firewood. Vacuum them up and destroy them. Keep your firewood outside and away from the house. Inspect each log carefully.

2. June bugs and May beetles fly at night. Replace white outdoor bulbs with yellow ones. Keep screens and storm doors tight.

3. Carpet beetles can damage many kinds of fabrics. Thoroughly vacuum rugs, dark corners, moldings, and under furniture, then remove and dispose of the vacuum bag. Clean pet bedding regularly and seal all floor cracks. Store clothes (dry-clean them first) in bugproof bags or boxes, along with some mothballs or flakes.

4. Garden beetles can be controlled; clean up debris to remove winter hiding places. Dust plants with diatomaceous earth or spray with kelp extract, soap and water, or various concoctions of onions, red peppers, and pungent herbs, steeped in water and strained. Or try planting beetle-repellent plants, such as mint and catnip, among your vegetables.

To protect developing melons and squash, cover with paper bags, stapled or pinned shut. Or use pantyhose sections tied off at both ends. (See also *Garden pests,* p.95.)

Bellows

Having trouble getting a campfire started? Use your lungs as a bellows. Blow through a hollow tent pole section or the rubber tubing from a medical kit. Both will enable you to direct and concentrate the air where it is needed.

Hold the tent pole section with a sock, glove, or washcloth to protect your hands from the heat, and blow through a cupped hand to avoid di-

rect contact with your lips. Blow gently so that the fire doesn't flare in your face—and *don't* breathe in through the tube.

Bicycle chains

1. Kerosene is the best cleaner for a greasy bicycle chain. To keep the chain from squeaking, clean it every 2 months and lubricate it with a lightweight bicycle oil or a spray lubricant designed for the purpose.

2. If your chain breaks and you can't fix it right away, lower the seat and push along with your feet.

Bicycle lock

You can make a lock from 6 feet of vinyl-covered steel cable, two U-bolts, and a padlock.

At each end of the cable, make a loop and secure it with a U-bolt;

strip or epoxy the threads so that the nut can't be removed (see *Nuts & bolts*, p.145). Run the cable through the frame and wheels and around the bike rack or a sturdy post. Padlock the loops together.

If you must leave your bike unlocked, remove the handlebars or front wheel and take it with you.

Bicycle riding

1. Keep a whistle on a chain around your neck and use it instead of a horn; it's louder and shriller.
2. Having trouble climbing hills? Maybe you're hunching over the handlebars; this constricts your breathing. Sit up tall instead.
3. On wet roads brake lightly now and then to whisk water off your brakes—especially after you've gone through a puddle and before you start down a hill.
4. If you skid, don't try to move your wheel; keep it in whatever direction you're going. Similarly, on a loose surface, let the bike drift the way it wants.
5. In the country, sharp curves often have loose gravel and holes. Brake to reduce speed *before* you get to a curve, not while you're on the loose surface. Keep as far to the right as possible to avoid cars that may move into your lane as they round the corner.
6. Use a winter hardhat liner, found in hardware stores, as a helmet liner in cold weather. For further warmth, push a folded section of newspaper up under your shirt to help block cold winds.

Bicycle tire

You can repair a tire—in no time flat—with two kitchen spoons, some fine sandpaper, contact cement, talcum powder, and a thin piece of rubber or soft plastic.

For patches, cut small squares of rubber from an old tire tube or swimming cap. Coat one side with contact cement and let it dry.

Remove the wheel and push in the tire with your thumbs just enough to angle the spoons, 5 to 7 inches apart, under its edge. Work them around, pulling the edge of the tire over the rim.

Take the tube out of the tire and look for the puncture. Check inside the tire for any sharp stones or debris. Put your ear to the tube; can you hear the air escape? If you can't find the leak, inflate the tube and submerge it in water; bubbles will locate the hole.

Dry the tube and rough up the area around the hole with sandpaper. Coat it with contact cement and apply the patch, sticky side down. Sprinkle talcum powder over the patched area so that the tube won't stick to the tire wall.

If you inflate the tube a little, it will be easier to put back in the tire. Begin remounting the tire by first inserting the air valve into the rim, then work the tire back onto the rim with your thumbs. (If this proves difficult, use the spoons—but with care. They could puncture your newly repaired tube.)

When the tire is back on the rim, inflate it and replace the wheel.

Bill paying

1. Many banks offer bill-paying services to their customers. You can use your computer to communicate with the bank, call in your merchant code numbers and the amounts to be paid, or punch the numbers into your Touch-Tone telephone.
2. Pay your bills at the office (on your own time, of course); you might even have them sent there.
3. Put everything you need (don't forget the stamps) in a large envelope and take it to a pleasant environment—a park or coffeehouse.

Binoculars

Want to see something far off more clearly? Close one eye and bring your hand, shaped into a circle, up to the other eye. Or look through one end of a cardboard paper towel roll. The small channeled opening acts as a lens.

Birdcalls

1. You can recognize many birds by their calls—whippoorwills, pewees, and phoebes, for example, repeatedly call out their own names.
2. A good way to attract birds is to make squeaking noises by kissing the back of your hand.
3. The time to hear the most birds sing is during the breeding season. Some birds (certain sparrows, warblers, and finches) also sing while they migrate. Most birds are quiet at midday and in midsummer.

Bird feeder

1. Make a funnel to load a bird feeder by cutting off the bottom of a plastic milk jug. Unscrew its cap and hold it upside down when you're ready to fill the feeder with seed.
2. Fill a nylon-mesh bag, the kind onions or grapes are packaged in, with suet and bread crumbs.
3. Tie a string around the top of a pine cone; roll the pine cone first in room-temperature bacon fat or peanut butter and then in birdseed or bread crumbs.

Birds as pests

Birds can devastate a fruit or berry crop in a twinkling. If you don't want to go to the trouble of covering your trees or bushes with the netting that's normally used to thwart them, try one or more of these tactics:
1. Let your cat wander loose among the trees or in the berry patch. Tie a bell to its collar so that it won't

bring home any dead birds.

2. Put a stuffed animal—a teddy bear, for example—in the branches. Move it every few days; birds quickly get used to stationary objects.

3. Plant a mulberry bush as a trap crop. Birds go for mulberries before hitting other fruits. Plant it well away from the house, however, since its fruits are messy.

4. Staple brown paper bags around bunches of ripening grapes; cut a vent hole at each corner.

Birth certificate

It's a good idea to keep a copy of your birth certificate in your home or office, as well as in your safe deposit box.

To get a copy, check with an agency of the state where you were born: the department of public health, the department of vital statistics, or possibly the county clerk. For a fee, you can get a certified copy of your birth certificate, bearing the stamp of the issuing agency. Otherwise, contact the hospital where you were born.

If no birth certificate exists for you—either because your birth was not registered or because the records were destroyed—obtain a letter from a state agency verifying that the state has no record of your birth. Then write to the U.S. Census Bureau for an application to receive a copy of your census record.

That transcript, together with the letter from the state agency, can substitute for a birth certificate. If you were born outside the U.S.A., you can use your naturalization papers as a substitute.

⟩ Bites

If someone has been bitten by an animal or by another person, your first priority is to stop any severe bleeding. Then wash the wound thoroughly with soap and water. Rinse under running water for 5 minutes and cover with a sterile dressing or clean cloth.

To prevent infection, immobilize the area of the bite with a bandage or a splint and take the victim to a doctor or a hospital emergency room for antibiotics and possible antitetanus treatment. (See also *Dog & cat bites*, p.64; *Insect bites*, p.116; *Stings*, p.196.)

Blackflies

Some insect repellents will keep blackflies away, but many campers and outdoor workers have found that a particular bath oil, Avon Skin-So-Soft (Original Formula) works better than any of them. Dilute it with a little water and apply directly to exposed skin. Frequent applications are necessary.

If you're working in the garden and the flies just won't leave you alone, wear a mosquito-net hat that covers the head and neck and ties under the shoulders. Make sure there are no openings in your clothing. Tuck in shirttails and tuck pants legs into socks.

Black tie

When an invitation says "black tie," the only article of a man's attire (other than a white shirt) that *doesn't* have to be black is—the bow tie! Whatever the tie's color, the cummerbund should match.

In summer he may substitute a white, print, or solid color dinner jacket. A woman can wear a long gown or a dressy short one.

A man can always rent a tux. At the height of the formal party season—that is, late spring, when there are a lot of graduations and weddings—and during the Christmas holidays, he'll need to book it well in advance. To buy a tuxedo at less than the cost of a new one, shop the rental agencies. One advantage: the adjustable-waist pants guarantee an adequate fit.

Bleach spots

1. If the garment is dark, disguise the spot by rubbing it with a permanent marker or a crayon that matches the fabric's color.

2. Dip a light-colored garment in diluted bleach to even the color.

3. Sew an appliqué over the spot.

4. Dye the garment a darker color or tie-dye it.

Blenders

1. If liquid leaks from around the cover, place strips of aluminum foil over the jar's edges before putting on the cover. The foil acts as a seal.

2. Prolong the life of your blender by whirling away any food particles caught under the cutting blades (a strain on the blades will eventually stop the motor from turning). Place a few drops of mild detergent and a cup of warm water in the blender jar and pulse at high speed for a few seconds. Repeat with clear water to rinse. If gummy food residue remains, bend the end of a bottle brush to reach under the blades.

3. When a blender no longer cuts it in the kitchen but its blades still turn, retire it to the workshop for such household and garden tasks as mixing paint or plant food.

Blood stains

1. Put a paste of water and cornstarch, cornmeal, or talcum powder on fresh spots; let dry and brush off. Or cover fresh or dried stains with meat tenderizer and add cool water. After 15 to 30 minutes, sponge off with cool water.

2. Fresh blood on leather? Dab on a little hydrogen peroxide. After it bubbles, wipe it off.

3. If you prick your finger while sewing and get blood on the fabric, quickly wet a long piece of white cotton thread with saliva and place it across the spot. The thread will absorb the blood.

Blushing

You can't control a blush; once it starts, it can't be stopped. (Fortunately, it usually lasts only a few minutes.)

1. You *may* be able to disguise a blush by combing your hair into your face, wearing lighter makeup, and dressing in blush-colored clothes so that there will be less contrast with your face.

2. Or you may get relief by meditating: close your eyes, relax, and think of some place far away.

3. If worst comes to worst, employ distraction—pretend you've lost your wallet or keys; look anxious and flustered while you search your purse and your pockets.

Board games

1. Bottle caps and coins make good checkers. Use different color crayons, tabs of adhesive-backed paper, or even child-sized round bandages to indicate the sides.

Check your candy drawer: roll candies or colored mints also work as checkers. Each player uses a different color to distinguish the pieces. And when you take an opponent's piece, you can eat it.

2. Lost dice? Mark sugar cubes with a ballpoint pen; they won't last long in play, but they're easy to replace. Be sure the numbers on opposite faces add up to seven.

Or you can substitute two cardboard spinners. Trace circles on a piece of cardboard, divide each into 6 equal sections, and number the sections. Make two arrows and attach them to the centers of the circles with metal paper fasteners, straight pins, or tacks. Spin both arrows for each turn.

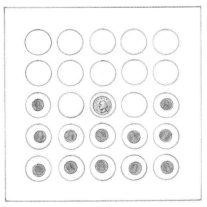

3. To make a simple board game called Indian and Rabbits, draw 25 circles in 5 rows of 5 each on a cardboard square. Place 10 pennies (the rabbits) across the bottom 2 rows of circles and 1 on each end of the center row. Put the quarter (the Indian) in the middle of the center row.

One player controls all the rabbits; the other controls the Indian. A rabbit or the Indian may move one circle up, down, or across on each turn. To win, the rabbits must corner the Indian, or the Indian must capture all but one rabbit. The Indian captures rabbits by jumping over them, as in checkers. The Indian may make more than one jump in a turn if all the jumps are in a straight line.

Boating mishaps

Tarpaulin

1. Sometimes the vibrations of high-speed power boats cause the powder in dry fire extinguishers to compact so tightly that they won't work even when the pressure gauge indicates they are ready. To make sure your extinguisher will work when you need it, occasionally hit it lightly with your hand or against the side of the boat several times to loosen the powder.

2. You may be able to plug a small leak temporarily with rags, cotton, or towels. It's better to carry an all-purpose damage-control device, resembling an umbrella, that will plug a hole until a permanent repair can be made.

3. For a larger leak or a hole, first try plugging from the inside with pillows or a mattress. If that doesn't work, make a damage-control device with a tarpaulin and four lengths of rope as shown above. Tie a rope to each corner of the tarpaulin. Secure three corners on the damaged side of the boat and bring the fourth rope under the craft and tie it on the other side.

4. You can also plug a large leak by running two ropes loosely around the hull and stuffing a mattress under them. Tighten the ropes to hold it fast.

Body bulges
WOMEN

1. Avoid tight-fitting undergarments; they can emphasize or even create bulges. Minimize bulges with a one-piece undergarment, such as a slip or body suit with a fitted top or built-in bra.

2. Add a bright scarf or large jewelry; accessories can deflect attention from bulges by drawing notice to themselves.

3. For a skirt that shows thigh bulges, try tying a large scarf (be sure to coordinate colors) around your hips. If your skirt buttons down the front, unbutton the bottom one or two buttons; the skirt will fall more gracefully.

MEN

1. To cover that paunch, wear full-cut rather than form-fitting clothes. A loose sweater is good for casual wear. A vest that matches your suit can have a slimming effect.

2. Pockets should not have flaps. Pants should have a belt. Stay away from heavy textures, such as nubby tweeds, and sharp color contrasts.

Bookcases

For a quick, attractive bookshelf, lay boards across bricks, glass blocks, or concrete blocks.

Plastic milk crates—the kind that milk cartons are carried in—can be stacked to make a colorful set of shelves for a child's room. Most of these cartons belong to dairy companies and must be paid for, but you can find similar units for sale in many home centers. (With diligence and a bit of luck, you may even locate some old-fashioned wooden milk crates at a flea market or country antiques shop.)

Some plastic milk crates are de-

signed to interlock. If yours aren't, secure them with twist ties, strips of cloth, or plastic tape. For neatness, choose a matching color.

Bookends

1. To make a bookend in a minute, snip off the hook of a wire coat hanger with wire cutters and bend it at a 90° angle. Slip one end of the folded hanger under the books.

2. Draw a line across an unwanted phonograph record just to one side of the label. With a hair dryer, heat the record on both sides along the line until you can bend it.

Books

1. Dog-eared corners? Put a sheet of paper on top and press with a warm iron.

2. Mend torn pages with gummed tissue, or glue rice paper or onionskin over the tears. Sandwich newly repaired pages between sheets of wax paper so that they won't stick to other pages.

3. Water spilled on a book's pages? A frost-free freezer will draw out the moisture and unstick the pages.

If water has damaged too many books to fit in the freezer, call a local wholesale meat distributor or food processor and arrange to rent freezer space.

4. Clean leather bindings with saddle soap, neat's-foot oil, or petroleum jelly. Apply sparingly and gently with your fingers or a piece of felt, cheesecloth, or chamois. Wait several hours, then repeat.

5. Protect your books with covers made of freezer paper. Shape the cover, then seal the edges with a moderately hot iron.

6. Clean books with your vacuum's dusting-brush attachment, a shaving brush, or a soft paintbrush.

7. Run a dehumidifier in a damp room containing books. Wipe mold and mildew off the bindings and pages with a clean soft cloth. If the pages are still moldy, wipe with an alcohol-dampened cloth, then fan out the pages to dry. Or sprinkle

some cornstarch on the pages and brush it off after a few hours.

8. To remember to return library books before you owe a fine, keep a running list of the due dates on your refrigerator. Do *not* remind yourself by removing the circulation card in the back of the book; if you lose it, you'll be charged a replacement fee.

9. If you lend a book to a friend, write "Please return to (your name)" on the inside front cover. Keep the jacket, along with a notation of the borrower and the date; it will remind you to ask for the book after a reasonable time.

10. If fire has damaged the outer edges of your books, remove the soot with a dry chemical sponge (available at janitorial supply stores).

Boots

1. To dry boots fast, heat a pan of clean round pebbles in the oven, pour them into the boots, and shake until the stones cool. (First test the boot lining by holding a hot pebble in one place for a few seconds.)

2. Blow warm air on wet rubber boots with a vacuum-cleaner blower attachment or your hair dryer.

3. To remove salt stains, wipe the boots with a solution of 1 cup water and 1 tablespoon vinegar.

4. Rub rain spots off suede boots with an emery board.

5. What to do when you're caught on a bad day without boots? Using a silicone shoe spray, make a sturdy pair of shoes water-repellent, and wear leggings made by cutting off the feet of old, worn-out knee socks. For walking a very short distance, fasten plastic bags over your shoes with rubber bands.

Bores

A bore has been defined as a person who finds himself more interesting than he finds you. If cornered by one, don't bother trying to be polite; he won't notice anyway.

1. Entertain yourself by asking irrelevant questions and counting the seconds until he manages to work his way back to his pet topic.

2. Create a diversion: spill a drink; get hiccups or the giggles; notice a long-lost friend across the room.

3. Smile, nod now and then, and recite poetry in your head. If the bore is someone important (your boss, for example), use the magic phrase "I see" from time to time.

4. Open a magazine, a book, your pocket calendar, or a small calculator. Give it your utmost attention.

5. Walk away.

Bottle & jar caps

1. Run hot water over a recalcitrant jar cap to expand it. Then, for additional grabbing power, wrap the cap with a rubber band.

2. To loosen the stop from a decanter, wrap a hot, wet cloth around the neck of the bottle. If necessary, let a few drops of water trickle into the neck and around the stopper to dissolve whatever might be holding it tight. Quickly drain off the water so that it doesn't touch the contents of the bottle.

3. To remove a bottle cap without an opener, use locking-grip pliers, a crescent wrench, or the strikeplate opening of a doorframe (the plate that receives the latch). Remember, too, that the handle of a corkscrew often serves as a bottle opener. Or you can use needle-nose pliers, a screwdriver, or the teeth of a key to pry up the folds of the cap, one at a time.

Bottles

To clean a narrow-necked bottle, fill it with equal parts water and detergent or ammonia. Add some uncooked rice and swirl the solution until the bottle comes clean.

For cloudy stains, pour in vinegar and some coarse sand. Every half hour for up to 5 or 6 hours, shake and swirl it around until the stain disappears.

Bra & slip straps

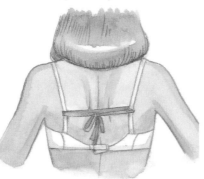

Straps keep falling down? Before you put your bra on, tie them together across the back with a shoelace, string, or ribbon.

For a permanent solution, sew a piece of thin elastic between them.

If you don't want straps to show with a wide neckline, sew small Velcro strips on the top of each one and on each inside shoulder seam of the dress or blouse. Or carefully pin your strap to your blouse with small brass safety pins.

Bracelet

1. Need a bracelet to match a special outfit? Wrap one of yours in matching fabric or ribbon.

2. Make your own bracelet by removing both ends from an empty tuna can, smoothing down any jagged metal with a metal nail file, and twisting or gluing on yarn, fabric, and ornaments. Use rubber cement or epoxy.

3. For a particularly festive look, dab papier-mâché on a band made from a strip of cardboard. When the papier-mâché is dry, paint it in bright colors.

4. Save old belts. For a bracelet that's sure to attract attention, fasten several buckles together on a single belt strap. Cut off the excess strap, and "fasten" your bracelet with the original belt buckle.

Brass

1. To remove the tarnish from unlacquered brass fittings, nameplates, and other small objects, submerge them overnight in a solution of equal parts water and ammonia; then rub with extra-fine steel wool or a soft brush.

2. For stubborn tarnish, rub with a paste of salt and vinegar or use a salted lemon rind. Toothpastes— both regular and gel—also work.

3. If the brass is covered with lacquer, clean it with mild detergent and water, then rinse and wipe dry. Avoid harsh abrasives, which can wear through the lacquer.

4. In all cases, rinse afterward in clear water and buff dry with a soft cloth or chamois.

Bread baking

1. Save the water when you boil peeled potatoes; it will provide food for yeast and make for a better-flavored bread. Heat the water to a temperature of 105°F–115°F before dissolving the yeast in it.

2. To get dough to rise, you need a draft-free spot with a temperature of 75°F–80°F. Try putting the bowl of dough, lightly covered, in a cupboard above a water heater, atop the refrigerator, on a heating pad at its lowest setting, or on a TV set or fish-tank light.

3. A quick fix for bread burned in baking or reheating is to rub off the black spots with a kitchen grater. For severe burns, simply cut off the damaged part and eat the rest.

Bread crumbs

1. Instead of relying on storebought dry bread crumbs, you can use crushed cornflakes, unsweetened bran cereal, or matzoh meal. Or make crumbs from toasted white bread; crush the slices with a rolling pin or an empty bottle, or buzz them to fine crumbs in an electric blender or food processor.

2. Cracker crumbs can also double as bread crumbs but contain more sodium, so taste for saltiness as you prepare a recipe.

3. Freshly made bread crumbs will keep for a week or more in a tightly closed jar in the refrigerator.

Breast-feeding

If full-time breast-feeding is impossible, the best substitute is expressed breast milk given from a bottle. Second best is a commercially prepared formula.

A good time to introduce a bottle is when the baby is 4 to 6 weeks old. Some babies may take 2 weeks or longer to become comfortable with a bottle-feeding.

Practice expressing your milk—manually or with a breast pump—before returning to work or other duties. In order to have adequate milk for bottle-feedings, you'll need to pump two or three times in the course of the day.

If you're away from home, take along a vacuum bottle filled with ice cubes; empty it when you want to store the milk. At home, store expressed milk in 4-ounce plastic (not glass) bottles.

If you plan to use the milk within 48 hours, place it in the refrigerator. For longer storage, use the freezer; it should remain good for at least 3 months.

When you're ready to use the frozen milk, thaw it in the refrigerator for several hours, use a microwave oven, or hold it under warm running water for a few minutes. Shake the bottle well before feeding.
Caution: Thawing in a microwave oven may overheat the milk; test it before giving it to the baby.

Breathing exercises

Increasing the volume of oxygen in your lungs can help relieve tension.

DIAPHRAGM BREATHING

Stand straight or lie flat on your back and place your hands flat against your diaphragm with your little fingers along your waistline. Inhale slowly and deeply through your nose, pulling the air down into your lungs. You will feel the bottom of your lungs fill, which concentrates airflow. Exhale through your mouth. Repeat five times.

Y MOVEMENT
Stand, or lie flat on your back, arms crossed in front, with each palm resting on the opposite thigh. While inhaling deeply through your nose, slowly raise both arms above your head, uncrossing them and turning the palms to face each other. As your shoulders open and your lungs expand, your arms will push outward at an angle. Reverse the movement as you exhale, bringing your shoulders forward to the starting position.

Brick & stone cleaning

1. Scrub paint specks and mortar smudges from brick surfaces with a piece of broken brick that's the same color as the brick you are cleaning. Don't use the face of the brick; it is harder than the core and can cause scratches. Use the broken surface.

This technique works for other masonry surfaces too. Use a bit of stone to clean stone and a concrete block fragment for concrete blocks.
2. Here's an easy way to rinse surface dirt and grime from a brick or stone wall. Position a lawn sprinkler to spray directly against the wall. Leave it on for several hours during 2 or 3 consecutive days.

---

3. Lift out fresh oil and grease stains with dry powdered cement or cat litter. Spread a layer of the material over the stain, allow it to soak up the oil, and sweep the area clean. Repeat if necessary.

On a vertical surface, hold a piece of plastic over the stain and attach the side and bottom edges with duct tape. Fill the pouch with powdered cement or cat litter and tape the top edge closed.

Brokers

1. If you own a home computer, you can trade stock through a discount broker and pay considerably lower commissions than you would at a full-service broker. This no-frills, no-advice service is safe and reliable, but it's useful only for well-informed investors. You can even arrange to access a broker's data base and can then research companies, check the latest market quotes, buy and sell stocks, and review your investment portfolio.

Under this arrangement, the brokerage will hold the securities you buy and will discount commissions on all transactions. There may be a monthly service fee and charges for the time your computer is connected to the data base.

2. Instead of buying through a broker, take advantage of the dividend reinvestment plan offered by many companies. You will pay no commission on the new shares, and you may even get a discount on the price of the stock.

3. Eliminate the commission altogether by selling a stock yourself.

Sign the back of the stock certificate, then ask your commercial bank to guarantee the signature (to protect against forgery). Fill in the name, Social Security number, and address of the new owner.

Get the name and address of the company's transfer agent from the stock certificate or the investor relations department of the company in which you hold stock. Send the certificate to the transfer agent by registered mail (keep a photocopy for yourself), along with a letter explaining that you are selling the shares. The transfer agent will issue a certificate to the new owner.

Bruises

A small bruise requires no special treatment, but if bruising is extensive, remember ICES: Ice, Compression, Elevation, and Splinting.
I. Place ice or cold packs over the bruise to help control bleeding and swelling and relieve pain.
C. Press your hand firmly over the injured area.
E. Elevate the bruised area to a level just above the heart.
S. Immobilize a badly bruised limb with a splint (p. 194).

Brushes

1. A soft-bristled baby brush is great for cleaning the delicate fabric on lampshades and curtains.
2. Place a wet towel or some damp newspaper under the radiator before using a radiator brush. The dust will stick to it. If you don't have a radiator brush, use the long

narrow brush meant for cleaning snow off your car.
3. Whenever you vacuum or dust, carry a whisk broom or a small unused paintbrush with you to get into the hard-to-reach places. (See also *Hairbrushes*, p. 102; *Paintbrushes*, p. 149.)

Bulbs

1. If you're the kind of serious gardener who plans for the long term, save money on expensive lily bulbs by harvesting bulbils, the tiny dark bulbs produced on the stem between the leaf axils. Pluck them just after the flowers have faded. Plant them in containers of potting soil just below the surface, spacing them well apart so that you won't have to thin them before they're established. They will take a long time to flower—3 to 4 years. Don't bother to propagate in this way from hybrid lilies, since the resulting blossoms are unlikely to resemble those of the parent plant.
2. Don't think of bulbs solely as spring bloomers. Plant the traditional tulips, daffodils, snowdrops, and grape hyacinths for that season, but also consider putting in dahlias and day lilies for summer, colchicums for autumn, and winter-flowering crocuses for the colder months. Cannas and gladiolus will bloom through winter in parts of the South. And even in the North, cyclamen, amaryllis, and other bulbs can brighten a windowsill on gloomy winter days.

Bumper stickers

Before you put that bumper sticker on your automobile, make sure you'll be able to remove it—apply it over a layer of car wax. You will also find it much easier to peel off if you remove it within a month.

Remove an old bumper sticker from chrome by scraping off the top layer of paper or vinyl with a sharp knife or a single-edge razor blade. (Try not to scratch the surface.) The adhesive beneath should come off with rubbing alcohol; if that doesn't work, use paint thinner. If the sticker is on a painted surface, test a tiny patch to make sure the paint doesn't dissolve.

Burglar alarms

1. Even if you don't have a dog, post a "Beware of the Dog" sign. Wire a recorded bark to your doorbell, or carry a small recorder with a taped bark to set off when you answer the door.
2. Hang a dummy alarm bell outside your home.
3. Slip a thin strip of plywood between the top and frame of a door. Pile tin cans, cowbells, or other noisemakers on it. When the door opens, the racket will alert you and frighten off an intruder.
4. Even if you can't afford an alarm system, paste security-system stickers on the windows. Instruct your children to tell no one that the system doesn't exist.
5. Turn on outdoor lights, or wire infrared or sound-activated detectors to switch them on if intruders come within range.

Burglaries

1. If you come home and see an open door or objects out of place, turn around at once and leave quietly. Notify the police from a neighbor's home.

Watch your home from a safe distance—don't try to stop the burglar when he leaves. Get a good description and write down the license number of his vehicle. (See *Witnes-*

sing a crime, p.233.) Stay out of your home until the police arrive to make sure nobody else is inside.
2. If you hear a burglar entering your home or prowling around, collect your family in a room with a strong door and a good lock; call the police if possible, or wait until the intruder leaves before seeking help.
3. If you confront a burglar face-to-face or wake up to discover one in your room, stay quiet and cooperate. Screaming may only frighten or anger an already scared or irrational burglar into violence.

AFTER A BURGLARY

The police need a full description of all stolen items. For that reason, it's wise to photograph and list all your valuables (including serial numbers) long before a crisis arises, and keep the inventory in a safe-deposit box. (See also *Insurance claims,* p.117; *Safe-deposit box,* p.176; *Valuables,* p.221.)

Burned cookware

To clean burned food from pots or pans, wet the burn, sprinkle with salt, and let stand for 10 minutes. Scrub well.

Or cover the burned area with a paste of baking soda and water. Leave it on overnight, then scour. (Be aware, however, that baking soda and other alkaline substances will etch the surface of an aluminum pan if they are left on for more than an hour.)

For stubborn burns, scrape off as much burned food as possible with a wooden spoon and fill the pot halfway with water. Add a strong detergent or scouring powder, boil for 10 minutes, and let stand overnight. Then scrub.

› Burns

The seriousness of a burn depends on three things: how deep it is, how much of the body it covers, and the age and health of the victim. Infants, children under the age of 5, and adults over 60 are especially vul-

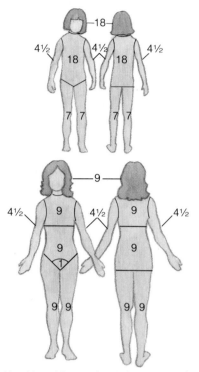

Use this guide to estimate the amount of burn damage; it divides areas of the body into portions or multiples of 9 percent.

nerable; a burn that's moderate to a young adult could be fatal to them.

First-degree burns are superficial; the skin becomes slightly reddened and swollen. The pain is similar to that of a sunburn.

Second-degree burns penetrate the first layer of skin and damage the second. The skin is red, mottled, and blistered; pain is intense.

Third-degree burns damage all layers of the skin, usually leaving charred, black areas or dry, white ones. There may be extreme pain or, because of nerve damage, very little pain after the initial acute pain. Such burns are always serious, as they are easily infected.
1. Wet down, remove, smother, or cut away any smoldering clothes. Pour cold water over tar, wax, or grease; don't try to remove it. If the skin and clothes are still hot, and the burn seems to be first or second degree, immerse the area in ice or cold water or apply a cool, wet dressing for no longer than 10 minutes.

If the burn appears to be third degree, immerse it in water only if it's still burning.

2. Facial burns or soot in the nose or mouth indicates that the person has inhaled smoke. Check that the victim has no breathing problems.

3. Apply a loose, dry, preferably sterile dressing to all third-degree burns and to second-degree burns over more than 9 percent of the body. If the burns are extensive, wrap the person in a clean sheet. *Don't put anything else on the burn.* Take the person to an emergency room.

If the burn is minor—second degree on less than 9 percent of noncritical areas of the body or first degree on less than 18 percent—apply a loose dressing, moistened only with cool water to help relieve the pain. Be careful not to break any blisters. If there's tar, grease, or wax on the skin, cover with a loose, dry dressing, and take the person to an emergency room.

Burping a baby

If your baby needs burping but you need to move around and keep one of your hands free, try one of these walking-burping techniques:

1. Set the baby on your hip, facing out, with one of your arms securely around his tummy. The slight pressure of your arm plus the movement of your walking will help bring up the bubble.

2. Strap on your "front pack" and put the baby into it, arranging a clean cloth to catch any milk that comes up with the burp.

3. If the baby is over 4 months old and can hold up his head, put him in a backpack carrier—the movement of your walking will help a burp develop.

Business lunches

When initiating a business lunch, especially with a new person, be sure to state the reason, even if it's only to share information and get to know each other. This will prevent misunderstandings and give both of you a chance to prepare.

The one who suggests the lunch should be ready to pay the bill. But if you're asked to lunch informally by someone who is obviously not on an expense account, offer to share the bill. No matter who had what, split it down the middle. Lunch is lunch.

To pay the bill unobtrusively, speak with the waiter or maître d' privately before lunch to make sure the check is given to you and not your guest. If you forget to settle this matter before lunch, excuse yourself to use the restroom and speak to the waiter on the way. You can even arrange to pay the bill while away from the table. (Paying by credit card is less obvious than by cash.)

If you entertain at one restaurant regularly, the staff will help make your lunches smoother. Call in advance for reservations. Give your name and company, the day and time, the number of people, and the table you'd like. After lunch, discreetly tip the headwaiter (between $2 and $10) and tip your waiter well. After doing this a few times, you'll find that you've bought and paid for especially good service.

Butter

1. Margarine can replace butter in most recipes, but not in those for shaped, rolled, or dropped cookies; its greater shortening power makes the cookies spread out over the baking sheet.

Vegetable oil or lard can substitute for butter in all dishes except baked goods, although the amounts will be different: 1 tablespoon butter equals ¾ tablespoon vegetable oil or lard; 1 cup butter equals ⅞ cup vegetable oil or lard.

2. Butter won't burn as quickly in a sauté pan if you add a drop or two of corn oil or olive oil.

Buttermilk

No buttermilk? Use plain low-fat yogurt. Sour cream works, too, but not in cakes—too much butterfat.

OTHER SUBSTITUTES

1. Stir a tablespoon of lemon juice or vinegar into 1 cup whole milk and let it stand for a few minutes.

2. Mix 1 cup milk with 1¾ tablespoons cream of tartar.

Buttons

TEMPORARY MEASURES

1. When a button pops, stay "decent" with a safety pin hidden under the buttonhole until you can replace the button.

2. Fasten a pretty brooch or pin in place of the missing button.

3. Tack the button to the fabric with the wire from a twist tie.

PERMANENT ALTERNATIVES

1. Use button-sized Velcro circles and squares. Position each piece with a pin, then hand- or machine-stitch around the edges.

2. Cut "buttons" any size you desire from iron-on Velcro tape. Follow the package directions for attaching them to the fabric.

3. Buy snaps or hooks and eyes that are anchored to tapes. Cut off as many fasteners as you need; stitch the tape edges to the fabric.

4. Try grommets; they're sold in lots of finishes. Attach them with a grommeting tool or a hammer.

Cabbage worms

To thwart these pests, slip sections of old pantyhose over young cabbage heads. Knot the tops and pull the hose down to soil level. They will expand as the plants grow.

Or lightly dust leaves with a powdered mixture of ½ cup salt and 1 cup flour; apply while the plants are wet with dew.

Cabin fever

Be imaginative when it comes to getting through a long, dark winter:

1. Host a cookie exchange. Tell your guests to bring enough cookies, wrapped in packages of six, so that everyone can take home a package from everyone else.

2. Invite a foreign exchange student to dinner. Many communities have visiting students attending high school or college. Often they are eager to meet new people and to tell about their native countries. Ask a local high school or college to put you in touch with a foreign student.

3. Find a class in a craft that you've always wanted to learn. Adult education programs and Y's have a wide range of arts programs that you can choose from.

4. Volunteer your services. Most hospitals, schools, literacy groups, town beautification projects, and scout programs welcome new helpers. Check with your library or town hall to get the names of local volunteer groups.

5. Did you play in your high school band or orchestra? Investigate whether any community in your area sponsors a town band you can join. There are usually no tryouts, and playing levels vary widely, so there's no need to worry if your skills are a bit rusty.

Cakes

1. Slip your hand inside a plastic sandwich bag before greasing a cake pan with shortening. No mess!

2. To find out if a cake is done, insert a wooden toothpick in the center. If it comes out clean, the cake is ready. Or press the center with your finger; the cake is cooked if the top springs back, leaving no imprint.

3. Cakes leavened with beaten egg whites—such as angel food, chiffon, and sponge cakes—often fall while cooling. To minimize the chances, invert the pan as soon as it comes from the oven and let the cake cool upside down. Don't worry about it falling out of the pan; egg white–based cakes have to be loosened with a spatula.

Most angel food cake pans have three "feet" at the top, so that the pan can be inverted without squashing a risen cake. If yours lacks feet or if the cake has risen too high, place the center of the inverted pan over a glass bottle.

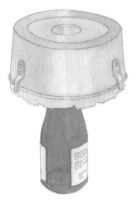

4. Because microwaved cakes often come from the oven sticky, uneven, and unbrowned on top, it's best to microwave only cakes that will be frosted or those that have crumb toppings.

5. To decorate a cake, turn a self-sealing plastic sandwich bag into a pastry bag. Store frosting in it, refrigerated, until the cake is ready. Then snip off a bottom corner and pipe away. For better control insert a plastic decorating tip.

6. Use a paper doily as a stencil. Position it atop the cake and sprinkle confectioner's sugar generously over it. Then carefully lift the doily.

7. When time is short, bake a sheet cake instead of a layer cake. It's quicker to frost.

8. A cut cake will stay fresh longer if you place half an apple inside the cake keeper or storage tin.

Calculators

A basic calculator is not just for balancing checkbooks and figuring out budgets—it has a wealth of helpful, perhaps unexpected, uses.

Before you begin, check your calculator's accuracy. Enter 9's all the way across. Divide by 81. The answer should be 12345678.

IN THE CAR

1. Figure your gas mileage. Note the odometer reading when you fill the tank; the next time you fill up, divide the number of gallons by the number of miles you've driven.

2. Check your speedometer's accuracy on a highway that has markers posted every mile. Driving at a steady speed, count the seconds between two signs. Divide that number into 3,600, the seconds in an hour, to get the speed in miles per hour.

IN THE SUPERMARKET

1. Curb impulse buying by tallying the amount of your grocery order on a calculator as you shop.

2. Comparison shop: you can compute the unit cost of an item by dividing the price by the number of ounces marked on the container.

AT SALES

1. Find out how much you'll pay on an item marked "reduced 60 percent," even if your calculator lacks a percent key. Multiply the price by the discount (.60); subtract the discount for the sale price.

2. Convert fractions to decimals by dividing the top number by the bottom number. If an item is ⅓ off, the discount is .33, or 33 percent.

IN HOME STORES

Figure the cost of new carpeting. Measuring in yards, multiply the length of the room times the width to get the square yards, and multiply that times the cost per square yard. If you're painting your walls instead, calculate the area in the same fashion in order to buy the right amount of paint.

IN A RESTAURANT

If friends want to split the bill, add up each person's share; to figure the tip, multiply the before-tax total by 15 to 20 percent.

IN A PHONE BOOTH

Use the calculator as a notepad to take down a phone number—but use the decimal point, not the minus sign, as the hyphen!

FOR FUN

Punch in .7734 and turn upside down to see HELLO.

Calendar

1. Coordinate family activities on a centrally located calendar with a big square for each day. Assign special colored pens or markers to different family members, or use them to differentiate specific activities: for example, red checks on the days you have the carpool, blue dots to indicate trash pickup days. Encourage everyone to record any activities affecting family life.

2. Use your home computer as a calendar; program it to display each day's activities, which you and other family members have previously entered into it.

3. Set up a countertop tickler file and keep it in the kitchen, hall, or other main area. Purchase a cardboard accordion file and number its compartments 1 through 31, or get a large-format (5- x 7-inch) file

box with 31 numbered dividers.

With this file you can organize many family activities: the list of items to buy at the hardware store on Saturday; dry-cleaner receipts; questions to ask the second-grade homeroom teacher; Tuesday's theater tickets. Drop the slips or tickets in the appropriate slot; then check the file each morning. Store next month's items in a separate compartment at the beginning or end of the file.

Calipers

To measure the outside diameter of a round object, use a C-clamp, a pair of locking-grip pliers, or an adjustable wrench. Set the jaws to the width of the object and measure the space between them.

If you have a couple of combination squares, slide both heads onto one ruler, face to face, as shown. Fit the heads against the object in question, then read the ruler.

Or use a cloth measuring tape to determine the circumference of a pipe or other cylinder; divide by pi (3.14) to arrive at the diameter.

Calorie counting

No more than 30 percent of your daily calories should come from fat. Study the labels of packaged foods and beverages and consult the nutritional analyses that accompany the recipes in some cookbooks. Then use this 9-4-4 formula to determine the sources of the calories:
1 gram fat is 9 calories;
1 gram carbohydrate is 4 calories;
1 gram protein is 4 calories.
Divide the calories-from-fat figure by the total number of calories to find out if it amounts to more than 30 percent.

Camera filters

Need a haze filter for that lovely scenic shot? You may already have the best one in your camera bag—a polarizer. Normally used to darken blue skies, polarizers also cut down haze in distant scenes. On a single-lens reflex camera, rotate the polarizer until you see the best effect.

A diffusion filter adds a dreamy feeling and soft edges to portraits and scenic shots. Don't have one? Lightly smear petroleum jelly on any ultraviolet or polarizing filter. Wipe it off later with tissue and rubbing alcohol.

Cameras

PROTECTION FROM THE ELEMENTS

Carry a supply of plastic bags in your camera pack. An inverted bag with the corners snipped off and the camera straps threaded through will give some protection against rain or snow. Let the bag hang over the camera, open end down; slide it

Protect your camera with a plastic bag.

Raise the bag for picture-taking.

up to take a picture. For more water-proofing, tape the edges of the holes to the strap with vinyl tape.

A self-sealing food storage bag, used as above, or a garbage bag, edges folded over and sealed with paper clips, will protect your camera from blowing sand and dust.

OVERRIDING AUTO EXPOSURE

Most modern cameras adjust automatically to give correct exposures. But sometimes the lighting will fool your camera into the wrong exposure—for example, if there's a strong backlight. If you suspect this (you get an abnormally high or low reading), review your camera's instruction manual; you can probably override the automation.

On some point-and-shoot cameras, you can change the film speed to fool the camera. For example, changing from a speed of 100 to 200 will reduce the exposure, giving you deeper blue skies in outdoor scenes.

Camp baking

An inexpensive 1½-quart ring mold (for gelatin) and a camp stove can be used to bake quick breads and biscuits. Mix the dry ingredients in a plastic bag at home. Add water in camp; hold the bag shut and mix the contents by squeezing and kneading. Slit the bag slightly and squeeze the batter into the greased mold.

Set the mold on the stove, centering its hole over the burner; to avoid burning the dough's edges, adjust the stove to the smallest possible blue flame. Cover with an upside-down frying pan or aluminum plate.

If your stove produces only a wide-spreading flame, nestle the ring mold inside another of the same size to distribute the heat more evenly. If wind keeps blowing the flame to the side, rotate the stove often.

Baking time depends on elevation but averages 80 percent of the baking time for a package mix—longer if you remove the cover often to check progress.

Camp cooking

1. A lightweight camp stove is faster, cleaner, and easier to cook with than a fire; it also causes less wear and tear on the landscape. If you do use a fire, spread the coals out for low, easily controlled heat.

2. You can devise cooking pots from 1-, 2-, and 3-pound coffee cans that nest inside each other. Pack pliers to lift the hot cans.

3. Supermarkets sell many freeze-dried foods at about half the prices charged by camping stores. Combine instant macaroni, noodles, or rice with instant soup mix for a satisfying camp meal. Other standbys, such as powdered fruit drinks, instant potatoes, individual oatmeal packets, spaghetti dinners, and puddings, work well too.

4. Remember that freeze-dried meat needs more cooking than other ingredients. Place the meat in cold water (20 percent more than the instructions call for) and bring to a boil; then add spices, if called for. Continue boiling for 5 minutes before adding other ingredients.

5. Because water boils at lower temperatures in high elevations (about 1 degree per 500 feet), you must boil foods longer. Experiment with cooking times.

6. Cooking with a stove inside a tent can cause headache, nausea, dizziness, or even death from carbon monoxide. In bad weather set the stove just outside the tent door under the rain-fly overhang while cooking from inside the tent. Some tents are designed with vestibules for this purpose.

Caution: Always refuel a stove outside the tent and away from all open flames. And don't ever throw used fuel canisters in the fire.

Campfires

Romantic though they may be, campfires are prohibited in many wilderness areas. Even where legal, they're dangerous and troublesome. If you must build an emergency fire and a fire ring is available, use it.

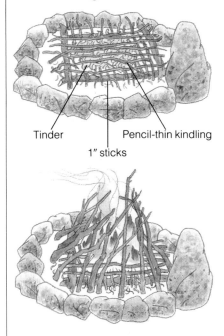

Tinder   Pencil-thin kindling
1″ sticks

Otherwise, clear away all organic material down to the bare dirt within a 3-foot radius. Assemble rocks into a circle that's slightly larger than the cooking utensils you intend to use.

Collect several dozen dry dead twigs and break them into kindling no more than a foot long. Use a pocketknife to slice two fistfuls of very thin shavings. Then assemble the materials as shown. Light the shavings from the windward side and feed more shavings into the flame, one at a time, until the fire is vigorous. (If it's windy, shield the flame with a flat rock.) Build a te-pee of larger wood pieces around the tinder, as shown.

Before you leave, be sure to return the rocks to their original locations, sooty side down. Douse the ashes with water until they are completely cold, then cover them with dirt.

Carry strike-anywhere matches in a waterproof tube and some old candle stubs or birthday candles. In wet weather a candle will help to sustain a flame.

Camping in rainy weather

1. Have your outer clothing water-proofed by a dry cleaner.

2. Rain gear works better and feels more comfortable when it fits loosely. Air spaces provide ventilation and allow your body to dry.

3. Any camper who has endured the tedium of a rainy day knows that a paperback book can be important first aid for boredom. Travel-size board games (checkers, chess, back-gammon, Scrabble) and a deck of cards are also lightweight, easy-to-carry protection against the dreary monotony of a soggy campsite. Writing postcards and letters helps you recall the best moments of your trip and takes your mind off the rain.

4. Suspend a waterproof tarp over a picnic table on a rainy day to create a welcome airy shelter for family activities outside the cramped confines of a tent or trailer. Anchor the corners with wooden pegs.

IN TIMES GONE BY

Weather forecasting

Most adages about the weather—many of them in rhyme—are grounded in centuries of observation by farmers and seafarers who were finely tuned to their surroundings. We can still take some of the old saws seriously today:

Sky red in the morning
  Is a sailor's sure warning;
Sky red at night
  Is the sailor's delight.

Dry air supports more dust than humid air and hence reddens the light. When the sky is red to the west—just after sunset—you can suppose that fair weather is on its way, since air currents in the Northern Hemisphere move from west to east. But when the pre-dawn sky looks red to the east, the dry weather has passed you by, and rain may be coming.

Swallows fly high,
  Clean blue sky;
Swallows fly low,
  Rain we shall know.

Low atmospheric pressure and high humidity, both harbingers of rain, make it difficult for insects to fly high; so swallows fly closer to the earth to prey on them. Other signs of low pressure and probable rain: smoke that curls down from a chimney, soot that falls into the fireplace, clouds forming at low altitudes, and strong ground odors rising from ditches and marshes.

A circle round the moon,
  'Twill rain soon.

Ice crystals in high cirrostratus clouds refract moonlight, so that there appears to be a halo around the moon. Those clouds, in turn, foretell advancing cold fronts that bring storms.

If groundhogs see their shadow
On February 2,
Men can take for granted,
Six more wintry weeks are due.

Though one of the best-known proverbs, this one has no basis in fact. You'd do better to flip a coin.

Camping meal planning

Eating outdoors is half the fun of camping, but it takes some planning. Consider not only the weight and bulk of the food you carry but also its caloric content (hauling a pack may burn 3,200 to 3,800 calories per day, more than twice what's needed to swing in a hammock).

Also consider storability. Among the foods that won't spoil if left unrefrigerated for a few days are hard cheese, hard salami, jerky, sliced carrots and celery, margarine, frozen bagels, and pita bread.

Try new camping foods at home; a campsite is a poor place to discover that an anticipated delight tastes more like sawdust.

Plan major meals in advance and pack all the ingredients in double plastic bags for extra protection. Use color codes to distinguish breakfasts, lunches, and dinners; place colored paper between the inner and outer bags or mark the bags with indelible pens.

If you are tenting, anticipate rainy days when you won't want to cook outside; take along a few one-pot, add-hot-water dinners to heat at the tent door. For cold, rainy mornings, fix a breakfast that doesn't need cooking: dried fruit, rich breads, cheese, and smoked fish.

Campsite lighting

When your trusty flashlight fails, you can fall back on these emergency short-term substitutes:

1. Car headlights can provide light for 10 to 15 minutes without the battery dying.

2. Make a lantern of an open tin can; punch a few holes for air and stick a candle on the inside seam. For a handle, thread wire through holes in the side opposite the seam.

BIRCH BARK TORCH

Take a strip of birch bark 1 foot wide and 3 feet long from the ground or a dead tree. Fold it in thirds lengthwise. Split a 3-foot pole to within 8 inches of one end. Slip the bark lengthwise into the slit and light the end.

As the bark burns, feed more up through the slit. For more light, point the burning end downward to ignite more bark. This torch will last 15 to 20 minutes and cast light for 20 feet.

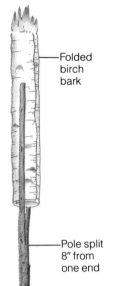

Folded birch bark

Pole split 8″ from one end

Campsite noise

Some campers seem to think that loud conversation is acceptable in the outdoors and that a loud radio is a welcome tie to civilization.

Try politely informing such folks that you are trying to learn the dif-ference between the songs of certain species of warblers. Ask them to let you know if they hear one.

Another subtle hint: In the evening, tell your noisy neighbors that you plan to rise early (for bird watching, of course) and that you'll try to be quiet. But you want them to know that if they do hear you stumbling about, it's just you, not a raccoon or a bear.

Campsite washing

Wear large latex gloves over wool gloves to keep your hands warm and dry while hauling water or washing clothes or dishes in cold weather.

LAUNDRY

1. In *Travels with Charley,* John Steinbeck wrote of putting water, detergent, and dirty clothes in a garbage can and securing the lid. Using an elastic rope, he hung it from a clothes pole in his camper and let road motion do the job. Later, he rinsed the clothes in a stream.

2. To dry socks, shut a car window on them and let them blow in the wind. Or tie wet clothes to a backpack; they'll dry as you hike.

DISHWASHING

1. Let fire-blackened pot bottoms stay black; they'll heat faster and more evenly.

2. Absorbent diapers are lightweight and make good camp towels.

3. Granular snow or sand stirred in greasy bowls and pans makes a good scouring powder.

4. Thoroughly rinse cookware and dishes to avoid digestive disorders.

Candle molds

Tin cans, cardboard milk cartons, heavy glass mugs, and plastic foam cups make good candle molds. Oil the inside of the mold lightly to make removing the candle easier; reinforce a milk carton with masking tape around the middle and across the top.

For a wick, knot a piece of light string to a pencil and lay the pencil across the top of the mold. Weight the loose end with split shot or with a bolt, nut, or paper clip so that it hangs straight.

Candles

1. To make a candle burn longer and drip less, give it a light coat of clear varnish.

2. Melting some wax into the holder is the usual way to get a candle to fit snugly. A cleaner method is to wrap the base of the candle with string or strips of paper towels, making sure they don't show.

3. To remove melted wax from candle holders easily, place the holders in the freezer for an hour or two.

Cane chairs

As a temporary measure, you can support the sagging seat of a cane chair by tacking padded plywood to the underside. Or try brushing water onto the underside to shrink and straighten the cane.

❯ Canes & crutches

CANES

A cane is the right height if the hand holding it is at hipbone level and the elbow is slightly bent.

For the best support, hold the cane on the side *opposite* the injury or weakness—6 inches to the right or left of the "good" foot, as shown.

6″

CRUTCHES

A crutch is at the right height if there's a three-finger-wide space between its top and the armpit.

The armpits and the shoulders shouldn't carry the weight—let the hands and the wrists do that. Keep your elbows slightly bent and rest your armpits on the crutches only briefly, when swinging the uninjured leg through.

EMERGENCY ASSISTANCE

1. Lay the arm on the injured person's good side over your shoulder, grasp the wrist, and put your other arm around his waist.
2. A push broom can serve as a crutch; a plain broom or mop handle, as a staff.
3. A thick stick, a sturdy umbrella, or a croquet mallet makes a serviceable cane.

Canker sores

1. To lessen the irritation, avoid citrus fruits, nuts, chocolate, spicy foods, and very hot foods.
2. To kill the bacteria that make the sore more painful and long-lasting, rinse with a mouthwash, hydrogen peroxide (diluted up to half-and-half with water), or aloe gel (from the center of a fresh aloe leaf).
3. To counteract the acid environment in which the bacteria thrive, rinse with milk of magnesia or a solution of baking soda and water.
Caution: Do not swallow any of the above solutions.

Can openers

1. Open canned liquids with the triangular punch end of a beer can opener; punch on *both* sides so that air can enter for easier pouring.

You can also use the triangular punch (with difficulty) all the way around a can, but be careful—there will be lots of sharp edges.
2. Puncture the can with a sharp rock, a pocketknife, or a screwdriver; then work it open a little at a time with pliers or some other tool (not your hands).

3. Multipurpose camping knives often have can openers. Plunge the sharp point of the U-shaped tool inside the rim, hook the other end on the outer edge, then work it, up and down, around the can. (The tool is made for right-handed people; lefties will have difficulty.)
Caution: Watch out for any metal scraps that fall into the can.

Canteen

An easy-to-clean plastic food bottle makes an inexpensive, lightweight canteen. Use a distinctive container, such as a ketchup bottle, to prevent mistakenly grabbing detergent or some other liquid when you want a quick drink.
1. A flip-top bottle cap may leak. Melt the flip top shut with a match or over a gas stove flame and then use the cap as a screw-on top.

2. A cord handle tied to the bottle neck helps prevent the canteen from slipping from your hands as you fill it in rushing streams.

❯ Car accelerators

If you let up on the accelerator, but the engine keeps racing, shift immediately into *Neutral* and brake gently until you can pull off the road safely.

Push the accelerator to the floor, then let it go. If the pedal is still stuck, turn off the engine; do not drive any farther.

Then look under the hood to see if something is stuck against the throttle linkage; free it if possible. Perhaps the throttle return spring has broken; if so, temporarily repair it by bending the end into a hook and reattaching it.

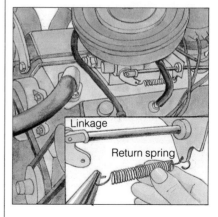

Linkage

Return spring

❯ Car batteries

If your car battery is dead, jumper cables and a working car (with a battery the same voltage as yours) can get you driving again.
1. Bring the cars nose to nose but not touching.
2. Set the cars' parking brakes; put both transmissions in *Park* or *Neutral;* turn off both ignitions and all electrical accessories.
3. Connect one jumper cable from the positive terminal of the dead car to the positive terminal of the live car.
4. Connect the other cable to the negative terminal of the live car and

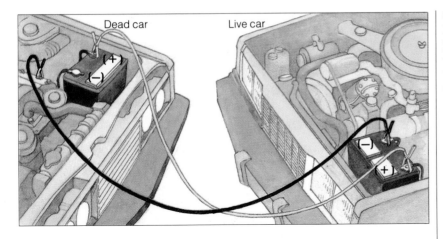

Dead car   Live car

to an unpainted bolt on the dead car's engine, away from the battery. Make sure that the cables are away from all fans, belts, and pulleys.

5. Immediately start the live car, then the dead one.

6. Remove the cables in the reverse order of the way you attached them.

7. Drive the car for at least half an hour to recharge the battery.

Caution: It is hazardous to smoke or to strike a match while jump-starting a car.

› Car brakes

If your brake warning light is on, check to see if the parking brake has been released.

If the light comes on when you hit the brake pedal, there may be something wrong with your car's main braking system. Don't panic. You probably have enough braking power to slow and stop the car.

1. Turn on the emergency flashers, then head off the road to stop. Keep in mind that you'll need more distance than usual for braking; you may have to press the brake pedal harder and it may depress farther.

2. Pump the brake pedal rapidly to build up pressure. If that doesn't work, use the parking brake or downshift so that engine drag slows the car. When in *Low* and slowed to a virtual stop, pull onto the shoulder of the road and turn off the ignition.

3. If none of these measures halt the car, you may have to sideswipe

something—a curb, a hedge, even a parked car—to stop it. Honk your horn and flash your lights to alert other drivers to your emergency.

Car camping

Popular campgrounds are usually jammed on summer weekends; for privacy, camp midweek. Check the facilities for cleanliness first.

During the colder months many campgrounds are nearly deserted, and there is seldom a fee. But water may be shut off and garbage may not be collected. Bring your own water supply and plenty of plastic bags to haul out your refuse.

COOKING ARRANGEMENTS

Most campsites have a fire ring or small fireplace. Where wood is scarce, you may have to buy firewood. Since it may be too large for a small cooking fire, carry a hatchet or other splitting tool.

Carry a small hibachi in case you are limited to burning charcoal. Portable gas stoves are useful for quick boiling and prolonged heating.

A large coffeepot has a variety of uses, including boiling vegetables and heating wash water.

OTHER AMENITIES

1. A reclining lawn chair is more comfortable than a picnic bench and is much easier to move.

2. A waterproof tarp draped over a rope will shelter your cooking area from rain and midday heat.

3. A soiled pillowcase makes a good laundry bag. Put several on each pillow and peel them off for use.

4. Sleeping bag liners extend the time between washings. To make one, fold a sheet lengthwise and sew the open side and bottom closed.

5. Sheets on top of the bags protect them from dirty footprints.

6. Quarters are handy for vending and washing machines, telephones, and showers. Stow them in 35mm film canisters.

Car doors

STICKING DOORS

Before going to the expense of getting a sticking door realigned, try lubricating its hinges with an aerosol penetrating solvent (sold in auto parts stores). This lubricant will also take the squeaks and groans out of the hinges.

WEATHERSTRIPPING

Don't wait until the rain is dripping into your car and the windows are difficult to move up and down before taking care of the weatherstripping. Instead, prevent it from cracking and tearing by applying a spray vinyl-and-rubber protectant every time you wash the car.

LOCKED BACK DOORS

Can't open a back door from the inside? Someone may have activated the child-safety lock. This tiny mechanical lever, hidden inside the jamb when the door is closed, is a special feature put on many cars to prevent small children from opening the door. Simply open the door from the *outside* and trip the lever to the open position.

Career advancement

1. Make yourself visible to the people who count; identify the influential people in your department or division (they may not be the ones with the formal power) and look for opportunities to work with them, even if it means extra hours.
2. When the boss is away, resist the temptation to slack off; work at your normal pace or even harder. You'll gain a reputation as a disciplined self-starter. If your boss gives you a job before he leaves, make it your business to have it completed upon his return. He'll be grateful for his lightened load.
3. People with contacts throughout the company have a better chance of promotion. Join in company-wide activities—the softball team, a charity drive, or the company picnic's planning committee.
4. Make your good work known to higher-ups by routing to them any complimentary letters you receive from customers or clients. If appropriate, include a cover memo with a good word about your boss and/or department. You'll make your team and yourself look good, and you'll reassure your boss that you're not trying to steal his spotlight.
5. Learn all you can about the business you're in. Don't limit your contribution to your own specialty.
6. Take night courses in a field outside your own discipline.

Career changes

1. What do you *really* like to do? You might be happy pursuing your hobby as a full-time career.
2. Which activities do you find most fulfilling? Do they involve working alone or with others? Solving new problems or making systems work? Negotiating or giving orders? The answers may help you find the ca-reer that you are best suited for.
3. Before leaving your company, ask the personnel department about jobs in other departments or divisions that you're qualified for.
4. If you want to investigate other fields, try to continue the work you've been doing on a part-time, freelance, or consultant basis.
5. Many colleges have programs geared toward older students, including those who work full-time. Some give credit for life experience (see *Continuing education,* p. 56).
6. If you're thinking about a new profession but you're not sure it's right for you, do volunteer work in the field to find out more about it.

❯Car fires

If you suspect a fire, pull off the road and turn off the ignition and lights; in so doing, you stop the flow of gas and electricity, which may be enough to stop the fire.

Get everybody out of the car. If the fire is near the gas tank, stay at least 500 feet away and warn approaching cars and pedestrians of the danger.

Call the fire department or emergency service (or ask a passing motorist to do so). Do not open the car's hood or try to fight even a small fire yourself.

IN THE PASSENGER COMPARTMENT

Every car should have a 2½-pound dry-chemical fire extinguisher (rated for class A, B, and C fires) to fight small interior fires that might be caused by a stray ash or an electrical malfunction. Keep the extinguisher *in* the car, under the front seat or in the glove compartment. In the time it would take to retrieve the extinguisher from the trunk, the fire could be out of control.

❯Car hoods

If the hood of your car suddenly flies up, don't slam on the brakes in panic; slow down carefully and pull off the road as soon as possible. Steer the car by sticking your head out the window or peeking through the opening between the hood and the dashboard. (It's a good idea to prepare for this emergency in advance by opening your hood to see which is the better vantage point.)

If the hood latch is broken, not just improperly closed, tie the hood shut with a piece of rope and get it fixed immediately.

Car horns

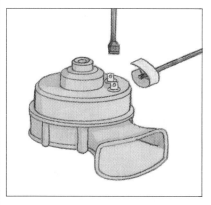

If your horn won't stop blowing:
1. Shut off the engine, open the hood, and locate the horn—the noise will guide you!
2. Disconnect or cut the wires leading to the horn and tape the exposed metal ends.
3. If you can't get at the horn wires and know where the fuse box is, pull the fuse.
4. Or *temporarily* disconnect the ground wire from the battery; reconnect before starting up the car.

Car jacks

It's best to jack up a car on level, firm ground. If you must do so on a slope, put large rocks or wedges on the downhill side of the tires.

In an emergency you can use a hubcap or wheel cover to support a jack on soft ground. Many newer cars don't have hubcaps, however, and others have wheel covers made of plastic or thin metal that may be ruined by such use. (Still, a wheel cover may be a small price to pay to get back on the road.)

A better solution is to carry a cou-

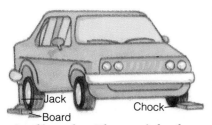

Jack

Board

Chock

ple of boards with you. Ask a lumberyard for scraps of ¾-inch wood: one about 1½ feet square to use as a base under the jack and another, about 6 x 8 inches, to use as a chock for the tire diagonally opposite the one being changed, to prevent the car from rolling off the jack. (If you're caught without a chock on the road, you can use a brick or a rock.)

Carpenter ants

These ⅜-inch pests don't eat wood as termites do, but they can still do serious damage to a house. They tunnel into moist wood, making complex nests. Deep inside, the queen lays vast numbers of eggs. The workers range afield gathering food for her and her offspring.

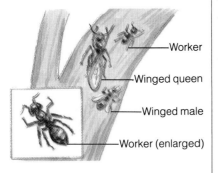

Worker

Winged queen

Winged male

Worker (enlarged)

The ants' presence is a warning that you have rotting wood in the basement, attic, or under floors. To find their nest, look for piles of sawdust left outside the entrance holes.

Drill deep, sloping holes above the infested area and, with a hand duster (see *Ants*, p. 10), blow a commercial insecticidal dust or boric acid powder inside. Effective ant bait is also available; look for the kind that contains disease virus—the workers carry it in to feed (and infect) the queen and the young.

Then see to replacing the faulty wood. To discourage future infestation, clear away wet and rotting wood in the yard, including tree stumps. Inspect all firewood before bringing it into the house; ants may hitchhike under the bark.

Carpenter bees

Carpenter bees, which bear a resemblance to big bumblebees, have a nasty habit: they bore tunnels into wooden doorframes, windowsills, outdoor furniture, siding, and the face boards of porches.

To control the pests, look for piles of sawdust under their entrance holes, which are about ½ inch in diameter. When you see a bee emerge from the hole, squirt it with rubbing alcohol from a hand pump sprayer. It kills quickly.

To repair damage to wood, first blow diatomaceous earth into the hole to flush out the insects. Then seal the hole with caulking compound or wood putty.

Carpets

1. To even out carpet wear, rearrange your furniture occasionally, redirecting the flow of traffic. Use scatter rugs in front of favorite chairs. Turn throw rugs and area rugs regularly.

2. To revive the dents left by furniture legs, hold a steam iron about 6 inches above the spot until the fabric is moist. Then work the fibers back and forth with the edge of a large coin or the back of a comb. Prevent such dents by shifting furniture a few inches often.

3. Prevent static shock by spraying carpets with a solution of 1 part liq-

uid fabric softener to 5 parts water. The solution can also be applied with a sponge or cloth.

4. To revive the color of a rug, first vacuum; then, using a sponge or cloth, apply a solution of 1 part white vinegar to 3 parts boiling water. Dampen only the nap, taking care not to wet the backing. When the rug is dry, rub it lightly with dry bread crumbs, then vacuum.

5. To make your own rug shampoo for nylon or other synthetic-fiber rugs, add 1 tablespoon ammonia and a generous amount of mild detergent to a large bowl of warm water; mix vigorously, preferably with an egg beater, to make suds. Rub the suds lightly over the carpet, let dry, then vacuum.

6. Cornstarch can also act as a rug cleaner. Sprinkle it on, let stand for 5 to 30 minutes, then vacuum.

7. To deodorize a carpet, liberally apply baking soda (4 or 5 pounds for a 9- x 12-foot rug). Let stand for at least 15 minutes (overnight for strong odors), then vacuum.

Carpet stains

Scrape off any solids. Blot up liquids quickly, dabbing lightly with a clean white towel or paper towel.

1. To remove greasy stains, apply a nonflammable dry-cleaning agent to the spot with a white towel; work from the edges toward the center. Don't scrub; dab gently until the spot comes clean. (Always pretest any cleaning agent on an inconspicuous part of the carpet and let it dry before continuing.)

Coat less stubborn greasy stains with aerosol shaving cream or carbonated water. Use a hair dryer to speed drying, then vacuum.

Or sprinkle a greasy stain with baking soda, cornstarch, cornmeal, or talcum powder. Leave on at least 6 hours, then vacuum.

2. To remove water-soluble stains, apply some detergent solution (½ teaspoon mild detergent per pint of water), working from the edges to the center of the stain. Place several layers of white tissues or paper towels over the spot and weight down with books or pots and pans; let stand about 1 hour. Replace with fresh tissues or towels and leave overnight. Then fluff up the carpet pile with your fingers.

3. To remove excrement, urine, or vomit stains, try this: After scraping off the solids, apply a detergent solution (½ teaspoon mild detergent per pint of water) and blot. Then use an ammonia solution (1 tablespoon per cup of water) and blot. Follow with a solution of equal parts white vinegar and water (pretest on an inconspicuous place; vinegar can remove some dyes). Blot, flush with water, and blot again.

Carpools

Carpooling saves money and time (many highways have high-occupancy-vehicle, or HOV, lanes), and many employers offer preferential or free parking to carpool vehicles.

FINDING A CARPOOL
1. Check with your employer to see if a service exists to match up employees with convenient carpools. If not, perhaps you could start one. Some employers provide company vehicles for carpools, and some will arrange transportation home in case of an emergency.
2. Call your county government or regional transportation agency to see if either one offers computerized carpool matchups.
3. Watch for highway signs with a central carpooling number to call.

CARPOOL RULES
To keep all members of a carpool happy, it's important to have a few ground rules: Music or not? If so, what type? Air conditioner on or off? Smoking or not? What if a person is always late? What about annoying personal habits—nonstop talking, whistling or humming, backseat driving, and so forth? Deciding on these issues beforehand goes a long way toward making a carpool peaceful and pleasant.

Car registrations

It's a good idea to order duplicates of your car registration card. Keep one at home in case the original is lost, and give one to each person who drives the family car.

Regulations vary from state to state on what you must do to obtain a replacement. Call the department of motor vehicles; find out if it's necessary to appear in person or if you can apply by mail.

Carrots

Mix a packet of carrot seeds with a cup of *unused* coffee grounds. Not only does the extra bulk make the tiny seeds easier to sow, but the coffee aroma is said by some gardeners to repel root maggots and other pests, too.

You can also add a few radish seeds to the blend. While the carrots may take 3 weeks to sprout, the radishes will be up in a matter of days to mark the rows. When you harvest the radishes, you'll be thinning the carrot seedlings and cultivating the soil at the same time.

Car security

1. Etch your automobile's identification number onto each window, including the sunroof. (Etching kits are available from the car's manufacturer, or your car dealer can do it for you.)
2. Don't leave valuables visible in the car.
3. Sharply turn the front wheels of the car to lock the steering wheel. Set the shift lever in *Park* on an automatic-transmission car; on a manual, leave the car in gear. Engage the parking brake.
4. Close all windows tightly, including the sunroof. Lock the car and pocket the key, even if you're only stepping away for a few minutes or you're parked in your own driveway.
5. Vary your routines—don't park in the same place every day, for the same length of time. Whenever possible, park your car in the middle of

a block so that it will be more difficult for a thief to tow away.
6. When leaving your car in a public lot or garage, give the attendant only the ignition key; don't say how long you'll be gone.
7. Avoid parking in a low-traffic, dimly lit area, such as the remote sections of a shopping mall, where a thief can work undetected.
8. Whenever you are traveling out of state, pack up any valuables and take them inside at night. Your license plates are a signal to potential thieves that your car may have salable contents.
9. Special locks, alarms, and assorted disabling devices are among the many antitheft devices available for cars today. Invest in one—and use it regularly (especially if you have a new or desirable car).

Carsickness

If you're prone to carsickness, get plenty of rest before you set out on an automobile trip. Eat a light, easy-to-digest meal and wear comfortable, light clothing.

To be on the safe side, carry waterproof plastic or paper bags (such as restaurant doggie bags) and a damp washcloth or premoistened towelettes.

Take along bland food and beverages: unbuttered popcorn, crackers or vanilla cookies, water, juice, or such nonsweet carbonated drinks as ginger ale and club soda.

Sit in the front seat and turn on the air conditioner to keep heat and humidity low. (Both are factors in motion sickness.)

If disaster seems imminent, open a window and breathe deeply. (See also *Airsickness*, p.9.)

❯Car-starting problems

1. Check the fuel gauge to make sure there's gas in the tank.
2. Try the headlights. If they seem dim or don't work at all, the battery may be either weak or dead. While this is a problem that usually occurs in winter, it can happen at

any time (see *Car batteries*, p.35).

If the battery is weak but not completely dead, you may be able to start a car with a manual transmission by getting it pushed; the working car should have bumpers the same size and height as your car's.
3. If nothing happens when you turn the key and the car has an automatic transmission, be sure the shift lever is firmly in *Park* or *Neutral*. Jiggle the shift lever in each position as you try to start the engine. If it then starts, you probably have a faulty safety switch; take the car in for service soon.
4. If you flood the engine trying to start the car (you'll smell gasoline), wait 5 minutes; then hold the accelerator to the floor and crank the starter 10 seconds. If this doesn't work the first time, wait at least 5 minutes and repeat the procedure. Never pump the pedal; you'll only flood the engine more.

› Car warning lights

OIL-PRESSURE LIGHT

If your car's oil-pressure light stays on longer than a moment as you start up or if it glows steadily as you drive, turn off the engine. This light is a warning that you may not have enough oil to lubricate the engine—a condition that can cause serious damage very quickly.

Check the oil level; add oil if it's needed. If the oil is at the correct level or the light stays on after you add oil, the problem probably is the light circuit. To be on the safe side, have the car towed to a gas station.

ALTERNATOR LIGHT

If the alternator light goes on, the battery is expending more energy than it is receiving; don't shut off the engine—you may not be able to restart it. Turn off any unnecessary electrical equipment and drive to a service station. In the meantime, keep an eye on the temperature gauge. If the car overheats, pull off the road to stop. (See also *Car brakes*, p.36.)

Cats

1. If your cat acts like an unwelcome alarm clock, feed it before you go to bed. Or install a bird feeder outside a window well away from your bedroom; your pet may become mesmerized by the birds and let you sleep.
2. In winter cats like to snuggle up in a warm place, such as a car engine. You might save your pet's life by banging on the hood or honking the horn before starting up.
3. Run a damp cloth along your cat's coat to pick up shedding hair. Or try your vacuum with the brush attachment; some cats love it.
4. To discourage your cat from jumping on beds, sofas, and other pieces of furniture, squirt it gently with a water pistol each time you spot it in a place that's off-limits.
5. A pine log makes a good scratching post. For toys, try balled-up aluminum foil, Ping-Pong balls, old knotted socks, paper bags, empty thread spools, and plastic pill bottles filled with rice. Avoid string, thread, yarn, and rubber bands—your cat may swallow them.
6. A clean cardboard box can serve as a cat bed. Cut an opening into one side for easy access. Then for comfort and warmth, line the box with a pillow, blanket, or towel.
7. To help prevent hair balls, add a teaspoon of bacon fat or vegetable oil to one meal daily.
8. To keep your cat from licking or biting at its wounds, isolate its head by securing a circular cardboard collar around its neck.

9. Trouble getting that pill down your cat's throat? Coat it with butter first. If the medicine is liquid, use an eyedropper to squirt it into your pet's throat.

Caulking compounds

1. Foam-rubber weatherstripping (actually made of vinyl or neoprene) is a good substitute for conventional caulking. Often sold as foam tape, it comes in square, rectangular, or round strips. Use a thin wood shim, a large screwdriver, or a dull putty knife to pack the strips into cracks and gaps.

Other usable materials include strips of Styrofoam (polystyrene), fiberglass insulation, and cotton rope. Seal holes and oddly shaped openings with wads of aluminum foil or well-chewed sugarless bubble gum.
2. When faced with cold-weather caulking chores, leave the caulk cartridges indoors, near a heating source, until ready for use. On extremely cold days you can wrap a household heating pad around the caulking gun. Set the control on *Low*. The surface to be caulked should be heated too; use a heat lamp, heat gun, or large floodlight.
3. Save the small plastic tip that you cut off a new caulking cartridge; it makes a perfect plug to seal a partially used cartridge. Insert it pointed end first into the

nozzle and cover with masking tape.

4. For a neat job of caulking around countertops, plumbing fixtures, and other interior surfaces, start by outlining the caulking area with masking tape. Apply a bead of caulking and smooth it with the back of a plastic spoon. Wait for it to get tacky (about 10 to 20 minutes) and remove the tape.

5. To apply caulking in hard-to-reach areas, use a length of clear plastic tubing. Force the tubing over the open nozzle of the caulking cartridge and secure it with duct tape. Hold the tubing as you would a pencil while you squeeze the caulking gun's trigger.

Ceilings

1. Acoustic ceiling tiles offer a decorative way to conceal an unsightly ceiling. Those that you staple in place are the simplest to install, but you must nail up furring strips first. A better solution is to install a complete system, in which a metal grid is fastened to the ceiling to hold the tiles.

2. A suspended ceiling is a good way to conceal wiring, pipes, and duct work. The panels can easily be removed to allow access for repairs. For a customized look, replace the drop-in panels with panels of hardwood-veneer plywood.

3. Wallpaper on the ceiling? Why not? First, patch all holes and cracks and remove peeling paint; then sand. Self-adhesive wallpaper makes the job easier. In any case, ensure a strong bond by pressing each wallpaper strip up against the ceiling with a clean, dry paint roller, working from the middle toward both ends.

4. It's hard to paint over water stains; they usually reappear within a few days. One solution is to seal the stained area with pigmented shellac or a stain-killing sealer before painting.

5. Use semigloss enamel for kitchen and bathroom ceilings; it's easier to clean than flat paint.

6. Wooden beams can lend a rustic charm to a living room that needs atmosphere. Fake beams of lightweight polyurethane foam are easy to install, and many look authentic. Or you can make your own beams using standard-dimension lumber. Screw a 1 x 4 mounting strip to the ceiling; then build a U-shaped box beam to fit snugly over it and nail it in place. For a weathered look, rough up the edges with a knife, chisel, or hatchet.

TEXTURED CEILINGS

1. The best way to clean ceilings that have a highly textured finish is with a vacuum cleaner; use the dust-brush attachment to avoid damaging the surface. Sweeping the ceiling will also work, but use only a soft-bristled floor brush.

2. Here's how to remove dust from small areas, such as those around light fixtures, that attract dust. Remove the crusts from several slices of fresh, doughy white bread, roll the bread into a ball, and roll the ball along the dusty surface.

Cellulite

If the skin on your thighs, knees, or buttocks looks dimpled—even if you aren't overweight—you have cellulite. Your best bet is a well-balanced diet and regular exercise—

Flex right foot; raise and lower top leg 10 times. Repeat with foot pointed.

Flex foot; raise and lower left leg 10 times. Repeat with foot pointed.

LOOK BEFORE YOU LEAP

Cellulite scams

Purveyors of expensive "solutions" to the cellulite problem sometimes say that the culprit is a different kind of fat from the stuff that is found elsewhere on your body. Or worse, that the condition is caused by "toxic" fat—a sort of swamp of suet trapped in abnormal, chronically inflamed tissue through which blood and lymph fail to flow as they should.

In fact, cellulite is caused by normal fat laid down unevenly under thin skin. The chief cause is heredity, which determines whether—and where—normal fat is to be deposited.

There is no sure cure for the condition, and no proof that special creams, scrubbers, or massage have any effect. Surgical liposuction may remove fat, but it may also create or worsen skin dimpling. If you have it, you probably have it for life, though you can improve the appearance of cellulite-dimpled skin.

Avoid "cures" designed to release the nonexistent "trapped toxins." Saunas to sweat them away, electrical devices to loosen them, crash diets to melt them, and body-wrapping tapes—all are equally ineffective.

to reduce body fat and to tone the skin. (The more fat you have, the more dimpling there will be.)

DIET

Avoid crash diets; when you regain the weight, your skin may stretch, making cellulite worse. Instead, cut back on fatty and salty foods and add fiber to your diet. Drink six to eight glasses of water daily.

EXERCISE

Aerobic exercise is best, especially walking and swimming. Spot calisthenics (p.41) may tone and shape problem thighs. Do 10 repetitions with each leg for each exercise.

Chair substitutes

You're having a party, but you have more guests than chairs. Aside from asking your neighbor for a loan, what else can you do?

1. Stacked two or three high, floor pillows can make a person feel like a raja. They stand up to hard use if you cover them with nylon, densely woven cotton such as corduroy, or other upholstery-weight fabrics.

2. For a children's party, make a picnic bench by nailing a 1 x 12 plank to two sawhorses or wooden crates. To prevent splinters, sand the board and cover it with a blanket or adhesive plastic, such as Con-Tact.

Or turn sturdy metal or plastic wastepaper baskets over; pad each "seat" with a towel or old throw pillow and decorate with crepe paper.

3. Don't forget the backyard. Patio chairs can be brought indoors and dressed up with pillows.

4. Use a coffee table for dining. With colorful placemats adding a festive touch, guests won't mind sitting on the floor (or on cushions). Let your guests know your plans beforehand so that they can dress appropriately.

5. Rent folding chairs.

Chandelier cleaning

You don't have to take a chandelier apart to clean it. First, turn the light fixture off and let it cool. Then cover the light sockets with plastic sandwich bags and secure with rubber bands or twist ties. Cover half the chandelier with a plastic sheet and spread another sheet on the floor. Spray the uncovered half with window cleaner or a commercial chandelier cleaner and carefully wipe each piece clean. Repeat for the other half.

A quicker, easier way: Liberally spray the chandelier with a solution of 2 teaspoons rubbing alcohol in 1 pint water, then let it drip dry over a plastic sheet.

Chapped lips

The skin on your lips is much more sensitive than the rest of your face; it cracks easily in cold air, sun, or wind. When this happens, resist the temptation to pick the peeling skin.

PREVENTION

1. Even though licking your lips seems to provide relief, resist the temptation; they're more likely to chap as they dry.

2. Apply a lip ointment at night; during the day use one that contains a sunscreen.

3. When reapplying lipstick, don't wipe off the old coat; doing so can cause irritation. At night gently remove traces of lipstick with petroleum jelly or cold cream.

Charcoal starter

Try this ignition sleeve for surefire charcoal lighting: First, punch holes around the lower edge of a clean gallon can with a beer-can opener; then remove both ends of the can. Punch two holes at the top and attach a handle of coat-hanger wire.

Set the sleeve in the barbecue and place one or two sheets of loosely wadded newspaper inside. Fill the sleeve with charcoal briquets and light the newspaper through the punched holes at the bottom. When the coals are aglow, lift the sleeve from the barbecue with tongs, leaving the burning coals behind. You can also use a 1- or 2-pound coffee can and surround

it with briquets; they'll light after the sleeve is lifted from the hot coals.

Or you can fill a milk carton with briquets and light it at the bottom. The briquets will be aglow by the time the carton burns away.

Checkbook balancing

Balance your checkbook as soon as your statement arrives. You have a limited time to notify the bank of any errors.

1. Compare each check with the statement, put the checks in numerical order, and mark them off in your checkbook.

2. Add up those checks that haven't cleared. Subtract this total from the bank's total, then add any deposits not on the statement.

3. Deduct any service charges from your checkbook total; add any interest payments.

If your checkbook and statement don't balance, try subtracting the smaller number from the larger. If the result can be divided by 9, you've probably transposed figures—written 142 instead of 124, for example. If you still don't come out even, recheck your math (see *Computations*, p.54).

Checks

Although banks resist substitutes, anything you can write on and take to the bank can serve as a check: a blank sheet of paper, a napkin—even a coconut—will do as long it's dated, says "Pay to the order of ------," names a dollar amount, includes the bank's name and the account number, and is correctly signed. (In all probability, a bank will charge a "special handling fee" for such a check.)

If you run out of checks, the bank can give you blanks while you wait for a new order.

SECURITY

Fill out checks carefully. Write the amount of the check tight against the $ sign; don't leave room between the figures. On the middle line, start writing at the far left; draw a line through any space before the word *dollars*. When depositing a check, write "for deposit only" with your endorsement.

BOUNCED CHECKS

Try to find a bank that will telephone when you risk an overdraft, so that you can cover the amount with a quick transfer of funds.

Avoid overdraft fees by taking advantage of the "ready credit" many banks extend to qualified customers. Instead of bouncing, the check becomes a loan against your credit. (But beware: the interest rate is high and nondeductible.)

STOPPING PAYMENT

Call the bank, give all details about the check, then confirm the stop-payment order in writing within 14 days. The bank will send you a form to fill out for their files. You must pay for each order.

DATING CHECKS

Most banks don't execute checks until the date written on them, and many will refer back to the payer before honoring a check that is more than 6 months old. However, many large banks don't examine the dates written on checks under $500 or $1,000.

Cheese grater

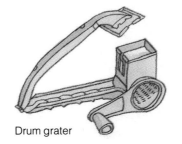

Drum grater

1. To avoid skinning your knuckles, use a hand-held cheese grater with a drum and turning crank.

2. In a pinch you can use a strong four-pronged fork as a cheese grater; just scrape away. Or place small cubes of Parmesan or other hard cheeses in a blender or food proces-

sor and buzz for a few seconds.

3. Brush a little cooking oil (or spray a little nonstick cooking spray) on a grater before using it; cleaning it will be a breeze. Keep an old toothbrush handy to scrub off any cheese that clogs the holes.

Chewing gum

1. To remove chewing gum from a rug or carpet, harden it with an ice cube and scrape it off with a dull knife. To avoid wetting the rug, put the ice in a plastic bag.

2. To remove gum from hair, work a little cooking oil or peanut butter into the gum and hair, then pick or comb the gum out. Or harden the gum with ice and "crack" it off the hair. Follow with an oil treatment.

Chicken cutlets

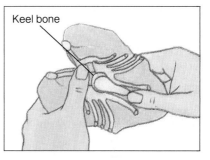

Keel bone

1. Don't give up if your favorite recipe calls for chicken cutlets and the store is out of them. Sliced turkey breast, pork scallops, or veal scallops are equally delicious in virtually any chicken dish.

2. Cutlets are expensive. Invest in a 6-inch boning knife and save money by boning chicken breasts yourself. First, wash and dry the chicken breast and place it, skin side down, on a cutting board. Cut down the center to expose the dark, spoon-shaped keel bone and the white cartilage.

With one thumb at the top of the bone and the other thumb at the base, bend the breast back until the bone snaps. Running your fingers under the cartilage and keel bone, pull out the bone.

Insert the tip of the boning knife

under the first long rib and gently free the meat from the bones, letting your knife slide flat along the rib cage. Repeat on the other side.

Pull up the wishbone and cut it free, slicing close to the bone. Cut the breast in half down the center and remove the white tendons underneath. Finally, pull off the skin and slice the cutlets. Freeze the surplus chicken and make stock with the bones.

Chicken pox

1. To relieve the irritating itch, apply calamine lotion to the affected areas of the body.
2. Or try a cool bath with several handfuls of baking soda or oatmeal in the water.
3. Smooth on aloe vera gel (slice a freshly cut aloe leaf lengthwise, or buy the gel in a health food store).
4. To keep children from scratching, put mitttens on their hands.
5. In severe cases, ask a doctor for an antihistamine prescription.

Children's crafts

Many household throwaways can be turned into children's crafts.

PUPPETS
Paint faces on worn socks for hand puppets; cut the fingers off old knit gloves for finger puppets.

For a milk carton puppet, cut off the carton top and slice the carton across the middle on three sides. Cut finger holes in the back. Make puppet hair and faces with yarn or markers, and glue on paper cutouts as ears.

VASE
Cover an empty bottle completely with irregularly torn pieces of masking tape. Rub over the surface with a crayon or wax shoe polish.

SPACE HELMET
Remove the bottom of a 1-gallon plastic milk jug and cut a face hole in the side. Make a cardboard visor with openings for the eyes; attach it to the helmet with bobby pins or

paper clips or, better still, a staple gun. Decorate with pipe cleaners, paper cutouts, and twist ties wound around the bottle's neck.

SPACESHIP
Cut one of the top flaps of a cardboard box into a T-shaped handle; remove the other flaps and cut them into the shape of tail fins. Glue fins on the sides; add buttons and bottle caps for a control panel; and attach paper cups or the rolls from toilet paper or paper towels for rocket exhaust pipes.

ETCHINGS
Save plastic-foam meat trays. Trace a picture on the tray and rub paint over the surface. Press a piece of paper onto the tray and lift it off.

FURRY ANIMALS
Draw an animal's outline on dark construction paper and fill in with white glue. Stick on plastic-foam packing beads, then spray-paint. Color individual beads for features.

TREASURE CHEST
Glue magazine pictures onto an old lunchbox, overlapping them to create a collage.

Milk carton puppet

Children's friends

1. Don't worry if your child is content with just one or two friends— we can't all be social butterflies. But if he's concerned, you can help

by making your home an inviting place for young people to gather.
2. If your child's "best friend" is "stolen" by a third child, help her realize that she shouldn't restrict her attachments, that she should get along with lots of people.
3. Young children sometimes invent imaginary friends—it's not a sign of mental instability but an indication of an active imagination. Don't squelch or ridicule it in your child; play along with it.
4. Even if you don't like how your child acts in the company of certain friends, don't criticize them. Consider inviting them into your home, feeding them, letting them sleep over, including them in family occasions. You will learn a lot about your child, and you will be able to show by example what kind of language and manners you find appropriate.

Children's parties

If you have qualms about giving a birthday party for an active 6-year-old, think about buying or hiring some of the vital party ingredients.

THE PLACE
Rent a room in a church or synagogue, YMCA, school, or day-care center. It will be more childproof than your home. In warm weather, have a picnic in a local park.

THE FOOD
Order in any or all of the food—pizza, fried chicken, birthday cake— or have the whole party handled by a professional caterer.

Take the guests out. Many fast-food and family restaurants provide birthday meals, including a decorated cake and special attention for the birthday child.

THE ENTERTAINMENT
Take the kids out to a movie, the zoo, a hockey game, a park where they can play softball or Frisbee, the ballet, or a skating rink. Lead them on a hike; take them bowling, fishing, or swimming.

Please come to a party for Evan. April 5, 1-3 Evan's house. R.S.V.P.

INVITATIONS

You can buy invitations, of course, but you and your child may enjoy making them together so that you can build up anticipation for the party. One simple design is illustrated above.

If sending by mail, make sure a cutout invitation fits your available envelopes. Or make fold-over invitations and seal them with stick-on dots (available at stationery stores in many colors). Use extra dots as "balloons" next to each address.

Children's quarrels

There's no doubt about it: young children enjoy fighting with their sisters and brothers. And children who learn to handle such quarrels may be better able to deal with challenges outside the home. Even so, you may wish to promote peace.

Don't even try to mediate routine squabbling—you probably won't be able to figure out who started it anyway. But if a fight sounds serious or if a child is being physically hurt, don't hesitate to separate the combatants. If a fight breaks out in the car, pull over, explain that you can't drive when you are being distracted by fighting, and park until the children are quiet.

Do try to understand the big picture of why the children fight and make adjustments as necessary. Is one of the children insecure? (Perhaps he needs a bit more time alone with a parent.) Do fights tend to erupt before suppertime? (Maybe they're just hungry.) Are they bored? (Try to keep them busier with more activities.) Do you need a few new rules? (No hitting; hands off Sally's toy cars!)

Do call a family meeting to draw up a list of rules of behavior that everyone agrees to live by.

1. Require two squabbling siblings to wash a window—one on the inside, the other on the outside—making faces at each other as they work.

2. Request a written report on the fight from each of the combatants. Write a response to each report.

3. Ask the combatants to imagine three better ways to settle an argument. Post the suggestions on the refrigerator and refer to the list when the next fight erupts.

Chili peppers

1. Wear rubber gloves when handling jalapeño, serrano, or other hot peppers. Never rub your eyes; oils in the peppers can irritate and burn your skin.

2. To peel fresh chili peppers, first roast them under a broiler or on a long fork over a gas flame. Turn often until the skin is charred all over, then immediately seal in a plastic or brown paper bag for 15 minutes. The skin will peel off easily under cold running water.

Chimneys

1. To prevent chimney fires, clean your fireplace chimney at least once a year and your wood-burning stove chimney at least twice a year. In both types, a buildup of materials (chiefly creosote) can pose a real danger. Most hardware stores carry chimney brushes; be sure to get the right size for your flue. Or you can hire a professional chimney sweep for a small fee. In some communities the fire department will clean the chimney of your wood-burning stove for free.

2. An open-top chimney is an invitation for trouble. Block out bats, birds, squirrels, and other animals with a chimney screen. Use a square of ½-inch galvanized steel mesh. With tin snips, cut out the corners to form a cross with four equal sides, as shown. Fold up the sides to make an open-ended box and wire the edges together. Then push the screen you've created, open end down, into the flue. Not only will it keep out animals, but it will also block airborne cinders and sparks—an especially important consideration for a home that has a cedar-shingle roof.

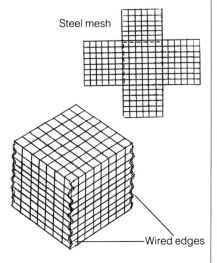

Steel mesh

Wired edges

Chipped porcelain enamel

1. To conceal nicks and scratches, use specially formulated porcelain paint. First, scrub the damaged area thoroughly to remove all traces of soap and grease. Then wipe with nail polish remover and let dry before applying the paint.

2. Repair large chips and cracks in a porcelain fixture with two-part epoxy resin designed for the job. When you can find it in the right shade, this does two things: it patches the surface and colors it to match the fixture.

First, scrub the area around the blemish with fine-grit emery cloth to remove all rust and soap deposits. Then, using a clean cloth, wipe with nail polish remover. Next, mix the resin and hardener and add the color (provided with the epoxy) until it matches the fixture. Using a single-edge razor blade, fill the crack with the epoxy compound.

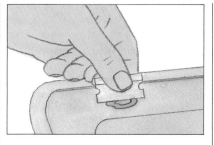

Pour alcohol on your finger and—using a very light touch—smooth the repaired surface.

Chocolate

Nothing but cocoa in the cupboard, and you need an ounce of unsweetened baking chocolate? No problem! Just blend 3 level tablespoons unsweetened cocoa powder with 1 level tablespoon vegetable shortening. (For an ounce of semisweet baking chocolate, use the same mixture with 3 tablespoons sugar.)

Chocolate stains

Blot up or scrape off the excess chocolate. Apply a solution of ½ teaspoon mild detergent in 1 pint water; blot with a clean white towel. If the stain remains, apply a solution of 1 tablespoon ammonia in 1 cup water; again blot with a clean white towel. If the stain *still* remains, use a 50-50 solution of white vinegar and water, then blot again. If the stain is on a carpet, dry it by stacking several white towels over the spot and weighting them down with a heavy object. Let stand for several hours.

Cholesterol

You can protect your arteries and lower your risk of heart disease by maintaining a cholesterol level of 200 milligrams or less (per deciliter of blood).

But beware: Your cholesterol level may vary naturally by as much as 20 percent—that is, a test that shows a level of 200 milligrams may indicate a high of 240 or a low of 160. Also, lab results are commonly off by about 10 percent, which could make the difference between a borderline and a serious problem. To be sure, have at least three tests done and compare the results.

For many people, a change in diet is enough to correct high cholesterol levels. The basic dietary strategy is low fat (*very* low saturated fat), low cholesterol, and high fiber (see *Low-fat diet,* p. 130).

1. Restrict the total fats in your diet to 30 percent of your daily calories and the saturated fats to 10 percent. Instead of fatty beef, pork, and lamb, eat salmon, tuna, mackerel, and herring, whose unsaturated oils may reduce cholesterol.

2. Cook with monounsaturated and polyunsaturated fats. Sauté with olive oil; bake with safflower oil; use olive or safflower oil in salad dressings. Avoid palm and coconut oils and hydrogenated vegetable oils—all saturated, all used in canned and packaged foods.

3. Use low-fat dairy products. Nondairy creamers may contain more saturated fat than half-and-half does; put powdered skim milk in your coffee instead.

4. Consume no more than 250 to 300 milligrams of cholesterol per day—about the amount in a single egg—or 100 for every 1,000 calories you take in.

5. Increase your consumption of oatmeal, oat bran, apples, oranges, carrots, and broccoli—each contains a special kind of fiber that helps reduce cholesterol.

6. A regular exercise program may also help. If all else fails, drug therapy may prove effective.

Chopsticks

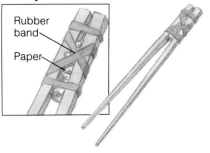

Rubber band

Paper

Do you find chopsticks unmanageable? Here's how to tame them: Wind a rubber band around the square ends, as shown, and slip a small wad of folded paper between them. Then slip a loop of the rubber band in front of the paper and you've created a hinge.

Chores

Start children young. Be patient, firm, and flexible. Praise generously as they do their share.

1. Ask the kids to help you make a list of what it takes to keep the household running smoothly, from cleaning the goldfish bowl to catching the dust "kitties" that gather behind the TV set.

2. Then parcel out the labor, considering everyone's skill levels, preferences, and outside commitments. Rotate the jobs everyone hates—and be sure to take your own turn.

3. Consign jobs that fall outside the weekly routine to a "chore jar," to be dipped into by family members in need of spending money. Write a job description and assign a "salary" for each chore.

Christmas trees

In general, balsam, Douglas, and Fraser fir trees retain their needles the longest; spruces, the shortest. Scotch pines are also long-lasting. Choose a tree with pliable needles and branches; test its freshness by dropping it on the cut end—few needles should come off.

To prolong your tree's freshness, saw off the bottom inch or two of the trunk and put the base in water as soon as possible. (Warm water will clean the sap off the cut and let the tree drink better.) Then spray the branches—be sure they are dry before you put on the decorations.

To help a tree absorb water better still, use a long drill bit to bore a hole up through the center of the trunk. Pack firmly with cotton balls; they'll act as a wick.

Keep the tree in the coolest part of the room, away from sunlight,

radiators, heaters, and fireplaces. When refilling the stand, use cool water with a few aspirins added. (See also *Christmas tree fireproofer*, p.390.)

If you buy a live potted tree, wrap wet towels around the root ball. Keep them moist. Protect the carpet, rug, or floor with a heavy plastic sheet. Keep the tree away from heat and drafts.

Chrome

1. Clean chrome with any of the following: club soda or seltzer, spray window cleaner, baking soda, vinegar (cider or white), or lemon peel. Or use a solution of 1 part clear ammonia to 16 parts water.

2. To remove insects from your car's bumper, rub with a soap-impregnated scouring pad moistened with cola. For rust spots, rub with crumpled aluminum foil.

Cigarette smoke

Allergic? Don't provide ashtrays. Politely explain your problem, then don't be afraid to get tough; ban smoking in your house, your office—and, of course, your car!

IF YOU SMOKE OR LIVE WITH A SMOKER

Buy special ashtrays that absorb smoke and stale odors, or invest in free-standing air purifiers. Better yet, install a permanent air ionizer or smoke filter and clean or replace its filtering mechanism regularly. Decorate with potpourris and houseplants (try the chlorophytum, or spider plant, said to be a natural air purifier).

FOR TEMPORARY TOBACCO ODORS

Before a party, set out bowls of vinegar or a mixture of 2 tablespoons ammonia in 1 cup water; their odor will help mask the smell of smoke. Burn scented candles; they will clear and perfume the air. Put solid room deodorizers near air vents or attach scented fabric-softener sheets over the grilles.

When your guests have gone, open the doors and windows and

whoosh out lingering smoke with a towel moistened with a vinegar-and-water solution. Turn on any exhaust fans and turn the air conditioner to *Vent*. Wash all ashtrays.

WHEN THERE'S SMOKE IN THE CAR

Empty the ashtrays after each use. Then put a layer of baking soda or pebbles in them to smother butts and ashes. Or make the ashtrays unusable; fill them with hard candy or tokens and change for tolls.

Clamps

1. A vise will stand in for clamps if you're gluing a small project. Protect your work from the jaws with plywood scraps. Another quick solution is locking-grip pliers; test the setting on same-size scrap.

2. Use weights—books or bricks, for example—to secure the joints of large projects such as bookshelves. Keep the work out of the way so that you don't accidentally knock it over.

3. Use a tourniquet to secure the corners of a newly glued drawer or the joints between rungs and chair legs. Canvas or heavy cotton fabric strips won't cut into your work as twine might. Stick a baton under the strip (a pencil will do) and twist it until the strip is taut. Tape one end to the strip to keep it tight.

4. For a homemade adjustable clamp, cut two 16-inch lengths of 2 x 3 hardwood. Drill two holes through each as shown—3 inches from one end and 9 inches from the other—both a bit larger than the diameter of a 12-inch-long machine

Adjustable clamp

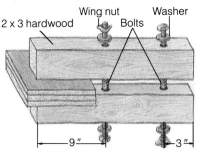

bolt. Insert two such bolts, one through each set of holes, using washers on both ends; the bolts should run in opposite directions. Secure with wing nuts. Position the open end of your clamp over the work and tighten the nuts.

Clams

1. Scrubbed clams will purge themselves of grit or sand if left an hour or so in cold salted water with a sprinkling of cornmeal.

2. To open clams, use a strong thin knife with a blunt rounded tip. Hold the clam in the palm of one hand and force the blade between the shells. Run the blade around the inner edge to sever both muscles, then twist it.

3. Here's a foolproof method for opening hard-shell clams that are to be cooked (not eaten raw): place them on a rack in a preheated 450°F oven; check often and remove each clam as soon as it opens.

Cleaning

1. Automatic-dishwasher detergent works well on refrigerators, stoves, floors, walls, and glass. Dissolve ¼ cup in 1 gallon of very hot water; wipe with a dry cloth afterward. Wear rubber gloves, and test first to make sure that what you're cleaning is colorfast.

2. Remove crayon marks from painted walls by scrubbing with toothpaste or an ammonia-soaked cloth. Rinse and dry.

3. Rubbing alcohol will clean the caulking around bathtubs; it also shines chrome and glass. Liquid chlorine bleach (¼ cup to a gallon of water) will also clean caulk.

4. Clean the toilet bowl while you're away by pouring in ¼ cup bleach and leaving it until you return. (Don't use bleach if you're already using a tank-held cleaner that's released when the toilet is flushed; the two may react chemically.) To avoid clogging and odors, pour 1 cup baking soda down the bowl weekly.

5. Can't get to that dirt in the corner? Make a pointed tool by cutting an old whisk broom at a 45° angle.

Clogged drains

First try a plunger (p. 159). If it fails, use a wrench to remove the plug on the bottom of the trap (or remove the trap itself) and try to dislodge the blockage with your fingers or a bent wire coat hanger. Don't forget to place a bucket under the trap before you open it.

Caution: Chemical drain cleaners are dangerous; they can burn your skin and damage the plumbing. If you use one and it fails to work, call a plumber—don't keep working on a drain with chemical cleaner in it.

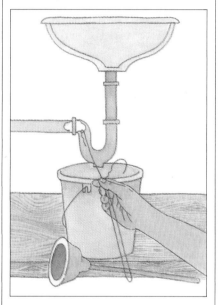

Clogged shower heads

If your shower has become erratic, spitting water in peculiar patterns, chances are that the openings in the shower head are clogged with mineral deposits.

Unscrew and disassemble the entire shower head, keeping the pieces in order for easy reassembly. Soak the parts in vinegar overnight, then scrub off the encrusted minerals with steel wool or a wire brush. Poke open the small holes in the faceplate with a pin.

Clogged toilets

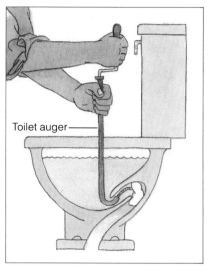

Toilet auger

1. If you think you can reach whatever is clogging your toilet, put on a rubber glove and try to fish it out. If necessary, reach in deeper with a bent wire coat hanger.

2. Next, try a plunger (p. 159). Give it several tries. If water rushes out, victory! Before flushing, pour in a bucket of water to make certain the toilet drains.

3. If the plunger fails, try a toilet auger, or snake—a tube enclosing a cable with a corkscrew on the end. Put the corkscrew end into the trap and crank the auger handle clockwise, forcing the cable around the bend of the trap as shown. When the tip bites into the blockage, continue cranking while pulling out the auger—the blockage should come with it. Or you may be able to break up the blockage by moving the auger handle back and forth.

Closet clutter

1. Use your closets for everyday things—not for long-term storage. If you haven't used an item for some time, get rid of it or store it in the attic.

2. Coats take up space; put them on a coat rack near the door.

3. Whenever you take a piece of clothing off a hanger, put the hanger in the center of the rod, where it

will be easy to find when needed.
4. To conceal open shelves at the top of the closet, install a decorative window shade.
5. To keep closets clean, dry, and fresh smelling, try placing open, empty perfume bottles or unwrapped bars of soap in them. Or make moth-repellent sachets from dried lavender, whole peppercorns, cedar chips, or a 50-50 mixture of dried rosemary and mint. (Try a pet store for cedar chips; a health food store should carry the others.) If you can't find sachet bags, make your own out of pantyhose, old clean nylons, or baby socks.

Closet doors

Want to hide unsightly or makeshift storage areas? Use your ingenuity to come up with decorative substitutes for closet doors.
1. Build shelves on bedroom walls and cover them with matching draperies. Or position handsome Japanese-style *shoji* screens at one end of a long room.
2. Hang bamboo or wooden roll-up blinds from the ceiling to conceal a Pullman kitchen. Or suspend a blind at the end of a long corridor and stow the ironing board and vacuum cleaner there.

Close-up photography

1. A cluttered background can spoil a close-up photo. One solution is to use a piece of black velvet or other solid-color fabric about 2 feet square. Drape it over unsightly dirt or branches to hide them; flowers, in particular, will stand out against the dark background.

Another alternative is a small wall mirror, angled to reflect blue sky as a background for flowers.
2. Inexpensive, lightweight alternatives to macro lenses and extension tubes are *close-up diopter lenses*. Like filters, they screw onto the front of a 35mm camera lens or onto a zoom lens. They come in a range of diopters, or magnifying powers: +1 allows a normal lens to focus on objects 20 inches away; +2 to about 13 inches. Coupling a +1 and +2 together yields a +3 diopter, focusing to about 10 inches.

Mirror angled to reflect sky

Clothes dryers

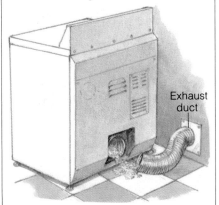

Exhaust duct

Dryer won't run? Check the plug, then the circuit breaker or fuse. Next, make sure that the electric or gas service hasn't been shut off.

The door safety switch may be stuck. This small button or lever, usually located in the rim of the opening, prevents the dryer from operating when the door is open. Jiggle it, then see if the dryer will run. If it doesn't, call for service.

DRYER FIRES
A dryer-related fire is usually caused by a dirty lint filter or exhaust duct or by drying such inappropriate items as foam-rubber pillows.

Keep the dryer door closed and shut the door to the room where it's located. Turn off the gas or electricity if possible. Call the fire department right away.

IF ALL ELSE FAILS
Speed up line-drying with a fan. A hair dryer works on thin fabrics, such as lingerie. If you have a hose-type hair dryer, slip a plastic dry-cleaner bag over the garment, put the hose in the bottom, and tie the bag around it. (See also *Hanging laundry*, p.104.)

Clothes shopping

You pay for the latest styles and for service in a department store. The markup is usually 100 percent—if the store pays $50 for a dress wholesale, you pay $100. Look for sales and end-of-season markdowns or try these alternatives:
1. Discount stores sell the current fashions (often without the manufacturer's label), but they provide few customer services. The markup is generally 65 to 70 percent; the $50 dress should cost about $85.
2. Off-price stores buy merchandise at the end of the manufacturer's selling season and may pay only $40 or so for the $50 dress. After a markup of 60 to 70 percent, you pay approximately $65.
3. Factory outlets sell leftovers, seconds, and some current styles. The policies vary, but that $50 dress probably would sell for $60 to $65.
4. Thrift shops or secondhand stores often sell quality clothing at the lowest prices of all. The asking price on the $50 dress you liked might only be $5 or $10.

Clothes washers

If the clothes washer doesn't run, check the plug first, then the circuit breaker or fuse. Next, see if both the hot and cold faucets are turned on. (Turn them off when the washer is not in use; constant pressure on the hoses eventually makes them leak.) Are the control switches properly set?

DRAINAGE PROBLEMS

1. If the washer isn't draining, the hose may be kinked or clogged—perhaps a sock has worked its way into the line. Refer to the owner's manual to see if you can correct the problem yourself.
2. There may have been a dip in voltage; wait 20 minutes for the motor to cool off and try again.
3. Otherwise, pull the plug, wring out the clothes, and bail or siphon out the water.

NOISY VIBRATIONS

1. Loud shaking during a spin cycle is usually a sign that the load is unbalanced, probably with bulky items. Stop the washer, rearrange the load, and continue the cycle.
2. Oversudsing can also cause such vibrations to occur. Use less detergent next time or switch to a low-suds soap.
3. Are the leveling legs properly set? If not, adjust them.

4. Is the drain hose secured? If not, tighten the clamp.
5. Inspect the floor under the machine; it may not be sturdy enough to give solid support.
6. If a new washer is noisy, look inside for packing materials that may have been left around the basket.

IF ALL ELSE FAILS

1. Fill a sink or bathtub with water and detergent. Imitate the washer's churning with a plunger.
2. Put white and colorfast cottons into a pot of simmering water and detergent for 15 minutes.
3. To remove excess water, wring out the clothes or place them on a towel on a firm surface and run a rolling pin over them. Roll delicate garments in a towel.

CLOTHING PROBLEMS

1. Undiluted chlorine bleach may damage fabric. Use it only as recommended on the container and by the washer manufacturer.
2. If there's lint all over your freshly washed clothes, you may be overloading your washer. Lint may also result from poor drainage (see above), too little detergent, undissolved granular detergent, or incorrect use of a fabric softener.

Clouds

Puffy white clouds sailing across a blue sky indicate continuing fair weather. But if they mass together to form tall, anvil-shaped clouds, be prepared for a lightning-filled thunderstorm, even if the sun is shining brightly.

Striped frosty clouds high in the sky indicate the probability of light rain; dark, layered clouds overhead mean steady rain or snow.

If you are ever lost at sea, look for the patches of stationary woolly clouds that usually form a little to the windward side of an island.

Clutter

1. Keep periodicals in baskets. Cull magazines and newspapers often; clip the recipes and articles you want to save and file them in folders labeled by subject.
2. Set out bedside baskets for reading material. Place dishes on bureaus to collect loose change, other pocket items, and jewelry.
3. Provide special bins for records, tapes, and games in rooms where the family relaxes; insist that users return these notorious clutter culprits to their "homes."
4. Throw out old medications and cosmetics. To keep bathroom countertops tidy, install bins for extra supplies—and any items that won't fit in medicine cabinets.
5. Outdoors, keep a plastic trash can in the garage or yard for playthings. Install pegboards in your garage or toolshed for gardening supplies and sports equipment.
6. Above all, "de-junk" your whole house. Room by room and in stages, go through all your possessions. Throw away, give away, or sell duplicates and anything else that you don't use or that is unusable.

Coasters

You can make your own coasters for furniture legs with the scrap ends of carpeting or cork samples from a flooring supply dealer. Nubby-textured carpet works best; it is more durable than plush or velvet and less expensive. Trace the shape from another coaster, then cut the coaster to size.

Cockroaches

Roaches lay their eggs in little brown satchel-shaped pouches that look like seeds. Look for the egg cases in dark, damp, warm places: under sinks, behind stoves and refrigerators, even in drapery pleats and inside curtain rods. Scrub them away or vacuum them up with the crevice nozzle of your vacuum cleaner and discard the dust bag.

To prevent infestation, dust cracks and crevices—especially under appliances, moldings, and cupboards—with boric acid, diatomaceous earth, or silica aerogel dust.

The most effective commercial

control is a bait that has hydramethylnon as the active ingredient. Place several bait traps in the kitchen and wherever roaches congregate; the pests are attracted to it, take some, and go off to die.

Coffee

1. Instant and freeze-dried coffees can taste and smell just like the real thing. The secret is to cover the cup or mug with a saucer after you've added the hot water, then let the brew steep for a full minute.
2. To preserve its fresh flavor, always store ground coffee in the refrigerator or freezer.
3. Freeze strong leftover coffee in ice cube trays. When you want a cup, put a couple of cubes in a mug, top up with water, and heat in a microwave.
4. Stretch a pound of coffee by adding 3 ounces of prepared chicory; it increases the yield by about 10 cups. If the pleasant bitterness of chicory suits your taste, add still more—up to half a pound.
5. Instead of decaffeinated coffee, try one of the coffee substitutes on the market. They are made from roasted grains, nuts, chicory, or dandelion root. Their taste can be mellowed by adding a vanilla bean to the grounds.

Coffee grinders

1. Grind only as many beans as you need each time you make coffee. For drip pots, including automatic coffee makers, grind them as fine as possible; for percolators, a coarse grind is better. Keep the grinder spotless, brushing out any stray bits of bean after each use.
2. While electric grinders do the fastest job, an old-fashioned metal or heavy ceramic mortar and pestle still gives the finest grind and will never break down or wear out. But be prepared to work hard; the process is slow and tedious.
3. Don't try grinding coffee beans in your blender or food processor; you'll more than likely dull and

bend the blades and possibly stall or burn out the motor.
4. In a pinch, wrap some coffee beans in a dish towel and pound them with a hammer. Use more beans than you ordinarily would—the "grind" will be quite coarse.

Coffeepots

1. Line a funnel or a strainer with a coffee filter (a white paper napkin, paper towel, or a double thickness of cheesecloth will do). Spoon in 2 level tablespoons of finely ground coffee for every 6 ounces of water, then set over a heatproof jar and pour the boiling water through.

Or simply use a jug or saucepan. First warm it with hot water and empty it; then spoon in the measured coffee. Pour in freshly boiled water, stir, cover, and allow to steep for about 4 minutes. Sprinkle drops of cold water on the coffee to get the grounds to settle.
2. You can serve Turkish coffee even without the traditional long-handled copper coffeepot. Grind the coffee beans—mocha is a good choice—to a very fine powder and spoon into a saucepan (1 heaping teaspoon per cup is about right). Add cold water and plenty of sugar and bring to a boil. Simmer until frothy, then serve in your smallest cups. Be sure to let the grounds settle in the cup before drinking.

Coffee stains

To remove a coffee stain from fabric or a rug, try one of these methods:
1. Dip a white cloth into a beaten egg yolk and rub the yolk into the

stain. Then rinse with clear water.
2. Work denatured alcohol into the stain, then rinse with water.
3. Apply a solution of ½ teaspoon mild detergent in a pint of water; blot with a white towel. If the stain remains, apply a 50-50 solution of water and white vinegar and blot.

Colds

1. If you think you're catching a cold, ask your doctor about taking zinc tablets to reduce its severity.
2. To relieve the dry throat that signals the start of a cold, dissolve 2 tablespoons of salt in 1 quart of very hot water; inhale the solution from a small dish or squirt it into your nose with an eyedropper.

THE FULL-BLOWN COLD
1. Take aspirin or an aspirin substitute for cold-related aches and fever. Give children under 18 acetaminophen (see *Aspirin*, p.12).
2. Rest as much as possible. Sleep helps recharge your immune system—and staying in bed prevents you from spreading your germs.
3. Avoid exercise; your strength and endurance are low, and you're more likely to injure a muscle. Exercising with a fever is especially dangerous because it can result in heat exhaustion.
4. Drink lots of fluids to replenish those you've lost. In addition to water, drink plenty of citrus juices; the acid they contain may make your throat inhospitable to the viruses causing your cold. Avoid colas, coffee, and tea; they contain caffeine, a diuretic that causes you to lose body fluids.
5. To soothe a sore throat and help shrink swollen tissue, gargle every 2 hours with a solution of ¼ teaspoon salt in 1 cup warm water.

NASAL CONGESTION
1. Saltwater nose drops may help relieve a stuffy nose. Boil ½ cup water, let it cool, and dissolve ¼ teaspoon salt in it.
2. If you prefer medicated nose drops or sprays, don't rely on them

for any longer than 3 days; longer use can cause the "rebound effect," which increases congestion.

3. Hot chicken soup helps dissolve mucus. In addition, the water and salt in the soup prevent dehydration, important when nasal tissue is unpleasantly dry.

4. A strong cup of peppermint tea has much the same effect. Pour 1 pint boiling water over ½ ounce dried leaves; steep for 5 to 20 minutes. (Adding honey helps soothe a sore throat.)

Cold-weather starting

If you're having trouble getting your car engine to turn over in cold weather, the problem is probably a weak battery. To forestall the problem, check your battery before cold weather sets in. At the same time, make certain that the clamps are securely connected and the terminals uncorroded.

To clean top-post battery terminals, first remove the clamps: loosen the bolts and twist the clamps

back and forth—you may even have to tap them lightly with a hammer before they'll move. Then plug the vent holes with a rag or cover them with masking tape. Scrub both the clamps and the terminals with a wire brush. Before you reattach the clamps, apply a thin coat of petroleum jelly at the connection to retard further corrosion.

To clean side-terminal batteries, loosen the retaining bolt until each cable comes off; clean all surfaces with a wire brush. Replace the cables and tighten the bolts.

If cold-weather starting is a constant headache, consider buying an engine heater (sold at auto parts stores). You can choose among several types; all plug into a standard 110-volt electrical outlet.

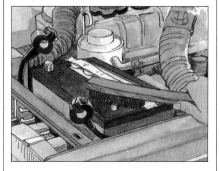

Colic

Some colicky babies seem to cry less if they sleep in a very quiet environment and are handled extremely gently. Others are soothed by monotonous sounds or motion, such as rocking.

Although not always convenient, a car ride is frequently effective treatment for a colicky baby. For times when this is impossible, many baby's accessories stores sell a small motorized device that attaches to the crib springs and simulates the vibration of a moving car.

Try giving the baby a fennel or anise solution. Boil 4 ounces water for 10 minutes; add 1 teaspoon fennel tea or aniseed and ½ teaspoon sugar; reboil for 1 minute, then strain into a bottle.

Collections

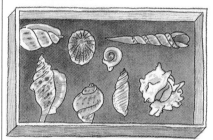

1. Look around the house to see if you already have the makings of a "pop culture" collection that can grow in value: *Star Wars* figures, teddy bears, theme glasses, or rock 'n' roll records. To add to your stock, check out flea markets and tag sales.
2. Pick a theme to organize a shell, rock, or pressed-flower collection: colors, interesting shapes, or geographic areas, for example.
3. A collection of small objects disappears against a white background. Paint shelf backs a dark color or line them with dark paper.

Small wooden flats—the kind that some nurseries still sell plants in—make attractive, if rustic, display frames. After cleaning, rub the sides with a furniture finishing oil and cover the inside with dark adhesive plastic, such as Con-Tact.
4. Stamps, coins, and antiques often grow in value, but they're easier to buy than to sell. Dealers seldom pay more than half the retail value.

College entrance

To improve your chances of getting into the college of your choice, consider the following strategies:

Start the process early. Sign up for the demanding classes that require extra work. College admissions directors are more impressed by good grades in difficult courses than by straight A's in easy ones.

Take as many advanced courses as soon as you can; you may even be able to skip some college courses as a result. Extra tutoring can help you bring up your grades and qualify for advanced courses.

Warm up for the college entrance

exams by taking them at least twice. You may raise your score by 25 percent. Cram courses and books of sample test questions may also help, but they're expensive.

College majors

How can you make the important decision of choosing a major when you haven't decided what you want to do with the rest of your life?

Begin your search by asking your guidance counselor for direction, by browsing through college catalogs, and by availing yourself of aptitude tests.

Ask yourself what broad area of study interests you the most. Is it the arts? The social sciences? Or the physical sciences?

When you get to college, take a variety of subjects in the area you're leaning toward. Use your electives to investigate other fields of study. By the time you must choose your major—usually not until the sophomore or junior year—you'll have a good idea of where your talents lie.

Consider taking some time off between high school and college to work in the field that interests you most. A teaching career, for example, can be evaluated first-hand by working as a teacher's aide. Or if you're attracted to a career in medicine, sign up for a job at your nearest hospital. You may not earn a lot of money, but the experience will help you size up the opportunities.

College tuition

1. The financial aid office at the college you apply to—as well as your high school guidance office—has information on all forms of help, including government programs.

Compile a list of all the grants and scholarships for which you may be eligible. Then apply to *each one*. Many scholarships go begging just because no one takes the trouble to apply. At the same time, check out all the loans that you or your family may be eligible for.

2. Consider the military alterna-tive. The Reserve Officers Training Corps (ROTC) pays tuition and other expenses in exchange for active duty in the armed services after graduation. The Army National Guard offers similar breaks.

3. Are you contemplating teaching as a career? Some states sponsor generous loan programs for those who agree to work in the public school system for a certain period of time after graduation.

4. Ask your parents to find out if their union, company, or fraternal organization offers scholarships for academic achievement.

5. No matter how much assistance you receive, your first stop after arriving on campus should be the student employment office; check its listings of part-time jobs on campus and with local companies.

Color in the home

The way colors are combined in a room sets a mood and sometimes creates illusions. Light colors on walls make a room seem larger; dark colors make it cozier. Reds, oranges, and yellows bring excitement and cheer; blues, greens, and purples are soothing and serene.

1. Start with the color of a favorite decorative element such as a rug, a chair, a vase, or even a painting. The simplest way to use that color is monochromatically—with shades or tints of the same hue.

2. You'd like more drama? Add other colors. Related colors (such as blue, blue-green, and green) yield natural harmony. Colors from opposite sides of the spectrum (red and green, perhaps) produce a complementary scheme that works best if one color predominates and the other provides accents. Since complementary colors are difficult to balance, test them out in smaller, proportional amounts first.

3. To ensure buying paints, wallpapers, fabrics, and carpets that coordinate, assemble a portable swatch book for each room. With each purchase, add a snippet large enough to show its color or mix of colors. Bear in mind that the colors in small or mat-finish samples will look darker in a big or sunny room.

4. Paint, stain, and home dyes can be mixed to the exact color you want. Paint can be custom-colored by the dealer, or you can mix "universal colorants" (sold in tubes at paint and art supply stores) and use the blend as the pigment for tinting white paint. Darker colors may require a tinted base paint.

Whichever color you use, test a small amount first. Don't judge it until it has had at least a day to dry. Then mix an ample supply—the color will be hard to duplicate.

5. Blend two or more commercial powders or liquid home dyes to create the exact shade you want. Fabric dyes work best on all sorts of natural fibers (cotton, linen, rayon, silk, wool, ramie), on nylon and acetate, and on blends. Polyester and acrylic do not accept dyes, but blends containing them will reach an even tint of the chosen hue, although not a deep shade.

Combs

1. To prevent static electricity, use a wooden comb.

2. In a pinch, use a plastic fork.

3. A hair pick works better than a comb for very curly hair, whether natural or permed. To provide lift for curly hair without a hair pick, use a comb handle, an unsharpened pencil, a pen, a toothbrush handle, or even a chopstick.

Comforters

A comforter is just a sandwich of fabric around a puffy filling. You can make one from two bed sheets and a fluffy blanket. You'll get the colors you want and can even match bedroom slipcovers or curtains.

The sheets should be at least 30 inches wider than your bed; stitch pieces together if necessary. Then cut the blanket an inch narrower and shorter than the sheets.

Put the two sheets together, right

sides facing, and sew up the sides and one end with ½ inch seam allowance. Lay the blanket on top, pin it to the seam allowance, and machine-baste in place.

Turn the assemblage right side out, turn in the raw edges of the remaining end, and stitch it closed.

To create tufts, push a large needle threaded with yarn through the layers and bring it up ¼ inch away. Double-knot the yarn and cut the ends. Repeat at regular intervals, working from the center outward.

Compass direction

To find your way without a compass, point your watch's hour hand toward the sun. South is a line equally dividing the smallest angle between the hour hand and 12 o'clock (1 o'clock during daylight saving time).

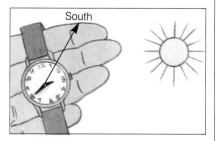

Compost bins

1. A 50-gallon drum makes a good compost container. First, remove both ends to make an open cylinder. Then set it upright in a corner of the garden and fill it gradually with compost material. When the drum is full, let the compost age for

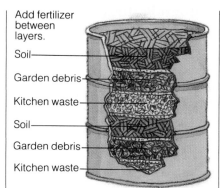

Add fertilizer between layers.

Soil
Garden debris
Kitchen waste
Soil
Garden debris
Kitchen waste

3 to 6 months, then lift it to release a pile of garden-ready humus.
2. In a small yard or on a rooftop or terrace, you can conceal compost neatly in odorproof plastic. Line a 30-gallon garbage can with a 33-gallon plastic bag. If the compost material is dry, such as autumn leaves, add a gallon of water and a pint of lawn fertilizer. Seal. The composting process should be complete in 3 to 4 months.

Compost material

1. Use your kitchen leftovers to feed your plants. Fill a compost bin gradually with alternating 6-inch layers of kitchen waste (no meat scraps, grease, or bones), garden debris (no weed seeds), and soil. Add a sprinkling of high-nitrogen fertilizer—a 10-6-4 formulation is ideal—to each layer. (A little lime will also help, but don't add it if you're going to use the compost to side-dress acid-loving plants such as azaleas.) Let the mixture age 3 to 6 months, dousing it regularly with a hose.
2. Such standard rural compost ingredients as animal manure and spoiled hay may be hard to come by for the average suburbanite. Look around your town for suitable industrial by-products instead: shredded cardboard and newspaper, weathered sawdust from the lumberyard, mill wastes of wool and silk, hair clippings from the barbershop. All can be prime fuel for the compost heap.

Don't use ashes from the barbecue, dog or cat droppings, or shred-

ded magazines; they may contain sulfur oxides, disease organisms, or inks that are bad for plants. And avoid cooking grease; it not only attracts animals but also slows the composting process.

Computations

Stuck without your trusty calculator? Here are a few easy ways to double-check your arithmetic.

ADDITION

A quick way to check your addition is to add up the digits in each number and then add up the digits in each sum; keep the process going until each number is reduced to single digit. Then add together the single digits above the line; their total should equal the single digit in your sum.

Example: $9,236 + 5,347 = 14,583$

$9+2+3+6=20$;	$2+0=2$
$5+3+4+7=19$	
$1+9=10$;	$1+0=1$
$1+4+5+8+3=21$;	$2+1=3$

It's even easier if you "cast out the 9's." Eliminate all 9's and digits adding up to 9—they (take this on faith!) don't affect the outcome.

Example: $9,236 + 5,347 = 14,583$

$\cancel{9}\ 2\ \cancel{3}\ \cancel{6} = 2$
$\cancel{5}\ 3\ 4\ 7 = 1$
$1\ \cancel{4}\ \cancel{5}\ \cancel{8}\ 3 = 3$

SUBTRACTION

To make sure you've subtracted correctly, add together the result and the number you subtracted—you should get the number you started with.

MULTIPLICATION

Divide the answer by one of the numbers being multiplied. You should get the other number.

DIVISION

Multiply the answer by the number you divided by; if you come up with the number you originally divided, you get an A!

Computers

When you can't get your computer to work, don't panic—the problem may be easy to remedy.

1. Check all cables and connections; one may have worked loose.

2. Did you turn everything on? the monitor? the printer?

3. Did you put a disk in upside down or backward? Quit the program and start it up again.

4. Did you skip a key step?

5. Is a special-function key in the wrong position?

6. If all else fails, refer to your user's guide.

DISKS

Treat your floppy disks with extreme care. Heat, fingerprints, magnetic sources (telephones, stereo speakers, televisions, motors), writing directly on or clipping something to a disk—all these things and more can destroy its contents.

FATIGUE

If you find it tiring to work (or play) at a computer for long periods of time, check these points:

1. Is the console placed too high, forcing your shoulders and upper arms into a strained position?

2. Is your chair the right height, with good support for your back?

3. Is there glare on the screen from the sun or room lighting, causing unnecessary eyestrain? (Wearing a visor may help if the problem is bright overhead lighting.)

Concrete floors

Here's how to remove dirt stains from a concrete floor: Spray with a garden hose and liberally sprinkle on scouring powder. Wait 20 to 30 minutes, then scrub with a stiff-bristled push broom. Rinse and sweep up the residue.

For grease or oil stains, cover with a layer of powdered portland cement and soak the powder with a solvent. Spread a sheet of plastic over the area and let stand overnight. The next day, sweep the powder away.

To make future cleaning easier, apply a liquid concrete sealer to the floor with a paint roller.

Constipation

Despite their popularity, laxatives and enemas are seldom the answer; they may even make constipation worse because many of them can be habit-forming.

1. Double your consumption of fiber-rich foods. But remember, all fiber is not the same. Wheat bran, whole-wheat bread, cereal, pasta, brown rice, and other whole-grain foods (except oats) contain the kind that works best on constipation. The fiber in oats, beans, apples, broccoli, and other fruits and vegetables helps somewhat less.

2. To get your system operating smoothly and help the fiber work, drink 1 to 2 quarts of water a day—at least a glassful with any whole-grain food. And take a daily half-hour walk, jog, or swim.

3. Whatever your normal pattern, don't ignore the urge to defecate; that in itself can cause constipation. So can antacids, diuretics, hypertension medication, or antidepressants.

Contact lenses

Many soaps leave an oily film on your hands that transfers to your lenses when you touch them. To check your soap, run a finger down a mirror after washing your hands. If you make a streak, use a different soap before handling your lenses.

For a cold disinfecting solution, use ordinary hydrogen peroxide. It is identical to, but less expensive than, the hydrogen peroxide solutions sold specifically for contact lenses. Soak for the usual 6 hours.

LOST LENS

If a lens falls into a sink, turn off the running water instantly and close or cover the drain. If it has fallen down the drain, act quickly. Place a bowl under the trap and open the clean-out plug with a wrench (see *Clogged drains*, p.48). With any luck, the lens will fall into the bowl with the other debris.

If your contact lens falls on the floor, darken the room and sweep a flashlight slowly and methodically back and forth across the area. The lens will glint in the beam, even if it has fallen into a pile rug. Or use a small lamp, as shown.

Contests

The chances of your winning a lottery, sweepstakes, or contest are remote—as high as one in a million. There are ways, however, of bringing the odds down.

1. If the rules permit, enter the contest over and over again. Send in each entry form separately, mailing them on different days and in different weeks.

2. To reduce your competition, enter contests that run for only a short time. The best time is summer, when a great many other potential contestants are on vacation.

3. Follow the contest rules to the letter—and be especially sure that your entries are postmarked before the deadline.

4. Watch for contests that allow you to send in a facsimile of the entry form. If you make yours on bright-colored cardboard, you will improve your chances of having it drawn. Pleat or fold your entry into an intricate shape so that it stands apart from the others in the drum.

5. Subscribe to one of the many newsletters that give tips and details on current contests.

CONTESTANT BEWARE

1. The value of all prizes is subject to federal, state, and local income taxes. You can, however, deduct the costs of winning, such as the postage and stationery.

2. Stay away from any contest that guarantees a prize to everyone; the prize is usually worthless.

3. Read the fine print. Some prizes aren't awarded for several years; others are of far less value than the purchase required for eligibility.

Continuing education

1. It's a rare college that doesn't offer a continuing education program, designed to allow working adults to earn college credits. The courses are given at various times: mornings, lunch hours, evenings, and weekends. Your employer may give you time off to attend job-related classes; some companies even provide tuition reimbursement.

2. You can earn credits by taking College Level Examination Program (CLEP) tests. They are given in four general areas—English composition, humanities, mathematics, and natural sciences—and some 30 specific subjects, ranging from accounting to Western civilization. CLEP test preparation guides are sold in bookstores.

3. More and more schools are giving "life experience" credits for knowledge and skills gained outside the classroom. Almost anything you've done may qualify for life experience credits, provided that it meets two important tests:

First, you must have increased your knowledge from the experience. Colleges will grant credits for foreign travel, for example, if you've learned something specific, such as a foreign language or the history of a country's art and architecture.

Second, you must show that what you've learned matches the content of a specific college course. If you've learned computer programming on your job, for instance, the experience may duplicate a course listed in the college catalog.

To obtain life experience credits, you usually must document what you've learned by preparing a portfolio with enough evidence to convince a review committee that you qualify for the credits.

⟩ Convulsions

Your companion suddenly becomes rigid and then begins jerking violently—he is having a convulsion. What can you do?

1. Assist him to the floor or the ground, away from potentially dangerous objects.

2. Loosen restrictive clothing.

3. Stand by to protect him from injury. Don't try to hold him down or place anything in his mouth. Most people neither bite nor swallow their tongues during a seizure, but they may break or choke on anything that's in their mouths (even objects as large as a small wallet).

A convulsion, whether epileptic or from some other cause, may last from one to several minutes. The victim may drool and foam at the mouth; his lips and face may turn bluish.

4. After the convulsion is over, remove any vomit from his mouth. Then keep him resting comfortably on his side, with his head down to allow him to breathe easier and to prevent choking.

Cookies

1. Let crumbly cookie dough—the kind made with a lot of shortening—rest and soften for an hour at room temperature. It will then be easy to roll.

2. To keep cookies from burning, bake them at a temperature 25°F lower than the recipe calls for and add a minute or two to the baking time. As extra insurance, double-pan the cookies: stack two baking sheets together with the cookies on the top sheet.

3. Need to soften tough cookies? Put them in an airtight tin or jar with a piece of fresh bread or a wedge of apple. Or wrap a wet paper towel in aluminum foil and place it in the tin on top of the cookies.

4. To keep cookies crisp, cool them on wire racks and transfer at once to an airtight canister.

5. When the kids ask for cookies and you're out, fake some in a jiffy by baking bits of marshmallow on graham crackers. Make them even better by adding some chocolate chips. Store extras in the freezer.

6. Use the crumbs at the bottom of the cookie jar as a tasty topping for ice cream.

7. To pack cookies for mailing, use unsalted popcorn in a cardboard box (fill it all the way to the top). It's great padding. Just mix the cookies in loosely.

Cooking oils

1. To cut down on cholesterol, substitute polyunsaturated vegetable oils and margarines for saturated fats and solid shortening. (Be careful of substitutes in baking, however; they don't always work.)

2. Look for soft tub or liquid margarine; the softer it is, the less saturated fat it contains. Choose one that lists corn, safflower, or soybean oil as the first ingredient. If the first ingredient is qualified as "partially hydrogenated," or if palm or coconut oil is an ingredient, choose another brand.

3. You can make French fries in

the oven by brushing potato slices with a little olive oil and baking them at 375°F for about 20 minutes. Turn three times during cooking, brushing each time with a little more oil. The "fries" will have considerably fewer grams of fat than the deep-fried kind.

Cookware

1. Some common items can do double duty in the kitchen. A wok makes an efficient Dutch oven or steamer. A plastic fruit basket or an old aluminum pie plate with holes punched in the bottom can serve as a makeshift colander.

Used coffee cans are perfect for baking banana and other quick breads. And a jelly-roll pan can stand in as a roasting/baking pan.

If you're caught without a fish poacher, use a roasting pan. Put a cake or cookie rack or an inverted saucer under the fish and cover the top with foil.

2. For minimum cleanup, nothing beats baking in foil packets; they're ideal for Swiss steak and for simply seasoned chicken breasts, ground beef, fish, and vegetables. Layer ingredients on one half of a large piece of heavy-duty foil. Dot with butter or margarine, add herbs or seasonings of your choice, and fold over the foil. Seal the edges tightly, then fold over once more. Seal again, leaving little room for expansion.

Try a favorite campfire dinner at home. Place a ground beef patty, two potato slices, a piece of carrot, a thin onion slice, and a pat of butter on foil. Season, seal, and bake at 350°F for 45 minutes to 1 hour.

Cooling

1. Install a ventilator fan in your attic. Under a blazing sun, attic air can be as much as 60°F hotter than the air outside—and some of that heat radiates downward.

2. Position portable or window fans to blow hot air *out*. For cross-ventilation, open windows at both the top and bottom and on all sides of the house.

3. Install ceiling fans. They're both nostalgic and practical as they stir up a gentle breeze.

4. Even on a windless summer day you can cool a house without air conditioning by taking advantage of the "stack effect"—a draft that rises through the house. The aim is to get the cool air from your basement or crawl space to replace the hot air that naturally rises and

---

IN TIMES GONE BY

The art of keeping cool

Those of us who routinely trek from an air-conditioned house to an air-conditioned car to an air-conditioned office, store, or factory may find it hard to believe, but before 1902—when Willis H. Carrier installed the first air-cooling system in a Brooklyn printing plant—people somehow managed to survive without air conditioning.

In hot climates, families learned to build shelters that shielded the sun's rays and took advantage of cooling breezes. Thatched huts, for example, kept out the sun overhead while filtering the wind through thinner wall weavings.

Tomb paintings tell us that the ancient Egyptians mounted what appear to be wind vanes above their roofs to catch breezes, a method still practiced in Pakistan. Several thousand years ago, East Indians hung wet grass mats over openings at night so that breezes could flow through, cooling interiors by evaporation.

In African lands bordering the Sahara, in many Mediterranean

locales, and in the American Southwest people built with adobe, stone, and stucco, which produced what is now called thermal lag. The masonry roof and walls were thick enough to absorb and retain the day's heat, keeping interiors cool. At night, when the air cooled, the masonry released its heat to warm the interior.

For many people, the best way to get relief from the heat was to take a trip to the mountains or the seashore. But the wealthy were sometimes able to buy comfort. Roman emperors, for example, imported snow from the Alps in summer, and Middle Eastern rulers had slaves fan them with palm fronds. And no less a consultant than Leonardo da Vinci was engaged by one Milanese duchess, who kept her boudoir cool with the inventor's foot-powered fan.

By the late 19th century, form had become as important as function. One cooling device, shown here, consisted of a metallic statue crowned with an urn. The urn was

filled with ice, which chilled the air just below the ceiling and dripped cold water through the statue into a basin filled with plants and fish.

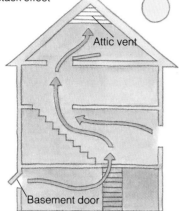

Stack effect

Attic vent

Basement door

passes through attic vents. Just keep your basement door open and open a path all the way to the attic.
5. Use awnings, solar screening, roof overhangs, or shutters to block sunlight. Interior shades, venetian blinds, draperies, and tinted glass are helpful, but don't work as well as devices that keep sunlight from getting through the window to begin with; heat trapped between the glass and interior shading will eventually circulate through the room.
6. Keep heat out by insulating to the maximum and caulking potential air leaks, just as you would to keep heat in during winter.
7. Deciduous trees on the south, east, or west help cool a house if they don't block breezes.
8. Choose white or light-colored roof shingles to reflect heat.

Cork retriever

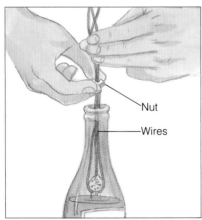

Nut

Wires

If a large piece of cork falls into a bottle of wine, twist three pieces of stiff wire together at one end and make hooks at the other ends. Push this "claw" into the bottle and grasp the cork with it. Tighten the grip by slipping a ring or nut down the wires as far as possible, then draw out the offending piece.

Corkscrew

1. Can't find your corkscrew? Open a bottle of wine with a large screw hook or eye; use a mixing spoon or sturdy stick to pull it out.
Or drive a plain screw into the cork and grip the head firmly with a pair of pliers.
2. To ease out a stubborn cork, dip a cloth in very hot water and wrap it around the neck of the bottle; it will expand the glass.

Screw eye — Wooden spoon

Coughs

1. For a cough from a cold, dissolve 1 tablespoon each of lemon juice and honey in a small glass of warm water and sip it.
If you prefer something stronger, combine equal parts of lemon juice and honey. Take ½ to 1 teaspoon at bedtime. Either mixture will help loosen irritating mucus.
2. Make a soothing "stew" by boiling quartered oranges and lemons in a little water and adding extra lemon juice and honey to taste. Take at bedtime.
3. To soothe the throat so that you can sleep, take 1 teaspoon honey at bedtime; let it trickle down your throat. (See also *Cough drops*, p.393; *Cough syrup*, p.393.)

Cracking walls

Joint tape
Crack

1. To conceal wall cracks that appear just below the ceiling, fill the crack and then cover it with a self-adhesive wallpaper border. These borders come in 6- or 8-inch widths and are available in a variety of colors and patterns.
Wood moldings—crowns, baseboards, chair rails, and so forth—can also serve this purpose.
2. To fill hairline cracks, use a quick-drying spackling compound. First, enlarge the crack slightly by raking it with the pointed end of a can opener. Brush away all dust and debris. Dampen the crack with a wet sponge and apply the spackling compound with a flexible-blade putty knife. Once the compound has dried, sand it flush with medium sandpaper.
Large or recurring cracks can be repaired the same way, but two additional steps are required. First, cover the crack with 2-inch-wide adhesive-backed fiberglass joint tape. Then force joint compound (not spackling compound) into the tape and crack with a 4- or 5-inch-wide putty knife. Allow this first application to dry, then apply a second layer of compound with an 8-inch-wide putty knife. Once the compound has dried, sand the repair with medium sandpaper.
3. Cover badly damaged walls with wood paneling or heavily embossed wallpaper, which hides surface im-

perfections much better than standard wallpaper.

4. Resurface with ½-inch wallboard. Nail directly into the studs or cement the wallboard in place with construction adhesive. Then tape and sand the seams (see *Wallboard*, p.223).

Crank calls

The most effective way to deal with a crank call is to hang up, depriving the crank of any satisfaction he may derive from harassing you. Instruct children and babysitters to do the same. If the calls continue, leave the phone off the hook for a while. The next time the caller disturbs you, blow a whistle into the mouthpiece.

If the calls persist or if they are threatening, record the time and date of each call. This will help the police apprehend the offender if you decide to file a formal complaint with the phone company.

Cream

For 1 cup of heavy cream, substitute ¾ cup whole milk and ⅓ cup melted unsalted butter. (Don't use in ice cream or mousse, however— the butter will lump.)

If you're counting calories, replace 1 cup of heavy cream (832 calories) with a cup of canned evaporated skim milk (176 calories). An extra bonus: evaporated skim milk has far less cholesterol, too.

Credit cards

1. Keep the number of your credit cards to a minimum to curb impulse spending and to reduce your risk if they're lost or stolen.
2. Make sure that the credit card you're applying for is a credit and not a debit card, for which payments are taken directly and immediately from your bank account.
3. Remember that a card's rate of interest doesn't necessarily indicate its true cost. You must also consider the cardholder fee and the grace period—if any—before in-

terest is charged. Make sure you pay interest *only* on the amount left unpaid at the end of a billing cycle; on some cards, unless your bill is paid up, interest is charged on all *new* transactions as well.

SECURITY
1. Sign new credit cards as soon as they arrive. Cut up the old ones.
2. Carry your credit cards separately from your wallet. Keep a record of their numbers and the telephone number of each company in a secure place.
3. Avoid placing credit card orders from a telephone in a public area.
4. Never sign a blank receipt.
5. Destroy all carbons and void all incorrect receipts.
6. Save all receipts to compare with your monthly statement.

Credit ratings

Avoid unpleasant surprises—check out your credit rating *before* you apply for a loan. A credit report costs little, and will give you a good idea of what your creditors think of you as a bill payer.

Look up "Credit" or "Credit reporting agencies" in the Yellow Pages; then call one of the listings and ask how to apply for your credit report. Or ask your bank for the name and address of the credit bureau it uses. Send a letter stating your purpose and giving your address, birthdate, and Social Security number; enclose a check for the required fee.

A typical report lists every bank, credit card company, and department store that has extended you credit and details your bill-paying history, including any missed or delayed payments.

If there's erroneous material in your file, correct it immediately. Write a letter to the credit reporting company; your claim must then be investigated and any inaccurate or unsubstantiated items removed.

There's nothing you—or anyone else—can do to remove accurate

information. You can, however, give your side of the story. Write a brief statement and insist that it be inserted in your record. It must accompany your credit report every time it's requested.

Beware of "credit assistance" or "credit repair" companies that claim to improve the information in your file. They can do no more than you can on your own—and they'll charge a hefty fee for this "service."

❯ Croup

1. A child with croup can breathe more easily sitting up.
2. A humidifier or vaporizer may help. For temporary relief, turn on a hot shower and sit with the child in the steam-filled bathroom.
3. If the child is having serious difficulty breathing, has secretions in his mouth, or is not relieved by the measures above, take him to an emergency room right away.

Cup stains

Remove stubborn coffee or tea stains from your china cups in one of the following ways. Then rinse thoroughly and dry.
1. Scrub with salt or a paste of baking soda and water or a 50-50 mixture of salt and white vinegar.
2. Place in a denture-cleaning solution and soak overnight.
3. Let stand overnight in a solution of ½ cup household bleach in 2 quarts water.

Curdling

Curdled cream sauce? Push it through a fine sieve with a spoon.

To save a Hollandaise sauce, add 2 tablespoons boiling water; beat with a wire whisk until smooth. Or set the pan in a bowl of ice water; whisk until smooth, then warm very gently over barely simmering water, whisking constantly.

Curfews

Children often perceive curfews as rules made to be broken, but in fact they should teach responsibility. Discuss the subject with your kids until you agree on a sensible, flexible policy. (It's OK to bend the rules for special events.) If you suspect you're being conned, consult other parents about their kids' curfews.

Insist that your children call if they'll be late. Five or 10 minutes past curfew doesn't really deserve a reprimand, but an hour or more requires an explanation and, possibly, corrective action.

If you want to enforce a curfew but also need your sleep, set an alarm clock in your bedroom; if the child gets in on time, he can turn it off with a quiet "Hi, I'm home."

Curtains

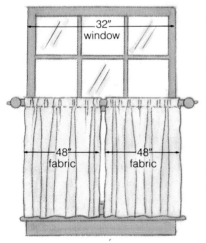

Bedspreads, tablecloths, quilts, and sheets can make good curtains and may well be cheaper than store-bought fabric. Choose a color and pattern to match the room's decor.

To determine how much fabric you'll need, measure the distance from the top of the window frame to where the hem will fall. Add 3 inches at the top for a 1½-inch pocket that the rod can slide through. Add another 2 to 4 inches for a hem (the heavier the fabric, the deeper its hem). For width, triple the distance across the area you plan to cover.

Customs

1. Find out about exemptions, allowances, and restrictions before you go abroad; contact your local office of the U.S. Customs Service.
2. If you're taking valuable foreign-made items abroad (furs, fine jewelry, cameras, binoculars, and so forth), bring proofs of purchase. Foreign-made items that have serial numbers should be registered at a customs office or at the airport before leaving the country.
3. If you take prescription medicine abroad, carry a sufficient amount; it may be difficult to get a prescription filled abroad. Leave it in its original labeled container and keep a copy of the original prescription with your travel papers.
4. Be wary of the terms "duty-free" and "free port." Items from duty-free shops are dutiable when brought into the United States.
5. Some items *are* duty-free, but with restrictions. Antiques, for example, must be certified to be at least 100 years old. Art must be original or a signed limited edition.
6. The United States allows many products to be brought in duty-free from developing nations that have Generalized System of Preference (GSP) status. Contact your local customs office for information.
7. If you think you've been unfairly charged, pay the duty, then write to your local customs office. Include a copy of the receipt.
8. When traveling with family members who live with you, you can make a joint declaration and combine personal exemptions.
9. If your property is damaged while being examined, apply for compensation at the customs office.
10. To reduce delays at the customs counter, keep your foreign purchases, along with their receipts, in a separate bag.

❯Cuts & abrasions

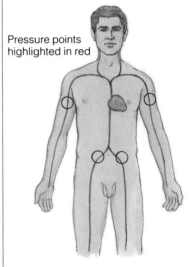

Pressure points highlighted in red

The seriousness of a cut depends on how large it is, how deep it is, and how much it bleeds.

Although painful, small cuts and abrasions are seldom dangerous. Wash them gently with mild soap and water, then apply an antibiotic cream if available; cover with a large adhesive bandage or a reasonable substitute (see *Bandages,* p.16).

SEVERE BLEEDING

When treating deep cuts, the first priority is to control bleeding.
1. Apply firm pressure directly to the wound.
2. Elevate an injured arm or leg, unless it is fractured or dislocated, something is impaled in it, or you suspect spinal injury.
3. If direct pressure and elevation don't stop the bleeding, locate a point between the heart and the wound where a major artery crosses bone near the surface (you can feel a pulse) and apply firm pressure to the artery.
4. When bleeding has stopped or

lessened considerably, place a clean cloth directly over the wound, completely covering it; put a clean bulky dressing on top. Wrap wide strips of cloth tightly over the dressing and on each side of the wound. Seek medical help.

Cuttings

A hanging bag of soil makes a space-saving medium for rooting stem cuttings from begonias, dieffenbachias, and other plants.

Mix enough peat moss and perlite or vermiculite (available at any garden center) in equal parts to fill a 4-gallon plastic bag. Moisten the mixture thoroughly and fill the bag with it. Poke small holes in the bottom for drainage.

Close the bag with stout cord and hang in an airy, well-lighted place with a waterproof floor; a shaded corner of a sun porch or a garage window is ideal. (In winter hang the bag over the drainboard of a sink in the laundry room.)

Poke holes in the sides of the bag and gently insert your stem cuttings. Mist the cuttings daily, letting water run down the stems to remoisten the rooting mixture. When the cuttings have rooted, slit the bag open with a sharp knife.

Cutworms

The usual method of foiling cutworms—placing a bottomless tin can or plastic cup around young plants—guards only against

worms outside the barrier. A better control is to wrap the stem of a seedling with aluminum foil before setting it out. Plant with 2 inches of foil below the soil surface and 2 inches above. Wrap loosely so that the stem has room to grow.

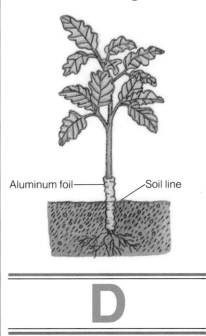

Aluminum foil————————Soil line

D

Dampness

Lingering dampness eventually leads to rot. Get rid of the source of water, then use one of these methods to dry out a damp area:

1. Vent moisture from a laundry room or bathroom with an exhaust fan. Fans are measured by the volume of air moved, in cubic feet per minute (CFM); you need 1 CFM per square foot of floor area. To be safe, buy a fan rated slightly higher.

2. In the kitchen, keep a window open and use the stove's exhaust fan when cooking or boiling water. If dampness is damaging walls made of plaster or gypsum board, paint them with an oil-based gloss or semigloss enamel.

3. Hang a dessicant (a moisture-absorbent chemical) near damp areas in small spaces like closets. The commonest dessicants, usually sold along with paint and hardware, are

inexpensive porous-cotton bags of calcium chloride. Buy two 2- or 3-pound bags. Hang one until it's saturated; then switch and dry out the first bag in the sun or your oven.

4. Install a dehumidifier. It works, but it's as expensive as a good TV set. Moreover, it throws off heat, and unless the collected water is piped to a drain, you have to dump the water pan once or twice a day.

5. If part of an exterior wall is damp, cut away nearby branches and shrubs. This will increase airflow and allow sunshine to keep the area dry and free of mildew.

Debt

Does more than 35 to 40 percent of your annual gross income go to cover your debt? For example, if you earn $30,000, are you paying more than $12,000 on a mortgage, installment loans, and credit card purchases? If so, you should consider taking immediate steps to reduce your indebtedness.

1. Stop the debt from growing—cut up your credit cards; postpone the purchase of that new car.

2. Cut back on open-ended lines of credit, such as bank credit cards or overdraft checking accounts, where the monthly payments vary according to the unpaid balance. Make all minimum payments on time, then add something extra to reduce the balance.

3. Apply windfalls, such as bonuses or tax refunds, toward paying off these open-ended accounts. If anything's left over, pay off as much principal as possible on other loans.

4. Evaluate consolidating all your debts into one big loan. You might even be able to convert your nondeductible personal interest into home mortgage interest to get some tax benefit. The interest rate on such debt is usually lower than credit card rates. Don't forget to factor in the costs of refinancing your mortgage or obtaining a home equity loan. (Ask your bank for the true costs of such financing.)

Decks

Rust spots caused by nails, screws, and corroding hardware will discolor a stained deck. Using a wire brush, remove as much rust as you can from the metal and the surrounding wood. If any rust spots remain on the wood, bleach them out by scrubbing with oxalic acid, available in paint stores.

Use a small artist's paintbrush to coat the metal with a rust converter. Let the repair dry thoroughly before you restain the wood.

Deer

Keep deer away from your garden and your valuable shrubs, fruit trees, and other plantings by using sounds, smells, tastes, or sights that are disagreeable to them.

SOUND

String twine across the deer trail, then suspend a metal bucket from it. Place a couple of old doorknobs in the bucket and tie metal scraps— small shelf brackets, large nails, or nuts and bolts—to the sides. When the deer hits the twine, the clatter will scare it away.

SMELL

Rather than commercial repellents that smell like rotten eggs, hang cloth bags of human hair, beef suet, dried blood (available at garden centers), or deodorant soap around your garden and in vulnerable trees.

TASTE

Make a spray of 2 tablespoons hot red pepper sauce to a gallon of water; add 2 or 3 tablespoons of liquid dishwashing detergent so that the mixture will stick to the plants.

SIGHT

Suspended pie pans that glint in the sun may work for a while. Use a blinking or rotating light at night.

❯ Dehydration

Heat, overexertion, illness, and long bouts of vomiting or diarrhea can cause the loss of body fluids and salt. Infants, small children, and the elderly are the most vulnerable.

If you suspect dehydration, drink lots of water or juice; in summer or after heavy exercise, drink cool water with enough salt to make it taste slightly salty. If these measures don't help, seek medical advice. (See also *Heat exhaustion,* p.106.)

Dentist visits

Fear of the dentist is old-fashioned. With today's techniques and materials, dentistry need not be painful. Seek out a dentist who seems sensitive to your fears and who will explain exactly what he's going to do before he does it.

To conquer anxiety in the chair, breathe slowly and deeply and focus on something else, such as counting backward from 100. Or try distraction—bring a cassette player with earphones to drown out the noise of the drill. Work out a hand signal with your dentist to indicate the onset of panic.

Try not to convey your anxiety to your children. Ask your pediatrician to recommend a dentist who specializes in preventing both cavities and fear of dentistry

Deodorant

1. Try plain baking soda. After you've dried off from your bath or shower, pat a little under your arms; the moisture still on your skin will help it stick. If it isn't soft enough, mix it with cornstarch.
2. Mash a sturdy dark-green leaf of romaine lettuce to extract a drop of

---

IN TIMES GONE BY

Common sense about common scents

It's not perspiration that causes body odor—it's the action of bacteria on our sweat and body oils. People didn't know this until fairly modern times, and so for centuries they tried to overpower their own smell by dousing themselves with stronger odors.

The ancient Egyptians, though they knew nothing of bacteria, understood all about countering the odors they caused. True, they regularly applied perfumes and oils made from citrus fruits, spices, and wood resins. But they also were fastidious about daily bathing, and they regularly removed their underarm hair—

which offers bacteria an expanded surface on which to grow.

Later cultures, in their own efforts to smell sweet, copied the Egyptian formulas and added powders and bicarbonate of soda to the deodorant roster. But somehow, with rare exceptions, cleanliness was overlooked by most of humanity.

Around the turn of this century, it even became stylish in some circles for women to flaunt a slight aroma of the upper body. It was romantically called *bouquet de corsage,* and these ladies believed men found it attractive. Perhaps. But the style soon passed.

chlorophyll. Spread the liquid under your arms and let it dry.
3. If you have persistent body odor, try a different brand of soap. Some soaps contain chemicals that cause odor when they react with certain people's body chemistry.

Depth gauge

Duct tape

Wrap a small strip of masking or duct tape around a drill bit so that the exposed part of the bit equals the desired depth of a hole. Or mark the bit with a grease pencil.

Alternatively, use a block of wood as a gauge; position it beside the bit so that the chuck will butt against it when the desired depth is reached.

❯ Diabetic emergencies

Insulin shock (too much insulin in the blood) starts very quickly. The symptoms are damp, pale, clammy skin; a strong, rapid pulse; sweating; dizziness; headache; hunger; aggressiveness; convulsions; fainting; or occasionally coma.

Give the person some sugar, honey, candy, fruit juice, or a soft drink right away—make sure that it is sweetened with sugar, not a sugar substitute. Do not try to give an unconscious person anything; get him to a hospital quickly or call an emergency medical service.

Diabetic coma (not enough insulin in the blood) develops more slowly than insulin shock, over several hours or days. The symptoms are thirst, abdominal pain, vomiting, restlessness, confusion, and a gradual lapsing into stupor and coma. The skin is dry, red, and warm. There may be a sweetish smell of acetone, like nail polish remover, on the breath. Whether the person is conscious or not, take him to an emergency room or call an emergency medical service.

If you're not sure whether a conscious person is in the first stages of diabetic coma or is going into insulin shock, ask. Most diabetics will know. If you're still in doubt, give sugar and call for help.

❯ Diarrhea

The cause may be a viral or bacterial infection, food poisoning, or an inflammatory disease. Or it could simply be stress or overindulgence in food or drink.

An infant under 3 months old can quickly become dehydrated from diarrhea; call a doctor immediately. A breast-fed baby should continue to be nursed; a formula-fed baby should be given half-strength formula thinned with water.

Give a child clear liquids and gelatin desserts. As the diarrhea tapers off, gradually introduce binding foods in the so-called BRAT diet (Bananas, Rice cereal, Applesauce, and Toast).

An adult should be treated in much the same way. If the diarrhea persists for several days, however, and the person hasn't eaten and drunk enough to balance the loss of fluids and nutrients, dehydration becomes a threat.

If thin, watery stools last longer than 3 days, contain blood or mucus, or are accompanied by fever and vomiting, call a doctor.

Dimmer switches

White neutral wires
Incoming black hot wire

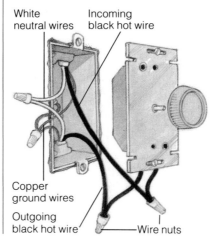

Copper ground wires
Outgoing black hot wire
Wire nuts

To replace a dimmer switch, first shut off the power to the circuit (see *Power shutoff,* p.162). Then pull off the dimmer knob and remove the cover plate screws and cover plate. Remove the screws fastening the switch to the box and pull the switch out, noting the wire connections. As in all switch loops, the switch should connect the hot (black or red) wires only. Undo the hot wires from the old switch leads and connect them to the new switch leads with wire nuts. Then fasten the new switch to the box and replace the cover plate. Finally, push the dimmer knob onto its shaft.

Dinner parties

For a dinner party with a different twist, try one of these ideas:
1. Throw a theme party featuring food, beverages, music, and decor from a foreign country or a distant region of America. Or, for the sake of variety, turn it into an international buffet.
2. Go co-op: ask each guest to prepare and serve one course at his or her own home. Your job will be to coordinate the transportation.
3. Serve elaborate but substantial finger food, such as stuffed croissants or chicken croquettes with a savory dip. In summer, prepare a cold alternative, such as ceviche or pickled shrimp with a spicy dip.
4. Have a potluck picnic: ask everyone to bring a favorite dish.
5. Supply the grill and beverages and ask each guest to bring one item for a barbecue.

Dishwashers

Your dishwasher stopped working? The timer may just be at a normal pause in a cycle; wait a few minutes to see if the action resumes.

Make sure you've latched the door and set the timer dial and cycle selector properly. Check the fuse or circuit breaker. See if the water is turned off anywhere on the line.

On a portable model, the electric cord may not be plugged in securely or the hot-water faucet may be off. Check the door latch. Look for a kink in the hose.

LEAKS

Many leaks are caused by objects blocking the water inlet. Remove and reposition them.

You may have used too much detergent, or your brand may generate excessive foam, forcing water out. Stop the machine and add a cup of vinegar to neutralize the foam. If that doesn't do the trick, remove the racks and bail out the water. Let the motor dry thoroughly before turning it on again.

DRAINAGE PROBLEMS

A little water at the bottom of a dishwasher is normal. (It keeps the seals from drying out.) If there's a lot of water, be sure the strainer at the bottom isn't clogged and the rubber drain hose isn't kinked. If the water drains through a garbage disposer, check that it's empty.

DIRTY GLASSES

The most common cause of spots or film on glasses is hard-water deposits. Soak the spotted item in white vinegar for 15 minutes; if the film disappears, hard water is the problem. To prevent a recurrence, increase the amount of detergent, be sure the water temperature is at least 140°F, and use a rinse additive to help water "sheet" off.

If the clouding can't be removed with vinegar, use less detergent, a lower water temperature, and a rinse additive; turn off the machine before the drying cycle.

› Dizziness & fainting

Fear, anxiety, pain, the sight of blood or injury, and a stuffy, overheated room can all cause dizziness and fainting.

To prevent fainting, have a dizzy person sit and place his head between his knees. Or if he has a heart problem, difficulty in breathing, or any serious injury, have him lie down with his feet elevated.

If a person faints, try to prevent him from injuring himself in the fall. Lay him on his back and raise his legs. If he doesn't revive in a few minutes, seek medical help.

Elderly people who faint should see a doctor right away; such an occurrence can be a sign of a serious medical problem.

› Dog & cat bites

Although a dog bite may look more serious, a cat bite is more dangerous—there are more bacteria in a cat's mouth.

Wash a dog or cat bite with soap and water, rinse under running water for at least 5 minutes, and cover with a dressing or a clean cloth. Try not to move the affected area until the bite has been treated by a doctor.

Although rare today, rabies can still be found in stray dogs and in such wild animals as squirrels, skunks, raccoons, and bats. It can even be transmitted if a rabid animal licks an open wound. Because the disease is fatal unless treatment begins at once, it's important to identify the source of a bite.

An animal's behavior won't necessarily offer any clue to whether or not it has rabies. If possible, check a dog's collar for a rabies vaccination tag or ask its owner about its shots. If it's an unfamiliar animal, arrange to have it impounded and observed. (See also *Bites*, p.22.)

Dog baths

1. Walk your dog before bathing it so that it won't go outside wet.
2. Put a steel-wool pad in the tub drain to collect hairs.
3. If your dog fears baths, let it watch you take one yourself. But be prepared—it may jump in with you.
4. To keep soap out of a dog's eyes, gently apply a thin layer of petroleum jelly over its eyebrows and around its eyes.
5. To minimize soap film, add vinegar or lemon juice to the rinse water. Rinse your pet thoroughly.

6. To prevent your dog from splattering you, wash its head last—a wet head makes the dog want to shake itself dry. Towel your dog immediately after its bath.
7. Use a blow dryer. Set it on warm, not hot, and hold it at least 6 inches away from your pet.

Dog chasing

Bicyclists and joggers can take a few precautions to protect themselves against being chased by dogs.
1. Speak to the dog in a commanding but calm tone.
2. Carry a stick and use it to keep the animal at bay. Don't hit the dog—just make it keep its distance.
3. If you can't outdistance a pursuing dog on your bike, dismount and use the bike as a shield. If necessary, try squirting the dog in the eyes with your water bottle.
4. Keep dog treats, such as biscuits, in your pocket. Throw one in the direction of an approaching dog—as far as you can.
5. Squirt highly diluted ammonia from a water gun.
6. Carry a pop-up umbrella to open in the animal's face.

Dog hair

1. To collect loose hairs, put your dog on an old sheet or towel before you brush it.
2. To remove burrs, crush them with pliers or soak the tangle in

vegetable oil, then just comb it out.
3. To get rid of sticky substances such as tar, saturate the area with vegetable oil. After 15 minutes apply dog shampoo; rinse immediately.
4. Allow paint or gum to harden, then snip off the hair that holds it.
5. To clean a dog brush, move a toothpick through the rows.

Dog leash

If you have to walk the dog and you can't find its leash, try one of these substitutes:
1. A rope or length of clothesline. Tie a secure bowline or other non-slip knot around the dog's collar. Make a loop for the handle and wrap it with electrical tape.
2. A long leather belt. Run the end beneath the collar and then through the buckle.
3. A pair of pantyhose. Pull one leg under the collar and tie the feet together with a square knot.

Dogs

If dogs are a nuisance:
1. Keep garbage cans tightly sealed and never put garbage out in un-protected plastic bags. Set cans out as close to pickup time as possible.
2. Erect a low-voltage electric fence (p.71) if local laws allow one. Kits are available in some gardening catalogs and at pet supply stores.
3. Catch the offender and note its tag. Trace the license through the local police or the courthouse. Talk the problem over with the owner before lodging a complaint.
4. Train your own dog to stay in bounds (or out of your garden) with an electronic boundary warning device. A buried wire transmits a harmless warning tone and shock signal to a tiny receiver attached to the dog's collar. Dogs soon learn to respect the warning tone. Check the phone book under "Fences" or "Pet supplies."

Doorknobs

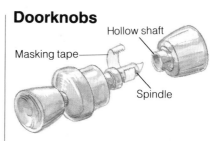

Hollow shaft

Masking tape

Spindle

A loose doorknob is probably the result of wear—the inside of the knob's hollow shaft has become slightly enlarged. Remove the knob, wrap the hollow shaft in a soft cloth, and tap it very gently with a hammer in several places to crimp it a bit; be careful not to crush it. Then slip the knob back onto the spindle and check for a snug fit.

You can also wrap the spindle with masking tape and then force the knob back onto the spindle. One or two layers of tape will usually suffice to ensure a tight fit.

Doors

1. When a door refuses to stay open, check the hinges. If one has shifted or a hinge screw has pulled loose, reset the hinge in its original position and tighten the screws. If a screw cannot be tightened because the hole has been stripped or enlarged, remove it, pack the hole with wooden toothpicks, reinsert the screw, and tighten securely.
2. To quiet a door that's a slammer, adhere a strip of foam rubber to the edge of the doorstop molding. Peel-and-stick foam weatherstripping tape works well. A short length of foam rubber near the top and bottom of the molding will often suffice. You can also try a narrow strip of cork or leather.
3. To keep a door from slamming against the wall when it opens, make a simple doorstop from window sash chain. Attach one end to a screw eye on the face of the door and the other to one on the top of the frame.
4. Here's an easy-to-make door bumper for a child's room: put a rubber ball in a sock and hang it

---

from the inside doorknob.

5. The self-closing hinges on many kitchen cabinet doors make them slam shut. Muffle the noise with bumpers made of silicone caulk:

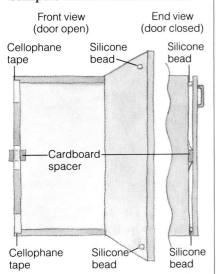

Front view (door open)   End view (door closed)

Cellophane tape   Silicone bead   Silicone bead

Cardboard spacer

Cellophane tape   Silicone bead   Silicone bead

Put two small dollops of caulk—each about the size of a pencil eraser—on the inside corners of each door, one at the top and the other at the bottom. Then place strips of cellophane tape on the cabinet where the silicone makes contact. Smear each tape strip with a thin film of petroleum jelly to keep the caulk from sticking when the door is closed. And, to act as a spacer, tape a small piece of 1/8-inch-thick cardboard to the cabinet between the tape strips. Close the door, let the silicone dry overnight, then peel off the tape and cardboard.

Down payments

To save money on a major purchase, pay for it outright or make the largest down payment you can afford. Because you'll need to borrow less, you'll pay less interest.

The savings may be greater than you realize. For example, if you buy a $12,000 car at 10.4 percent and make a 10 percent down payment, you'll pay $1,818.36 interest over 3 years. But if you make a 50 percent down payment ($6,000), you will pay only $1,010.10 interest over

the same period—a savings of $808.26, or almost *45 percent.*

Few, if any, investments offer a higher rate of return than the interest you pay on a loan. Therefore, when making a major purchase, if you can withdraw money from your savings account without incurring a penalty, consider using it to make a larger down payment.

Drafts

Cold convection currents drop to the floor from windows, uninsulated walls, and glass doors, then move across your feet. To prevent them, insulate walls and ceilings to the maximum and add storm panes to single-glazed windows. Plastic interior storm windows help too, including the type that you staple over the window and "shrink-tighten" with hot air from a hair dryer.

Air leaks are the other source of drafts in the house. There are six vulnerable spots:

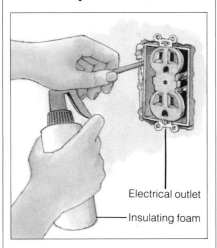

Electrical outlet

Insulating foam

ELECTRICAL OUTLETS

Remove the switch and the outlet plates; fill the openings around the box with foam insulation.

WINDOWS AND DOORS

Caulk between casings and sidings around all windows and exterior doors. Use silicone, Butyl, or acrylic for durable protection. Install weatherstripping around all windows and doors.

UNUSED ROOMS

Close off the room; stuff the crack under the door with old towels or a strip of carpet.

UNDER THE WALLBOARD

Caulk the baseboard to fill the crack between the drywall and the floor.

FIREPLACES

Shut the damper after you are certain the fire is out.

ATTICS

Insulate around the access door. Use foam or fiberglass to insulate around plumbing vent pipes and other openings.

Drainage testing

1. To test how well your garden soil drains, dig holes 2 to 3 feet deep at different locations around your yard and fill them with water. Then observe what the water does.

If it drains away immediately, your soil is too sandy for most plants; dig in some compost, peat moss, or other organic matter to help it retain water.

If it stands for 30 minutes to 1 hour, the drainage is ideal for vegetables and flowers.

If it remains in the hole for several hours, your soil is poorly drained—a heavy clay or fine silt. Either dig in some sand, peat moss, manure, or compost, or construct raised beds (p. 169) of improved soil.

2. An easier, though less reliable, drainage clue is natural vegetation. Such water-loving plants as willows, sweet gums, and purple loosestrife suggest poorly drained soil; junipers, sassafras, common milkweed, and other dryland plants indicate good drainage.

Drawers

1. When a drawer won't pull out, the chances are that something inside is projecting above the sides. Simply remove the drawer above, then empty and repack the sticking drawer.

2. A loose nail in the drawer frame

may also be the culprit; if so, hammer it down.

3. If a wooden drawer drags, sand its runners lightly and then rub them with a candle or a bar of soap. Or if the wood has swollen in damp weather, lightly sand or plane the front lip of the drawer and along the tops of the sides and back.

4. If a wooden drawer pulls out too far, the chances are that you need to reattach or replace either the glue blocks that secure the bottom or the stop that is on top of the rail—below the drawer—at the front of the chest.

5. When the bottom of a wooden drawer sags, flip over the drawer. If nails hold the bottom to the back, pull them out with pliers. Break the glue blocks from the bottom with a chisel and mallet. Slide out the bottom and return it upside down. Then renail the bottom to the back and glue the blocks back in place.

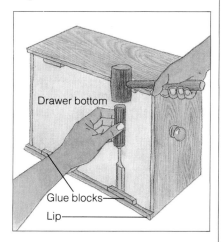

Drawer bottom

Glue blocks

Lip

6. If the sagging bottom fits into a groove in the back of the drawer, you must disassemble the frame to fix it. Wrap a cloth around a mallet and tap apart the dovetail joints at the corners of the drawer. Slide the bottom out, scrape off the old glue, and reassemble the drawer with the bottom upside down.

7. Replace a split bottom with thin plywood, or mend it with a canvas strip and white glue.

Drawstrings

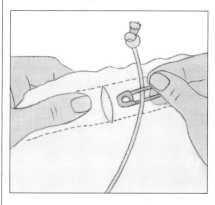

1. If a drawstring frequently does a disappearing act into its casing, double-knot the tips. Or harden the tips with a few drops of household cement for easy retrieval.

Play it safe—tie the drawstrings together before laundering.

2. If you lose a drawstring, substitute a shoelace, ribbon, or fabric tubing; attach a safety pin on one end to help feed the replacement through the casing.

Drills

If you don't have an electric drill, use a finishing nail or push drill to make a pilot hole and then try one of these alternatives. All make for slow work, but they'll do the job.

1. Lock the shaft of a bit upright in a metal vise. Position the starter hole over it and turn the work.

2. If you lack the appropriate bit for a pilot hole, snip the head off a finishing nail and use it instead.

3. Insert the bit into the collar of an old-fashioned doorknob and tighten the setscrew.

Bit   Setscrew

Dripping faucets

Modern hot-and-cold combination faucets seldom leak, but when they do, the entire central cartridge usually needs replacement. Use a re-

pair kit made specifically for your model of faucet. It should come with a complete set of instructions.

The model number of your faucet may be engraved at the base, under the spout. If you can't find it, try to take the faucet apart—look for pry-off caps or setscrews recessed under the lever—so that you can take the innards to the hardware store for identification and replacement. If all else fails, take a snapshot of your faucet to the store with you.

STEM FAUCETS

A single faucet—hot or cold—is prone to leaks, but you can usually fix it by replacing the washer.

Shut off the water under the sink and remove any decorative cap over the faucet handle. Then unscrew the handle counterclockwise. Next, unscrew the packing nut or lock nut that holds the faucet stem in place, and lift out the stem.

For a quick fix, you may be able to reverse the washer at the end of the stem. But it's best to replace it with one the same size. Use a soft washer for a cold-water tap, a harder one for hot. (Keep a packet of assorted washers in your tool kit.)

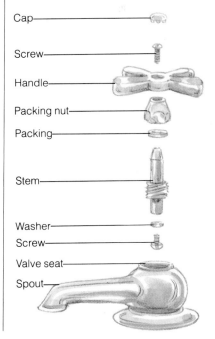

Cap

Screw

Handle

Packing nut

Packing

Stem

Washer

Screw

Valve seat

Spout

Driver's license

If you lose your driver's license, phone your local department of motor vehicles right away and ask how to obtain a replacement. (The regulations vary from state to state.) Don't just go in—you may find after a long wait that you lack the necessary papers.

〉 Drug interactions

Anyone who takes more than one drug at a time—prescription or over-the-counter—or who drinks alcohol while taking medication may suffer side effects from their interaction or cumulative effect. The elderly are especially vulnerable. Here's how to help prevent this problem:

1. Keep an updated list of all the drugs and vitamins you take; go over it with your doctor whenever a new medication is suggested.

2. If your doctor uses a computer, ask her to check with the American Medical Association's drug interaction data base before prescribing a new medication. The service shows all known interactions with other drugs, food, and alcohol, as well as possible allergic reactions.

3. If you develop new symptoms at any time, especially after starting a new drug, call your doctor or put all your drugs into a bag, take it to her office, and ask her to review your medication.

4. Ask for a full drug review at every checkup—and take samples of all your drugs along whenever you see a new doctor.

5. Look for a pharmacist who will keep a complete record of all the drugs you take, your allergies to foods and drugs, and your doctors' names and addresses. When a new medication is prescribed, a check of this record will identify incompatible drugs.

Drunk drivers

1. If you intend to drink alcoholic beverages at a party, designate someone else as the driver. If you're going alone, arrange a ride home.

2. If an intoxicated person is about to get behind the wheel of a car, reason firmly with him not to drive. If that doesn't work, take his car keys away and call a cab for him or find someone who will give him a ride home. If you're already in motion when you realize the driver is drunk, insist that he stop the car and let you or someone else drive. If he refuses, get out at the first opportunity and call the police. Give them your location, a description of the car and driver, and the license plate number. You may lose a friend, but you may also save a life.

3. If you see a car weaving toward you, assume the driver is drunk and be prepared to take evasive action.

Dry-cleaning odors

It's your dry cleaner's obligation to deliver your clothes odor-free. The petroleum-based solvents once used in the process *did* cause an unpleasant aroma, but that day is long gone.

If your garments smell, take them back and complain. It may not be the operator's fault; fabrics are often treated with a resin sizing to give them body—but it gives them an odor, too. Have the clothes recleaned; if the problem isn't solved, return them to the store.

Occasionally, dry-cleaned clothes smell because the unit malfunctions or because the drying cycle is too short. Again, have the clothes recleaned. If the condition persists, change cleaners.

In all cases, remove the plastic covering. Nearly all odors evaporate quickly with an airing out.

Dry skin

1. The best remedy is also the easiest to find: water. Drink six to eight glasses a day and eat foods high in water content, such as fruits and leafy vegetables. Use a humidifier in winter.

2. Bathe in mildly salted water (½ cup of salt per tubful) to rehydrate your body, then apply a cream or lotion that will act as a moisturizer.

3. For an easy facial, mash a banana, add a tablespoon of honey, and smooth the mixture on your face. After 15 minutes, rinse with warm water.

Dual careers

Do you and your working spouse spend too little time together? Why not try this:

Choose a day when you're both free—Sunday is probably best—and go over your respective calendars, looking for times when you can schedule dinner, a movie, or a romantic evening at home. Make a date and don't cancel unless there's a good reason.

Not only will this private time together let you relax and enjoy each other's company, but it will lend both of you energy and emotional support for facing your professional challenges.

HOUSEHOLD TIMESAVERS

You and your spouse will find more time to devote to each other if you take the following shortcuts:

1. Do one-stop shopping whenever possible, seeking out supermarkets that sell clothing, rent videos, provide automated banking machines, sell stamps, and so forth.

2. Stock up on nonperishables.

3. Shop by mail for items such as clothing, cosmetics, and books.

4. Look for stores that take phone orders and deliver.

5. Enlist the kids to help you with the chores around the house (see *Chores*, p.47).

6. Hire neighborhood teenagers or retirees to do chores and run errands. Give the babysitter some extra money to wash dishes, iron clothing, and such.

Dusting

Your aim is to pick up dust, not displace it. For dustcloths, spray discarded undershirts, diapers, or old towels with silicone. Cheesecloth moistened with diluted lemon oil also works fine. Avoid feather dusters; get the lamb's-wool variety.

Starting at the top and working downward, use slow, even strokes. If you'll be dusting for some time, coat your nostrils with petroleum jelly to prevent a scratchy throat.

Wear a multipocketed apron or carry a cleaning supplies tray—a cheap, compartmented plastic box with a handle makes a good one—to keep supplies within reach. Include a bag for collecting debris.

Treat an old sock with silicone and wear it as a glove to dust tables and chairs.

Don't bother dusting knick-knacks one by one. Just soak them all together in a dishpan with detergent. Use your hair dryer to blow them dry.

Use eyeglass-cleaning tissues to dust small picture frames.

Wax your dustpan so that dust won't cling. Shake mops and dustcloths inside a sack or outdoors.

Hard-to-dust things and places—pleated lampshades, carved furniture, and crevices—are a snap if you blow the dust out with a hair dryer. An empty squeeze bottle used as an air pump also does the trick.

To get at narrow spots behind radiators, in louvers, or under the refrigerator, dampen an old sock, slip it over one end of a yardstick, and secure it with a rubber band.

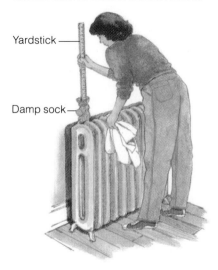

Yardstick

Damp sock

Ear popping

Avoid traveling by plane if you have a cold, flu, or allergy; you may develop painful ear or sinus problems. If you must fly, take an oral decongestant an hour before takeoff and landing, or use a nasal spray before and during descent.

If your ears start to pop or you get an earache, try one of the following: swallow, chew gum, suck on a piece of hard candy, sip a liquid, or yawn. Don't sleep during takeoff and landing; you won't swallow often enough to keep your ears clear.

For babies, nursing or sucking a bottle or pacifier will help, especially during ascent and descent.

Earrings

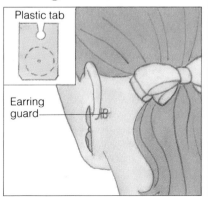

Plastic tab

Earring guard

1. To keep pierced earrings from flopping forward and to balance heavy ones, make an earring guard. Fold a small piece of transparent tape so that the sticky side is covered. (You may want to cut it into a circle.) Or cut a circle from the plastic tab that seals a loaf of bread. Poke a pinhole in the center of this tab; then insert the earring through your earlobe and the tab. Finally, secure it with the earring back.
2. If you lose an earring, put the remaining one on a chain to wear as a pendant, turn it into a pin or a

stickpin with supplies sold in crafts stores, or make a ring out of it.
3. To keep track of your pierced earrings and display them at the same time, attach a piece of burlap to a dowel and hang it next to your dresser or vanity. Your earrings will slip easily into the burlap, and you'll have a pretty wall hanging besides.

Ears

1. Something in your ear? Don't probe it—you may drive the object deeper and damage the eardrum. Instead, ask someone to look inside the ear with a flashlight or strong light. If there is no bleeding and the object is small, irrigate the ear with tepid water from a syringe. If it is large or embedded, seek medical help.
2. If there's an insect in the ear, shine a flashlight in to attract it. An alternative is to float the insect out by pouring warm mineral, olive, or baby oil gently into the ear.

EARWAX
Never probe your ear canal with anything smaller than a clean fingertip. If wax builds up, lie on your side and put a few drops of lukewarm water into your ear; after 10 minutes, shake the water out. Repeat with hydrogen peroxide; leave it in for 10 minutes, then, using an ear syringe, rinse with water. Follow with several drops of warm mineral or baby oil; drain your ear after 15 minutes—the softened wax should have worked its way out.

RINGING IN THE EARS
1. Check for earwax buildup.
2. Eliminate caffeine and stop taking aspirin.
3. Avoid loud noises.
4. If the ringing persists for more than a day or two, see a doctor.

WATER IN THE EAR
To rid your ear of water, gently clap the heel of your hand against the side of your head several times or insert an eyedropper of rubbing alcohol into the ear canal.

EARACHES

For temporary relief, take aspirin or acetaminophen and lie with your head raised and your ear resting on a hot-water bottle or hot compress.

PIERCED EARS

To prevent infection, swab newly pierced earlobes with alcohol twice a day. Apply a nonprescription antibiotic ointment with a cotton swab nightly. To avoid an allergic reaction, make sure the posts are gold or surgical steel.

❯ Earthquakes

IF YOU'RE INDOORS

Stay indoors. Get under a table, desk, or bed, or stand in a doorway or an inside corner next to an interior wall. Keep away from windows, mirrors, glass, bookcases, light fixtures, tall cabinets, and fireplaces.

IF YOU'RE OUTDOORS

Get into an open area; avoid buildings, walls, power lines, and trees. If you're in a car, stop—but stay inside until the tremors stop. Avoid bridges and power lines.

AFTERWARD

1. Be on guard for smaller aftershocks that can cause additional damage.
2. Apply first aid to any injuries.
3. Check the house for structural damage, fires, and damage to utili-

ty lines and appliances. Open doors and cabinets carefully.
4. If you smell gas, open all doors and windows, turn off the main gas valve, leave, and report the leak to the gas company.
5. If electrical wires are shorting out or fixtures have loosened, shut off the power (p.162).
6. Until public water supplies are declared safe, boil all tap water for 10 minutes. If water pipes are damaged, shut off the water supply (see *Water leaks*, p.226). Get emergency drinking water from the toilet tank (not the bowl), water heater, or ice cube trays. Don't flush the toilet until you know that the sewer lines are intact.

Eating utensils

UTENSILS FOR THE DISABLED

Specially designed eating utensils are available for the disabled. These include built-up flatware for those who have difficulty gripping and a rolling knife for people who have the use of only one hand. For more information on these products, contact the American Association of Retired Persons.

SUBSTITUTE UTENSILS

In a pinch a number of items can serve as eating utensils. Before using any item, clean it thoroughly.
1. As a knife: a seashell edge, a nail file, a letter opener, the serrated edge of an aluminum foil box, a single-edge razor blade, scissors, or even a sharp-edged rock.
2. As a fork: a twig, a skewer, a hair pick or comb, your fingers, or a pair of chopsticks.
3. As a spoon: a seashell, a small stone with a hollow, a coffee scoop, or molded aluminum foil.
4. As a plate: a napkin or paper towel, a piece of cardboard, aluminum foil, a plastic coffee can lid, or a flattened coffee filter.
5. As a bowl: a jar, a coconut shell, a seashell, a coffee filter, a Frisbee, a thermos top, or a hollowed stone.
6. As a cup: Fold a square piece of

paper as shown; turn corner *A* over to meet corner *B* and crease. Then turn corner *D* up to meet line *BC*, so that the new edge is parallel with the bottom edge. Turn corner *C* over to corner *E*. Fold the two top corners (at *B*) outward and down. Tuck in *A*. Squeeze gently to open.

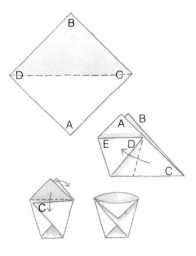

The evolution of eating utensils

The earliest spoon undoubtedly was a cupped hand. The discovery of fire and cooking, however—and the danger of burning one's hands—led people to shape clay, carve wood and stone, and utilize the natural shape of shells.

The earliest knives, dating back 35,000 years, were chipped from stone. Because of their crudeness, they were used mainly to hack up food rather than to eat with.

Forks were originally one-pointed, like knives. The Romans invented the two-tined form, but eating with forks was still considered an affectation as late as the 16th century. The colonists brought forks to America, but most Americans preferred to eat with knives until the mid-19th century.

Eggs

1. Test eggs for freshness by placing them in a bowl of cold salted water. Discard any that float to the surface or turn their broad ends up—they're stale.

2. Don't discard an egg just because its white is cloudy. Most likely it's the freshest egg of all, since 1- or 2-day-old eggs still retain a little carbon dioxide. The gas is harmless and tasteless.

3. For a perfect poached egg, add a tablespoon of vinegar to the water. It helps set the white.

4. When you cook eggs in a microwave oven, prick the yolks first to keep them from bursting. And *never* microwave eggs in their shells—they'll explode and make a mess.

800 numbers

1. Save the price of a postage stamp or long-distance call: use toll-free 800 numbers whenever possible. Many businesses maintain these numbers to take orders and handle questions and complaints. A number of government agencies also have 800 "hot lines."

2. If you don't know a specific 800 number—or if you're not sure the company or agency has one—dial 1-800-555-1212 and ask.

3. If you know what you want but don't know the name of the company, refer to the classified section in an 800 directory (sold in both consumer and business editions). Not every 800 number is listed in the directory, however.

4. Why doesn't someone pick up the phone? Because not all 800 lines are manned around the clock; consider time-zone differences when making the call.

5. When placing an order, have your credit card number and all product information at hand. Make a written record of the order, including the name of the person you talked to, the date, the amount, and the estimated delivery date.

6. Don't confuse 800 and 900 numbers; the latter are not free.

Elastic

1. To substitute a drawstring or cable cord for worn-out elastic, cut the cord 24 inches longer than the casing and knot both ends; brush clear nail polish or household cement on the tips to prevent fraying. Pin one end to an open seam and feed the other through the casing. (See also *Drawstrings*, p.67.)

2. To replace a waistband that has lost its stretch, snip open a seam across the casing and pull out the old elastic. Cut a piece of new elastic 1 inch smaller than your waistline. (Use nonroll elastic with vertical ribs to prevent twisting.) Pin one end at the open seam and work the other through the casing with a safety pin. Smooth out the elastic; then overlap the ends ½ inch, sew them together, and close the seam.

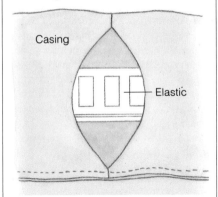

Casing

Elastic

Electric blankets

An electric mattress pad is more efficient and comfortable than an electric blanket. Because the heat is under you, little is lost to the air.

If you prefer nonelectrical warmth, try an old-fashioned hot-water bottle, which does a good job of heating the bed before you climb into it. Cotton flannel sheets help, too; even without a hot-water bottle, they warm your skin more than smooth sheets do.

Electric fence

An electric fence keeps dogs, rabbits, and other small animals off your property or out of your garden. But before you install one,

check your local laws; they are banned in many communities and strictly controlled in others.

1. Control weeds and prune away overhanging branches to keep them from touching the wires and causing a short circuit. Keep weeds down with well-anchored plastic mulch; herbicidal sprays may corrode the wires.

2. Check the fence occasionally for cracked or broken insulators; they can cause a short circuit, especially when fence posts are wet.

Electronic banking

1. No matter how technically proficient you may be, before you make your first transaction at an automatic teller machine (ATM), ask a bank official for a full explanation and demonstration of how it works.

2. Select a personal identification number or code that's really secret: not your birth date, address, telephone or Social Security number, since those are public knowledge. Memorize the code—don't write it anywhere.

3. Wait until the ATM has turned itself off and you have received your bank card and printed receipt before walking away. Check the receipt to make sure that neither you nor the computer made a mistake.

4. Record each transaction in your checkbook as soon as possible so that you can balance your bank statement more easily. If the statement shows any inaccurate ATM transactions, notify the bank within 60 days. The bank must resolve the problem within 45 days.

5. Lost your bank card? If you tell the bank within 2 business days, you're only liable for $50.

Elevators

Holding an elevator button in or pushing it repeatedly may satisfy you but does nothing at all for the elevator. Its electronic circuity can register only the first call.

The same is true when a car passes you by. Modern elevators

have load sensors that cause them to bypass floors once they've reached load capacity. Be patient; the car will stop for you on its return.

Newer elevators have devices that are sensitive to pranks. If a prankster pushes all the buttons on his way out of your car, the newer models will automatically cancel the calls. Just rekey your floor to get moving again. Older elevators may have to stop at all floors.

Employee health insurance

To prevent surprise medical expenses, learn how your company health insurance works. Find out the answers to these questions:
1. What does your policy cover? What about pregnancy? Dental care? Psychotherapy? What coverage is available for dependants?
2. What is your deductible (the medical expenses you must pay per year before your insurance plan kicks in)?
3. How much more must you pay toward your medical bills after the deductible has been satisfied?
4. What are the limitations on the payment for or the duration of a hospital stay? On other coverage? Is preadmission approval required?
5. Does your company offer a plan that provides all services for one fee?
6. Must you have a second opinion before undergoing surgery?

If you have special health benefit needs, check with your company's personnel or benefits department. You might be able to pick and choose among the benefits offered. And make your needs and wants known to your employer; if enough people need certain coverage, your company might redesign its plan accordingly.

Employee testing

A prospective employer may require you to take job-related tests to make certain that you have the skills you need to do a job. The most common tests include typing and stenography for secretarial positions, math

tests for accounting jobs, and various tests in computer programming languages.

If you're required to provide blood and urine samples as part of a pre-employment physical exam, you can ask what you are being screened for. In most states you cannot be tested for drug use or AIDS without your knowledge.

If a drug test is required, ask the company to explain its policy and procedures regarding drug tests; to tell you the test method being used; to assure your right to a retest in the event of a positive result; and to show you the test results. Remember that, except in states where laws offer some protection, the employer can refuse to hire you if you don't take the test. Also keep in mind that the chemicals in some foods and medications can show up positive on a drug test.

Pre-employment polygraph (lie detector) tests are banned or carefully regulated in many states. Some companies use psychological and paper-and-pencil honesty tests. You can ask what the purpose of the test is before you agree to take it. It is rare, and in some states considered discriminatory, to reject a candidate based upon such tests.

Employment agencies

Don't expect an employment agent to provide career counseling. His business is filling vacancies for clients, not helping individuals find the right vocation. Take the agent's assessment of your skills and potential with a grain of salt; he may even belittle you or mislead you about the job market so that you'll take the job he has available. If this happens, try another agency.

To help an agency find the right job for you, write a letter stating
1. Your job objective, target industry, desired salary range, and the geographical areas you'd consider.
2. Several of your proudest accomplishments (with the dollars-and-cents results of each, if possible).

3. A description of your personality traits that make you ideal for the job, with examples.

You'll have to fill out an application form and submit a résumé.

When you get a job offer, negotiate the salary on your own; to serve his client, the agent may try to convince you to take less money. And don't be afraid to turn down a job if it's not right for you; the agent won't drop you—on the contrary, he will assume that if you've received one offer, you'll get another. (See also *Headhunters*, p.105; *Job hunting*, p.119; *Job interviews*, p.119.)

Empty-nesters

Some survival strategies if your children have left home for good:
1. Move into a smaller space; sell or store the excess furniture.
2. Expand your environment. Convert a former child's room into a den, home office, or workroom.
3. Fill the void. Some young people who have left their homes in distant cities may need not only a place to live but a family to live with. You may gain a "perfect" substitute son or daughter who will gladly do household or other tasks in exchange for rent. Draw up a written contract so that expectations are clear on both sides.
4. Extend your family. Develop new relationships, drive senior citizens, do volunteer work with children.
5. Expand your horizons—don't just sit home waiting for the kids to pay a visit. Enroll in a continuing-education course (p.56), take up a hobby, travel.

Endurance building

Badly out of shape? Recuperating from an illness? Start rebuilding yourself slowly by walking up and down your block for 2 minutes. Walk 5 days a week, a little longer each time, until you can walk 15 minutes without stopping.

Gradually increase your speed until you can walk a mile in 15 minutes. Start your workout by walking slowly until your body is warm; slow down again toward the end to cool off. Finish up with stretches for flexibility (see *Warm-up & cool-down exercises*, p.224).

Gradually increase distance until you're walking 3 miles in less than 45 minutes. (This should take about 12 weeks after you achieve a 15-minute mile.)

THE GOAL

Now you're ready to start jogging, aerobic dancing, rowing, or cycling three to five times a week for 30 minutes or so. Or just keep walking; aim for 4 to 5 miles at 4 m.p.h.—when you reach 20 miles a week, you'll be in good shape.

Ultimately, your heart rate should increase to between 70 and 90 percent of your maximum rate (calculated by subtracting your age from 220). If you're sedentary, aim to increase your heart rate to 60 percent of your maximum.
Caution: If you're over 35, overweight, or have a family history of high blood pressure or heart disease, see a doctor before beginning any exercise program.

If at any time you feel an irregular heartbeat or pain or pressure in your chest; if you're dizzy or lightheaded or if you vomit during or after exercise; if, after finishing your workout, you can't catch your breath in less than a minute, *stop at once and seek medical help.*

To measure your walking distance, wear a pedometer on a belt or waistband.

Eraser

1. Twist a rubber band around your finger to erase pencil marks. Or roll some rubber cement into a ball.
2. For special jobs on colored pa-per—hand-lettered invitations and school projects, for example—cover errors with a dab of the acrylic paint used for model airplanes. Choose low-gloss paint and mix the colors until you have an exact match for the paper.

Evening attire

Going straight from the office to an evening affair?
1. If you're a woman, wear a simple dress or ensemble to work and bring accessories—earrings, bracelets, necklace—a pair of dressy shoes, and an evening wrap, such as a brightly colored shawl or silk blouse to wear as a jacket. A length of black satin ribbon, 1½ to 3 inches wide, can serve as a last-minute evening belt or hair tie. The finishing touch: a showy silk tassel (you can buy one

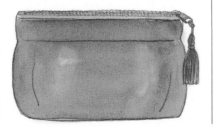

at a drapery store) attached to the zipper pull of a leather handbag.
2. If you're a man, wear a dark suit to work and bring a clean shirt, fresh tie, and perhaps a silk handkerchief, if that's your style. A flower in the lapel does wonders, too.

Exchanging currency

Learn a country's official exchange rate before you go; check with the consulate, a large bank, or the business section of a newspaper. You'll usually get a better rate in the country itself, but take the equivalent of $100 with you—order it from your bank or exchange it in the airport before departure—for immediate incidentals such as tipping, phone calls, and taxi fare.

In your host country, hotels, shops, and independent exchange agencies generally offer the worst rates; airports and downtown banks, the best—although in some countries officially tolerated black markets offer the best of all. Traveler's checks often get better rates than cash. If there is a difference of more than 5 percent between the posted buy and sell rates, you are

---

DID YOU KNOW . . . ?

The tuxedo rebellion

The year: 1886. The place: Tuxedo Park, New York.

As the story goes, tobacco tycoon Pierre Lorillard was bored with the formality of traditional tails. And so, for the annual Autumn Ball, he had his tailor make him several tailless jackets in the mode of the British riding coat popular among fox hunters. It was a daring idea, but Pierre lost his nerve and donned the standard formal costume.

His son, Griswold, however, possessed the audacity that Pierre lacked. He and his friends astounded the cream of society by appearing in short dinner jackets. Tongues wagged for a while, but the desire for change must have lurked beneath the staid surface of society—or perhaps the famous Lorillard name worked some magic—because others were soon wearing the tailless "Tuxedo suits" that eventually became standard attire.

Accessories to the tuxedo also have their histories. A forerunner of the cummerbund, for instance, was worn in India as part of Hindu formal attire. The British liked the look and adopted the style for themselves. The pleats were worn facing up, probably because dress trousers lacked pockets and, after all, one needed a place to carry theater tickets.

probably getting cheated.

You must show your passport during transactions, and you may be required to show your receipts when you exchange your currency back into dollars. Coins are usually not exchangeable.

Be aware of bank hours and holidays in the country you're visiting. Large train stations and airports often have longer banking hours.

The exchange rate on a credit card billing is based upon the rate in effect when the charge clears in the United States, not when you make the transaction.

A pocket calculator is handy for converting prices when you shop.

Exercise cramps

WHILE RUNNING

1. If you feel a twinge in your abdomen, slow both your pace and your breathing rate; if necessary, stop. The pain should disappear when breathing returns to normal.
2. For relief of a cramp in your calf or thigh, do a "wall stretch": stand 2 to 4 feet away from a tree or a wall and lean into it, bending your front knee while keeping your back heel on the ground. Hold for a count of 50 or until the cramp disappears. (See also *Stitch in the side*, p.197.)

WHILE SWIMMING

1. If you're in a pool, get out or go to the shallow end and do a wall stretch.
2. In a lake or an ocean, float on your back or stomach, straighten the cramped leg, and extend your toes forward as far as you can. Hold and count to 30 slowly, then relax. Repeat until the cramp disappears.

Exercise equipment

1. One-pound cans of soup or vegetables make good hand weights for arm exercises. So do 1-liter soda bottles. (Don't open them immediately after use.) Hold one item in each hand and, with both arms at your sides, alternately raise each arm to shoulder level.
2. For ankle weights, fill socks with dry sand, raw rice, dried lentils or beans, or clean cat litter. Weigh them (start with 2 pounds) and tie them shut, leaving room in the toe so that you can fasten them around your ankles.

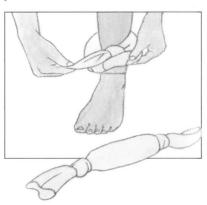

Lie on your back, with one knee bent and the other leg straight. Raise the straight leg as high as you can. Switch the position of both legs and repeat.
3. Squeeze a tennis ball or tightly rolled-up pair of socks in each hand to strengthen your grip.

4. To stretch your calves, sit on the floor with your legs straight, loop a bath towel around the ball of one foot, and pull, resisting with your foot; repeat with the other foot.
5. Stand, holding a towel above your head, and pull on the ends.
6. Rest your ankle on the back of a chair in front of you, keeping the leg straight. Bend over, getting your face as close to your knee and your hands as close to your ankle as possible; hold for 5 seconds. Repeat with the other ankle.

Exercise mats

1. If you're not doing heavy tumbling, a bath or beach towel on a rug or a folded cotton or wool blanket will work just fine as a mat.
2. Or exercise on a firm mattress, preferably one resting on a bedboard, a platform bed, or the floor.

Exercising gently

IF YOU'RE CHAIR-BOUND

1. Raise first one arm, then the other straight up over your head. With both arms overhead, reach for the sky with your right hand, then your left, five times each. Relax.
2. Let your head fall forward. Slowly tilt it to the right and let it rotate back, to the left, and then to the front. Repeat in the reverse direction. Don't force the action.
3. Shrug your shoulders high, then let them drop four times. Pull them backward, then push them forward four times.
4. With your feet firmly on the floor about a foot apart, hold your arms straight out in front of you. Bend forward as far as you can, stretching out your arms. Return to the starting position. Twist to the right and bend as far as you can, then to the left. Repeat.
5. Hold the seat of your chair. Raise your right leg from the knee, wiggle your toes, and move your foot in a circle, first one way, then the other. Return the right foot to the floor and repeat with the left leg.
6. Raise one knee as high as you

can, then let it drop and raise the other one. Repeat this action as vigorously as you are able to, "marching" in place 10 times.

IF YOU'RE BEDRIDDEN

1. Lie on your back on a firm mattress. Raise your head; with your chin close to your chest, turn your head slowly from side to side.

2. Lie on your back with your arms comfortably at your sides. Raise your right arm, cross it over your face, then return it to your side. Repeat with your left arm, three to five times each.

3. Lie on your left side, with your legs straight, your head resting on your left arm, and your right hand flat on the mattress at chest level. Bend your right knee and pull it up toward your chest. Hold it there, resting on the mattress, for 2 to 3 minutes. Then roll over and repeat the action with the left leg.

Exercising on the go

1. Whenever possible, walk, jog, or bicycle to work. Carry your work shoes in a tote. (You can even carry a change of clothes in a small backpack and change at the office.)

2. If you take a bus or train, get off a mile before your stop and walk the rest of the way.

3. Use the stairs instead of riding the elevator.

4. Walk a mile before lunch.

WATCHING TV

Ride an exercise bike, bounce on a mini-trampoline, jump rope, or run in place while you're watching your favorite programs.

ON THE PHONE

Use wrist and ankle weights to do leg lifts and arm raises while you're talking on the phone.

DOING HOUSEWORK

1. For aerobic housecleaning, warm up with a light activity such as dusting or washing dishes, then proceed to vigorous vacuuming, sweeping, or floor polishing for 20

to 30 minutes. Upbeat music may help keep you moving.

2. To pick up light items from the floor, stand with your feet apart, arms at your sides. Bend slowly from the waist and touch the floor, flexing your knees if you have to. Count to 10 before straightening.

3. To dust a high shelf, stand with your feet apart and hold the dustcloth in both hands, bending from side to side to wield it.

AT YOUR DESK

1. While sitting, lean slightly forward, grip the sides of your chair, and alternately raise your left and right knees to your chest.

2. While reading, put your foot through the handle of your handbag or briefcase; lift until your leg is horizontal. Repeat 10 times without touching the floor. Then do it again with the other foot. (See also *Office exercises*, p. 145.)

Exposure meter

If you've left your exposure meter at home or your camera's meter is faulty, use the "Sunny 16 Rule." On a sunny day with distinct shadows, set the f-stop at f/16, then match the shutter speed as closely as possible to the film's speed; that is, 1/60 second for 64 ASA/ISO film or 1/125 for 100 ASA/ISO.

If it's cloudy but fairly bright with soft shadows, set the stop at f/11 and use the same formula. On a day without shadows, set at f/8.

Extension cords

Be careful when you choose an extension cord. Just because it happens to have several receptacle ends, don't take that to mean that it can carry more amperage than the outlet it's plugged into.

And be aware that the longer the cord, the greater the amperage drop. A 100-foot cord, for example, has to be heavier than a 10-foot cord performing the same task. If an extension cord feels warm, consider that a stern warning. Replace it with a heavier cord or jettison an appliance or two.

Eyeglasses

1. When buying a pair of reading glasses, whether over-the-counter or prescription, keep in mind that glass lenses are less likely to scratch than plastic, but they will shatter and they weigh more. Shop for tempered lenses that fit securely in the frame.

2. If you lose the hinge screw that holds an earpiece to the frame, use a small safety pin or paper clip for a quick fix.

3. Make your glasses fit more securely on your face by tightening the hinge screws with a jeweler's screwdriver, the tiny screwdriver that comes with a sewing machine, or the point of a paring knife or letter opener.

4. If a lens breaks cleanly, you can hold it together temporarily with a little transparent tape at the top and bottom of the crack.

5. Clean lenses with soapy water or a drop of vinegar, vodka, or rubbing alcohol. To prevent scratches, do not rub plastic lenses until you've rinsed off all dirt.

6. Do your glasses fog up when you come in from the cold? Before heading out on a chilly day, just rub a thin coat of soap on the lenses. Then polish them until clear—instant waterproofing!

7. Do the lenses tend to pop out of your half-glasses? In an emergency, put chewing gum or any other sticky substance in the corner of the lens to hold it in place.

8. To secure a loose lens in a pair of full-frame glasses, look for a set-screw near the hinge; if your glasses are so equipped (some are not), tighten it as you would the hinge screw described in **3** on p.75. (See also *Magnifying glass*, p.131.)

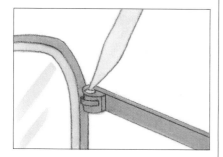

› Eye problems

STIES

A sore lump on the edge of your eyelid is a sty. Apply a hot, wet compress several times a day to bring it to a head, then squeeze gently to release its contents. If it remains for several weeks, see a doctor.

RED EYE

A bright red blotch in the white of your eye is usually a harmless hemorrhage caused by coughing, choking, or rubbing the eye. It should disappear by itself in about a week; if it occurs again soon or if you are bruising easily or experiencing headaches, see a doctor.

PINKEYE

If one (or both) of your eyes is red, teary, and sticky, you may have pinkeye, or conjunctivitis. Wash the eye with warm water twice a day and apply an over-the-counter ophthalmic ointment, such as bacitracin or boric acid, to the eye. Put a warm compress over the eye several times each day.

The disease is contagious. Wash your hands before and after touching your eyes and keep your towels and washcloths separate from those of the rest of the family. Throw out all your old eye makeup. (Replace with new products once the infection is over.) See a doctor if the infection persists.

If your eyes are red, itchy, teary, and feel sandy but are *not* sticky, you may have noncontagious pinkeye. This condition may be due to allergies; use cold compresses to relieve the itching and avoid the allergen if possible. The condition may also be the result of chemical irritation; if so, use "artificial tears" (available without prescription at a drugstore), avoid the chemical, and wear goggles while swimming.

BURNED EYES

If you burn your eyes, close them immediately. Ask someone to put moist, preferably sterile pads (in a pinch, use handkerchiefs, sanitary napkins, or any other clean soft cloths) over your eyes and secure with a bandage. Seek medical help right away.

CHANGE IN VISION

If all or part of what you see appears hazy, blurry, wavy, or distorted; if you see spots or clouds, sudden flashes of light, or black specks or threads drifting across your field of vision; if you experience a sudden partial or complete loss of vision, however brief, see your ophthalmologist *immediately* or go quickly to the closest emergency room. If the doctor finds nothing wrong, get a second opinion.

Eyestrain

PREVENTION

1. Do not position your computer screen under a bright fluorescent light or opposite a window.

Install an antiglare screen; reduce blur by cleaning it often and tuning the display so there's a high contrast between the characters and the background.

2. When reading or writing, light should come from over your shoulder—the right shoulder if you're left-handed, the left shoulder if you're right-handed.

3. Turn on a low light when watch-ing TV and sit directly in front of the screen, 6 to 7 feet away.

4. Wear gray polarized sunglasses in sunlight, particularly when sunbathing, boating, skiing, or driving long distances.

RELIEF

1. If your eyes feel tired and achy after prolonged close work, refresh them by refocusing on a distant object for several seconds.

2. Rest your eyes for 15 minutes every hour or so.

Eyewinker

1. Even an infinitesimal foreign object—a speck of soot or a grain of sand—can irritate your eye. If you refrain from rubbing it, your tears may wash the object away.

2. If an object is on the surface of the white of the eye or under the lower lid, irrigate gently with sterile water, if available; otherwise, use tap water. Tilt your head and pour from the inner corner of the eye so that the water drains down toward the outer corner and out. A small, irritating scratch may remain after the object has been removed.

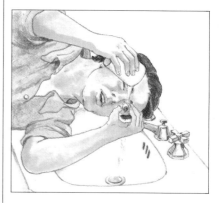

If the object doesn't wash out, it may be stuck to or embedded in the eye. Don't try to remove it; get to a doctor as soon as possible.

3. If the object is under the upper eyelid, grasp the lashes with your thumb and forefinger and fold them up over the tip of a cotton swab. If you can see the object, remove it with a moist, sterile cotton swab.

Fabric care

1. Read and follow all care labels. If you buy your own fabric, make a note of its content and use only those cleaning agents recommended as safe for it.

2. Wash or clean all the pieces of a matched set together every time—the jacket *and* the trousers, *all* the living room slipcovers, *all* the bedroom draperies, and so on. Exceptions are sets in which one piece is a solid color and the other a print.

3. Bleach generally whitens and brightens a washable fabric, but check the label to see whether chlorine or a milder oxygen bleach is called for. Permanent-press white fabrics, for example, often yellow when exposed to a chlorine bleach.

4. Always remove stains before laundering, or tell the dry cleaner where and what the stains are. Light-colored liquids such as ginger ale and perfume may leave no mark but in time or with heat may turn brown and stubborn. Blot up food spills on washable fabrics at once and sponge from the wrong side with club soda. Wash or dry-clean the article promptly.

Family relationships

A close-knit family? If you make your home in Idaho and Grandma lives in Atlanta, Brother Bill and his kids in California, and Sister Sue in Japan, it may be a long time between visits. But there are ways to build a family support system.

THE MAIL POUCH

Use a sturdy manila envelope to circulate messages among the family. Each recipient puts in something: a letter, snapshots, newspaper clippings, 3-year-old Lisa's portrait of the family dog, a great new recipe, or even an audio or video tape. (Who

but the family can truly appreciate a tour of the old homestead, the baby's gurgles, or the spring peepers back on the farm?)

To keep the packet moving through far-reaching branches of the family tree, provide a routing list and preaddressed labels. As you add your latest contribution, remove material that has made the rounds, preserving it for your own personal archives if you like.

ALBUMS AND SCRAPBOOKS

1. Start a new photo album at the beginning of each year to provide a visual diary of your family life; add snapshots or school photos sent by distant relatives.

2. Keep a scrapbook of notes, photographs, and birthday cards from grandparents, aunts, uncles, and cousins to remind your children of happy family relationships.

3. When youngsters go out on their own, give them an album of family photographs as the cornerstone of their own family archives.

STORIES

Telling tales—and preserving them on audio or video tape when possible—about relatives, distant and long gone, builds a sense of family and may create surprising relationships between the subject of the story and the audience. Black sheep Uncle George may really have been a rotter, but the spunk he showed in emigrating to Australia may serve as inspiration to a descendant yearning to follow her own star.

Family snapshots

If your family pictures are all forced smiles and stiff poses, try these tips to improve them:

1. Avoid poses. Everyone is uncomfortable in front of a camera. To make sure your subjects look relaxed, snap them while they're active. At a family cookout, sneak up on someone cooking hamburgers or setting the table. If he stiffens, ask him to describe what he's do-

ing. Take his mind off the camera.

2. Use a zoom lens. A camera at close range can be intimidating. A zoom lens lets you stand back while zooming in for a tight portrait.

3. Watch the details. It takes only a second to check for cluttered or distracting backgrounds.

4. Beware of light. Bright sunlight is harsh and causes squinting and ugly shadows. Shade is softer and more flattering to skin tones.

5. Take two or three quick shots of the same person. Pros know that it's rare to get a perfect picture on the first try. Shooting several increases your odds of capturing the peak of action or the perfect smile. So bring plenty of film on family trips or outings.

6. To keep full-length shots from looking amateurish, include the *whole* figure; be careful not to cut off the subject's feet.

7. Turn your snapshots into postcards by gluing them to index cards with rubber cement; trim with scissors, a razor blade, or a utility knife. Your friends and family will love finding pictures of themselves in the mailbox.

Fashions

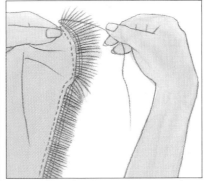

For a budget fashion accessory, make a fringed scarf from a length of fabric. Loosen thread at the edge of the fabric and pull; for longer fringe, remove more threads.

1. No matter what the latest fashion is, ignore it until you determine what basic lines are becoming to you. If you can't tell by spending some time in front of a mirror, ask

a friend for an honest appraisal.
2. Experiment with color. Hold fabric swatches next to your face to see which colors are most flattering. Don't be a slave to fashion—if this year's colors don't look good on you, don't wear them.

3. To play it safe, choose classic styles for expensive items such as coats; go trendy with less costly separates and sportswear.

4. An alternative to making a big commitment to this year's styles is to follow the fashions only with accessories: shoes, belts, purses, and jewelry. Scarves in particular can give clothes a fashionable lift. Make them from any lightweight fabric, new or old, and tie them at your neck or waist, or use them as turbans or shawls.

Fastening into concrete

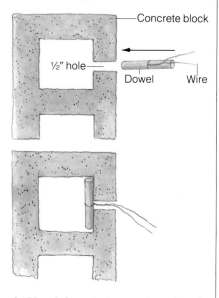

Concrete block

½" hole
Dowel
Wire

1. Here's how to improvise a toggle bolt to fasten an object to a hollow concrete-block wall. Make the "toggle" by wrapping a 12-inch-long piece of flexible wire around the center of a 3-inch length of ⅜-inch hardwood dowel, as shown, or even around a pencil stub. Then, using a carbide-tipped masonry bit, bore a ½-inch hole into the block and force the dowel into it. Hold onto the wire's loose ends so that, after

the dowel is trapped inside the concrete block, you can use them as twist ties to secure an object.

2. When screws driven into plastic or lead anchors loosen from solid concrete walls or floors, replace them with wood screws. First remove the anchor and clean out the hole. Then whittle a softwood plug to fit tightly into the hole. If necessary, wrap it with masking tape to ensure a snug fit. (A section of hardwood dowel, sanded to fit, can also be used.) Drive the plug into the hole with a hammer and cut off the protruding end flush with the surface. Bore a small pilot hole and drive in a wood screw.

3. If a screw loses its grip in a lead anchor, replace it with a larger screw. Or insert one or two lengths of lead solder into the anchor and then redrive the screw.

4. To fasten wood furring strips to a concrete wall, make glue-in-place nail fasteners. First cut a 3-inch-square piece of sheet metal and drive a 6d common nail through the center. Then spread a generous amount of panel adhesive or construction adhesive on the back of the metal square and on the nail's head. With a twisting motion, press the plate onto the wall with the pointed end of the nail protruding. Install one such fastener every 16 to 24 inches. Once the adhesive has cured, hold the furring strip against the row of nails and hammer it down. Bend the nails over to secure the furring strip.

Fastening into metal

1. If a sheet-metal screw strips its hole, replace it with a larger screw or with a blind rivet.

2. Metal parts fastened together with nuts and bolts often loosen as a result of vibration. To prevent this, coat the bolt's threads with shellac or clear nail polish before threading the nut onto it.

A more permanent way to secure the nut is to crush the remaining threads with a hammer and punch

or cold chisel after the nut is tightened in place.

3. To hang light objects from metal columns or beams, use heavy-duty magnets and string or wire.

4. Here's how to replace a threaded fastener in a metal component when you don't have the right size replacement: Insert into the tapped hole a plastic expansion anchor that accepts machine screws and bolts. Then drive in the appropriate fastener for the anchor.

5. Fasten objects to metal studs with self-tapping sheet-metal screws. Drill a small pilot hole for each screw.

To hang a heavy object from a metal stud wall, use a strong magnet to locate a stud, then drill through it and insert a toggle bolt.

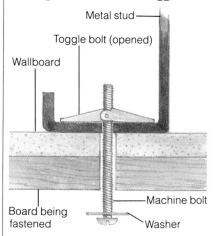

Metal stud
Toggle bolt (opened)
Wallboard
Board being fastened
Machine bolt
Washer

Fastening into wallboard

1. If you must attach an object to wallboard where there is no wood backing, such as a stud or joist, use hollow wall fasteners: plastic anchors, mollies, expansion anchors, or toggle bolts.

2. Hot-melt glue—the quick-setting kind dispensed from an electric glue gun—is ideal for adhering wood, plastic, and small metal pieces to wallboard.

3. To hang a lightweight item, such as a small picture frame or a calendar, make a hanger from an 8-inch length of wire clothes hanger. File a sharp point at one end of the wire

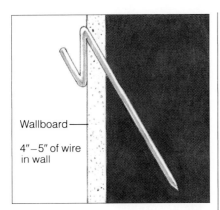

Wallboard

4″–5″ of wire in wall

and use pliers to make two bends at the other end, as shown. Then force the point into and through the wallboard at a sharp downward angle. Push about 4 or 5 inches of wire into the wall.

Fastening into wood

1. Save some elbow grease by rubbing a candle or a piece of soap on the threads of wood screws.

2. When nailing into hardwoods, bore pilot holes to prevent splitting the wood. If you don't have the appropriate bit, use a finishing nail as a drill bit (see *Drills*, p.67).

3. If you must screw into end grain, reinforce the joint with a hardwood dowel. Drill a hole and insert the dowel as shown.

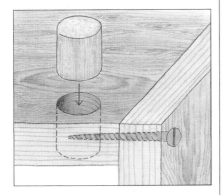

4. If a wood screw strips its hole, replace it with a larger screw. Or insert a few wooden matchsticks or toothpicks and drive in the screw.

Or whittle a tight-fitting wooden plug. Apply glue around the inner edge of the hole and then drive in

the plug with a hammer. Bore a pilot hole before driving the screw.

5. When fastening into wood, drive nails at a slight angle to increase their holding power. About two-thirds of the nail's length should enter the second board.

Fatigue

1. Tired all the time? See your physician for a checkup; there may be a medical reason for your fatigue.

2. Give aerobic exercise a try. It can combat the fatigue caused by insomnia, anxiety, stress, premenstrual hormonal changes, and—believe it or not—inactivity. It tones up your body, pumps oxygen to your brain, and revs up the production of "feel-good" body chemicals.

3. Cut down on caffeine and alcohol; eliminate both after dinner. Caffeine may appear to give you energy, but the lift is short-lived; it will also keep you awake. Alcohol makes you drowsy but interferes with normal sleep patterns.

4. Review your eating habits; crash diets cause fatigue by producing nutritional deficiencies. The cure: a well-balanced diet.

5. Check out your drugs. Antihistamines, diuretics, tranquilizers, pain relievers, and antihypertensives can all cause fatigue. So can many drug interactions (p.68). Discuss the problem with your pharmacist and doctor.

6. If you're one of the many who are prone to midafternoon energy slumps, try to schedule challenging, creative projects in the morning and save your routine chores for the afternoon. Alcohol-free, protein-based light lunches also combat afternoon fatigue.

Fences

1. A living screen of fast-growing flowering vines offers a low-cost summertime alternative to conventional fencing or hedges. Dig a strip 2 feet wide along the perimeter of the area you want to enclose and set rough poles at 6-foot inter-

vals along the center line. Staple a strip of chicken wire or plastic netting from top to bottom. Around the base of each pole, plant several seeds of a fast-growing flowering vine: scarlet runner beans, morning glories, sweet peas, and vining nasturtiums are good choices. As the tendrils grow, fasten them to the wire with twist ties.

2. Instead of topping off a hollow metal fence post with an expensive cap, cram it with wadded newspaper or styrene chips; then fill the top 2 inches with concrete.

3. When painting a fence with a roller, hold an old dustpan at the bottom of the posts to keep the roller from touching the ground and picking up dirt. If necessary, use a shoe polish dauber to touch up the posts at ground level.

4. If you're spray-painting a fence, protect plants by dragging a large piece of cardboard along the fence as a backdrop; a large appliance carton is ideal.

5. To treat an already painted fence post with a wood preservative, drill holes at a sharp angle on all four sides at the top, middle, and bottom of the post. Use the longest drill bit you have—at least 10 inches. Pour the preservative into the holes until it overflows and let it soak in for a few hours. Then patch the holes with wood putty.

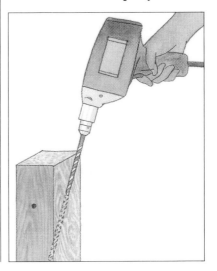

IN TIMES GONE BY

Old-time fertilizers

Before today's high-powered synthetic fertilizers came along, gardeners made do with what they found around the house and farm. Ashes from the fireplace were stashed away in a dry place, then worked into the soil a couple of weeks before planting time. (Not a bad idea today; hardwood ash is about 40 percent potash, a major plant nutrient.)

New England gardeners who lived near the coast harvested seaweed to plow directly into the soil; they found that the high salt content killed weeds and hastened decomposition. Farther south, guano (the accumulated droppings of seabirds and bats) was imported by the shipload from the Peruvian coast; it provided a plant-boosting yield of 10 percent nitrogen and 10 percent phosphorus. When New Mexico's Carlsbad Caverns were discovered, a ready market was found for the 100,000 tons of prized bat guano that was mined from the caves.

The standby of every gardener a century ago was "manure tea," used as a liquid fertilizer for houseplants, flowers, shrubs, and trees. To make it today, fill a 100-pound burlap bag with equal parts fresh cow, horse, and chicken manure, then sink it in a 60-gallon steel drum of water. Let it stand for 30 to 45 days; remove the bag and top up the drum with fresh water. The resulting tea-colored extract has yet to be improved upon.

Fertilizers

1. Make your own fast-acting tonic for garden plants. Mix 1 teaspoon Epsom salts, 1 teaspoon baking soda, and ½ teaspoon household ammonia in a gallon of warm water. Apply at a rate of 1 quart for a rosebush-sized shrub.

2. Mow regularly to keep grass clippings short. Leaving such clippings in place as a mulch not only saves the trouble of raking them but also returns nutrients to the soil, reducing the need for fertilizers by about 30 percent.

3. "Shampoo" your lawn with a spray of biodegradable liquid detergent (1 ounce in 10 gallons of water for every 1,500 square feet of turf) to reduce surface tension in the soil and allow fertilizers to penetrate more effectively. Apply when the ground is dry—after snow melts in the North or when winter rains stop in the West.

4. To rebuild garden soil naturally, plant a "green manure." Hairy vetch, a legume that manufactures its own nitrogen fertilizer, is a good choice. Sow 30 to 60 pounds of seed per acre, in the spring up North and in the fall elsewhere. The following spring, mow and till into the soil.

❯Fever

Except in a very young or a very old person, a fever up to 101°F is not ordinarily serious; aspirin or an aspirin substitute (p. 12) will usually bring it down to the normal 98.6°F. In the meantime, get plenty of rest and drink lots of fluids. If body temperature rises higher than 101°F, consult a doctor.

A sick child can develop a high fever very quickly; temperatures of 103°F are common in infants and small children but should be reported to a doctor nonetheless.

Fiberglass tubs

Never use harsh abrasive cleansers or scouring pads to scrub fiberglass; they scratch the surface, making it harder than ever to keep clean. Instead, use a special fiberglass cleanser or a mildly abrasive powder or liquid cleanser. Or rub with baking soda and a damp sponge. Then, for a nice shine, rinse the tub thoroughly and dry it.

For stubborn stains, let the cleanser stand for a minute or so before removing it. Or apply paint thinner, then wipe it off with a dry cloth and rinse thoroughly.

Files & rasps

1. Coarse tungsten-carbide sanding sheets with steel backing provide a workable stand-in for files and rasps. Coarse aluminum-oxide sandpaper also works but won't last as long. Both types will reduce wood, plastic, or metal. To shape flat surfaces, try attaching a sheet to the workbench, nailing it to the sides to keep the nailheads out of the way. To reproduce the action of an angle file, wrap the sandpaper around a tapered stick.

2. For rough wood texturing or heavy stock removal, cut and flatten a section from the side of a tin can. Puncture the metal liberally with a 6d nail, then turn it over and nail it to a block of wood. It won't last long, but it does the job until you can buy the right file.

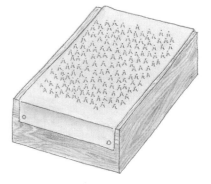

Fingernails

1. No emery board? Try the striking part of a matchbook.

2. For nail-mending paper, cut off a bit of a coffee filter or a tea bag.

3. When applying polish, rest your hands on an upside-down bowl.

4. To dry polish in a hurry, dip your fingers in a bowl of ice water (don't touch the cubes or the bowl). Or stick your hands in the freezer.

5. Do you tend to polish your finger as well as the nail? Moisten the end of a toothpick, wrap cotton thread or toilet paper around it, and saturate it with nail polish remover. Then dab away the polish.

6. To remove the yellow stains caused by some polishes, try soaking your nails in lemon juice.

7. Ragged cuticles? Lubricate them with lip balm (p.311). Or put a few drops of mineral, baby, or vitamin E oil into a bowl and soak your fingernails. (See also *Hands*, p.104.)

› Fire damage

1. Photograph or videotape all damage immediately to document the extent of the fire.

2. If firemen have broken doors or windows, have them boarded up.

3. Contact a loss-control consultant or public adjuster to assist you with your insurance claim.

4. Collect receipts for all costs related to your fire damage.

5. If it's cold, rent portable heaters or call for a mobile steam unit. If you can get neither, drain the plumbing system and pour antifreeze down the toilets and drains to prevent the pipes from freezing.

6. Before using electricity, have a licensed electrician check that everything is in safe working order.

7. Move damaged household goods to a safe place so that the insurance adjuster can inspect them.

8. Use fans, blowers, or dehumidifiers to dry out the house.

9. Move all rugs and carpets (and their padding) outdoors to dry and eliminate odors.

10. Wipe off wood furniture; vacuum loose sooty residue from upholstery and all horizontal surfaces.

11. Don't let wet fabrics dry in place. Move them to an undamaged room to dry at room temperature.

12. Transfer art, books, and other porous valuables to a freezer (if yours is too small, try a local frozen-food company) until you can hire specialists to restore them.

13. Discard all food, beverages, and medicines that have been exposed to high heat or otherwise damaged.

14. Send clothing to a dry cleaner with an ozone chamber; improper cleaning can set the smoky odor permanently.

Fire extinguishers

There are three categories of fire; each is extinguished differently.

1. *A* fires burn to *ash*. They are fueled by wood, cloth, paper, and some plastics. Water quenches them.

2. *B* fires *bubble*. They involve flammable liquids and grease. Most kitchen fires are of this type; do not use water on them—it will only splatter and spread the flames.

For oven or broiler fires, turn off the heat and shut the door. If meat catches fire, put a lid over it.

If the fire is on top of the stove, turn off the burner, leave the pan where it is, and smother the flames with a lid. Or douse the fire with handfuls of baking soda or salt.

Caution: Never put baking powder, sugar, or flour on a fire.

3. *C* fires have a *charge*. They occur in electrical wiring or appliances. Unplug the appliance or shut off the power (p.162). Extinguish the fire with an all-purpose, or ABC, fire extinguisher. (This can be used on all types of fires.) Pull its pin, press the handles, point at the base of the fire, and spray with back-and-forth passes.

Fireplace mess

Keep a whisk broom with your poker and shovel to make it easier to sweep up little bits and pieces of bark and firewood.

Remove ashes from the fireplace as soon as they're cold to prevent their being spread throughout the rest of your home. With the damper closed, gently sweep up as much as possible into a dustpan. To make the job easier next time, spread aluminum foil beneath the grate; when the ashes are cold, simply gather up the foil and discard it.

Vacuum the fireplace occasionally, using the crevice tool to clean out the corners. Wipe the andirons with a damp cloth or buff them with a metal cleaner; clean glass doors with a window cleaner or a solution of 1 tablespoon ammonia per quart of water.

Fireplaces

Fireplaces are inefficient because most of the heat rises up the chimney. In fact, furnace-heated house air may go with it, making the house even colder than it would have been without the fire.

Installing glass doors with an adjustable air vent over the fireplace opening gives the fire enough air to burn while controlling the loss of furnace-heated air. And the doors guard against flying sparks. Close the air vent whenever the fireplace is not in use and before retiring.

Raise efficiency another notch by putting in a fireback—a cast-iron plate, often embossed, that covers the back of the firebox. It reflects heat into the room.

You can increase efficiency by as much as 40 percent by installing a heat-circulating fireplace inset, complete with glass door, that warms and redistributes cool room air.

› Fires

If you decide to put out a small fire, position yourself between the fire and your escape route. If after 2 minutes you can neither contain nor extinguish the flames, don't waste critical time. Close the doors and windows to confine the flames, gases, and smoke, get out of the house, and call the fire department.

MAKING AN ESCAPE

1. Test each door for warmth (use the back of your hand). Do not open a door if it feels hot or if smoke is seeping in. Otherwise, proceed quickly and cautiously, staying low if there's smoke.

2. If you're in bed when the smoke

alarm goes off, roll out and crawl to the door. If the door is not hot, proceed as above. If possible, cover your mouth and nose with a damp cloth.
3. Try to escape through a first- or second-story window if the exit is blocked. If there's no rope or chain ladder, straddle the sill, then hang by your hands before dropping to the ground. If you must break a window, use a chair or drawer—anything but your hands.

AWAITING RESCUE

1. If you're trapped above the second floor, try to keep smoke and flames out by stuffing the cracks around the door, the heating ducts, and the air ducts with damp sheets or curtains. (Do not use paper.) If a faucet is nearby, fill a wastebasket and douse all doors and walls between you and the fire.
2. Position yourself near a window and signal by waving a brightly colored cloth or a flashlight or by turning a light on and off rapidly. Keep the windows closed to prevent a fire-attracting draft. If necessary, crack a window at the top to let smoke out, at the bottom to admit fresh air. Do not break the window—you may need to shut it if there's smoke outside.

Fire safety

1. Be prepared: Draw a plan of your home (including stairs, windows, and doors) and plot two escape routes from each room. Study the

plan with household members; assign someone to help young children, the elderly, or the disabled. (As an extra precaution, apply special decals to the windows of their rooms so that firemen can locate and rescue them.)
2. Hold regular fire drills and designate a place to meet outside for a head count.
3. Make sure everyone needing to use a window for escape is able to reach and unlock it, remove the screen or storm window, and reach the ground safely.
4. Purchase chain ladders (available from locksmiths) and store them next to upstairs windows.

❯ Fires in public places

1. Note the location of the fire exits any time you're in a high-rise office building, theater, restaurant, or any other public place—no matter how brief the visit.
2. Don't use an elevator if a fire breaks out; heat or power failure can make it stall or go to the floor that's burning.

IN HOTELS AND MOTELS

1. Immediately after checking into your room, go into the hall and locate the exits and fire-alarm box. Count the number of doors between your room and the exits.
2. Buy a portable smoke detector to hang on your door.
3. In case of fire, roll out of bed, take your keys and flashlight (make it a habit to keep them on the night-

stand), and crawl to the door. Check to be sure that it isn't hot, open it cautiously, and follow your escape route. If the exits are blocked or filled with smoke, stay in your room.

Firewood

1. For the hottest, cleanest fire, burn hardwoods rather than softwoods. Hickory, apple, black locust, beech, oak, yellow birch, ironwood, and sugar maple produce the most heat. For scent, throw a cedar log or two onto the fire.
2. Brittle frozen logs are the easiest to split. But don't use a frozen ax or maul; the steel may crack.
3. Use a forked branch as a prop if you have trouble keeping a log upright on the chopping block.
4. If you have a lot of wood to split, save time and muscle by renting a gas-operated log splitter; they're available at low daily rates and do the job in a fraction of the time.
5. If you don't have a woodshed, stack the split wood in layers alternating in direction, log cabin-style. Store it bark side up so that the wood sheds rain.
6. Save money by buying slabwood from a sawmill or discounted culls, ends, and warped boards from a lumberyard.
7. Tightly roll a stack of newspapers to log size and tie the roll with twine. (Avoid color pages; the ink may release chemicals.) These "logs" may lack the romance of glowing embers, but they burn cleanly and last almost as long as hardwood.

Fireworks

1. Buy only labeled, top-quality fireworks; store in a cool, dry place well away from all flammable materials.
2. Light fireworks outdoors, one at a time, in an open area. Never ignite a firecracker indoors or in a can or bottle. Avoid high-explosive firecrackers; some are equal to a quarter stick of dynamite or more.
3. Keep everyone at a distance and out of harm's way when lighting fireworks; aim rockets and set off

Roman candles, wheels, or snakes away from people and houses.

4. Never pick up a "dud"; it could explode at any moment. Keep a water bucket nearby for emergencies and for disposal of used fireworks.

WATERWORKS

As an alternative to fireworks (especially if they're illegal in your state), present a nighttime display of colorful waterworks. Ask your guests to wear swimsuits and hand out flashlights covered with colored cellophane. Turn on your sprinklers, then light up the water as it sprays in all directions; play recorded patriotic marches—or Tchaikovsky's *1812 Overture*, which actually ends with cannon fire.

Fish bait

1. You can substitute cheese balls, bread balls, or pieces of lunch meat for live bait. A bit of aluminum foil—even a gum wrapper—makes a convincing minnow.

2. Trick night crawlers, the best bait worms, into emerging from their holes by pounding a small stake into the ground and rubbing vigorously across the top with another piece of wood. The vibrations will drive the worms to the surface.

3. Ensure a steady supply of bait by starting your own worm farm. Line a wooden box 2 to 3 feet long with leaves and grass and fill it halfway with soil. Add another layer of dry grass and leaves and a cup or two of chopped garbage. (Coffee

grounds and vegetables that rot quickly are good choices.) Top with a final layer of leaves and wet the mixture down before adding the worms. Feed the worms monthly with chopped garbage and sour milk and they'll multiply rapidly.

4. Grubs and mealworms also make good bait. You can raise mealworms by filling a 2-gallon jar three-quarters full of flour mixed with sawdust. Put in the mealworms and punch tiny holes in the lid. Don't be surprised when you see that the mealworms, which are actually beetle larvae, have matured inside the jar into full-grown beetles. They will, in turn, produce more mealworms.

5. Freeze unused minnows. But don't defrost them completely when you use them again; they'll be too soggy to stay on your hook unless they are partially frozen.

Fish cleaning

1. Before cleaning a fish, wipe it instead of washing it; water causes a slick coating to form. If you do have to handle a slippery fish, rub your fingers first with salt.

2. You can remove the innards of a fish with one quick jerk, since the tongue, gullet, gills, and intestines are connected.

First, using a small, very sharp knife, cut through the gristle that holds the gills to the skull at the roof of the mouth. Then feel for the bony ridge next to the gill plate on the outside of the fish; cut along the outside of this ridge, extending the cut all the way to the tip of the lower jaw. Repeat on the other side of the head.

Again insert the knife into the fish's mouth, this time cleanly severing the strip of gristle that connects the tongue to the jawbone.

Next, keeping your cut very shallow, slit the belly cleanly from the gill line to the anal vent.

Finally, holding the fish lengthwise, put your fingers into the slit under the jaw, grab the tongue,

and pull downward stongly and quickly. The innards should all come out in a clump. If necessary, cut around the anal orifice to disconnect them.

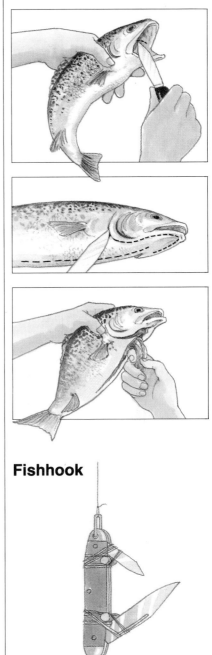

Fishhook

Need a fishhook? In a pinch, even a pocketknife can become a hook for a large fish. Prop the blade partly open with a piece of wood and tie it in place. Use a smaller blade at the other end to form a barb.

For smaller prey, try a safety pin, wire, bent finishing nail, or even a paper clip. Or carve a hook from bone or hardwood as the Indians did, binding on a thorn or sharp sliver for a barb.

Fish poaching

1. You don't need a poaching pan to poach fish; your roasting pan will do fine. Place the fish on the rack, cover with water or stock, and barely simmer for 10 minutes per inch of thickness at the middle.
2. To keep a poached fish from breaking as you transfer it from cooking pan to serving dish, cook it on cheesecloth or greased aluminum foil. Cover the rack of the poacher or roasting pan, making sure enough material extends over the edge so that you can get a good grip. Hold the material taut as you lift the fish from the pan and slide or roll it onto a serving dish.

Fish stuffing

To dress up a fish, stuff it with your own mixtures of chopped mushrooms, bread crumbs, or cheese. Pieces of shrimp, crab, and lobster also make a good filling. If a big enough cavity is left after cleaning, simply stuff the fish and close with skewers or sew shut with heavy-duty thread.

1. If you must make more room for stuffing in a cleaned fish, take out the spine and ribs. Make a slit along the length of the spine with a sharp knife, cutting on the thicker side (often the darker side) of the fish. Lift the flesh with your fingers and, with the tip of the knife, release it from the ribs. Turn the fish over, cut down the other side of the spine, and repeat. If you haven't already removed the head and tail, cut through the bones at the head and just above the tail, then remove the spine and ribs in one piece. Close the openings with skewers or heavy-duty thread.

2. To prepare fillets or steaks for baking, simply sandwich the stuffing between two of them; top with more stuffing if you like. Or spread the stuffing on a thin fillet and roll it up like a jelly roll; secure with toothpicks or poultry pins.

Fish tanks

To keep tropical fish happy, change about a third of the water in their tank every week. The simplest way is to make a siphon from an old hose or plastic tubing. Pinch the bottom tightly with your fingers and fill the tube with water from the faucet; pinch the top closed and carry it to the tank. Insert one end in the tank and the other in a pail a few feet below it. The water will flow from the tank to the pail. When you've removed enough water, refill the tank with water that has been sitting at room temperature for several hours.

To start the siphoning without filling the tube with water, suck sharply on the loose end of the tube before putting it in the pail. But do this carefully, lest you get a mouthful of fishy water.

Fitness for the elderly

1. If you're not exercising regularly, ask your doctor if it would be advisable. If he thinks you should exercise, choose an activity, such as

---

walking, biking, or swimming, that won't cause stress to your joints or tendons—and don't start out too strenuously (see *Endurance building*, p.72). Check with your local senior center or health club for classes in aerobics and calisthenics tailored for older bodies. Whatever exercise you select, in order to reduce the chances of injury, warm up and cool down gradually (p.224).

2. If you have difficulty walking or are otherwise disabled, rent or buy exercise cassettes to guide you in less strenuous fitness routines. Or seek out an adult activities center where a physical therapist leads special exercise sessions.

3. To keep fit mentally, stay involved. Church, family, and volunteer activities; crafts, puzzles, and games; and especially a wide circle of friends—all contribute to sustained mental alertness.

4. If you live alone, adopt a pet, preferably one that's easy to look after. If a dog is too much to handle, consider a cat instead or perhaps a bird or fish.

Fitness on the road

ON AN AIRPLANE

1. Check to see if the airline magazine or "fitness channel" provides an in-seat exercise program.

2. Exercise in your chair (see *Office exercises*, p.145; *Exercising gently*, p.74).

3. Walk up and down the aisles for 15 minutes every hour or so; take the opportunity to stretch in the open spaces next to the rest rooms.

ON A DRIVING TRIP

1. Stop every 2 hours for 5 minutes of strenuous stretching and a brisk 15-minute walk.

2. Walk for at least 15 minutes before eating lunch and dinner.

AT HIGH ELEVATIONS

The first day just take a stroll; after that, do your usual exercises but reduce the time by 15 percent for each 5,000-foot gain in elevation. If it's hot, don't exercise outdoors between 10 A.M. and 4 P.M.

AT THE HOTEL

1. If there's no exercise room or pool, ask at the desk for a list of local health clubs or get a street map so that you can walk or jog.

2. To find an aerobics class, look under "Exercise and physical fitness programs" in the Yellow Pages.

3. Bad weather? Walk or jog in the halls. Or stair walk: up for 1 minute, down for 30 seconds.

IN YOUR ROOM

1. Pack a jump rope, exercise tape, and cassette player.

2. Run in place to the morning news or dance to radio music.

3. Stretch for 10 minutes morning and night, or pack 100 paper clips or bobby pins, throw them in the air, and bend to retrieve each one.

Flashlights for camping

1. A flashlight that throws a short, wide beam is adequate for most camping needs. Long beams use up battery power faster.

2. To keep your flashlight from being turned on accidentally in your pack or glove compartment, reverse one battery; reinsert it when needed. Or place a strip of duct tape over the switch.

3. Attach a loop of string to your flashlight so that it can be hung inside a tent or from a branch.

4. Headlamps are often more useful than flashlights. They leave your hands free, and you are far less likely to drop one of them.

5. Cold drains battery power. If the light beam fades in cold weather, warm the batteries next to your skin. Keep your flashlight warm by carrying it inside your jacket; at night keep it in your sleeping bag.

6. Even if your flashlight is waterproof, always carry a backup light in a plastic bag.

Fleas

Attack fleas on two fronts: on your pet and in your house.

Comb your pet with a flea comb to remove adult fleas and eggs. Bathe the animal in a mixture of orange oil (available at health food stores) and shampoo. If you can't find orange oil, buy a shampoo containing citrus extracts (limonene). As an extra measure, spray the animal's bedding with a nontoxic insect growth regulator, such as methoprene, which keeps flea larvae from developing into adults for up to 3 months.

To keep fleas out of the house, steam-clean all rugs and pet bedding; wash pet bedding at a high temperature to kill eggs and larvae. Vacuum the furniture, rugs and bedding, and baseboards.

Flood damage

1. Before dealing with the effects of flooding—whether from an act of nature, a burst pipe, or an overflowing bathtub—shut off your home's power (p.162).

2. Remove standing water with a submersible pump. (If the power is still off, rent a gasoline-powered pump.) Then scrape all remaining debris into piles with a squeegee or a 4-inch-wide strip of ½-inch plywood screwed to a push broom. Shovel the piles of mud and debris into pails and deposit them outdoors. If there's a lot of debris, shovel it out a window into a trash can, wheelbarrow, or pickup truck.

3. To dry out a room quickly, place fans in windows at the opposite ends of the room; put one on intake, the other on exhaust. You can also dry out a room with portable heaters fueled by kerosene or propane; they can probably be rented from a local contractor.

4. If trapped water has caused a ceiling to sag, punch drainage holes at the low points with an awl, an ice pick, or a small screwdriver.

❯Floods

If time permits, move portable valuables to the upper floors of the house.

1. If your home is susceptible to flooding, backfill soil against the foundation so that the land slopes gradually away from the house. Plant grass or shrubs to absorb water and prevent erosion.

For extreme situations, dig around the foundation and lay perforated PVC drainpipe on a gravel bed. Slope it so that the water will drain off.

2. Photograph and list all your household belongings (see *Valuables*, p.221); keep this inventory in your safe-deposit box.

FLOOD WATCH

1. As soon as you hear of a flood watch, prepare for evacuation. Fill the gas tank and stock the car with food, water, warm clothes, blankets, flashlights, and a first-aid kit with essential medications.

2. Rinse bathtubs, sinks, and jugs with household bleach and fill with clean water for drinking.

3. Shut off the electric power (p.162) and gas valve.

4. To prevent fast-rising floodwaters from lifting your house off its foundation, open the windows and doors to let out the water.

DURING THE FLOOD

1. Listen to a portable radio for information and instructions.

2. Don't drive through water; if the car stalls, abandon it and make your way to high ground.

3. If you're trapped at home, go to the top floor and wait for help. Take emergency food and water, warm clothing, and a flashlight.

AFTERWARD

1. Check your home for structural damage.

2. If you smell gas, open all the doors and windows, leave, and report the leak to the gas company.

3. Throw out all food that has been touched by floodwaters.

4. Boil all drinking and cooking water for 10 minutes. (See also *Flood damage*, p.85.)

Floors

1. To remove stains from resilient flooring, use a detergent that contains ammonia. Scrub lightly with a plastic scouring pad. If that fails, rub lightly with extra-fine (No. 000) steel wool. Then wax or polish.

2. "Erase" light scratches in resilient flooring by rubbing with a soft cloth moistened with paste floor wax. Or try rubbing with the edge of a large coin. If the flaw remains, place two layers of aluminum foil over it and press with a hot iron.

3. If you spill nail polish on resilient flooring, allow it to dry until tacky, then peel it off. Clean up any residue with nail polish remover.

4. Chewing gum stuck to the floor? Put an ice cube in a small cup and turn the cup upside down over the gum. When the gum is brittle, gently pry it up with a butter knife.

5. Never clean a wood floor with water; it can cause warping, and even worse, wood rot. Instead, use a dry dust mop. If necessary, wrap the mop with a damp, soft cloth that's thoroughly wrung out.

Flour beetles

If a package of flour, cornmeal, nuts, cereal, or birdseed is seriously infested, discard it immediately. To get rid of a minor infestation, place the foodstuff in the deep freeze for 4 days or in the oven long enough so that the internal temperature remains at 120°F for 30 minutes. (To prevent overheating, prop the oven door open a few inches.)

To guard against reinfestation, clean out cabinets by vacuuming and scrubbing. Remove and replace shelf paper. Keep foodstuffs in tightly closed clear containers so that the pests can be seen without removing the lid.

Flour sifter

The flour labeled "presifted" is so uniform in texture that it doesn't need sifting again—just a good stir to lighten it. Unbleached flour needs sifting, and so do those that you use in delicate pastries and cakes. If you don't have a sifter on hand, try one of these alternatives (*before* you measure).

1. Put the flour in a medium-size fine-meshed kitchen strainer and shake or stir until it sifts through.

2. Your food processor will give you extra-fluffy flour; use the metal blade and pulse two times for 5 seconds each.

Flower boxes

Wooden flower boxes provide far better insulation than plastic or metal planters, helping to protect roots against summer heat and unseasonable frosts.

Rot-resistant cedar and redwood are the best materials. Less expensive spruce and pine must be treated after the box is assembled. Avoid commercial wood preservatives;

their fumes may kill plants. Instead, char the interior of the box by painting it with kerosene and setting it afire for 30 seconds. Smother the flames by turning the box over or covering it with a piece of plywood.

Exploded view of flower box construction.

Flower drying

Would you like to keep your house full of flowers right through the winter? You can do it by drying your favorite blossoms in your microwave oven. Roses (including buds), geraniums, marigolds, and zinnias dry well; impatiens and petunias don't. Whatever you use, cut the flowers late in the morning, after the dew has dried. And be aware that your dried flowers will come out a couple of shades darker; red roses become almost black, pink or coral ones become red.

1. Line a microwave-safe container with a bed of silica gel crystals (available at craft stores) and heat at *High* for 3 minutes to make sure the crystals are as dry as possible.
2. Pour an inch of warm crystals into a heavy glass tumbler wide enough to accommodate the flower you're drying.
3. Snip the flower stem so that only an inch remains attached to the flower, then stick the stem into the crystals so that the blossom stands upright.
4. Gradually pour the remaining warm crystals down the side of the glass until the blossom is completely covered.
5. Microwave at *High* for 1 minute 45 seconds for rosebuds or up to 4 or 5 minutes for large, fleshy blossoms (experiment with imperfect blossoms to judge precise timing).

6. Cool for 20 minutes, then gently pour off the crystals. Clean the flower petals carefully with a fine paintbrush, then mist lightly with an acrylic spray. Tape to florist wire to make a new stem.

Flowerpots

1. Look around the house for containers that would make good flowerpots. Pretty coffee mugs fit on a windowsill and make the perfect holder for herbs or small plants. Drill a drainage hole in the bottom with a carbon-tipped glass or masonry bit, or place an inch of gravel and some charcoal in the bottom of the container to keep the roots from becoming waterlogged.

Larger kitchen containers, such as bean pots, ceramic milk pitchers, and the Crockpot that sits abandoned at the back of the cupboard, are good choices, too.
2. Cleaning a plastic flowerpot requires nothing more than a stiff brush and hot soapy water, but the stains and ground-in dirt on an old clay pot may prove more stubborn. Soak the pot in a solution of ½ cup bleach per gallon of hot water for 5 minutes, then remove, rinse, and scrub; repeat as necessary.
3. If a pot has housed a diseased plant, sterilize it before reusing by soaking it in boiling water or running it through a complete cycle in the dishwasher.

Flowers

You can make your own preservative to keep cut flowers fresh. To each quart of water add 1 tablespoon sugar, 1 teaspoon vinegar, 1 teaspoon mouthwash, and 3 to 4 drops dishwashing detergent. An alternative is to add a drop of chlorine bleach to the water.

Before setting flowers in the water, remove 1 to 2 inches of stem by making a diagonal cut with a sharp knife (scissors crush the stems). Wash bowls and vases with hot soapy water before reusing; fill them with lukewarm water.

Keep flower arrangements out of direct sunlight; store them in a cool room (40°F to 50°F) until ready to display. Although florists keep cut flowers in a cooler, the home refrigerator is not a good storage place, especially if it contains fruit; fruit releases ethylene gas, which will cause the flowers to age prematurely. (See also *Tulips,* p.217.)

Flyswatter

Because flies are sensitive to air currents, a rolled-up newspaper is a poor substitute for a porous flyswatter. Instead, put some rubbing alcohol in a plant mister and spray the fly. The stuff kills on contact—but be aware that it may mar some finished surfaces.

Or zap the fly with hairspray to immobilize its wings; then you can swat it with a newspaper.

Folding laundry

1. To reduce wrinkling, remove clothes from the dryer and hang them up as soon as possible. Since most of the laundry is stored in or near the bedroom, do your sorting on the bed. If the seams or pockets on jeans or other sportswear are slightly damp and puckered, pull on them and flatten them with your fingers; then let them air-dry before putting them away. This can often save you ironing time.
2. Fold towels lengthwise first so

that you don't have to refold them when you hang them on the rack in the bathroom.

3. Try this method for folding contour sheets: (1) Fold in half, bringing the contoured ends together; at each corner align the contoured edges and invert one into the other. (2) Fold in half again, bringing one matched set of corners to the other; invert one set into the other set. (3) Then fold as usual, smoothing the edges as you go.

Reverse side of contour sheet

Step 1   Step 2

Food odors

1. To rid a plastic container of food odors, freeze it or expose it to sunlight for several hours. Or drop a lemon wedge into it, close it, and let it stand until the odor disappears. (It may take a few days.)

2. Freshen a lunchbox by moistening a piece of bread with white vinegar and leaving it in the closed box overnight.

3. Eliminate lingering food odors in the kitchen by baking orange peels at 350°F for several minutes.

4. Fast cooking may be the cure for the powerful aroma that Brussels sprouts, cabbage, and broccoli can leave. Put them in a pot of rapidly boiling water and return it quickly to the boil. A few drops of vinegar in the water helps, too.

5. For a natural room deodorizer, keep an open jar of vanilla beans in the kitchen.

Food processors

1. Don't ignore your food processor because you can't face cleaning it. Check the instruction manual; many models can be cleaned in the dishwasher.

2. The bowls of food processors have been known to crack right in the middle of processing. Don't remove the food; just tape the crack temporarily with several layers of masking or duct tape, then finish processing. Replace the bowl at the first opportunity.

3. To prevent leaks between an average size bowl and its cover, never use more than 2 cups liquid.

4. Don't think something's wrong with your processor if food is left on top of the disc after slicing or shredding. It's normal.

5. Avoid overprocessing foods: use the pulse button to chop. Check the food frequently to make sure that it's not getting mushy.

6. Pastry scraps? Throw them into the processor along with some sesame seeds, honey, brown sugar, or a zesty spice. Both kids and adults love cookies made this way.

Food safety

1. Bacteria love to lurk in the cracks and little knife nicks on your cutting board. Use a brush to scrub the board vigorously with hot soapy water after each use. And don't let any meat, fish, or poultry—raw or cooked—sit on the board for more than a few minutes.

2. Before freezing uncooked poultry, remove it from the store package, rinse well, and rewrap with your own plastic wrap or freezer paper; this reduces the bacteria accumulated between processing and purchase. It's also a good practice to rinse chicken under cold running water before you cook it.

3. If you're grating lemon, lime, or orange peel, scrub the fruits first under cold running water; they may have a residue of insecticide.

4. Don't leave homemade custards or other milk-based dishes in the refrigerator for more than 2 days. Yogurt is an exception.

5. It's safer to thaw frozen foods, including the Thanksgiving turkey, in the refrigerator than outside it.

6. In a hot climate carry an insulated cooler in the trunk of your car to make sure cold foods get from the supermarket to the kitchen without spoilage.

7. Stow a freezer gel pack in a lunchbox. Or freeze the sandwiches overnight before you pack them in an insulated lunchbox—they'll thaw nicely by the time lunch rolls around. (See also *Picnics*, p. 155.)

Food storage for campers

1. Remove powdered foods from their original containers and repackage small quantities in double plastic bags. Between the two layers, slip in an identification label and the mixing instructions.

2. Transfer spices from large containers into clean prescription bottles or plastic film canisters; label the containers *and* lids.

3. To protect eggs, carry them in a container filled with pancake mix or flour.

4. Snowbanks provide cool storage; put food in secure containers and bury it deeply.

5. A stream can serve as a refrigerator; put the food in well-anchored waterproof bags.

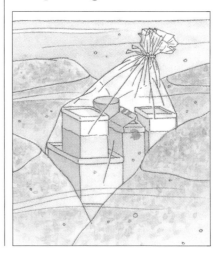

6. In camp remove food from backpacks and tents and leave zippers and flaps open. Otherwise rodents will gnaw through them to investigate aromas.

Football jargon

Here's your guide to what the gridiron announcers are saying on television and radio:

Audible. A play called at the line of scrimmage, nullifying the play that was called in the huddle. Also called an automatic.

Blitz. A defensive play in which one or more linebackers rush the passer. It's a gamble, since the rushing linebackers leave holes in the defensive formation.

Bomb. A very long forward pass.

Bullet. An extremely forceful forward pass thrown so that it travels in a straight line.

Bump and run. A defensive maneuver in which a cornerback hits or bumps into a potential pass receiver as he leaves the line of scrimmage, hoping to upset his timing, and then runs with him. Only one such bump is allowed.

Clipping. An illegal block in which an offensive player hits a defensive player from behind.

Completion. A forward pass that's caught by an eligible receiver.

Conversion. The scoring of an extra point after a touchdown, made by kicking the ball from a set position so that it clears the crossbar between the goalposts. In college ball only, a team can score a 2-point conversion by running or passing the ball into the end zone.

Fair catch. An option of the receiver of a punt. By raising his hand before catching the ball, he indicates he will not run with it; defenders may not tackle him.

False start. A violation committed by an offensive player who, after having assumed a set position on the line of scrimmage, moves before the ball is snapped.

Interference. Preventing an opposing player from catching a pass by holding or pushing him intentionally; an illegal maneuver.

Line of scrimmage. An imaginary line upon which the forward point of the ball rests; it separates the offensive and defensive forces.

Offside. A 5-yard penalty called when a player has any part of his body beyond the line of scrimmage as the ball is put into play.

Onside kick. A deceptive kickoff in which the ball skitters along the ground just far enough so that the kicking team may recover it.

Pocket. An area protected by blockers behind the line of scrimmage, within which the quarterback sets up to throw a pass.

Reverse. A play in which an offensive back running in one direction hands off to another moving in the opposite direction.

Sack. To tackle the quarterback behind the line of scrimmage.

Safety. A 2-point score awarded the defense for downing the ball in the offense's own end zone.

Shotgun. An offensive formation, used primarily for passing, in which the quarterback stands several yards behind the center to receive a long snap.

Two-minute warning. An official time-out, called when 2 minutes of play remain in each half of a game, during which commercials and promotional spots are aired.

Footgear for sports

1. Your old-fashioned sneakers are still fine for boating as long as they have a nonslip tread.

2. Try high-top basketball shoes for canoeing (and portaging); they'll provide extra ankle support when you need it.

3. It's OK to play tennis in aerobic shoes (they give support for quick side-to-side movements), but don't do aerobics in tennis or running shoes—they lack sufficient cushioning under the ball of the foot.

FIT

1. Be sure your shoes have enough room for your toes to spread under your full weight; allow ½ inch between the end of your big toe and

---

DID YOU KNOW . . . ?

Footgear favorites: the story of sneakers

Although actor Dudley Moore (whose feet are two different sizes) bought 30 custom-made pairs in one day, and singer Mick Jagger got married in them, and comedian Woody Allen was spotted wearing them with a tuxedo, these modern miracles of comfort are really nothing new. When—as Indian lore has it—members of a Brazilian tribe dipped their feet into the liquid latex of rubber trees some 300 years ago, they created what were, in effect, the world's first sneakers.

The vulcanizing process, developed in the 1860's, made it possible to manufacture rubber shoe soles. But it wasn't until just before the turn of the century that canvas-and-rubber sneakers appeared, and Keds didn't become popular until 1917. For years sneakers (named for their noiselessness) were white or black, low or high cut, and maligned as unhealthful and informal.

In 1962 the first modern running shoe, with a comfortable wide front, a rippled sole, and a shock-absorbing wedge, was marketed. Innovations followed: designer colors, new sole patterns, "breathable" nylon uppers, and more. Now technology has caught up with the running shoe. One model has a built-in microchip that measures speed, distance, and calories burned. Another, when plugged into a computer, tracks long-term performance.

the tip of the shoe when you are standing on both feet.

2. Shoes should be snug and supportive in the heel, but not tight. If you have narrow heels, buy shoes with extra lacing holes. Or loop each shoestring through the last hole on its own side and thread the opposite string through the loop.

Foot odor

1. Soak your feet every night for 10 minutes in cool Burow's solution (1:40 concentration), keeping your toes separated to ensure penetration; air-dry. If foot odor persists, double the strength of the solution. If you can't find Burow's at your drugstore, use a solution of 1 ounce vinegar in 1 gallon water. Once the problem is under control, soak two or three times a week.

2. Dust your feet with talcum powder or baking soda every day.

3. Wear clean, absorbent, light-weight wool or cotton socks and leather shoes; steer clear of synthetic fibers—they don't breathe.

4. Rinse socks in a solution of 1 ounce vinegar in 1 gallon water.

5. Avoid wearing the same pair of shoes 2 days in a row.

6. Air your feet as much as possible by wearing open sandals.

Foot problems

ATHLETE'S FOOT

Soak your feet in cool Burow's solution (1:40 concentration) and rinse your socks in a solution of 1 ounce vinegar in 1 gallon water.

Apply an over-the-counter anti-fungal solution or cream between your toes and on reddish, scaly areas of your feet twice a day for a month. Sprinkle antifungal powder in socks and shoes daily.

To prevent a recurrence, keep your feet dry and clean; if they tend to sweat, dust the inside of your shoes with antifungal powder and change your socks twice a day. Wear shower sandals in the locker room.

BLISTERS

Leave blisters alone to break spontaneously. Twice a day apply a compress of Burow's solution (1:40 concentration), then cover the blister with antibiotic cream.

BUNIONS

Elevate your feet and apply an ice pack: 10 minutes on, 10 minutes off, until swelling and pain dissipate. Or run cold water over your feet for 2 minutes at a time.

CALLUSES AND CORNS

Use a pumice stone to smooth off calluses right after bathing.

Don't cut corns away—rub them with an emery board. Cover a stubborn one with a pad on which you've put several drops of 10 percent salicylic acid solution or use a 40 percent salicylic acid plaster; after 4 or 5 days soak the foot in water and check to see if the corn has dissolved enough to lift off. Repeat the treatment if necessary.

Caution: If you're a diabetic, seek professional foot care for calluses and corns.

INGROWN TOENAILS

Soak the foot in a basin of lukewarm water with 1 tablespoon Epsom salts twice a day. Insert a piece of cotton soaked in mineral or baby oil under the nail and cover with a gauze pad. Repeat daily until the ingrown toenail has healed.

SORE FEET

Soak weary feet in a basin of hot water with 2 tablespoons Epsom salts or a handful of plain salt. Or rub them with ice cubes, towel-dry,

and splash with cologne. Elevate them whenever possible.

Massage sore feet by rolling them over a tennis or golf ball. Or knead them, pulling each toe for 10 seconds, and run the knuckles of a fist along the midsoles.

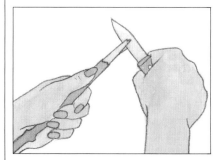

Forcing flowers

For a springtime display in midwinter, you can force flowers from a few branches of forsythia, redbud, pussywillow, or witch hazel.

1. Anytime after the first of the year, choose branches with the fattest buds (these are flower buds—the smaller ones produce only leaves). Cut the branches off with sharp pruning shears.

2. Scrape the bark from the lower 3 to 4 inches of each branch and split the end lengthwise for 2 to 3 inches.

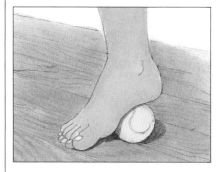

3. Plunge the whole branch into a bathtub full of room-temperature water for a few hours.

4. Arrange the branches in a vase or bowl of cold water and set it in a sunny room. (Ideally, the temperature should be 60°F to 65°F.) Mist the branches twice a week to protect the buds from drying out. They should bloom within 2 weeks or so.

You can also force apples, crab-apples, pears, dogwoods, and lilacs, but they'll take 3 to 4 weeks to bloom; don't cut them until 6 weeks before their normal flowering time.

Foreign phrases

Before visiting another country, it's best to learn the language; take a course, buy tapes, or borrow them from the library. But if there isn't time, take along a phrase book and dictionary or at least learn a few basics such as *Please, Thank you, Good day, Where is . . .* , and *Help, I need a doctor.*

Don't be afraid to use these phrases; a few words can go a long way toward making friends and getting assistance. Gestures and pantomime also help. Or carry a pocket-size electronic device that translates your phrase. For a real treat, hire an interpreter.

In a country that uses a different alphabet (Japan, for example), buy a map with both foreign and English place names. Before leaving your hotel, have someone write your destination in the native language. Carry the name, address, and phone number of your hotel with you at all times (a printed matchbook or the hotel's business card is good for this). Keep a list of emergency phone numbers handy, including the police, local tourist board, and American embassy or consulate.

For a list of English-speaking doctors in various countries, call the International Association for Medical Assistance to Travelers (716-754-4883).

›Fractures

Even a slight force can cause a broken bone. Fracture victims often feel the bone break or hear a snapping sound.

There may be intense pain and tenderness—especially when there is pressure on the area of the break—with swelling and discoloration; the limb may look deformed or oddly angled. Or swelling and pain may not occur for hours.

Many fractures are impossible to detect without an X-ray. If any of these symptoms are present, however, assume there's a fracture and seek medical help.

WHILE AWAITING TREATMENT

1. Relieve swelling by placing an ice pack near the break (not on it).
2. Immobilize the injured part and move as little as possible.
3. If an ankle or a foot appears to be broken, take off shoes and socks and elevate the leg.
4. If bone has pierced the skin, cover the wound with a dry, clean dressing and apply pressure to control severe bleeding. (See also *Slings,* p.188; *Splints,* p.194.)

Freckles

1. If you don't like your freckles, stay out of the sun; it darkens them. And *don't* put lemon juice on them; it just increases the skin's sensitivity to the sun.
2. Cover them with liquid makeup.
3. Flaunt your freckles! Even them out by dotting on rose-brown lip pencil and wear copper-toned lipstick, blusher, and eyeshadow to set them off.

Free information

1. For information on a specific subject, look it up under "Associations" in your telephone directory or go to your public library and use the *Encyclopedia of Associations.* This extraordinary three-volume resource contains details on more than 25,000 health, sports, religious, and other organizations. Chances are that one or more of them will give you the basic information you need and connect you to other qualified sources. Because many of these groups work on a low budget, if you expect a prompt reply, send in your request with a stamped, self-addressed envelope.
2. Call on the government. Its numbers are often listed in a separate section of blue pages in your phone book, or if you know the name of the appropriate government agency, call directory assistance. When you're connected, ask for public information.
3. Check your local newspaper and library for reference services.
4. To learn more about a city you're going to visit, contact the local visitors bureau or chamber of commerce. For facts about a foreign country, contact the public information department of its tourist bureau, the United Nations mission, or the embassy.
5. If you want to know what to raise on your land and how to raise it, call upon your local Cooperative Extension Service; its number is in the telephone directory.
6. Send for a copy of the *Consumer's Resource Handbook,* a free paperback published by the federal government. It lists many businesses' customer service numbers, Better Business Bureaus throughout the country, trade associations, government consumer protection agencies, and other sources of free information. For a copy, write to Handbook, Consumer Information Center, Pueblo, CO 81009.

The *Consumer Information Catalog* is also valuable; it describes dozens of government publications available free of charge or at very low prices. To request a free copy, write to Catalog, Consumer Information Center, Pueblo, CO 81009.

Freelancing

Selling your art, writing, or photography is difficult, but successful freelancing can be a rewarding full-time job, or it can be a good supplement to a more stable source of income.

To find a pro who can assess your talent and possibly help you break into the freelance market, take a course that relates to your chosen field at a local university or adult learning center. Also join a writers', artists', or photographers' group;

use ads to find fellow hopefuls to form a support group; or consult the *Encyclopedia of Associations* at your library for the names of appropriate organizations.

The easiest places to break in are local newspapers, penny savers (free papers supported by advertising), and regional magazines. Submit your work for no fee at first, then photocopy your published work to send to larger publications.

Writer's Market, Artist's Market and *Photographer's Market* (check your public library or the research section of a bookstore for copies) contain the names, addresses, phone numbers, and fee scales of publications that buy freelance work, along with the names of contact people. Many will send you samples and freelancers' guidelines if you provide a stamped, self-addressed envelope big enough for the publication you've requested. Subscribe to magazines for writers, photographers, or artists for tips and names to know.

Once you've targeted a publication, submit several ideas for stories, photos, or illustrations; you might even get an assignment and a cash advance.

Be professional. Use appropriate business cards and letterhead. Do your best on every project and include a bill with each assigned submission. Be cordial but persistent as you follow up on projects you've had no word on or payments that are tardy.

Freezer odors

To prevent odors, package all foods in moistureproof, vaporproof materials that are labeled for freezer use—do not use old bread wrappers, wax paper, margarine tubs, or plastic supermarket bags.

CURE

1. Spread baking soda or activated charcoal (available at drugstores or hardware stores) on pans and place them on the freezer shelves.

2. Remove all food from the freezer and pack crumpled, slightly dampened newspapers on each shelf. Replace the newspapers every day or so until the odors disappear. (It may take 5 or 6 days.)

3. When defrosting, clean and deodorize the freezer with a solution of 2 tablespoons baking soda in 1 quart warm water. If you have a frost-free freezer, wash the interior with a baking soda solution at least once a month.

4. To get rid of the smell of spoiled food after a freezer failure, place bowls filled with used or unused coffee grounds inside the freezer.

Frost

1. An easy way to protect plants from light frost is to sprinkle them the night before. Before you go to bed, wet them with a fine spray from the garden hose. (If you have an automatic sprinkler system, set it to spray once or twice more during the night.) The mist will crystallize on the surface and insulate the plant's foliage.

If you awaken to find that there was a frost you didn't expect, minimize the damage by spraying plants before the sun strikes their leaves.

2. To protect tender seedlings from a late-spring cold snap, cover them with miniature greenhouses; just

cut the bottoms off plastic bottles or jugs and mound soil around the base of each container to hold it in place. On cold but sunny days, unscrew the caps for ventilation.

› Frostbite

1. Superficial frostbite, or frost nip, can develop very rapidly in a cold wind. The skin turns whitish or mottled and feels firm to the touch. Warm the skin directly against the body and go indoors immediately.

2. If the flesh feels hard and cold and the skin turns grayish yellow to grayish blue, get medical help as soon as possible. Do not rub the frostbitten tissue or try to rewarm it or put any pressure on it.

3. If you're hiking, get to a warm shelter right away and call for help. While waiting, immerse the frostbitten area in warm water (no hotter than 110°F), being careful not to let the flesh touch the container. When the skin begins turning red or blue, gently pat it dry and cover with a clean cloth—preferably a sterile one—making pads between fingers and toes if they're affected. (See also *Hypothermia*, p.112.)

› Frozen tongue

If your child's tongue sticks to the frosty metal of his sled or any other very cold object, the first thing to do is calm him down and prevent him from jerking his tongue away.

If a warm (not hot) liquid is available, pour it slowly over the spot where the tongue and the metal are joined until the tongue comes free.

Or ask the child to breathe out through his mouth; his warm breath should melt the connection. If he's a very small child, breathe on the sticking point yourself.

Fruit flies

These tiny flies are attracted by fermenting or overripe fruits and vegetables, vinegar, fruit juices, and yeast breads. To trap them, insert a paper or metal funnel into the mouth of a quart jar baited with bits of overripe fruit. They'll fly into the jar but won't be able to find their way out. Outdoors, promptly collect fallen tomatoes and other fruit from the garden and keep garbage cans tightly closed.

Fruit

1. If you have a big bunch of bananas or other fruit that you're afraid may ripen all at once, place a few in a brown paper bag with holes poked in it. The bag traps ethylene gas, making the fruit inside ripen almost twice as fast.

2. Fully ripened nontropical fruit belongs in the refrigerator. Unripe fruit is best kept at room temperature in an open-weave basket that allows air to circulate.

3. If fruit has gotten overripe, don't throw it away. Purée it in a blender or food processor with a little lemon juice and spoon the result over ice cream.

4. Strawberries retain more juice and absorb less water if you wash them *before* hulling. And always rinse the berries quickly in running water instead of soaking them.

Funnel

1. A better substitute than a rolled-up, taped piece of cardboard is an empty food can—a 16-ounce one will do fine—with a hole punched near the joint between the bottom and the side. (Don't punch the hole in the center of the can or you'll have less control over the flow.)

Hold the can at an angle while you pour through it.

2. Cut the bottom off a plastic soda bottle and turn it upside down.

Furniture polish or wax

Avoid buildup; apply polish or wax sparingly and no more than a few times a year. To prevent a buildup in the crevices of carved or decorative areas, put a small amount of polish or wax on a cloth before you wipe it onto the furniture.

If a buildup does occur, you can remove it by wiping the furniture with a soft cloth dampened with a little mineral spirits; then apply fresh wax or polish.

HOMEMADE POLISHES

1. Use mineral oil. If you prefer a lemon-scented polish, add 1 teaspoon of lemon oil for every 2 cups of mineral oil.

2. Mix 1 quart boiled linseed oil with 2 cups turpentine. (Store in a covered container.)

3. Combine 1 part lemon oil and 3 parts olive oil.

Furniture scraper

If you don't have a steel-blade furniture scraper, you can use a scrap piece of window glass. Cut or break it into a rough rectangle about 4 x 5 inches. Cover three edges with masking tape to protect your hands.

To scrape, set the cutting edge on the wood and, using long strokes, pull the glass toward you at a 75° angle. Keep the pressure even so that the corners don't gouge the wood and the glass doesn't break in your hands.

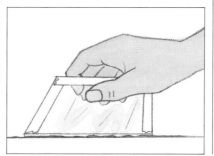

Furniture stains

1. To remove the white rings left by cups or glasses, rub with an abrasive. First, try cigarette or cigar ashes moistened with a little cooking oil; apply with your finger. If that doesn't work, try successively stronger steps: use table salt and a drop of water; silver polish or car polish; and, finally, pumice or rottenstone and oil.

2. Erase superficial ink spots with oiled pumice or steel wool.

Fuses

1. If your fuses blow only occasionally, the cause is probably the surge that occurs when you start up an appliance. A time-delay fuse will allow the appliance to reach its normal running rate.

2. Never replace a fuse with one of a higher rating, and never use a penny, a piece of aluminum foil, or any other object in place of a fuse. Doing so could cause a fire.

3. If fuses blow regularly, call an electrician. It may be time for an electrical upgrade.

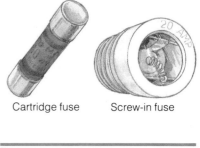

Cartridge fuse   Screw-in fuse

G

Games for grown-ups

1. Badminton volleyball. Play badminton over a volleyball net using volleyball rules.

2. Frisbee golf. Use trees, poles, and rocks as holes and designate tee-off spots. Throw a Frisbee and keep throwing it from where it lands until you hit the hole. The person who takes the fewest throws to hit all holes is the winner. Assess a penalty point whenever the Frisbee lands on a spot from which it can't be thrown.

3. Word spell. One person says a letter and the next person adds another letter to logically spell a word. Play continues around the room, with the object being *not* to complete a word; giving the last letter of any word costs you a point. For example, if the existing letters are *t* and *a*, add a *c*, perhaps (for *tack*), or an *i* (for *tail*). A *b (tab)* or *g (tag)* would complete the word and penalize you 1 point—5 points and you're out. In case of a challenge, you must identify the word you have in mind or lose a point. The winner is the last person left.

4. Dictionary. The player who is "it" picks an obscure word from the dictionary and writes its definition on a card; the other players write what they think the word *might* mean. The cards are shuffled and the definitions read aloud by the "it" player; then each player guesses which definition is correct. The "it" player keeps score, awarding 1 point for guessing correctly and 1 point for fooling someone with a false definition. He, himself, gets 5 points if no one guesses the word. The game continues until each player has had a turn being "it."

5. Gomuku. This Japanese tic-tac-toe game uses a grid of 19 horizontal and 19 vertical lines. One player places *X*'s, the other *O*'s on the intersections of the lines. The first to have 5 letters in a row wins.

Garbage cans

Prevent back strain: use your child's skateboard or wagon to take the filled cans out to the curb.

CLEANING

1. Wash with ½ cup ammonia in 1 gallon water. To disinfect, substitute ¾ cup bleach for the ammonia; let stand 5 minutes, then rinse.
2. To fight mold and bacteria, sprinkle ½ cup borax in each can.

PREVENTING ANIMAL RAIDS

1. Pour bleach over the garbage to eliminate the odor of food.
2. Stretch bungee cords across the lids, hooking them onto the handles of the can.
3. Strap or tie the cans to a sturdy fence or post.
4. Slip broom handles or stakes through the handles and drive them into the ground.
5. Tie the cans together—they'll be harder to knock over.
6. Put the cans in a box with a lid fastened by a hasp.
7. Suspend the cans from a frame so that they are 18 inches above the ground. If an animal tries to break in, the can will simply swing away.

Garbage disposers

1. "Sweeten" your disposer by running lemon or orange peels through it from time to time. Or, to sharpen the blades at the same time, make ice cubes (½ cup vinegar per tray of water) and run them through.
2. Never put your hand in a disposer to free a jam. Instead, turn off the power and use a dowel or broom handle to turn the flywheel rotor in both directions. Remove debris with kitchen tongs.

—Flywheel

Garden hose

1. You can temporarily plug a pinhole leak by jamming a round wooden toothpick into the hole. Snap the toothpick off flush with the hose's outer skin. Then wrap the hose with plastic electrician's

---

IN TIMES GONE BY

Haste makes waste

Garbage disposal has always been a problem. The residents of ancient Troy left their wastes on the floors of their homes or dumped them in the streets. In some ancient African cities, garbage piled so high that street levels rose and new houses had to be built on higher ground.

The ancient Greeks organized the first municipal dumps in the Western world, and Athens was the first city known to prohibit throwing refuse into its streets.

Still, as late as the 14th century, Parisians were allowed to cast garbage from their windows.

It is believed that Benjamin Franklin was the first American to begin a drive for municipal garbage disposal; he suggested hiring men to dump waste into the Delaware River. However, it wasn't until much later, in the 1850's, that some American cities initiated collection services. Until then, even in the nation's capital pigs were the primary garbage disposers.

Since 1960, Americans have gone from generating 2.6 pounds of refuse per person per day to more than 3.5 pounds; it is projected that by the year 2000 we will each be contributing 4 pounds of waste to the world every day. In the meantime, the scarcity of landfill space has become a national crisis. As a result, it's very likely that recycling will be a mandatory form of trash disposal by the end of the century.

tape for 2 inches on either side of the leak. Stretch the tape tight over the hole but looser toward the ends, so that the bandage can flex as the hose bends. As the wood absorbs water, it will swell to seal the hole.

2. Never store a garden hose by hanging it over a nail or peg. The hose will sag and kink, and repeated kinking will crack the vinyl or plastic skin. Instead, mount an old auto tire rim on the garage or toolshed wall to serve as a hose rack.

Gardening

You can get more plants out of your vegetable plot—and reduce pest damage at the same time—by interplanting a crazy quilt of vegetables in a wide row. Choose plants that can be sown in the same season and, for the fun of it, follow a theme. A salad row, for example, might consist of radishes, garden cress, red and green leaf lettuce, chicory, dill, and parsley.

First, prepare a row at least 3 feet wide. Combine all the seeds in a small jar (a peanut butter jar is ideal). Then punch a dozen or more holes in the lid and screw it on. Using the jar as a shaker, sprinkle seeds sparsely over the whole row. Scratch the surface lightly with a hand cultivator to cover the seeds, then water with a gentle shower.

Thinning will be the only real chore. Widen the intervals between plants only as they actually need the room, since the less soil you leave bare, the less chance there is for weeds to invade. A thick blanket of foliage also shades the soil, acting much as a mulch would.

The interplanting also helps keep garden pests in check; in traditional row gardens, insects find the crops they like and race down the rows, jumping from plant to plant. In your crazy quilt garden, they're more likely to concentrate on one plant at a time.

Be imaginative and choose other themes: a spaghetti sauce row, with tomato and pepper seedlings, basil, and garlic; or a soup row, with kale, carrots, leeks, and beets.

Garden pests

You need look no further than your pantry, medicine chest, or seed catalog for an arsenal of rough-and-ready remedies for many pests.
1. Aphids, mealybugs, and other soft-bodied insects succumb instantly to a spray of full-strength rubbing alcohol. But don't spray young or tender plants or you may damage them.
2. Bait slugs with jar lids filled with at least ½ inch of beer or dry yeast mixed with water—they love the stuff and drown in it.
3. Kill mites with a spray of buttermilk from a plant mister.
4. Control onion maggots and bean beetles by scattering wood ashes around plants or on the foliage.
5. Queen Anne's lace, fennel, sage, and buckwheat attract beneficial insects such as hover flies, lacewings, stinkbugs, and parasitic wasps and flies. Sit back and let them do some pest-control work for you. (See also specific pests.)

Garden produce

1. To save mature green tomatoes from an early frost, pick them and set them on top of the refrigerator to ripen at room temperature. Or wrap them individually in newspaper and store in a cool spot.
2. Keep bean weevils from ruining your dried kidney beans or limas: just dip the freshly shelled beans in boiling water for 1 minute before you spread them out to dry.
3. Instead of thumping your watermelons to check for ripeness, look for brown tendrils on the stem near the fruit and a yellow area instead of white where the fruit touches the ground. Both are signs that the melon is ready to pick.
4. When you harvest winter squash, leave a 4-inch stem on the fruit to ensure that it stays succulent until cooking time.
5. Test potatoes before you store them by rubbing the skin; if it rubs off easily, the potato is probably too green for storage.
6. Don't wash or blanch freshly harvested peas before freezing them. Just shell them directly into a plastic freezer bag; they'll stay separated, allowing you to dip into them as you need them.

Garden tools

1. For jobs too big for a trowel but too small for a spade or shovel, use an army entrenching tool. You can usually find them at camping supply or army surplus stores.
2. An electric drill will keep your garden tools polished and sharp. Use a wire brush attachment to scour rust from neglected tools; a coarse aluminum oxide disc (No. 36) can put an edge back on a nicked ax or mower blade much faster than a file and whetstone. Do it quickly, so that the high-speed sanding doesn't heat the steel and ruin its temper. After polishing

and sharpening, keep blades and teeth bright with a coat of oil; dirty oil from your car or power mower is as effective as any and costs nothing (see *Motor oil*, p.315).

3. A wide putty knife is great for scraping earth from shovels and trowels. And it's unbeatable for transplanting seedlings from flats, weeding between closely planted vegetables, and cultivating the soil in the crevices of a rock garden.

Garlic

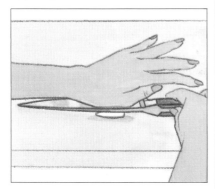

1. You can peel a garlic clove by placing the flat side of a knife over it and giving it a sharp rap with your hand or a utensil. The skin will come away easily.

2. If you want a subtle garlic taste, mince the cloves with a knife. Putting garlic through a press or mincing it in a food processor makes it considerably stronger because more oil is released.

3. If you don't have fresh garlic, substitute ½ teaspoon garlic salt for each clove and omit ½ teaspoon salt from the recipe.

4. To tame your breath after a garlic-rich meal, munch fresh parsley.

Gas burners

A professional should check your burner before each heating season. In addition, you can take these steps at any time to ensure safety:

1. Run the dust-brush attachment of your vacuum cleaner over the opening between the gas manifold and the burner heads to remove dust and carbon particles.

2. With the burner turned off, open the access door and examine the firebox and heat exchanger for soot deposits. If soot is present, either the burner or something in the gas lines is malfunctioning. Call a service center to locate and fix the problem, as well as to remove the soot (a dirty job).

3. With the burner switched on and the thermostat turned up for heat, the burners should ignite. If the pilot light is on and the burners fail to ignite, don't try a second time. Call for service. If the pilot is out and doesn't relight after three or four tries, call for service.

4. If the burners come on as they should, open the access door and inspect the flames; they should form a solid blue bank. Significant amounts of yellow—especially yellow tipping—indicate a poor air-fuel mix. Something in the lines is at fault. Turn off the burner and gas. Call for service.

5. Examine the mechanical vent damper, if there is one. It should be located in the flue at or near the point where it leaves the furnace. Spray the damper shaft ends (visible through the flue) with a lubricant. With the damper closed, turn on the burners. The damper should open immediately. If it fails to do so, it could cause a dangerous malfunction; turn off the burners and call a service center.

› Gas odors

1. If a strong whiff of gas awakens you or greets you at the door, leave your home at once. Do not use your telephone or turn on any light fixture or appliance—an electric spark can cause an explosion. Call the gas company from a pay phone or a neighbor's home; don't return home until a service representative says it's safe to do so.

2. If you smell a faint odor of gas near your range, open the windows to clear the air and open the oven door. See if any burners were left on and turn them off. Check to be

sure that all the pilot lights are lit.

When you're sure the smell is gone, carefully relight all pilot lights. If your stove has pilotless ignition, turn on each burner to test it. If a pilot won't stay lit or the smell persists, call for service.

› Gasoline

1. The fuel gauge reads *Empty* and you think there's a service station within a few miles. Here's how to conserve fuel by coasting: Turn on the emergency flashers and move into the slow lane or onto the shoulder of the road. If your car has an automatic transmission, slowly accelerate to 30 m.p.h., then shift into *Neutral* and coast until your speed reaches 10 m.p.h. Then repeat the process. With a standard transmission, coast downhill whenever you can, but don't let the car slow to the point where you must shift into a lower gear.

2. If your engine is sputtering to a stop, turn on the emergency flashers and try to coast off the road to a safe spot. Leave the flashers on and use a distress signal, such as a raised hood or a white cloth on the antenna, then call or wait for help.

3. Keep an *empty* gas can in the trunk in case you run out of fuel and can hitch a ride or walk to a service station. *Never* carry gasoline in it as a "safeguard." The risk of fire or explosion is too great.

4. Carry a siphon pump so that another motorist can give you some gas. But first find out what kind of gas it is—leaded fuel will damage a car that requires unleaded fuel, although unleaded gas will not harm an older car.

5. After running out of gas, your refueled car may be difficult to restart. Depress the accelerator once, then release it. Turn the ignition without pumping the accelerator; you may have to run the starter motor for 15 seconds or more. If the first attempt fails, wait 2 minutes and try again. If a third attempt fails, call for help.

Getting & giving directions

You're lost in a strange place and you ask a stranger for help. She, familiar with the territory, gives you directions that only confuse you further. It has happened to all of us, but how do you make sure it doesn't happen next time?

1. Carry a map. It's easier to mark out a route than to describe it.

2. State your destination clearly. If possible, write down the name and address. Ask the person to locate it on the map, along with the place where you are. If you don't have a map, ask her to sketch the route.

3. Write down all instructions, including landmarks, and repeat them back. Don't be embarrassed to admit you don't understand a direction; ask for clarification.

GIVING DIRECTIONS

Remember that the person you're helping doesn't know the territory.

1. Be sure you understand where the person wants to go. If he speaks a foreign language, use a map or have him write down the address or name of his destination.

2. Use large, obvious landmarks as references rather than those that require familiarity with the place.

3. Estimate distances as best you can, whether in city blocks or country miles.

4. Make sure that the person understands. Have him repeat your directions back to you.

5. Draw a sketch.

Gifted children

1. Boredom and lack of challenge can be major problems for a gifted child. If your child's school has no special program for the gifted, ask his teacher, counselor, or principal to suggest alternatives. Correspondence courses are available, and a number of colleges offer courses or early-admissions programs for gifted children.

2. Look for gifted children's groups; your child will probably feel more comfortable with others like him-self. Consider joining (or perhaps starting) a parents' group; contact your state education department for information.

3. Classmates—and even adults—may perceive your child as odd. Be sure to let him know that you're proud of his achievements and that he shouldn't be embarrassed by his intelligence. Let him express and test out his ideas at home.

4. Never use a gifted child's intelligence against him ("How could someone as smart as you do something so stupid?").

5. Emphasize that he doesn't have to do everything perfectly. (Gifted children can be overly demanding on themselves.) Make sure that he knows you love him for himself, not for his brains or talent.

6. Even though your child may sound like an adult, he's still a child who needs guidance. Don't be afraid to set limits and don't be intimidated or manipulated—gifted children tend to challenge authority out of a need to learn.

7. If your gifted child has siblings, keep in mind that each child is unique and all are special. Avoid comparisons; help each to succeed in his or her own way.

Gifts at work

Occasional business lunches or inexpensive holiday gifts are usually acceptable; expensive, personalized gifts are best refused. Report them to your boss, then return them with a gracious thank-you note stating that accepting such gifts is against company policy.

If you're offered a gift from an organization you feel might be trying to buy your influence, ask your boss for guidance. Or check your company's personnel manual; it may instruct you to refuse certain gifts, to make a written declaration of gifts over a certain value, or to report all offers of gifts.

If your employer requires you to influence customers or suppliers through gifts or lavish entertain-ment, you'll be wise to move on; your own reputation may be at stake. The most appropriate and commonly accepted gifts to give and receive are samples of your company's products.

Gift wrap

1. If your wrapping paper is a bit too short to cover your package, turn the package at an angle and try wrapping it that way.

2. To premeasure a length of gift wrap from a roll, wrap string around the package and use it as a guide.

3. Aluminum foil is a good substitute for gift wrap; for a textured look, press it gently against a rough surface such as a stucco or brick wall.

4. Make your own printing block by cutting a simple design on a bar of soap or a halved potato (p.378). Then use it to decorate newspaper, paper bags, or white shelving paper. Use an ink pad or pour out some paint on a paper plate or a clean plastic foam meat tray.

5. Save wrapping paper. When you have a large carton to cover, use different pieces of your stored paper to create a patchwork look.

Glare on the road

To eliminate hazardous glare, extend your car's sun visors. Secure adhesive-backed Velcro to the visors and to pieces of cardboard or opaque plastic. Attach the extensions to the visors and move them around until you can comfortably see the road.

Glass

Never pick up broken glass with your bare hands—or approach it in your bare feet. Carefully sweep it into a dustpan, wrap it in newspaper, and throw it out.

To pick up tiny flecks of glass, wipe all around the breakage area with a paper towel smeared with moist bar soap. Rinse with a water-soaked paper towel and wipe dry.

Glassware

1. Use the bartender's method for speedy stemware washing: Holding the base, pump the glass vigorously in very hot sudsy water, then quickly pump it in hot clear water (cooler water may shatter it); dry upside down on a cotton towel.

2. For extra-shiny, streakless glasses, add a little vinegar or borax to the final rinse water.

3. If glasses have hard-water stains, rub them with a scouring pad dipped in vinegar.

4. Never use hot water, harsh soaps, ammonia, or washing soda on silver- or gold-rimmed glasses.

5. A well-lathered shaving brush cleans deeply etched or hobnailed glass especially well.

6. If eggs have dried on your patterned glass tableware, rub off the residue with a slice of lemon.

7. Handle glass ovenware very carefully. Avoid hard knocks and sudden exposure to heat or cold and keep it away from water (even a moist countertop) while warm.

8. If glass cookware remains stained after washing, boil a solution of 1 part vinegar to 3 parts water in it for about 20 minutes.

Gloves

1. Need gloves in a hurry? Slip a sock over your hand and move your thumb away from your index finger; cut through the material in that space. Remove the sock and stitch along the cut edge.

2. Remove fresh spots from leather and suede gloves by rubbing them with stale bread.

3. Clean white kid gloves with powdered starch or tailor's chalk. Apply with a piece of silk, then shake the loose powder off.

4. For a stain on black kid, dab on indelible black marker, then rub in a few drops of olive oil.

5. To dry out wet plastic or rubber gloves, hang them by their fingers or put them over propped-up wooden spoons.

6. Instead of wearing plastic or rubber gloves while painting, apply liquid latex (available at hardware stores), which dries to a flexible film; wash it off with the paint. For quick touch-ups, just coat your hands with hand or face cream.

Glue

1. Replace the cap to a tube of glue with a cuphook or screw eye. Then you can hang it up for storage.

2. Substitutes for glue on such lightweight materials as paper, fabric, and cardboard include flour and water mixed to pancake-batter consistency; plain egg white (no yolk) applied with a brush; double-stick tape, which adheres to almost any clean, dry surface; and iron-on tape, which forms a surprisingly strong bond on fabrics.

3. When disassembling furniture, soften the old glue with warm distilled white vinegar. Drip it directly into the joints with an eye dropper.

4. To unclog a tube, don't try to poke through the hardened glue with a nail or needle. You may damage the tube. Instead, bore into the clogged nozzle with a small drill bit. (Soak the bit in lacquer thinner or nail polish remover first and clean off all the glue afterward.)

5. Most white glue and carpenter's glue are water-based. To clear a nozzle, unscrew it and soak it in warm water. (Tape the bottle closed so that the glue won't harden.) Once the glue in the nozzle softens, clean it out with a wooden toothpick.

IN TIMES GONE BY

For love of a glove

Power, wealth, nobility, and even love—all these things and more were once symbolized by gloves. They seemingly carried the aura of the hands that wore them.

Not until early in the 17th century were gloves commonly worn by the average woman—but fine ladies had begun to sport fancy gloves as early as the Middle Ages. Still warm from a soft hand, a glove would be given to a knight as a token of love. And off he would ride into battle, the intimate favor in his helmet, its mate with his mistress awaiting his return.

Dainty though it was, the feminine glove became a sign of strength to him—an amulet to ward off evil, an incentive for brave deeds, and a reminder of the sweet reward that would be his should he survive.

His own armored glove, or gauntlet, was a different matter entirely. There was nothing dainty about it; its aura embodied strength, power, and honor. It might be offered as a pledge in a court of law. And to "throw down the gauntlet" at another man's feet was to challenge him to combat, often mortal combat. It was a meaning that lasted for centuries; long after the knightly gauntlet had faded into history, perfumed dandies were challenging each other to duels at the drop of a soft kid glove as dainty as any lady's of the time.

Glued fingers

1. Quick-setting cyanoacrylates (Superglue and Krazy Glue, for example) bond instantly. If your fingers get stuck together, dissolve the bond with a little nail polish remover or acetone. Most epoxies can also be dissolved this way.

2. If your skin is stuck with contact cement, dissolve the bond with lacquer thinner. Let it soak the cement for a couple of minutes and then slowly pull your fingers apart. If necessary, apply more thinner.

Golf jargon

Here's a guide to what the television announcers are saying:

Ace. A hole in one.

Address. To prepare to hit the ball.

Approach shot. A shot made from the fairway toward the green.

Back nine. The last 9 holes of an 18-hole golf course.

Birdie. To score 1 shot under par.

Blast. A hard trap shot.

Blind hole. A green that the golfer cannot see when driving or making an approach shot.

Bogey. To score 1 shot over par.

Bunker. A sand trap.

Carry. The distance a ball stays in the air after being hit.

Chip. A short, low approach shot.

Divot. A piece of sod dislodged by the player's stroke.

Dogleg. A fairway that bends.

Double bogey. To score 2 over par.

Double eagle. To score 3 under par.

Drive. The first shot toward the green, generally from a tee.

Eagle. To score 2 under par.

Fairway. The area of well-mowed, hazard-free grass between the tee-ing-off area and the green.

Flagstick. A marker on the green indicating the location of the cup and the number of the hole.

Gimme. An easy putt conceded to an opponent.

Green. The area of short, well-tended grass surrounding the cup.

Handicap. The number of strokes that are deducted from the score of a weaker player when competing against a more skillful opponent.

Hazards. The bunkers and water obstacles on the golf course.

Hook. A ball that veers in mid-flight to the left for a right-handed golfer, to the right for a lefty.

Iron. A club with a bladelike metal head; used for accuracy.

Lie. The position in which the ball stops after a stroke.

Links. A golf course (from the Scottish word for the undulating land by the sea where the early courses were built).

Par. The score an expert player in good weather is expected to make on a particular hole.

Putter. The club used for making short, accurate shots on the green.

Rim. To have a ball go around the edge of the cup and not drop in.

Shank. To hit the ball poorly.

Slice. The opposite of a hook.

Tee. The peg used to raise the ball off the ground before it is driven, or teed off.

Trap shot. A shot from a bunker.

Wood. A club with a hardwood head, used for long shots.

Graduate school entrance

1. To improve your chances of getting into a graduate program, start planning early—freshman year isn't too soon. A plan can always be changed, but without one you might overlook courses and qualifications you need.

2. Compile a list of universities that offer the type of program you're considering. Write for their graduate catalogs and applications; ask about their requirements and possible financial assistance. For fast results, telephone—you'll also be able to discuss the details.

3. Take advanced courses in your field whenever possible; strive for especially good grades in them.

4. If the Graduate Record Examination (GRE) is required, buy test preparation guides and see how well you do. If you're weak in any area, enroll in courses that will help you correct the weakness.

FINDING A FELLOWSHIP

1. Ask your adviser and professors what kinds of fellowships may be available in your chosen field.

2. Don't spread yourself too thin; focus your attention on three or four possibilities at most.

3. Get your application and portfolio of supporting documents (transcripts, recommendations, financial and academic records) in on time—the deadline may be a year before you intend to start graduate school. For best results, begin preparing the application 6 months before this deadline.

Grandparenting

1. Set aside a closet or a room as a "family museum" to focus the younger generation's attention on their heritage; fill it with old pictures, letters, clothes, toys, and furniture.

2. If you can't see your grandchildren regularly, call and write often to remind them of their "roots." (Don't wait for them to call you and don't be offended if they fail to—you're the one with the job to do.) Or bridge the distance by recording personalized bedtime stories that describe the family's past.

3. When it comes to gift giving, it's natural for grandparents to be generous. But parents, the generation in between, should have some say about what you give their children. They must deal with such problems as favoritism, sibling rivalry, competition between two or more sets of grandparents, or just the feeling of being outdone by their own parents. Don't undermine their efforts by going overboard with extra treats.

Grants

Do you need money or equipment for a photography project, a community garden or theater, a youth recreation hall? Grants for an amazing variety of projects are available from government and community agencies, foundations, corporations, and other organizations.

Here are a few tips on getting one:
1. Consult the many excellent reference books available at your public library, including the *Annual Register of Grant Support* and *The Foundation Directory.*
2. Once you have decided which grant to apply for, find out as much as you can about the organization providing the funds. Call and ask for a brochure or an annual report. Try to make personal contact with someone at the organization, especially if it's a local donor.
3. Keep your grant proposal clear, simple, and brief, with the most important information at the beginning. Explain how you're going to make the best possible use of the money. Include information on the support you already have for your project. Try to get endorsement letters from people well known in the community or in your field. Once you have submitted your proposal, make an appointment to discuss it in person.
4. If you're turned down, consider applying to the same donor again. It often takes three or four tries to gain approval.
5. Apply for many grants. If you're lucky enough to be approved by two donors, decide which offer is better. Explain the situation to the other source—you may be able to receive both grants, either in succession or at the same time.

Grass

1. To speed germination, pretreat your grass seed: Mix 2 tablespoons of cold, strong brewed tea into each pound of seed; cover, then set in the refrigerator for 5 days. Before sowing, spread the seed to dry for a day or two on newspapers on the garage or basement floor.
2. Native American prairie grasses (Sharp's Improved and Texoka strains of buffalo grass are two good examples) make an interesting, if unconventional, lawn in northern climates. They have an attractively rough texture, are re-

sistant to drought and pests, and need mowing only once a month.
3. Little bluestem, another native American, can enliven your lawn in autumn, when it turns a rich reddish-brown. Mix some of the seed into your regular grass seed but confine the mixture to parts of the lawn that are off the beaten path, since little bluestem tends to be clumpy. (See also *Lawns,* p.123.)

Grass stains

1. Rub the stain with liquid detergent, naphtha soap, or a pad soaked in diluted alcohol; rinse thoroughly. If the stain persists, try a little vinegar on it, a mild solution of hydrogen peroxide, or—if safe for the fabric—bleach.
2. If you're in a hurry, dab the stain with a cotton swab soaked in water and a little bit of bleach. Be patient—it may take a few minutes for the stain to fade.
3. Cover a permanent stain with an appliqué or a patch.

Gravy

1. For extra flavor, stir a handful of diced carrots, celery, and onions and a pinch of herbs into the drippings as they simmer; strain before serving. Or, if you don't have time to cut and chop, just add a bouillon cube. Or turn the gravy into an epicurean treat with a splash of port, Madeira, sherry, or white vermouth.
2. Brown flour in the oven before using it to make gravy. It adds flavor and color.
3. If gravy lacks body, stir in 1½ teaspoons of cornstarch for every cup of liquid. Cook and stir until the mixture bubbles, thickens, and clears (about 3 minutes—no longer or the gravy will begin to thin).
4. Remove fat from the surface of gravy with a bulb-type baster. Or, time permitting, refrigerate the gravy overnight, then lift off the congealed fat. If you need the gravy right away, quickly chill it on ice or in the freezer. You can also blot up fat by placing several thicknesses

of paper towels flat on the surface of the gravy. Repeat as needed.
5. Freeze leftover gravy in ice cube trays. Wrap the frozen cubes tightly in aluminum foil and reheat as needed or add to soups.

Gray hair

1. Since gray hair tends to be dry and wiry, keep it well trimmed for manageability and to prevent split ends. For a more youthful look, avoid a rigid, overdone hairstyle.
2. If you're just beginning to turn gray and would like to conceal it, try highlighting your hair; the gray will blend in with the newly lightened strands.
3. Downplay the gray by lightening your original hair color a shade or two. A general rule of thumb: lighten rather than darken as you age; it's more flattering, less harsh.
4. A quick way to help cover gray: Stir 1 tablespoon cider vinegar into 1 gallon warm water. Use as a final rinse after shampooing.
5. Your gray hair may look better than you think. Try to enjoy it rather than change it.

Gray market goods

The gray market—as opposed to a black market—deals in legally imported goods that have passed through customs but not through normal distribution channels. The lack of middlemen makes for lower prices, but there may be problems.
1. More than likely, you'll receive a retailer's—rather than a manufacturer's—warranty. It's important, therefore, to shop at a reputable store and to get a copy of the warranty to safeguard your rights.
2. Instructions may be in a foreign language, the measurements may be in metric, or the item may contain ingredients that are banned in the United States.
3. The item may not have been shipped in the manufacturer's protective container. (Check your purchase to make sure it hasn't been tampered with or damaged.)

4. You may not be eligible for any rebate the manufacturer offers.

5. In the case of a car that you have bought overseas and brought back to the United States, you won't be able to drive it or recover the import bond fee until it has met federal safety and emission-control standards. Find out how much the modifications will cost; then add on the shipping and insurance costs to get the total price of the car.

Grease spots

1. In a hurry to remove a grease stain? Apply shampoo, then rinse and blow-dry.

2. Absorb the grease from a rough-textured fabric with cornmeal; for a smooth fabric, use cornstarch. Leave on the spot for up to 12 hours, brush off, then wash the fabric.

3. Use club soda to remove grease stains on double-knit fabrics. Talcum powder works on polyester; rub into the spot with your fingers, let stand for 24 hours, then brush off. Repeat if necessary.

4. Get rid of grease stains on white shoes with nail polish remover. (Be careful not to remove the shoe's finish.) For other colors, rub on cleaning fluid with a soft cloth.

5. Wash auto grease from hands with laundry detergent and water. Kerosene works, too—but wash immediately with warm, soapy water.

6. To remove greasy heel marks from vinyl or linoleum floors, try silver polish or white appliance wax.

Greeting cards

1. To preserve a greeting card, coat it with a light film of hair spray.

2. Use last year's Christmas cards to make this year's postcards. Tear a card apart and cut the front to postcard size. Glue it to a blank card if it is not thick enough. Draw a line down the middle of the back and write your message on the left side and the address on the right.

3. If you find a card with the perfect message but you don't like the art, glue gift-wrapping paper or your favorite photo over the front.

4. Make gift tags by cutting down last year's greeting cards, folding them, and punching a hole in the corner for a ribbon.

5. For an attractive greeting card, use a leaf as a stencil. Affix it to a sheet of stiff white paper or a note card, then spray-paint. After the paint dries, just strip away the leaf.

Grills

1. Line a grill with heavy aluminum foil to reflect heat upward; it also makes the cleanup easier.

2. A wire cake rack can replace a light camping grill. Stove or refrigerator shelves can support pots over a fire, but don't let them touch the food—some shelves contain poisonous cadmium.

3. Use an old Boy Scout trick to make a "tennis racket" grill. Find a green forked stick and wire the ends of the fork together (or use long shavings from green wood). Use short green sticks to lace the meat into this circle before holding it over the campfire. If the meat is going to take a while to cook, use stones to prop the grill over the fire.

4. Rub a cooking grate with fat trimmings or bacon to keep meat from sticking to it.

Grommets

1. A sewing machine buttonholer will reinforce a fabric hole, though not as securely as a grommet does.

2. For temporary reinforcement, try sticking small strips of duct tape around the edges of the hole.

3. You can recycle the grommets from old sneakers. Cut them off, then open them with needle-nose pliers. Slip the grommet into the hole in the fabric and pound it closed with a hammer.

4. Two washers of the proper size can serve as a grommet set. Put one on a solid surface—an anvil or a brick will do—and center the grommet on it. Then position the other washer atop the grommet and hammer it down.

Grout

1. Remove old grout with a beer can opener. Use the pointed end to scratch out the grout, taking care not to damage the tiles.

2. After regrouting, use a spray bottle to apply liquid silicone sealer to the dried grout lines; it helps prevent staining and makes the grout more water-resistant.

Guarantees & warranties

1. Before making a major purchase, read the guarantee or warranty (the terms are interchangeable).

2. Store all your warranties, along

101

with proofs of purchase and dated receipts, in a separate file. If you misplace a warranty, call the store where you bought the merchandise and ask for a copy or have them read the terms over the phone.

3. You needn't send in a warranty card to be covered by its provisions. (You won't be notified, however, if the manufacturer recalls the item.) Even if you lose the warranty, your merchandise is covered, as long as you have proof of purchase.

4. If a manufacturer fails to honor a warranty or if, even after repair, you still feel you're stuck with a "lemon," call your local Better Business Bureau, your state department of consumer affairs, or your local consumer hot line.

Gum disease

1. To prevent this major cause of tooth loss, clean your teeth after every meal and at bedtime with a soft, rounded, nylon-bristled brush; work in circles, keeping the bristles at an angle to the gum line. Instead of toothpaste, you can use a pea-soup-thick mixture of baking soda and water once a day.

2. If you can't brush after every meal, rinse with a mouthwash or a solution of 1 teaspoon baking soda in 4 ounces water. At the very least, swish water around your mouth.

3. Floss at least once a day (preferably at bedtime) to remove plaque and food particles from between the teeth.

4. Massage your gums regularly with a toothbrush or a clean fingertip to stimulate blood flow.

5. Eat a low-sugar diet rich in calcium and vitamins A, B, and C.

6. If your gums bleed, are swollen and sore, or contain puss, see a dentist immediately. (See also *Dentist visits*, p.62; *Toothbrush*, p.213.)

Gutters

1. Try clearing debris-clogged gutters and downspouts with a garden hose. First push it up the downspout and turn the water on hard to loosen any blockage. Then move to the roof and, with another high-powered blast, push debris along the gutter toward the downspout.

2. No need to climb onto the roof to inspect gutters. Instead, tape a hand-held mirror to the end of a garden rake or other long-handled tool.

3. To prevent gutters from clogging, cut leaf guards from steel-wire mesh (hardware cloth) or plastic mesh, both sold at hardware stores. Use tin snips to cut the mesh into strips about 6 inches wide, then bend the strips lengthwise down the middle to bow them slightly so that they will fit into the gutters.

4. L-shaped aluminum flashing, or drip edge, can be used to divert rainwater from a section of roof directly above a doorway. Slip it under the second course of shingles and angle it to one side to direct water away from the door. Hold it in place with a couple of nails; cover the heads with roofing cement. Be sure to position the flashing so that it extends at least 2 feet beyond the doorway on each side.

H

Hacksaw

1. If you don't have a hacksaw and need to cut a thin piece of metal, use the edge of a file or wood rasp to make a groove, then bend the metal back and forth until it breaks.

2. Grind through hard metal with an abrasive wheel in your electric drill. (Wear eye protection!)

Hair

1. No time to shampoo? Put a clean nylon stocking over your brush and run it through your hair to remove dirt and oil. Or work a mixture of ½ cup bran and 1 tablespoon baking soda into your hair and brush out.

2. To cure hair spray buildup, work 1 tablespoon baking soda into your lathered hair when shampooing.

3. Rinse oily hair with a 50-50 mixture of water and lemon juice or vinegar.

4. Out of cream rinse? Add a little fabric softener to your final warm water rinse.

5. For a conditioner, saturate dry hair with warm safflower or corn oil. Cover with a plastic bag and hot damp towel; leave on for 2 hours and rinse off. Or try a rum and egg conditioner: beat 2 yolks, add 1 tablespoon rum, and beat again; leave on 30 minutes, shampoo, and rinse.

6. Prevent sun and saltwater damage by applying a small amount of coconut oil, wheat-germ oil, or petroleum jelly to hair ends.

7. If your hair is limp after conditioning, rinse with 1 cup water mixed with ¼ cup vinegar.

8. Make an aromatic hair spray from a lemon or, if you have dry hair, an orange. Boil 1 piece of fruit (quartered) in 2 cups of water until 1 cup remains; cool and strain. Keep in a spray bottle in the refrigerator.

9. Did chlorine turn your blond hair green? Rinse with club soda, tomato juice, or several aspirin in warm water. (See also *Gray hair*, p.100.)

Hairbrushes

To clean hairbrushes (and combs too), soak them in about a quart of warm water with a few tablespoons of ammonia, then rinse and let dry. A mixture of a tablespoon of borax, a tablespoon of detergent, and a quart of water works well too. Pull hair from the brush with a comb.

Hair dryers

1. If your dryer suddenly stops working on you, it may have just overheated; wait a few minutes and try it again.

2. In summer use the *Vent* setting on your air conditioner to dry your hair; in winter the hot air ducts of your heating system will do the job.

3. Put a net over your hair and sit in front of a fan.

4. Attach the hose to the exhaust port of a canister vacuum cleaner.

Hairstyling

1. No hair rollers handy? Cut narrow strips of cloth from an old shirt or clean rag and knot them in the middle. Roll a section of damp hair around the knot and use the loose ends of the cloth to tie the curl in place, or secure it with a bobby pin. For larger curls, cut a paper towel roll into four sections and roll the hair around them.

2. To revive a perm, spray it with water from a plant mister and fluff with your fingers. For setting lotion, put flat beer in the mister and spray on damp hair.

Halloween costumes

Use household items and cast-off clothing to create Halloween costumes that don't cost money.

1. Transform old colanders, bowls, and plastic containers into helmets and other hats. Cut a deflated volleyball in half and spray-paint it silver for a robot's, spaceman's, or knight's helmet. Turn thick work gloves into gauntlets by spraying them silver.

2. Use shredded cellophane from Easter baskets as a wig.

3. A ski mask makes a good start for a lot of costumes; attach animal ears, yarn, or jewelry. For a small child, use a one-piece sleeper in the same way.

4. Make white clown makeup by mixing 2 tablespoons of cornstarch with 1 tablespoon of solid shortening. Add some color, if you like, with a few drops of food coloring.

5. For facial decals, cut stars, flowers, or hearts from brightly colored tissue paper. To make the glue, cook one large potato, with skin, until it's soft; let it cool. Rub decals on the potato and then stick them on dry, clean skin.

6. If you need extra padding for a costume, wear large pantyhose and stuff with cushions or rags.

7. Care to go trick-or-treating dressed as a slice of pizza? It's easy to do. Start with a piece of carpet foam padding; cut it into a triangle as tall as you are. Spray the "crust" at the base of the triangle tan (allow for plenty of crust, because you'll have to fold some of it over your shoulders), then spray the rest of the triangle tomato-sauce red (or red and yellow if you like your pizza with cheese). Cut mushroom slices, green pepper strips, and onion rings from plastic foam meat trays and paint them the appropriate colors. For pepperoni, cut circles from a brown paper bag and paint them reddish-brown; they curl up just like the real thing and look wonderful. Glue the pieces on the pizza slice or, better still, attach them with Velcro glued to the slice and to the backs of the various pieces. Fold over the crust, cut a hole for your head, and staple the crust together at your shoulders.

IN TIMES GONE BY

Battling the bane of baldness

☐ The Egyptians, in an attempt to stimulate hair growth, used to anoint their heads with fat from snakes or crocodiles.

☐ In Greece, Hippocrates applied a mixture of opium, rose oil, and unripe olives in an effort to reforest his pate. (The fringe of hair over the ears and around the back of a bald man's head is called the Hippocratic wreath even today.)

☐ Romans who were too poor to buy wigs painted hair on their scalps—evidence of the desperate measures men will take.

☐ Men through the ages have massaged their scalps with rum, vodka, red pepper, ginger, the boiled flesh of moles, and even horse manure. For all their ingenuity, their hair remained as sparse as ever. Even minoxidil, the locally applied drug approved for distribution in the late 1980's, can't guarantee results, although its introduction was celebrated by worried men the world over.

Hands

1. For dry hands, rub petroleum jelly or baby oil on at bedtime and sleep in cotton gloves or socks.

2. To wash away the grime of gardening or housework, sprinkle a little sugar on your hands as you lather with soap and water.

3. While rearranging items in the freezer, wear oven mitts to protect your hands from the cold.

4. When you wash your hands with soap, counter the drying effects of the alkali by adding a few drops of cider vinegar to the water.

5. To avoid soap, wet your hands, rub plain bran all over them, then rinse. On sensitive hands try a mixture of cornmeal and lemon juice.

6. Remove light stains with a piece of grapefruit or lemon peel, heavier spots with powdered pumice stone and lemon juice.

7. Protect chapped fingertips with fingercots (small latex caps available in drugstores). Dab cream or ointment on each fingertip before donning them, then wear them as you go about your daily tasks.

Hanging laundry

1. No clothespins? Try clip-on earrings, tie clasps, hair clips, paper clips, or the pocket clasps of pens. (To avoid rust, put wax paper, plastic, or cloth under metal clips.)

2. If you need a clothespin bag, use a hanging plant pot. Its drainage holes will keep rain from collecting and waterlogging the clothespins. An onion or potato bag—the mesh kind—will do the same. (See also *Plastic jugs*, p.320.)

3. To keep your hands warm on a winter day, put a hot-water bottle in the clothes basket for occasional squeezes. Or wear cotton gloves covered with rubber gloves.

Hangovers

PREVENTION

1. In anticipation of a big night, take a gram or more of vitamin C for a couple of days; it may help clear the alcohol from your body.

2. Just before you go out—and also while you're partying—line your stomach with milk products.

3. Fill up on bulky foods, such as bread and pasta, to slow the absorption of alcohol into the blood.

4. Avoid red wine and such dark liquors as bourbon and rum; they contain more congeners, the impurities that intensify a hangover.

5. Mix your drinks with fruit juice or plain water—carbonated water speeds the absorption of alcohol—or down a glass of water after every alcoholic drink.

TREATMENT

1. Before going to bed, take a B-complex supplement (50 to 100 milligrams) and drink at least 1 pint of water or juice.

2. The morning after, drink more water and juice. (Sauerkraut juice neutralizes congeners.) Avoid caffeine; it dehydrates. Eat easy-to-digest foods for breakfast—cereal and milk, toast, and fruit. (Skip difficult-to-digest eggs.)

3. Honey is a specific remedy for an alcohol-induced headache; take two tablespoons. Aspirin or acetaminophen helps, too. For an upset stomach, try mint tea or an antacid.

Hatchets & axes

A sharp hatchet or ax is safer than a dull one; it cuts cleanly, whereas a dull one may ricochet from a log to your leg. Use a fine, flat file or a grinding wheel to sharpen the blade before each use, then clean and oil the metal before you put the hatchet away. Store with the blade covered in one of these ways:

1. Make a wood or leather sheath and secure it against the blade with a heavy rubber band or strip of inner tube.

2. Sink the blade into a sturdy block of softwood.

3. Wrap a burlap bag around the blade and tie it with twine.

4. Slice open a short scrap of garden hose and cover the cutting edge of the hatchet with it.

Hazardous waste

Leftover paint, household cleaner, bug spray, and weed killer are all hazardous wastes. Flushing them down the drain can damage sewage treatment systems; putting them out with the garbage sends them to the landfill, where they eventually seep into groundwater.

If you can't use up a potentially hazardous product, think of someone who can. Schools, neighbors, or churches may be pleased to accept your extra paint, insect spray, or cleaning solution.

Call a local health department, recycling center, or environmental agency to see if they organize collection drives. If they do, make sure the wastes are in sealed, watertight containers. If a container is rusting or leaking, put it in a larger, secure container.

If your community doesn't have a collection drive, call the health department or Cooperative Extension Service to find out the best way of disposing of a hazardous product.

Headaches

1. At the first sign of a headache, stop what you're doing and, if possible, lie down in a dark, quiet room with an ice bag or a cold pack on your forehead for 30 to 45 minutes.

2. Relax: Ask someone to massage your neck, shoulders, and upper back; take a hot bath; do relaxation exercises (see *Stress*, p.198).

3. Take aspirin or a substitute (p.12). To prevent a rebound headache, don't overdose the medication or take it after the pain is gone.

4. As long as the pain persists, eat very lightly and abstain from alcoholic beverages.

5. To identify and remove the cause of recurring headaches, keep a record: the date and time of each occurrence, what you were doing and with whom, what foods or beverages you had consumed, and any recent change in habits.

6. Most headaches are not serious. But if yours doesn't respond to simple self-treatment; if it includes fever, facial soreness, and a nasal discharge; if it's accompanied by other symptoms or follows an accident or injury; or if it's piercing or localized, seek medical help. (See also *Migraine headaches,* p.135.)

Headboards

If your bed doesn't have a headboard, you can make your own and hang it on the wall.

1. Cut a piece of ½-inch hardboard to size. Paint or stain it, then hang it with heavy-duty picture wire or mount it with screws or toggle bolts. Dress it up, if you like, by gluing on a geometric design in wood lath.

2. To make a padded headboard, start with a base of ½-inch plywood or hardboard. Cut a 3-inch-thick layer of polyester batting 2 inches larger all around and a piece of tightly woven fabric 3 inches larger all around.

Lay the fabric wrong side up, place the batting over it, and put the wood on top. Every 10 inches or so, snip both the fabric and the batting from the edge of the material to the edge of the wood. Then, starting at the center of a long edge, pull the batting over the wood and staple it in place, working alternately on opposite sides. Then do the same with the fabric, smoothing it as you staple it down. Mount the construction with picture hangers or bolts.

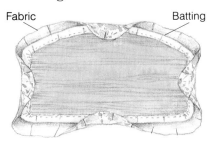

Fabric   Batting

3. For a still softer effect, mount a pair of café curtain rods, one above the other, behind the bed and stretch fabric between them. To create generous folds, sew enough widths of fabric together to form a panel three times wider than the length of the rods.

4. If you trust your artistic talents, you can paint a *faux* headboard on the wall. Add black to the paint to put in gray shadows and give your creation dimension. If you'd like striations similar to wood grain, use a feather to brush on vinegar paint—1 part powdered pigment to 2 parts white vinegar.

Headhunters

A headhunter, or executive search specialist, is not an employment agent. He's a recruiter, hired by companies to seek out candidates for high-level positions or specialized jobs. He finds people through research, networking, and discreet telephone calls.

FINDING ONE

1. Ask industry colleagues to recommend you to the headhunters they work with.

2. Call a headhunter directly (it's best to say who recommended him), but be sure you're clear about the kind of job you want and what you have to offer.

3. Join an industry association and get published in its magazine or newsletter; headhunters often scan association directories and magazines for names.

4. Send your chronological résumé (see *Job interviews,* p.119) to headhunters specializing in your field.

5. Don't be surprised if they won't see you. They're paid by the companies who hire them and may not have time to spend counseling you.

USING ONE

1. Discuss your background and experience (don't lie about your salary or misrepresent yourself), and ask for an evaluation.

2. Question the headhunter in depth about any companies to which he sends you. (But do your own independent research as well.)

3. Discuss your career goals and ask for feedback on your résumé.

UNSOLICITED CALLS

1. If a headhunter telephones you, ask for his firm's name, address, and phone number right away. (Be suspicious if he won't tell you.) Check out the firm with your colleagues and look it up in a directory of executive search firms.

2. If the headhunter is vague concerning job information or asks a lot about your present firm and little about you, be suspicious—he may be trying to pump you for information about your employer.

3. If he uses high-pressure sales tactics or seems unresponsive to your needs, don't work with him.

Head lice

If you or the school nurse finds lice in your child's hair, eradicate them with an over-the-counter shampoo or rinse that contains pyrethrin, a safe, natural insecticide. Avoid self-medication with any product that contains lindane, a powerful chemical that can cause headaches or even brain damage.

Wash, dry-clean, or spray with pyrethrin everything the child has come in contact with.

With a fine-toothed comb dipped in vinegar, check your child's hair, strand by strand, every night until you find neither lice nor their eggs, or nits. To prevent a reoccurrence, tell the child not to share combs, brushes, hats, or earphones.
Caution: A child allergic to ragweed may also be sensitive to pyrethrin. Consult your doctor.

Hearing loss

1. Safeguard your hearing—keep the noise down. To protect yourself from excessive noise made by others, carry earplugs or improvise with cotton or tissue paper. Wear earplugs or antinoise muffs when operating noisy power equipment.

2. Keeping your diet low in fats may help prevent age-related hearing loss due to atherosclerosis, the accumulation of fatty deposits in the arteries, including those that lead to the ears (see *Cholesterol,* p.46). **3.** Check your medications. Too much aspirin can cause ringing in the ears, as can antibiotics whose names end in *-mycin.* Talk to your doctor about the problem.

› Heat exhaustion

When you overexert yourself or wear heavy clothing in hot, humid weather, you run the risk of heat exhaustion. Among its symptoms: cold, clammy, gray skin; heavy perspiration; dizziness, nausea, and headache; rapid breathing and pulse; and faintness that may lead to unconsciousness.

If you see someone with these symptoms, have him sit or lie down in a cool spot immediately. Loosen his clothing and remove extra layers. Fan his skin. If he's alert, get him to drink up to a quart of water; if he's groggy, don't force fluids— you could cause choking.

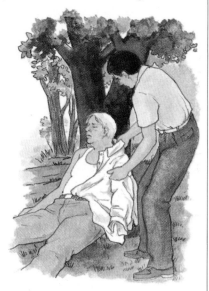

HEATSTROKE
If the condition doesn't improve within 30 minutes, there is risk of heatstroke. Its symptoms: hot, dry, flushed skin; deep, then shallow breathing; rapid, strong pulse, followed by rapid, weak pulse; dilated pupils; unconsciousness; twitching muscles; and convulsions.

If you suspect heatstroke, get the person cooled off as fast as you can. Take extreme measures: soak towels and sheets in cold water and wrap them around his body. If ice is available, put it in plastic bags and place under his armpits, behind each knee, in the groin, on the wrists and ankles, and on the sides of the neck.

Call an emergency medical service or rush the victim, wrapped in wet cloths, to a hospital emergency room. If hospitalization must be delayed, immerse him in the coldest water possible; stay with him to prevent drowning.

Heat pumps

A heat pump is a highly efficient combination furnace and air conditioner. In winter it extracts heat from outside air, water, or the ground and moves it indoors. In summer it pumps heat out. It performs both functions through two linked units of coils and compressors, one inside and one outside.
1. The sound of rushing air from the outdoor unit is normal; you can muffle it with a double-sided picket fence, the inner row overlapping

the outer as shown. If the noise still seems excessive, call for service.
2. Keep the outdoor unit free of leaves, lint, twigs, and trash. Clear snow from around and on top of it. Never hang anything on the refrigerant tubing.
3. Change or clean the filter once a month for peak efficiency.
4. A clanging or rattling sound from your heat pump is a signal that it's time to call for service.

Hedges

There's no instant cure for an overgrown hedge. It takes hard pruning and a few growing seasons to bring it under control. But there are ways to do the job while keeping the hedge healthy looking.

IN TIMES GONE BY

Forerunners of the furnace

For those of us who merely have to turn a dial to warm our homes to a cozy and precise 72°F, regulated room temperature is easy to take for granted, but it was a long time coming.

The ancient Greeks built their rooms over flues that were warmed by outside furnaces. Wealthy Romans refined this system by placing their rooms on pedestals so that heat from a fire could circulate beneath cold floors. They also installed networks of terra-cotta tubes to distribute hot air, produced by basement fires of wood or coals, throughout their houses.

With the fall of the Roman Empire, central heating disappeared, and it wasn't rediscovered until some 1,500 years later. For much of the Middle Ages, people built indoor log fires that sent smoke billowing throughout their houses. The fireplace, which became popular in 11th-century castles, allowed smoke to escape up the chimney; unfortunately, a great deal of the heat went right up the chimney with it.

In the 18th century fireplaces gave way to stoves, which gave way, in turn, to furnaces in the 19th century. The 20th century, however, would witness a return to the most natural heating system of all: solar energy.

1. If the hedge has grown too dense, shear it back right next to the main stems *on one side only*. Let the hedge recover and put forth new growth for a year. Then shear back the other side.

2. If the hedge has gotten too tall, cut back every second shrub to within a few inches of the ground. A thicket of new shoots should sprout around the severed trunks. Then cut back the remaining shrubs the following year.

3. Don't prune a hedge into a vase shape, wider at the top than at the bottom. The lower part will be shaded, and the foliage will fall off while the upper growth flourishes and spreads. The result: a leggy hedge. Instead, prune so that the base is broader than the top.

Note: Privet, yew, holly, barberry, forsythia, roses, honeysuckle, and spireas respond well to hard pruning. Needled evergreens, such as hemlocks and pines, do not; replanting is the only way to rejuvenate such a hedge.

Hemorrhoids

1. Avoid constipation (p.55); a high-fiber diet—rich in fresh fruits and vegetables as well as wholegrain or bran breads and cereals—and plenty of nonalcoholic liquids every day will soften the stool and eliminate the need to strain.

2. Wash and dry yourself gently with soft tissues.

3. Apply a cloth or tissue soaked with cold water or witch hazel to the affected area for 5 to 10 minutes; to soothe the pain of a partic-

ularly severe attack, use an ice bag.

4. Soak in a hot bath to relieve painful muscle spasms.

5. Buy over-the-counter astringent suppositories to help soothe and shrink the hemorrhoids.

Hems

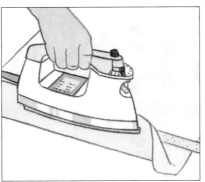

1. Instead of sewing a hem, use iron-on fusible web tape. Turn up the hem, press it, and trim the edge, then insert the tape about ¼ inch from the hem's top edge. "Baste" it with light touches of a warm dry iron; to secure, press the hem with a steam iron (use the *Wool* setting).

2. For a temporary fix, attach a drooping hem with transparent, masking, or adhesive tape. Or try a dab of chewing gum.

3. When lengthening a garment, sponge away the crease with equal parts white vinegar and water. If the crease leaves a dark line, try to eradicate it with spot remover. A white line is permanent; hide it under lace, braid, or trim.

4. Instead of pinning up a hem, use paper clips—they won't prick your fingers. And for easy measuring, notch a piece of cardboard at the desired hem width; place the turned-up hem in the notch and move it along as you sew or pin.

Herbs

1. For a quick *bouquet garni* for soups, stews, or sauces, use a tea ball instead of the usual cheesecloth bag. Fill with parsley flakes, dried thyme, and a crumbled bay leaf (the traditional mix). Or try cel-

ery seed, fennel seed, and dried basil, marjoram, or tarragon. Taste the dish often as it cooks and remove the herbs when you like.

2. When you're substituting dried herbs for fresh, use less. A rule of thumb: 1 teaspoon dried herbs replaces 1 tablespoon fresh.

3. Crumble dried herbs between your fingers to release their flavor.

4. No tarragon? Use parsley or chervil—but increase the quantity by about 50 percent. If you're out of thyme, use marjoram, oregano, or a bay leaf.

5. Thyme on your hands? If you have too many home-grown herbs at the end of summer, dry whole plants upside down in perforated paper bags; then use them to make herb wreaths or sachets. Or tie the dried bunches with ribbon and hang them from hooks for a country kitchen atmosphere.

Dried herb and flower wreath

Hiccups

If all your standard remedies for hiccups don't seem to be having an effect, give one of these a try:

1. Stand in front of a mirror and—taking short, shallow breaths—slip a cool spoon handle into your mouth and touch the uvula, the small lobe hanging at the back of the throat, until your hiccups stop.

2. Lie down with your head tilted as far back as possible and your mouth open.

3. Ask someone to gently press the protruding skin directly in front of your ear canals while you drink a glass of water. The hiccups should subside within a minute.

4. To help stop alcohol-related hiccups, eat a lemon wedge saturated with bitters.

Hiking boots

1. In an emergency you can make a hiking boot water-resistant by dripping candle wax onto the welt where the sole joins the upper. But to do the job right, use boot wax.

Set the boots and the tin of wax in the hot sun until they are warm, or you can warm them with an electric hair dryer. Then apply the wax evenly and rub it in with your bare hands; put an extra-thick application all around the welts. Warm the boots again until the leather has completely absorbed the wax. Repeat the procedure, then remove excess wax with a dry cloth. If the boots will be exposed to moisture often, reapply boot wax frequently. (A small amount can be carried in a 35mm film canister.)

2. To make boots warmer, use insoles. Or put heavy wool socks on *over* the boots. The bottoms of the socks will wear out quickly, but what remains will add considerable warmth. (See also *Boots*, p.24.)

Hinges

1. Here's an easy way to silence a squeaky hinge. Cut a washer out of felt and saturate it with light oil. Then remove the hinge pin, put the washer on it, and reinsert it. Add more oil if the squeak ever returns.

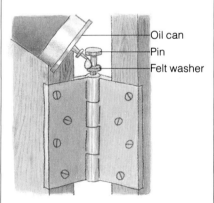

Oil can
Pin
Felt washer

2. For a quick fix, nail a short piece of leather belt over a broken hinge— it's flexible and surprisingly strong. Apply mink oil to keep the leather from drying and cracking.

3. Replace a damaged or lost hinge pin with a snug-fitting common nail or a machine screw. Coat the replacement pin with lubricating oil.

4. Hinge screws often pull loose

and lose their holding power. To repair, whittle a wooden stick to fit tightly into the screw hole. Coat it with glue and jam it into the hole. When the glue is dry, cut the stick off flush with the hole and drive the screw. As an alternative, jam several toothpicks into the hole and cut off the excess; glue is not needed.

Holes in knitwear

1. Repairing a knitted garment? Place the unraveling part over the bristles of a brush—they will hold the knit and prevent stretching.

2. To repair holes in a sweater, place mosquito netting on the wrong side of it, then darn right through its holes.

3. For a quick fix when your sweater snags, pull the loose loops to the inside and secure them with a bobby pin or paper clip until you get home and can restitch.

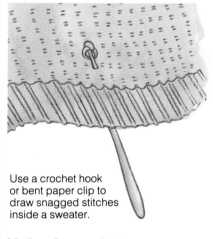

Use a crochet hook or bent paper clip to draw snagged stitches inside a sweater.

Holes in pockets

1. For an emergency repair on an inside pocket, fold the torn edge under and secure it with safety pins or staples.

2. If a patch (exterior) pocket gives way, attach it with double-faced tape. (Don't put anything in the pocket until you can make repairs.) Or, if you can fold under the loose section, fasten it from the inside with safety pins.

3. For a permanent repair, instead of stitching, insert fusible web tape between the two seam allowances of an inside pocket or between a garment and its patch pocket; press with a warm dry iron.

Home equity loans

A kind of second mortgage, this is the least expensive way to borrow money because your house is the collateral. For the same reason, it is also among the most dangerous.

A home equity loan is a good way to finance a college education or an addition to your home, but don't use it to back a risky investment— if you can't meet the payments, you can lose your home.

Before signing up for such a loan, ask your banker these questions:
1. What is the annual percentage rate and what is it based on? The prime rate is the best base, rather than a narrower, less stable guide.
2. How much of your house will be mortgaged?
3. How often and how much can the interest rate change annually? Over the life of the loan?
4. Are there closing costs? (Some banks absorb these.)
5. What other fees will add significantly to the actual cost of the loan?
6. Is there a conversion clause that allows you to change from a variable- to a fixed-rate loan to protect against high inflation?
7. Are there prepayment penalties?

Homeowners insurance

1. How much insurance do you need for your home? Probably about 80 percent of what it would cost to replace it. If your home is totally destroyed by fire, you'll collect the face value of your policy, minus the deductible. However, total loss is rare. And, in the event of partial loss, you get 100 percent of the replacement cost—*if* you're carrying insurance equal to 80 percent or more of the value of your home.
2. Although separate coverage is available, your best bet is a homeowners package that covers theft, liability, fire, and other perils. (Par-

ticularly valuable possessions may require a floater policy.) Include an "inflation guard endorsement" in your policy, as well as coverage for living expenses if your home becomes uninhabitable because of fire or flood. And don't forget to increase your coverage for any major improvements you make.
3. To save money, comparison shop, increase your deductible, and look for special deals—some companies offer discounts for smoke detectors and alarm systems.
4. To find a company that pays claims fairly, call local contractors, roofers, and carpet cleaners. Ask who pays *them* promptly—and without a hassle.
5. Figure out how much your home is worth in terms of rebuilding and refurnishing it—not recouping the original price or the amount of the mortgage. Enlist the assistance of a reputable appraiser or builder, not a real estate agent.
6. Take a detailed inventory of your possessions (see *Valuables*, p.221), then get a replacement-cost rider on your policy so that you'll be reimbursed at full value if they're lost. (See also *Insurance claims*, p.117.)

Home pollution

Modern houses are so well sealed that they may keep pollutants trapped inside. Radon gas, formaldehyde, tobacco smoke, bacteria, fungi, pollen, and combustion byproducts such as soot and carbon monoxide can cause illness—even death—if they are present in high concentrations. The danger is greatly reduced or eliminated with good ventilation (which older, leakier houses encourage naturally).
1. Install a small exhaust fan over a gas oven. Kitchen, bath, laundry, and attic fans help, too. Do not, however, install a large exhaust fan upstairs if a conventional gas burner, oil furnace, or boiler with a chimney is in the basement. The fan could suck air down the chimney and bring dangerous combus-

tion products into the house.
2. Consider installing a heat-recovery ventilator (also called an air-to-air heat exchanger) to reduce the amount of gas, fungi, smoke, bacteria, and formaldehyde (present in particle board and some ceiling tile) in the home; you'll lose only 20 to 50 percent of the house heat— considerably less than with most ventilator systems.
3. Repair all pipe leaks from furnaces, wood stoves, space heaters, and gas clothes dryers.
4. Don't heat a closed space with an unvented device such as a kerosene heater (besides, it's against the law to do so in most places).
5. If you live in an older house and discover that you have asbestos insulation in walls, ceilings, stoves, or furnaces, don't touch it. Call a professional to remove it.

Home study

Complete your high school requirements, earn a college degree, learn how to run a business, or pursue a new career just by studying at home. Many universities and professional schools offer correspondence programs at about half the cost of on-campus courses. And you can work at your own pace.

To find out what programs are available, write to the National Home Study Council (NHSC) at 1606 18th Street NW, Washington, D.C. 20009. This is the official accrediting agency for correspondence schools; request a complete list of programs in your field.

Some reputable correspondence schools, however, are not listed with the NHSC. Before you apply to one of these, check its reputation with your state department of education or with the Better Business Bureau closest to its headquarters.

Beware of schools that claim that all their graduates get high-paying jobs or that require large up-front payments. Make sure that you fully understand the tuition policies before you enroll.

Horseradish

Folk wisdom holds that planting horseradish at each corner of a potato patch repels Colorado potato beetles. Even if you don't have a potato patch, grow horseradish anyway; the sauce you'll make from it is far zestier than anything you can buy at the supermarket.

Just scrub and peel the roots and purée them in a blender with an equal amount of white vinegar. Add a pinch of salt and refrigerate.
Caution: The plant is very invasive. To keep it from taking over your garden, enclose its bed to a depth of at least 1 foot with bricks or sheet metal. Or grow it in a tub.

Hospital stays

1. If you have a choice of hospitals, consider your own needs. A large teaching hospital usually provides state-of-the-art care, but for simpler procedures you may feel more comfortable and get more individual attention at a smaller institution. Before making your decision, get the advice of your physician and any family members or friends who have received treatment at the hospitals you're considering.
2. When you enter the hospital, you'll be given a copy of the Patient's Bill of Rights, issued by the American Hospital Association. If you don't get a copy, ask for one. Read it carefully so that you know your rights and privileges while you're in the hospital. You have the right to all the information you need in order to give informed, written consent to your treatment—to examine your medical records, for example, to know what medication you're given, and to ask what your temperature is. Review the consent form in the relaxed atmosphere of your physician's office, if possible; you have the right to delete any clause to which you object.
3. Find out if the hospital has a patient advocate and learn how to get in touch with her.
4. Remember to bring your insur-

ance identification cards along with your robe and toilet articles. If your coverage requires preadmission approval, call several days before your scheduled hospitalization or, in an emergency, no more than 48 hours after admission.
5. Bring a couple of small plastic shopping bags; they're handy for keeping things organized.
6. Ask your spouse, a relative, or a friend to be there for you. Besides lending emotional support, they can see that you're comfortable by getting fresh water or pillows; they can even question the advisability of prescribed tests or drugs for you.
7. Don't feel you must play host to unexpected visitors when you're tired; ask them to come back another day—and to call beforehand. (See also *Surgery*, p.201.)

Hotels & motels

1. Nearly everyone qualifies for some sort of hotel or motel discount. When making reservations or checking in, ask if your age, employment situation, professional or fraternal affiliation, motor club, or frequent-flyer membership qualifies you for a cut rate. (If not, ask what does.) At big city hotels, inquire about seasonal savings and weekend discounts.
2. For low rates at downtown locations, check into a YMCA/YWCA. If you're under 21, try a youth hostel.
3. Consider bed-and-breakfast alternatives; many guidebooks describe the ever-growing options, from a room with a shared bath in a private home to a nicely appointed suite with a private bath in a grander, less intimate inn.
4. Traveling abroad? For information on such unique accommodations as castles, villas, farmhouses, and canal boats, contact the country's tourist board in New York City.
5. House or apartment swapping is a possibility for a longer trip; put an ad in the classified section of the newspaper of your intended destination. Or take advantage of

listings from the tourist board. Travel agencies can often help you find approved listings, too.

Hot-water bottles

1. Half-fill a self-sealing, heavy-duty plastic bag with hot (not boiling) water. Seal it inside a second bag and wrap in a towel.
2. Fill a screw-top glass jar with hot water, tighten the lid, and wrap in a towel.
3. Heat a clean brick in the oven and wrap in a towel.

House guests

1. When inviting house guests, let them know what time you expect them to arrive *and* to leave. Mention in your invitation any activities that call for special clothes, such as tennis or swimming.
2. If someone is notorious for staying longer than scheduled, arrange an activity for the day after the preset departure time and inform the guest of your other plans.
3. Ask your guests if they have food and drink preferences or allergies.

THE ROLE OF GUEST

1. Bring a small gift—wine, flowers, or a homemade cake. Or bring toys to leave behind for the kids.
2. Adjust to the schedule of the house. If you're an early riser, try to remain in your room until your hosts are up and about. If you really *must* have a cup of coffee, move very quietly around the kitchen.
3. Instead of asking if and how you can help, simply observe. Figure out what needs to be done and do it. A good guest pitches in by helping clean up after meals, sweeping sandy porches, and occasionally buying the groceries.
4. Offer to bring or buy one night's dinner. If you plan to visit for 3 nights or longer (usually not a good idea), take your hosts out or cook for them, but give them enough warning so that they won't already have planned that meal.
5. Keep the guest room neat and

clean even when the door is closed. On the last day of your stay, remove and fold your soiled linen and remake the bed with just the blanket so that the guest room looks presentable after you leave.

6. Ask permission before making any long-distance calls and arrange to reimburse your host.

7. Don't overstay your welcome.

Houseplant food

To supplement complete fertilizers with an extra dose of nitrogen, add a little gelatin to the water once a month. Just empty an envelope of *unflavored* gelatin into 1 cup of boiling water, stir until the gelatin dissolves, and mix with 3 cups of cool water. Apply immediately; discard any leftover liquid.

Houseplant pests

Control spider mites, whiteflies, aphids, and thrips with a spray of 2 tablespoons biodegradable liquid detergent in a gallon of water. Coat the leaves top and bottom. One treatment may not kill all the invaders, so spray a second time in 3 to 7 days. Small plants without flowers can be dipped into the solution for better coverage.

For a persistent infestation, purée two hot peppers and two or three cloves of garlic in a blender; add 3 cups water and 2 tablespoons biodegradable liquid detergent, then strain into a spray bottle.

Caution: Soap can injure leaves in very hot weather; don't use these treatments during a heat wave.

Houseplant polish

Plant polish, whether store-bought or homemade, plugs leaf pores and does your indoor greenery more harm than good. For a healthier luster, bathe plants twice a month in the detergent solution recommended above for pests. Wash both sides of the leaves to remove dust and grime. Mix a small dose of mild tea into the bath water to strengthen leaves and deepen their color.

Housing for the elderly

A nursing home is not necessarily the next stop when you're no longer able to live on your own at home. There are many housing arrangements that will let you retain your independence.

1. For those who are slightly disabled, living at home may still be feasible with help from housekeepers, paid companions, and visiting nurses. Meal-delivery and transportation services are also available in many places.

2. If you choose to remain at home, take the time to enroll in an emergency response system. You'll receive a lightweight wearable alarm that, when pressed, will signal a central operator, who will then call a relative or an ambulance.

3. If loneliness is more of a problem to you than frailty is, consider a group living arrangement. Shared housing services exist to help match up compatible older people; check the Yellow Pages for one. In some group houses, people have their own rooms, but meals and laundry are furnished.

4. You may prefer living on your own in a retirement community. Many such communities—ranging in size from single apartment buildings to mobile home parks to whole villages—offer hotel-type services and limited medical care.

5. Or you may choose to live with relatives or to move into a private home offering foster care. In some areas day-care centers can provide outside contact and stimulation while family members are at work or school.

6. Some retirement communities provide lifetime "continuing care," with accommodations that range from independent living to 24-hour nursing care. Residents can move from one level of care to another according to their needs. Contracts for lifetime care can be complicated and expensive; consider them carefully and have a lawyer review them before you sign anything.

Humidifiers

1. To add moisture to the air in your home, place pans of clean water on top of your radiators or other heat sources.

2. For a temporary infusion of moisture, shower with the bathroom door ajar.

3. Install a special accessory to vent your clothes dryer indoors during cold weather. It can add more than a gallon of water to the air per load—and it gives off heat, too. (Don't just unhook the dryer vent hose; lint will spew into the room, and the concentrated hot, humid airflow may cause furniture to warp and wallpaper to peel.)

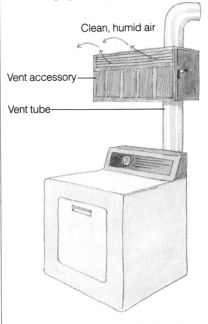

Clean, humid air

Vent accessory

Vent tube

Caution: Do not install the dryer vent if you live in a mobile home (because outdoor venting is required) or if you have electric or hot-water heat (because extensive humidity may cause a problem).

› Hurricanes

THE WATCH

1. Fill your car's gas tank and stay tuned for weather bulletins.

2. Make sure you have adequate emergency food supplies, containers of water, a radio, a flashlight, extra batteries, candles, and a first-aid kit stocked with the family's special medications.

3. Have masking tape ready to cover small windows; plywood or shutters for large panes and doors.

THE WARNING

1. Bring all loose, heavy outdoor objects inside or anchor them.

2. Tape or cover windows; wedge sliding glass doors shut.

3. Moor your boat securely or bring it onto land and fill it with water to weight it down.

4. Stay indoors, away from windows and glass doors.

5. Leave low-lying areas that may be caught by high tides and waves.

EVACUATION

1. Take food, water, warm clothing, blankets, a first-aid kit, a battery-operated radio, and important papers, such as birth certificates and insurance policies.

2. Leave pets with food and water; shelters won't admit them.

3. Lock all doors and windows. Shut off gas, water, and electricity if told to do so by authorities.

AFTERMATH

1. Don't be fooled by the calm in the eye of the hurricane; the powerful winds will return after it passes. Listen for the official all-clear and for other emergency information before venturing out or going home.

2. Avoid loose or dangling wires;

report them to the power company, the police, or the fire department.

3. If the power has been off, make sure that refrigerated and frozen food has not spoiled (see *Power outage*, p. 162).

4. Do not drink the water from faucets until it has been officially declared safe. Then boil tap water for 10 minutes before drinking it.

5. Save the receipts for all repair expenses for insurance and income tax purposes.

Hypertension

1. Learn to check your blood pressure at home. Buy an inexpensive blood-pressure monitor (available at drugstores or by mail order), then take it to your doctor's office to check its accuracy as well as your own technique.

2. Keep a running chart of your readings to show your doctor. Record the date, time, location, body position (standing or sitting), circumstances (stress, medications, and other special factors).

3. To maintain a normal weight, eat a well-balanced diet and exercise regularly.

4. Limit your sodium to 3,000 milligrams a day. (A can of soup or a frozen entrée may have 1,000!)

5. Ration your alcohol. Drink no more than two 12-ounce beers, two 4-ounce glasses of wine, or 3 ounces of 80-proof liquor per day.

6. Eliminate caffeine for a couple of weeks to see if it affects your blood pressure.

7. Get a pet. Caring for, playing with, talking to, and even watching pets can reduce stress and blood pressure. Birds and fish are particularly soothing.

›Hypothermia

If you're out in the cold and one of your companions begins to shiver violently and then becomes lethargic and drowsy, call for medical help immediately.

In the meantime, keep the person sheltered and out of the wind.

Remove wet clothing and replace it with dry. If he's fairly alert, feed him candy and, if available, hot, sugary, nonalcoholic liquids. Cover him with blankets or get him into a sleeping bag; if possible, get into it with him and hug him—a person on each side is even better. (See also *Frostbite*, p. 92.)

Ice cream

1. Ice cream retains its texture and quality best at 0°F; put a thermometer in your freezer and adjust the setting accordingly.

2. Ice cream picks up freezer odors easily, so store the carton in a sealed plastic bag.

3. To soften a quart of ice cream for serving, put the carton in a microwave on *Defrost* for 40 seconds.

4. Be aware that if you replace ice cream with ice milk or sherbet, you'll be eating less butterfat but consuming more sugar.

Ice cream cones

Before you scoop ice cream into a cone, drop a jelly bean in the bottom; it helps forestall drips.

With a bit of ingenuity, you can serve up an ice cream treat without relying on store-bought cones. Here are some ideas:

1. Make an ice cream sandwich by putting a scoop between two oversize cookies or splitting a brownie in half and filling it.

2. Hollow out a cupcake to make a little edible bowl.

3. Use a flour tortilla to make an ice cream *burrito* (hold one end tight to keep it from dripping).

4. Enclose the scoop in a pita bread pocket. It's better than you think; just make sure the bread isn't the garlic-flavored kind.

5. Surprise the kids with cones shaped from fruit leather (sold as

I scream for ice cream

No one really invented ice cream—not even Dolley Madison (who, as every schoolchild knows, served it at the White House long before it became the nation's favorite dessert). Rather, ice cream evolved.

History records that iced drinks were served in King Solomon's time. Later the Roman Emperor Nero is said to have had snow retrieved from the mountains and served with fruits, juices, and honey. At the end of the 13th century Marco Polo returned from the Far East with a recipe resembling today's sherbet. Most historians believe it was probably this recipe that evolved into ice cream in Italy sometime during the 16th century.

Ice cream was first served to the general public at Café Procope in Paris in the late 1600's (the café, like the dessert, is still there). But almost 200 years passed before the stuff was really made available to all; it happened after the invention of insulated ice houses and the hand-operated ice cream freezer.

The first wholesale ice cream appeared in Baltimore in 1851, and before long, ice cream vendors were setting up shop. By 1874 a soft drink concessionaire in Philadelphia had introduced the ice cream soda.

If an ice cream vendor at the 1904 World's Fair in St. Louis hadn't run out of bowls, we might never have seen the birth of the ice cream cone. As the story goes, he had some Middle Eastern waffles at hand, and when he folded them into cornucopia shapes and filled them with ice cream, he started a fad that's still going strong.

roll-ups). Roll the cones and store them upside down in the freezer for at least 15 minutes before adding the ice cream. Warn the kids that this cone loses it shape quickly, and they'll have to clean up the mess unless they eat fast. For less mess, put a small scoop on an unfrozen sheet of fruit leather and roll it into a cylinder; fold the ends over.

Ice cubes

1. Need extra ice cubes for a party? Freeze water in clean egg cartons, then transfer the ice to sandwich bags and store in the freezer.
2. You won't get bubbles in your ice cubes if you use bottled spring water—noncarbonated. Or if you boil tap water, cool it, then freeze.
3. A full freezer works best, so fill up the empty spaces. Giant ice cubes, made by filling loaf pans or plastic bags with water, do the job. They're great for picnics, too; just pop them into the cooler.

Ice hockey jargon

Here's a guide to what the TV announcers are saying:
Blue lines. The two 1-foot-wide lines drawn 60 feet from and parallel to the goal lines, dividing the rink into offensive, defensive, and neutral zones.
Body check. To block an opponent by hitting him above the knees from the side or front—a legal maneuver, provided that no more than two strides are taken first.
Butt end. To jab an opponent with the butt of the stick; an infraction.
Center ice. The neutral zone between the blue lines.
Crease. The 4- x 8-foot area in front of the net where the goalie stands; an offensive player is allowed to skate here only when he has possession of the puck.
Down a man. The status of a team when one of its six players is in the penalty box and it must play without him; also called shorthanded.

Face-off. A formal competition for the puck; the referee drops it inside a face-off circle, between the sticks of two selected opponents.
Glove save. The accomplishment of a goalie who blocks the puck with his glove, preventing a goal from being scored.
Goal lines. The red lines extending across the width of the ice, behind which the goals are centered.
Goalie. The goalkeeper.
Hat trick. The scoring of 3 or more goals by one player in a game.
High stick. To hit a man with the stick held above shoulder level (4 feet in college play); an infraction.
Icing. Shooting the puck from your defensive zone across the opponent's goal line; if an opposing player touches it first, a face-off ensues (unless your team is down a man).
Kill a penalty. To use up the time while your team is down a man without giving up a goal.
Offside. An infraction that occurs when one of the attacking team crosses the blue line into the offensive zone before the puck does; a face-off then occurs.
Penalty. The punishment for an infraction. The guilty player must leave the ice and wait in the penalty box for a set period of time (up to 5 minutes for a major infraction such as fighting), causing his team to be down a man.
Power play. A concentrated attack on the goal when the defending team is down a man or more.
Slapshot. A shot in which the puck is hit hard toward the goal, usually from some distance.
Spear. To jab an opponent with the blade end of the stick; an infraction.

Icy walks

1. Use sand, sifted ashes, or cat litter to improve traction.
2. Spread rock salt *before* snow or sleet falls; this helps keep ice from bonding to a concrete surface. Or spread granulated urea fertilizer; it melts ice and helps plants in spring.
3. Keep a walk relatively dry and

ice-free by digging shallow trenches along both sides. They'll trap rainwater and melting snow.

4. On an icy walk, tilt your body slightly forward and set your feet down flat. Short steps also improve stability. If you fall, don't tense up; go limp and try to roll as you land.

Illness away from home

1. Planning a foreign vacation? A month or so before you leave, have thorough physical and dental examinations, get all the required inoculations, and request copies of all your prescriptions, including those for your eyeglasses. As an additional safeguard, ask your doctor to write out the generic names of all your medications so that a foreign pharmacist can recognize them.

2. Pack a small first-aid kit with bandage materials, disinfectant, antibiotic ointment, diarrhea medicine, motion sickness pills, and aspirin or a substitute (p.12).

3. Carry a short medical history in your wallet and wear a tag indicating any life-threatening allergies or conditions such as diabetes.

For a small fee you can give your medical history to the Medic Alert Foundation International (800-344-3226); you'll receive a membership card and a bracelet or necklace engraved with your identification number, any critical medical conditions you have, and the organization's internationally recognized symbol and phone number. Should someone find you ill or unconscious, she or a doctor can call the foundation collect from anywhere in the world.

4. Ask your travel agent about special insurance that will help you get a doctor, a prescription, money, or transportation home. Carry your insurance card, your agent's name and phone number, and several claims forms.

5. If you get sick abroad, American embassies and consulates can usually supply you with the names of English-speaking doctors.

Income tax returns

To help keep your tax return problem-free, take these steps:

1. Double-check your math—one error is one too many (see *Computations*, p.54).

2. Remember to include your Social Security number and to sign your return and your check.

3. Answer all questions. If you have no response to a question, write "None" or "N/A" (not applicable).

4. Do not claim dependents who had more than half their support from another source. Make sure that those you claim as dependents don't take an exemption on their own returns.

5. Make sure you haven't omitted any sources of income. Attach the appropriate copies of your W-2 wage statements to your return. The IRS cross-checks your figures with those provided by your employer, your bank, and other sources.

6. Make sure you have the same figures on the return and on the supporting schedules.

7. File your return on time even if you can't pay the taxes; otherwise you will be subject to late-payment penalties and interest. Or send your payment along with Form 4868 for a 2-month extension.

8. Happily, if you make any mistakes, you can correct them—even on April 16—by filing Form 1040X.

Incontinence

This once-forbidden subject is no longer taboo, nor should it be a cause for embarrassment. In most cases incontinence can be successfully managed or even cured.

1. The first step is a medical diagnosis of the underlying cause. If the pelvic and bladder muscles are weak, they can be strengthened with a regimen of simple exercises or biofeedback methods. If the prostate has become enlarged, surgery may restore proper bladder function. In addition, medications and bladder pacemakers can sometimes aid in regulating the bladder.

2. For incontinence that can't be managed medically, absorbent pads, lined underwear, collecting bags, and catheters are available.

3. Support groups such as the Simon Foundation in Wilmette, Illinois, keep members abreast of new developments and help them learn to live more comfortably.

Indigestion

1. To relieve gas, drink peppermint tea. Steep ½ ounce of fresh leaves in 1 pint of boiled water for 20 minutes.

2. Instead of a commercial antacid, try 1 teaspoon baking soda in a glass of water (not recommended for those who must restrict their intake of sodium).

Caution: A heart attack may be mistaken for indigestion. If you are in doubt, seek medical help fast.

PREVENTION

1. Stop smoking and chewing gum. Cut out aspirin, alcohol, caffeine, and carbonated drinks. Forgo foods that don't agree with you.

2. Make time for stress-free meals. Try eating four or five small meals slowly instead of gulping two or three large ones.

3. Relax, sitting up, for 15 to 30 minutes after every meal.

4. Sleep with the head of your bed slightly elevated.

Indoor plants

You don't need expensive and temperamental houseplants to add greenery to your home. Many of the vegetables you bring home from the supermarket will sprout and brighten a windowsill. And kids love to watch them grow.

1. Cut the top inch or two off a beet, parsnip, rutabaga, or turnip and completely trim off the greens. Line an earthenware ashtray or other low container with pebbles and fill it with water. Set the flat cut end of the vegetable on the pebbles. Over the next few days, change the water whenever it gets cloudy.

LOOK BEFORE YOU LEAP

Are your houseplants killers?

You may find it merely annoying when your cat chews on the houseplants. Your poor cat may find it fatal.

Most people know that oleanders are poisonous, but so are some innocent-looking favorites: caladiums, dieffenbachias, elephant ears, monsteras, philodendrons, and even English ivy.

Not only cats, but also toddlers, can be attracted to houseplants—especially those with flowers or berries. Besides oleanders, hazardous flowers include angel's-trumpets (*Datura candida*), every part of which is toxic, birds-of-paradise, and lantanas, which bear berries that are poisonous while they are green.

Two plants popular at Christmastime also pose hazards. Mistletoe and the Jerusalem cherry (*Solanum pseudocapsicum*) have berries that look invitingly edible—but don't partake! And keep these plants well out of the reach of pets and children.

Many of the spring bulbs we raise on windowsills are also toxic: daffodil, narcissus, hyacinth, and amaryllis bulbs may look like onions to a child but are dangerous if ingested.

If you have any doubt about a plant's toxicity, ask your florist or nursery owner for its botanical name. Then call the nearest poison control center (you'll find the number at the beginning of the white pages of your telephone book) to find out if it's safe.

The resultant forest of greens will last for a month or more.

2. Slice the leaf crown and 1 inch of flesh off the top of a pineapple. Set it in moist sand and keep it watered. When roots form, plant in potting soil that has some peat moss mixed in and—presto!—you have a bromeliad that will last for years.

3. To germinate apple, orange, lemon, or grapefruit seeds, sow them in small flats of potting soil and keep well watered. When they're a few inches tall, transplant them to larger pots and watch them grow into lush (but probably fruitless) trees. Kiwifruits, loquats, pomegranates, and such tropical fruits as papayas, litchis, and mangoes can also be started this way.

4. You can easily turn a carrot into a hanging display of fernlike feathery foliage. Just cut the top inch or two off an extra-large carrot, along with the leaves. Hollow out the center, leaving the outer wall intact. With a stout needle, run a thread through the wall of this "basket" and hang it, leaves down, in a sunny window. Fill it with water and keep it filled—if it dries out, it will shrivel. Before long, delicate foliage will emerge and all but hide the carrot.

5. That old standby, the indoor tree grown from an avocado pit, usually turns into a slender stem weighted down by a little pom-pom of leaves. The reason: it's not pinched back and pruned hard enough. Don't be afraid to start over occasionally; cut the plant back to a 3- or 4-inch stem. You'll force new root growth and get a bushier, healthier plant.

Influenza

1. For achiness, fever, or a headache, take some aspirin or acetaminophen (p.12).

2. Drink 8 ounces of fluids every 2 hours to prevent dehydration from fever. Dilute apple juice or flat ginger ale with water. Avoid citrus juices if you feel nauseated; milk if you are vomiting or have diarrhea.

3. *Don't* starve a fever. Eat small, bland meals—cottage cheese, yogurt, applesauce, bananas, dry toast, baked or boiled potatoes. Don't worry if you're not hungry for 3 or 4 days, but when your appetite returns, eat a high-protein, high-calorie diet rich in vitamins B and C (see *The Balanced Diet*, p.254).

4. If you have a sore throat (p.192), drink hot liquids, gargle with salt water, and chew cloves.

5. For a runny nose, sip hot tea with a bit of honey and take a decongestant if you wish.

6. For a dry cough, use a humidifier (p.111) and suck on cough drops or hard candy (see *Coughs*, p.58).

7. Stay in bed—or at the very least reduce physical activity—as long as you can (at least until your temperature returns to normal); resuming your regular activities too soon will encourage a relapse.

8. Don't drive; flu impairs reaction time almost six times as much as moderate alcohol intake.

9. If you're over 65; if you have a chronic disease; if you feel especially ill or the fever lasts more than 4 days; or if your fever is accompanied by a stiff neck, severe headaches, irritability, and confusion, see a doctor. (See also *Colds*, p.51.)

Informal attire

1. A woman who gets an invitation for an evening party that says "informal" should wear a cocktail dress; a man, a dark suit.

2. If the invitation says "casual" or is for a daytime event, and you're unsure what to wear, call your host and ask. If the answer is vague, ask what the host plans to wear.

Ink stains

1. To clean ink from skin, moisten the white tip of a safety match and rub with it, then rinse.

2. For ballpoint pen marks on fabric, try a pen eraser. If this doesn't work, saturate the spot with hair spray or nail polish remover (test on an inconspicuous part of the fabric first); then blot, first with a cloth dampened with the solvent and then with a dry cloth. Or apply petroleum jelly, then soak in a detergent solution. As a last resort, if the fabric is bleachable, use chlorine bleach.

3. For felt-tip pen marks on fabric, place the stained area over a piece of clean, absorbent fabric and sponge with another cloth dampened with cleaning fluid. Then place the fabric in sunlight, which will lighten the stain further.

FROM LIQUID INK

1. If the ink is still wet, pour salt on the stain and brush off after a few minutes; repeat if necessary.

2. Soak the stain with rubbing alcohol, then blot with cheesecloth.

3. Work concentrated ammonia into the stain, then vinegar; rinse with water.

4. Sponge the stain with water, then with a solution of mild detergent and a few drops of vinegar; let it remain for 30 minutes.

5. Rub liquid detergent over the stain, then rinse.

In-laws

1. Get the jump on potential conflicts. As soon as you become an in-law, circulate a questionnaire— make it as humorous as possible—

covering potentially thorny issues, such as what to call your in-laws, where holidays will be celebrated, who will help after a grandchild is born, and whether attendance at family weddings is mandatory.

2. Some relationships are permanent. Your son is your former mother-in-law's grandson, no matter how many times you divorce and remarry. The same is true of aunts, uncles, and cousins. Don't discourage such family relationships, however you feel about your former in-laws. They can enrich the lives of your children.

Insect bites

To relieve the itch of a mosquito, blackfly, no-see-um, or other insect bite, apply an ice pack or ice cube four times a day for 5 minutes or a cold Burow's solution (1:40 concentration) for 10 minutes. Let the skin dry, then smooth on an over-the-counter hydrocortisone cream.

If the bite is especially itchy, swollen, or uncomfortable, or if you have many bites, take an antihistamine.

Insect repellents

1. Natural substitutes for commercial repellents include oils of citronella and pennyroyal, available at health food stores. Mix them with vegetable or baby oil—a few drops to about an ounce of oil.

2. To make yourself less attractive to insects, wear light-colored clothing and skip the perfume or cologne. (See also *Blackflies*, p.22.)

Insomnia

1. Cut back on smoking, chocolate, caffeine, and alcohol, especially in late afternoon and evening.

2. Avoid heavy meals close to bedtime—a snack of hot milk and crackers may be helpful—and all meals in the middle of the night.

3. Do not exercise strenuously just before going to bed.

4. Spend less time in bed. Get up at the same time every morning, but go to bed later. Start with a half

hour later; if necessary, keep pushing back your bedtime until you can doze off readily.

5. Don't sleep late or take naps during the day.

6. Turn your alarm clock toward the wall so that you don't keep checking the time.

Installment loans

1. A rule of thumb: Never buy anything on credit whose value won't outlast the payments.

2. Ask your bank if it charges lower interest when monthly payments are deducted directly from your checking account. If you have a CD at the bank that equals or exceeds the amount of the loan, try to negotiate an even lower rate.

3. Figure out how much you will actually pay—including service charges, fees, and points.

4. Beware of added features you don't really need or want, such as insurance to protect the loan; a "balloon," or oversize, final payment; or the dread acceleration clause— if you default on one payment, the entire balance comes due.

5. Find out in advance what penalties the contract specifies in case you miss a payment. (It's usually a flat fee of 5 percent, plus interest.)

6. Ask if there's a penalty for paying off a loan earlier than scheduled; if so, try to negotiate better terms. (See also *Credit cards*, p.59; *Debt*, p.61; *Down payments*, p.66; *Home equity loans*, p.109.)

Insulation

Sand-filled sealer

1. Make sealers for the cracks at the bottoms of doors by filling socks three-quarters full of sand or cat litter. Knot the tops and decorate, if you like, as mice or dachshunds.
2. On a particularly cold night, insulate a window by taping clear plastic—even food wrap—to the frame. (See also *Drafts*, p.66.)

Insurance claims

1. Inventory everything covered by your homeowners policy. Photograph each item, note its serial number, and keep the sales slip to show its cost and date of purchase. In case of loss, phone your insurer right away, then follow up with a letter. If the loss is the result of a crime, report it immediately to the police to validate your claim.
2. After a fire, make a detailed description of the damage done to your home; the insurance company's appraiser will prepare an alternate list. Get bids for repairs from several reputable contractors. If your home is unlivable and your clothing is beyond repair, save the receipts for lodging and new clothing to get reimbursed. (See also *Homeowners insurance*, p.109.)
3. To avoid filling out detailed health insurance forms, laying out cash, and waiting for reimbursement, try to negotiate with your doctor, dentist, or other provider of services to accept an "assignment of benefits." This way, someone else does most of the paperwork and waits for the insurance money.
4. Be sure to disclose any preexisting conditions on your health insurance application; the policy may be invalidated if you make a claim for treatment of a condition you haven't previously reported.
5. To get the best settlement on an automobile insurance claim, keep all receipts for maintenance; take periodic photographs of the car to demonstrate its condition before the accident.
6. Keep the information on how to file claims with all your policies.

Insurance costs

To save on carrying charges, pay all your premiums annually.

AUTOMOBILE

1. As a car loses value, decrease the collision and comprehensive coverage and raise the deductible.
2. Ask about discounts for the following: an accident- and summons-free driving record; automatic seat belts and air bags; and insuring both home and car with the same company.
3. Insure your children on the family policy. Ask about a discount if they pass a safe-driving course, earn good grades, and demonstrate responsible behavior. If your child is away at school, uses the car for less than 10 percent of its total use, or is in the service, find out about an "occasional driver" discount.

MEDICAL

1. If you don't have an employer to pick up the tab, get group rates by joining a professional or special-interest organization that has a medical insurance plan.
2. Choose a higher deductible so that you can apply your premium to purchasing expanded coverage.
3. Find out if the company offers a nonsmoker's discount. (See also *Homeowners insurance*, p.109; *Life insurance*, p.126.)

Ironing

1. When ironing a variety of fibers, start with the iron at its lowest setting and work up to the highest. Go with the weave of the cloth so that you don't stretch the fabric. To prevent a shine, iron dark fabrics, rayons, and acetates on the wrong side.
2. If you're traveling and don't have an iron, hang your just-unpacked clothes in the bathroom and run hot water in the shower. Close the door and let the steam smooth out the wrinkles. This method works especially well with wool.
3. If you have an iron but no board, cover a counter with newspapers and then a towel. Or put newspapers into a pillowcase and use it as your ironing board. Or place a towel over the corner of the bed.
4. Place a piece of aluminum foil, shiny side up, between the ironing board and cover pad; it will reflect heat for a faster job.

IN TIMES GONE BY

This is the way we pressed our clothes

Ironing is still a chore, but today's lightweight, thermostatically controlled irons make the task a lot easier than it used to be.

In ancient Greece, where crisp clothing was a sign of status (and permanent-press fabrics did not exist), a heated rod resembling a rolling pin was used to put pleats in linen robes. The Romans fought wrinkles as fiercely as they fought their foes—they hammered them out with a flat metal mallet, usually wielded by slaves.

By the 10th century, the iron had evolved into a mushroom-shaped glass object that the Vikings rolled back and forth on dampened fabric. Europeans in the 15th and 16th centuries used either a flatiron heated over a fire or, in wealthier homes, a hot box iron containing coals or a hot brick. Gas-heated irons were introduced in the 19th century, but they sometimes leaked or exploded, setting a house on fire.

Although most of the United States was not yet electrified, the first electric iron was patented in 1882, followed by ones that were temperature controlled. But the real breakthroughs in the war against wrinkles came in 1926, when the steam iron hit the market, and in the 1960s, when easy-care permanent-press fabrics were introduced.

5. Interrupted from your ironing? Throw sprinkled clothing into a plastic bag and put it in the refrigerator or freezer. The bag holds in moisture and the low temperature prevents mildew. (Let frozen clothes thaw before ironing!)

6. To press a pesky ribbon, keep the iron stationary and pull the ribbon underneath it.

Itching

1. For quick relief, place a wet tea bag or a cold witch hazel compress directly on the itchy area.

2. If skin is not broken, apply a cooling lotion made from ½ cup water, ½ cup rubbing alcohol, and 3 to 4 drops oil of peppermint. Store in a tightly capped bottle and shake well before using.

3. For allover relief, crumble 1 cup uncooked oatmeal into lukewarm bath water as it flows from the tap. Be careful getting in and out of the tub—it will be extremely slippery. Soak 15 to 20 minutes and gently pat-dry so that a thin coating of oatmeal remains on your skin.

4. For itchy, dry, or chapped skin, a mineral oil bath (2 to 3 ounces per tub of lukewarm water) or a salt bath (½ to 1 cup per tub) works wonders. (Mineral oil or salt will also make the tub slippery, so be careful.) After the bath, smooth on aloe vera gel from the center of a freshly sliced aloe leaf—you can also buy it at a health food store.

Japanese beetles

Control Japanese beetles in your garden in one of these ways:

1. Knock them from plants onto a sheet on the ground in early morning, before they're limber enough to fly. Then dump them into a pail of warm soapy water or kerosene.

2. Turn a can of fruit cocktail into a Japanese beetle trap. Open it and let it ferment in the sun for a week. Then set it on bricks inside a light-colored pail 25 feet from the plants you want to protect. Fill the pail with water to a level just below the rim of the can. The beetles, drawn to the sweet fruit, will fly to the pail, fall in the water, and drown. Cover the trap when it rains.

3. Spray the pests with insecticidal soap, alcohol, or pyrethrum.

4. For a long-term solution, apply milky spore disease (*Bacillus popilliae*) to turf areas; it will take a couple of years to eradicate the grubs.

Jellyfish stings

If you're stung by a jellyfish, take the following steps:

1. Quickly rinse your skin with rubbing alcohol (vodka or other spirits will do), vinegar, diluted ammonia, or urine. Or you can apply moist sea or beach sand for 20 minutes. Or rub with fresh papaya or meat tenderizer. (Do not use water.)

2. Remove any bits of tentacle stuck to your skin with tweezers or gloved hands, *not* your bare fingers.

3. Lather the skin with shaving cream and remove any embedded stinging cells with a razor or sharp knife, then rinse as described above for 15 minutes.

4. Slather the affected area with over-the-counter hydrocortisone cream 3 to 4 times a day until the redness disappears.

5. To reduce swelling, take oral antihistamines; to relieve pain, take acetaminophen (not aspirin—it promotes bleeding, which is a problem with these stings).

6. If dizziness, nausea, vomiting, or other signs of shock develop, get medical help right away.

Jet lag

1. Alternate a "feast day" (high-protein breakfast and lunch, high-carbohydrate dinner) with a "fast day" (soup and salad) for 3 days before departure; during those days don't drink any caffeine except between 3:00 and 5:00 P.M. On flight day eat sparingly and drink caffeine only in the morning if you're flying west, between 6:00 and 9:00 P.M. if you're headed east.

2. Preadjust your bedtime. If flying east, go to sleep an hour earlier each day for each time zone you're crossing; if flying west, move bedtime later in the same fashion.

3. When flying east over several time zones, try to take a morning flight instead of an overnighter. On arrival your "body time" will be midafternoon; local time will be early evening. Eat dinner and go to bed late by local time. The next morning you'll feel rested.

4. Flying west is easier. In fact, you may avoid jet lag altogether if you take a late flight, stay awake during the trip, then go to bed as soon as you reach your destination.

5. For a short coast-to-coast trip, try staying on your own time.

6. Drink lots of fluids before and during the flight, but avoid alcoholic beverages.

7. Go outside into sunlight as soon as possible after arriving. Take a brisk walk or jog; moderate exercise may help your body adjust faster (see *Fitness on the road*, p.85).

Jewelry allergies

1. To prevent inflammation when having your ears pierced, make sure a stainless-steel needle is used. Wear only stainless-steel post earrings until the earlobes heal.

2. If you have a reaction to a ring, earrings, or metal eyeglass frames, clean them with rubbing alcohol, then use clear nail polish to coat the part that touches the skin. Reapply the polish when it wears off. Another way to lessen irritation is to apply over-the-counter hydro-

---

DID YOU KNOW . . . ?

A few nuggets about gold

☐ To produce 1 troy ounce of gold (about 1/15 pound) nearly 2½ tons of rock must be processed.

☐ All of the gold ever mined could fit into a cube with 53-foot sides.

☐ Gold is so valuable that refineries clean their roofs and chimneys periodically to recover the specks that have accumulated there.

☐ The Romans serrated the edges of gold coins to prevent people from shaving off tiny bits.

☐ Gold doesn't tarnish or corrode. Coins from sunken ships often are as shiny as new, even after centuries beneath the sea.

☐ Gold is so malleable that 1 ounce can be hammered into a gold leaf that covers 1,400 square feet, or pulled into an extremely fine wire 50 miles long.

☐ Pure gold (24 karat) is so soft that it must be mixed with another metal to make it durable enough for jewelry. It turns reddish when mixed with copper, bluish when mixed with iron, and it forms white gold when nickel is added.

☐ Gold is important to the space program. During astronaut Edward White's historic space walk, a gold-plated cord was his lifeline; today gold wire and tubing are vital to the space shuttle.

cortisone cream before you put on the jewelry or frames.

3. Nickel, a component in some jewelry metals, causes an allergic reaction in some people; if you suspect you're one of them, wear pure copper or nonmetal jewelry.

4. Don't wear tight-fitting metal watchbands or bracelets. Wrap a handkerchief or other fabric under a watch or bracelet during humid weather or exercise.

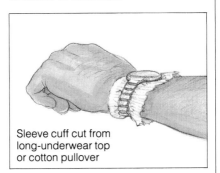

Sleeve cuff cut from long-underwear top or cotton pullover

Job burnout

Have you reached the point— whether from overwork, stress, or just plain boredom—where you don't enjoy your job anymore? Here are some ways to get the zest back:

1. Redefine your job. Write up a realistic job description and discuss it with your boss, stressing that you want to adjust your duties so that you can be more productive.

2. Develop and sell a new project. Write a memo to your boss explaining why your idea is worthwhile, what kind of help you would need, and how long it would take. Even if the project doesn't pan out, you'll have done something different, and you'll probably be remembered for your earnest attempts.

3. Develop a life outside work— take up a hobby or do volunteer work. If necessary, take some time off to gain perspective.

4. If you're still burned out, perhaps it's time to find a better setting for your skills or to consider a career change (p.37).

Job hunting

1. A good career counselor can be a great help. Choose one who has excellent references and charges by the appointment. Watch out for high-pressure "marketing shops"

that charge steep up-front prices and prey on your insecurity.

2. Invest in an answering service or machine so that you can get messages from prospective employers.

3. Inform friends, business associates, acquaintances, and former employers that you're job hunting. (See also *Networking*, p.142.)

RESEARCHING A PROSPECT

1. If you hear of an interesting job, investigate the company—read newspaper and magazine articles about it; study its annual and quarterly reports; look it up in reference books from Standard and Poor's, Dun and Bradstreet, or Moody's.

2. If possible, talk to people who work for the firm. Find out its position in the industry, what its main problems are, and what it's like to work for. Does it promote from within? Does it educate employees? Help them advance?

3. Visit the company if it is practical to do so. Do the employees look enthusiastic? Do they talk positively about their work?

4. Write a letter to whoever is in a position to hire you. Indicate your knowledge of the company, state how you could help it reach its goals, and request an interview. Say that you'll follow up by phone in about a week. Then do so.

IF YOU HAVE A JOB

1. Ask agents or prospective employers to leave only their first name if they call you at work. Or have them call you at home.

2. Do not look for work on company time. Schedule interviews for before or after work or during your lunch hour.

Job interviews

1. Prepare a customized résumé for each interview, tailoring your stated objectives to suit the available job. (It's easier to customize a résumé if it's on a computer disk.)

2. Create two basic résumés—a chronological one if you're working through agencies and a functional one, organized around your skills and experience, if you've had a number of jobs or are returning to work after several years.

PREPARATION

1. Choose four or five incidents from current and past jobs that show your accomplishments and work style. Create a success story for each one to help answer such questions as "What are your major accomplishments?" or "What is your relevant experience?"

2. Rehearse the interview with a friend or family member. Anticipate likely questions and practice telling your success stories without rambling. Ask for feedback.

3. Give yourself an extra hour or so to dress and get to the interview. If your hands tend to be clammy, use antiperspirant on your palms.

THE INTERVIEW

1. Look the interviewer directly in the eye and follow her lead in shaking hands.

2. Remember that you are making a choice as much as she is. Ask any questions necessary to decide if this is a job you really want.

Job loss

A job loss is almost always an opportunity disguised as a disaster. Keep in mind that you have several priorities: to handle the immediate crisis, to reevaluate your career, and to make plans for your future.

1. Press for severance pay—many employers offer as much as 2 weeks' pay for each year of service. Find out about continuing group health insurance at your own expense.

2. Losing a job can feel like losing a loved one. Allow yourself to feel depressed and angry. Tell your family what you're experiencing and ask them for extra moral support during this difficult time.

3. Don't panic. If you can afford to take a vacation, do so—it may lend perspective. If you can't, give yourself little treats: eat lunch at a new restaurant or escape to the movies.

4. Then get busy. Reevaluate what went wrong—be honest, but don't torture yourself. Did you hang on too long when you knew things were going badly? Was there poor chemistry between you and your boss or your colleagues? Were you less than fully committed to your job?

5. Make use of any outplacement services your company offers. (See also *Job hunting*, p.119.)

Jogging

1. Before you buy a new pair of running shoes, check the soles of your worn-out pair. If the outer edge of the heel is worn, your running style is to roll your feet outward; if the inner edge is worn, you roll your feet inward. Take the old pair to the store and ask a knowledgeable salesperson what kind of shoe suits your style best.

2. If your cotton socks are lined with terry cloth, wear them inside out to reduce friction and help prevent blisters. Smearing petroleum jelly on your feet before running also helps; rub it on your inner thighs to keep your legs from chafing.

3. If you find jogging too jarring, try walking briskly on a regular schedule; it gives comparable benefits. Start moderately: walk a mile in 15 to 20 minutes five times a week. Gradually increase distance and time over the next few weeks (see *Endurance building*, p.72).

Juicer

1. Gently squeeze cut citrus fruit over an inverted cup, using a saucer to catch the juice. (A demitasse cup works best for lemons.)

2. Put the halved fruit in a sealed plastic bag and squeeze it between the hinges of a door.

3. Try pliers or a nutcracker.

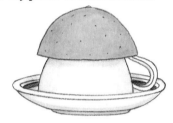

LOOK BEFORE YOU LEAP

The jeopardies of jogging

Every form of exercise has its risks, but jogging may be the only one in which buzzards pose a health hazard. According to a letter to the *New England Journal of Medicine,* 12 joggers in Switzerland were attacked by European buzzards in a 2-year period. Such behavior seems to be a threat only during breeding season, when the birds protect their nestlings—but there are plenty of less dramatic, year-round dangers that joggers face. Consult a doctor before you start jogging, and take these precautions to avoid injuries:

☐ Wear running shoes with thick, flexible soles or use shoe inserts (orthotics), especially if you have flat feet or high arches. Replace shoes every 500 to 800 miles.

☐ Run on a resilient surface, such as grass, wood, or asphalt, to prevent shinsplints, an inflammation of the tissues in the front of the lower legs.

☐ Strengthen the muscles in the calves and in the front and back of the thighs to prevent runner's knee, a painful stiffening of the area around the kneecap.

☐ Stretch the muscles and tendons in the backs of the legs to prevent Achilles tendonitis, an excruciating inflammation of the heel cord.

☐ Avoid excessive running to prevent stress fractures, slight cracks that form in the bones of the foot or lower leg.

Jumping rope

A brisk 10-minute workout with a jump rope can be as good an exercise as a 30-minute jog. You can use a piece of clothesline (about 10 feet will do—measure it by stepping on the middle; the ends should come to about midchest).

For handles, tie knots in the ends and wrap plastic electrical tape 4 to 5 inches in front of each knot. In a pinch (but only if you jumped rope as a child and remember how), you can jump with a phantom rope—no rope at all.

Always jump on a carpet or mat, and always wear cushioned aerobic or jogging shoes with good arch support. Start with the rope hanging to the floor behind you, your arms angled out 6 to 10 inches from your hips. Twirl the rope forward from the elbows. Start out jumping with your feet together; as you gain skill, try alternate-foot jumps. Your feet should come only a few inches off the floor. For variation, lift your knees high in front or kick up high behind.

Jump for 30 seconds, then rest for 30 seconds. Do this 10 times. Gradually increase the jump and rest times to 60 seconds each, for a total of 20 minutes, then gradually lengthen the total time until your heart rate is in your aerobic target range for 20 minutes (see *Endurance building*, p.72).

Ketchup

1. Don't just pound on the bottom of a stubborn ketchup bottle. Run the blade of a table knife around the inside of the neck; then tip the bottle and watch the ketchup flow.
2. When you've finished a bottle of ketchup, make use of the residue: add a little water or vinegar and shake, then use the liquid to enliven soups, stews, or salad dressings.

Keys

1. Carry two sets of car and house keys just in case one set gets locked inside. Keep a third set at home in something that can't be locked.
2. Color code the faces of your keys so that you'll instantly know what lock each one opens.
3. If a duplicate key is difficult to insert or remove, try filing down its rough spots with an emery board.
4. To straighten a bent key, put it on an overturned iron skillet and hammer it lightly.
5. If a key breaks in a lock, you may be able to extract it with a pair of needle-nose pliers or a fine, stiff wire. An alternative method is to insert a coping-saw blade into the lock as shown.

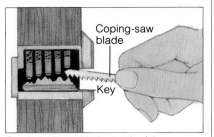

Catch the key with the teeth of the blade, then pull it out, keeping the blade parallel to the top of the keyway.

6. When a house key is hard to turn, squeeze a little powdered graphite into the lock and spread it around by jiggling the key back and forth. If you don't have any powdered graphite, scrape the point of a soft-lead pencil over the teeth of the key and insert it into the lock. Don't ever use oil—it will gum up the lock.
7. If you've lost the key to a locked drawer, first see if the drawer above is unlocked; if it is, remove it to get into the locked drawer below. If this approach is impossible, minimize damage by taking off the back of the desk or chest.
8. Copy the manufacturer's code number imprinted on a new car key or its attached tag and keep it in a safe, handy place so that a locksmith can easily make a duplicate key in an emergency. If you lose the code, your car dealer may have a record; find out before asking a locksmith to make a car call.

Knee problems

If God had intended humans to be perfect, goes an old saying, he wouldn't have given us knees. Despite the fact that the knee is the body's biggest, heaviest, and best-protected joint, it is injured more often than any other. Many injuries can be prevented by taking these precautions:
1. If you're overweight, slim down to reduce stress on the joint, especially if you engage in such activities as jogging or playing tennis.
2. If you sit in one place for long periods, change the position of your legs often. Whenever possible, stand up and stretch your legs or take a short walk.
3. Avoid climbing stairs or bending your knees any more than is necessary. When working on something below waist level, sit on a stool or on the floor.
4. Avoid wearing high-heeled shoes or those that have thin, poorly cushioned soles.
5. When gardening, kneel on an

old sofa pillow or a piece of foam rubber; shift your weight frequently from one knee to the other.

6. Relieve wear and tear on your knees whenever you exercise. Use a resilient surface for walking, jogging, playing tennis, or doing any kind of aerobics. Wear fins while swimming so that your calves and ankles will do much of the work. Avoid cycling in high gears.

7. To strengthen your knee muscles, do a set of knee curls daily. Lie on your stomach on an exercise bench or a bed so that your lower legs extend over the edge. Turn one foot inward to an angle of about 45°, slowly bend your knee to a 90° angle, and lift your upper leg as high as you can. Hold this position for 10 seconds, then lower your leg slowly and let it straighten. Repeat 10 times with each leg.

8. Never ignore any knee injury, however slight it may seem. See a doctor as soon as possible. Meanwhile, follow the RICE rule: Rest, Ice, Compression, and Elevation.

Knitting

1. You can use a pair of chopsticks or wooden dowels as substitutes for knitting needles in a pinch. Just sharpen the tips in a pencil sharpener and smooth them off with an emery board.

2. Similarly, you can renew the blunted tips of wooden knitting needles with a pencil sharpener or by rubbing them with fine sandpaper or an emery board.

3. Wooden knitting needles will work more smoothly if you rub them with a soap-filled scouring pad.

4. No stitch holder? Use a plastic straw.

5. To keep a ball of yarn from unrolling while you work, put it in a potato chip can; poke a hole in the lid to draw the wool through.

6. For stitch and row markers, attach the little plastic tabs used to close packages of bread.

7. Instead of yarn, knit or crochet with one long fabric strip cut from

an old T-shirt. Starting at the hem, cut the T-shirt horizontally into a continuous 1-inch-wide strip. Tug on the strip and the cut edges will curl under neatly.

Ladders

1. Spray-paint the top two steps of a stepladder bright orange or red as a visual reminder to keep off them.

2. As a safety precaution, always keep your hips within the vertical rails of the ladder.

3. Before climbing an extension ladder, jump up and down lightly on the bottom rung a few times to make certain that the legs are firmly planted.

On muddy or frozen ground, drive a 2 x 4 stake into the ground behind the ladder, as shown. Then tie a rope around the second rung from the bottom, knot it tightly, and secure it to the stake.

4. When working high on a ladder against the house, lash the ladder through an open window so that it can't fall over. Tie one end of a rope to a rung about two-thirds of the way up, and the other end to a radiator or other solid object inside. Or use a 2 x 4 long enough to bridge the inside of the window.

5. Because the hollow rungs of alu-

minum extension ladders weaken with wear, reinforce them before they fail. Insert a hardwood dowel into each rung; make sure it's long enough to extend ¼ inch past the rail on both sides. Wrap tape around both ends to ensure a snug fit. (If you're painting, replace a dowel with one that extends a foot or more—it makes a great place to hang the paint can.)

Lamps

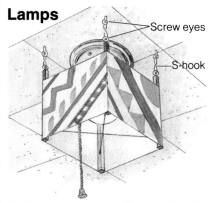

Screw eyes

S-hook

1. Dress up a bare ceiling bulb with a colorful box kite. Cut off one end of the assembled kite and insert screw eyes into the ends of the spines. Keep the sides at least 3 inches away from the bulb.

2. Need light fast? Clip photographers' lamps to a shelf, cabinet, desktop, or wherever you need it.

3. If a light bulb shatters, turn off the switch or unplug the cord, press a wad of putty over the sharp edges, and twist the stub with it. A cut potato works, too.

Lampshades

Here are a few ways to spruce up an old shade:

1. Using a toothbrush, lightly spatter the surface with a shade of paint that matches or accents the color of the room. (Practice your technique on newspaper first.)

2. For a rustic touch, glue on dried flowers or leaves.

3. Create silhouettes of recognizable shapes or free-floating patterns by gluing noodles, rice, or paper stars inside the shade. Keep these objects well away from the bulb,

which should be 60 watts or less.
4. Custom decorate a flat-surfaced shade with stencils (p.349). Or glue a colorful old map around the outside and lacquer it when dry.
5. Transfer a needlepoint design directly onto a cloth shade. Use heavy yarns and double-tied knots.
6. To remove spots from a paper shade, use an art-gum eraser. Plastic or nylon shades can be washed in a tub with mild liquid detergent and water. Send silk and other fabric shades to the dry cleaner.
7. Repleat a shade by simply gathering every two or three pleats with a decorative stitch or tassel.

Laryngitis

1. Rest your voice; don't even answer the phone. Carry a pencil and paper to replace conversation.
2. Give up smoking.
3. Eat mild, easily swallowed foods; drink plenty of nonalcoholic liquids.
4. Stay in a humid atmosphere. Use a humidifier or inhale steam— sit in the bathroom with the door closed and the hot shower on, or fill a bowl with boiling water, lean over it with a towel over your head, and breathe in the vapors.
5. If laryngitis lasts longer than 48 hours or is accompanied by a high fever, call your doctor. (See also *Sore throats*, p.192.)

Latchkey children

Fear, loneliness, and boredom can be afternoon demons for children staying home alone after school. But careful preparation and training can help you and the child feel more comfortable.

TRAINING
1. When you go out together, let the child lock and unlock the door. Leave him alone for short periods, making sure he locks the door behind you.
2. Give the child a small task to accomplish while you are out so that he gets used to functioning independently.
3. As you near the day when the child will be home alone after school until you return, you can both gain confidence with a regular "What would you do if . . .?" quiz. Keep this up even after the child is staying alone; it will help uncover lurking anxieties or problems.

SUPPORT SYSTEM
1. Identify which neighbors the child can call for assistance, companionship, or a spare house key.
2. Call home at a set time each day or have the child call as soon as he gets home. If you can't be available by telephone, arrange for a relative, friend, or neighbor to receive this check-in call and chat.
3. Post a list of important phone numbers or enter them in the memory dialing system of the telephone.
4. Leave the radio playing the family's favorite station.
5. Install an answering machine to monitor incoming calls.
6. Assign a necessary but unburdensome task that will help the flow of family life: setting the table, making a salad, putting away laundry. This helps remind the child that family members are soon to return.

Lawn patches

When you dig a new planting bed or vegetable garden, use the upended turf to patch bare or damaged spots in your lawn. Such homegrown sod may not be as flawless as the commercial product, but it will match your lawn perfectly, making mends invisible.
1. Strip the turf from the new planting area by cutting it into 1-foot squares with a sharp spade

and turning it over right in place. With an old butcher knife or machete, shave most of the soil from the roots so that the pieces of turf are no more than 2 inches thick.
2. Store these patches grass side up in a shady spot; keep moist until needed. They should stay fresh for 3 to 4 weeks in cool weather.
3. Prepare bare spots for patching by loosening the soil to a depth of 4 inches. If the gap in the lawn was caused by an herbicide or gasoline spill, remove and replace the loosened soil. If salt or the neighbor's dog did the damage, neutralize the soil with a handful of gypsum.
4. Cut the turf pieces to size and fit them into the gap, sifting compost into the cracks to protect the roots from drying out. Water well.

Lawns

1. A lawn looks best when it forms a sweeping, unified background to trees, shrubs, and other elements of the landscape. If you stud it with island beds of flowers and shrubs, it loses much of its esthetic appeal.
2. Aerate your lawn often, not just once a year, by wearing golf spikes as you mow it.
3. Don't mow too short. Blades of grass are the turf's leaves, converting sunlight into food; if you leave them a little long, you'll significantly reduce the need for fertilizer.
4. If you have a large, high-powered rotary mower, another adjustment can save hours of labor in the fall. Tape a piece of cardboard over the exit chute to block it; then mow the newly fallen leaves instead of raking them. They'll be pulverized, sifting back into the turf to serve as organic fertilizer.
5. Who says you have to plant grass? For a part of the yard that is usually only seen and not used, consider ground covers such as Ajuga, English ivy, euonymus, pachysandra, thyme, or vinca. Not only are they ornamental, but they also don't need regular mowing. (See also *Grass*, p.100.)

Lawsuits

Did your used car turn out to be a lemon? Is your brand-new wall-to-wall carpeting falling apart at the seams? Instead of hiring a lawyer, consider turning to Alternative Dispute Resolution (ADR), a money- and time-saving device that helps people settle their disagreements through mediation or arbitration. (In *mediation* both parties sit down with a mediator to work out a solution. In *arbitration* both sides agree to tell their stories to an arbitrator and let him resolve the dispute.)

To find an ADR center near you, look in the Yellow Pages under "Mediation services," ask a local social service agency, or write to the American Arbitration Association in New York City or to the Special Committee on Dispute Resolution of the American Bar Association in Washington, D.C. (See also *Small claims court,* p.189.)

Lawyers

1. If you qualify, free legal services are available from such organizations as the Legal Aid Society. In addition, many bar associations keep a list of lawyers who do *pro bono* work at no charge.

2. You can buy do-it-yourself legal kits that supposedly contain everything you need to draft a will, buy and sell property, or incorporate a business. If you decide to use one, it's still a good idea to have a lawyer examine your completed papers. (Because it will take less time, this will cost much less than having the lawyer prepare the papers herself.)

3. For a simple, routine problem, consider a low-cost legal clinic. But if your case requires complicated analysis, your needs may be better served by a private lawyer.

4. Ask your lawyer for a letter specifying his fee, what services it will cover, and the payment schedule. If you think the fee is too steep or you simply can't afford it, don't be reluctant to negotiate for a lower rate or more time to pay. Or shop around for a lawyer who can accommodate both your legal needs and your financial situation.

Learning disabilities

Some children of average or above-average intelligence have difficulty learning and retaining information in the traditional fashion. Some early warning signs: hyperactivity; inability to concentrate; problems with discipline and changes in routine; lack of coordination; memory problems; and difficulties in speaking, reading, and writing.

If your child exhibits any of these "symptoms," contact your family doctor to be sure there's no medical cause. If there isn't, ask your child's school to test him. If he has a learning disability, federal law requires that the school provide a special educational program for him. The law also gives you the right to be informed of and to appeal all test results and plans for your child.

For more help or support, ask your school administration about local parents' groups or contact the Association for Children and Adults with Learning Disabilities in Pittsburgh, Pennsylvania, or the Foundation for Children with Learning Disabilities in New York City.

Leather

MAKING GARMENTS

1. For skirts, pants, and vests, buy 2- or 3-ounce leather or suede. It's easy to machine-sew with a No. 14 needle and heavy-duty cotton or polyester thread.

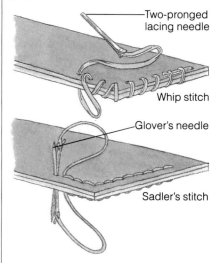

Two-pronged lacing needle

Whip stitch

Glover's needle

Sadler's stitch

For sturdy outdoor garments, belts, and handbags, buy 4- to 10-ounce leather. Rent a professional sewing machine or put pieces together by punching holes along their edges with an awl and lacing thongs through the holes.

2. Before cutting leather or suede, check the hides for scars so that

---

DID YOU KNOW . . . ?

Famous people with learning difficulties

☐ Leonardo da Vinci. Some believe the mirror writing in his notes was a code; others say it was a symptom of dyslexia.

☐ Hans Christian Andersen. The manuscripts of this writer contain amazing variations in spelling.

☐ Thomas A. Edison. This brilliant inventor was taught by his mother after schools were unsuccessful.

☐ Albert Einstein. This genius didn't talk until he was 4 or read until he was 9.

☐ Woodrow Wilson. This president couldn't read until he was 11. His relatives considered him "dull" and "backward."

☐ Auguste Rodin. "I have an idiot for a son," the sculptor's father once said. He did poorly in spelling and arithmetic—but his most enduring work is "The Thinker."

☐ Winston Churchill. A duplicate of his original application, sent anonymously to his old school, was rejected as not up to the school's standards.

you can avoid them in laying out your pattern. If you find thin spots, reinforce them with fusible tape.

3. Stroke suede to find the direction of the nap, mark it on the wrong side with a felt pen, then cut the pattern pieces so that the nap all goes one way. Otherwise, adjoining pieces won't match.

4. Instead of basting seams on a leather garment, "pin" them with paper clips 3 inches apart. After you've finished stitching them, brush a little rubber cement onto the underside of the seam allowances and onto the adjacent leather. Let it dry, then press the seam allowances flat with your fingers; flatten further by tapping lightly with a wooden mallet.

MAINTENANCE

1. If a leather coat gets wet, hang it on a padded hanger—not a hook—and let it dry away from direct heat. Wrinkles will generally hang out overnight, but if they don't, press on the wrong side with a dry iron set on *Low*, using heavy wrapping paper as a pressing cloth.

2. Clean small spots on smooth, glossy leather with a damp sponge.

3. Erase scuff marks with wax shoe polish or mink oil. On suede use a gum eraser, a terry cloth towel, or a sponge.

4. When restitching leather gloves or slippers, use dental floss instead of thread. It lasts longer.

5. To clean a combination bag, such as canvas and leather, clean the nonleather portion first. Make suds with liquid dishwashing detergent and rub them into the material with a sponge or soft cloth (use only suds—don't immerse the sponge). Work on heavily soiled spots with a soft brush, such as a vegetable or nail brush. To rinse, dampen a sponge in warm water and rub the surface until the suds are gone. Use saddle soap to clean the leather portions, then apply a neutral shoe wax or a wax the same color as the leather.

Leaves

Sending leaves to the landfill is a time-consuming nuisance and the waste of a valuable resource. Instead, "chunk mulch" the leaves. Stack them in an inconspicuous corner of the garden, wet them down, and trample them. Over the winter they will settle further, compacting into a tight, solid mass. In the spring break the mass up into small chunks with a garden fork and spread it among shrubs, flowers, and vegetables. It will serve as an attractive mulch for at least one season, then decompose to fertilize and condition the soil.

Leftovers

1. Don't throw out stale bread and rolls. Use them for bread crumbs, melba toast, and croutons to serve with soups and salads.

2. Freeze leftover cooked fish until you want to use it in a salad. Thaw, flake, and toss with onions, salad vegetables, and a dressing.

3. Keep a special bag in the freezer for leftover vegetables. When you have enough for soup, thaw and purée in the blender with a cup or two of chicken or beef stock.

4. Or turn leftover vegetables into a salad. Toss with a vinaigrette dressing or mix with chopped onions, mayonnaise, and herbs before mounding onto lettuce leaves.

5. For a terrific sandwich spread, grind beef scraps and mix with mayonnaise or cream cheese; enliven it as you like with mustard, horseradish, or pickle relish.

Leg cramps

1. If you wake up with a painful cramp in your leg, try to flex first your toes and then your whole foot upward, toward your knee. Or bend your knee, grab your toes, and flex them toward you while pushing back with your foot. If this gives only partial relief, massage the sole of your foot under the arch, pressing firmly.

2. For a calf cramp, straighten your leg and flex your foot as far up as you can. Or put your toes on the floor and slowly lower your heel.

PREVENTION

1. If you sleep on your back, use an open-ended box or a frame to keep the weight of the covers off your feet. If you sleep on your stomach, let your feet hang free over the end or the side of the bed.

2. Drink lots of water (some people find quinine water is beneficial) and keep your diet rich in calcium, potassium, and the B vitamins (see *The Balanced Diet*, p.254).

3. Do wall stretches nightly: stand 2 to 3 feet from the wall and lean toward it, keeping your heels firmly on the floor; hold for 1 minute.

Lemons & limes

1. You can substitute ½ teaspoon vinegar (any kind) for 1 teaspoon lemon or lime juice in a recipe.

2. To get just a few drops of juice from a lemon or lime, prick one end with a fork or toothpick and squeeze. The fruit can be refrigerated and used again.

Letters

The art of letter writing, as practiced by previous generations, is rare in today's electronic world. But there are some occasions when only a letter, note, or card will do. When you must write, keep these tips in mind:

PERSONAL

1. Don't write only about yourself and your family. Ask questions, even rhetorical ones. Even if you don't expect a reply, at least express interest in the recipient's welfare and activities.

2. Avoid dwelling on dreary topics such as a minor personal illness.

3. Choose plain white blank cards for letters of sympathy. Don't be mawkish, but do say that your thoughts are with the bereaved and then recall a fond personal memory of the deceased. Offer specific help, if possible—babysitting or shopping, for example.

4. Wait 24 hours before mailing an emotion-packed letter—whether written in love or anger. Read it over and then decide if you really want to send it after all.

BUSINESS

1. If you're writing a corporation, address your letter to a specific person. Call the headquarters and ask who's in charge of the department you want to reach.

2. Letters of complaint should be straightforward, factual, and polite. Expressing too much indignation will merely antagonize the reader. If possible, work a touch of humor into the letter; it can be effective in getting results. (See also *Letters for Various Occasions*, p.284.)

Lettuce

1. Reviving wilted lettuce is easy. Just give it a quick dip in hot water, then a rinse in ice water that has a little salt or sugar added. Shake, then refrigerate for an hour.

2. Always make sure lettuce leaves are absolutely dry before tossing them with dressing; it won't cling to moist leaves.

3. If you have to dry a lot of lettuce—say, for a party—put the washed leaves in a clean pillowcase, tie it shut, pop it in a clothes dryer, and set on *Air Fluff*.

4. Use your fingers to tear lettuce into bite-size pieces; a knife can cause the edges to turn brown.

5. Use extra lettuce leaves as a hot vegetable. Braised, sautéed, or stir-fried, they make a surprisingly good side dish.

Level

1. To make sure a picture or mirror is level, hold a half-full glass of water against the top edge. The water surface will be level no matter how you tilt the glass.

2. For long-distance leveling, use a length of plastic tubing attached to a bottomless plastic jug, as shown.

Pour water into the jug until it reaches the desired height at both ends; mark the spot on the tube. No matter how far apart the ends are or how irregular the terrain is between, the water, when aligned with the mark, is at the same level.

Liability

1. The best precaution: an umbrella policy that gives you additional coverage if an accident occurs on your property.

2. Inspect your property regularly for hazards, such as broken railings or deeply cracked sidewalks. Fix them as soon as you can; meanwhile, do your best to warn and protect others against harm. This does not guarantee you against a lawsuit—anyone can sue anyone for anything—but it greatly improves your chances of winning.

3. If you have an "attractive nuisance," such as a swimming pool or a sledding hill, put up warning signs and a fence with a locked gate.

4. Clear ice and snow from sidewalks and driveways as soon as possible (see *Icy walks*, p.113). If you have guests, warn them that the walkways may be slippery.

5. Keep family pets inside or within a fenced-in area.

6. If, despite your efforts, a guest has too much to drink, drive the person home yourself, call a taxi, or make him stay until he sobers up.

Life insurance

How much life insurance is enough? You can still follow the old rule of thumb that says coverage should equal four to five times your annual salary. Or, for greater precision, you can use this formula:

1. Set an income objective for your survivors—perhaps 70 percent of your current yearly income. Multiply this by the number of years you want them covered.

2. List all other financial resources your survivors can use, including your current assets—cash, securities, pension, Social Security benefits, and so forth—as well as their own income. Subtract this amount from the amount required.

3. What remains is the amount of life insurance you should obtain.

Life preserver

1. Anything with buoyancy—a Styrofoam ice chest, even an empty 1-gallon jug, tightly sealed—can help a nonswimmer stay afloat.

2. If your trousers are made of a natural fiber—cotton or wool—take them off and knot the bottoms of the legs. Holding the waistband,

Inflating trousers as a buoy gives arms a temporary rest from treading water.

swing the pants over your head and down onto the water. Then tuck the air-filled pants legs under your armpits to serve as a buoy.

Light bulbs

1. The familiar incandescent bulb is the commonest but least efficient kind, although some types are better than others.

Low-wattage bulbs will give you the same output as regular bulbs for about 12 percent less power.

Long-life incandescents are more expensive to buy and use, but last about 3,000 hours—an advantage in hard-to-reach places.

For extra efficiency and longer life, try *halogen* bulbs. They cost about double but give nearly twice the light—and they last roughly 3,500 hours. They require special fixtures, however.

Most efficient are *fluorescent* tubes. They and their fixtures are costly, but a tube lasts an average of 9,000 hours and gives triple the light per watt of an incandescent.

2. For easy removal of an outdoor bulb, coat the threads with silicone spray before you screw it in.

Lighting

Add drama to a drab room by "painting" with light.

1. For an element of surprise, vary the light sources throughout the room. Mount small fixtures under a row of wall cabinets, inside a china hutch, atop a bookshelf, and so forth. Bounce light both upward and downward.

2. Vary the intensities as well; a 25-watt bulb here and there provides a nice, subtle touch. Or for real flexibility replace your lamps' on-off switches with dimmers.

3. Warm up a cold room with a floor lamp or a pendant fixture hung over a chair or sofa.

4. Picture lights lend a soft glow while accenting works of art.

5. In a child's bedroom, glue or paint glow-in-the-dark stars or creatures on the ceiling.

6. To make the most of a blank wall, project a floor spotlight up through the leaves of a large plant.

Lightning

Lightning tends to strike the tallest object around, then arc off to the side. If you get caught in a lightning storm and you're the tallest thing on the terrain, get to a low spot, squat down (preferably on something dry), and make yourself compact; hug your knees and tuck in your head (most fatalities occur when lightning strikes the head and exits through the feet or arms). Stay clear of hills, trees, fences, barns, automobiles, and other conductors.

If you're playing golf, quit and go home. If you're in your car, stay there; don't touch any metal parts. Lightning will arc across the metal shell, but you'll be safe inside.

Often you'll get advance warning of a strike. If your skin begins to tingle and your hair stands on end, stoop down immediately. If someone near you is struck, keep her warm and dry and try to revive her breathing as quickly as possible.

Linen closets

1. To keep table linens from creasing, install a rod just beneath a low shelf and hang the linens on hangers padded with paper towel tubes.

DID YOU KNOW . . . ?

Lightning lore

☐ Lightning can and does strike the same place twice—at least. The higher the structure, the more likely it is to be hit. Statistically, an average home on moderately flat terrain in a moderately active thunderstorm region might be hit once in 100 years. But a structure 1,200 feet high might be struck 20 times each year.

☐ It is perfectly safe to touch a person who has been struck by lightning—he no longer holds an electrical charge.

☐ To learn how many miles away a thunderstorm is, count the seconds between a lightning flash and the ensuing thunderclap, then divide by 5. That's how much slower sound travels than light.

☐ Lightning helps fertilize the soil. It converts nitrogen into an oxide, which, coupled with rainwater, forms a weak nitric acid (a compound of hydrogen, nitrogen, and oxygen). Added to the minerals in the soil, this acid forms nitrates, which nourish plants.

2. Fold and store bed or bath linens by sets, not by size. That way, you can grab a complete set when you want it instead of having to pick through several stacks.

Lint

Since lint is highly contagious, remove it *before* you put a garment in the closet.

1. No clothes brush? Wrap a strip of masking or cellophane tape around your hand, adhesive side out, and move it across the garment. Or use a damp sponge.
2. You'll find that lint is much easier to remove with a damp clothes brush than with a dry one.
3. To remove lint from velvet, a sponge powder puff works well; on wool use a dry cellulose sponge.

Lipstick stains

Before washing a smeared garment with extra detergent, try one of these pretreatments:
1. Rub in some cold cream or shortening, then rinse the stained area with club soda.
2. Use rubbing alcohol or salad oil.
3. Rub the stain with a generous amount of petroleum jelly.
4. Wipe with a slice of white bread, then brush away the crumbs.
5. If the garment is white, soak it in lemon juice; if it's colored, dilute the lemon juice by half with water.
6. Place the stained area over a white towel and sponge on a mixture of powdered soap and water.

Litter for cats

1. Instead of commercial cat litter, you can use sand, wood shavings, or peat. Don't use peat for long-haired cats, however; it sticks to their coats.
2. To deodorize any type of litter, mix 1 part baking soda into 3 parts litter; cover the bottom of the pan with straight baking soda.
3. Use cut-up plastic lawn bags as pan liners.
4. Better still, make a "pillowcase" for your litter pan: slip the whole pan into a heavy-duty garbage bag (or two thin ones—claws can punch tiny holes) before filling it with litter. When it's time to dispose of the contents, simply turn the bag inside out over the litter and lift it off.

Locks

1. If your outside door has a window in or near it, install a double-cylinder dead-bolt lock, which must be opened with a key from either side. That way, even if a burglar breaks the window, he won't be able to open the door.
2. To prevent a sliding glass door from being opened, place a pipe or stick in the bottom track as shown.

To prevent anyone from lifting the door out of its track, set protruding screws in the top groove.

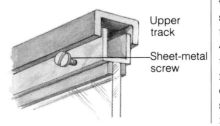

Upper track

Sheet-metal screw

3. Burglarproof your basement windows by installing two or more strong bars across each one.

ON CARS

1. Don't try to force a frozen car lock open—the key may break off. Check the lock on the passenger side. It may not be frozen.
2. Or heat the key with a match or lighter, then insert it into the lock. Repeat until the lock thaws.

Long-distance parents

Though you and your child may live far apart, whether because of divorce or some other cause, there are ways to ensure that the bond between you stays strong.
1. Regular phone calls are a necessity, not a luxury. Phone every few days at least—often enough to know what tests are coming up in school and how the child does on them; to share her excitement over an upcoming birthday party or field trip and then get a full report after the fact; to discuss current movies and TV shows. Prepare for each call: think about what was said the last time and have a list of fresh things to talk about. It's a good idea to call at set times so that your child can be prepared, too.
2. If the child can read, send cards and newspaper or magazine clippings that amuse and provoke. These small gestures remind the child that she is in your thoughts.
3. Arrange for the child to visit you as often as possible. Then let her share your daily routine. Don't try to cram every minute with a special activity; having to keep up with a "Disneyland daddy"—one who tries too hard to entertain—can be hard work for a kid and is ultimately less satisfying to both of you than quiet time spent together.
4. Develop a set of rituals and routines that only the two of you share: reading favorite books at bedtime, eating at a neighborhood diner, strolling in a nearby park, attending Sunday school.

5. Keep a "treasure box" for the child's knickknacks: polished stones, stickers, souvenirs, and whatever small items she chooses to keep. Reexamining her treasures each time she visits will help give her a sense of continuity and make her feel all the more at home.

Lopsided houseplants

All plants grow toward the light. To keep one that sits on a windowsill well rounded, rotate it 90° every 4 or 5 days. Always turn it *counterclockwise;* rotating it clockwise will retard its growth.

Caution: Do not rotate a flowering plant that is about to bloom. The drastic change in light may cause the flower buds to drop.

Lost child

Getting lost is a part of nearly everyone's childhood. To keep it from becoming a tragedy, prepare your children for the experience.

1. Teach them a family whistle, an easy-to-learn tune involving a phrase and a response. This can reduce panic and help you find each other in the aisles of a supermarket or in the woods.

2. Teach them early how to use a public phone to call home collect. Have them practice it.

3. Introduce them to a new environment (the mall, the state park) by showing how to get help. (Where's the policeman? The ranger? A telephone?)

4. Make sure they always carry a copy of your address and phone number—both at home and at work. (See also *Runaways*, p.175.)

Lost friends

Can't find an old friend? Try one of these methods:

1. Call directory assistance (1-area code-555-1212) in the cities where you think your friend might be living. If you're looking for J. A. Smith, for example, and the phone company has a long list of subscribers by that name, call all of the numbers and explain that you're looking for the John Adam Smith who grew up in, say, Philadelphia in the 1940's and attended St. John's High School. Most people will be polite and obliging.

2. Towns and cities keep open records of marriages and deaths, and the tax department has an open file of everyone who owns property, even if it's only a car.

3. A college alumni director will forward a letter to an alumnus. Some colleges will give you an alumnus's address over the phone if you attended the same institution.

4. Professional organizations, such as the American Dental Association, keep extensive directories of all people currently in practice.

5. Trade unions keep rosters, too. If you know your friend's trade, call the union's headquarters.

6. Sororities and fraternities keep national directories of past and present members.

Lost in the woods

The first impulse of any lost person is to keep moving. Wrong! The best strategy is usually to stay put and signal for help. Find a way to give three consecutive signals—shouts, whistle blasts, or smoke columns, for example—to serve as an SOS. On a sunny day use a mirror to flash signals at low-flying planes; if you don't have a mirror, use a knife blade, a piece of glass, or any reflective surface.

If you must find your way out of the woods, first sit down and get your bearings. Try to remember the last spot where you knew where you were. Then try to recall landmarks, such as a distinctive rock or tree, between that spot and where you are now. Ask yourself, Which way do the streams run? The roads? In which direction am I most likely to find help?

Choose a direction and stay on course by using a compass (p.54) or by walking from landmark to landmark. Within your line of sight, find two landmarks a good distance apart in the direction you wish to go. Before you reach the first, look for a third one that lies beyond the second.

As you set out, glance behind yourself to keep track of how things look in case you have to backtrack. If you stop to rest, sit or lie down facing the direction you've chosen. If you take a nap, scratch an arrow in the dirt to remind yourself of that direction.

Lost luggage

Of the more than 480 million pieces of luggage handled by airlines annually, less than 2 percent are lost. But when you're searching desperately for your luggage on an airport conveyer belt, this rosy statistic is little consolation.

There is no way to guarantee that your luggage won't be lost or stolen, but there are ways to rig the odds in your favor—and to improve your chances of recovery.

1. Check in early; last-minute arrivals often mean lost baggage.

2. If you are making a connecting flight, try to use the same carrier. Choose a flight that allows adequate time for your luggage to be transferred. Consult the airline, your travel agent, or the *Official Airline Guide* (OAG) for a minimum connecting time.

3. Use durable luggage with combination locks.

Standard suitcase locks are easily pried open. A combination lock is more secure.

4. Put your name, business address, and business phone number inside and outside each bag. (A home address is an invitation to burglars.) Enclose a copy of your itinerary in each bag so that the airline will be able to locate you.

5. Remove tags from other flights.

6. Carry a list of each bag's contents. Keep valuables, important documents, prescription medicine, and eyeglasses in carry-on luggage.

7. If your homeowners insurance doesn't cover away-from-home losses, consider buying baggage insurance. (If you buy your tickets with a credit card, it may be included automatically.)

8. If a bag doesn't show up, file a claim immediately at the baggage service desk; produce your list and demand reimbursment for out-of-pocket expenses for essential items. If your bag isn't located within 3 days, chances are slim that it will ever turn up. Even so, hold on to your claim form, baggage check, and ticket receipt for at least 6 months; it may take you that long to get reimbursed.

Lost pets

1. Have your name, address, and phone number engraved on a tag and make sure your pet wears it at all times. Or make an ID collar: write the information on a white elastic band with indelible ink, sew on a snap, and fasten the band to the animal's neck—loosely but securely. Or have your pet tattooed with your name and address when it visits the veterinarian.

2. Keep on hand a clear color photograph of your pet and a list of its distinguishing markings.

3. If your pet is missing, search the

neighborhood, call the local animal shelters and veterinarians, post notices with a photo and description, and check the lost-and-found section of the local newspaper. If your pet is a purebred, contact local pedigree clubs; they may have their own rescue committees.

4. If you find a pet with a tag but no owner ID, contact the agency that issued the tag. Call the police and local shelters in case the owner has notified them, and check local newspapers for notices. Insert a notice of your own, describing the pet but leaving out a detail that only the owner will know.

5. The Pet Club of America offers a service called Petfinders, which registers pets and provides tags inscribed with a toll-free number.

Low-fat diet

1. Buy ground beef labeled "extra lean." It has about half the fat of regular ground beef.

2. Avoid well-marbled beef. The lower grades tend to be less fatty, and the fat is more easily trimmed off.

3. Make soups and stews a day ahead so that you can extract the fat. After overnight refrigeration, it will be solidified on top.

4. The white meat of chicken has about half the fat of dark meat.

5. Avoid products that list palm oil or coconut oil as an ingredient. Both are high in saturated fat.

6. Skim milk has less than ¼ gram of fat per cup, while whole milk has more than 8 grams. Skim milk is also considerably lower in fat than 1 percent and 2 percent low-fat milk.

7. Instead of sautéing onions in butter or oil, poach them in a little chicken stock or beef stock before adding to a dish. (See also *Calorie counting*, p.31; *Cholesterol*, p.46; *The Balanced Diet*, p.254.)

Low-sodium diet

1. The salt in ham and other cured meats can push your sodium consumption way above the daily recommended level of 1 to 3 grams

(about 1½ teaspoons), so avoid the deli counter. Make sandwich fixings of cold home-cooked meats and poultry or use canned salt-free tuna packed in water.

2. Beware of canned or dehydrated soups, almost all of which are sky-high in sodium. Instead, make your own chicken or beef stock and freeze it for use in soups. A few cups boiled down to a glaze make handy bouillon cubes when frozen in an ice cube tray.

3. Substitute lemon juice, vinegar, wine, aromatic bitters, herbs, and spices for salt (dill weed, especially, has a vaguely "salty" flavor). Experiment with your own herbal blends in the kitchen as well as at the table. Throw out saltshakers and use pepper mills to grind whole mustard seeds or black peppercorns over soups and salads. (See also *Salt substitues*, p.177.)

Lubricating oil

1. All out of oil? Try mineral oil—but *not* in your car's engine. Cooking oils may also do for short-term projects but soon turn rancid.

2. For lubricating parts underwater—in a toilet tank perhaps—petroleum jelly is long-lasting.

3. To remove rust or corrosion, use vinegar, lemon juice, or hot pepper sauce instead of penetrating oil.

Magazine subscriptions

1. If you didn't get the most recent issue of a magazine you subscribe to, or if someone has given you a subscription to a magazine you already receive, write the magazine's subscription department for an adjustment. If you get no cooperation, write the Magazine Action Line (MAL) in Port Washington, New York; they may be able to get you a replacement issue, a refund, or an extension of your subscription. **2.** If you're moving, notify every magazine you subscribe to at least 4 weeks in advance. Use the change-of-address form in the publication or send the address label from a recent issue and your new address.

Magnifying glass

1. Turn a rounded wineglass or goblet on its side and hold it over the material you want to enlarge. Rotate the glass slightly to bring things into focus.
2. Poke a small hole in a piece of paper and bring it up to your eye; things will appear larger. (See also *Binoculars*, p.21.)

Mailboxes

Mailbox bashing, whether done intentionally by vandals or accidentally by a snowplow, is a problem for rural dwellers. Here are two ideas for protecting your mailbox:
1. Mount it on the arm of a 2 x 4 frame as shown, then hinge the frame to a post set back from the road. Secure the frame with a small hook and eye or with a string; either will give way easily under a violent assault, allowing the mailbox to swing free.

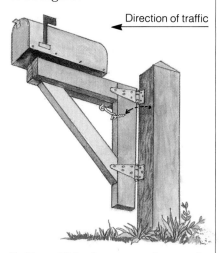

Direction of traffic

2. Pour 12 inches or so of concrete into an old milk can and set the post into it. To prevent the post from rotting, drill drainage holes in the side of the can above the con-

crete. When hit, the can will probably right itself; at worst, you'll have to stand it up again.

Mailing

1. When you need to express an item, ask about the cost of 2-day versus overnight delivery. It's much cheaper and usually takes only 24 hours anyway.
2. If you have a lot of mailing to do—at Christmas, for example—look in the Yellow Pages for a mailing service. For a fee, many will address the envelopes, stuff and stamp them, and send them off. They also offer cartons, packaging, faxing, overnight delivery, and so on.
3. Before you go on vacation, type addresses for postcards on gummed labels. You'll be more likely to send the promised cards.
4. A cigar box is perfect for mailing small items. Most tobacconists will give you one for free. (See also *Postal service substitutes*, p.161.)

Mail-order buying

1. Be wary of imitations of brand-name products. What you see in a catalog may look better than what you get. If it's an unfamiliar brand, read the description carefully and study the illustration closely. If it's a brand name, be sure you know the model number you want.
2. Order by phone—especially if there's a toll-free number. Your order will get into the system faster, and you'll be able to ask questions about the merchandise and delivery dates. (Be sure to get the name of the person you talk to.)
3. Ask about the return policy before you order. You should have the right to a full refund as long as you have not damaged the product.
4. Use a credit card whenever possible. You'll have a separate record of your order, and if there's a problem, the credit card company won't require you to pay until the matter is settled, provided you notify them of the dispute.
5. Is your order lost? Federal law

requires that the advertiser ship your merchandise when promised or within 30 days of receiving your order. If not, the advertiser must notify you of the new shipping date in writing and give you the option to cancel and receive a full refund.
6. To protect yourself in case of disagreements, keep a copy of your order, noting the date it was placed and the name of the company representative, the original advertisement, canceled checks or credit slips, and all correspondence with the advertiser.

Male menopause

Men don't really go through menopause, of course (p.134). But many experience some kind of psychological crisis in their 40's or 50's. The urgent awareness that there are goals yet to be reached and pleasures yet to be enjoyed—and that time will, indeed, run out—can lead to anxiety, depression, self-doubt, and marital discord.

If you're having such feelings, remember that they are perfectly normal and that they, too, shall pass. Here, nevertheless, are a few tips to help you get through:
1. Don't become a cliché. The trappings of youth don't make you look younger, just faintly ridiculous.
2. Don't leave your wife for a younger woman. It's usually a mistake, and it's not really dealing with the cause of your unhappiness.
3. Don't worry about sex. You may not be 17 anymore (and aren't you glad?), but your body still works; problems in the bedroom are often the result of worrying about them. Consult your doctor to be safe.
4. If you hate your job, don't just sit around complaining. Either quit or don't—then get on with your life (see *Career changes*, p.37).
5. Get involved in volunteer work. Find out how you can teach reading to underprivileged people or English to immigrants. For a real change (if you can afford to draw a tiny salary), consider joining the

Peace Corps; older, experienced volunteers are highly valued.

6. Can a therapist help? Make an appointment with one and see.

7. Jog, walk, or join a gym so that you get at least 30 minutes of heart-pumping exercise at least three times a week (with your doctor's permission, of course). You'll look better, feel better, and probably add years to your life in the bargain.

Maple syrup

Go easy on your food budget by substituting this mock maple syrup for the genuine article.

In a glass or enamel saucepan, bring 2 cups water to a fast boil. Add 4 cups dark brown sugar and stir until it dissolves into a smooth syrup. Remove it from the heat and let it cool, then stir in 2 teaspoons maple extract. Mix well.

Pour the syrup into a clean glass jar and let it stand at room temperature for at least 24 hours before using. It will keep for up to 6 months in the refrigerator.

Marking gauge

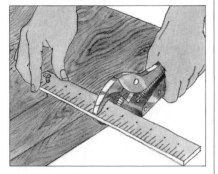

Make your own marking gauge from a wooden yardstick and a pair of locking-grip pliers.

Insert a small wood screw through the 1-inch mark on the ruler. Then, if you want to mark a parallel line 3 inches from the edge of your work, for example, set the pliers at the 4-inch line. Hold the nose of the pliers against the edge of the work with one hand; hold the end of the yardstick with the other. Keeping the yardstick square with the edge,

pull it evenly toward you across the work surface, so that the screw scratches a line.

Marshmallows

1. To freshen stale marshmallows, seal them in an airtight can or plastic bag with a slice of fresh bread for 2 or 3 days.

2. If a recipe calls for marshmallows by weight, use this guide: 16 large marshmallows or 1 cup melted marshmallows equals ¼ pound.

3. Marshmallows are easier to cut with scissors than with a knife. Dip the scissors repeatedly in hot water so they don't gum up.

Matches

1. Starting a fire without matches is hard work, so carry reserves. If you must do so, however, first gather some dry tinder, such as the inner lining of a bird nest, lint from clothing, bits of rope end, or punk (the rotted portion of dead logs). Form the tinder into a nest and shelter it from wind and moisture.

Hold the flint edge of a waterproof matchbox or a dry hard stone as close to the tinder as possible. Strike it downward with the back of a knife blade or a small piece of steel to send sparks into the center of the tinder. Fan the smoldering tinder into a flame; add fuel gradually, starting with small, dry twigs.

2. On a sunny day use a magnifying glass, a camera or binocular lens, or a pair of strong reading glasses to focus the sun's rays on the tinder.

3. When lighting a fire in windy or rainy weather, use a candle stub to conserve matches.

4. To waterproof "strike anywhere" kitchen matches, dip them in melted candle wax or paraffin.

5. To dry matches quickly, pull them through your hair.

6. If you're short on paper matches, you can double your supply. Insert the point of a sharp knife in the base of each match and slowly pull the halves apart.

Math in your head

1. A quick way to do calculations is to drop the 0's at the ends of numbers, then replace them for your final answer. For example, to add 120 and 90, get the sum of 12 and 9 and then add one 0.

2. Similarly, to break down complex problems, start with the big numbers. To multiply 6 times 348, for example, first multiply 6 times 300 (1,800), then 6 times 40 (240). Add the two to get 2,040 and tack on the result of 6 times 8 (48) for a total of 2,088.

3. Change kilometers to miles by dropping the last digit and multiplying by 6: thus, 72 kilometers is *approximately* 42 miles. Or consult your car's speedometer; most of today's models have both scales.

4. Want an easy way to multiply by 9? Assign each finger a number, beginning with the little finger of your left hand (1) and ending with the right pinkie (10). Then, to multiply 3 times 9, for example, turn down the number-three finger, making a space on your left hand. Count the fingers to the left of the space (2); then count the fingers to the right (7). The answer: 27. (See also *Computations*, p.54.)

Mattresses

1. To keep a mattress from sliding around on its foundation, put a nonslip rug pad between the two.

2. To even out the wear, flip a new mattress over and reverse it end to end every 3 weeks for 3 months—every couple of months thereafter.

3. Don't use the handles on the mattress to lift it. They're not designed to take the full weight but only to move the mattress around while it's on the foundation.

4. Air a mattress in the sun occasionally for a fresh, clean odor.

Measuring

1. If there's no one to help you measure a long stretch with a tape measure, secure the end of the tape with masking tape or anchor it

with a brick or a heavy wood block.
2. To find the circumference of a round object when you don't have a flexible tape measure, try this simple trick: Cut a strip of paper and wrap it around the object. Mark the spot where the end of the paper overlaps itself. Then lay the strip out flat and measure it with a ruler.
3. Here's how to divide a board into equal parts lengthwise. Lay a ruler diagonally across the width of the board so that the beginning (0) is at the left edge. Then adjust the other end of the ruler until the right edge of the board aligns with the number of parts desired. Mark off each of the inch graduations.

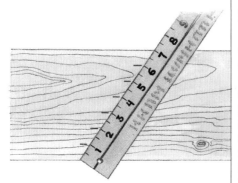

4. To lay out an exact 90° angle, use the 3-4-5 ratio. From a common point, stretch out two long strings perpendicular to each other. Mark one string at 3 feet from the common point and the other at 4 feet. Stretch a tape measure from the 3-foot mark on one string to the 4-foot mark on the other and adjust the strings until the distance between the two marks is exactly 5 feet. The angle between the two strings will be 90°. (This method works for any unit of length and for any variation of a 3-4-5 ratio.)
5. For fast, approximate measuring, use your own body. If you're of average size, the first joint of your index finger is about 1 inch long, your fist is about 4 inches wide, and the span from the tip of the thumb to the tip of the pinky on your outstretched hand is about 9 inches. Your shoe is about a foot long.

Measuring cup

1. No measuring cup? The plastic dipper that comes in a can of coffee holds 2 level tablespoons.
2. Use your pint jars (2 cups), quart jars (4 cups), and milk cartons.
3. An 8-ounce can holds 1 cup.
4. The standard juice glass holds 4 ounces, or ½ cup.

Meat grinder

1. Clear clogged holes in a meat grinder by rapping the grinder plate several times against the edge of the counter.
2. If your grinder is dirty or extra greasy, run a piece of bread through it, then wash it.

Medication schedule

1. Make up a week-by-week chart: write the days of the week down the short side of a large piece of paper, the hours of the day across the long side; fill in the dosages in the appropriate hours. Hang the chart near or inside your medicine cabinet and check off each marked box right after you take the medication.
2. Label the compartments of an ice cube tray for all your waking hours. Each morning place pills or small slips of paper (representing liquid medicines) in their appropriate compartments. Discard the slips after taking the medicine.

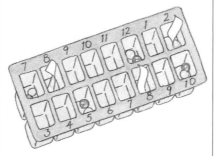

3. If you're away from home, wear a digital watch set to beep every hour. Carry your medications and schedule in your pocket or purse. When the beeper sounds, check your schedule and take your medicine.
4. To prevent confusion, write the name of each medication in bold, bright letters on the biggest self-sticking label that will fit on the container. If possible, color-coordinate the labels on your morning, afternoon, and evening medicines.

Meetings

1. When it comes to meetings, keep in mind that less is more. Any meeting will be shorter and more productive if you invite only those people who are directly involved in the matters under discussion.
2. Whenever possible, schedule a meeting in the morning, when people are more alert. But avoid "first thing in the morning" sessions. The day before or after a weekend or holiday is also a bad time.
3. A few days before the meeting, put your agenda in writing and distribute it to all participants. Tell them how much time will be devoted to each topic, and allow extra time at the end just in case some topics run overtime.
4. To stay on schedule, refer to the agenda as the meeting progresses. If someone gets long-winded, wait until he takes a breath and say, "I'm afraid we've run out of time on this topic, so let's summarize."
5. To keep participants on their toes, ask each one to give a brief presentation.
6. To draw out a creative but shy person, tell her in advance that you'd like her ideas on a particular topic, then call on her. Or go around the table, asking each person in turn for a comment.

Memory

1. To remember the name of a person you've just been introduced to, first make sure that you've heard it properly. (Ask to have it repeated or spelled if you're not sure you understand.) Then call the person by name in your conversation and again when you say good-bye.
2. If you find it hard to keep the names of your friends' children straight, jot them down next to the friends' names in your address book.

Do the same with business contacts you don't deal with often.

3. Establish a place for putting such easily misplaced items as gloves and keys. Much of what people think is bad memory is just bad organization.

4. Keep a pad and pencil handy near your telephone and in your purse, pocket, and car. If you write something down, you won't have to worry about remembering it. Make a habit of going over your list at a set time every day—say, right after breakfast.

5. Don't be afraid to talk to yourself. If the telephone rings while you're on your way out, put your car keys down and say out loud, "OK, keys, I'm putting you on the kitchen table." It might sound silly, but it will also help fix their location in your mind.

6. Use the same technique if you have medicine to take daily. Before you swallow your pill, say out loud, "I'm taking my pill now," and you won't wonder in an hour whether you've taken it or not. Or establish a signal to yourself; move a straight pin from your left lapel to your right, shift your watch from one wrist to the other, or transfer a spe-

cific object from pocket to pocket.

7. Give your memory a regular workout by playing quiz games that demand quick recall or card games (such as bridge or concentration) that require keeping track of the cards played.

8. To remember the main topics of a talk you're to give, associate each one with a room in your house. As you give your talk, picture yourself moving from one room to the next.

Memory loss

Although older people are often forgetful, aging itself is not the cause. Memory can be affected by medications, illness, alcohol, depression, stress, or isolation. If you or an older relative becomes increasingly forgetful, go to a doctor to see if there is a physical cause and if it can be remedied.

You can make life easier for someone whose memory is failing by organizing the household:

1. Label cabinet doors and drawer fronts with lists of their contents.

2. Paint hot-water faucets with red nail polish.

3. Hang a large-type list of emergency numbers by the phone. Or buy a phone with a memory.

4. Place an oversize hook next to the door for keys.

5. Put up a big wall calendar and mark it with reminders of important dates.

6. Talk over upcoming events just before they occur.

Menopause

For most women the "change of life" is a brief, relatively painless event. Some, however, endure several years of hot and cold flashes, emotional upheaval, and even occasional mental confusion.

If you're having such difficulties, be honest with your family and friends. Tell them what you're experiencing; they can't be supportive if they don't understand the problem. It might be especially helpful to discuss what you're feeling with an older woman.

1. Stay cool during hot flashes— lower the thermostat and wear easy-to-remove layers of loose, cotton clothing.

2. For nighttime hot flashes, buy absorbent cotton sheets and nightclothes. Keep a spare nightgown and a thermos of ice water at the ready on the night table.

3. Keep two athlete's cold packs in the freezer; hold them against your cheeks when a hot flash begins.

4. Continue or, after checking with a doctor, start regular aerobic and relaxation exercises.

5. Ask your doctor about estrogen replacement therapy. (See also *Osteoporosis*, p.146.)

Menstrual cramps

1. At the first sign of cramps, start taking ibuprofen; it works much better than aspirin. (Some women get prompt relief from ibuprofen; others may find they must take it for 4 to 5 days.)

2. Instead of going to bed when you feel the pain, get some exercise—take a walk, ride a bicycle, or do a few minutes of yoga.

3. Give yourself a heat treatment: a warm bath or a hot-water bottle on

---

DID YOU KNOW . . . ?

Develop that memory!

☐ "I'M NO WIMP," answered the boy when the teacher asked him to name all nine states that border on the Great Lakes. Actually, the student was simply using a mnemonic device to aid his memory. His response contained the first letter of each state.

☐ To remember the names of the Great Lakes themselves, try HOMES—the lakes' initials are all there. Want a quick way to recall the planets in order? Take the first letter of every word in this sentence: My Very Educated Mother Just Served Us Nine Pickles.

☐ Mnemonics can be more than just a game. You can use them to help your own memory. Make up a sentence using the first letters of all the items on your shopping list, for example: Eagles Become Panicky Before Showers for a list of eggs, bread, peanut butter, and sugar. Or for errands at the cleaners, the market, the post office, and the gas station, try Clever Mothers Prepare Orange Gravy.

☐ And how can you remember how to pronounce *mnemonics*? Think of the title of this article. It's a mnemonic for Drop The M.

your lower back or your abdomen.

4. Some women get relief by taking B complex vitamins, vitamins C and E, zinc, calcium, and magnesium. Check with your doctor.

5. Get a lower-back massage. Or ask a friend to apply acupressure: rub the midback, 1 inch to the right of the spine, for 3 to 4 minutes. (You may get 3 to 6 hours of relief.) If you're alone, press on a point two thumb widths above the wrist joint on your inner arm, in line with your middle finger.

6. Eat a low-fat, low-salt, high-carbohydrate diet with plenty of fiber. (See also *PMS*, p.159.)

Mice

1. If you have a mouse problem, move objects around periodically to disorient the creatures; they're easier to trap as they move about investigating the rearrangement.

2. If you use standard snap traps, don't fall for the old cartoon cliché of baiting them with cheese. Use bits of peanut butter, oatmeal, or cooked bacon instead; mice seem particularly fond of them.

3. To catch a mouse alive, try this trick: When you see the beast running around a room, open a black umbrella and hold it on the floor at an angle that allows the mouse to run in (it helps if someone else can chase the mouse). Your prey, drawn to dark places, will probably head straight for the umbrella. Then quickly close it, go outside, and set your prisoner free.

Microwave ovens

1. Find the hot and cold spots by spreading a layer of trimmed white bread slices edge to edge over the microwave floor. Set on *High* and watch the browning process through the glass door.

2. To test whether a dish is microwave safe, place it in the oven next to a glass measuring cup of water; turn on *High* for 1 minute. If the water is warm, you know the oven is working. If the dish is cool, it's OK to use; if it's hot, don't use it in the microwave.

3. To get full cooking power, wipe out the oven after each use—especially around the door seal—using a mild detergent or baking soda solution. Soften stubborn soil with steam by boiling a cup of water in the oven; then clean with a plastic (not steel wool) scrubbing pad.

4. To give microwaved meat an appetizing browned look, brush it first with soy sauce mixed with a little water.

5. To get rid of lingering food odors or a stale smell, place a thick slice of lemon on a paper towel and microwave it on *High* for 1 to 1½ minutes; let stand overnight.

6. If greasy residue or food inside the oven catches fire, keep the door closed, turn the oven off, and disconnect the cord at the plug or shut off the power (p.162).

7. If you're worried about high electricity or gas bills, economize by preheating food in a microwave on *High* before completing the cooking in a regular oven. (See also *Microwave do's & don't's*, p.257.)

Migraine headaches

The warning: flashes of light, dizziness, and nausea. The affliction: an intense, throbbing pain on one side of your head.

1. If you sense the warning stage, take your medication and drink a cup of hot coffee (not decaffeinated).

2. When pain strikes, pour cold water over your head, take a cold shower, or use an ice or cold pack.

3. Lie down in a dark, quiet place and imagine a beautiful scene. Listen to soothing music. (To develop a "relaxation response," do this exercise for 30 minutes twice a week for 5 weeks, whether you have a headache or not.)

4. Give yourself (or ask someone to give you) a gentle scalp, neck, and shoulder massage.

PREVENTION

1. Try to discover and eliminate the cause of your migraines by keeping a diary (see *Headaches*, p.104). Common culprits are red wine, hot dogs, bacon, pork, salami, MSG, yeast, chocolate, aged cheese, and cigarettes.

2. Maintain a routine: wake up at the same time each day, eat regular meals, and exercise daily.

3. Wear sunglasses in the sun and avoid looking directly at bright lights. (See also *Pain relief*, p.148.)

Mildew

To prevent mildew, keep things clean and dry.

BASEMENTS

1. Close the windows and use a dehumidifer to reduce moisture.

2. Check the drainage around the outside of the house and seal up all cracks so that moisture can't get in.

BATHROOMS

1. Use an old toothbrush to scrub the mildew from grout. For stubborn stains, cover with a paste of scouring powder that contains bleach and let stand for several hours; scrub and rinse off.

2. After using the shower, keep the shower door or curtain open while you wipe down the walls and let them air-dry. Then close the curtain or door so that it, too, can dry.

3. To clean a fiberglass shower stall, gently scour the walls with baking soda on a damp sponge, then rinse and dry.

4. Got a mildewed shower curtain (p.185)? Just soak it in the tub in water softener.

BOOKS

1. Put a piece of charcoal in a closed bookcase to absorb moisture.

2. For damp pages, sprinkle cornstarch throughout the book; brush it off several hours later, after the moisture has been absorbed. If the pages are mildewed, brush the cornstarch off outdoors to keep mildew spores out of the house.

CLOSETS

1. To increase air circulation, keep the door ajar. Consider replacing a solid door with a louvered one.

2. Keep items susceptible to mildew, such as shoes and luggage, on wire racks or perforated shelves so that air can circulate around them.

CLOTHES

To remove mildew from a washable fabric, wet the area and rub it with detergent. Launder in the hottest water recommended for the fabric, using chlorine bleach if the fabric will tolerate it. If not, soak in an oxygen bleach solution, then wash.

MATTRESSES

1. If possible, take a mattress outside and brush off the mildew; if not, vacuum it and throw away the bag. Lay the mattress in the sun for several hours until thoroughly dry; if drying indoors, use a fan.

2. Platform beds often mildew. Buy one with slats, or drill a few holes in the platform for air circulation.

REFRIGERATORS

1. Wipe interior walls regularly with baking soda to keep them clean.

2. If your refrigerator has a pan underneath, clean it regularly and sprinkle some baking soda inside.

Milk

1. If you're out of milk and need some for baking, try using the same amount of fruit juice. It works surprisingly well for many quick breads and butter cakes. Or use buttermilk (add ½ teaspoon baking soda per cup). If you use skim milk, add 2 teaspoons of vegetable oil per cup.

2. Milk in paper cartons picks up refrigerator odors. Close the carton flaps with a paper clip—the spring type works best.

3. If milk starts to go sour, salvage it for use in cake batter, pancake batter, or cookie dough; just add ½ teaspoon baking soda to the dry ingredients. Sour milk also makes a good substitute for buttermilk.

Mirrors

1. Never spray cleanser directly on a mirror—the drips could seep onto the silver backing and damage it. Instead, spray the cleanser on a clean soft cloth or paper towel and wipe the mirror.

2. Make your own cleanser. Fill a spray bottle with water and a little vinegar, rubbing alcohol, or ammonia. Avoid strong ammonia solutions and abrasives, both of which can damage mirrors.

3. To hide a scratch in the silver backing of a mirror, cover the spot with a piece of aluminum foil, shiny side forward. Paint with clear shellac and let dry.

Moles

1. Discourage these little diggers by removing the main attraction: soil-dwelling grubs, especially Japanese beetle larvae (p.118).

2. Repel moles by dropping such noxious items as dog waste or rags soaked in olive oil into their tunnels. They hate it.

3. Moles can damage roots as they tunnel through the garden. Worse still, mice use their tunnels to gain access to tender bulbs and root vegetables. Protect plants by lining planting holes with hardware cloth.

The mystique of mirrors

The reflected image—it entranced Narcissus in a pool of still water, and it has lost none of its fascination since. But mirrors serve more than vanity. They've inspired superstition and ingenuity throughout history.

☐ The Chinese hung mirrors on their front doors so that evil spirits, seeing their horrid reflections, would be frightened away.

☐ The Greek mathematician Archimedes used huge mirrors to save his native city of Syracuse. They reflected the sun onto an attacking fleet of Roman ships, which burned in the intense heat.

☐ In wealthy Venetian homes during the 16th century, homeowners encouraged servants to be careful by telling them that breaking a mirror would result in 7 years bad luck—and they had the power to make the curse come true.

☐ Silver is used in mirrors because it reflects about 95 percent of the light that falls on it. Also, its neutral color accurately reflects skin tones and makeup hues.

☐ The Select-A-Size mirror, patented in 1974, has an adjustable lower half that permits the viewer to appear as slim as he wishes.

☐ NASA's Edwin P. Hubble Space Telescope contains a 94-inch (diameter) mirror, ground to a tolerance of nearly two-millionths of an inch.

Moonlighting

Need a second job to make ends meet? You'll have more zest for moonlighting if your part-time job is built on hobbies or interests you already enjoy.

Try to find work you can do on your own time, perhaps even at home. Some possibilities: selling, fund-raising, or conducting surveys over the phone; babysitting; selling cosmetics or home products; tutoring or giving lessons; teaching a course at a community college or trade school; selling real estate; proofreading; word processing on your home computer; bookkeeping for a local company; boarding or grooming pets; growing plants; running a bed-and-breakfast inn.

Check with your employer first. If there's no conflict of interest, you're not legally or ethically obliged to tell your boss about your outside activities—but he'll probably appreciate your candor. And some firms forbid employees to freelance, particularly for competitors.

Mops & brooms

1. Always clean a dry dust mop before you store it. To avoid making a dust cloud, put a damp paper bag over the head of the mop before shaking it. Wash a very dirty mop in sudsy water and rinse. Or, if the head is removable, put it in a mesh bag and toss it into the washer. Hang to dry in an airy place.
2. Rinse and squeeze a wet mop after each use. Store with the head up; a string mop can be hung head down if its strings are well off the floor. Keep the door to the storage closet open slightly until the mop is dry. For best results, hang a sponge mop outside in the shade to dry, a cotton string one in the sun.
3. Never store a wet mop in a pail; it may sour or mildew. If this happens to a cotton string mop, soak it for a few minutes in a weak bleach solution (½ cup chlorine bleach in a gallon of water). Rinse several times and let dry.

4. Trim a cotton mop occasionally with a pair of strong scissors.
5. When you store a broom, hang it so that there's no pressure on the bristles. You don't need a special broom and mop holder; just attach screw eyes to the tops of the handles.
6. To prevent a mop or broom handle from marring furniture as you clean under it, wrap the lower part of the handle with velvet ribbon.
7. To neaten an old, frayed broom, soak the bristles in warm water for a few minutes, then wrap several heavy rubber bands around them until the broom is dry.

Mortar repairs

1. To prevent mortar from crumbling, brush on a masonry sealer. It will repel water, which damages mortar by freezing and expanding.
2. If patches of mortar need repointing and you can't find a mason willing to do such a small job for a reasonable price, try this. Wait until you see a new building going up in the neighborhood and ask one of the masons if he'd like to earn a few extra dollars during his lunch hour.
3. To save yourself a trip up to the roof, ask the chimney sweep to inspect the condition of the chimney and the mortar joints during his annual cleaning.

Mortgage default

You've always paid your mortgage on time but suddenly you can't— perhaps you've fallen ill or lost your job. Tell your lender the situation; you'll probably be allowed to delay payments on the principal for up to a year, as long as you pay the interest, taxes, and insurance. (If you're regularly tardy with your payments, however, you may be in trouble— most foreclosure laws tend to favor the lender.)

If your mortgage is foreclosed, your house will be sold at auction (probably to the lender) for the amount outstanding on the mortgage plus any incurred costs. You'll get nothing. The prudent thing to do, therefore, if foreclosure is a real threat, is to sell your house, pay off the lender, and put the leftover cash in an interest-bearing account.

Mosquitoes

1. Check such innocent indoor breeding places as flower vases; change the water daily. And don't forget the humidifier and the catch pan under the refrigerator.
2. If you're camping in a mosquito-infested area, you may want to invest in a "bug suit," available at sporting goods stores. Worn over your clothes, the pants and jacket are made of mesh cloth treated with an insect repellent.

Mothball odor

1. Hang clothes outdoors on a windy day. To prevent a garment from blowing away, place it on two hangers with the hooks facing in opposite directions; secure with clothespins.
2. Let the clothes air for a few hours, then tumble them in a warm dryer for 15 minutes.
3. Keep sachets or empty perfume bottles in drawers or closets.

Mothball substitutes

1. Try cedar in your closets and chests. It's nonpoisonous and comes in blocks, chips, shavings, hangers, and drawer liners.
2. Use cheesecloth bags, clean baby socks, or nylon stockings to make moth-repellent sachets. Fill with any combination of the following: cedar chips, dried lavender, aro-

matic pipe tobacco, whole pepper-corns, or a mix of equal parts dried mint and rosemary.

Mother's helpers

If you have to hire a mother's help-er, whether a full-time *au pair* or a high school student who babysits on weekday afternoons, consider these pointers:

1. Interview the candidate. You should be able to tell fairly quickly whether he or she will fit in.

2. Clearly establish salary and hours, days off, level of responsibil-ity, and duties. Write these out in detail and give the candidate a copy to consider, then make any agreed-on changes. This serves as an in-formal contract after both of you have signed it.

3. Carefully check all references, by telephone if possible. Quiz prior employers and interview the par-ents of a teenage candidate. (What guidelines do they set?)

4. Arrange a trial run: ask the pro-spective helper to spend an after-noon or weekend with your child. Then observe your child's behavior afterward. If grouchiness, quarrel-ing, disobedience, irritation, or si-lence holds sway, extend your search for your Mary Poppins.

5. Before clinching the agreement, have a candid talk: will the helper be happy with your child, require-ments, family, and neighborhood? You don't want to start interview-ing again in 3 months.

Moving heavy objects

The key to moving something heavy by yourself is to use more brain than brawn. First make sure the item—including any protruding parts—will fit through openings and around corners. Then give care-ful thought to how you can do the job with the least strain. Once you decide on a strategy, be patient; go-ing slowly may take time, but it may also prevent injury. If neces-sary, get help. Here are some tips:

1. In general, pushing is easier and more effective than pulling.

2. Make a big box lighter by remov-ing all or some of its contents.

3. If you are throwing the object out or if you can reassemble it, take it apart and move it piece by piece.

4. When pushing something across the floor, put newspapers, blankets, or cardboard under it. You'll pro-tect the floor and the thing will slide more easily.

5. To move a large object, such as a refrigerator, get behind it, lean it toward you, and walk it slowly from side to side.

6. To carry a box on your back, wrap a strap around it; a belt, beach towel, or blanket will do. Or make a loop of strong rope; put one length around the box and hook the other around one bottom corner so that it passes under the box. Put your hands in the free ends of the loop.

7. Invest in an inexpensive hydrau-lic barrel jack, available at most hardware stores. They do wonders.

STAIRS

1. To get an object down a flight of stairs, use two boards as a ramp; slowly slide the object down the boards as you back between them.

2. Or lay the burden on a quilt or heavy blanket; control the descent with your shoulder as you back down, lifting the leading edge of the "skid" slightly with both hands.

3. If circumstances permit, slide the object down the banister.

DOLLIES

1. To get a dolly under a heavy ob-ject by yourself, put the dolly against the wall, then walk or slide the ob-ject to it; the wall will keep the dolly from scooting away.

2. Improvise a dolly with a shop-ping cart, a child's wagon, a skate-board, or roller skates.

3. Instead of a dolly, use pipes, poles, or unopened tin cans. As those in the rear become free, move them to the front.

FURNITURE

1. To move a couch or anything else with legs, lay it on its back or side and slide it.

2. Take the drawers out of a desk or dresser.

3. To move a bulky chair, put the seat on your head and stand up-right with the back on your back.

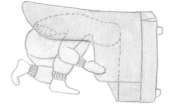

Muffler noise

A small hole in your muffler proba-bly won't do any damage, but the noise is offensive and probably ille-gal. Worse, poisonous carbon mon-oxide can seep into your car. Get the leak fixed as soon as possible.

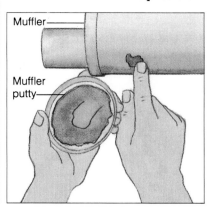

Small holes (no larger than ⅛ inch) in the muffler or tail pipe can often be repaired with muffler putty (available at auto parts stores). For larger holes (up to 1 inch) you can buy inexpensive heat-resistant "bandages." In a pinch you may be able to cover the hole temporarily by slicing open a tin can and holding the material in place with wire or clamps, but such a patch probably won't last more than 50 miles.

⟩ Mugging

1. If you think you're about to be mugged, stay calm and consider your options: acquiescence, stalling for time, talking your way out, screaming ("Fire" may get more response than "Help"), or—as a last resort—resisting.

2. If resistance appears to be your only choice, don't be squeamish about it—hurt your attacker any way that you can. Kick the groin or the instep; scratch at the eyes (a handful of keys or the teeth of a comb can do a lot of damage); bite; or go for the hands (the thumb and the pinkie are especially vulnerable). But don't get too involved in the battle; all you want is a chance to get away.

PREVENTION

1. If you live in a multiple dwelling, put just your first initial and surname on the mailbox or door buzzer; if you live alone, add a fictitious roommate's name. If a threatening stranger follows you into the entryway, push all the buzzers to summon neighbors.

2. Lock all the windows and entry doors. Install a peephole (p.152). Ask meter readers and repairmen for identification before letting them in; if you still have any doubt, call their place of business to double-check their identity.

3. Travel with a companion and steer clear of dark, empty buildings, poorly lit streets, and dangerous neighborhoods.

4. Walk confidently at a steady pace,

close to the curb and facing traffic. If you think someone is following you, cross the street. If the suspicious person does the same, walk quickly to a busy, well-lighted area or go to an occupied house or store and phone the police. As a last resort, throw a rock through a store window to set off its burglar alarm.

5. Drive with your doors locked. If your car breaks down, raise the hood and put a white cloth on the antenna. Get back in your car and lock it; if strangers approach, roll down your window slightly and ask them to call the police. Wait inside until help arrives.

6. Park in a well-lighted area; look around before getting out and check inside before getting in. (See also *Rape*, p.170.)

Mulching

To make black plastic sheeting even more effective as a mulch in your vegetable garden, add a coat of aluminum paint. By reflecting sunlight away from the soil and onto the plants' foliage, this shiny coating keeps the soil as much as 6°F cooler, even in the heat of the summer, and promotes stronger growth. (In trials, it has increased the yield of squash plants by 60 percent and corn by 200 percent.) It also repels aphids and thrips.

A coat of red paint has a similar effect on tomatoes, boosting their yield 20 percent over plants mulched with ordinary black plastic. A white mulch is good for potatoes and bell peppers. Green plastic is best for early spring crops.

Mushrooms

1. Keep mushrooms from molding or getting mushy during storage by leaving them *unwashed*. Wrap them loosely in paper towels, refrigerate in plastic or paper bags, and use as quickly as possible.

2. Slicing mushrooms is a cinch if you use an egg slicer. Cut downward from the rounded side of the cap. The fresher the mushrooms

are, the better this method works.

3. A rule of thumb for substituting canned mushrooms for fresh ones: a 6-ounce can equals ½ pound of fresh mushrooms.

Musical instruments

Homemade musical instruments can be more fun—and easier to construct—than you think. Make them with your friends and organize a little rainy-day band. Who knows? It may be your ticket to fame and fortune.

1. Make a rhythm bass—the kind you see in bluegrass bands—from a metal washtub, a broom handle, and some sturdy twine. Turn the tub upside down and punch a nail hole in the center of the bottom. Push a small bolt through and secure it with a nut, using washers top and bottom. Tie one end of the twine to the top of the bolt.

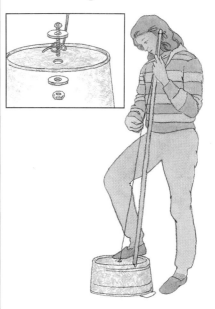

Notch one end of the broomstick and groove the other about an inch from the end. Fit the notched end over the tub edge, then tie the free end of the twine around the groove. As you hold the broom handle upright, the twine should be fairly taut. Now put one foot on the edge of the tub and pluck away, varying the tone by changing the tension on the twine. As you gain virtuosity, you can also change the pitch by holding the twine at various places along the broomstick.

2. For a simple rubber-band zither, use four 6d nails, a 6-inch length of 1 x 6 wood with a hole cut in the center, and a pie pan. Drive one of the nails about an inch from the edge, centered on one side of the wood, then hammer the remaining three along the other side. String rubber bands of different thicknesses from each of the three nails to the single nail. Put the instrument on top of the inverted pie pan to give it a resonating chamber.

3. A few ballpoint pens can yield a homemade harmonica. Take out the ink cartridges and use the plastic casings. Plug the small holes at the points with clay; add more clay for a high note, less for a lower one. Line the "pipes" up and fasten them to two ice cream sticks with a couple of rubber bands. Then play a tune; it takes a bit of practice, but keep trying.

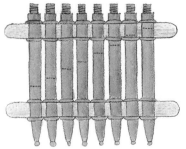

4. Play the jug. A large earthenware one looks best and gives the most resonant tone, but you can also use a large glass soda bottle or even a ketchup bottle.

Hold the jug straight up and pucker your lips against the neck; arch your upper lip slightly over the opening. Then blow gently across the opening, adjusting your lips until you get a sound. One note is all you can play—the jug is a rhythm instrument. To change the note, add or remove water.

With practice, your group can play real songs, but you're probably better off letting a piano or guitar carry the melody and using these instruments as accompaniment. (See also *Xylophone*, p.236.)

Mussels

1. If a shell isn't tightly closed, test to see if the mussel is alive. Thump the shell with your fingers or insert the tip of a knife; the shell should close immediately. Discard any mussels that stay open or have cracked shells.

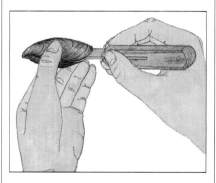

2. To clean mussels, scrub with a stiff brush, then pull off the beards or remove them with a sharp knife or kitchen shears. Place the mussels in very cold water and rub the shells together to remove any remaining debris. Or scrub with a vegetable brush.

Mustaches & beards

1. To help you decide which style of mustache or beard suits your face, have a black-and-white portrait taken, get several 8 x 10 prints, and draw various styles of facial hair with a felt-tip marker. Be aware, however, that nature will also have a say—your whiskers will grow the way they want to, so make the most of your own attributes.

2. Since wet hair stretches, always trim your mustache when it's dry.

3. To give your mustache a nice flat appearance, cut the top hairs shorter than those at the bottom.

4. To shape your mustache more easily, apply mustache wax or a little hair-styling mousse.

5. Remove after-meal crumbs from your mustache with a toothbrush. A firm-bristled toothbrush also works well for grooming beards.

Mutilated money

1. Your puppy chewed up a $20 bill? Your bank should redeem it if it's in fairly good shape. If it's badly mauled, mail the scraps, along with your name and address, to the Office of Currency Standards, Department of the Treasury, Bureau of Engraving and Printing, Room 344, P.O. Box 37048, Washington, DC 20013. Specialists will try to put the pieces together; if they can assemble more than half, they'll send you a check. (If they're satisfied that fraud is not involved, they'll sometimes redeem a bill even when less than half remains.)

2. If your stash of cash gets burned or otherwise mutilated, wrap the remains in cotton or styrene chips so that they don't jiggle around or crumble further, and send the package by registered mail with a letter of explanation to the address above.

3. If you pick up a few ravaged coins while beachcombing or you own corroded or charred coins, take them to a bank for redemption. Or if there's more than a pound, separate the coins by denomination and send them by registered mail, along with your name and address, to the U.S. Mint, P.O. Box 400, Philadelphia, PA 19105.

N

Nail biting

1. When you're tempted to nip at your nails or cuticles, keep your hands busy—doodle, knead an eraser, or finger some worry beads.

2. Give yourself a weekly manicure; the neat appearance may deter you from biting your nails.

3. Buy your young nail biter a manicure set as well.

Nailing

1. Caught without a hammer? Pound home a nail with the back end of a hatchet. Or try using a small crowbar. Or hold a flat metal plate (a hinge, perhaps) on the nailhead and hit it with a piece of 2 x 4.

2. A quick solution to the problem of driving picture-hook nails into plaster or plasterboard has been used by generations of homemakers: find an old steel-tipped, high-heeled shoe and pound the nail home with the heel.

3. Don't hammer with wrenches, planes, or other shop tools. You could render them useless. A nail can gouge a smooth metal surface and crack a cast-iron wrench body.

4. To keep from mashing your fingers, hold a brad or tack with tweezers, a bobby pin, or a paper clip until you get it started.

Nail set

For a homemade nail set, lock a 10d nail in a vise (without crushing the head), point up. Using a hacksaw, cut the tip off at an exact 90° angle; then smooth the cut sur-

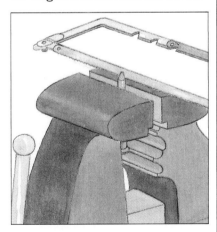

face with a metal file. You now have an instant nail set that does a good job of embedding 6d finishing nails or larger, since the diameter of the shaft matches that of the head of the finishing nail.

To drive smaller finishing nails, reduce the diameter of the cut end with a metal file and emery paper.

Neckache

1. If you feel an ache coming on, shrug your shoulders several times.

2. Take a hot shower, letting the spray hit the back of your neck for 10 to 15 minutes.

3. While reading or watching TV before bedtime, rest a heating pad against your neck.

4. Using your fingertips, knead the back of your neck from the earlobes down to the shoulders; lightly massage the vertebrae. Finish off with brisk chopping movements, using the little-finger side of your flat, stiff hands—but not too hard.

5. Exercise your neck. Stand or sit erect, with your arms relaxed, or lie flat on your back, with your knees bent. Slowly turn your head to the right as far as you can without feeling strain or pain; hold for 5 seconds, then turn to the left. Repeat the exercise five times.

Necklaces

1. To prevent metal costume jewelry from tarnishing, store a piece of white chalk with it.

2. To avoid tangled necklaces, hang them from adhesive-backed plastic hooks on your dresser mirror or from a tie rack on the inside of the closet door.

3. Make a necklace from fishing swivels. String them together with satin cord, knotting the cord between each swivel.

4. To clean nonplastic costume jewelry, immerse it in rubbing alcohol for 5 minutes. Then rinse in warm water and dry with a lint-free cloth. Soak rhinestone pieces in straight liquid detergent for 15 minutes; rinse in warm water and dry with a flannel cloth. Do the same for metal jewelry, but dilute the detergent with warm water.

Neckties

1. Don't throw away a tie just because its width is no longer in style; fashions being as fickle as they are, your old tie is bound to make a comeback sooner or later. Mean-

while, pair a wide tie with a wide shirt collar and a narrow one with a narrow collar.

2. Having trouble tying your bow tie? Pretend it's a shoelace. Practice by tying it around your thigh.

3. You can knot a four-in-hand tie around your thigh, too; then slip it off and pull it over your head.

4. To keep the narrow end of your tie in place, slide it through the label in back of the wide end. If there's no label, attach a strip of cloth tape. Or make a loop of masking or transparent tape, sticky side out.

5. If a restaurant requires a tie and you lack one, borrow a scarf and wear it as an ascot. Wrap it around your neck, one end shorter than the other; cross the long end over and bring it up behind, so that it comes out on top.

6. When packing ties, fold them over thick cardboard and wrap a rubber band around the middle.

7. No tie rack? Stretch a thick rubber band between two cup hooks on the closet door or wall. Or shape a wire coat hanger into a circle.

Needle & thread

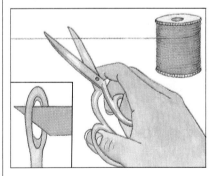

1. To make threading a needle easier, cut the thread diagonally.

2. Keep your needles extra sharp by storing them in a steel-wool pad.

3. All out of thread? Use dental floss or, on heavy clothing, 6- to 10-pound fishing line.

4. If you can't quite match the color of a fabric, buy thread a shade lighter than the cloth.

5. Try unraveling an edge of the fabric you're about to mend to get some thread that is a perfect match. **6.** There's no need for a needle and thread with iron-on fusible tape; use ¼-inch tape for basting (p.18), ¾-inch for hemming (p.107). If you change your mind, press to reheat the tape and peel it off.

Needlecraft

1. Knit an American classic, a rag rug, from pieces of old fabric cut lengthwise into thin strips. Sew the ends together and press the edges in for a neater look. Use a simple knit stitch, wielding needles that are about ½ inch in diameter.
2. To make a patchwork quilt in jig time, arrange your patches on panels of fusible web (sold by the yard in fabric stores) and iron them down. Peel the paper backing from the web panels and iron them onto a bedsheet. Use the zigzag stitch on your sewing machine to conceal the patches' raw edges. Add filler and backing (see *Comforters*, p.53) and quilt as usual.

Neighbors

Neighbors need not be nuisances. Here are some tips on building good relationships:
1. If your neighbors are willing, exchange home phone numbers and find out how to reach them at work in case of emergency.
2. Invite your neighbors over occasionally. Make sure they know the layout of your house or apartment and make an effort to learn theirs. Such knowledge could be important in a crisis.
3. When a new family moves in, welcome them with a basket of cookies and a list of the names and phone numbers of their new neighbors and nearby stores. Offer to collect mail and newspapers and to keep an eye on their home while they're on vacation. Be friendly, but don't make a nuisance of yourself; some people prefer to keep their distance from neighbors.
4. Organize an annual block party or neighborhood family day. (Ask the police if the street can be closed to traffic for a few hours.) Have everyone bring something—food, beverages, or entertainment. Make an effort to chat with neighbors you don't know well.
5. To smooth year-round relationships, establish a council with the authority to consider such neighborhood problems as roaming dogs, loud parties, and unkempt lawns.
6. Start a neighborhood newsletter (the kids can be reporters).

Networking

This is the modern term for what your parents meant when they said, "It's not *what* you know, but *who* you know." Whether you're trying to find a job, change careers, or get a promotion, the fundamental thing applies—you need help to achieve your goal. Here are some tips:
1. Ask friends, neighbors, relatives, and former colleagues if they know anyone who works in the field you're interested in. If so, write or phone the person to request a brief interview (be sure to mention the name of your contact). If she's too busy to meet with you, invite her to lunch.
2. When you meet, don't simply announce that you're networking or looking for a job. Instead, ask about her work, her company, and how she got where she is.
3. Avoid getting too personal. Your attitude should make it clear that your interest is in business.
4. Mention your skills in passing, but don't sell yourself. Bring a résumé in case it's requested.
5. At the end of the conversation, ask for the name of another person you could contact. Follow up with a thank-you note.
6. Remember that whenever a person recommends you, she is putting her reputation on the line. Never abuse the privilege, and always offer to return the favor.
7. If someone's lead pans out, treat her to lunch. And make it clear that you know you owe her one.

IN TIMES GONE BY

A labor of love

(From *The Standard Book of Quilt Making and Collecting*, by Marguerite Ickis)

That kindly, ancient lady reminisced as she passed work-worn fingers over a quilt she had pieced together while her family was growing up: "It took me more than twenty years, nearly twenty-five, I reckon . . . in the evenings after supper when the children were all put to bed. My whole life is in that quilt. It scares me sometimes when I look at it.

"All my joys and all my sorrows are stitched into those little pieces.

When I was proud of the boys and when I was downright provoked and angry with them. When the girls annoyed me or when they gave me a warm feeling around my heart. And John, too. He was stitched into that quilt and all the thirty years we were married. Sometimes I loved him and sometimes I sat there hating him as I pieced the patches together. So they are all in that quilt, my hopes and fears, my joys and sorrows, my loves and hates.

"I tremble sometimes when I remember what that quilt knows about me."

New baby

Forestall jealousy among siblings before a new baby arrives.

1. Discuss the responsibilities of keeping a helpless infant alive, the resultant changes in daily routine, and the ways the kids can help. Emphasize that the situation won't be permanent, but will gradually change as the baby develops into a self-sufficient human being.

2. Make sure the older children know that they'll have certain perks and powers along with their new responsibilities.

3. Make a scrapbook of baby pictures clipped from magazines; borrow videotapes from other families with new babies. Do a sales job, not a con job—show crying and messy diapers as well as the cute stuff.

4. Ease into talking about the sex of the baby. Start out with his personality: though helpless, he'll be a distinctive new person—not a copy of anyone and not an object to be molded. Make a game of imagining who he might turn out to be.

5. Involve the children in choosing a name for their new sibling (see *Babies' names,* p.14). Let them help make birth announcements.

6. Before you confront the kids with the new baby, let them welcome Mother. They'll have missed her.

New pet

1. Don't take home a puppy or kitten less than 8 weeks old or you may encounter some behavior problems later in your pet's life.

2. When you're picking up a puppy or kitten that you've bought from a breeder, take a soft piece of fabric with you. Rub it on the fur of the animal's mother and siblings to catch their scent. Then put the fabric in your new pet's bed.

3. If your pet cries at night, it may still miss its mother. Wrap a ticking clock in a towel and put it in the animal's bed. Or wrap a hot-water bottle for it to cuddle against.

Newspaper clippings

1. To prevent yellowing, dissolve a milk of magnesia tablet in a quart of club soda. Let the mixture stand overnight. Stir well and soak your clipping in the solution for 1 hour; blot with a paper towel and place on a screen to dry.

2. If clippings have been stored in a damp place, remove mildew by drying them in the sun. (On a rainy day try the low setting on a hair dryer or an electric fan.) Then sprinkle cornstarch over them to absorb what moisture remains. (See also *Photographs,* p.154.)

Night blindness

Avoid bumping into the furniture when you step into a dark room. Wait a minute or so to let your eyes adjust to the dark. Then focus your gaze slightly off-center—your eyes' light receptors are concentrated on the sides of the retina, so peripheral vision is better than direct vision in dim light.

Noise

1. If you're regularly awakened by early-morning traffic, garbage trucks, or barking dogs, make use of white noise—a low, constant sound that screens the din but isn't loud enough to keep you awake. An air conditioner does the trick in summer, an electric fan or a hu-

midifier in winter. Or make a continuous tape loop of chirping crickets, running water, or another soothing sound. Machines made for the purpose, called white noise generators, are available, too.

2. For white noise in your yard, install a splashing fountain.

3. If you work in a place where you must shout to be heard 3 feet away, the noise around you may be causing permanent hearing loss. Wear antinoise muffs or earplugs.

4. Don't listen to headphones for more than 3 hours at over 100 decibels, which is about the loudness of a car horn. (See also *Hearing loss,* p.105.)

Noisy pipes

1. If a loosely mounted pipe vibrates against a basement beam or a wall stud, wrap it with felt or secure it with extra pipe hangers or a U-shaped strap cushioned with a piece of rubber.

2. If you hear rattling when the water turns on and off quickly in your clothes washer or dishwasher, the problem may be a loose washer. Turn off the water supply, remove the faucet, and replace the washer (see *Dripping faucets,* p.67).

3. Sometimes the hammering and clanging can be stopped only by installing shock-absorbing air chambers on top of the pipes leading to your fixtures. If you already have them, you may need to restore air to the chambers by draining your plumbing system; call for professional help. (See also *Pipes,* p.157.)

Nonstick cookware

To remove grease buildup and stains from a nonstick pan, mix one of these solutions: ½ cup coffeepot cleaner in 1 quart water; 3 tablespoons nonchlorine bleach and 1 teaspoon liquid dishwashing detergent in 1 cup water; or 3 tablespoons automatic-dishwasher detergent in 1 cup water. Simmer for 20 minutes in the pan; then wash, rinse, dry, and reseason the pan.

Nosebleeds

1. Sit down, lean forward, and firmly pinch the fleshy part of your nostrils shut for at least 10 minutes.
2. If the bleeding doesn't stop after 20 minutes, hold an ice pack or athlete's cold pack to your forehead and the bridge of your nose while continuing to pinch the nostrils.
3. As a last resort, pack the bleeding nostril with sterile gauze for 30 to 60 minutes.

No-see-ums

These invisible insects—also known as sand flies, biting midges, and punkies—are so tiny that they can pass through window screens, but their bite is extremely painful. Other than wearing an insect repellent (p.116), here's how to thwart the pests:
1. During the evening and early morning hours in summer, stay away from their breeding grounds: dead or decaying plants along rivers, lakes, and seashores.
2. When camping, pitch your tent in an area open to the wind; avoid shining a flashlight inside the tent. (See also *Insect bites*, p.116.)

›Nuclear power plants

Many nuclear power plants have installed special sirens to notify surrounding areas of an emergency. If you hear such a siren sounding without interruption for 3 to 5 minutes, tune your radio or TV to the local Emergency Broadcast System station; it will give you official emergency information and instructions. Avoid using your telephone except to call for help.

In anticipation of such a situation, learn your community's plan for responding to a nuclear power plant accident; review evacuation routes and learn where all reception centers and shelters are. If possible, arrange to stay with a friend or relative outside your area. (See also *Radioactivity*, p.169.)

Nursing homes

Guilt feelings may keep you from placing a loved one in a nursing home long after the move is needed. But remember that even love and care can run to excess; if keeping your aging relative at home causes severe deprivation and ruins your family life, it is not good for either of you.

Perhaps the most difficult problem you'll face will be bringing up the subject in the first place. But it is imperative to face this emotionally charged situation honestly.

Listen to your relative's concerns; he will be more reassured if you let him air his fears. His major worry is likely to be abandonment. You must be very firm about the nursing home being part of your continuing care—not the end of it.

Another key step is to come to terms with any revulsion you yourself feel for nursing homes. Visit several homes in your area, keeping in mind that they are designed to help severely disabled people and must be judged on that basis. Try to focus on how well they keep their patients functioning.

If possible, take your relative along. First reactions will probably be negative, but in time you both are likely to see which of the homes will be most suitable.

Since people in nursing homes live in close quarters, find one that offers a compatible environment. Note the religious, ethnic, and cultural groups in each home that you visit; if religion is important to

---

IN DAYS GONE BY

Accommodating the aged

Old people in some nonindustrialized societies have had it better than their counterparts in the rest of the world. Aged members of the Hottentot tribe in Africa, for example, have long been valued for the advice they could offer to the active food producers in the group. In Bali the oldest people enjoyed the highest rank because they were living repositories of information; their knowledge of religion, social customs, and history earned them unquestioned control over the community.

The Yakut nomads of Siberia, on the other hand, were not so generous to the aged. Living on the edge of starvation, parents tended to neglect their young children; when the children grew up, they in turn were hostile to the needs of their aging parents.

In the Western world, old people reap the benefits of their years of work through pensions from their governments and former employers. (Germany started the ball rolling by initiating old-age pensions in 1889. The United States was relatively late; the Social Security Act was passed in 1935.) But the value of the accumulated experience of the elderly is too often discounted as new technology makes the old ways of doing things obsolete.

Still, oldsters in the West can probably be glad they live where they do. Some Eskimos, after all, faced with food shortages and harsh winters, still abandon old people who become too feeble to care for themselves.

your relative, give priority to homes run by his denomination.

Another important consideration is proximity to family members. Frequent visits will be the best way to reassure your relative that your love and concern are as strong as they always were. (See also *Housing for the elderly*, p.111.)

Nutcrackers

No nutcracker handy?

1. Wrap a nut in a towel and pound it with a rock, hammer, or mallet.

2. Squeeze the nut with a wrench, a pair of pliers, or a vise.

3. Put it on the hinge side of a door, then shut the door slowly.

4. Hold the nut at the top edge of a drawer and slam the drawer shut, but watch out for your fingers.

Nuts

1. Mature nuts usually fall by themselves; if necessary, gently shake the tree, but protect your head. Gather no more than you need—leave some for the wild animals.

2. Eat or freeze butternuts soon after they fall; they turn rancid quickly. Dry other nuts for about 21 days in a shady place, safe from animals.

Pecan

Butternut

English walnut

3. Nuts will crack more easily and won't break up as much if you heat them in a covered glass dish of water in a microwave oven for 2 minutes. Drain, cool, then crack.

Nuts & bolts

1. To keep a nut from working loose, slip a locking washer over the bolt before applying the nut or tighten a second "jam" nut over the original one.

2. Another method: Crush the exposed threads with pliers or a cold chisel. Or coat them with silicone caulk, epoxy glue, or a proprietary nut-locking chemical before tightening the nut.

3. The best way to remove a rusted or "frozen" nut is with penetrating oil, sold at hardware stores. Let the solution seep in and then, using a wrench large enough to give good leverage, work off the nut with a series of short, sharp jerks rather than an extended pull. (See also *Lubricating oil*, p.130.)

4. Or heat the nut with a propane torch or even a few kitchen matches. It may expand enough to let you work it loose.

5. To prevent nuts from rusting and freezing to bolts in the first place, dip them in shellac before use. They will always come apart.

6. If you find there's no way to remove a nut, destroy it. Rent or buy a nut splitter, a kind of ring-held cold chisel. Position the ring over the nut and turn the screw with a wrench. Or hold a cold chisel against the nut and give it a few hefty blows with a hammer. Though split, the nut may still have to be wedged off with a crowbar.

7. Here's how to shorten a bolt with a hacksaw without ruining the threads: First, screw a nut well up the shaft of the bolt. Then, before putting the bolt in a vise, put a spring-type clothespin on it to protect the threads from the steel jaws. Finally, after sawing the bolt off to the desired length, unscrew the nut to restore the threads.

Office exercises

Exercising at your desk or computer terminal will help relieve tension. Whenever time permits, try one or more of the following:

1. Inhale deeply through your nose and then exhale through your mouth. Repeat six times.

2. Raise your arms high above your head; stretch one hand toward the ceiling, then the other, and then both together; relax. Repeat twice.

3. Clasp your hands behind your head to keep it still and press back your neck muscle to loosen and stretch it. Hold for 10 seconds and relax. Repeat five times.

4. With your arms by your sides, push your shoulders back as if to make your shoulder blades meet; hold 5 seconds and relax. Now push your shoulders forward; hold 5 seconds and relax. Repeat three times.

5. Hold your arms straight out at the sides, with your palms up, and slowly rotate them in small circles; do 20 forward, then 20 backward.

6. For your hands, wrist, and fingers, hold both arms straight out in front with the palms down. Keeping your fingers straight, gently bend your hands back at the wrists as far as you can, then bring them forward. Now spread your fingers as wide as you can; hold for 5 seconds, then make a tight fist.

Office politics

1. The best way to deal with the office rumor mill is to listen with interest but never pass on what you hear. That way you can benefit from inside information without getting a reputation as a gossip. In fact, people will be more likely to confide in you.

2. To prevent colleagues from stealing credit for your ideas, put them in writing; send a copy to your boss.

3. Even if you dislike a colleague, never let it show. The ability to get along with coworkers—including those you don't care for—is a measure of your professionalism.

4. Though flattery may get you somewhere, in the long run it usually backfires. If someone is shallow enough to reward an employee for buttering him up, he probably won't last long—and neither will you if you become his yes-man.

Office romance

Depending on how you look at it, the office may be the best or the worst place to find someone special. On the one hand, it's an ideal setting in which to get to know someone well. On the other hand, mixing business and pleasure can jeopardize your job, your relationship, or both.

1. Before getting involved with a coworker, weigh the risks carefully—a relationship with the boss is especially dangerous. If you do decide to start dating a coworker, keep your behavior at work strictly professional—don't call each other by pet names, don't display affection publicly, and don't spend hours chatting on the phone or in the halls. And don't discuss your romance with coworkers.

2. No matter how discreet you both try to be, sooner or later teasing or gossip is bound to begin. If you're not prepared to accept this, don't start a relationship.

3. Bear in mind that romances often go sour, and if this one does, you and your coworker will still have to face each other every day.

4. Also bear in mind that if you get married, your company may forbid you to work in same department.

Oily skin

1. To help normalize skin, avoid spicy foods, reduce oils and fats in your diet, and drink six to eight glasses of water daily.

2. For a refreshing facial, fill a spray bottle with tepid water and 1 teaspoon of salt, then spray the solution on your face. Blot dry with a towel. For a quick steam, heat a wet towel in the microwave and form a tent over your face.

3. Here's a quick facial mask: Mix 3 tablespoons each of mineral water and fuller's earth and apply the paste to your face. After 20 minutes rinse with warm water. Or try a paste of warm water and oatmeal for 10 minutes.

4. If you're out of astringent, mix cider vinegar or lemon juice with a little cool water and splash some on your face; cover your hair and close your eyes. Wipe with a cotton ball. During the summer, freeze the solution in an ice cube tray; run a cube over your face when you feel hot.

5. To remove makeup, mix a teaspoon of powdered skim milk with warm water; apply with cotton balls, wipe with tissues, and blot dry.

Older drivers

1. If you're worried about your own driving ability, enroll in a special defensive-driving course that teaches you to cope with such age-related changes as slowed reflexes and limited vision. The course may even save you money; many insurance companies give graduates a break on premium rates. Contact your state highway department, the American Association of Retired Persons, or your county cooperative extension office for information on courses for senior citizens.

2. Steer clear of potentially dangerous situations. Devise alternate routes to shopping centers and doctors' offices to avoid busy intersections and highways. If you're in the market for a new car, buy a white, beige, or yellow one so that other drivers can see you more easily.

3. When you've stopped driving, don't give up your independence. Look for alternatives: explore bus routes and scout out dependable taxi services. Many churches, senior centers, and clinics provide transportation for older people, and local agencies for the aging can recommend pickup services.

Only child

1. Take extra care to see that an only child has plenty of opportunities to play with others. Ask friends and relatives who have children to come over often and make sure your child gets to spend a lot of time with them. Make young friends feel like part of the family; put an extra bed in your child's room to encourage sleep-overs.

2. Don't gang up on an only child when disciplining or criticizing him; it tends to make him feel he's one against the world and to envy children who have siblings to side with. Instead, you and your spouse take turns at the unpleasant chore. (Praise, on the other hand, is reinforced when both parents join in.)

3. Make time for silly behavior now and then: a pillow or water pistol fight can be fun for everyone.

Osteoporosis

Just ingesting calcium may not prevent bones from growing thinner during and after menopause. What seems to work is calcium—1,500 milligrams a day—combined with regular exercise. (Although men are less prone to osteoporosis than women are, they should also follow these suggestions.)

1. Dairy products, sardines, salmon, broccoli, collard greens, and kale are excellent calcium sources (see *The Balanced Diet*, p.254). If your diet doesn't fulfill your needs, take a supplement.

2. To absorb calcium, you need 400 units of vitamin D daily; a quart of milk or 15 to 60 minutes in the midday sun will do the job. It's best to avoid calcium supplements containing vitamin D, which can be toxic in high doses.

3. Avoid smoking, alcohol, and caffeine, and cut down drastically on salt; all interfere with the absorption of calcium. So do some drugs; check with your doctor. (Women should also ask about estrogen replacement therapy.)

4. Weight-bearing exercise—walking, jogging, dancing, tennis—for half an hour three times a week prevents loss of bone mass and may increase it. Before starting an exercise program, check with your doctor; then, if she approves, begin slowly and build up gradually (see *Endurance building*, p.72).

5. Prevent falls and possible broken bones by "trip-proofing" your home—nail down throw rugs, provide adequate lighting, and install grab bars and nonskid decals in the bathtub.

Outdoor cooking

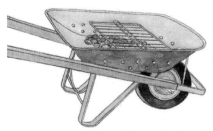

1. You can turn an old metal wheelbarrow into a mobile barbecue. Punch ½-inch holes in the bottom and sides, line with a layer of stones, and cover with charcoal. An old oven shelf can serve as a grill (don't use refrigerator shelves; they might contain poisonous cadmium).

2. Season a new iron hibachi to prevent rust. First, check that there are no wooden parts. Then rub all surfaces with vegetable oil and set

the hibachi on a baking sheet in a 250°F oven. Leave for half an hour, turn off the heat, and let the oven cool. Remove the hibachi and wipe off excess fat.

3. To find out if the coals are hot enough to barbecue steaks, hold your hand an inch above the grill for a count of three. If the heat's unbearable, the fire is ready.

4. To prevent flare-ups when you barbecue, make a drip pan from aluminum foil and set it atop the coals under the meat.

5. Another way to prevent flare-ups: spread lettuce leaves on the hot coals before you barbecue fatty meat (the outer leaves from the head you're using for the salad will do nicely). The lettuce will blacken but won't ignite.

6. Don't forget that you can barbecue vegetables as well as meat. Wrap onions, corn on the cob, or sliced potatoes (all dotted with butter or margarine or brushed with barbecue sauce) in heavy-duty foil. Grill onions and corn over medium coals for 30 minutes, turning often; place foil-wrapped potatoes directly on the coals for 45 minutes, turning once. Put chunks of zucchini or eggplant on skewers, brush with oil, and grill for 10 minutes over medium coals, turning often.

7. Flies hate basil, so keep a pot of the herb close to the dining table. Crush a few leaves to release the oils. A bonus: fresh basil leaves to chop into your salad.

Ovens

1. If your electric oven isn't working, check to see that all the controls are set properly. If they are, see if a fuse has blown or a circuit breaker has tripped.

2. Never use a commercial oven cleaner in a self- or continuous-cleaning oven. If you accidentally apply one, clean the oven thoroughly before using it again: Apply full-strength white vinegar to the oven surfaces with a sponge, then rinse with warm water. Next, for a self-

cleaning oven, run a full self-clean cycle. For a continuous-cleaning oven, heat the oven to 400°F for 1 hour. Rinse either type with warm water after it has cooled.

Oven thermometer

You can check your oven's accuracy with this simple test: After preheating, lay a sheet of plain white paper on the center rack and leave it for 5 minutes. The paper's color will now correspond to the stove's temperature: pale biscuit, 300°F or less; light brown, 350° to 400°F; golden brown, 400° to 450°F; dark brown, 450° to 500°F; black means the temperature is over 500°F.

To determine the temperature in a wood-burning oven by the same method, let the fire burn for 20 minutes to preheat the oven.

›Overheated engine

Overheating can ruin a car engine very quickly, so if the temperature gauge starts edging up, take immediate action. (By the time the warning light comes on, the problem is already serious!)

Turn off the air conditioner and turn on the heater (it draws off engine heat). If you stop for a minute or more in traffic or at lights, shift into *Neutral* and rev the engine. Stay as far behind the car ahead of you as possible to keep its hot exhaust away from your radiator.

If this doesn't stop the temperature rise, get off the road at your first opportunity. Raise the hood (be careful; the hood and under-hood areas are hot) and see if there is something obviously wrong, such as a snapped belt, a broken fan, a coolant leak, or insects or other debris coating the air conditioning condenser or the radiator.

If there are no obvious reasons for the overheating, wait at least an hour for the engine to cool, then check the coolant level in the radiator. If it is low, let the engine idle while you top it up (plain water will do in a pinch). If there is no cap on the radiator, add coolant to the reservoir if it's empty. As soon as possible, have the system drained and filled with the appropriate coolant. (See also *Radiator hose*, p.168.)

Overindulgence

Afraid you may eat or drink too much at a party? Here are some survival strategies:

1. Never go to a party hungry. Eat a light, high-carbohydrate snack (salad and pasta or whole-grain bread) beforehand so that you won't be tempted to overeat.

2. At a buffet, put only one course on your plate at a time, beginning with the salad. You may be full before dessert is served.

3. If you are offered a drink, ask for just a little alcohol in a tall glass of water or fruit juice; find out if there is alcohol-free beer or wine, or drink club soda with a twist.

4. When your alcoholic beverage is half gone, refill the glass with ice.

Overspending

The compulsive spender is often the last to recognize that he has a problem, but if your checkbook refuses to balance or your total debt is more than 20 percent of your annual take-home pay, here are some constructive actions you can take:

1. If shopping is your social exercise, look for new friends who play cards or golf.

2. When you feel a sudden urge to go on a spending spree, telephone a frugal friend and ask her to talk you out of it.

3. Go on a crash "spending diet" for a month. Shun shopping malls; shut off TV commercials; avoid glossy "consumer" magazines and catalogs. Then count all the cash you've saved.

4. Cut up your credit cards and close your checking account. Make all purchases with cash, money orders, or certified checks.

5. When shopping is absolutely necessary, make a list and buy *only* the items that appear on it.

6. Once you've got your spending under control, open a savings account and deposit 15 to 20 percent of your pay; restrict yourself to withdrawing the accrued interest.

Oysters

1. Don't worry about eating oysters when there's no *r* in the name of the month. They're edible year round (but in summer they're more palatable cooked than raw).

2. You can tell if an oyster is fresh because its shell is firmly closed or snaps shut when tapped. If it's already shucked, check for a clean, sea-sweet odor and clear liquid.

3. A "drunken" oyster is much easier to open than a sober one. Carbon dioxide does the trick; after 5 minutes in carbonated water, its muscles relax and the shell is a cinch to open.

4. Caught at the shore without a knife? Set oysters on hot rocks close to the fire—they'll open right up. Or wrap them in wet seaweed and lay them on hot coals for a minute or two.

5. Cook shucked oysters quickly on low heat so that they don't become tough. The best way is to poach them gently in hot milk or sauce, just until the edges curl.

6. If you're broiling oysters, steady them in the pan by setting them in rock salt or propping them with crumples of aluminum foil.

P

Packing clothes

1. To reduce wrinkles, fold your garments in tissue paper or wrap them in plastic bags. For shirts or blouses, wrap several layers of them around a piece of cardboard.

2. Or interfold clothing; place one end of a long garment face down and even with an inside wall of the suitcase and let the other end hang

out. Then lay shorter items vertically on top of it and fold the end over. Alternate layers so that the garments cushion one another.

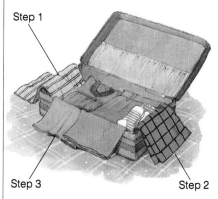

Step 1

Step 3   Step 2

3. Tuck small items, such as socks and handkerchiefs, into collars and along fold lines.

4. Don't fold clothes that are going into a duffel bag; roll them.

5. In a three-section suitcase put the heaviest items in the middle.

6. In any bag make sure that heavy items are on the bottom when the luggage is upright. Don't overstuff.

7. In a hanging bag put the delicate clothes in first. Center garments on hangers and bring their sleeves slightly to the front.

8. Need an extra bag? Use a department store or dry cleaner's garment bag as a hanging bag. Use a child's book bag or knapsack for personal items. On short trips a picnic basket is handy for carrying frequently used items.

Pain relief

1. Laugh. Really! A hearty laugh causes the release of endorphins, the body's natural pain relievers. If you're lacking humor in your life, rent comic videotapes or read humor magazines or joke books. Invite friends over to tell jokes or go to a comedy club.

2. Tension and stress tend to intensify pain. Take up meditation or join a meditation group. Get a massage or do relaxation exercises (see *Stress*, p.198), but don't strain the painful part of your body.

3. Explore hypnotherapy; it teaches you to screen out pain with pleasant images. (See also *Aspirin*, p.12.)

Paintbrushes

1. To keep from flooding the rim of a paint can, remove excess paint by tapping the bristles against the inside of the can. Also, if you punch several nail holes around the groove inside the rim, any paint that does drip in will drain back into the can.
2. If you take a short break while painting, you needn't clean the brushes or rollers. Just wrap the wet bristles in plastic food wrap.
3. To store brushes overnight, wrap them in plastic food wrap or aluminum foil and pop them into the freezer. Remove them about an hour before you resume painting.
4. To soften a paintbrush that's stiff with dried latex paint, soak it in a 50-50 solution of vinegar and water for 10 minutes.
5. To protect cleaned brushes for long-term storage, wrap the bristles in brown paper cut from a grocery bag and secure with a rubber band or tape. Store brushes flat or hang them by their handles; standing them up will bend the bristles out of shape permanently.
6. For hard-to-paint objects, such as wrought-iron fences and narrow pipes, make a painting mitt. Put a plastic bag over your hand and cover it with an old towel. Secure with a rubber band around your wrist—not too tight!

7. Don't throw away an old paintbrush with ruined bristles. Snip about an inch off the tip and use the brush for dusting. Or cut the bristles to stubble—about ¾ inch long—for a handy scrub brush.

Painter's tray

Need a tray for a roller?
1. Try a shallow baking pan. Line it with aluminum foil for easy cleanup. Or use a foil baking pan.
2. Line a shallow cardboard box with a plastic garbage bag.
3. Coat the roller with a brush.

Painting

1. To mask adjacent surfaces while painting trim or molding, use an old metal venetian blind slat. A piece of sheet metal or thin cardboard also works.
2. For a drop cloth, use canvas or heavyweight cloth instead of plastic; it will absorb paint that might otherwise be tracked through the house. If you must use plastic, cover it with old newspapers.
3. Before painting a window frame, rub a bar of paraffin on the glass next to the woodwork. Then scrape dried paint off with a putty knife or a single-edge razor blade.
4. If you use tape to mask a painted area, remove it *before* the paint dries. If you forget, cut along the edge of the tape with a single-edge razor blade or utility knife; otherwise you'll peel off the fresh paint.
5. When touching up small areas with spray paint, mask them with

rubber cement. Peel away the rubber film after the paint has dried.
6. To prevent "skin" from forming on the surface of paint, seal the lid tightly and store the can upside down. The paint will form an airtight seal around the lid. Or lay a sheet of plastic food wrap or aluminum foil on the paint's surface before closing the can.

Paint roller

1. To make use of a roller encrusted with dried paint, wrap a terry cloth towel tightly around it. Secure each end with a rubber band.
2. If a roller is coated with latex paint and you plan to use it the next day, don't bother to clean it. Wrap the roller in plastic food wrap and put it in the freezer. Give it an hour or so to thaw before using it.
3. If you don't have a roller, make a painting pad by gluing a piece of thick carpet to a block of wood.

Paint solvent

Solvents such as paint thinner, mineral spirits, and alcohol can easily be reused. Pour the used solvent into a large jar and cap it tightly. In a couple of days, when the paint solids and resins have settled to the bottom, carefully pour the clean solvent into another container.

Paint stains

1. To make cleanup easier, apply a thin layer of petroleum jelly to your hands and face before painting.
2. To remove dried latex paint from clothing, soak the garment in a solution of warm water and detergent for 2 hours. Then brush gently with a toothbrush. Repeat if necessary.
3. As a last resort for a paint-spattered carpet, carefully snip off the stained fibers. (See also *Brick & stone cleaning*, p.26.)

Pants

1. To keep your pant legs smooth while away from home, lay them between the mattress and the springs and press them as you sleep. Or hang them in a steamy bathroom. (Don't forget to pack clothespins for converting ordinary hangers into pants hangers.)

2. Before buying new pants, make sure they fit properly. If they wrinkle upward, the crotch length is too short; if they wrinkle horizontally, they're too tight across the front.

3. To keep knees from wearing out, put iron-on patches on the insides before wearing pants the first time.

4. Iron-on fusible tape will secure a split seam temporarily.

5. When hemming pants, finish one leg completely, then use it to mark the length of the other. Double-check by measuring the length at the inseam.

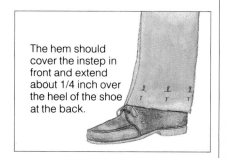

The hem should cover the instep in front and extend about 1/4 inch over the heel of the shoe at the back.

Pantyhose

1. To prevent snags, soften rough hands with lotion before handling pantyhose or wear cotton gloves while putting them on.

2. Tie the ankles of pantyhose that have runs so that you can quickly recognize them as "for slacks only."

3. If your pantyhose seem a bit short as you put them on, wet your hands and smooth the legs upward. Next time stretch the legs first.

4. Do your pantyhose tend to tear at the toe? Before putting them on, stretch out the toe area. Or spritz it with hair spray or rub it with paraffin after each washing.

5. Pantyhose tend to last longer if you hand-wash them; for an extra-thorough cleaning, add 2 tablespoons of ammonia to the water and detergent in the basin. When machine-washing, put hosiery in a mesh bag and use the *Gentle* set-

ting. It's best to let hosiery drip-dry, but if you must use the dryer, set it on *Low* and remove the pantyhose as soon as the legs and top are dry; the elastic may still be damp, but it will air-dry quickly.

Parked cars

Keep a bright cloth in the glove compartment of your car so that, when parking, you can tie it to the radio antenna. Or carry a distinctive device attached to a suction cup for the roof. It's also helpful to jot down your vehicle's location on a slip of paper. But don't write "next to the big van"—it may be gone when you return.

CHILD SAFETY

Toddlers have been known to release an emergency brake, put a car in gear, and even start one. Never leave a child alone in a parked vehicle, even for a moment.

SUMMER DANGERS

On an 85°F day, the temperature inside a closed car can rise to 102°F within 10 minutes, presenting serious hazards.

1. Audiotapes and camera film may deteriorate. Remove them if it's hot or if you will be parked for more than a few hours.

2. Perishable foods will deteriorate within an hour, and milk-based dishes can spoil even faster (see *Food safety*, p.88).

3. To keep interior fabrics from fading, cover the front windshield with cardboard shades. The side windows can be shielded with louvers; they come in kits, are easy to install, and can reduce the temperature by as much as 30°F. There are also covers for sunroofs.

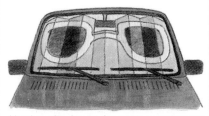

Use imagination to decorate a sunscreen.

4. Never leave your pet in a parked car in warm weather—even in the shade with the windows open. The animal can die from the combination of heat and stress.

Part-time jobs

1. Consider turning one of your skills into a part-time business. Are you a good baker? You might supply cakes to a local restaurant. If you're good at fixing things, you might find work doing odd jobs.

2. If you know someone else who is also looking for part-time work, see if the two of you might be able to split a full-time job. (See also *Moonlighting*, p.137; *Temporary employment*, p.207.)

Party crashers

Try politeness first: ask the unwanted person to leave, explaining that he is intruding on a private party. If he refuses, *tell* him to leave; until you have done this, the police cannot legally take action.

Avoid physical confrontation. Enlist the help of a guest in keeping the crasher quiet and away from the rest of the party. If he is drunk, phone for a cab. If he insists on driving, immediately contact the police with the license number, make of car, and location.

Party decorations & favors

1. For a special birthday or anniversary, decorate the room with enlargements of old photos of the guest of honor.

2. If you're serving foreign cuisine, ask a travel agency or the local consulate or tourist board of the appropriate country for posters and travel fliers and spread them out as a tablecloth. Add little flags to flower arrangements.

3. If you forget to buy decorations, a platter of colorful fruits or vegetables can make any table festive.

4. For a children's party, how about an arrangement of stuffed animals or toys down the middle of the table? (The arrangement probably

won't last very long, of course.)
5. Throwing a shower? Use a shower curtain as a tablecloth and a watering can filled with flowers as a centerpiece.

6. For help or ideas, look under "Party supplies" and "Party planning services" in the Yellow Pages.

Party guests

1. Keep three lists: an A list of fascinating people, a B list of good listeners who can also converse easily, and a C list of people to whom you are personally or socially obligated. Then, when you plan a party, draw from all three lists to balance personalities and interests. Recombine old friends and always invite someone new to keep things interesting.
2. If there is a guest of honor, tailor the guest list to her personality.
3. If you're entertaining a newcomer, try to have at least one other person present whom he knows, and invite guests who share common interests with him. Give everyone some information about the newcomer so that they will have points of departure for conversation.
4. Never invite a roomful of people who share the same occupation unless you want an evening given over to shop talk.
5. If you are having a special group—office people, fellow golfers, or the like—tell your other friends so that they won't be offended at not receiving an invitation.
6. At a small dinner party arrange

the seating for complementary personalities and interests. Place people with opposing views next to each other for lively conversation (but only if you're sure they'll restrain themselves).
7. A host has the right to stand firm against people trying to bring uninvited friends or children. If they say, "I can't come unless I bring my child" (or my poodle, for that matter), tell them that you'll miss them and that you hope they can come next time.

Passports

1. Need one in a hurry? You can get a passport in a day if you show up at the passport office carrying an airline ticket with a confirmed reservation. Otherwise it will take 2 to 3 weeks between September and December; up to twice as long from late April through the summer. Remember that you must present proof of citizenship, such as a birth certificate, naturalization papers, or a previous passport.
2. In case of extreme emergency, the State Department may ask an airline to carry someone without a passport, but don't count on it.
3. Passports are worth a lot of money on the foreign black market. Don't ever leave yours with anyone or use it as collateral. If a hotel requires you to leave it overnight, get a receipt from the desk clerk.
4. To prevent theft, always carry your passport in a front inside coat pocket or in a document pouch worn under your shirt. Or leave it in a hotel safe-deposit box. Never leave it in your hotel room or carry it with your money.
5. Make several photocopies of your passport in case of theft or loss. Leave one stateside, another in a separate section of your luggage. And carry extra copies of your passport photo.
6. If you lose your passport in the U.S., report it to the nearest passport office; if abroad, to the nearest U.S. embassy or consulate.

Pattern cutting

1. If you can't find a tracing wheel to transfer a pattern, check the kitchen drawers—a pizza cutter or a pastry wheel may do the job.
2. Protect the cutting surface beneath the pattern with felt, a flattened cardboard box, a magazine, or thick newspapers. An added bonus: you can pin the fabric and pattern down to prevent slippage.
3. To strengthen pattern pieces you want to preserve for frequent use, iron fusible interfacing onto the edges. Store them, rolled up, in cardboard tubes.
4. Create your own pattern: take apart a favorite worn-out garment with a seam ripper and press each piece out carefully.

Peeling paint

1. Scrape off peeling paint with a wide putty knife, a kitchen spatula, or even an outdated credit card. Then sand to a feathered edge. Apply a prime coat and let it dry. Then apply two finish coats.
2. To reach peeling paint on ceilings, tape a wide putty knife or spatula to a broom handle. Replace it with a paintbrush or roller to paint.

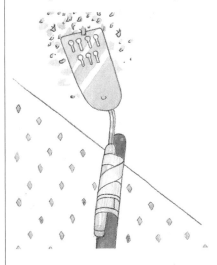

3. Remove peeling paint from metal with steel wool or a wire brush. Then apply a metal primer and two coats of rust-resistant paint.
4. To scrape away peeling paint and

dispose of it at the same time, use the bare end of your vacuum cleaner's extension wand.

Peepholes

Don't depend on a door chain when checking to see who's at the door; most aren't strong enough to prevent a forced entry. The safest way to find out who's outside is with a peephole, or door viewer.

Although you can simply install a swinging cover over a hole in the door, you're better off with a wide-angle peephole that gives you a 180° view of the exterior. Position it at a convenient height for the shortest adult in the family.

If you don't want to put a hole in your door, you can mount a mirror above or beside the door or on a nearby window frame at an angle that reflects a visitor's image.

Peer pressure

Although we experience peer pressure throughout our lives, it is strongest during childhood, especially adolescence. It takes a secure, independent person to "just say no"—whether to drugs, alcohol, petty theft, or other dangerous group activities. You can help.

1. Remember that peer pressure has its positive side; it can help instill generosity, empathy, and social skills.

2. Encourage your child to asso-

ciate with friends who share your family's values and standards. Once identified with one peer group, a child may find it difficult to break away and join another.

3. Don't argue over things that are superficial and harmless. If your son wants an outrageous haircut so that he "fits in," let him have it. Save your energy for more important issues.

4. Try to remember what you went through when you were young. Tell your child about your experiences, even if they're embarrassing.

5. Stay in touch with the parents of your child's friends so that you can work together to set standards.

6. Tell your child she can use you as an excuse if she doesn't want to go along with the group.

7. Some circumstances—the divorce of parents or the death of a grandparent, for example—can be extremely stressful; at such times a child may be more in need of peer support and therefore more susceptible to peer pressure. Help your child talk about his feelings with you or a counselor. Encourage him to spend time with friends, and provide them with space, privacy, and time for conversation.

Pencil & paper

If you have to take down a phone number, address, or message and can't find a pencil or paper, try one of the following:

1. Use your fingernail, a paper clip, or a bobby pin to scratch the message on the top sheet of a multicopy deposit slip in your checkbook. It will appear on the next sheet.

2. Write with lipstick, eyeliner, nail polish, or a spent match on napkins, newspaper, lens tissue, or gum wrappers.

3. Try "braille": use a pin to poke tiny holes in a piece of paper to form letters or numbers.

4. If you have a pen or pencil but no paper, write the number on an inconspicuous part of your clothing— the back of your tie, the label of

your jacket, the clean instep of your shoe sole.

5. Trace the number on a dirty or frosty windowpane until you find a pencil to write it down. Or wet your finger and dip it in dust or dirt to use as "ink."

6. If you're near a phone, call your own answering machine and tell it whatever it is you're trying to remember. You'll have it on tape.

7. Try singing a phone number or address to a familiar tune. Sing it over and over in your head until it gets stuck there. (See also *Calculators*, p.30; *Memory*, p.133.)

Pencil sharpener

1. No pencil sharpener? Use a wood plane. Pull the pencil against the blade, turning as you go.

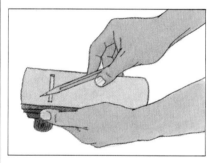

2. Try a potato peeler.

3. To hone the point of the lead itself, rub it across sandpaper, an emery board, or the friction strip of a matchbook.

4. If you're desperate, break the pencil in two. You'll probably be left with a usable, if jagged, edge.

5. Glue a small plastic pencil sharpener to the bottom edge of your workbench or telephone table. This way, you can sharpen a pencil one-handed, leaving the other hand free.

Perfume

1. Be careful of "nose fatigue." If you've been wearing the same perfume for a long time, you may not smell it as easily as others do. If the scent is obvious to you 30 minutes after application, you've probably overdone it; dab alcohol or a paste of baking soda and water on the perfumed area, then wash off.

2. For a light touch, spray your perfume in front of you, then walk through it.

3. To make your fragrance last longer, apply it after your shower or bath, while your skin is still damp.

4. To coordinate scents, spray a little perfume onto your bath powder, close the container tightly, and allow to dry.

5. Lost the stopper for your perfume bottle? Try a pencil eraser.

6. Never leave perfume in direct sunlight; keep it in the refrigerator to help prevent evaporation and deterioration.

Permanent press

1. To prevent wrinkles, wash permanent-press garments in warm water and rinse in cold water. Place a dry towel with the wet clothes in a half-filled dryer. Hang or fold the clothes as soon as they're dry. If you accidentally forget about them, run them through the dryer again on *Permanent Press* for 15 minutes.

2. No dryer available? Remove the clothing from the washer before the final *Spin* cycle and let it drip-dry on rustproof hangers.

3. If white wash-and-wear items turn yellow, make a solution of 2 gallons hot water, ½ cup automatic-dishwasher detergent, and ¼ cup liquid bleach; soak clothing in it for half an hour. Launder and rinse in water to which you've added ½ cup white vinegar.

4. You may not have to iron creases caused by sitting. Go over the wrinkles in your pants or skirt with a washcloth or sponge moistened in warm water, then hang to dry.

Pesticide residue

1. The wax on supermarket apples, cucumbers, and bell peppers is not as harmful as the pesticide it often seals in. Washing in soapy water reduces some of the residue; peeling usually eliminates all of it, but it also reduces vitamins and other

nutrients. Your best bet is to shop at farmer's markets and roadside stands for unwaxed produce; then wash it well.

2. Fruits that have to be peeled (bananas, oranges, grapefruit, and the like) are safest, although it's possible that a tiny amount of pesticide may have been absorbed by the pulp. If you don't want to ingest even what is considered a harmless amount of pesticide, find a food co-op or market that shares your views and shop there (be aware, however, that "organically grown" produce may have a residue of organic pesticides that are just as toxic as chemical ones).

3. Because of stringent U.S. laws governing pesticide use, domestically grown produce is safer than imported fruits and vegetables.

Pet allergies

1. Allergic? Brush your pet outdoors or ask someone else to do it.

2. The animal should be wiped down daily with a damp towel, and its living quarters or box thoroughly cleaned. If you must do these things yourself, wear a dust mask and wash your hands afterward.

3. If possible, connect an air filter to your furnace or buy a portable unit for the pet's room. Make your bedroom a pet-free sanctuary.

4. Don't keep a cat's litter box in your bathroom (urine contains allergens); put a hooded box in an empty closet.

5. If your allergy to cats or dogs gets the best of you but you can't live without a pet, consider a bird, a fish tank, or a terrarium with frogs, toads, lizards, or snakes.

Pet odors

1. In many cases, regular bathing with a shampoo formulated to reduce odors will do the trick.

2. Tartar buildup can cause bad breath. Take your dog or cat to the vet for dental cleaning.

3. Ear infections, anal gland infections, and dermatitis can also pro-

duce bad odors; check with your vet.

4. The problem may be hormonal odor—designed by nature for sexual attraction. Altering the animal is the only solution.

5. If carpeting or upholstery smells after a pet "accident," sprinkle it with baking soda or cornmeal and let it sit for several hours. Brush off the excess, then vacuum. If that fails, try one of the new bacteria-enzyme solutions available at your vet's office or pet stores. But note that they can be used only on water-safe fabrics.

6. The sight of other cats in your yard may be causing your male to spray. Close the curtains when you go out or spot an interloper.

7. If your cat tends to spray the furniture, protect the upholstery with a finishing spray so that it won't absorb the odor. If he favors one spot, attach a matching piece of fabric that you can detach and clean. (Recurrent spraying may be a sign of a medical problem; check with your vet. She may also be able to suggest effective behavioral modification training.)

8. If possible, keep all pet paraphernalia—beds, toys, litter boxes—in rooms with hard floors and hard-surfaced furnishings. Upholstery and carpeting absorb odors.

9. A cat will pick up the scent of other animals when it stays at the vet's, and your other cats may attack it when it returns home. Put some kind of natural fragrance on all of your pets for several days.

Pewter

1. If you don't have pewter polish, use wood ashes moistened with water. Or rub with raw cabbage leaves and buff with a soft cloth.

2. Remove corrosion from old pewter with fine steel wool (No. 0) dipped in linseed, olive, or vegetable oil.

3. If pewter cookware doesn't come clean with soap and warm water, try a paste of denatured alcohol and whiting (a fine abrasive powder available in hardware stores).

Phobias

1. All phobias represent a fear of losing control. To conquer yours, don't flee from it or the situation that brings on an anxiety attack. Accept it and control it; watch it happen and rate its intensity on a scale of 1 to 10.

2. If you feel an attack coming on in a public place, try to act as though you're not anxious at all. Breathe normally but more slowly; focus intently on something specific, such as a window display or the directions printed on a package.

3. Develop a ritual that gives you the illusion of being in control. If you're afraid to fly, for example, always carry a good-luck charm and sit in the same seat on the plane.

4. Find a sympathetic person, preferably a recovered phobic, to help rid you of your phobia.

5. Get an audiotape designed to counter your fears through self-hypnosis or relaxation. Do relaxation exercises (see *Stress*, p.198).

Photo film

1. You can keep your film supply fresh in a sealed plastic bag in a refrigerator. Or put the bag in the freezer—you'll actually extend the film's expiration date by a few months. Let it warm to room temperature before using.

2. Take prepaid processing mailers with you on vacation. As film gets shot, mail it in for developing (don't drop it in outside mailboxes that get hot in the sun—heat damages film). Your pictures may be waiting when you get home. For easy cataloging and identification, code your return address labels in the upper corner: Y = Yellowstone, D = Disneyland, CO = Colorado, and so on.

3. If film gets jammed in your camera, you can rescue the pictures already on the roll by making a "darkroom" with a dark-colored jacket or coat. Put the garment on back-to-front so that your hands stick through the ends of the

sleeves. Then turn it inside out and lay it on a table in front of you without removing your hands. Place the camera inside and have someone pile clothing or pillows around the edges to further block the light. Open the camera, remove the film, and rewind it by hand.

Photo flash

1. For softer lighting (especially for portraits), make your own flash diffuser from translucent white plastic shopping bags or coffee can lids. Hold the plastic over the flash with tape or a rubber band; leave the flash sensor uncovered so that the automatic exposure will work. For manual operation, exposure correction is necessary; it's usually an increase of one f-stop, but run some tests to be sure.

2. Slide-type switches for flash units sometimes get nudged to *On* in a camera bag, resulting in drained batteries. Put a strip of electrician's tape over the switch. Then peel it partway back to use the flash.

Photographs

If your photos are fading, your album itself may be the culprit. Cheap albums have high-acid paper that eventually disintegrates and gives off harmful fumes; the effect is increased if plastic sleeves enclose the page. Moreover, the adhesive that holds the pictures to the page can also cause fading.

Keep important pictures in sealed polyethylene bags (don't use other kinds of plastic) with a small bag of moisture-absorbing silica gel (like the one that came packed with your new camera) in each. Store color prints in a dark place; light accelerates fading, as do heat and humidity. Protect slides in the same way.

Where you store pictures is important, too. Avoid attics (too hot) and basements (too damp). A closet in the middle of the house has the most stable and moderate temperature and humidity.

Pickpockets

1. Carry cash and credit cards in separate wallets and pockets. If possible, divide your cash between your wallet and pocket.

2. Keep your wallet in an inside coat pocket or a front pants pocket.

3. Keeping your hands in your pockets keeps a thief's hands out.

4. The smaller your handbag, the smaller target it is for a pickpocket. Grip the bag tightly, close to your body and in front of you; if it has a flap or outside pocket, keep that toward your body. An open-top handbag invites trouble.

5. Make a list of the identification numbers for your credit cards, driver's license, employee badge, check-cashing cards, and so on, as well as the numbers to call in case of theft. Keep one copy at home and another in a locked compartment at work.

6. Never flash money or jewelry in public—at a newsstand or bus stop, for example.

7. When shopping, be especially alert at store entrances, on escalators and elevators, in bargain or demonstration areas, or anywhere large crowds gather. Also be on the lookout at the checkout counter, where you might lay down your purse and parcels.

8. Before using a cash machine, take a good look around. If you see someone suspicious, go elsewhere. While using one, stand close so that no one knows the extent of your transaction. And when you leave, walk half a block or so in the wrong direction, then reverse yourself to see if you've been followed.

COMMON SCAMS

Pickpockets often work with accomplices who create distractions while the thief robs the "mark." Here are some common ruses:

1. "Watch out for pickpockets!" Be wary when you hear someone shout this; your natural response, to reach for your money, alerts the pickpocket to its location.

2. The accident: Perhaps someone's foot slips getting off the bus in front of you, or perhaps she drops packages in a crowded lobby; in either case, the momentary confusion is all the pickpocket needs.

3. The fight: An argument breaks out and people jostle each other getting out of the way; when it's all over, you're the loser.

4. "Oh, I'm sorry!" Someone rushing through an airport or train station bumps into you or spills food on you, then stops to help you up or brush you off; then he rushes off again—with your wallet.

Picnics

1. No cooler? Line your picnic basket or box with cold beverages and pack the food in the center. But remember that the cold cans are no substitute for ice; use this trick only if you have a short way to travel and your food is unlikely to spoil.

2. Oilcloth or a clean shower curtain makes a good picnic spread. Spills are easy to wipe up.

3. Carry your food to the picnic site in cardboard boxes; turn them upside down after removing the contents, line them up, and cover with your oilcloth or blanket. *Voilà!* A miniature table.

4. A good picnic table for the beach is a card table with the legs cut off.

5. To keep ants out of food, use dome-shaped screens to cover your plates between servings; they are available at hardware and kitchen stores. Or use foil or plastic wrap.

6. Concerned about food poisoning? Avoid egg salad, potato salad, fish, and pasta dishes, especially on hot days. Instead, make sandwiches out of lunch meats, canned meats, or cheese. And use mustard (a fairly good preservative because of its acid content), butter, or margarine instead of mayonnaise.

7. For greater protection against contamination, freeze the sandwiches. You can freeze puddings and yogurt, too—stir first to distribute the fruit. Keep your cooler filled with ice (replenish if necessary) and keep your traveling time short. (See also *Food safety,* p.88.)

8. Want some boiled corn or hot soup without a fire? Lift the hood of your car, start up the engine, and put a pot of water on top. It will boil fairly soon.

Picture frames

1. Make back-to-school frames for portraits of the kids. Mount each photo on stiff cardboard with double-stick tape, leaving a ¼-inch margin all around. For a frame, glue wooden pencils to the margins.

2. To make random frames look like a set, spray-paint them all one color or use coordinated mats.

3. Reinforce a wobbly frame with a staple gun; drive two staples across the back of each mitered joint.

4. For a substitute picture frame, try a shallow wicker basket with the center cut out.

Pictures

Anything that will hang fairly flat can take the place of a picture.

1. Quilts, rugs, and flags make attractive wall hangings. Tack or staple the top edge to a strip of lath or a lightweight batten. Or wrap it around a dowel and slip-stitch the back hem. Hang with picture wire, a decorative cord, or Velcro.

LOOK BEFORE YOU LEAP

Watching out for scams and swindles

To protect yourself from con artists, remember a simple rule: if something sounds too good to be true, it probably is. Here are some common come-ons.

☐ Lucky winner: A telephone caller informs you that you've won an expensive prize, but he needs your credit card number to "verify" your identity. On your next bill you discover that you've been charged several hundred dollars for the "free" prize.

☐ Vacation sensation: A letter offers you a free trip, but when you call for reservations, you learn that all the "free" days are booked. For a small fee, however, your trip can still be arranged. By the time the charges are totaled, you've taken an expensive vacation.

☐ Make a million: A "financial adviser" touts a surefire investment, often in commodities or precious metals. But once you put up your money, the cash vanishes, along with the counselor.

☐ Something for nothing: That's what the letter promises. But you must visit a new resort community to pick up your prize. When you arrive, you get a high-pressure sales pitch to buy a vacation home. What's more, the "free gift" often turns out to be far less valuable than promised.

2. Do you enjoy jigsaw puzzles? When you've finished one, slide it onto a glued sheet of ¼-inch plywood. Using two boards, force the pieces tightly together, first from the sides, then from the top and bottom. Cover it with wax paper, another piece of plywood, and some weights until the glue sets. Then varnish the surface or apply spray fixative before framing.

3. Let the room's decor suggest appropriate decorations. In an entryway, for example, you could use hats or canes. In a living room musical instruments, historic newspapers, or antique embroidery tools might work. In the dining room display doilies, baskets, or napkin rings. In the kitchen hang decorative pots, a spice rack, or a shelf of glass canning jars. In the TV room hang maps to locate places that are in the news. Add interest to a child's bedroom with colorful kites or a bookcase filled with dolls, model airplanes, or stuffed animals.

Pie crust

1. To prevent the edge of a pie crust from browning too quickly, fold narrow strips of aluminum foil over it. Another trick is to trim the edge off a disposable aluminum pie plate that's a little larger than the pie you're baking. Place this collar over your pie crust and bake.

2. The liquid in fruit pies can make the crust soggy. Prevent the problem by brushing the bottom crust with beaten egg white and letting it air-dry for 10 to 15 minutes before filling. Set the pie on a piping hot baking sheet in a preheated 400°F oven and bake for 10 minutes; then reduce the heat to the specified temperature and continue baking.

3. To keep pie crusts from baking unevenly, leave ample space between the pans and make sure they are at least 2 inches from the oven walls. Never block airflow by covering the baking rack with aluminum foil; instead, partially cover the rack below to catch any drips.

Preheat the oven to the correct temperature and resist the temptation to peek before baking time is up.

4. For flakier crusts, keep everything cold. Use ice water and well-chilled shortening for mixing. Chill the dough before rolling it out (a marble slab is best for rolling because it stays cool). Use two knives or a pastry blender to cut shortening into flour—not your warm fingers.

Pigeons

Get tough with pigeons. Forget noisemakers and inflatable cats, owls, or snakes (they don't work with these urban pests) and try one of these methods:

1. Stir a tablespoon of oleoresin capsicum (sold at pharmacies) into a quart of rubbing alcohol and paint ledges and other perches with it. It irritates the birds' feet.

2. Screen the birds out of wall recesses and window ledges with hardware cloth or plastic netting, sold at hardware and garden stores.

3. Run a strand of wire across a ledge at about half the height of a pigeon's breast. This will halve the amount of usable space, and the birds will hate it.

Pills

1. A pill that sticks in your throat may be caught in the tiny fleshy pocket between the upper throat and the larynx. To prevent this from happening, drink a full glass of wa-

---

Pigeons in peace and war

☐ Airmail service started long before the airplane. Some 2,500 years ago, Cyrus the Great of Persia used homing pigeons to carry messages. Guided by an uncanny ability to find their way (which a modern ornithologist called "one of the classic puzzles in all of biology"), these tiny feathered messengers have played important roles in history ever since.

☐ In the first Olympic games, in 776 B.C., a victorious athlete sent news of his triumph to his father by tying a purple ribbon to a pigeon's foot. Romans later used pigeons to relay the results of gladiatorial contests—and possibly to place bets before word of the results arrived by foot.

☐ Caesar conquered Gaul with the help of these small but sturdy avians, who can fly as far as 600 miles without food or water.

☐ During the World War I Battle of the Argonne Forest, a pigeon named Cher Ami lost an eye and a leg while carrying a message that saved an American unit from being fired on by its own troops. The intrepid bird was awarded the Distinguished Service Medal, and its body was later stuffed and displayed at the Smithsonian Institution in Washington, D.C.

☐ In World War II the pigeon G.I. Joe flew 20 miles in 20 minutes and saved a British battalion, despite being shot through the wing. This feathered hero won a medal from the lord mayor of London.

☐ The French Army still keeps a pigeon corps in case communications are disrupted by nuclear holocaust. The birds can deliver a message some 500 to 600 miles in a day. U.S. Postal Service—take note!

---

ter each time you swallow a pill.

2. Coat pills with butter or margarine to help them slip down more easily. Or crush them and mix into applesauce or ice cream.

3. If your child is having difficulty swallowing a pill, coat it with a bit of banana or embed it in a bite-size piece of the fruit. Or have her eat a few bites of banana immediately after taking the pill. (See also *Medication schedule*, p.133.)

Pimples

1. Clear up a sudden single blemish quickly with an over-the-counter benzoyl peroxide gel (5 percent).

2. To treat bigger breakouts, wash your face gently with warm water and a mild soap; rinse thoroughly and pat dry. Apply a benzoyl peroxide gel once a day (start with 2.5 percent). If after 2 weeks you see no improvement, apply it twice a day or use a 5 percent concentration.

3. Here's some single-pimple camouflage: use a little green eye shadow to neutralize the redness, then cover with foundation.

4. When shopping for new skin products, look for water- or glycerin-based moisturizers, sun lotions, and foundations that won't clog your pores. Check the labels for the worst oils: any compound with lanolin or isopropyl myristate. If you're in doubt, test a product by dabbing it on a clean brown paper bag or a piece of bond paper; wait 24 hours and check for an oily ring.

PREVENTION

If you are subject to skin blemishes, here are some hints:

1. Do not touch—or allow objects, such as the telephone, to touch—your face.

2. Avoid foods containing iodine (iodized salt, asparagus, kelp, and shellfish, for example) or hormones (beef, liver, and kidneys, for example). Watch out for the word *iodide* on multivitamin labels.

3. Prevent flare-ups by learning to relax (see *Stress*, p.198). Exercise also reduces stress, but take a shower soon afterward to prevent workout breakouts.

› Pipes

Did winter burst your water pipes? Don't thaw them until you've put temporary patches on the damaged sections.

1. For an emergency patch on drain lines, slit a rubber hose and slip it over the pipe. Cover it with a metal sleeve (you can make one by cutting a tin can open along its seam) and secure with pipe clamps or automobile hose clamps (or use two blocks of wood and a C-clamp).

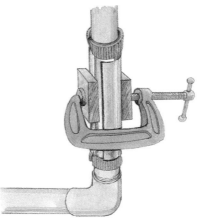

2. For a semipermanent patch, use a pipe repair clamp (available at plumbing supply stores); its inner rubber liner is covered by a metal sleeve that bolts around a pipe.

THAWING

After you've patched the broken spots, open the faucet nearest the frozen area. Then melt the ice.

1. If the pipe is metal, thaw it slowly, using a hair dryer, a heat lamp, a household iron, electric heating tape, or an electric heating pad. Always start at the open faucet and work toward the frozen area. Never let the pipe get too hot to touch—it may explode if the water inside boils. Keep looking for cracks and fix them as you go.

2. If the pipe is inside a wall, set a heat lamp 6 inches from the wall.

3. With plastic pipe, wrap towels or rags around the affected area and pour boiling water over them until the ice melts.

LEAKS

First, shut off the water supply (see *Water leaks*, p.226). Then clean and dry the pipe.

1. Patch a leaky joint in a waste pipe with two coats of epoxy. Let the first harden before applying the second; let the second harden before turning on the water.

2. Repair a pinhole leak in a waste pipe by wrapping plastic electrician's tape around the pipe, extending it about 6 inches on both sides of the hole.

3. For a larger leak in a waste pipe, cut a section of rubber hose and wrap it around the pipe; secure at 1-inch intervals with automobile hose clamps or heavy-duty wire.

Caution: Any repairs to leaky pipes are temporary. Replace all defective pipes, valves, and fittings as soon as possible.

Planing wood

1. If your plane isn't working as smoothly as it should, it may be that gummy wood resin has collected on the sole. Remove it with paint thinner. To keep the resin from collecting in the first place, apply paste wax regularly to the sole.

2. Always plane *with* the grain, not against it. To determine which way that is, look at the edge of the wood; the grain's pattern will be angled, not straight. "With the grain" means in the uphill direction of this pattern.

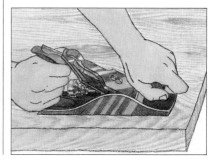

3. To keep from splintering the edge of your work, clamp a scrap board to it and plane them together.

4. To ensure a square edge, attach a guide to the sole of the plane. Choose a piece of wood at least as long as the plane and position it flush with the edge of the plane iron so that it forms a square that can ride along the face of the work. Clamp it in place or drill two holes through the sole and screw it on.

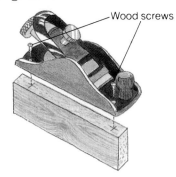

Wood screws

Plant markers

Instead of marking rows with the traditional empty seed packets on stakes, make far more durable labels out of plastic picnic knives. Use the plain white kind; their blades offer a good flat surface for inscriptions. Record plant variety and planting date with an indelible marker; then push the knife, handle downward, into the soil at the head of the row.

TOMATO-ROMA 4-15

Plants in winter

Snow, a good insulator, can help protect your plants from the repeated freezing and thawing that is winter's greatest threat. Pile it high on perennial beds, rock gardens, and berry patches to keep them at an even, moderate temperature and to shield them from killing winter winds. As the snow melts, it supplies not only moisture but also a little fertilizer in the form of nitrogen compounds and minerals that it picked up as it fell through the atmosphere. (See also *Frost*, p.92.)

Playground equipment

1. Children can jump and slide on a 12- x 15-foot sheet of 4-mil polyethylene wetted down with a garden hose. Spread it on a slope and leave the hose running at the top corner. Move the sheet every hour to prevent damage to your lawn.

2. A section from a big log makes a fine play horse. So does a section of large ceramic water pipe; children can crawl through it, too.

3. For maximum fun as well as good drainage, build a bottomless sandbox. Make a frame of 2 x 10's; reinforce the joints by driving stakes on both sides of each corner. Within the frame dig a pit 2 feet deep and line the sides with cedar siding, but leave the bottom uncovered. Fill with beach sand. Cover with plastic or canvas when not in use to keep pets and water out.

Pleats & creases

1. Before washing pleated clothes, turn them inside out; remove them before the final spin.

2. To drip-dry a garment quickly, roll it up lengthwise in a towel and squeeze out excess water from one end to the other; then hang to dry.

IRONING

1. To hold pleats in place while pressing them, put a sheet of coarse sandpaper beneath.

2. For sharp creases, turn pleats inside out and iron them over a damp cloth, moving from top to bottom. For longer-lasting pleats, lightly spray the edges with starch before ironing.

3. To prevent pleats underneath

from marking the fabric on top, insert strips of brown paper and fasten them under the folds with paper clips, being careful not to snag the fabric.

4. In a pinch, you can press pleats by keeping the garment under your mattress overnight. (Keep in mind that the sides of the garment will also be creased.)

5. To pleat curtains without ironing, fold them while they're wet and hang them from trouser hangers.

Plumb bob

1. Use a child's toy top as a plumb bob. Suspend it point down on a string; add weight by dropping a few metal washers over the string.

2. Or make a plumb bob from an empty frozen juice can. Mark dead center on the bottom; puncture it and insert a brad through the hole as your marker. Poke two holes exactly opposite each other at the top of the can, just under the rim, and form a short yoke with a piece of string. Fill the can with sand and suspend it from a string.

Plunger

Can't find your plunger? Try one of these remedies to unclog your sink:

1. Bail the water out, then pour lots of boiling water down the drain.

2. Cup your palm over the clogged drain and "squoosh" it up and down until the sink clears.

3. Shove a hose down the drain as far as it will go. Then attach it to a faucet and turn the water on full blast for just a second or two. Bail out the sink if necessary and repeat. (See also *Clogged drains*, p.48.)

Plywood

1. Store plywood flat to deter warping. If you must store it on edge, rest it on wood blocks so that the bottom edge won't absorb moisture.

2. To keep all edges from absorbing moisture, rub with a bar of paraffin or a candle.

3. When cutting plywood with a handsaw, place the finished side face up so that any splintering will occur on the bottom. If you're using a circular saw or saber saw, place the finished side face down.

4. To prevent splintering, cover the cutting line with masking tape, then mark the line on the tape.

5. Or score the cutting line with a utility knife—just deep enough to penetrate the top veneer. Then make the cut; any splinters will break off cleanly at the scored line.

6. Finish plywood edges with veneer tape. Or use adhesive plastic, such as Con-Tact.

7. Plywood occasionally blisters as the top veneer delaminates from the core layer. To fix this, slit the blister with a single-edge razor blade and squirt a little glue inside. Spread the glue under the blister with a toothpick. Then cover the area with wax paper and weight it down overnight with large books.

8. Don't toss out a sheet of plywood just because it's warped. First try moistening the concave side, then lay the sheet flat with weights on top. If that doesn't work, save it for small pieces.

PMS

1. If you're beset by premenstrual syndrome, or PMS, keep a symptoms diary for 2 to 3 months; record when your periods begin and end, how you feel (bloated? headachy?), and what foods you crave. Report your findings to your doctor.

2. To combat mood swings, irritability, and fatigue, eat a low-fat, high-carbohydrate diet (p.130). Include four helpings of whole-grain breads and cereals a day and plenty of leafy green vegetables and fresh fruits; replace fatty red meat with fish and poultry.

3. Instead of three large meals a day, eat a small meal every 3 hours to stabilize your blood sugar level. Cut out sugar and caffeine; they cause volatile blood sugar levels.

4. Even if you crave potato chips, pretzels, and ham, skip them to limit your intake of salt and prevent bloating; use herbs, lemon juice, and vinegar as seasoning (see *Low-sodium diet*, p.130).

5. Do aerobic exercise—take a brisk walk, dance, or jump rope—for 20 minutes every day or for 30 minutes four times a week.

Poisoned pet

Drooling, panting, vomiting, persistent diarrhea, burns on the mouth, lack of coordination, convulsions, and coma are all signs of poisoning.

1. Be prepared. Buy a pet book that lists common poisons and their antidotes, and also keep a supply of activated charcoal and hydrogen peroxide, both of which are available at drugstores.

2. Try to determine what your pet ingested. The container's label may list an antidote.

3. Call your vet immediately. If you can't reach him, call a veterinary hospital or a poison control center, which should be listed inside the front cover of your phone directory.

4. If you're unable to reach professional help and you don't know the antidote, give 2 teaspoons of activated charcoal mixed with water or milk. See a vet as soon as possible.

5. If the substance is corrosive (contains acids, alkalis, or petroleum distillates), do not induce vomiting. Give your pet milk, whipped egg whites, or water to dilute it.

6. If you're sure that the poison is noncorrosive and you need to induce vomiting, give your pet a dose of hydrogen peroxide (1 ounce per 20 pounds of body weight). Or use a solution of warm water and 1 teaspoon of salt.

7. Let your pet drink as much water as it wants. However, don't give it anything by mouth if it's unconscious or convulsing.

8. When you go to the vet, take the toxic substance and any packaging that has a label. If you don't know what the animal ingested, take any suspect material—loose pills, solvents, pesticides. If your pet has vomited, bring a sample.

Poison ivy, oak & sumac

Direct contact with these plants may cause a red, itchy, burning rash with small blisters that ooze if broken. Only rarely does a more severe reaction occur.

1. If you find you've been exposed, quickly rub the crushed leaves and stems of the orange- or yellow-flowered jewelweed, or touch-me-not, over the area. (Ironically, this plant often grows in the same habitat as poison ivy.) Its juices counteract

159

the irritant, but they won't cure a rash once it has begun.

2. As soon as possible, flood the affected area with rubbing alcohol to remove the plant's juices from the skin. If alcohol isn't available, use running water.

3. Rinse or wash all contaminated clothing and tools as well.

4. Once the rash appears, apply compresses soaked in cold water or Burow's solution (1:40 concentration) for 10 minutes three times a day. After air-drying (do not rub with a towel), soothe the rash with calamine lotion or over-the-counter hydrocortisone cream.

5. If the rash affects the face or genital area or if it spreads widely, seek medical treatment.

Poison ivy

Poison oak

Poison sumac

Considered a single species with variable forms, poison ivy and oak can be a vine, a shrub, or a small plant. Poison sumac, a shrub or small tree, thrives in wet areas.

ELIMINATION

1. Mix 3 pounds salt with 1 gallon soapy water; spray the solution on the plant's leaves and stems.

2. To pull out a few small shoots, slip your hand into a plastic bag; after uprooting the plant, carefully cover it with the bag. Close and toss into the trash.

3. Never burn these plants or their leaves; smoke carries the irritant.

› Poisons

The symptoms of oral poisoning are burns or stains around the mouth; abnormal breathing; foaming at the mouth; pain in the mouth, throat, or stomach; nausea; vomiting; diarrhea; convulsions; and shock.

Call a poison control center (look on the inside cover of your phone book) or an emergency medical service immediately. Be ready to tell the size, weight, and age of the victim; the name of the substance ingested; how much and when; and whether the person has vomited.

ON THE SKIN

If a dry chemical, such as an acid, gets on skin, brush it off thoroughly, then flood the exposed flesh with a gentle stream of cold water for at least 10 minutes. Remove all contaminated clothing, jewelry, and shoes and wash the skin beneath with soap and water. Go to a doctor or to an emergency room.

IN THE EYE

If a chemical or caustic agent gets into an eye, immediately flood it with cold water for 20 minutes. Run the water from the inside corner of the eye toward the outside, holding the lid open (see *Eyewinker*, p.76). If only one eye is affected, be careful not to let the water run into the other eye. If both eyes are affected, flood both by pouring water straight down onto the bridge of the nose. After washing, cover both eyes (even if only one is affected) with moist pads and get to an emergency room.

FOOD POISONING

Prolonged vomiting and diarrhea 2 to 18 hours after eating generally indicate food poisoning. The symptoms continue until the digestive system is empty, usually not longer than 24 hours after eating. The victim may feel ill for another 24 hours. If he develops a fever over 101°F, if vomiting and diarrhea persist for 48 hours, or if at any point he becomes unresponsive or has a seizure, seek medical help.

CARBON MONOXIDE

Headache, dizziness, nausea, and drowsiness are the first signs of carbon monoxide poisoning. Get yourself or the victim outside into fresh air, or open all doors and windows and turn off the source of the fumes. If the victim remains groggy, call an emergency medical service and request oxygen.

Popcorn

1. Popcorn won't pop? The kernels may have dried out. Soak them in water for about 5 minutes, then drain and try again. Or freeze them for a day or so.

2. In fact, the freezer is the ideal place to store popcorn—don't even thaw the kernels before putting them in the popper; the additional moisture will actually improve their performance.

3. Unbuttered popcorn has fewer calories than most snack foods. Try sprinkling it with crushed herbs or spices.

4. You can also keep calories down if you use a hot-air popper; it pops without oil.

Portaging

1. A canoe can be carried by one person more easily than by two, since no two people have exactly the same gait. When two people are sharing the job, the one with the shorter stride should take the lead.

2. Before a long portage, pad the center thwart with foam rubber to reduce shoulder discomfort. You can also wear your life jacket as extra padding.

3. To relieve your shoulders without setting the canoe down, rest its end in a tree crotch or on a stump or large rock for a few minutes.

4. To lift a canoe, roll it on its side with the interior facing away from you. Then lean over, grasp the center thwart with both hands (your stronger arm reaching farther), and lift the canoe onto your thighs while rolling it toward you. Straighten your knees and face forward as you

Gunwale

Thwart

raise the canoe above your shoulders, ducking your head in front of the thwart. Settle the canoe on your shoulders and firmly grasp the gunwales. Periodically shift the weight from shoulder to shoulder.
5. If you have a partner, have her lift one end of the canoe while you back into the carrying position.
6. To lower the canoe, reverse the lifting procedure.

Positive reinforcement

To get the response you want from people and pets, give them what they want: praise and rewards.
1. Compliment your child regularly for good behavior. Favorite foods, special activities (perhaps a trip to the movies or the video store), and inexpensive toys can all be used as rewards. Some parents use tokens, such as stars or stickers, that can be exchanged for a treat—for example, 20 tokens for a doll or a board game. You can even use positive reinforcement when your child misbehaves; after a tantrum, for example, praise him for being back in control.
2. Don't take your spouse for granted. If he or she has agreed to take on an unpleasant chore or done a special favor, show your appreciation: put a note under a pillow or in a briefcase, plan a special dinner,

or buy tickets to a play or a movie.
3. Try positive reinforcement in the form of a compliment, a cup of coffee, or a small gift to your mail carrier, coworkers, and friends.
4. Pavlov's dog wasn't the last animal to respond to conditioning. Praise, petting, and treats will teach your pet appropriate behavior.
5. Don't forget yourself! If you're having trouble finishing a project or sticking to an exercise program, promise yourself specific rewards (a new sweater, a dinner out) for goals met.

Postal Service substitutes

Looking for fast delivery at a reasonable price?
1. Shop all the services—United Parcel Service, Federal Express, and any others. Then do test runs to see which is best.
2. A private mailing service center can do the job for you (see *Mailing*, p.131). You can also have your mail sent directly to them.
3. Fax machines are the quickest way to transmit words and images around the world: 20 seconds via ordinary phone lines. Your easiest access to a fax machine is through a copy shop, which can send your material to another copy shop in the recipient's city. Most mailing services have fax machines, too.

Just be sure to include the recipient's telephone number on the item you're faxing so that she can be notified immediately.

Potato blight

If blight attacks your potato plants every year, delay planting. It's moisture on the leaves that promotes the destructive fungus—and since foliage dries more quickly in warm weather, later planting may help you beat the blight. Just be sure to select a variety, such as Homestead Hybrid, that thrives in summer weather. Blight-resistant varieties are available as well, with Kennebec leading the list. Cherokee, Alamo, and Sebago are among the several moderately resistant varieties that are well worth trying.

Potato skins

Slices of baked potato skins can be crisped in the oven for a healthful snack. Or try stuffing halved skins with cheese, meat, fish, or vegetables; if you wish, mix the filling with the potato pulp.
1. Plan ahead. Before you bake the potatoes, prick the skins only where you plan to cut them into slices or halves. Then there won't be extra holes for the filling to leak through.
2. When you scoop out the pulp with a spoon, leave a little next to

---

IN TIMES GONE BY

Getting the mail through

"Neither snow nor rain nor heat nor gloom of night stays these couriers from the swift completion of their appointed rounds."

Though many Americans think of that well-known quote as the motto of the U.S. Postal Service, it is not. But it does appear on the General Post Office in New York City, where it was inscribed by the building's architects, McKim, Mead, and White. The line was borrowed from the Greek historian Herodotus, who was describ-

ing the undaunted Persian messengers who delivered the mail on horseback.

Horses aren't the only animals man has enlisted for help to deliver the mail. During the 19th century cows hauled mail wagons in some German towns. In Texas, New Mexico, and Arizona, camels were used. In Russia and Scandinavia, reindeer pulled mail sleighs. The Belgian city of Liège even tried cats, but they proved to be unreliable.

the skin so that the skin won't burn or tear when recooked.

3. To store cooked potato skins (filled or not), freeze them on a cookie sheet. Then stack them in freezer bags, seal, and keep frozen until you're ready to use them.

Power outage

Given advance warning, you can do a lot to ease the problems of sudden power loss. Even without warning, an outage need not be a disaster for your household.

BEING PREPARED

1. Stock up on flashlights and batteries, including at least one high-power lantern. Have a transistor radio on hand.

2. Make sure you have plenty of candles (in hurricane-type holders to minimize the danger) and perhaps some oil lamps and a camp stove. Don't keep fuel in the lamps or stove, but know where to find it.

3. Keep two ½-gallon milk cartons filled with water in your freezer.

4. If you don't have a fireplace or wood stove, learn how to operate your oil or gas furnace manually. If you depend on electric heat, invest in a safe nonelectric heater and be sure it can be properly vented.

5. Maintain an emergency supply of canned and dry foods, as well as a few gallon jugs of fresh water. Replace them regularly.

6. If you cook with electricity, have a substitute stove on hand—a charcoal grill or wok, a camp stove, even canned heat—but make sure you have adequate ventilation whenever you use it.

WHEN AN OUTAGE OCCURS

1. If you receive advance warning of an outage, go grocery shopping and gas up the car. Clean your bathtub and fill it with fresh water. Even if you don't depend on an electric well pump, public service may be interrupted.

2. Fuel your oil lamps or lanterns; make sure they work properly. Place them, as well as candles in holders,

throughout the house, making sure they're in the open on noncombustible surfaces. For safety, place each on a "doily" of foil.

3. Move one of the ½-gallon cartons of ice from the freezer to the refrigerator; leave the other in the freezer. At the same time, remove enough food for immediate needs— fresh for today, frozen for tomorrow. Then leave both appliances closed for the duration.

4. Shut off all air conditioners, ovens, microwaves, computers, television sets, stereos, and so forth. Such devices could draw a sudden rush of excessive amperage when power is restored, tripping circuit breakers, blowing fuses, and possibly damaging circuitry.

Power shutoff

Know where to find the electric service panel in your house. It's usually in the basement, the garage, or a utility room, and it should be easily accessible. It will be equipped with a main disconnect switch that will take one of three forms, depending on the type of panel.

CIRCUIT BREAKER PANELS

These have no fuses and are the easiest to shut off. Simply open the panel door and flip the main disconnect switch at the top of the vertical row of breakers. It should be marked *Main.*

SCREW-IN OR CARTRIDGE FUSE BOX

If your service panel has Edison-type screw-in fuses, look for a lever. If you see it on the side of the panel cover, move it to the *Off* position. If no lever is there, open the panel door and trip the switch at the top of the fuse board.

PULLOUT FUSE BLOCKS

These are easily identified by their square shape and small front-side handles. To shut off the power, grasp the block handle and pull the entire block out of the panel. This procedure is safe so long as you keep your fingers out of the opening after the block has been removed. To restore power, just press the block back into its slot.

Pregnancy exercises

1. Because your joints are looser and your center of gravity is off, avoid strenuous activities such as high-impact aerobics, squash, and jumping rope.

2. Swimming, walking, and stationary bicycling are all good exercises if not done too strenuously. Check your pulse rate to be sure that it stays at a safe level (consult your doctor).

3. You can jog if you are accustomed to it, but watch out for back strain. Drink plenty of water, don't get overheated or overtired, and don't exceed the pulse rate suggested by your doctor.

4. Here's a pelvic tilt to strengthen abdominal and back muscles: Lie flat on your back, knees bent, feet comfortably apart. Rest your hands on your lower abdomen. Inhale; feel the floor with your lower back. As you exhale, gently pull in with your abdominal muscles, squeeze your buttocks, and raise your pelvis from the waist, keeping your upper back on the floor. Return to the flat position, inhale, and repeat. Work up to 10 repetitions. You can also do bent-leg curl-ups (see *Abdominal flab,* p.8).

5. After the fourth month add this

Cat-stretch exercise: Exhale as you slide forward from the starting position. Then gently press your chest down.

cat-stretch exercise: Kneel with your buttocks resting on your heels, your torso folded over your knees, your forehead resting on the floor, and your arms stretched out in front of you. Inhale. Then exhale, raising your hips high and sliding your chest and arms forward as you do so. Gently press your chest down, keeping your hips still. Resume the original position. Repeat five times.

6. This exercise to tone your pelvic muscles can be done as long as you're comfortable: Sit on the floor, legs crossed, back straight (against a wall if you like), and hands draped loosely over your knees. Close your eyes, relax your jaw, and tighten the vaginal muscles deep inside your pelvis. Hold for 5 seconds; release. Repeat 5 to 10 times. Do 30 to 40 repetitions per day.

7. Always do exercises that are specially designed for pregnant women. With your doctor's approval, you can do stretching and conditioning exercises throughout your pregnancy if you don't have complications. After the fourth month, change your position (from back to side, for example) every 10 minutes.

8. If you experience swelling in your legs and ankles due to water retention and increased weight, avoid high-heeled shoes and don't sit cross-legged. To counter the condition, do ankle circles: Lie on your back with your knees bent; raise one leg perpendicular to the floor, the knee slightly bent; rotate your ankle five times in each direction. Repeat with the other leg.

Pregnancy tests

There are two types of home test kits, and both use urine samples. One, which claims to work within a day of a missed menstrual period, turns a dipstick blue if a hormone secreted in the urine after conception is present. With the other, done 9 days after a missed period, a dark brown ring appears in the test tube if the results are positive. Although both are reliable, most doc-

tors prefer the former test because its results are easier to interpret.

Both tests can be affected by heat, cold, vibrations, and foreign materials. So, whichever test you choose, repeat it a few days later.

Price stickers

Can't get a price sticker off? First, peel away as much paper as you can. Next, soften the residue. On glass apply vinegar, hair spray, or nail polish remover; on plastic or painted surfaces, a hot rag or hair dryer; on fruits and vegetables, vegetable oil. Scrape off the softened residue with a dull knife, a coin, a letter opener, or your fingernail.

Privacy

Don't feel guilty if you regularly require some time alone to relax and refresh yourself.

1. Keep hours that are slightly different from those of the rest of your family: rise earlier to recharge your energy and clear your head, or stay up a little later at night.

2. Invest in an answering machine and turn it on to screen calls even when you're at home.

3. Set aside your own private area in the house as a sanctuary.

4. Arrange a "Do not disturb" signal—a sign on the door, a special hat on your head—to let your family know you're in a private mode.

5. Go for a long walk. Or if you prefer to be alone in a crowd, go to a concert, a movie, or a museum.

6. Learn to respect other people's privacy as well. Knock before opening a door; never open others' mail, read their diaries, or listen in on their phone conversations. (See also *Quiet time,* p.167.)

Product failure

1. Avoid the problem by shopping carefully. Many products fail because people purchase the wrong model or have unreasonable expectations. (A weed whacker light enough for a child to use may not have the power to trim heavy un-

derbrush.) Before making a purchase, read the operating instructions and warranty to make sure the item will do what you want. You won't be able to return it if it did its job, even though it was not the job you had in mind.

2. If you have a legitimate complaint and get no satisfaction from the store where you bought the product, write to the president of the company that manufactured it. Enclose a copy of the sales receipt and warranty, if you have them, along with a letter detailing the problem and identifying the store. As a last resort, write to the local Better Business Bureau; enclose a copy of the letter you sent to the manufacturer. (See also *Guarantees & warranties,* p.101; *Sales slips,* p.177; *Small claims court,* p.189.)

Profanity

1. Since "Darn!" and "Gosh!" hardly make the grade as satisfying substitutes for profanity, rack your brain for creative euphemisms. Like W. C. Fields, who coined "Godfrey Daniel!" you can probably come up with a curse that amuses rather than offends.

2. If you feel that you must occasionally use real profanity to underscore something you say, remember that your expletive will carry more weight if it's the only one in a given diatribe; repeated use makes the word lose its power.

3. If you're talking with someone whose profanity offends you and there's no easy escape, try facial language first—look mildly shocked or troubled. If that doesn't work, laughingly say, "I don't know if my ears can take that language!" If *that* doesn't work, ask him directly to curb his tongue.

4. If your child uses profanity, explain to him why he shouldn't. Tell him that swear words are usually a crutch for not-so-smart people who can't think of a more precise word to express what they mean. If he continues to use it, discipline him.

Don't play cute games with him, like charging him a quarter every time he swears; that's only likely to make the problem more of an issue than it should be.

Property taxes

You can get your taxes reduced if you can prove that the assessment on your property is exorbitant.

1. Go to the assessor's office and get a copy of your record. It will list the factors used to arrive at the valuation of your home.

2. Look for similar houses in your neighborhood (don't go too far afield; market values can vary widely from one area to another); get copies of their assessments and compare.

3. If you find that your assessment is indeed out of line, find out the procedure in your community for presenting your case at the next assessment review hearing.

4. Prepare your case well. Most people think their taxes are too high. You must present clear, factual evidence either that your assessment is higher than that of comparable homes in your neighborhood or that the valuation was based on inaccurate information—the wrong square footage, for example, or an extra bathroom.

Prostate enlargement

After a man nears his 50's, the walnut-size prostate gland around his urethra may begin to grow, sometimes enlarging to the size of a lemon or lime and blocking the urinary tract. Symptoms include a frequent urge to urinate and a diminished stream of urine. If your doctor suggests surgery, ask him about such alternatives as hormones, radiation, or balloon dilatation.

Pruning shears

1. Your pruning shears will cut more efficiently if you clean the blades after each use with a toothbrush dipped in kerosene, then wipe with a light lubricating oil.

2. To restore the cutting edge, dis-assemble the shears by unscrewing the pivot nut and removing the pivot bolt. Sharpen by stroking a medium-grit oilstone along the cutting edge of the blade. Move from the pivot end to the tip, matching the original bevel as closely as possible (never hone the inside face of the blade, except to remove the burr left by sharpening). Repeat the process with a fine-grit stone.

3. Use bonsai shears for pruning roses and other small ornamentals. The unusual configuration of their blades leaves a concave cut that heals more quickly than the flat cut of regular shears.

Bonsai shears

Public speaking

Are you afraid to give a speech? Most people are. Here are some ways to cope with the anxiety:

1. Be well prepared but don't try to memorize your speech. Whether you read it (10 double-spaced typewritten pages equal about 20 minutes of speech) or make notes and speak extemporaneously, rehearse your speech once or twice.

2. Grab the audience's attention by opening with a joke, a moving personal story, or a relevant anecdote. Don't make it too controversial; if you antagonize your audience right away, you may never win them back.

3. Organize your speech by asking yourself, "If I could leave my audience with one main idea, what would it be?" Then focus on that idea, supporting it with no more than four secondary points. All of your facts and anecdotes should relate to at least one of these points.

4. When you arrive at the room, make sure that the sound system is working properly.

5. Take advantage of your pumping adrenaline. Use the energy and excitement to help project your ideas forcefully. But calm yourself with a few deep breaths before you start speaking.

6. Oddly enough, if you acknowledge your nervousness to the audience, there's a good chance that you'll defuse it.

7. Don't worry about being boring. Focus instead on the importance of what you're saying. You're there to communicate ideas—not to be judged on your performance.

8. Watch your posture. If you stand straight, you'll automatically feel and look more self-assured.

9. A comforting fact—most audiences report that they notice little anxiety in speakers. So don't compound your anxiety by thinking everyone can see your trembling legs.

Puffiness

1. If your hands are puffy, hold them over your head for a couple of minutes; repeat at least three or four times a day. Elevate swollen feet for a minimum of 15 minutes.

2. If too much sun causes your lips to swell, use a sunblock (SPF 15) specifically designed for lips.

AROUND THE EYES

1. Since moisturizers plump up the skin, apply them sparingly around your eyes or use a specially formulated eye cream.

2. The culprit may be water retention (p.227); cut down on salt and eat more bananas and grapefruit, which are natural diuretics. Raise the head of your bed or sleep on two pillows to keep your head elevated.

3. Apply soothing compresses of cold milk, borage tea, or a mild astringent.

4. Throw away your frosted eyeshadow—it accentuates puffiness.

Pulley

1. Make your own clothesline pulleys by slipping short lengths of vinyl pipe over smaller steel pipes or wooden dowels or even large spikes driven into trees or posts.

2. The same pipe-over-pipe trick works as a weight-hoisting pulley. In this case, the inside pipe must be strong, smooth, and solidly mounted—between rafters in a garage, for example. Drop your rope over the outside pipe, attach a strong hook, and haul away.

Pumpkin

1. It's easier to peel a pumpkin *after* it's been cooked. Cut the pumpkin into large cubes; cover and steam over boiling water for about 7 minutes. Then peel the rind.

2. Easier still, especially if you're going to mash the pulp, is to bake a whole pumpkin on a baking sheet (1½ hours at 350°F for one that's 12 inches in diameter). Then cut off the top and scoop out the seeds.

3. Save pumpkin seeds for a healthful, iron-rich snack. Wash the fibers off, spread the seeds on a cookie sheet, and toast in a preheated oven at 325°F for 15 to 20 minutes.

4. To microwave the seeds, spread half a cup of them in a ring around the bottom of a 9-inch glass ovenware pie plate. Microwave on *High*, uncovered, for 2½ to 3½ minutes.

Punch

A 10d nail can serve as a punch for most sheet metal work, although some jobs may call for different sizes. A nail set will also work, but only if you want a large hole.

Punching bag

1. For a lightweight bag, put a soccer ball or volleyball in the waist section of a pair of nylon pantyhose and knot the waist. Using the legs, tie it to a hook or beam.

2. For a heavy bag, stuff a duffel or heavy-duty laundry bag with rags or laundry and hang it securely from a beam or firmly mounted ceiling hook. Or use a tightly rolled foam mattress.

Quackery

1. Be wary of exaggerated claims— a guaranteed, fast, easy, painless, miracle cure that sounds too good to be true probably is.

2. Question claims that a product is ahead of its time or that the medical establishment is trying to suppress it or persecute its promoters. Think twice about traveling to a foreign country to spend a lot of money for a "cure."

3. Suspect unspecified "scientific studies" and testimonials by "satisfied users."

4. Don't assume that an advertisement in a reputable publication is an endorsement; most publications don't screen their ads.

5. If you have questions about dubious drugs and mail-order devices, call your doctor, the foundation or society for a particular disease, the local consumer protection agency, the state attorney general's office, or the Food and Drug Administration.

6. On your first visit to a doctor, inspect his office walls. A licensed doctor will display a diploma from an accredited medical school and certification by the American Medical Association, the state medical society, and other professional groups. Check unfamiliar or suspicious credentials.

IN TIMES GONE BY

Quacks who got rich quick

Quackery, noted the French philosopher Voltaire, has existed since the first knave met the first fool. Here are some knaves who met enough fools to get rich:

☐ In the late 1700's Elisha Perkins, a Connecticut doctor, made a fortune selling his "metallic tractors" at $25 a pair—many times their cost. These metal rods were supposed to "draw out" disease as they were moved across the ailing part of the body.

☐ A 19th-century Florida physician named Bosso concocted a recipe to prevent yellow fever. He named the wondrous potion Bosso's Blessing for Mankind and did well for a while. But sales must have dropped off dramatically when Bosso himself contracted the disease and died.

☐ During the 1920's Frank Rollins, a court reporter, marketed B & M External Remedy in Boston as a cure for tuberculosis, rheumatic fever, pneumonia, and just about everything else. Originally intended as a liniment for horses, it consisted mainly of ammonia, turpentine, and raw eggs.

☐ Also in the 1920's John Romulus Brinkley convinced thousands of impotent men that he could restore their potency by implanting in them the sex glands of male goats. "Goat Gland Brinkley," as he came to be called, later ran for governor of Kansas.

☐ Dinshah Ghadiali actually formed an institute based on his invention, the spectochrome. The gadget, which he claimed healed afflictions by using "attuned colored waves," required the patient to be naked while facing north. He was convicted of fraud in 1947.

Quack grass

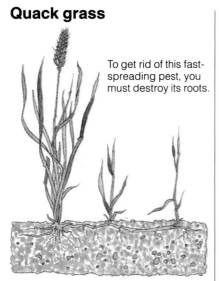

To get rid of this fast-spreading pest, you must destroy its roots.

1. Pulling or digging up this obnoxious weed will probably only help it spread, since every piece of rootstock or stem left behind will develop into a whole new plant. Instead, mop a systemic herbicide such as glyphosate directly onto the leaves with a paintbrush or a sponge tied to a stick. (Don't spray—you may damage nearby plants.) The poison travels directly to the roots. Spring, when the plants are at least 8 inches tall, is the best time to apply it.
2. Quack grass won't bother tomato plants; their roots secrete a substance that is toxic to the weed.

Quarantining pets

1. Many countries (including Australia, England, Ireland, and Israel) require that an animal be quarantined for 2 to 6 months before entering. This experience can be very stressful to a pet. If your pet is old or sickly, consult a vet to see if it can withstand quarantine. If at all possible, leave the animal at home with a trusted friend.
2. If you must take your pet with you, contact the foreign consulate well in advance to reserve a space in a quarantine facility. Try to arrange for one that will be near you and allows visits. Find out whom to contact in case problems arise.
3. If allowed, provide your pet with

a toy and something that has familiar scents on it—a blanket or a pillowcase stuffed with old clothing from each family member.
4. When your pet is released, take it to a vet for a checkup. Find out what it has been eating. An abrupt change in food could make the animal sick—the vet may suggest a transitional diet.

Quarrels

If you're about to quarrel with a loved one, try one of these releases:
1. Stop and count how many deep breaths you can take in 3 minutes.
2. Call someone—it doesn't matter who it is so long as you trust her—and talk about your feelings. The point is not to involve an outsider in the quarrel but to give yourself a release and perhaps a fresh perspective.
3. Escape to the bathroom for at least 15 minutes with an apple and a good book. Chewing often relieves tension, and so does reading.
4. Write down everything you're feeling. Try to express your frustration on paper. If you find it difficult to write, try singing, painting, or molding clay.
5. If you still want to fight, beat up a pillow, go for a fast walk, or engage in some other vigorous physical activity. (See also *Children's quarrels*, p.45.)

Quartz

If you come upon natural quartz crystals (Arkansas has the richest deposits in the United States), they'll probably be covered with a layer of yellow iron oxide. To see the real beauty inside, you can soak the crystals for a few days in oxalic acid or, in a pinch, rust remover.

Questionnaires

Many questionnaires ask for more information than you're legally required to give. Here's what you do and don't have to answer:
1. On warranty cards you don't have to answer the questions about

income, age, and housing. This is just market research. In fact, you don't even have to send in the card—all you need for your guarantee is proof of purchase (see *Guarantees & warranties*, p.101).
2. If you don't want unsolicited telephone calls, don't include your telephone number.
3. Telephone surveys? Again, this is market research. If you want to spend your time answering questions for free, go ahead. But you don't have to give any information at all.
4. When you apply for a mortgage, a scholarship, credit, insurance, or a bank loan, be prepared to answer fully all questions about your health and finances. If there's a personal question you're not comfortable answering, consult a lawyer.
5. On job applications you must answer questions about past employment truthfully. But you don't have to answer questions about race, religion, sex, or national origin. Nor must you answer personal questions that don't relate to your ability to perform the job. These include marital status or future marriage plans, number of children, age or date of birth, weight, handicaps (unless they would affect job performance), the person with whom you live, home ownership or rental status, and outstanding debts. If you feel that your refusal to answer such questions has cost you the job, you can file a complaint with the Federal Equal Employment Opportunity Commission.

Quicksand

1. If you ever get caught in quicksand, don't panic. Fall onto your back as gently as you can, spread your arms, and try to float. If you're carrying a walking stick, maneuver it under you as you fall.
2. Try very slowly to get your feet back to the surface; if necessary, dig them out with your hands. (You may have to sacrifice your shoes.)
3. Grab any nearby vegetation on

solid ground or "swim" a very slow backstroke to safety. Don't hurry— quick, jerky movements will suck you down deeper; if you need to rest, lie still with your arms and legs spread wide.

Quiet time

1. Noise pollution, once mostly an urban problem, has become a major source of stress in modern life, no matter where you live. To help protect your health and sanity, set aside an hour or so—early evening is probably best—when there will be no electronic amplification allowed in the house: no stereo, no TV, no radio, no video games, no robots, no toy fire engines. Unplug the phone, turn off the bell, or install an answering machine to intercept the outside world. You and your family will feel better for it, and perhaps you'll learn to talk to one another.

2. For some quiet time on the way to work, walk or get off the bus several blocks early. Or take an entertaining book; you'll be less aware of noise if you're absorbed. If you drive, stop for a quiet cup of coffee before going in to work.

3. To discourage an overly friendly seatmate on public transportation, carry a cassette player and put on the headphones; no one will know

if you haven't turned on the tape. Or just wear antinoise muffs. (See also *Noise*, p.143; *Stress*, p.198.)

Quitting a job

Be very careful not to alienate your boss when you leave. You may need his reference down the road.

1. Give at least 2 weeks notice—3 or 4 if you have been at the company for some years. If you're in the middle of an important project, ask your new boss if you can stay until it's finished. Whether she says yes or no, she'll certainly respect your commitment to your old employer.

2. Your letter of resignation is part of your permanent personnel file. Keep it simple and factual. If you're quitting because you are unhappy, don't put your gripes in the letter.

3. Offer to train your replacement. If a new person has not been hired, leave a list of things she should know. Make copies for your boss and your successor.

4. Tell your most important contacts you're leaving and give them the name of your replacement.

Quiz shows

To get on your favorite quiz show, keep an eye out for ads for potential contestants or call the local TV station and ask for the address and phone number of the show's production company.

Potential contestants are usually screened in Los Angeles or New York. (The big shows sometimes hold auditions in other parts of the country.) The first screening often involves a written test. The second may feature a mock version of the game; while playing it, smile a lot and be energetic. You may be asked to deliver a brief autobiographical speech; be outgoing and as humorous as possible, maintain eye contact with the tester, and be sure to mention any unusual hobby, interest, or experience that would set you apart from other contestants.

Once selected, watch the show as often as you can, get the rules down

pat, and figure out a strategy. Then practice: sit under a bright lamp to simulate the studio lights and ask your family to take pictures of you while you rehearse so that you'll get over being camera shy.

Within weeks or months you may be invited to return to Los Angeles or New York at your own expense. On taping day be prepared to be confined to the studio for 10 to 12 hours under strict security. Be sure to bring a change of neckties and accessories—usually several shows are taped on one day to be televised on consecutive days.

If you lose, you'll get a compensatory gift—but you'll be out the cost of your trip. If you win, you must immediately report anything over $600 to the IRS and your state's tax agency; you can deduct the cost of the trip, however. Anything you win—whether cash or merchandise—is taxable income.

Gifts are valued at the manufacturer's suggested retail price; if you can prove you could buy something for less, you can use that figure on your tax return. Donating merchandise to charity will lower the tax bill, provided you itemize your deductions; you may also be able to sell some prizes to obtain the tax money, but you'll have to advertise them as "used."

Quotation marks

Here's how to use these helpful punctuation marks:

1. When you write, use quotation marks to enclose a cited speaker's or writer's exact words; use them to set off the titles of short works, such as stories, magazine articles, poems, and songs, as well as words and phrases used in a special way (irony and jargon).

2. For a quotation within a quotation, use single quotation marks. For example: John said, "I wonder who wrote 'To be great is to be misunderstood.' Rachel thinks it was Emerson." If the first and second quotations end together, put a sin-

gle quotation mark, then double quotation marks: John said, "I wonder who wrote 'To be great is to be misunderstood.' " Do just the reverse—double followed by single quotation marks—if the first and second quotations begin together.
3. Where should other punctuation go? A period or comma should always be placed *inside* quotation marks. When you use an exclamation point or question mark, however, it's a different matter; if the punctuation is part of the quoted matter, it goes inside; otherwise it should follow the quotation marks.
4. If a quotation has more than one paragraph, begin each paragraph with quotation marks but use them to close only the final one.

R

Rabbits

1. Fool rabbits into thinking that one of their mortal enemies is around: spray your garden soil with fox urine, available from sporting goods stores.
2. Or make a homemade rabbit repellent in your blender. Purée two peeled cloves of garlic, three hot peppers, and 1½ cups water for 2 minutes. Let the mixture steep for 24 hours, strain, and add 1 tablespoon liquid detergent. Dilute with 7 cups water and spray the plants that attract rabbits.
3. Put up a 2-foot-high fence of 1½-inch chicken wire. Plant the posts deeply and make sure the bottom of the wire extends at least 6 inches below the soil line.
4. Surround your garden with a double row of onions; rabbits hate the smell and won't cross the rows.

Raccoons

1. Hang an electric bug zapper above the corn patch just as harvest time approaches. The sizzling,

popping, and flashing will scare raccoons away for a while. But don't leave it hanging there too long; once raccoons get used to the sound of the zapper, they may be *attracted* by the dead bugs.
2. Or you can place a radio in the garden to repel the masked marauders; it, too, will probably work for a while. But tune it to an all-news station. Music doesn't bother them; constant chatter does.
3. Interplant your corn with pumpkins and squash. Raccooons have tender feet and hate to step onto the prickly foliage.
4. Circle the garden with an 8-inch band of lime when the corn is just beginning to ripen; it burns their feet a little. Replenish the lime after every rainfall.
5. To fence raccoons out, use ½-inch chicken wire. Staple the mesh tightly to 3-foot fence posts at ground level but let it project 12 to 15 inches above the tops of the posts. Or simply add such a 12- to 15-inch overhang to your existing fence. When raccoons try to scale it, they'll pull the overhang down on top of themselves.

Radiator hose

If a leaky radiator hose is causing your car to lose coolant and its engine to overheat, you can usually fix the leak temporarily so that you can drive to a service station.
1. Let the engine cool thoroughly. The coolant is well above the normal 212°F boiling point, and opening the radiator cap prematurely will release a scalding geyser.
2. When the radiator cap is cool to the touch (20 to 30 minutes), place a thick cloth over it and turn counterclockwise until you hit a stop—about one-quarter turn—then let go. This will release the remaining pressure, and the cloth will catch any steam and hot coolant.
3. If the leak is at the hose connection, retightening the clamp may do the job temporarily. If looseness was the problem, you're home free.

4. If not, look for the leak in the hose and patch it, using duct or electrician's tape or even tied rags.

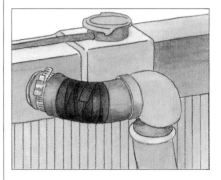

5. Then start the engine and fill the radiator with plain water. Replace the radiator cap, but tighten it only to the first stop so that pressure won't build up.
6. Put the heater on *High* (see *Overheated engine,* p.147) and drive at moderate speed to a garage or service station.

REPLACING A HOSE

You may find that the clamp is "frozen" to the hose (or the hose to the hose neck) by scale or rust. Don't try to pry it loose—you could damage the connection at either end, causing a leak.
1. Put some penetrating oil on the clamp.
2. If it's a squeeze- or spring-type clamp, squeeze and wiggle it with pliers. It should come loose.
3. For a screw-type clamp, insert the tip of a screwdriver beneath the clamp and gently work it around.
4. If the hose is stuck to the hose neck, don't pull. Twist it left to right until it releases. If that doesn't work, cut the hose off beyond the hose neck, slit the remaining hose lengthwise, and peel it off.

Radiators

1. Hammerlike knocking in a hot-water radiator means that water is trapped. Use a spirit level to make sure the radiator is tilted slightly toward the return pipe. If it's not, put a shim under the free end so

that gravity can solve the problem.
2. Gurgling is a sign of trapped air. Purge it by opening the bleeder valve with a key or slotted screwdriver; have a container handy to catch the water that will spurt out once the air is purged. Then close the valve.

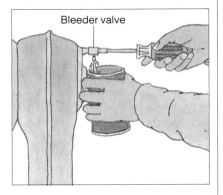

Bleeder valve

3. If gurgling persists or if the system constantly needs to be purged of air, it means that the expansion tank needs draining or that there is a leak in the system. Call for service.
4. If the air vent in a steam radiator gets clogged, stick a needle or stiff wire into its opening. If that doesn't work, apply vinegar to the opening with an eye dropper. If the vent stays clogged, buy a new one.
5. If the valve handle won't turn, use a strap wrench or improvise one from a belt (p.289).

Radioactivity

If you're worried about radioactivity in your area, plant purple spiderworts. The stamen hairs on these sensitive wildflowers change from blue to pink when exposed to as little as 150 millirems of radiation.

Radio antenna

1. Antenna broken? If there is a hollow end protruding, you can make a substitute from a wire coat hanger. Using pliers, disengage the coiled joint beneath the hook. Then cut off the hook, straighten the hanger, and jam the coiled end into the antenna hole.
2. If the reception on your car ra-

dio is getting weak or ceases but the exterior portion of the antenna is not broken, it's one of three problems: a defective antenna, a bad antenna connection, or a broken radio. To find out which, use this test: Pull the antenna cable plug out of the jack in the back of the receiver. (If it's not accessible from under the dash, remove the molding, take out some of the screws, and pull the radio forward.) Then insert a straightened hanger or a 2- to 3-foot piece of wire through the center of the antenna hole and lean it against the outer edge of the hole. If the radio begins to pick up AM stations, however poorly, the problem is in the antenna, its mounting, or the connection. If there's no improvement, the problem is the radio.

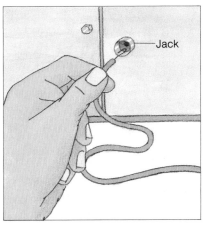

Jack

Radon testing

1. When using a radon detector, put it in the lowest accessible place in your house, preferably the basement or crawl space. Before testing, close all windows, doors, and vents in the test area for 24 hours.
2. Before you hire a company to test radon levels, contact your state health department or environmental protection department and ask for recommendations.
3. Before you begin making any radical changes in your home, perform repeated tests. Radon levels can vary widely according to weather and seasonal temperatures.

Raincoats

1. In an emergency you can transform a plastic garbage bag into a poncho. Cut a hole in the bottom for your head and openings in the sides for your arms. Use a smaller plastic bag as a hood.
2. Remove spots from slickers with baking soda or scouring powder; rub on with a moistened cloth and rinse well.
3. To make a water-repellent finish last longer, hand-wash rainwear instead of dry-cleaning it. You'll know it's time to renew the finish when even a light rain soaks in (usually after a couple of dry cleanings).

Rain spatters

Rainy day? Carry a few paper towels so that you can moisten them and wipe those dirty splotches off stockings and pant legs before they have a chance to dry. Or wear dark patterned stockings. Keep extra stockings at work for days when the damage is beyond remedy.

Raised-bed planting

If your raised vegetable beds are infested with slugs and snails, it may be because you've enclosed them with boards or stones—ideal havens for the pests. Build the beds the Chinese way instead.
1. Using stakes and string, divide your garden into 5-foot-wide beds separated by 2-foot-wide paths.
2. Turn or rototill the soil inside the beds to the depth of about a foot, removing all stones and roots. Work in plenty of compost, manure, peat, and sand so that the beds rise above the surrounding ground.
3. Rake the beds flat and smooth and shape their sides. Do *not* frame them with boards or stones. Dig narrow trenches between them and the paths to catch water runoff.
4. You can remove the string from around the beds, but leave the stakes in place; they'll keep the hose from dragging across your plants as you water.
5. Unlike a conventional garden,

these raised beds won't need annual tilling. Just add a layer of compost and, if necessary, a dose of lime every autumn and turn it under with a spading fork.

Raises

Do you want a raise but don't know how to ask?

1. Try to determine what your job is worth. Ask friends in similar positions if they're willing to swap information in confidence. Check the want ads and consult any professional organizations you belong to. Make allowances for factors that affect salary: your geographic location, your education (an advanced degree may be worth more money), the number of people you supervise, and the budget for which you are responsible (salary is usually commensurate with responsibility).

2. Lay the groundwork. Routinely give your supervisor any memos or documents that demonstrate your achievements. Pass on any compliments you get (but don't overdo it).

3. Always ask for slightly more money than you think you can get. You'll allow the boss to feel she's saved money by giving you slightly less, and you'll probably come out about where you want. You may even get what you ask for.

4. Time your request wisely. Obviously your chances are better after you've scored some kind of success or when the company is doing well; certainly not when it's doing poorly. (Although, surprisingly, many people have gotten big raises during shake-ups, when a company was anxious to keep things stabilized and didn't want to lose valuable employees.) If a performance review shows that your work has improved, take it as an opportunity to ask for extra compensation.

5. Sometimes it's best to take on new responsibilities or projects and wait to ask for a raise (and perhaps a new title) until after you've performed successfully.

6. If a raise is less than you want,

ask for a review in 6 months. If possible, set goals that, when met, will entitle you to the increase.

Rakes

1. When your bamboo rake dries out and gets brittle, soak it overnight in a pan of soapy water. If you live in an arid climate, repeat the process every 2 or 3 months.

2. To fight rust on your steel rake and make it easier to clean, spray-paint it with metal paint. Spray on an undercoat of metal primer first.

3. A little wire mesh over the head of a garden rake keeps stones from bouncing over the top; tack or staple it about a foot up the handle.

4. As a substitute for a lawn rake, secure wire mesh to a push broom. Or use your power mower (see *Lawns*, p.123).

Ranges

1. If the reflector bowls on your electric range have turned brown or black, soak them in hot sudsy water; if they're porcelain-coated, soak in a solution of baking soda and water. Then scrub with a mild abrasive or soapy steel-wool pads.

2. To prevent this problem, clean up spills and spatters as soon as the range top has cooled. Use a spatter shield for messy cooking such as frying or cover unused units with overturned disposable pie plates.

3. Hobs—solid cast-iron electric heating elements—require that the bases of all pots and pans be perfectly flat. To check, rest a ruler across the bottom of an overturned pan. If you can see light at any point, the bottom isn't flat and

cooking will be slow and uneven.

4. To prevent cast-iron hobs from rusting, clean them after every use, wipe dry, then heat on *Medium* for 2 minutes. Season periodically with unsalted cooking oil.

5. If the flame is uneven on a gas burner, some of the ports may be clogged. Clean the holes with a straightened paper clip, a pin, or a pipe cleaner—do not use anything that could break off and get lodged in the port, such as a toothpick.

❯Rape

If you're ever raped, do not touch anything, change your clothes, or wash. Call the police, someone you trust—a friend, family member, doctor—or a rape crisis center and ask to be taken to a hospital. The hospital staff will provide medical assistance and collect evidence that will support legal action if you choose to take it.

If you are threatened with rape and there are people nearby, screaming or running may improve your chances of escape. Other than that, it's impossible to make specific recommendations. A woman must assess her own situation—each offender's reactions will be different. (See also *Mugging*, p.139.)

Rats

1. Bait several traps but don't set them. Just leave them out for a few days, replenishing the bait as needed, until the rats in a basement or barn get used to them as a food source. Then set them.

2. Secure garbage cans so that they don't leak or lose their lids when pushed over. Keep them on a rack 1 to 1½ feet off the ground and at least 2 feet away from walls.

3. Plug cracks and holes in outside walls with wads of steel wool, then permanently seal with hardware cloth or heavy-gauge sheet metal.

4. Here's an old-fashioned barrel trap for getting rid of a barn full of rats: Fill a barrel or oil drum halfway with water; stretch heavy, stiff

paper over the top of the open barrel and secure with staples or duct tape. Place the barrel next to a table or some other object that rats can climb on. Spread food on the paper for 4 or 5 nights running until the rats expect a nightly meal. Then cut an *X* in the paper with a razor blade. The unsuspecting rats will fall through the paper into the barrel and drown.

Caution: Keep barn cats or other climbing pets penned on the night you set your trap.

Razor bumps & nicks

1. To prevent them, shower before shaving or steam your face over a basin of hot running water before applying shaving cream. Shave in the same direction the hair grows, using a light touch and long strokes; avoid going over the same area more than twice.

2. Rinse a nick with cold water, then press hard. If the bleeding persists, apply a styptic pencil or hydrogen peroxide on a cotton swab. (In a pinch, use lemon juice or a baking soda paste.) For deep nicks apply an antibiotic ointment or cream.

3. To loosen ingrown hairs that can cause bumps, clean your face with a loofah sponge. If you have just one or two such hairs, pluck them out with a sterilized needle or tweezers; if you have more, consider using a depilatory.

4. No shaving cream? Use soap or baby oil instead.

Reaching things

1. Can't reach something on a high shelf? Use barbecue tongs.

2. Push and pull objects out of tight spots with a yardstick, radiator brush, or straightened wire coat hanger. Place sticky tape or gum on the end to pick up light items.

3. If a regular match won't reach the wick in a hurricane lamp, light a strand of uncooked spaghetti.

Reading

1. If you haven't enough time for the reading you'd like to do, scan the first and last paragraphs of an article or the first and last pages of a book's first chapter to decide if it's worth your while to read what's in between.

2. Set time limits on your reading material and sort it accordingly: a high-priority pile for newspapers and news magazines that become useless quickly; a medium-priority pile for material that should be read for your job or your investments; a low-priority pile for material that has no time frame, such as cookbooks, novels, or travel magazines.

3. Don't try to read everything—sometimes it's enough to know that you have an article on file in case you need specific information in the future.

4. Make an appointment with yourself to do your reading; if necessary, get up a half hour earlier, go to bed a half hour later, or schedule reading for your quiet time (p. 167).

5. If you're looking for something other than a best-seller, ask your librarian for advice; he may ask about your interests or refer you to one of several guides to the classics.

6. Don't throw away all those paperback books; set up an exchange at work. If you find you don't like a book you borrowed, there's no need to feel guilty—you haven't spent a dime; just return it for another.

7. If your child resists "good" books, consult a children's librarian or a sympathetic, well-informed bookseller. She may be able to interest him in books you don't know about.

SCANNING FOR SPEED

1. Let your eyes follow your hand as it brushes down each page. Practice focusing on a line as a whole rather than one word at a time.

2. Run your fingertip or a bookmark under every line as you read it, to focus your attention and prevent your mind from wandering.

3. As you scan, mark the passages you'd like to return to with pencil checks or a highlighter. Or jot down the page numbers in the back of the book.

Recordkeeping

Is tax season a nightmare? If you keep good records, you'll find everything in order when you need it.

1. Find out what you can deduct; check with a CPA or tax lawyer.

2. Then buy a spiral-bound calendar. Every night jot down any tax-deductible travel, entertainment, and meal expenditures; note the time, date, and place and the nature of the business conducted. If you spend $25 or more, you'll also need the receipt.

3. Keep all your receipts in 8 x 10 envelopes organized by category: medical expenses, office supplies, and so forth.

4. Pay all your bills by check. When you balance your bank statement, place the canceled checks for deductible expenses in the appropriate envelopes.

5. Keep a separate envelope for records of any stock sales or other capital gains. (See also *Income tax returns,* p.114.)

References

1. If you didn't get along well with your former boss, ask someone else with whom you've worked for a reference—preferably someone with a managerial title.

2. If you know that a former employer had reservations about certain aspects of your work, tell him that you've improved in those areas. He might be willing to think again and give you a recommenda-

tion on the basis of your strengths.

3. If you've never held a paid job, ask former teachers or supervisors on internships or volunteer work.

4. To avoid alienating a reference, always call first and ask if she would be willing to recommend you. Follow up with a thank-you note.

Refinishing

1. To darken bare wood, soak a plug of chewing tobacco in a pint of ammonia for a week. Strain the liquid through an old pair of pantyhose before mopping it onto wood.

2. You can turn bare oak from light brown to driftwood gray by rubbing it with household ammonia; the tannic acid in the wood reacts with the solution to change the color permanently.

3. Never apply shellac in high humidity. The finish clouds as vapor condenses on the surface.

4. To disguise an ugly furniture scratch, rub bits of pecans or Brazil nuts into the wood.

Refrigerators

1. If your refrigerator or freezer conks out, check for a loose plug, a tripped circuit breaker or blown fuse, or a temperature control accidentally turned off. If these check out, test the outlet with a lamp. If it

lights, the problem is in the appliance or its cord; if not, the outlet or house wiring is at fault. Until you can get it fixed, plug the unit into another outlet, but be sure any extension cord you use is rated the same amperage as the unit.

2. Water on the floor? Perhaps the drain tray is placed incorrectly or is cracked and needs replacing. Or maybe the drain tube is clogged; if so, flush hot water through it with a meat baster.

COOLING PROBLEMS

1. Make sure the temperature control is turned on. If it is, change it to a colder setting; wait 24 hours before adjusting it again.

2. Check the condenser coils at the base or the back of the refrigerator; if dust has collected on them, the

The iceman cameth

The almost mythical iceman was a familiar neighborhood figure during the early part of this century. On hot summer days, as his horse-drawn wagon came dripping down the street, he was trailed by children who knew him by name and were often treated to slivers of ice.

Sporting a rubber apron aglisten with ice crystals, the iceman stopped at house after house, where cards or slates in the windows told him how much to deliver.

This muscular man carried ice into each home with tongs, and if someone ordered a heavy block—say, 75 or 100 pounds—he slung it over his back. Sometimes a block was so big that its sides had to be chipped off so that it would fit inside the tin-lined icebox.

The electric refrigerator, introduced in 1916, eventually put the iceman out of business. But his spirit lives on in the memory of all those who still fondly refer to their refrigerators as "the icebox."

unit won't cool properly. Clean with your vacuum's crevice or brush tool.
3. Check to see that the door is sealed tightly. If the gasket is torn, dried out, or obviously damaged, replace it. If it's in good condition, the refrigerator is probably improperly positioned on the floor; adjust the leveling legs or rollers.

Reservations

1. Avoid spending time on hold: call for reservations early in the morning or late at night.
2. Hotels aren't legally bound to honor reservations, but in case of overbooking, they must obtain comparable lodging for you elsewhere, and they must pay for your transportation there. To protect yourself when making reservations, always get a confirmation number and write it down. Find out if the hotel belongs to the Assured Reservations Program; if so, give your credit card number when you book your room, and your reservation will be guaranteed—for a room category but not for a specific room.
3. Ask about the cancellation policy. You can be charged for late cancellations.
4. If you've booked a room for a week and paid only a night's deposit, it's all right to leave after the first night if you're not satisfied.

IN A RESTAURANT

1. To avoid getting a bad table, find out the number of a table you like and ask for it specifically when you phone for a reservation. If you haven't been to the restaurant, specify your preferences and hope for the best.
2. If your table isn't ready when you arrive, you may get it faster by becoming a slight pest; rather than going to the bar to wait, stay put and keep asking when your table will be ready.
3. If you're not happy with your table, ask for a better one. If the restaurant is crowded, it helps to tip the maître d'.

Restaurants

1. If you dine out frequently, join a discount dining program. Enroll through your company or through a participating restaurant.
2. When dining out with the kids, consider a buffet. It will probably be cheaper than a full-course meal and will be more likely to please a variety of tastes and appetites.
3. If a waiter spills food or a beverage on you, you're entitled to be reimbursed for any dry-cleaning expenses; be sure to get the name of the waiter and one witness.
4. To get a waiter's attention, wave your hand or call "Waiter!" *Never* snap your fingers.
5. If a waiter is taking too long to bring the check, as soon as he looks in your direction, stand up as though you are going to leave.
6. If you complain to the waiter about something and you're still not satisfied, insist on speaking to the manager or owner.

Retirement

Are you considering early retirement? Experts estimate that you'll need 70 to 80 percent of your current income. Here's how to figure your potential assets. (See also *Ready for Retirement?*, p.246.)
1. Check with your company's pension plan administrator to find out how early retirement would affect your pension.
2. Also check with the Social Security Administration. Their rules are constantly being adjusted; however, at this writing you will receive full benefits if you retire at age 65. Benefits are reduced 20 percent if you retire at 62, $13\frac{1}{3}$ percent at 63, and $6\frac{2}{3}$ percent at 64. (Don't forget that the money you would have earned between the ages of 62 and 65 won't be calculated in determining your benefits, lowering them slightly more.)
3. See how your investments could be rearranged to provide income instead of long-term growth.
4. Figure out how much money you

would have if you started spending your savings and selling off your capital assets. To decide at what rate, look at a life-expectancy table. If you're 65 and expect to live 15 more years, you should plan to sell or spend $\frac{1}{15}$ of your capital per year; if you estimate 25 more years, plan to sell off $\frac{1}{25}$.
5. Add in the money you would save if you kept just enough life insurance to allow your survivors to maintain their standard of living and pay estate taxes, any leftover debts, and your funeral expenses.
6. Now add it all up. Could you live comfortably on the results?

DELAYING RETIREMENT

1. If you delay retirement, your Social Security benefits will be raised $\frac{1}{4}$ of 1 percent for each month, or 3 percent per year, between the ages of 65 and 70. (Most companies cannot force you to retire before 70.)
2. If you want to start collecting benefits between the ages of 65 and 70 and continue working, there is a limit to the amount of money you can make and still collect full benefits. When you subtract increased income taxes, it may not be profitable. However, after age 70, you can make as much money as you want without affecting your benefits.

Rice

1. To keep rice from clumping, add a few drops of cooking oil or a teaspoon of butter or margarine to the cooking water.
2. For snowy white rice, add a few drops of lemon juice or vinegar to the cooking water.
3. If your rice turns out like wallpaper paste, use it in a casserole, in soup, or to stuff peppers. Try again, using less water. Fluff the rice gently with a fork before serving.

Roof gardens

Before starting a garden on the roof of your apartment house, consult your landlord and offer to share the cost of an architect's or engineer's inspection to make sure the roof can take the extra weight. Here's how to keep the weight down:

1. Lay a thick sheet of plastic on the roof to protect it from seepage and plant roots. Then construct a box frame of 2 x 4's on edge and set it on top of the plastic. Reinforce the corners with angle irons.

2. Fill the frame with organic matter—grass clippings and finely shredded corncobs are suitable; vermiculite or perlite will serve in a pinch. (Beware of peat moss, which becomes very heavy when wet.)

3. Water thoroughly and add 5 pounds of 10-10-10 fertilizer per 100 square feet. Water again lightly, then set out plants and sow seeds. (Herbs, onions, radishes, lettuce, collards, kale, green beans, peas, strawberries, peppers, and dwarf varieties of tomatoes will all thrive in this garden in the sky.)

4. Keep the surface of the "soil" evenly moist until germination, then increase watering to 2 gallons daily. Feed with a soluble fertilizer every fourth or fifth watering.

Roof leaks

1. To catch water dripping into an attic from a leaky roof, nail a small wood block to the bottom of the rafter nearest the leak. Then place a bucket under the block. As rain-

water runs along the rafter, the block will interrupt its flow and redirect it into the bucket.

2. In an emergency, protect a damaged roof with a plastic drop cloth. Lay the plastic over the damaged spot, tucking its top edge *under* a course of shingles above that spot. Tack the plastic down or weight it with bricks or sandbags.

3. You can patch a small damaged spot with sheet metal or an asphalt shingle. Spread some roofing cement on the underside of the patching material, then force the patch under the shingle course directly above the leak and press it in place.

Roofs

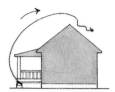

1. Here's how to give yourself secure footing when working on a steep roof. Secure one end of a long rope to a sturdy, stationary object, such as a tree or porch, on the far side of the house. (If you use a car bumper, make sure the keys are in *your* pocket!) Then tie the other end to a weight, such as a large bolt, and toss it over the roof ridge. Lay a ladder on the far side of the house, from the roof ridge to the gutter. Thread the rope between the top two rungs and tie it to the bottom rung.

2. When working on any pitched

roof, use a safety line. Secure a rope as described above and tie the loose end around your waist, allowing enough slack to let you work freely but not so much that you could fall over the roof's edge.

3. For traction when working on a roof, wear soft rubber-soled shoes or sneakers.

4. To move about the roof most safely, crawl on your hands and knees.

5. During winter the best time to work on a roof is on a sunny afternoon. In the morning the roof may be covered with a thin layer of ice. **Caution:** Never work on a roof on a windy day, in rain or snow, or when a thunderstorm threatens. Stay clear of overhead power lines.

Roommates

1. Looking for a roommate? When you interview a stranger, take along a friend whose judgment you trust. Have a talk about smoking, neatness, TV, music, and your social activities to make sure your habits are compatible.

2. When you move in with a new roommate, work out rules for bathroom times, overnight guests, shut-off times for the TV and stereo, division of expenses and housekeeping chores, and refrigerator use.

3. Separate telephones and answering machines will probably do more than anything to ensure that things run smoothly.

4. If you live with more than one person, post weekly maintenance duties for each. The refrigerator door is a good place for the list.

5. Develop a civilized method of airing problems and don't let annoyances fester. Humor can go a long way toward working things out.

Rose propagation

To start a new rosebush from your favorite variety, snip a perfect rose along with a foot of stem that has at least five leaf clusters. Set the stem immediately in water and leave it there for an hour or longer (up to 2 days if you want to enjoy the bloom).

Prepare a bed in a sheltered, shaded spot. Dig to a depth of 18 inches and add 1 part builder's sand to each part soil.

To prepare the cutting for rooting, snip off the blossom and cut off the top of the stem at an angle ¼ inch above a bud. Cut the bottom of the stem off square ¼ inch below the bottom leaf cluster. Strip off all but the topmost leaves, then dust the bottom of the cutting with powdered rooting hormone for softwood (available at most garden centers).

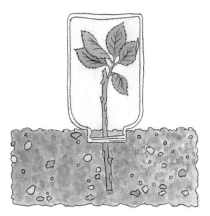

Plant this almost-bare stick in the prepared soil to a point just below the second leaf scar from the top. Firm the soil around the cut-ting, water well, and cover with an inverted fruit jar. If water droplets gather inside the jar, prop it on stones so that air can enter.

The appearance of a *second* new leaf means that the cutting has started to root. Let it grow undisturbed for 8 or 9 months before transplanting; tip the jar up or remove it entirely in warm weather.

Ruler

If you're caught without a ruler, use a penny to make small measurements; it's exactly ¾ inch across. Here are some other common items you can use:

1. U.S. currency is 6⅛ inches long by 2⅝ inches wide

2. A standard paper clip is 1¼ inches long; a giant clip, 1⅞ inches.

3. Nails: The shank of a 2d nail is 1 inch long; that of a 6d nail is 2 inches; a 10d nail is 3 inches; a 20d nail is 4 inches; a 40d nail is 5 inches; and a 60d nail is 6 inches. (See also *Measuring,* p.132.)

Runaways

1. Little runaways, newly independent first- and second-graders, usually head for the woods behind the house or to a friend's house, and they generally make it home by sup-pertime or bedtime. In fact, you may miss the drama of the occasion and think they're just visiting.

2. An older runaway presents a more serious problem. You, the parent, may have little or no warning, especially if communication has gotten shut off during the turbulent early teen years. Watch for such signs of discontent as loss of interest in schoolwork, withdrawal, depression, and unexplained bursts of anger. And pay special attention to your teenager when there is a major change in the family: death, remarriage, impending divorce, or a move to another town.

3. To make sure the police will take you seriously, do not emphasize that you think your teenager is a runaway—state only that he is missing. If the child has left home of his own choice, the police may not mobilize the same resources as they would for a kidnapping, and by the time they finally act, clues that could help them find your child may have grown cold.

4. A number of nationwide organizations maintain hot lines offering help; through them parents and children can exchange messages and arrange transportation home. Among them are Covenant House; Child Find; Adam Walsh Child Resources Center; and the National Center for Missing and Exploited Children (see *800 numbers,* p.71).

Rust

The best defense against rust is prevention. The second best: treatment as soon as spots appear.

1. To protect your metal workshop equipment or any metals exposed to the elements, apply two coats of clean synthetic resin mixed with lamp black or any colored pigment. Black asphaltum varnish is also very good.

2. Rub small patches of rust with a typewriter eraser. It removes spots and won't scratch the surface.

3. To keep iron and cast-iron garden furniture rust-free, scrape or

---

DID YOU KNOW . . . ?

Roses in myth and history

☐ Myths about roses abounded in ancient Greece and Rome. One was that roses were originally white until Venus, the goddess of love, pricked her foot on a rose thorn as she hurried to save her imperiled lover. A drop of her sacred blood fell on the bush's flower, dying it forever red.

☐ The rose gave its name to the cycle of prayer known as the rosary, literally "a rose garden." Rose petals may actually have been joined together to form the first rosary "beads."

☐ The 15th-century conflict between the English royal houses of York and Lancaster is known as the Wars of the Roses because the men of York supposedly wore a white rose as their badge while those of Lancaster wore a red one. But, in fact, Lancaster did not adopt the red rose as its badge until the wars were over.

☐ In 1986 Congress adopted the rose as the official flower of the United States, despite Senator Everett Dirksen's long campaign for the marigold.

use a wire brush to get down to the bare metal. Paint with a rust-preventative primer followed by a premium top coat. Renew the top coat where needed each spring. Pay particular attention to any metal that is in contact with plants or soil.

CARS

1. Most new cars have extensive rustproofing. Beware if your dealer tries to sell you more. It's rarely needed.

2. To protect your car from road salt, winterize it. Wash the underbody with a hose to remove road film. Then check the underbody box sections and clean out all mud or leaves with a stiff wire brush. Finally, flush the box sections with water. Repeat the underbody clean-up at winter's end.

3. Place the car on a lift or safety stand and make sure that all drain holes are clear; they're on the underside of each door and in the frame or unit body. Also, to keep water out, make sure access holes placed in the sides of doors and in rocker panels are firmly plugged.

4. Chips and scratches let moisture under the paint surface. Fix them immediately. Scrape away loose paint and rust with the corner of a single-edge razor blade, then wipe the spot with rust converter (a product that combines a rust inhibitor with a primer, thus eliminating a step). Wash with a mild detergent, rinse well, and dry thoroughly. Then, using an artist's brush, apply the primer that is recommended for your car's model and color. Let dry, then apply the correct paint. Don't be worried if the color doesn't match exactly— that's a minor problem compared to rust damage.

Rust stains

Nonwashable garments must be dry-cleaned, but washable fabrics with rust stains can be treated in one of several ways:

1. Rub a paste of salt and vinegar into the stain; let stand for 30 minutes, then launder as usual.

2. Soak the rust stain in lemon juice, then dry the garment in the sun to bleach out; rinse thoroughly.

3. Work a paste of cream of tartar and hot water into the stain; let set, then launder as usual.

4. Boil five stalks of rhubarb (cut into ½-inch pieces) in 1 cup of water until soft; pour the hot liquid over the stain. Launder as usual.

Safe-deposit boxes

1. Keep all valuable or hard-to-replace documents in a safe-deposit box: birth, adoption, marriage, divorce, and death certificates; real estate deeds; military papers; car titles; stock, bond, or savings certificates; a *copy* of your will; a household inventory; and all insurance policies except those for life insurance. Keep an up-to-date list of the box's contents at home.

2. If you lose one of the keys to your box, the bank will provide a new one for a small fee. If you lose both keys, the bank must have the lock drilled; they'll charge a hefty fee.

3. Check your homeowners policy to see if it covers the contents of your safe-deposit box, or ask the bank if it offers insurance.

4. For more privacy, space, and accessibility, consider renting a vault in a private safe-deposit company. It will also cost more.

5. When a box renter dies, many states mandate that the box be sealed until officially inventoried. If this is true in your state, keep all documents that your family will need immediate access to—your will, cemetery plot deed, and life insurance policy—in a safe place at home or in your lawyer's vault. (See also *Getting Organized*, p.238; *Valuables*, p.221.)

Safes

When looking for a place to stash cash, jewelry, or other small valuables, avoid the obvious.

1. Put them in a frozen vegetable box in the freezer or in a cream carton or the cavity of a green pepper in the refrigerator. (Avoid the foods thieves are likely to sample, such as ice cream or fruit.)

2. Wrap them in plastic and store in a vacuum cleaner bag.

3. Hide them in a hollowed-out hardcover book (p.343).

4. Keep them in detergent boxes stashed under the sink or in the laundry room.

Safety gates

1. If you don't like the look and inconvenience of safety gates in your home, hang Dutch doors between rooms instead; close the bottom section whenever you want to restrict your toddler's travels.

2. You can substitute a screen door for a solid door in your child's room; just make sure that the lock is on the outside. That way you'll be able to see what the child is up to, even though her getaway will be thoroughly blocked.

3. When a friend brings a crawler or toddler to visit your normally child-free home, you can improvise temporary safety gates from mattresses or tables turned on their sides. Or for a longer visit, hinge window screens or pieces of plywood to the doorjambs; equip the unhinged side with a hook and eye.

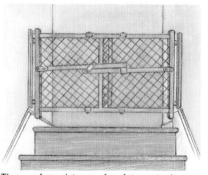

The preferred type of safety gate has a straight top edge and rigid mesh screen.

Saffron

Dried marigolds

Substitute marigolds from your garden for expensive saffron. They have a similar pungent flavor and the same yellow color. Let the flower heads air-dry or dry them in a microwave (p.87), then grind the petals into a fine powder with a mortar and pestle. Use in pastries, fish stews, and the classic Spanish *paella*, adding just a pinch more than you would of saffron.

Sagging porch

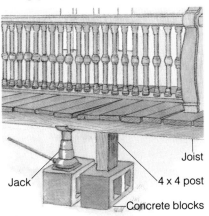

Joist

Jack

4 x 4 post

Concrete blocks

With the help of a car jack, you can install a temporary brace until you have a chance to make proper repairs on a sagging porch. Place the jack on a concrete block and hook it securely under the header joist. Make sure the jack remains plumb as you raise the porch until the floor is level (stand clear in case the jack slips). Then cut a 4 x 4 post to fit between the bottom of the joist and another concrete block. Put the post in place and remove the jack.

Sales slips

Lost the sales slip for merchandise you want to return?

1. If the price sticker is intact, it will sometimes be accepted in lieu of a receipt.

2. If you have a charge account, most stores will let you return the item in exchange for credit.

3. Stores where you don't have a charge account will usually give a credit voucher for the amount of your purchase.

4. Exchanging a gift can be a problem, but if you keep the container and packing material, they might help you convince the store manager to refund the purchase price.

Salt substitutes

Try this blend of herbs: 1 teaspoon garlic powder and 1 teaspoon each dried basil, oregano, and powdered lemon rind. Use a mortar and pestle to grind them together; transfer to a saltshaker. Add a few grains of rice to keep the mixture dry.

For a spicier blend, use 1 teaspoon each ground cloves, black pepper, and crushed coriander seed, plus 2 teaspoons paprika and 1 tablespoon rosemary.

Sanding

1. Use fine sandpaper to roughen finished wood before applying new enamel or varnish. Sand between coats, too.

2. To sand chair rungs and table legs, cut a strip of sandpaper and apply masking tape to the back as reinforcement. Then pull the paper back and forth around the rung, shoeshine-style.

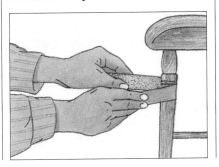

3. At carvings and turnings, fold the sandpaper and fit the folded edge into the curve so that the grit smooths both faces at the same time. Use fine steel wool (No. 0) to get all the way into deep crevices.

4. When you sand, wear rubber gloves or fingercots—the kind designed for office use—to protect your skin and keep oily fingerprints off the wood.

5. Make a tack rag to wipe sanded wood clean: Dip cheesecloth in water, wring it out, dip it in turpentine, and shake it dry. Then drip varnish onto the cloth from a brush, fold it, and knead until the varnish is evenly spread. Store the rag in a covered jar or in plastic wrap. If it dries out, moisten it with water and turpentine.

Satellite dish

A black mesh or smoked chrome satellite dish is less of an eyesore than the original white fiberglass kind. But it's still worth hiding or dressing up somehow.

1. Paint the dish green—perhaps even in a camouflage pattern—to help it blend in with the landscape.

2. Screen it with plants or a hedge. But make sure that no foliage arches in front of the dish; it will interfere with reception.

3. Turn it into a giant happy face, landscape scene, or abstract painting—or have an artist do it for you. Or, if you're bold enough, paint it to look like a huge dinner plate and have a sculptor create a giant fork or spoon to go with it.

4. To keep adventurous children from climbing on and possibly damaging your dish, plant thorny, low-growing shrubs beneath it. Barberry or a well-trimmed hedge of roses should do the job.

Saving money

1. Treat your savings as a necessity like food and clothing. Aim to build a readily available emergency cash reserve—enough to cover such essentials as groceries, mortgage

177

and car payments, and utility bills for at least 3 months.

2. Instead of relying on your self-discipline, enroll in your company's payroll savings plan or arrange with your bank to automatically transfer a specific amount every month from your checking account to an interest-bearing account.

3. If you get 26 paychecks a year, use 24 of them—2 a month—for the family budget; put the 2 extra paychecks in your savings account.

4. Or use the "loose money" system. At the end of each day, put all your loose change in a jar; once a week, deposit the coins in your savings account.

5. Try not to supervise your children's saving and spending too strictly. Letting them learn lessons with small amounts will save them expensive lessons later in life.

Savings bonds

Are you looking for a safe, worry-free investment vehicle? If you don't need to get your hands on the money for a few years, consider savings bonds. Sold at most financial institutions and through payroll savings plans, Series EE U.S. Savings Bonds are available in denominations of $50 to $10,000; you pay half the face value and collect full value at maturity. (There is an annual limit of $30,000 face value per person.)

Keep a record of the serial numbers, issue dates, names, and addresses on all savings bonds. If your bonds are lost, stolen, damaged, or destroyed, write for replacement to the Bureau of the Public Debt, Parkersburg, WV 26106-1328. Be sure to list the above information, as well as your Social Security or employer identification number.

INTEREST

1. Series EE Bonds held 5 years or longer earn interest based on current U.S. Treasury market rates, with a guaranteed minimum. Any bonds redeemed during the first 5

years earn interest on a fixed, graduated scale. Interest accrues until you redeem the bond; it is not subject to state or local income taxes.

2. Bonds earn interest from the first of the month; you can delay purchase until late in the month, however, and not lose interest.

3. For the first 2½ years, interest is credited monthly; twice a year thereafter. Don't cash in just before a crediting date—you could lose up to 6 months' interest.

4. New interest rates take effect each May and November. Call your bank or 1-800-US BONDS for the current rates (in metropolitan Washington, D.C., call USA-8888).

Scale insects

Get rid of a scale infestation on your houseplants by dabbing the insects, which look like tiny brown army helmets, with rubbing alcohol on a cotton swab. (Mealybugs, scales' woolly white relatives, suc-

cumb to the same treatment.) Then set the plants in the sink and wash gently with a spray of tepid water to eliminate any newly hatched insects that may have escaped your notice.

Scissors

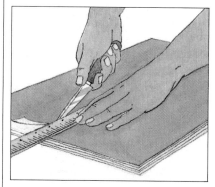

1. No scissors at hand? Hold a metal-edge ruler firmly on the paper and draw a sharp knife or single-edge razor blade along it. Be sure to have padding underneath to protect the tabletop.

2. Never cut paper with your barber scissors or dressmaking shears; it dulls the keen edge needed for cutting hair or fabric.

3. If your scissors are binding, tighten the screw.

Scratches in wood

1. To keep lamps and other table-top accessories from scratching furniture, line the bottom with felt, cork, or another soft material; attach it with rubber cement, double-stick tape, or white glue.

2. A scratch on bare wood can be rubbed out with medium sandpaper. Sand *with* the grain, not across it.

3. To hide scratches on furniture, use a crayon that matches the color of the finish.

4. To hide scratches and fill nicks in shellac and other clear finishes, use clear nail polish.

5. For shallow scratches on a wood floor, buff the area lightly with extremely fine (No. 0000) steel wool, rubbing with the grain. Then apply two coats of paste wax; buff each coat with a soft cloth. Rewax three or four times a year to prevent future scratches.

Screen door spring

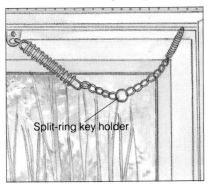

Split-ring key holder

Don't throw out a broken spring. You can probably repair it.

1. If the break is in the snubber (the length of chain between the spring and the door), replace the broken link with a split-ring key holder or a bit of wire coat hanger.

2. If the problem is a broken brack-

et on the jamb or the door, replace it with a large screw eye. After screwing it in, pry it open slightly, insert the end of the spring or chain, and pinch the eye shut with pliers.

3. If the mounting bracket is pulled out, don't try to drive the screws back into the old holes. Reposition the bracket and drive larger screws into a new spot.

4. In a pinch, replace an irreparably broken spring with a large rubber band or piece of elastic until you can get a new one.

Screens

1. If you don't want passersby looking in, apply a coat of white paint thinned with turpentine to your screens. You can still see out.

2. To prevent moisture from rotting wood frames, remove the molding and apply caulking compound to the rabbet. Replace the molding and remove any excess caulking.

3. To keep metal frames shiny, apply a coat of clear lacquer.

4. Fix a dented screen by pushing the strands back in place with a pencil, an awl, a knitting needle, a chopstick, or an ice pick.

5. If one or two strands are broken, seal the hole with several coats of shellac or clear nail polish; let each coat dry before applying the next.

6. To repair a large hole, cut a patch out of the same type of screening 1 inch wider and longer than the hole. Unweave each edge for about ½ inch, then bend the wires at right angles to the patch. Push

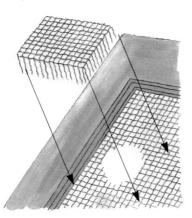

the bent strands into the screen holes and fold them toward the center. Sew the patch in place with nylon thread; seal with a few coats of shellac or clear nail polish.

7. Mend a long rip by sewing it with thin wire or nylon thread.

8. Repair plastic and fiberglass screens with patches of the same material; seal with clear cement.

9. Repair tent screens by sewing on patches of netting or pantyhose.

10. In fact, pantyhose can make a good temporary patch on any type of screen; secure it with tape.

Screwdriver

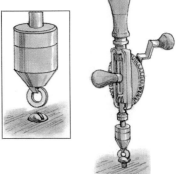

Here are some make-do solutions for those occasions when you lack a screwdriver.

1. Tighten a steel washer into the chuck of a hand drill or brace and insert the edge into the screw slot. (This is a good idea as well when you want to exert some leverage on a screw.) You can use a variable-speed power drill, too.

2. Check out pocketknives around the house. Some may have a screwdriver blade. Or you can break the tip off an old knife blade.

3. A nail file can tighten a tiny screw—in eyeglasses, for example.

4. House keys will sometimes fit a slotted screw. But use them only on loose screws because key metal bends easily under pressure.

5. Or try a used hacksaw blade, the blade of a small pry bar, a paint scraper, a putty knife, the back of a skate key, or the blade of a can opener or bottle cap opener.

Screws

1. Can't remove a screw because the slot is ruined? If the head is above the workpiece, use a hacksaw to cut a new groove at a right angle to the original slot. Exert pressure evenly, not jerkily, with a screwdriver to ease out the screw.
2. Or remove the screw by gripping the head with locking-grip pliers.
3. To remove a broken flathead screw, slice a new slot with a small drill and a tiny abrasive wheel. (Some hardware stores will rent this tool and bit.) Or cut a new slot with a few sharp blows on a cold chisel the same width as the screw.
4. If a screw is rusted in place, try dropping a little kerosene or hot paraffin on it.

Sea stings

1. In preparation for a trip to the ocean, assemble a first-aid kit containing 0.5 percent hydrocortisone cream and antibiotic ointment; rubbing alcohol, soap, calamine lotion, and papaya-base meat tenderizer; cotton swabs, waterproof plastic bandages, and sterile gauze pads; over-the-counter antihistamine tablets; pointed tweezers; and, if possible, disposable hypodermic needles.
2. If you're stung and didn't see what got you, ask lifeguards or local people what is native to the area and treat your sting accordingly.
3. Sea urchin spines can penetrate sneakers and flippers. If one breaks your skin, it will probably cause redness, swelling, and burning pain. Pull out any visible spines with tweezers or a sterilized hypodermic needle; wash with soap and water, then apply a hot-water compress and an antibiotic ointment. If several spines are embedded or you feel intense pain, see a doctor.
4. If you've brushed against stinging coral and it has reddened your skin, apply rubbing alcohol. (You can also use cologne or liquor.)
5. If true coral has caused the irritation, apply calamine lotion. If your skin is broken, cleanse the

wound thoroughly with soap and water, then let hydrogen peroxide bubble on it for several minutes; apply antibiotic ointment and 0.5 percent hydrocortisone cream several times daily. If the wound doesn't appear to be healing, see a doctor.
6. Treat a sea anemone sting like a jellyfish sting (p.118).

Security blankets

Don't worry if your small child develops a close attachment to a special object, even if it's worn and ugly. Make sure it's available when he needs it—at Grandma's house, in a shopping mall, or on vacation. Don't try to take it away or substitute a newer, cleaner version. Your child likes the way his old blanket, diaper, or stuffed animal smells, tastes, and feels; its familiarity is what makes it appealing. But to be on the safe side, get a duplicate in case the original gets lost.

If you accidentally leave the treasured object behind on vacation, explain that a vacation is a special time and that it will be waiting when you get back. Then help your child find a substitute that will give some degree of comfort, especially at bedtime; try making a doll or puppet out of a sock or glove (p.307). Perhaps cuddling in your jacket or a cozy comforter will do the trick. (See also *Bedtime rituals,* p.19.)

Seed germination

1. For fast germination, soak seeds in water overnight before planting. To speed the process even more, add a drop or two of detergent; it reduces the water's surface tension, helping it to penetrate the seed's coat. An easy way to soak is to empty each seed packet into a different cup of a plastic egg carton, then fill each with the detergent solution.
2. Heating bean and pea seeds in the microwave not only increases the chances of germination but also enhances subsequent growth. The recommended power level varies with the oven, but it's always at the

low end of the scale—four 15-second treatments with a cooling period after each, for example. Never warm the seeds to more than 120°F or they won't germinate at all.

Seed planting

Ensure proper spacing and eliminate the need for thinning with a homemade seed tape. An added bonus: the seeds will sprout faster.

Lay a strip of damp paper toweling on top of a strip of plastic wrap, then set out the seeds at the intervals recommended on the seed packet. Cover with another strip of damp toweling, roll the paper and plastic up together, place in a plastic bag, and store in a warm place (the top of the refrigerator is ideal).

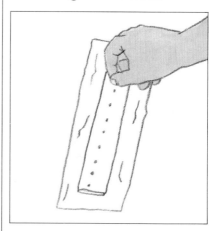

As soon as roots begin to emerge, take the tape to the garden and unroll it onto a well-tilled bed, peeling the plastic away. Cover with a fine layer of soil or sand and water thoroughly but gently. Don't worry about the paper—it acts as a mulch to inhibit dehydration, then soon dissolves to reveal a perfectly spaced row of young seedlings.

Self-adhesive mounts

To remove a self-adhesive hook, drip vinegar behind it. Scrape any residue off the tile with your fingernail or a dull knife. On a painted or plastic surface soften stubborn residue with a warm rag or hair dryer. On unpainted surfaces use alcohol, mineral spirits, cleaning solvent, lacquer thinner, hair spray, or nail polish remover (acetone); test first on an inconspicuous area.

Sensitive skin

If your skin is easily irritated by the elements, by alcohol and other cosmetic ingredients, by chemicals in synthetic fabrics, or by shaving, consider these recommendations:

1. Stay away from alkaline soaps, facial masks, grainy cleansers, alcohol-base astringents, acetone products such as nail polish remover, and anything with fragrance.

2. Bathe in tepid or cool water, using mild superfatted soap; pat dry (no rubbing!), then apply a moisturizer containing urea or lactic acid to your damp skin.

3. "Breathable" natural fabrics are the best choice for clothing, but if you prefer synthetics, launder them several times before wearing to remove potential irritants.

4. Give extra protection to your hands when washing dishes or clothes by wearing cotton liners inside your rubber gloves.

5. Don't assume products labeled "for sensitive skin" are necessarily safe for you. Test a new product on a small area of your inner arm daily for a week; if your skin reacts, don't use it. Look for products containing nonirritating allantoin, petrolatum, and zinc oxide.

Septic tank backup

Is the grass greener over your septic tank? Worse still, are your drains backing up or smelling foul? If so, call a cleaning service and have your tank pumped out immediately.

If it's too late and your system backs up, whatever you empty or flush down a drain will back into your lowest plumbing fixtures. (Don't add water—it will only make matters worse.) Your second-floor bathroom drains may seem clear, but if you use them, you'll cause an awful mess in the basement laundry sink or first-floor lavatory.

If the cleaning service can't come at once, a plumber may be able to dig down and break up the layer of semisolid scum blocking the inlet pipe, giving you temporary restricted use of the plumbing.

PREVENTION

1. If possible, measure the level of solid waste in your septic tank regularly by removing its cover and probing with a long towel-wrapped pole. The sludge will leave a dark stain on the end; a layer more than 12 to 18 inches deep requires pumping. Generally, the tank should be emptied every 2 to 5 years (depending on the size of your tank and your family's plumbing demands).

2. Keep all chemicals, including drain cleaners and commercial tank-cleaning compounds, out of your septic system.

3. Instead of chemical bowl cleaners, add a gallon of white vinegar to the water in the commode; let it sit for a few hours, then flush it down.

4. To keep the decomposition process active, flush an ounce of dry yeast down the drain monthly.

5. Don't pour liquid fat or grease down the kitchen drain.

6. Never introduce facial tissues, newspaper, paper towels, sanitary napkins, or any kind of wrapping material into your septic system.

Sex education

1. Give short, simple answers to the questions your child asks about sex. Let her reaction to what you say determine whether to provide additional information. Be factual and to the point; don't overload her with facts she didn't ask for.

2. Listen carefully to your child's questions. If she asks where she came from, find out—before you launch into a lecture about how babies are made—if she just wants to know the name of the hospital where she was born.

3. As time goes on, don't restrict your answers to factual information; also communicate your atti-

tudes and values. Children need help in coping with their sexual feelings and defining responsible sexual behavior.

4. An easy way to introduce your children to the mystery of sex is to arrange for them to witness the birth of a litter of puppies or kittens.

5. For children over the age of 8, use the plots of TV programs and the lyrics of songs as springboards for conversations about sex. "What does the woman find attractive in that man?" "What do those lyrics mean to you?"

6. If you and your adolescent find it difficult to discuss sexual matters, write her a letter describing the risks and responsibilities involved in sexual behavior and stating your personal values.

Sexual harassment

ON THE STREET

1. People who shout obscenities, whisper unwanted endearments, or make obscene gestures may be capable of physical violence. The best response is to ignore them completely and keep moving to a safe, well-lighted place. If the offender pursues you, call the police.

2. If you are constantly harassed at a particular building site, contact the contractor or the company constructing the building.

ON THE JOB

1. Confront the harasser. Appeal to his or her professionalism and make it clear that you object to the advances. If they continue, send your tormentor a letter by certified mail, expressing your feelings and mentioning that such behavior is against the law and that you may have to make an official complaint.

2. Keep a dated, written record of all incidents. Save all notes or letters.

3. If necessary, file a written complaint with your employer; if you work for a corporation, address it to the human resources department or the president of the company. Include the date, place, and details of all incidents. If you're a union member, your representative may handle the problem for you.

4. If there is no immediate investigation, if the harasser is your employer or a responsible official, or if the behavior persists, contact the Equal Employment Opportunity Commission, listed in the phone directory under U.S. Government.

IN AN APARTMENT BUILDING

1. If a building employee is harassing you, send a letter of complaint to the landlord, the superintendent, and the managing agent; keep a copy. If nothing is done or if one of the above is the problem, contact your town's housing authority.

2. Document your case meticulously; write down exactly who said what to whom and when.

3. Talk to your neighbors; this may be happening to others. Perhaps you can take action as a group.

Shaded garden

If your garden lacks sunshine, don't give up on color. Just think in terms of foliage rather than flowers.

Coleus, familiar as houseplants, make a brilliant massed display in a shady corner. Hostas, hardy perennials of the lily family, bear leaves in muted shades of blue, gold, green, and white; they thrive in a damp, cool, woodland setting.

Caladiums, a southern favorite, are at their brightest in filtered sun, sporting arrowhead-shaped leaves marbled and veined in red, pink, green, and white. Though not winter hardy in the North, they adapt well to hanging baskets or tubs and can overwinter indoors.

Vivid ground covers include dead nettle, a type of mint whose green leaves are splashed with silver, and variegated lilyturf (*Liriope muscari* Varietaga), with grasslike green-and white-striped leaves. Two other lilyturf varieties, Big Blue and Munroe White, offer less dramatic foliage but bear showy flowers of blue or white in late summer.

Shaded lawns

The right choice of grass seed and a little extra care are all it takes to keep a shaded lawn full and green.

1. Plant chewings fescue, creeping red fescue, or turf-type tall fescues if you live in an arid area. If you live in a region of high rainfall or if your soil is poorly drained, plant rough-stalk bluegrass.

2. To fill in bare spots, overseed with a fast-growing ryegrass. You'll have to reseed every spring, since rye won't last from year to year in the shade.

3. Thin trees instead of removing them. A good tree surgeon can remove 40 percent of a tree's leaf surface without harming it, and the extra light will do wonders for the grass underneath.

4. Raise your mower blade to a height of 2½ inches before mowing a shaded part of the lawn; you'll leave more leaf surface to trap light.

5. Water no more than once or twice a week—and water deeply. Wetting only the surface of the soil encourages tree roots to grow upward, where they compete with grass for water and nutrients. (See also *Grass,* p. 100; *Lawns,* p. 123.)

Sharks

Although shark attacks are extremely rare, it's still a good idea to call the local newspaper and ask if there have been any recent sightings or talk to the lifeguards before going into a body of salt water.

1. Stay out of the water if you have an open cut or scratch; sharks are thought to be attracted to blood.

2. Avoid swimming near drop-offs or too far from shore; sharks are more likely to congregate there.

3. To discourage an inquisitive shark, use a shark billy—a thick, 3-foot-long stick with a loop for your wrist at one end and a circle of nails, pointing outward, at the other; keep the shark at bay by poking it on the snout.

4. Swim with at least one other person to keep a watch for danger.

Sheet metal

If you lack tin snips, try one of these methods for cutting sheet metal:

1. Use a hacksaw. Put the sheet on a flat bench or table with the saw line slightly overlapping the table edge. Position the blade at a 45° angle and keep the teeth in constant contact with the metal. If the waste section is sizable, support it on another table or bench or have a partner hold it. Wear work gloves—the edges of newly cut metal are sharp.

2. Use a cold chisel to cut a small piece. Lock the metal in a vise with the cut line level with the top of the jaw. Hold the chisel against the edge of the metal at a 45° angle to the jaw top and hammer it along the length of the piece. The waste will curl back like an orange peel.

3. You can also slice a large piece with a cold chisel. Lay the metal on a hardwood bench or table with the cut line even with the edge; then clamp a length of straight steel or hardwood on top. Hold the chisel at a 45° angle to the bench or table edge and hammer along the length of the metal. Scrap should peel down toward the floor.

Shelves

1. A clear pine 1 x 12 should be able to span 48 inches without sagging under a light load such as clothes, toys, or pans; 26 to 30 inches under a heavy load such as books or records. For ⅜-inch plywood the limit is 26 inches on a light load, 16 inches on a heavy one; for ¾-inch plywood, 46 and 29 inches.

2. To make a removable shelf, mount folding brackets on the wall. Pull them down and place a board on top when needed.

3. Build a set of shelves from boards and coffee cans. Paint the cans or cover them with matching wrapping or wallpaper.

4. Clay flowerpots work well for medium-weight loads. They look especially nice if you top each "column" of pots with a potted plant.

5. For a colorful look, use glass blocks or large jars as shelf supports, filling them with marbles or some other bright objects.

6. Hang shelves with rope from a beam or hooks attached to the ceiling or wall. Drill pairs of holes at the ends of the boards and at all support points, 1 inch from the edges. Knot the end of a length of rope for each hole and slip a washer onto it; then feed the ropes up through the holes in the bottom shelf and knot them again on top.

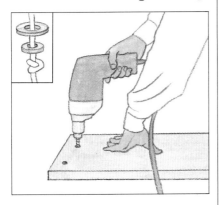

Measure up for the next shelf and repeat the process. Just be sure that when you hang the shelves the ropes are firmly anchored; they may have to bear a lot of weight.

7. Or instead of using rope, hang the shelves with punched metal plumber's tape. Screw or nail two or three strips to each end of the shelves and suspend from a beam.

8. For lighter-duty shelves, use heavy cord or fishing line; instead of knotting the line, double-wind it through each pair of holes like a sewing stitch.

Shiny clothing

1. If the knees or elbows on worsted-wool garments become shiny from wear, try steaming them; hang them in the bathroom while running hot water in the shower.

2. To prevent sheen, always press heavy cotton, wool, acetate, rayon, linen, permanent-press, and dark fabrics on the wrong side. Or use a pressing cloth.

3. To get a high sheen on polished cotton, add half an envelope of unflavored gelatin to the last rinse.

Shoe heels

1. Touch up scuffed heels quickly with a felt-tip pen or use a cotton swab to dab on ink, acrylic paint, or auto paint. On white heels, use toothpaste.

2. Protect and shine wooden heels with lemon oil or clear nail polish. If they're badly scratched, sand and stain with furniture finish.

3. Rebuild worn rubber heels with athletic shoe repair material (available at sporting goods stores). Make an outline of the original shape of the heel with masking tape, angling the tape outward slightly to make sure the material will cover heel edges. Fill with the repair material and let dry. Trim with scissors or a razor blade. The stuff will dry clear, so you'll have to color it with shoe polish or a felt-tip marker.

Shoehorn

No shoehorn? Use a tablespoon, a soupspoon, or a rubber spatula. Or use the narrow end of a silk tie to ease your heel into the shoe.

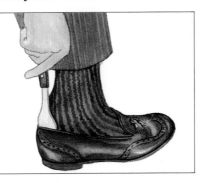

Shoelaces

1. If you're not sure what size shoelaces your child needs, count the pairs of holes in one shoe and multiply by 3. For adults, multiply by 6.

2. If the plastic tip of a shoelace is broken, wrap the tip with transparent tape. Or dip it in glue, hot paraffin, or clear nail polish.

3. No shoelaces? Use string, yarn, or twine. For women's shoes, ribbon makes a pretty substitute, especially if it's lace or satin.

4. Here's how to retie a broken shoelace. Remove the lace, join the two pieces together with a square knot, and estimate where the knot will fall in the laced shoe. Put the knot there and lace from that point outward in both directions.

Shoe polish

1. In a pinch, you can shine your leather shoes with floor wax, spray furniture polish, or spray window cleaner; you can even use a banana peel (p.288). On rubber overshoes use vegetable shortening; on patent leather try petroleum jelly, spray window cleaner, or castor oil.

2. For a high shine, squeeze a few drops of lighter fluid into your solid boot wax—it will spread more easily and penetrate better. Or rub lemon juice into the leather after it's polished, then buff.

3. To get an even shine on white shoes, wipe them with rubbing alcohol, then polish.

4. To keep fresh polish from smearing clothing, let it dry, then rub with wax paper or spritz with hair spray.

5. If you don't have a soft cloth for

applying polish, use a powder puff or a sheet of fabric softener.

6. Hard to get polish in that space between the uppers and the soles? Use a cotton swab.

7. To clean suede shoes, first remove the dust with pantyhose or your vacuum cleaner's dust-brush attachment. Then hold the shoes over steam to raise the nap; brush lightly and let dry.

8. Cover spots on black suede by sponging a little black coffee on them; on white suede, use chalk.

9. Remove stains from kid leather with a cloth and cleaning fluid.

10. Take spots off the white rubber on sneakers with steel wool dipped in detergent.

11. To remove salt rings from your boots, brush with a solution of 1 tablespoon vinegar in 1 cup water.

12. Clean up buckskin shoes by going over them with fine or medium sandpaper. Or touch up with an emery board.

13. If your shoe polish brush becomes caked, soak it overnight in paint solvent.

14. If your polish gets hard, heat it in the oven or add a few drops of turpentine or mineral spirits to soften it.

15. To keep your hands clean while polishing shoes, wear old gloves or cut the pockets out of old trousers and use them as mitts.

Shoes

1. Slippery soles? Sand them or apply bathtub appliqués, strips of adhesive tape, or repair patches for bicycle tubes.

2. Cold feet? Make liners from pieces of sturdy quilted fabric, felt, or scraps of thin carpet. First, make a pattern by tracing your feet on paper, then cut out the liners and slip into your shoes or boots.

3. Keep canvas shoes smelling sweet; sprinkle a little talcum powder, baby powder, or baking soda into them occasionally to absorb any moisture.

4. Deodorize any type of shoe with a little baking soda.

5. Make your shoes water-repellent with a light coat of floor wax. Use petroleum jelly for galoshes. (See also *Hiking boots*, p.108.)

6. If the sole of your shoe separates from the upper, reattach it temporarily with a silicone or plastic sealer used for weatherstripping.

7. To prevent leather shoes from cracking after they've been wet, apply a liberal coating of saddle soap while they're still damp. Let it dry away from the heat, then remove any excess saddle soap.

8. Soften dried leather shoes by wetting the outside with warm water and rubbing with castor oil, glycerin, or kerosene.

Shopping addiction

Don't let "Born to Shop" bumper stickers fool you into thinking that compulsive shopping is something to be laughed off. It's not. A steady flow of credit card charges can put you in serious debt more quickly than you can imagine.

If you find yourself buying things you neither need nor can afford, get in touch with a support group for help. Debtors Anonymous conducts meetings throughout the country. Look in the phone book.

If you're not a compulsive shopper but still feel that you should pull the reins in, try these tips:

1. Don't ever shop without a list— and stick to it.

2. Avoid sales; the temptation to overbuy is too great.

3. Keep a small notebook where you list everything you buy, even the morning paper. You'll find it harder to spend if you know you must write each purchase down.

Shopping lists

Here's an easy way to speed up your weekly grocery shopping—and save money by curbing impulse buying.

Make a permanent list of the items you regularly buy; arrange them in the order in which they're set out in the supermarket, proceeding from aisle to aisle. If the produce area is normally your first stop, for example, list the fruits and vegetables you routinely buy, such as apples, oranges, carrots, and lettuce; then leave some blanks for less frequently purchased goods.

Make lots of photocopies of the list and always keep one on the refrigerator door; mark items as soon as a need arises. When you go to the store, take the list; your shopping is organized as soon as you walk in.

IN TIMES GONE BY

Magic slippers

Since the earliest times, people from various cultures have regarded shoes as symbols of fertility and prosperity.

□ In ancient Egypt, Palestine, and Assyria, the seller of land gave a sandal to the buyer as a gesture of goodwill and a seal of purchase.

□ In India an old shoe placed upside down on the roof assured a couple good fortune.

□ Childless Chinese women borrowed shoes from the shrine of the mother goddess to help them become pregnant.

□ For good luck, the Scots threw a shoe after a sailor departing for his first voyage or after anyone starting a new venture.

□ In ancient Anglo-Saxon weddings the father of the bride transferred his authority to the groom by handing him one of his daughter's shoes—it was this ritual that gave rise to the modern-day custom of attaching old shoes to the bridal carriage.

Shovel

1. Plenty of garden tools are handy for breaking up the soil—a hoe, cultivator, pickax, metal rake, tiller, edger, or pitchfork—but not much good for moving earth into a wheelbarrow. That takes a shovel. If you don't have one, lay out a square of burlap or heavy plastic; then, once the soil is loose, use a hoe or edger to heave dirt onto the square. Pull up the four corners and empty the soil into the wheelbarrow.

2. You can make a snow shovel from a round 5-gallon can. Remove the top and cut out the bottom with tin snips, a saber saw, or a hacksaw. With the same tool, slice the can, top to bottom, into quarters, each a potential snow shovel. With screws and washers, fasten one of the quarters to a broomstick or dowel. For support, fasten most of the metal to the stick and bend the cut edges over like hems. If this shovel bends from the weight of too much snow, you'll still have three more.

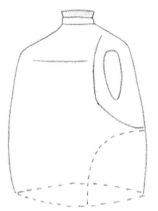

3. Simpler still, make a snow scoop for quick jobs like clearing steps. Cut the bottom out of a 1-gallon plastic milk jug, then cut out the side beneath the handle. Now you have a durable scoop that's easy to grab hold of.

Shower curtains & doors

1. Make your plastic shower curtain more pliable by dipping it in warm water to which you have added a few drops of mineral oil.

2. Protect your new shower curtain by hanging the old one behind it to take the soaking. Wash both frequently to prevent mildew.

3. Shower curtains will dry faster if you spread them out.

4. To remove mildew (p. 135) from duck (light canvas) shower curtains, use a solution of chlorine bleach and water.

5. To remove water and soap marks from glass shower doors, rub with a sponge dampened with vinegar. Or gently scrape with a single-edge razor blade.

6. If the doors don't slide smoothly, first clean the tracks with a brush and dull knife or screwdriver; use a cotton swab or toothbrush to reach nooks and crannies. Then wash with ammonia or a strong detergent solution. After the tracks dry, spray with a silicone lubricant. (Shield the tub—the spray will make it slippery.)

Sibling rivalry

1. To encourage affection between siblings, arrange for them to enjoy things in common, such as holiday traditions and summer trips. Shared experiences and memories help build friendship that can withstand occasional angry flare-ups.

2. After a new baby arrives, give each older child some private time with you every day, away from the younger sibling and free from household distractions.

3. Encourage older children to use their experience to help younger ones. Commend their cooperation.

4. To prevent feelings of resentment and competition, never compare one child with another or hold one up as an example to another.

5. Give undivided love and attention to each child at scheduled and unscheduled times, focusing on each one's strengths and individual accomplishments.

6. Designate special days other than birthdays—half-birthdays, for example, to mark the 6-month plateaus—for each child. Hold a fam-

ily celebration, complete with little gifts, and serve the favorite dessert of the center of attention.

7. "Who gets to ride in the front seat?" "Which TV program will we watch?" To eliminate competition, have each child take turns making these decisions for a week.

Siding

1. To clean and rinse siding in one step, tape a garden hose to the head of a wide push broom, using duct tape at two or three places along the handle. Position the nozzle near the top of the broom head, just above the bristles.

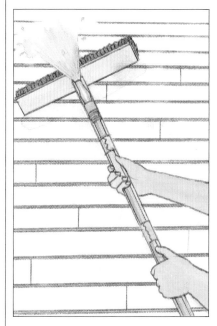

2. Mildew can discolor any siding, particularly wood. It usually grows in the shade, appearing as dark gray or black spots that spread over larger areas. To treat a mild case, scrub with a solution of 1 part water and 4 parts household bleach. For a more stubborn case, use 1 cup trisodium phosphate (TSP) and 1 cup bleach in 1 gallon of warm water; scrub the surface with a stiff brush, let dry on the surface, then hose it down.

3. Stained-wood siding fades and discolors after exposure to sun and rain. To get an even tone, restain it, let it dry, and apply a clear wood preservative.

4. Warped siding can often be pulled tight to the house with galvanized thin-shank screws. Be sure to bore pilot holes to prevent splitting the siding. Or nail the warped siding back in place with galvanized spiral-shank nails.

Sieves & colanders

1. Improvise a makeshift strainer for liquids from the legs of clean pantyhose. Stretch the fabric across the bottom of a wide-necked funnel, hold it in place, and pour.

2. No colander? Punch holes in the bottom of an aluminum pie plate.

3. Use a fine sieve to smooth out the lumps in confectioner's sugar; just push it through with a wooden spoon. The same remedy works for lumpy custard, sauce, or gravy.

Silk flowers

1. To get more for your money and greater flexibility in your arrangements, buy stems with more than one flower. Cut off the blossoms and make a stem for each by twisting wire onto the cut end and covering it with green florist's tape.

2. For fragrance, hide a perfume sample card in the arrangement.

3. To clean, dust each blossom with a soft brush or wipe it off with a damp cloth.

4. For a more thorough cleaning, disassemble the arrangement and swish each flower in warm water and mild detergent. Rinse well and stand in tall vases or jars to air-dry. Or have the flowers dry-cleaned.

Silver

With proper care, you can safeguard silver against tarnishing, pitting, or scratching. Be especially gentle with silver plate, as the plating wears off easily.

1. Always wash silver and silver plate by hand with mild detergent—never in the dishwasher. Then dry with a chamois cloth or soft towel.

2. Don't leave silver overnight with food on it. If you can't wash it right away, at least rinse off all the food. You can let it stand in clear water overnight, but don't add detergent.

3. If you don't have specially treated cloth bags or a silver chest for storage, thoroughly dry each piece, then wrap airtight in plastic wrap. Place alum or camphor in with the silver to discourage tarnish (keep it away from children and pets).

4. Never let rubber come in contact with silver—it causes tarnish.

5. Don't let egg, fruit juice, olives, perfume, toilet water, salad dressing, salt, sulfur, or vinegar stay on silver for any length of time—they cause stains and corrosion.

6. Clean silver saltshaker lids frequently to keep them from corroding. To remove corrosion caused by salt, soak for 5 minutes in a solution of hot vinegar and salt, then wash and dry.

7. If you put cut flowers in silver bowls, change the water often to prevent deposits at the water line. Remove the flowers as soon as they begin to wilt.

8. If you keep fruit in a silver container, use a liner.

9. If you run out of silver polish, use one of the following homemade substitutes: a paste of water and

cornstarch, cigarette ashes, or baking soda; toothpaste; lump starch rubbed on with a damp cloth, allowed to dry, and rubbed off with cheesecloth. Or let silver stand in sour milk or buttermilk overnight (you can substitute 1 cup whole milk mixed with 1 tablespoon white vinegar or lemon juice).

10. Polish with brisk up-and-down strokes, not across or in circles. For hard-to-reach crevices, use a soft brush.

11. Use a pipe cleaner with polish on it to clean between fork tines. Or put polish on a string and pull it back and forth between the tines.

12. To remove scratches, make a paste of putty powder and olive oil; rub on with a soft cloth and polish with a chamois cloth.

13. If silver-plated objects are too badly worn to withstand more polishing, you can give them a bright, hard gloss that looks something like porcelain by painting them with refrigerator enamel.

Skewers

1. If you sometimes turn a barbecue skewer and find that the food doesn't turn with it, solve the problem by using two-pronged skewers. Or simply thread the ingredients onto two skewers instead of one.

2. You've prepared the ingredients for shish kebab but the skewers can't be found? Cut new ones from unpainted wire coat hangers. Or look in the toolbox for some heavy-gauge wire. Or slice the food into small pieces and stir-fry it instead. (Just be sure to cook the meat—especially pork and chicken—longer than the vegetables.)

3. When camping, improvise skewers by peeling thin green branches and sharpening the ends.

❯Skidding

Don't slam on the brakes—it only makes the skid worse. Instead, take your foot off the gas pedal and turn the wheel gently in the direction of the skid. When the front wheels start gripping, begin to steer again (be prepared to counter another skid in the opposite direction). Very gently apply light accelerator pressure.

Ski goggles

To keep lenses from fogging up, try one of these tricks (on the inside):
1. Spray with shaving cream or furniture polish, then wipe clean.
2. Wet with a 50-50 mixture of liquid detergent and water; wipe dry.
3. Rub with a cut raw potato.
4. Spread a thin layer of toothpaste, then wipe it off.
5. For a quick defogging, spit into the lenses; rub the spittle around.

Skiing

1. You don't need an expensive ski rack to carry your skis to the slopes. If your car has a standard roof rack, you can fasten skis to it with three bungee cords, one at each end and one in the middle. Hook the cords to one side of the rack, then circle them completely around the skis and hook to the other side. To keep the skis from scratching the car

roof, tape kitchen sponges on the underside at each end.
2. If you lack a lock to protect your skis from theft while you're in the lodge, leave one ski and pole in one place, the other set in another.
3. Remove boot liners and dry them before storing boots at the end of the season. Wash the outsides of the boots, replace the dry liners, and fasten the boots before you put them away (fastening helps them keep their shape). Mice and spiders like to nest in ski boots, so stuff yours with plenty of tightly packed, wadded-up newspaper.

CONDITIONING EXERCISES

A few weeks before ski season, use these exercises to get in shape:
1. Chair sit: Press your back against a wall and lower yourself down as though sitting on an imaginary chair; hold the position for 15 seconds. Repeat six times a day.
2. Knee stretch: With your feet together, bend your knees to a half crouch. Hold for 30 seconds. Repeat several times a day.

Skunks

1. If you live in an area where your pet is likely to encounter a skunk, buy a chemical called Neutroleum Alpha from a hospital supplier or pest-control service. Then, on that awful day when the pet comes home reeking, mix a tablespoon of it into the animal's bathwater. It's the most effective deodorant you'll find, but be sure to keep it out of your pet's eyes.
2. You may also have some success washing out the odor with vinegar or chlorine bleach, diluted 1 to 10 with water. Add some laundry soap as a wetting agent.
3. For a quicker fix, rub tomato juice into the animal's fur. It won't get rid of the skunky smell completely, but it will help.

Sleds & toboggans

1. Flatten some large corrugated cardboard cartons to create instant sleds. For a toboggan that seats several people, use a refrigerator-size carton.
2. Or you can slide down a hill on a cafeteria tray, a garbage can top, or an inner tube.
3. If your inflatable plastic raft developed a leak after a summer in the water, don't throw it away; uninflated, it will make a perfectly good sled.
4. Sheets of sturdy plastic, like old shower curtains, can also be used.
5. In very cold weather you can soak an old blanket in water and set it outdoors to stiffen. It will be good for a few exciting rides before it begins to thaw.
6. For a sled that ensures a good laugh as well as a speedy ride, just tie a large plastic garbage bag around your bottom like a diaper.

Sleeping bag

If you have two blankets, you can improvise a sleeping bag. Fold one in thirds lengthwise and pin the free edge with large safety pins. Then fold up 3 or 4 inches at the bottom and pin it. Lay it on the oth-

---

IN TIMES GONE BY

Ski story

☐ Remnants of skis up to 4,000 years old have been found in Finland, Sweden, and Norway. The long wooden boards were originally used strictly for transportation. In the 10th century Norwegian tax collectors used them to reach outlying districts (or maybe to catch up with recalcitrant taxpayers). By the 12th century Norway had ski troops armed with bows and arrows. By the 15th century Sweden, Finland, Russia, and Poland had followed suit.

☐ It wasn't until the 19th century that skis were used for fun. The Norwegians took the lead, racing one another down snowy hills—often trying not to spill the mug of beer they held in one hand!

☐ When skis first appeared in 19th-century California mining towns, they were called Norwegian snowshoes. Racing was popular among the miners, and betting was heavy. The idea was to shoot down the hill without turning, and each skier had his own secret speed-wax formula. In 1870 Tommy Todd was clocked at 87 miles per hour.

☐ The first ski tow in America was built in 1934 in Woodstock, Vermont. Before long, people realized they didn't have to climb up the hill anymore, and the sport suddenly gained popularity. A major resort was built a few years later at Sun Valley, Idaho, and the ski boom has been on ever since.

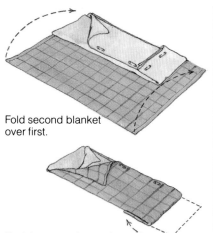

Fold second blanket over first.

Tuck bottom edge under.

er blanket, as shown, and fold the second blanket over the first, pinning the edges together. Tuck the bottom under.

Slides

1. You can scan your slides more easily if you store them in plastic slide sheets instead of boxes. Just make sure they're made of polyethylene (see *Photographs*, p.154). The sheets hold 20 slides and are punched to fit three-ring binders.
2. For safe storage, slides should be kept in a cool, dry place—*not* the attic or the basement. Heat and humidity are the enemies of color dyes in slides and prints.
3. Dusty slides? To prevent scratching, use a soft camel's-hair brush, the kind that's used to clean camera lenses. Dust lightly and gently, starting from the center.

Sliding glass doors

1. To prevent children and guests from walking into closed doors, apply two rows of decals 30 to 40 inches above the floor.
2. To protect birds from flying into the glass, attach decals of diving sparrow hawks, available from the Audubon Society. Or hang wind chimes outside the door.
3. To insulate glass doors, install lined curtains. Use rods that extend well beyond the sides of the frame so that you can just pull

the curtains back to enjoy the view.
4. To replace a glass door panel, lift the old panel up into the empty headspace in the top of the frame, then tilt it and remove the bottom first. Reverse the procedure with the new panel.

Slings

1. Loop a towel or long scarf around an injured arm; pin or tie the ends securely around the victim's neck.
2. Put a fairly tight jacket on the victim, leaving the injured arm out of its sleeve. Then button or zip the jacket around the arm, elevating the hand 3 inches above the elbow.
3. Put an oversize, long-sleeved shirt, jacket, or cardigan sweater on the victim; support the injured arm by pulling up the bottom of the garment as shown and buttoning it at the top.

Slipcovers

1. Save yourself the trouble and cost of matching up different pieces when making a slipcover: choose a solid-color fabric or one with a small overall pattern. Avoid stripes, plaids, large patterns, and fabric with a one-way nap.
2. Don't use your old sheets as slipcovers; get new ones with sizing to protect them from soil and stains. Buy all that you need at one time so

that you can be sure the sheets come from the same dye lot and match perfectly.

3. Hide worn upholstery under a bedspread, quilt, sheet, or drop cloth. For a more finished effect, drape the fabric over the frame, tuck it into the inside crevices, and safety-pin in place. At the outside corners, cut quarter circles to remove the excess cloth; stitch down the cut edge, then attach grommets or ties to pull the remaining cloth tight. Wrap loose cushions separately.

Slips

1. If your full slip has become worn at the top, cut it in half; sew elastic into the waist and presto!—a new half-slip.
2. In a pinch, you can improvise a full slip, albeit a short one, by pulling a half-slip up above your bust or by pinning it to the bottom of your bra.
3. If your white slip is dingy gray and bleach doesn't help, darken it. Soak it in hot, strong tea until it's a shade darker than you want. Rinse in cold water and let dry.
4. Prevent nylon gray with proper washing—use hotter water, more detergent, and always separate all whites from colors.
5. Does your slip constantly ride up? Sew felt or trim around the inside hem to give it weight. Or wear it inside out. (See also *Static electricity*, p.195.)

Slugs & snails

1. If you live near the coast, try using salty seaweed as a slugproof and snailproof mulch.

2. Spread a circle of marble dust in a circle around seedlings. The soft bodies of slugs and snails can't tolerate it.

3. Sprinkle salt on slugs to kill them. Stage an evening raid in the garden, saltshaker in hand; sprinkle each slug once, then again in 5 minutes. Or spray them with a 50-50 solution of vinegar and water.

4. Keep snails out of trees by wrapping a 3-inch band of thin copper sheeting around the trunks; the pests get a weak electrical shock when they crawl on it. Or wrap a band of sticky tanglefoot adhesive around the trunks. (See also *Garden pests,* p.95; *Ashes,* p.287.)

Small claims court

Do you have a small legal claim that isn't worth the time and expense of a lawsuit? In small claims court you can act as your own lawyer and collect damages ranging from $500 to $3,000, depending on the state where you live. Here's how:

1. You must sue in the same county where the defendant does business.

2. Get a complaint form from the court. In some localities small claims courts are known as magistrate's courts, municipal courts, or justice of the peace courts. Check in the phone book under City or Municipal Government Offices or Courts. There will be a fee ranging from $2 to $10.

3. After you've filled out the complaint, the clerk will assign you a hearing date and notify the defendant by mail.

4. Prepare your case. Gather pertinent receipts, letters, and any legal agreements; if the issue is a damaged item, bring it or a picture of it. If witnesses can help, ask them to attend the hearing. If they're unable, see if the court will accept a written statement.

5. If possible, go to court before-hand and watch what goes on there.

6. When you arrive, you may be asked if you will agree to go to arbitration rather than wait for a judge. This means your case will be decided by an uninvolved third party, usually an attorney; the advantages are that your case will be heard sooner and that there's an opportunity to negotiate a compromise solution—but you won't be able to appeal the outcome. The judge's decision, on the other hand, may be subject to appeal in some states. (See also *Lawsuits,* page 124.)

7. As the plaintiff, you testify first. Tell your story to the judge or arbitrator in as straightforward a manner as possible. If cross-examined, answer questions directly and honestly, offering no information that isn't asked for. If you can't remember something, say so. And don't be bullied into agreeing to anything that isn't true.

8. Both you and the defendant will be notified of the decision by mail. If you've won and the defendant doesn't pay when asked, the court will advise you on the legal steps to take next.

Small talk

If you get tongue-tied at parties and in other social situations, try these tips to make chitchat easier:

1. Start with a compliment—it gets the ball rolling on a pleasant note.

2. Ask the other person about her hobbies—people like to talk about what interests them.

3. Here's a good opener to use at parties: Ask how the other person knows the host.

4. Or draw him out by asking his opinion of something (nothing too controversial, of course). Sports, movies, books, and celebrities are good. The weather's a bit dull unless you're in the middle of a heat wave or just survived a hurricane.

5. A good exit line is also a necessity. Explain that you want to refresh your drink, get a second helping of food, or talk with your spouse.

Smoke detectors

1. The best location for a home smoke detector is on or near a ceiling close to the sleeping area, away from corners, windows, and doors. The top of a stairwell is also good.

2. If cooking causes false alarms, put a shower cap over the detector while you're in the kitchen. It's obtrusive enough that you'll remember to take it off right after you've finished eating.

3. Never paint your smoke detector. Twice a year (perhaps at the same time you change your clocks for daylight saving time), dust or vacuum it and change the battery.

Smoking

Quitting smoking isn't easy, but it may be the most rewarding thing you ever do. If you've failed before, the following suggestions may help you succeed:

1. Investigate your options—from "cold turkey" and nicotine gum to videotapes and group programs. Be prepared to try several methods or combinations of methods (prescription nicotine gum, for example, works best in conjunction with a group program).

2. Be prepared for withdrawal symptoms: Anxiety, restlessness, irritability, lethargy, impatience, confusion, and lack of concentration are common. So are coughing, headaches, insomnia, and appetite swings. Take a brisk walk or do aerobic exercises to make you forget about your withdrawal symptoms and to burn energy.

3. Use the buddy system. Join forces with another smoker who wants to quit and give each other moral support.

4. Enlist a former smoker to help you through the rough times and focus you on the benefits of quitting.

5. Get rid of all ashtrays, matches, and lighters. Spend more time in places where you can't smoke.

6. Get your teeth cleaned; resolve to keep them free of nicotine stains.

7. Keep your mouth and hands busy: chew sugarless gum, nibble raw vegetables and fruits, drink liquids through a straw, play with a lucky coin.

8. Put the money you used to spend on cigarettes in a special bank account; use the proceeds to reward yourself for every week you succeed.

9. If you fail, try again. Most smokers need three or four tries.

❯Snakebites

Take the following steps if you think someone has been bitten by a poisonous snake:

1. Wash the bite with soap and water. Don't put ice on it.

2. Immobilize the bitten limb with a splint (p. 194), and keep it at or below heart level.

3. Carry the victim to an emergency room; if some walking is unavoidable, move slowly.

4. Only if you can't reach medical help within 30 to 45 minutes should you tie constricting bands on each side of the bite. Use two lightweight bands, such as folded handkerchiefs. Don't tie them too tight; the poison moves just under the skin, not through the blood, so you need not cut off circulation. You should be able to slip a finger under the bands. For a bitten finger, put the band around the wrist. If the bite is

on an elbow, knee, or foot, use just one band above the joint. Leave the bands on until you reach help.

5. If you're in the wilderness and severe symptoms (extreme pain, weakness, nausea, and shortness of breath) occur, apply the constricting bands, slit the puncture marks with a sterilized knife, and remove the venom with a rubber suction cup (found in commercial snakebite kits).

Snaps

1. An easy way to position a metal snap is to "baste" the ball half to the overlapping edge of the garment with a dab of fabric glue. Run a pin through the ball to mark where the center of the socket should be on the garment. Dab glue on the spot and press the socket to it. When the glue dries, stitch on the snap.

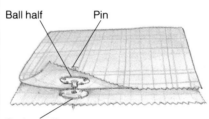

Ball half   Pin

Socket half

2. Instead of laboriously sewing on one snap at a time, buy tape with a row of snaps attached. Preshrink it, then baste it to the garment with fabric glue, putting the ball strip on the overlap; machine-sew in place.

3. If your snap pops and you're far away from a needle and thread, hold the opening together with a pin (safety or straight), paper clip, or tape (masking or transparent).

Snoring

1. Caused by an obstruction of your breathing passages, snoring can sometimes be prevented by raising the head of your bed on bricks or concrete blocks (extra pillows won't work). An alternative method of keeping your airway open is to sleep on a cervical pillow or with a cervical collar or a rolled towel pinned around the neck; use no pillow.

2. Don't take anything that might relax the muscles in your airway, including alcohol, tranquilizers, sleeping pills, and antihistamines.

3. If you snore only when sleeping on your back, sew or tape a large marble or a tennis ball to the back of your pajama top. Or add a pocket in which to put such an object.

DID YOU KNOW . . . ?

"A little night music"

☐ The British novelist Anthony Burgess once noted: "Laugh and the whole world laughs with you; snore and you sleep alone."

☐ Almost half the adult population snores occasionally; a quarter are habitual snorers. Problem snoring is more common in men, but women and children snore, too. And so do cats, dogs, horses, and many other animals.

☐ Historically, snorers are in good company: Plutarch, Winston Churchill, and 20 of the first 32 U.S. Presidents were known to be nocturnal nuisances. Once when

hospitalized, Teddy Roosevelt snored so loudly that most of the patients in his wing asked to be moved.

☐ In Silver Spring, Maryland, a woman struck her stertorous husband with a billy club and was found guilty of assault and battery. A Denver fireman once shot a coworker in the leg during an argument over snoring.

☐ While snorers have tried everything from surgery to self-hypnosis to chin straps, a dependable cure for the sonorities is yet to be found.

4. If you or your loved one gasps and snorts while snoring loudly, consult a doctor.

Snorkeling masks

1. To prevent your mask from fogging over, spit in it; rub the spittle around and rinse the mask.

2. To clear the snorkel tube of water as you ascend after a breath-held dive, tilt your head well back and exhale just as your mask breaks the surface of the water. Keep exhaling as you roll your head forward to continue snorkeling.

3. If your breathing tube fills with water, don't breathe in. Wait until the top of the tube is above the surface, then blow the water out.

Snow blindness

1. If, 6 to 8 hours after you're out in the snow, your eyes feel irritated and gritty or you're having difficulty detecting variations in the level of the ground, you may be suffering from snow blindness, or sunburn of the cornea; stay out of the sun for a few days.

2. If your eyes hurt so much that you don't want to open them, cover them with cold compresses and rest in a dark room for 12 to 24 hours—long enough to let the pain subside. To prevent infection, don't rub your eyes.

PREVENTION

Whenever you're out in the snow—even on cloudy or foggy days—wear specially coated sunglasses (preferably with side shields) that keep out ultraviolet rays. If you get caught without them, make some cardboard "sunglasses" with narrow eye slits (p.200), or blacken your cheeks, nose, and the area around your eyes with soot.

Snowed-in car

If you're ever trapped in a blizzard, stay in your car and wait for help.

1. Before the snow gets too deep, clear a space around the tailpipe to let carbon monoxide escape when you run the heater.

2. Get whatever you need from the trunk into the passenger compartment; look for a tool, such as a jack handle or an umbrella, to clear an air passage if snow buries the car.

3. Keep warm. Put on all available clothing and cover yourself and the other passengers with blankets or carpeting; for more insulation, stuff newspaper inside clothing. Run the heater for no longer than 10 minutes per hour to conserve fuel. (Crack a window on the side away from drifting snow to let the carbon monoxide escape.) The rest of the time, get emergency heat from a large votive candle in a coffee can.

4. Stay awake. Don't drink alcohol; it causes drowsiness. Be active—stretch, flex your muscles, wiggle your fingers and toes.

5. Limit your use of the radio and lights to conserve battery power.

6. If other cars are snowbound near you, join forces. More people in a car will keep it warmer, boost morale, and encourage wakefulness.

Snow shoveling

1. Right before a snowfall, spread a little sand, rock salt, or cat litter on steps, sidewalks, and driveway to prevent snow from sticking (see *Icy walks*, p.113).

2. Don't lift snow; push it. If you must lift, bend your knees and keep your lower back straight. Carry the loaded shovel close to your body.

DID YOU KNOW . . . ?

The cold, hard facts about igloos

For most of us, snow is snow. But to an Eskimo, snow is so important that his language contains more than a dozen words to describe its various forms.

Perhaps the most useful form is created when snow from a single storm freezes into a solid sheet of ice, for only that kind is suitable for building an igloo. Once the Eskimo finds such a sturdy layer of ice, he clears away the soft snow on the surface and draws the outline of his

house—a circle measuring 9 to 15 feet in diameter.

Standing inside this circle, he cuts blocks of ice and places them along the outline in spiraling rows upward, pressing them together to ensure a snug fit. Meanwhile his wife plasters any cracks on the exterior with fine, soft snow. After an entrance has been made, he adds the finishing touches: an air vent in the ceiling and a window of clear, freshwater ice to admit light.

3. Start shoveling as soon as 1 or 2 inches of snow are on the ground and never let more than a couple of inches accumulate.

4. To avoid pulling a back or shoulder muscle, warm up indoors with a few minutes of light calisthenics and stretching exercises (p.199).

5. Use a small shovel (p.185) or fill only half of a large one. For hard-packed snow use a garden shovel.

6. To keep snow from sticking to a shovel, spray with silicone lubricant. Or apply two thick coats of car wax.

Socks

1. If holes always appear in the same place on your socks, check your feet for rough spots—pumicing them may save your socks. Check your shoes, too.

2. Socks won't stay up? You may be drying them on too hot a setting, which damages the elastic fibers.

3. Where do socks disappear to so mysteriously? We don't know, but here are a few ways to cope. Some get stuck in an inaccessible part of the washer or dryer. Check with the manufacturer on how and where to look for them. Better yet, before washing, put all your socks in a zippered net bag or tie the pairs together. Or buy socks of the same style and color in quantity— you may even get a discount. Then you'll never have to worry about pairing them up.

4. If several people in your household wear socks that look just alike, mark the toes with small colored stitches or initial them with indelible ink.

5. Athletes are less likely to get blisters if they wear high-quality socks made of high-bulk synthetics like Orlon and polypropylene. They cushion the foot and draw perspiration away from the skin. Or buy socks specially designed for your sport. Aerobic socks are padded at the heel, ball of the foot, and toes; ski socks have a protective pad along the shin.

Soft drink can

If the pop-up tab breaks off and you don't have an opener, don't despair. Because the hole in the can's top is scored, you can open it by lining up the tip of a spoon with the hole and pressing down with your thumb. No spoon? Do it with the tip of a screwdriver or house key. (See also *Can opener,* p.35.)

Soil erosion

Use plants to stop soil erosion. They're cheaper and longer-lasting than a retaining wall.

MODERATE INCLINES

Plant a ground cover. First, sow annual ryegrass for an almost instant cover, then plant a fast-growing perennial like Bishop's weed or a creeping shrub like Bar Harbor juniper through the rye. The next spring treat the rye with a crabgrass preventer so that the ground cover can grow unimpeded.

STEEP SLOPES

Wattle the ground. Take pencil-thick, 1- to 3-foot cuttings of willow, alder, honeysuckle, forsythia, ivy, or any other easy-to-root plant and tie them in bundles about 6 inches in diameter, alternating the tips and the cut ends. Lay the bundles flat in shallow trenches dug across the slope wherever there is evidence of runoff. Cover with no more than an inch of soil and place

rocks around the cuttings to hold them in place. When they sprout, they will form a soil-holding thicket of roots and stems.

Soil testing

The type of soil in your garden determines how much water and fertilizer you should apply and even what kinds of plants you can grow. Plants in sandy, or light, soil need plenty of water and nutrients; those in heavy clay may well be killed by overwatering. To figure out what kind of soil you have, try this simple test:

1. Fill a quart jar two-thirds full of a solution of 1 teaspoon commercial water softener in 1 quart water.

2. Add soil until the water level rises to the jar's lip. Screw on the cap and shake vigorously.

3. Set the jar down and watch the particles settle. The larger sand grains will fall to the bottom of the jar almost immediately; finer silt particles will take a while longer; and tiny clay particles will settle only after several hours.

4. Now "read" the layers. Equal layers of sand, silt, and clay indicate loamy soil—ideal for plants. A thick layer of sand means light soil; dig in some organic matter. A thick layer of clay shows heavy soil; dig in sand and organic matter.

Clay—
Silt—
Sand—

Sore throats

1. Avoid irritation—if you smoke, take the opportunity to stop.

2. To numb the pain, make this icy honey-lemon drink: squeeze the juice of one lemon into 4 ounces of water and mix in plenty of honey or sugar; add lots of ice, stir well, and sip through a straw. Other soothers: gargle with ½ teaspoon of salt in 8 ounces of water three times a day or suck lozenges containing benzocaine or phenol.

3. Keep the mucous membranes moist: drink plenty of nonalcoholic liquids and run a vaporizer in your bedroom.

4. Take aspirin or a substitute (p.12) to relieve pain.

5. Call a doctor if you have a fever of 101°F or higher, white spots on your tonsils, swollen lymph nodes for longer than 2 weeks, great difficulty swallowing or breathing, or pain on opening your mouth wide—also if you have recently been exposed to strep throat or have ever had rheumatic fever. (See also *Pain relief*, p.148.)

Soundproofing

1. In a rumpus room, carpet the floor, cover the walls with cork, and install acoustical ceiling tile.

2. Insulate heating and air-conditioning ducts. Hollow, uninsulated metal ducts carry sound throughout the house.

3. Insulate a noisy water heater.

4. Place a clothes dryer, washing machine, or dishwasher on a thick pad of carpeting or rubber.

5. Put a television or stereo against an outside wall so that it won't transmit noise to an adjacent room.

6. Put stereo speakers on foam rubber on shelves or low tables.

7. Use lined curtains to block out street noise.

8. Carpet stairs to quiet footsteps.

Sour cream

1. Use plain low-fat yogurt in dip recipes that call for sour cream. To thicken the yogurt, spoon it onto a piece of cheesecloth and suspend it over a bowl in the refrigerator overnight to drain off the whey.

2. For a less calorie-laden potato topping, whirl low-fat cottage cheese or ricotta in a blender to smooth out the lumps, then stir in chives or chopped parsley. Or use low-fat yogurt mixed with chopped basil, Parmesan cheese, and freshly ground pepper.

Soy sauce

1. Dilute soy sauce with an equal quantity of water to lower the sky-high sodium content. Or buy reduced-sodium soy sauce.

2. If sodium isn't a concern, a good soy sauce substitute is *tamari*, made from fermented soybeans.

3. As a substitute in cooking, use 3 parts teriyaki to 1 part water.

Spelling

1. Remember the old rhyme "*I* before *E*, except after *C*, or when sounded like *A*, as in *neighbor* and *weigh*"? Well, even this rule has its exceptions—many are in the sentence "Sheik, seize the weird words *either* and *neither* at your leisure."

2. Ask a skilled speller to check what you've written; see if there's a pattern to your misspelling.

3. Use mnemonic aids to remember difficult words. For example: There's *a rat* in sep*arat*e; there's an *end* in fri*end*; the princi*pal* is your chief school *pal*; but a princi*ple* is a r*ule*.

4. Play word games and hold family spelling bees to help your children improve their spelling.

5. But note: some scholars believe that good spelling isn't a measure of intelligence and application but rather is an innate neuromuscular skill—that is, it can't be acquired. If, after trial and many errors, you still can't spell, the problem may be in your genes. If so, keep a dictionary always at hand: at home, on your desk, in your computer, in your briefcase or handbag.

6. No dictionary? Try looking up a word in the Yellow Pages, an encyclopedia, or the index of a book.

Spiders

1. You don't have to see a spider to kill it. Just spray its web with insecticide. Some spiders constantly rebuild their webs by eating the old silk, and they'll ingest the poison along with it.

2. Spiders are among a gardener's best friends. If you see a wolf spider

---

DID YOU KNOW . . . ?

Spelling bee stumpers

Even champions have been stumped by the words on this list. Try holding a spelling bee at home to see how many of these tricky, tough-to-spell words will baffle your family as well.

afflatus	condominium	ichthyology	mnemonic
atelier	dentifrice	incandescence	persiflage
baccalaureate	encomium	lavender	quidnunc
badinage	esoteric	meringue	quietus
cedilla	exorcism	minuscule	ratiocination
codicil	hemorrhage	miscible	sarcophagus

or some other large species on your basement wall, don't smash it; screw up your courage and capture the creature in a wide-mouth jar. Then release it in the garden, where it will feast on crickets, sow bugs, and other such pests.

3. Don't spray insecticide on a spider that's directly overhead, lest it drop down and bite you. If a spider does fall on you, prevent a bite by quickly brushing it off instead of swatting it.

4. Outdoors, paint the inside of a tire swing white so that you can see a spider before it sees you. And before using an outdoor toilet, run a stick under the seat to knock off any lurking spiders.

Splinters

1. Can't see a splinter? Use a magnifying glass (p.131) or apply a drop of iodine to stain it. Then remove it with tweezers and cleanse the area with soap and water or hydrogen peroxide.

2. If the splinter resists or a bit of it remains, soak the wounded area in water and dry; then dab on some white glue and gently press on a bit of gauze. When it's dry, peel it off; the splinter should come with it.

❭ Splints

Almost anything can serve as a splint. The lighter in weight it is, the better, so long as it can keep the fractured limb immobile.

1. A magazine works well; wrap it around the limb and secure it with cloth strips, tape, or rubber bands. A thick newspaper will also do.

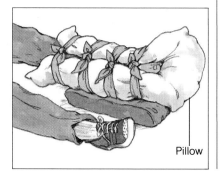

Pillow

2. Other usable objects include pieces of lumber, plywood, or stiff cardboard; broom handles, umbrellas, or ski poles—even such soft items as pillows or blankets. Using a roller bandage or wide strips of cloth, fasten the splint snugly (but not so tightly that you cut off circulation) in several places above and below the fracture. Or wrap continuously upward from the end of the affected limb.

3. If nothing is available, bind a fractured arm firmly to the victim's chest, a broken leg to the uninjured one. In all cases, get the victim to a doctor or an emergency room as quickly as possible. (See also *Fractures*, p.91; *Slings*, p.188.)

Spring fever

Does the end of winter leave you feeling lazy, listless, and depressed? Here are some ways to cure the blues and put you in harmony with the new season:

1. Get plenty of extra rest and make a special effort to eat a low-fat, low-carbohydrate, high-protein diet (see *Low-fat diet*, p.130; *The Balanced Diet*, p.254).

2. Change out of your winter clothing; spring's lighter fabrics and colors may give you just the psychological lift you need.

3. Alter your daily routine: get up earlier than usual, take a different route to work, discover new places to eat lunch.

4. Instead of saving your vacation days for summer, use one or two now to do something fun that you don't ordinarily have time for.

5. Brighten up your environment: wash the windows, pull back the curtains, buy something new for your home.

6. Start to work on your garden: plant seeds indoors, lay out vegetable beds, begin tilling the soil as soon as it's dry enough.

7. Find other excuses for getting outdoors more: make time to walk to work, watch the sun go down, count the stars at night.

Squaring a corner

No framing square? Try one of these methods to check for square:

1. To check a bookshelf or cabinet, measure diagonally from the upper left-hand corner to the lower right-hand one, then from the upper right corner to the lower left. If the work is square, the two measurements will be exactly the same.

2. Place a large book in the corner. If the work is square, both edges of the book will be exactly parallel to the two sides they touch.

3. Use a level and plumb bob. Make sure the top of the work is exactly level, then hang the plumb bob from the top. A visual check should tell you whether the side is perpendicular to the top.

4. Use math—the 3-4-5 ratio—to check for an exact 90° angle (see *Measuring*, p.133).

Squeaking floor

1. For a quick fix, sprinkle talcum powder or powdered graphite between the squeaking boards. Or if that doesn't work, squirt in some liquid wax.

2. Rearrange some furniture in order to change the traffic pattern in the room.

3. To silence a squeak from above, drill pilot holes and drive spiral-shank flooring nails through the floorboards into a joist.

4. If the floor is accessible from below, drive thin wood shims (cedar shingles work best) between the underside of the squeaking boards and the top of the joist.

To keep wood shims from shifting, spread glue on both sides.

Squeegee

1. If the blade is nicked or damaged, reverse it. If it cannot be removed, smooth the edges with some fine sandpaper.

2. To clean car windows, cut a section of windshield wiper blade and hold it with a large paper clamp.

3. You can also use an old rubber dish-draining mat. Cut off the end several inches back from the lip so that you can hold it comfortably.

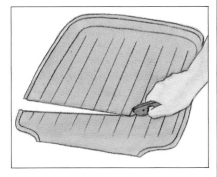

4. Clean rinse water from window glass or glazed ceramic tiles with balled-up newspaper.

Squirrels

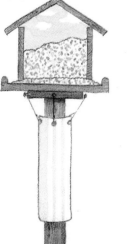

1. To deter these acrobatic interlopers, install a bird feeder on a 6-foot pole. First slip a 12-inch length of 4-inch plastic pipe over the pole, then suspend it from the bottom of the feeder. Squirrels won't be able to scale it or climb inside. But keep the feeder away from trees, or they'll find a way to drop down onto it.

2. Or hang the bird feeder from a long wire strung between two poles. Cut the bottoms from eight plastic bottles and string the wire through the bottles, four on each side of the feeder. They'll spin under the squirrels' feet, dropping the would-be seed thieves to the ground.

3. Keep an active dog or cat near the vegetable garden to discourage squirrels.

Stairs

1. To put a slip-resistant surface on concrete stairs, mix sand into masonry paint and coat the treads with it. Stir often as you work.

2. On uncarpeted steps, apply a nonslip adhesive-backed strip about 1 inch from the front edge of each tread.

3. When carrying a large object, such as a basket of laundry, it's safest to back down the stairs; drag the load behind you with one hand and hold the banister with the other.

4. To silence squeaky stairs, nail the treads to the top edge of the risers with spiral-shank nails. Be sure to bore pilot holes first.

5. For a temporary tread, cut a piece of ¾-inch plywood to fit and nail it in place.

6. If a staircase has very little headroom, install a small mirror on the front of the low spot. When people see their reflection, they'll duck.

Stamps

1. If your postage stamps get stuck together, place them in the freezer for an hour or two. They'll usually come apart and be usable.

2. To remove a stamp from an envelope for collecting purposes, put it in the freezer overnight; then take it out and slide a knife between it and the envelope.

3. Or cut off the corner of the envelope with the stamp and float—don't immerse—it in lukewarm water until the paper comes off. Dry the stamp on blotting paper, then flatten it between the pages of a book. Or lay a thin paper over the stamp and run a moderately hot iron over it.

Caution: Never put an antique stamp in water because the ink might run. And don't use steam to loosen such a stamp: it might be ruined as a collector's item.

Staples

1. If you don't have a working stapler, fasten papers at the corners with a dab of rubber cement or small squares of double-stick tape.

2. If you're missing a staple gun, tap staples into woodwork or upholstery with a tack hammer.

3. To remove stubborn staples from a wall or bulletin board, try needle-nose pliers, tweezers, or a fingernail clipper.

Static electricity

1. Take the crackle out of your carpet with a mixture of 1 part liquid fabric softener and 5 parts water. Put it in a spray bottle, mist the carpet, and let dry.

2. To fight static electricity in clothing, add fabric softener to the final rinse. If a clinging slip is the problem, starch it.

3. If you're already dressed, rub your slip or stockings with a fabric softener sheet or a wire hanger. Or spritz with hair spray.

Staying awake

1. Get up and move around; talk to other people.

2. Splash your face with cold water. Open the windows and let in some fresh air.

3. Drink beverages that contain caffeine and eat high-protein foods. Stay away from potato chips, muffins, cookies, crackers, cake, and candy; far from being a "quick energy fix," these high-carbohydrate foods will make you sleepier.

4. Chew on a peppermint or a hot pepper; your body may rouse itself to the irritation.

5. If it's absolutely necessary to

stay up for a couple of days, it may work to take a nap during the first 24 hours; a nap on the second day, however, will probably leave you feeling groggy.

6. If you feel drowsy while driving, open the windows and let the fresh air blow on your face. Sing along with the music on the radio or talk back to the disc jockey. If you're still not alert, pull over, get out, and jog around the car.

7. If you have to change from one work shift to another, keep the same daily routine, regardless of what the clock says; eat breakfast before you go to work, break for lunch in the middle of your shift, and have dinner at the end of your work "day."

Stereo systems

1. If your tapes don't sound as good as they used to, it's probably time to clean the playback heads on your tape player. (A once-a-month cleaning is wise.) Although you can use rubbing alcohol on a cotton swab, it's best to buy a special cleaner from an electronics supply store.

2. To clean the stylus on your turntable, put a little rubbing alcohol on a fine camel's-hair brush and move it *gently* along the cartridge from back to front—never sideways or front to back.

SPEAKERS

1. If a speaker stops working, make sure that all the connections are secure. If it's still dead, detach the jack or wire that goes into it from the back of the amplifier or receiver and connect it to the working speaker (after removing its own connection). If that speaker continues to work, the silent speaker needs to

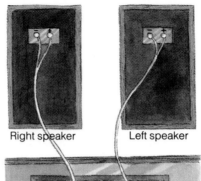

Right speaker   Left speaker

be repaired. If the second speaker ceases to work, the problem is in the wire or the amplifier; to find out which, reconnect the speakers and reverse the jacks or wires on the back of the amplifier. If the dead speaker now works, your amplifier needs repair; if it doesn't work, replace the jack or wire.

2. Does the speaker go out when you're using the turntable? Check the stylus while a record is playing; if it veers to the left or right, it may be missing one of the channels from the record. Replace it.

TURNTABLES

1. Does your turntable hum? See if the grounding wire (a thin black or green wire) is securely attached to the grounding post on the back of the receiver or amplifier.

2. Or try moving the turntable away from the speakers and other stereo components; it may be picking up vibrations. If you can't move it, place it on a piece of foam rubber.

Stings

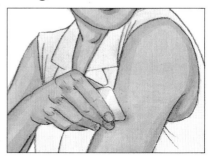

Insect stings—even multiple stings—are seldom very serious. The only notable exception (most often caused by a bee or wasp sting) is allergic, or anaphylactic, shock (see *Allergies*, p. 10).

Remove the stinger by gently scraping it with the dull edge of a knife blade or with a credit card—do not use tweezers. Apply a paste of meat tenderizer and water to the sting site as quickly as possible to reduce pain and swelling and to slow the rate of absorption of the poison. To relieve the itch, apply ice packs, followed by 0.5 percent hydrocortisone cream; if not available, use calamine lotion. (See also *Insect bites*, p.116.)

Stitch in the side

1. Breathe deeply in and out to oxygenate your blood and energize the cramped muscle.
2. Dig your fingers into the muscle at the point where you feel pain—usually just at the bottom of the rib cage—then massage the spot by digging and rubbing.
3. If the stitch was caused by fatigue, rest is the best cure.
4. Mineral depletion is often the problem. Prevent a recurrence by eating a banana and some salt in the morning (for potassium and sodium). Pay attention to your calcium intake; it helps regulate muscle contractions. Drink lots of water.

Stitch removal

1. In a chain-stitch seam, cut a single loop and unravel the whole line of stitching.
2. The quickest way to remove a conventional machine stitch is with a seam ripper—or in a pinch, a single-edge razor blade—but be careful not to cut the fabric. The slow but sure way is to snip the individual stitches with tiny sharp-pointed scissors.
3. Overlocked, or serged, seams look complicated, especially those using four or five threads in ladders of chains and loops. But you can cut them simply by running a seam ripper along the fabric's edge, under the outer row of loops.

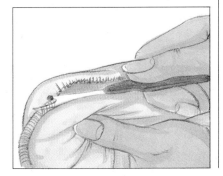

Stolen car

1. Thieves often repaint cars and change the vehicle identification number (VIN) so that owners can't identify them. Foil them by having the VIN etched onto all the windows—a thief is less likely to steal a car on which all the windows would have to be replaced. You should find the VIN on the left front side of the dashboard.
2. To help identify your car should it be stolen, drop business cards down the window channels and under the backseat.
3. In order to report the theft to the police, keep a record of the year, make, and model of your car, as well as the VIN; make copies of the license and registration.

Storage space

1. In one section of your closet install two rods, one 3 to 4 feet above the other. Use them for short items such as shirts and skirts.
2. Suspend shower curtain hooks from the rods to hold belts, purses, and scarves.
3. Place storage boxes in the wasted space at the closet bottom. Make your own from bureau drawers; add hinged tops to keep out dust.
4. Storage boxes also work well under the bed. They'll be easier to pull in and out if you put them on rollers.
5. Store frequently used items in clear plastic boxes or wire baskets on closet shelves.
6. Attach hooks, towel racks, or shoe bags to the closet walls or door for miscellaneous items.
7. In children's closets place rods within the kids' reach and use the upper space to store out-of-season clothing. To encourage neatness, use plastic storage bins or label boxes with pictures of what's supposed to go in them.
8. Make a child's closet from an old chest with a hinged top. Screw short legs to whichever end will be the bottom. Stand the chest up and put a rod across the inside and a knob on the "door." For safety, re-

move all locking devices; use a friction catch to keep the door closed.
9. In an entrance hall where there's a staircase, hinge the tread of the bottom step; use it to store boots, umbrellas, and sports equipment.
10. If there's space above or below your kitchen cabinets, enclose it and install sliding doors. Use the upper "mini-cabinets" for rarely used items, the lower ones for things you use all the time.
11. In your vacation home use metal storage compartments to keep out mice and other pests. Or line wooden compartments with aluminum sheeting or foil.
12. In the basement make a rack to fit under the steps and use it to store window and door screens.
13. In the dining room turn a windowsill into a bar and build a storage chest under it.
14. In the attic build triangular storage units to fit under the eaves.
15. If your living room fireplace sticks out into the room, build in a set of floor-to-ceiling bookshelves or cabinets on both sides.
16. If your basement has exposed joists overhead, turn them into storage bins by nailing sheets of ½- or ¾-inch plywood under them. Put hinged doors on each one and use them to store lumber and painting supplies.
17. Where there are closets under stairways, install a small shelf under each step. Use the shelves for storing small articles.

Storm windows

1. A broken storm window? For an energy-efficient quick fix, carefully knock out the rest of the glass and staple a sheet of 4-mil polyethylene to the frame, inside and out. Or cover the screen window with a double thickness of polyethylene and put it in place while the storm window is being reglazed.

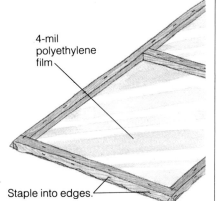

4-mil polyethylene film

Staple into edges.

2. Or you can just use the plastic instead of storm windows. Staple it to the exterior window frame, then secure it with a frame of lath.
3. To make interior storm windows, trim the window frame with two or three adjacent strips of clear double-stick plastic tape. Then cut a plastic sheet slightly larger than the frame and press it onto the tape; start at the top, stretching the plastic to eliminate wrinkles.
4. If you've installed a traditional storm window and condensation forms on the house window, the storm window needs caulking. Apply latex caulk around it to form an airtight seal.
5. Before taking down storm windows in the spring, mark each one with a letter or number keyed to its proper place. This will simplify installation next fall.

❯ Strains & sprains

Both strains and sprains hurt. To tell the difference between them, look for swelling and discoloration; a sprain will have both.
To treat either injury, elevate and

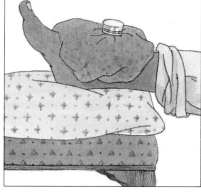

immobilize the affected part and apply ice as continuously as it can be tolerated for about 24 hours; after that time, substitute heat for the cold. If swelling and pain persist, see a doctor. (See also *Fractures*, p.91; *Pain relief*, p.148.)

Strengthening exercises

1. For arms and shoulders: Do hip raises. Lie on the floor on one side. Raise your upper body, supporting it with your arm. Push your hip up to straighten your body, then bend your elbow as you lower yourself to the floor. Repeat three to six times on each side.
2. Or do modified push-ups. Stand 3 or 4 feet away from a strong desk, table, or counter—preferably one that has a rounded edge. Lean forward and support your weight with your hands on the edge, keeping your arms straight. Then bend your arms, keeping your body straight until your chin or chest touches the edge. Push back to the starting

position and repeat 5 to 20 times.
3. For legs: Try semi-squats. Stand with hands on hips directly in front of a straight chair. Bend your knees slowly until the backs of your thighs just touch the front edge of the chair at midthigh (or as low as you can without pain), raising your arms straight in front as you bend. Rise to the starting position. Repeat 5 times; work up to 30 or more rapid repetitions. As you get stronger, remove the chair.
4. For the calves: Hop, first with feet together, then on alternating legs, then stepping forward on alternating legs as if walking. Repeat each 5 times; work up to 25 times.
5. To build up endurance for hiking, walk with a weighted backpack, increasing the poundage as you grow stronger. Five-, 10-, or 25-pound bags of cat litter or dry pet food work well.

Stress

Feeling tense, restless, anxious, or irritable?
1. Clear your mind. Sit comfortably away from noise and distractions, close your eyes, and focus on a peaceful thought, a tranquil setting, or a neutral word. Try to recall, minute by minute, the finest hour of the happiest day of the best vacation you ever had. Or just listen to yourself breathe. After 5 to 10 minutes, you'll feel refreshed.
2. Schedule at least 30 minutes daily for relaxation—listen to soft music, read, write, think, or dream.

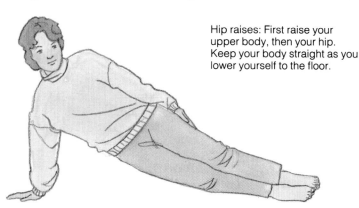

Hip raises: First raise your upper body, then your hip. Keep your body straight as you lower yourself to the floor.

3. Breathe deeply for a few minutes several times a day or whenever you begin to feel tense. Clasp your hands over your abdomen and inhale slowly and deeply through your nose, extending your abdomen as far out as it will go. Hold your breath for several seconds, then exhale slowly through your mouth. (See also *Breathing exercises*, p.26.)
4. Loosen up tense muscles by doing stretching exercises.
5. Practice progressive relaxation. Sit in a comfortable chair or lie on your back with your arms at your sides; close your eyes. One by one, tense up and relax each muscle area in your body, beginning with your head and working your way down to your toes. As you progress, try to isolate individual muscles. (See also *Insomnia*, p.116; *Noise*, p.143; *Quiet time*, p.167.)

›Stretchers

In an emergency you can use a table leaf, door, surfboard, or blanket as a stretcher. Or you can make do with one of these:
1. Place approximately 150 feet of rope on the ground and make 16 loops about as long and as wide as

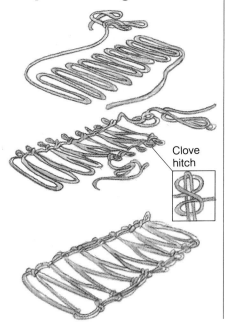

Clove hitch

the person to be carried. Work the rope ends down the sides as shown, using a clove hitch to tie the loops together; thread what's left of the rope ends through the closed loops, then tighten all the loops.
2. Button or zip a coat or several jackets; turn inside out and run two poles (or broom handles, pipes, or oars) through the sleeves.
Caution: Before using a makeshift stretcher, test it with an uninjured person. It may need more padding or support.

Stretching exercises

To reduce muscle tension and feel more relaxed, try these stretching exercises. Do each one slowly and stop when you feel tension in the muscle—but before the onset of pain. Hold a position, but never bounce; you could injure a muscle.
1. Arms, shoulders, and back: Kneel down, bend over, and rest your forehead on one forearm on the floor. Reach forward with your other arm, grab a couch leg or other firm object, and pull, feeling the tension in your arms, shoulders, upper back, and sides. Hold for 15 seconds and release. Repeat with the other arm.
2. Arms and shoulders: Raise your arms straight above your head, with your wrists intertwined and your palms together, so that the right palm faces right and the left palm faces left. Inhale as you stretch your arms up and back. Hold for 5

seconds, then lower your arms and relax. Repeat up to 10 times.
3. Sides: Stand with your feet a shoulder width apart. Raise one arm straight above your head, palm in. Rest the palm of your other hand against your thigh. Bend sideways from the waist, sliding your hand down your thigh and bringing your raised arm over, until you feel a pull from hip to shoulder. Hold for a count of five. Straighten. Alternate five times on each side.
4. Hamstrings: Stand with your feet shoulder width apart and your knees slightly bent. Bend over slowly, letting your arms and head dangle; keep your belly pulled in. Stop when you feel tension in your back or in the backs of your thighs and knees. Hold and count to 30, letting yourself relax. Imagine that the backs of your legs are turning to soft butter.
5. Calves: Stand at arm's length from a wall, hands flat on the wall, arms straight. Bend your elbows and lean toward the wall, keeping your back and legs straight, until you feel tension in your calf muscles. Hold for 20 seconds, then push upright. Repeat three times. The goal: to hold for 1 minute with your head against the wall.
6. Groin: Lie flat on your back with your legs raised, the heels resting against a wall, and your buttocks about 4 inches away from it. Slowly separate your legs, letting your heels slide apart and down the wall until

Groin muscles: Support your legs against a wall as you spread them apart.

you feel a stretch in your groin and inner thighs. Hold for 30 seconds; then relax and pull your legs together. Repeat twice.

String

1. To loosen a knot, twist the string to compact it while pushing toward the knot from both sides. If necessary, ask someone to open the knot with a pencil tip or nail while you push. Or use your teeth.
2. Keep string neat by putting it in a dispenser. Make your own from a can or jar; punch a hole in the lid for the string to feed through. Or use a watering can or teapot, pulling the string through the spout. Or use a heated nail to melt a hole in one end of an egg-shaped pantyhose container.
3. Wrap short lengths of string around a fishing reel. Or use a toilet tissue tube with a notch cut in one edge to secure the loose end.

Stringing beads

1. For heavy beads use fine fishing line or monofilament leader.
2. If you're using string, dab clear nail polish on one end. Let it dry before starting to string.
3. To keep the whole strand from coming apart if the string breaks, tie knots between the beads.
4. To keep beads of varying sizes in order while restringing, stick them to a strip of tape. Or lay them in the crack of an open book or magazine.

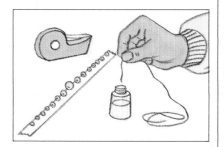

Stuck car

1. If you're stuck in mud or snow, don't gun the engine; you'll dig yourself in deeper. Put metal mesh traction mats, pieces of old carpet (the

twisted or knotted type works best), gravel, sand, cat litter, or branches under the drive wheels for traction (front wheels in a front-drive car, rear wheels in a rear-drive). Then, keeping the front wheels pointed straight ahead, rock the car gently by shifting quickly from *Low* or *Drive* to *Reverse*. If you're not out after rocking 12 times, stop. You don't want to deepen the grooves or damage the transmission.
2. If you're stuck in sand, let a little air out of the tires. Drive immediately to a service station to reinflate them. But be careful; pressure below 20 p.s.i. can cause rim slippage and air leaks. If the pressure has gotten that low, have the tires carefully checked and reinflated.

Studs

1. No studs for your dress shirt? In a pinch, use brass or gold paper fasteners; you could even paint the round part with black liquid shoe polish or a felt-tip pen.
2. Or substitute attractive buttons. Take a strip of cloth, put it under your shirt, and mark where the buttonholes are. Sew the buttons onto the strip, slip it under your shirt, and button up.

Sunburn

1. For quick relief, take a cool oatmeal bath (see *Itching*, p.118), then smooth on a thin layer of 0.5 percent hydrocortisone cream, followed by a soothing moisturizing lotion. Apply cool compresses for 10 to 15

minutes several times a day; repeat applications of the hydrocortisone cream, avoiding the eye area.
2. To prevent dehydration, drink lots of nonalcoholic liquids.
3. To relieve general discomfort, take aspirin or a substitute (p.12).
Caution: If you feel intense pain or if you have blisters, swelling, or fever, see a doctor.

Sundials

The advantage of a sundial: it doesn't have to be wound or plugged in. The drawback: it can't be used at night or on cloudy days.

To make one, plant a straight or forked stick firmly into the ground at high noon; tilt it slightly northward (in the northern hemisphere) so that you get a shadow. Put a line of pebbles at the tip of the shadow. Then set an alarm clock for each hour; when it rings, place another line of pebbles at the shadow's tip. Repeat until sundown, then resume at sunrise until you've come full circle.

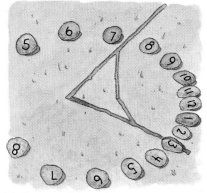

Ideally, a sundial should be laid out on the day of the vernal or autumnal equinox. It will be accurate only on those 2 days.

Sunglasses

1. For maximum protection, look for the label "Absorbs UV up to 400 nm"; this indicates that the sun's most damaging ultraviolet rays will be blocked.
2. Caught without your sunglasses? Make Eskimo-style goggles: Bend a strip of cardboard lengthwise, then cut two slits along the

fold for your eyes and a nose slot. Attach with ribbon or string. (Don't pull your "sunglasses" flat; the triangular shape shades your eyes.)

Sunscreens

Sunscreens should be used regularly from early childhood to prevent skin damage (altered texture, wrinkling, discoloration, pronounced blood vessels, and cancerous lesions) that may be caused by prolonged exposure to the sun.

1. Here's a formula for judging their effectiveness: Determine how many minutes it takes your skin to begin to burn when unprotected. Multiply that number by the sun protection factor (SPF) printed on every commercial lotion. Divide the result by 60 to find how many hours of protection you can expect. If you would normally burn in 30 minutes, for example, an SPF 8 lotion should protect you for about 4 hours.

2. The most protective sunscreens are also the most expensive—one with an SPF of 50 may cost four times as much as one with an SPF of 25. To economize, buy a sunscreen with an SPF of 25 and apply it more often. If you burn easily or must be out in the sun for a long time, consult your dermatologist; she may recommend a complete sunblock such as zinc oxide.

3. Also take into account the sun's intensity; the higher in the sky it is, the more direct the rays are. You need a higher SPF number at midday than you do in the morning or evening, a higher number in the tropics than farther north.

4. What ingredients should you look for? At one time many dermatologists recommended PABA (para-aminobenzoic acid) derivatives; however, many people have developed allergic reactions to them, so doctors now suggest you look for PABA-free sunblocks. Sunscreens should also be waterproof and non-stinging and give broad-spectrum protection (not just against UVA and UVB rays).

5. Even a sunscreen labeled "waterproof" may come off while swimming. Remember to reapply it.

6. Never use a sunscreen that is more than a year old. Some have expiration dates—go by them.

7. Don't rely on "natural" lotions like sesame oil, cocoa butter, or mixtures of vinegar and olive oil. They're not effective. (See also *Burns*, p.28.)

Support groups

You no longer have to be alone with your problems; for almost every difficult personal situation, physical affliction, fear, and addiction, there is a mutual help or support group. By joining one, you'll gain the understanding of others who have gone through similar experiences and get practical help in dealing with your problem.

FINDING ONE

1. Some of the larger organizations are listed by subject in the phone directory. The names of many more are available from local churches, hospitals, and health and social service agencies. (See also *800 numbers*, p.71.)

2. Check to see if your state has a self-help "clearinghouse" that can refer you to an appropriate group. Or contact the National Self-Help Clearinghouse in New York City. (If there's no group nearby, there are some that can be networked by mail, telephone, or computer.)

3. Or start your own group after getting some guidance from a self-help clearinghouse. Recruit members who'll help you from the start; don't try to do it all yourself.

Surgery

1. Be sure there are no alternatives to surgery. Talk to your doctor and, to be on the safe side, get a second opinion—perhaps from an internist or nonsurgical specialist—even if your insurance company doesn't require one.

2. Choose your surgeon with care. Get recommendations from local medical societies, hospitals, doctors, nurses, and former patients. Interview each candidate. Be sure they're certified by the American College of Surgeons and the appropriate specialty board. (A specialist should perform a common procedure 100 to 200 times a year, a complex procedure with some regularity.) Ask about the extent of the operation, its risks, and its probable results.

3. Ask how much the surgery will cost; find out how much your insurance will cover. If your insurer feels the fee is too steep, try to negotiate a lower amount.

4. Go over the surgical consent form in your surgeon's office *before* entering the hospital. Make sure that the names of your surgeon and anesthesiologist are included and that the operation described is exactly what you expect; you have the right to delete permission for more extensive surgery. Don't sign until you're satisfied. And don't sign another form after you've been given medication.

5. Ask your surgeon for the names of others who have had similar operations. Call one or two and ask how you'll feel afterward; they'll probably offer suggestions for what you can do beforehand to prepare yourself for the experience.

6. Arrange to meet your anesthesiologist (physician) or anesthetist (nurse) before the operation—preferably before you're admitted to the hospital—to discuss any allergies or other physical conditions you have, any drugs you take, and any previous negative reaction to anesthetics. If you smoke, don't forget to say so; it could affect your breathing during surgery.

7. If you know well in advance that you'll need blood during and after an operation, donate your own and have it frozen and saved for you.

8. Request that any IV tubes be placed in your nondominant arm, away from the elbow, so that you'll be able to maneuver more easily.

9. Ask your doctor exactly where the incision is to be made; then, if you wish, use a felt-tip pen to mark that place on your body before you go into surgery. (See also *Getting Well*, p.251; *Hospital stays*, p.110.)

Sweaters

1. Cotton sweaters absorb a lot of water when washed, which makes them heavy and easily pulled out of shape if improperly hung or handled. You can hasten drying by turning them inside out and putting them in the dryer on *Tumble Dry* or *Air Fluff* for 15 minutes—no more. (Make sure the heat is set on *Low*.) Then spread flat to air-dry. **Caution:** Never put a wool sweater in the dryer.

2. If your cotton or synthetic sweater is out of shape, dampen it and pop it in the dryer on *Tumble Dry* or *Air Fluff* for a few minutes. If only the cuffs have stretched, soak them in hot water and dry with a hair dryer set on *Hot*.

3. You can speed up the drying of any sweater by putting wrapping paper or a paper bag inside it before spreading it flat. Or put the sweater on a towel, place another towel on top, roll everything up, and carefully step on the roll with bare feet to extract excess water.

4. To keep a sweater from getting baggy, mark the shape with pins on a towel before you wash it. Then block it to your outline for drying.

5. Never dry a sweater over a shower curtain rod or on a hanger. Don't pull on the bottom to even the front and back. Just straighten the seams and carefully smooth out any wrinkles.

6. "Shave" off those annoying pills with a razor, electric shaver, or medium sandpaper. Or wipe them off with a dry sponge.

7. If your angora sweater sheds, put it in a plastic bag, then into the freezer for an hour before wearing.

8. Give an old sweater new life or cover holes by sewing on appliqués.

› Swimming emergencies

1. If you tire far from shore, don't panic. Float on your back. If there are people around, wave one arm slowly from side to side to attract attention. Start for shore when you regain strength. Don't push yourself; float when you need to rest.

2. If you're tangled in weeds, relax, gently shake your arms or legs, and move slowly away—with the current. If you're stuck, roll the weeds down your arm or leg like a sock.

3. Let heavy surf help you get to shore. As a wave approaches from behind, turn your body sideways to it, so that you can watch its progress while you tread water. Try to ride with the wave's upward movement. If the wave breaks on you, hold your breath until it passes over; then either resume a back float or ride behind it toward shore.

4. Bodysurf on smaller waves: Start swimming as one approaches. As it catches you, straighten your body, thrust your arms out in front, and hold your head up, tucking your chin in. Ride the wave, kicking to

keep up with it. Rest when the crest passes.

5. If you get caught in an undertow, take a deep breath, relax, and let it carry you under and out. You'll bob up in time to breathe again. Bodysurf back to shore.

6. If you get caught in a riptide (a current moving out to sea), let it carry you out. As soon as it slows down, swim sideways (riptides are usually only about 20 feet wide). Then swim toward shore, moving at a wide angle away from the tide.

RESCUING OTHERS

1. Never get close enough to a panicked swimmer for him to be able to grab you. Instead, reach out with a long stick or your leg while maintaining a firm hold on dry land. Or throw a coil of rope or something that floats, ideally a life buoy.

2. If the victim is beyond reaching or throwing distance, try to go out with a floating support, such as a canoe or surfboard; a rowboat is best. When near the victim, turn the boat and approach stern first. Let the victim hold on to the stern as you row to safety.

3. Only as a last resort should you attempt a swimming rescue—and then only if you are a very good swimmer. If you have a shirt or towel, swim to the victim while holding it in your teeth. When you are just beyond arm's reach, take the shirt in one hand and flip the other end to the victim. Tow him to shore.

If all else fails, grasp his hair, collar, or chin. If he grabs you, try to break his hold. Or take a deep breath and sink with him—he'll let go. Kick away before trying again.

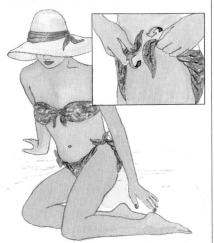

Swimming pools

1. To save wear and tear on an above-ground pool with a plastic liner, cut up a rubber dish mat and put the pieces under the legs of the ladder where they meet the liner.

2. If your child's pool has a small hole or crack, let it dry and then patch both sides with duct tape.

3. Attack the mud and gravel problem by placing a small plastic tub of water next to your pool. Ask children to step in it before jumping in the pool.

4. If your fence isn't keeping trespassers out of your pool, try planting thorny plants around it.

5. Want an easy way to inflate a child's plastic swimming pool? If it has a wide fold-type opening, you can use a vacuum cleaner; place the vacuum hose in the opening and turn the machine on *Exhaust.*

POOL GAMES

1. Float an inflated bicycle inner tube in the water and use it as a target for balls. Or fly-cast into it, using a bolt or a practice plug instead of a hook.

2. Enjoy water basketball? Just bolt a standard backboard, equipped with a hoop and nylon net, to 1½-inch angle irons. Attach them to the end of the diving board with two C-clamps.

3. Let small children go fishing. Make fish out of metal canning lids; tape over sharp edges and tie on bright plastic tails. Give the kids poles that have magnets for hooks. **Caution:** Don't let children play around any pool unattended. Always empty a small pool when not in use; remove game equipment from any pool.

Swimsuits

It's easy to make your own bikini. All you need are three sizable scarves and a little ingenuity. A sewing machine helps, too, or at least a needle and thread; but in a pinch, you could probably make do with small safety pins.

The world's smallest bathing suit

In 1946 French couturier Jacques Heim created "the world's smallest bathing suit"—two tiny cloth triangles joined at the hips and topped by a narrow bra. That same year the United States announced that it would begin peacetime nuclear testing by dropping an atomic bomb on a small island in the Pacific known as Bikini.

Both events, though unrelated, inspired French manufacturer Louis Réard, who had copied Heim's design, to dub his creation the bikini, hoping its impact on the fashion world would be as explosive as an atomic bomb.

Before long, American GI's stationed in Europe brought bikinis home for their wives and girlfriends—who were thrown off beaches for wearing them. Not until the 1960's did the teeny-weeny garments become socially acceptable on U.S. shores.

THE BOTTOM

Fold two scarves in half to form triangles. Then fold back the tips (the bottom of the *V*) about 2 inches and sew them down. Sew both sections together to form the crotch. Tie the loose ends at the sides, as shown.

THE TOP

1. Fold the remaining scarf into a triangle, then a wide band. Place it against your back, then tie it in front; adjust the width as needed.

2. If the scarf is long enough, you can make a halter top. Put the scarf around your neck, cross it over your bust, then tie the ends in the back.

For proper contour, twist the front end up and the back end down; knot the ends at each side.

T

Table linens

1. Stored linens will discolor if all of the soil—especially food or body oils—isn't removed first with proper laundering. Use hot soft water and adequate detergent and make sure all stains are completely out.

2. Sun-drying helps reduce discoloration in linens.

3. If your linens have discolored, a mild solution of chlorine bleach and water will do wonders.

4. To remove wax, place a white facial tissue, folded four times, over the spot and press with a warm iron. Repeat with a clean tissue if necessary.

5. Instead of ironing linen napkins, just smooth them out, still wet from the washer, onto a table or counter shelf. They'll dry crisp and neat. Spread a damp tablecloth over a nonwooden table.

Table manners

1. If you can't get at your food with a knife or fork without making a mess—when eating ribs, corn on the cob, or lobster, for example—go ahead and use your fingers.

Otherwise, when in doubt, follow your host's example or consider the formality of the situation.

2. If you've bitten into something that can't be swallowed—gristle, a pit, or a fish bone, for instance—remove it from your mouth the way it came in (generally with your fork) and put it on the side of the plate.

3. Hair in your soup? Bug in your salad? In someone's home, either remove the interloper and eat your food, or leave it untouched—but refrain from commenting on it. In a restaurant, send the food back.

4. If ashtrays are on the table, you can assume it's all right to smoke; otherwise, ask if anyone minds. Never smoke while others are eating; only between courses.

Tables

1. If the sides of your drop leaf table rattle on the legs, put a small adhesive bandage or foot pad at each point of contact. (If they're visible, paint them to match the wood.)

2. For a toddler's birthday party, use a long coffee table and short stools. If necessary, put books under each leg to elevate it. Cover with a stainproof tablecloth.

3. Reconditioned steamer trunks can make interesting coffee or occasional tables.

4. Or use two stained or painted sawhorses to support an old but attractive door.

5. Or place a sheet of heavy glass on top of a matched set of sturdy pedestals such as inverted urns, clay flowerpots, or heavy baskets.

6. Shade your redwood picnic table with a big outdoor umbrella. Drill a hole in the center of the tabletop, put the umbrella through it, and secure the bottom in a weighted umbrella stand.

Talcum powder

Either cornstarch or fuller's earth makes a good substitute for talcum powder. So does rice powder, which is especially good for use in place of a face powder.

Tangled cords

1. To store extension and appliance cords neatly, fanfold each one separately, wrap it with masking tape, and label it. You can also keep folded cords in napkin rings or toilet paper tubes.

2. Or hang your extension cords from a tie rack.

3. When storing appliances that have cords permanently attached, avoid kinks by fanfolding the cord. Hold it together with a twist tie or a rubber band.

4. Pivoting connectors are available at most electrical or electronics supply stores to keep your telephone cord from snarling.

IN TIMES GONE BY

Minding your manners

□ "Refrain from falling upon the dish like a swine while eating, snorting disgustingly, and smacking the lips," cautioned one 13th-century etiquette book.

□ Another warned, "A number of people gnaw a bone and then put it back in the dish—this is a serious offense." (The proper way to discard a bone, as all refined folk knew, was to throw it on the floor.)

□ Scratching while at the table was pointedly frowned upon, even though fleas and lice were everywhere. "Thou must not put either thy fingers into thine ears, or thy hands to thy head. The man who is eating must not be cleaning by scraping with his fingers at any foul part," wrote Fra Bonvincino da Riva, in *The Fifty Courtesies for the Table* in 1290.

□ Other etiquette writers in the Middle Ages frowned on the common practice of blowing one's nose into a tablecloth or coat sleeve. They also advised their readers not to blow their noses into their fingers while seated at the table.

□ Then, as now, propriety at the dinner table was a concern of the upper classes. But the proprieties put forward by medieval makers of manners differ sharply from today's codes of conduct. Among the worst offenses in modern times are talking with a mouth full of food, waving a fork or spoon in the air for emphasis, and eating with elbows on the table. And one more: It's considered rude to look down upon a person whose manners are less than perfect.

Tape

1. If you're having trouble finding the end of a roll of tape, just slide a credit card along the roll until it catches. A knife or single-edge razor blade will also work.

2. If tape is difficult to peel off a roll, put a drop of paint thinner on the end and wait 30 seconds.

3. To mark the end of a roll, insert a paper clip under the sticky side of the tape.

4. Need a lot of short pieces of tape that are the same length? Use a single-edge razor blade to cut into the roll through several layers of tape. Then peel off one piece after another.

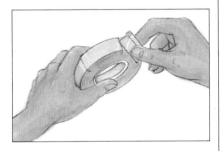

Tapes & CD's

1. Don't touch audio or video tapes with your fingers; you'll leave grease marks and particles of grit.

2. Don't store tapes on top of televisions, amplifiers, speakers, or VCR's. All these machines generate magnetic fields that could erase the recordings.

3. In the car keep tapes off a hot dashboard; they'll get brittle.

4. If you bring a videotape in from the cold, let it warm to room temperature before you play it. This gives condensed moisture a chance to evaporate. VCR's are sensitive to moisture, and even a small amount can do damage.

5. If a compact disc gets warped, heat it with a hair dryer until it's flexible; then put it on a flat surface between two pieces of wax paper. Weight it down with a heavy book or two and leave it in place for several hours. Repeat the process if necessary.

Tape splicing

1. The most foolproof way to edit or repair an audiocassette tape is with an inexpensive kit sold in electronics supply stores; it includes picks for retrieval, splicing tape, and a rewinding device. But if you find that the tape is badly tangled in the cassette, don't force it; seek professional help.

2. Splicing videotapes is *not* recommended; even professionals won't try it. So use an ounce of prevention: make a copy of valuable tapes and play only the copy. "Exercise" the master tape twice a year by running it fast forward through the player, then rewinding.

Taxicabs

1. To avoid being cheated on airport runs, ask at the information counter what the fare should be. Then ask the driver what it will cost—if his estimate is way off, use another cab.

2. If a driver tells you there's a surcharge to an outlying destination (permissible in many cities) and you aren't sure he's being truthful, ask him to verify it with the dispatcher over the radio.

3. Always make sure the driver restarts the meter when you get in so that the previous fare isn't added on to yours.

4. To ensure that you won't be stranded at the last moment, reserve a cab a few days ahead; call a few hours before your departure to confirm the reservation.

5. So there are no unpleasant surprises, always check the price over the phone. And ask if there's a surcharge for an extra passenger and any baggage

6. When a crowd of people are trying to hail cabs in one spot, walk two or three blocks up the street and then flag one down.

7. If you're vying with someone else for the same cab, suggest sharing—it usually works.

8. Any place that gets a lot of traffic is a good place to find a cab—restaurants, hotels, bus terminals, and, we're sorry to report, hospital emergency rooms.

9. Always look for cabs on streets where traffic is moving opposite the flow during the rush hour.

10. Never wait for a cab on the side of the street where the bus stops—the cabdriver can't see you.

11. Don't ignore off-duty cabs. If you're really desperate, hold up five fingers, signifying you'll pay $5 over the fare; ten fingers for $10. Money talks.

Teachers

1. Among the biggest turnoffs for teachers: talking in class, disrespect for school property, sloppy schoolwork, habitual tardiness, snapping chewing gum.

2. If your child says, "The teacher hates me," don't merely brush off the comment; discuss the situation sympathetically and get the facts. While it is true that children often exaggerate, the teacher may have had a bad day or may be more demanding than most. It is also true that personality conflicts sometimes exist. If so, your child needs your help and support.

3. Don't just storm into the teacher's classroom. Write a note asking for a conference and indicating the topic you want to discuss. During the meeting, focus on identifying and solving your child's problem, not on correcting what you think the teacher and the school are doing wrong. If possible, have your child participate in at least part of the conference.

4. If things still don't improve, you can go to your child's counselor and, if necessary, the principal.

5. If you decide to drop the matter, explain to your child that you're not abandoning him but are backing off to see if the situation will work itself out. Be prepared to help him cope—and to get involved again if things don't improve.

Teething

1. Rub a little over-the-counter anesthetic gel on the baby's gums or, if your pediatrician permits, dip your finger into some cognac, then rub it on your infant's gums.

2. Dip your finger in ice-cold water and massage the baby's gums.

3. Let the baby chew on something cold: a chilled teething ring; a washcloth soaked in cold water, wrung out, and twisted; a frozen bagel; or a large, cold carrot.

Telephone calls

1. Can't hear the bell when you're in the basement or yard? Put the phone in a metal pan or on top of a ceramic tile.

2. If someone rings you by mistake and asks who you are or what number he has dialed, don't say—you never know who it is or what he really wants. Instead, ask what number he was trying to reach and tell him his mistake.

3. What to do if you have call waiting service and another call comes in? Out of courtesy to the first caller, tell the second you'll call her back unless it's an emergency.

4. If you enjoy long phone chats but worry about wasting time, keep some busywork near the phone.

5. If you have a toddler who loves to dial the phone but doesn't know the meaning of "expensive long-distance call," hold the receiver buttons down with a rubber band. (See also *Crank calls*, p.59.)

Telephones

1. If your phone doesn't work, make sure that all the cords are properly connected: at the wall jack, on the telephone, and between the handset and the phone. If the phone is a plug-in type, test it by switching it with a working phone in your house or a neighbor's; if the instrument then works, call your local phone company for service on the line.

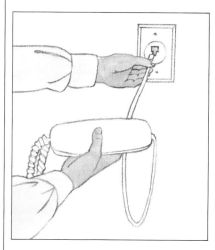

2. During flu season or anytime someone is ill at home, wipe the mouthpiece, receiver, and handpiece with rubbing alcohol.

3. To prevent electrical shock, never use the phone while you're in the tub, shower, or swimming pool.

4. When making a long-distance call away from home, don't be surprised by the cost; ask the operator which company is handling the call, what the rate will be, and how you'll be billed.

5. If you find it difficult to read the numbers on your push-button phone, write larger numbers on white masking tape and stick them on the buttons.

Telephone sales calls

1. Never invest money in stocks or anything else strictly on the strength of a telephone call. The rosier the prospects and the more fantastic the promised profits, the more likely it is that the caller is a con artist. If you're interested in the offer, ask the caller to send you information through the mail—then check it out as you would any other investment. If you think you've encountered a swindler, contact your state attorney general or one of these federal agencies: Commodities Futures Trading Commission, Federal Trade Commission, or Securities and Exchange Commission. They'll check out your report and may even be able to help you get back some of your money.

2. If you're tired of having your dinner interrupted, learn to spot telemarketing calls quickly. The caller usually repeats your name

---

DID YOU KNOW . . . ?

Telephone tunes

□ For a clever birthday greeting, call on a push-button phone and play "Happy Birthday" by pushing the following buttons in the appropriate rhythm:
1-1-2-1-#-6; 1-1-2-1-#-3;
1-1-#-#-8-4-1; #-#-6-4-2-1

□ Here are a few other telephone tunes you can play—but always dial someone's number first, or you may find yourself paying for a call to Brazil or Singapore:

America (My Country 'Tis of Thee): 5-5-6-1-5-9;
0-0-9-0-8-4; 8-4-2-4

Oh! Susanna: 4-8-6-9-9-#-8-7;
4-8-#-#-8-1-8; 4-8-6-9-9-#-8-7;
4-8-6-6-0-0-4

Old MacDonald Had a Farm:
6-6-6-7-8-8-7; 9-9-0-0-4;
4-6-6-6-7-8-8-7; 9-9-0-0-4

Old Folks at Home (Swanee River): 3-2-1-3-2-1-#-4-5;
6-1-4-2; 3-2-1-3-2-1-#-1-4;
6-5-4-2-2-4

frequently: "Hello, Mrs. Smith? Might I ask you a few questions about your purchasing habits, Mrs. Smith?" If you don't want to buy anything, simply hang up with a polite "No, thank you"—you don't have to wait to hear more. Telemarketers seldom make repeat calls to people who cut them off quickly.

3. If you get a telemarketing call from a computer, wait 15 seconds after you hang up, then try your telephone line. If it isn't free, the call has not disconnected; report the company to the telephone company, your local Better Business Bureau, or state attorney general.

Telephoning for services

How do you select a repair service, contractor, or other company from all the listings in the Yellow Pages?
1. Most people simply ask how much a company charges and how soon someone can come. Then they take whatever they get. Instead, try to determine the company's experience and professionalism: Does the owner do the work or is it done by employees? How are the employees trained? How long has the company been in business? Is it a member of a local trade association? Is it insured in case a worker is injured on the job? Did the owner learn his trade on his own or did he have professional schooling? Is the company licensed? (If so, get the license number.) What is its policy if you're dissatisfied? Finally, ask, "Why should I do business with you?"
2. After weeding out unqualified and unprofessional companies, ask about price and availability—then make your decision. When the repairman arrives, be sure to get a written estimate to back up all verbal claims.

Television addiction

Here are some tips on kicking the boob-tube habit:
1. Don't flick aimlessly around the dial. Select specific programs to watch, and just as soon as they're over, turn off your television set.
2. Unplug the thing. Store it in a closet or back room and bring it out only when there's something special to watch.
3. To help judge the quality of your viewing time, write yourself a brief report on each show as soon as it's over. Say what it was about, what you learned from it, and what satisfaction it gave you. Be honest. Then read the reports weekly and write down what else you could have been doing with your time.
4. Instead of watching your local team's game on television, attend it in person. You'll rediscover the thrill of crowd participation and be reminded that TV makes much of life seem secondhand.
5. Don't use TV as a babysitter. Help your kids select the programs they can watch each day and don't be swayed if they beg for more.
6. Have other entertainment handy when children plead boredom. Play cards or board games with them until they get used to the idea of generating their own fun.

Televisions

1. Broken TV antenna? You can substitute a straightened wire coat hanger for a single-rod type (see *Radio antenna*, p.169); wrap a bit of aluminum foil around the tip. Or improvise rabbit ears from several feet of lightweight zip cord; split and strip one end and attach it to the connectors on the back of the set where the antenna leads go. Then split 3 or 4 feet of the other end, strip the tips, and hook them to something high up; you'll have to move them around to get the best reception on various channels.
2. Do you see snow on your TV when you play a VCR tape? Tack or glue a sheet of aluminum foil to the shelf between your VCR and your TV to reduce interference.
3. For clearer viewing, spray the TV screen at least once a week with window or eyeglass cleaner; dry with a soft tissue or paper towel.

Temper tantrums

Normal and inevitable, your child's occasional temper tantrum has more to do with frustration than with temper in the usual sense.
1. Keep calm; getting angry will only make things worse.
2. Sometimes it's best to ignore the tantrum. Tell your child that you can see she's angry and that you'll talk about the problem once she calms down. Then pick up a magazine or do a chore, but stay within sight in case she needs comforting. And as soon as the tantrum subsides, keep your word.

PREVENTION

1. Children's frustrations are often rooted in their own helplessness. You can give your child more control over her life by letting her make certain decisions: which cereal to eat, which sweater to wear, which stuffed toy to sleep with, and so on.
2. Sometimes, however, decision-making itself leads to tantrums; if this is your child's problem, simplify her life by making matter-of-fact statements. Say, for example, "When we have our coats on, we'll go to the store," rather than "Would you like to wear your blue coat or your red jacket?"
3. Try to anticipate some of the situations that provoke tantrums. If they happen when she's hungry, give her an extra-nutritious snack or serve her meals earlier; if they occur when she's tired, encourage her to take a longer nap or help her to find a quiet activity such as looking at books or coloring.

Temporary employment

1. Although many people aren't aware of them, most cities have employment agencies that specialize in temporary jobs, from clerical work to manual labor. Some agencies even provide training in skills such as word processing.
2. Think seasonally. Hotels and restaurants hire extra employees during peak tourist periods. Farms

need help at harvest time; department stores need people at peak holiday periods.

3. Look for businesses with high employee turnover—fast food places, telemarketing services, taxi companies. (See also *Moonlighting*, p.137; *Part-time jobs*, p.150.)

Tennis jargon

Here's a guide to what the television announcers are saying:

Ace. A serve that is not returned.

Advantage. The first point scored after deuce.

Approach shot. A hard-hit ball deep into the opponent's court, giving the hitter a chance to rush the net.

Backspin. The effect on the ball when a hitter's stroke makes it rotate in the opposite direction of its flight, causing it to bounce backward or to stop suddenly.

Baseline. The line marking the end of the court, behind which a player must stand to serve.

Baseline strategy. A plan in which the player avoids the forecourt, staying close to the baseline.

Chip. A short, slicing return, often aimed at an opponent's feet; frequently used in doubles.

Chop. A sharp spin given the ball by slicing down and under it with the racket.

Crosscourt shot. A ball that is hit diagonally across the net from one side of the court to the other.

Deuce. A tie score on the last point of a game; since a game must be won by 2 points, a player must win 2 consecutive points to prevail.

Dink. A softly hit ball that falls just beyond the net.

Double fault. A point lost by a server for hitting two consecutive faults.

Down-the-line shot. A ball hit along the sideline deep into the corner of the opponent's court.

Fault. A service that fails to clear the net or that lands outside the proper service court.

Foot fault. A fault called when the server's foot touches or goes beyond the baseline while serving.

Forecourt. The section of the court nearest the net.

Lob. A ball that is hit high above the opponent's head.

Love. Zero.

Match point. The point that, if won, will give a player the match.

Net point. A ball that hits the net and goes over; it remains in play except on the serve.

Net serve. Net point on service; not a fault if it hits the proper service court—the ball is served again.

Rush the net. To move quickly forward, in hopes of volleying.

Seeding. The ranking of competitors by actual or potential ability.

Service court. The two subdivisions of each forecourt; a server must place the ball within the opponent's crosscourt service court.

Set. A unit of a match; to win a set, a player must win at least six games with a margin of at least two games.

Smash. A ball hit hard with an overhand motion.

Volley. To return the ball before it bounces.

Tennis rackets

1. Have your racket strung to the tension that suits you best. The lower end of the tension range gives more power; the higher gives more control. If you're not satisfied with your racket tension, try moving it up or down in 3-pound stages.

2. Check the tiny plastic grommets in the racket head. A cracked or broken one will cut into the string that goes through it, causing it to snap. Have faulty grommets replaced when your racket is restrung.

3. At the end of every game, examine your racket strings and adjust them with your fingers if they are out of line. Strings that aren't properly aligned are more likely to break.

4. Look for an old wooden racket at a tag sale to start a beginner playing tennis; it will give better ball control than a metal one.

Tent pegs

1. Carry pegs in a separate bag to avoid damaging the tent.

2. For lightweight, inexpensive pegs, use 6-inch aluminum spikes.

3. To anchor lines in snow or sand, tie them around sticks, rocks, or sacks of sand. Then bury them.

4. To reduce wind stress on a rain fly, tie elastic cord between the pegs and the guy lines.

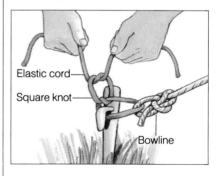

Elastic cord
Square knot
Bowline

Tents

You can improvise a fair-weather tent with a 10- x 10-foot waterproof tarpaulin, a 10-foot rope, and a couple of poles, ponchos, and shoe-

laces. Keep in mind that this tent is a fragile one, unable to withstand high winds or heavy rain.

1. Drive a pole (a straight, sturdy 5- or 6-foot stick will do) into the ground so that it stands erect.

2. Center the tarp over the pole and lash a shoelace around the top.

3. Weight one edge of the tarp down with rocks.

4. Place the other pole under the opposite edge of the tarp to form a door; lash with the other shoelace.

5. Guy the top of the front pole to the ground with the 10-foot rope. (If you don't have a peg to secure the guy rope, tie the end to a stick and bury it.)

6. Secure the sides of the tarp with more rocks.

7. Drape both ponchos over the door, hanging them by their hoods from the pole.

Test taking

1. Get a good night's sleep, eat a high-protein meal, and bring some hard candy to suck on when your energy flags.

2. Read all instructions *twice* before you begin, just to be on the safe side. When reading the questions, underline such key words as *not* and *except.*

3. Budget your time. Divide the total number of questions by the allotted number of minutes to determine how long to spend on each question. If you find you're taking too long on one, leave it and go on.

4. If you can make an "educated guess" between two or three choices on a multiple-choice question, do so; the odds favor you—even if the exam has a penalty for incorrect answers. But if you haven't a clue, don't guess wildly between five or six choices.

5. On true-or-false quizzes, questions that contain an *always* or a *never* are likely to be false; those that say *usually, sometimes,* or *often* are likely to be true.

6. Begin with the easiest essay question and work up to the most

difficult. (Sometimes a bit of incubation time helps.) If you don't have time to complete an essay, try writing an outline with the explanation "Ran out of time."

Theater tickets

1. If you order your tickets by phone, ask which rows and seats are available. If the ticket agent can't tell you, you're better off going to the box office, looking at the seating plan, and choosing the seats that *you* consider the best.

2. When you pick up phone-ordered tickets at the box office, you'll probably have to show your credit card as identification.

3. Once you've purchased tickets, you can't get a refund unless a show closes unexpectedly. Try selling them to friends or putting a notice on your office bulletin board.

Thermometers

Wonder what the temperature is? In summer you can use an insect "thermometer" to find out:

1. Count a cricket's chirps for 14 seconds and add 40 to get the degrees in Fahrenheit.

2. Are the cicadas singing? If so, it must be at least 83°F.

3. Listen for a katydid. If it says "Katy-did-it," the temperature is at least 78°F; "Katy-did," 72°; "Kaytee," 65°; "Kate," 58°.

Thermostats

Most of what you do to fix a balky thermostat depends on its age.

1. Behind the cover of a unit made before 1973 are open contacts that may be dirty. Clean both contacts

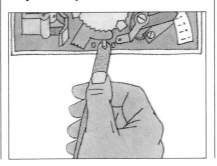

with an emery board and blow the dust away with a dry-air canister (available in photo stores).

2. A thermostat made between 1973 and 1983 may have a mercury switch sealed in glass and a bimetallic coil. The unit must be level to operate accurately; check its mount with a spirit level and reposition if necessary. Dust on the coil can also cause problems; using a light touch, clean it with a soft artist's brush.

3. The newest thermostats contain solid-state controls; dust is unlikely to affect their operation. If the unit doesn't work properly, you probably need a replacement.

Throw rugs

1. To keep a throw rug in place, put a rubber bath mat under it.

2. To make a scatter rug lie flat, shellac the underside. When dry, apply a mild solution of laundry starch; let dry before using.

3. Prevent rag rugs from curling by rinsing them in a mild solution of starch and water.

4. To wash throw rugs, place them in the bathtub with warm soapy water and scrub with a broom. Place smaller rugs in a washtub and use a long-handled plunger to agitate the water.

5. If nylon bathroom rugs are matted, wash with soap or detergent, then add ½ cup vinegar or fabric softener to the rinse water. Comb the tangles out with a wire dog-grooming brush.

Thunderstorms

1. Is your preschool child afraid of thunder? Buy him a drum and tell him to bang it every time a thunderclap sounds or just have him yell "Boom!" back at the thunder. It will give him a sense of power.

2. Condition him by occasionally playing "thunderstorm." Turn on a recording of thunder, dim the lights in the house, and let him imitate lightning with a flashlight.

3. If your child is old enough, explain the connection between lightning and thunder; tell him how to figure how far away the storm is (see *Lightning lore*, p.127) and make a game of tracking it.

4. If your dog is afraid of thunder, the following routine may calm its fears. First, have the dog sit or lie down and give it a treat. Then turn on a recording of thunder very softly and give another treat. Increase the volume gradually, rewarding the dog with a treat or praise with each raise. Finally, decrease the volume slowly until there's no sound. Repeat the artificial storms often.

5. When a real thunderstorm occurs, have the dog sit or lie down and reward it with treats for non-fearful behavior, just as you did in the practice sessions. If it shows signs of anxiety, don't discipline it; just ignore it completely.

Tiles

CERAMIC TILES

1. Before cleaning bathroom tiles, run the shower on *Hot* for 5 minutes to steam the dirt loose.

2. For stubborn stains, apply a paste of scouring powder and water and let sit for 5 minutes. Scrub with a nylon scrub pad, rinse, and wipe dry.

3. To keep the grout joints on countertops clean longer, wash with a solution of 1 to 2 tablespoons chlorine bleach in 1 quart of water. Dry thoroughly, then apply an acrylic sealer or three coats of lemon oil (let dry 1 hour between coats).

4. Remove mildew and make tiles sparkle by sponging with a solution of ammonia and water.

5. Remove soot from fireplace tiles with a mixture of lemon juice and salt, then wash.

PLASTIC TILES

1. If bathroom walls are dull, wash the tiles with a solution of vinegar and water; polish with a towel.

2. Has a tile come loose? For a quick fix, put a little piece of chewing gum on each corner; use a warm iron to press it back in place.

ACOUSTICAL TILES

1. Clean with the dust-brush attachment of your vacuum cleaner.

2. Remove stains and dirt with mild soap and water; don't let the tiles get too wet.

ASPHALT TILES

1. If smudges don't come off floor tiles easily, rub with superfine (No. 00) steel wool and soap.

2. For easier cutting, heat tiles for 1½ minutes under an infrared lamp. Heat rubber tiles 1 minute.

Timers

If you haven't got a timer and your watch is broken, don't give up; as long as you have a television, radio, record or tape player, or telephone, you have plenty of substitutes around the house.

1. TV programs are usually ½ hour, 1 hour, or 2 hours long. Prime-time shows generally run 12½ minutes between commercials.

2. Most commercials on TV and radio are 30 seconds long, with an occasional 15- or 60-second one. Many program breaks are four commercials, or 2 minutes, long.

3. Music videos and popular songs usually last 3 to 4 minutes; an album or tape side, about 20 minutes.

4. A telephone ring and pause is about 3 seconds. (See also *Alarm clocks*, p.9.)

Tire changing

1. Can't loosen frozen or rusted lug nuts? Apply penetrating oil, vinegar, lemon juice, or hot pepper sauce. The next time you rotate the tires or change one, coat the threads with an antiseize compound.

2. If one wheel has lost its lug nuts, borrow one nut from each of the other tires; replace them as soon as possible.

3. Be sure to turn the wrench in the proper direction. In most cars it's counterclockwise. In some cars, however, the nuts on the driver's side are left-threaded. These are usually marked with an *L* and

are loosened by turning clockwise.

4. More force can be applied by pushing a wrench down, not pulling it up. If possible, try using your foot.

5. A cross-shaft lug wrench, available at auto supply stores, gives more leverage than a single-shaft wrench. For additional leverage, fit a piece of pipe over one arm of the wrench. (See also *Car jacks*, p.37.)

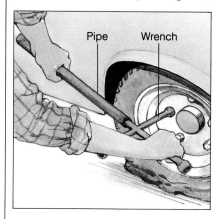

Pipe   Wrench

Toasters

1. If you can't reach that broken English muffin in the toaster, use dry wooden chopsticks.

2. If your toaster's broken, use the broiler in your stove or hold the bread with tongs over a surface burner or heating element.

3. Or prop the bread against an electric heater (set on *High*), as close to the coils as possible without touching.

4. Or wrap buttered bread in foil and iron both sides; it doesn't brown, but it's warm and crunchy.

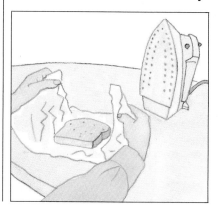

Toilet-flushing problems

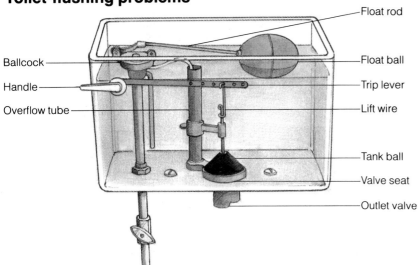

Ballcock

Handle

Overflow tube

Float rod

Float ball

Trip lever

Lift wire

Tank ball

Valve seat

Outlet valve

If the toilet fails to flush, remove the tank lid and study the linkage from flush handle to flush valve.

1. If the handle is loose, use a wrench to tighten it on its shaft and at the setscrew holding it to the trip lever. (You can temporarily replace a broken handle with locking-grip pliers or a C-clamp.)

2. Reconnect or replace the lift chain or wire if necessary. Fishing line is a temporary expedient.

3. Make sure that the tank ball or flapper is securely screwed or hooked to the lift chain or wires.

INCOMPLETE FLUSHING

The water in a toilet tank should be ¾ inch lower than the top of the overflow tube.

1. If it's too low, raise the level by bending upward the rod that connects the ball to the ballcock. With a float-cup ballcock, pinch the spring clip on the pull rod and lift the cup to raise the water level.

2. If the water level is correct, check as you flush to see if the lift wires pull the ball clear of the outlet valve; if not, reposition the wires. If the ball is porous and soggy, replace it.

CONSTANTLY RUNNING WATER

1. If the tank doesn't fill, gently scour the valve seat (the outlet to the bowl) with fine (No.0) steel wool and wash the ball. Replace a sod-

den ball or flapper. Make sure that the lift wires are properly aligned.

2. If the tank is full and water still runs down the overflow tube, lower the water level by bending the float rod or adjusting the float cup downward. Unscrew the float ball and shake it; if it leaks, replace it. (First, drain the tank by turning off the water and flushing the toilet.) If, after filling the tank, water still runs, the ballcock leaks. Replace its diaphragm or washer or the ballcock; follow manufacturer's instructions.

Toilet leaks

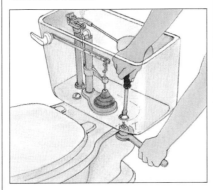

1. Condensation may be the cause of moisture around the bolts from the tank to the bowl. Or perhaps the bolts are loose. To check, put food coloring in the tank; after an hour, dab the bolts with white tissue. If it colors, drain the tank by

turning off the water supply (see *Water leaks*, p.226) and flushing; then tighten the bolts—hold the head of each with a screwdriver and turn its nut with an adjustable or socket wrench.

Caution: Overtightening may crack the toilet tank.

2. Moisture at the base of a toilet may mean that the bowl is cracked or that the wax ring sealing the bowl to the drain is faulty or worn. While waiting for the plumber, you can minimize the leakage—drain the tank and bowl as directed above.

3. An older toilet with a wall-hung tank may leak around the slip nuts at either end of the pipe joining the tank to the bowl. After draining the tank, unscrew each nut with a large wrench. Wrap the exposed threads in self-forming packing, then retighten the nut.

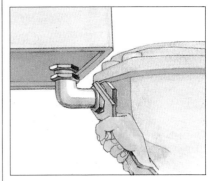

Tomatoes

1. Make the most of bland supermarket tomatoes by buying them a few days ahead of time and ripening them, stem side up, at room temperature. Never store them in the refrigerator.

2. To speed ripening, place tomatoes in a paper bag with a banana. Punch a few holes in the bag first.

3. You can use your own vine-ripened tomatoes for cooking right through winter. Just quarter the newly harvested, washed fruits and freeze them on cookie sheets. Then store in freezer bags. When you defrost the little morsels, their skins will peel right off.

4. To make peeling ripe tomatoes a breeze, plunge them into simmering water for 20 seconds and remove with a slotted spoon. Plunge into cold water and pull the skin away with your fingers. To microwave, bring 1 cup hot water to a boil on *High*, then add a tomato for 30 seconds; peel as above. (See also *Vegetable varieties*, p.222.)

Tomato paste

1. In a pinch, substitute a tablespoon of ketchup for a tablespoon of tomato paste. Or use ¼ cup tomato sauce, reducing the liquid in the recipe by 3 tablespoons.
2. Buy tomato paste in a tube to avoid the problem of what to do with a half-used can.
3. If you do have leftover paste, it can be saved and refrigerated in a camper's reusable squeeze tube. Or spoon it into an ice cube tray, freeze it, and store the cubes in a freezer bag.

Tomato plants

1. Prevent common problems by buying varieties with the letters *V*, *F*, *N*, or *T* on the label. *V* means resistance to (but not immunity from) verticillium wilt; *F*, to fusarium wilt; *N*, to nematodes (root-knot eelworms); and *T*, to tobacco mosaic virus.
2. If you smoke, dip your hands in milk before handling tomato plants. It retards the growth of tobacco mosaic virus, which may have been left on your hands.
3. For plants that keep producing throughout the growing season, choose an *indeterminate* variety. For a heavier crop in the space of a few weeks (for canning, for example), choose a *determinate* variety.
4. When you buy at the nursery, look for seedlings with thick stems and large root systems (the clues are a deep container and dark green leaves). Avoid plants that are already in bloom; they've been in pots too long and are stunted.
5. To help transplants get off to a quick start, trench-plant them. Remove the young plant from its container and pinch off all but the top clump of leaves. Then lay it on its side in a shallow trench and cover the roots and stem with soil, leaving the tuft of leaves exposed. The sun will warm the shallow soil to encourage faster growth, and the heat-loving tomatoes will respond by sprouting roots along the stem.

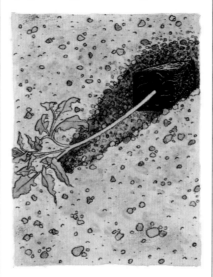

6. Encourage bigger yields by injecting fertilizer into the root zone. Use 1½-inch plastic pipe to stake your tomatoes—a 6-foot length if you intend to train the vines to a single stake, two 5-foot lengths to anchor a tomato cage. Fill the pipes with water to irrigate; add a soluble fertilizer when the first fruits form and repeat at 3-week intervals. (See also *Vegetable varieties*, p.222.)

Tool grips

1. To make hand grips for a shovel or spade, slit two pieces of radiator hose lengthwise, slip them over the wooden handle, and hold them in place with duct tape. (You can probably get used hose free from a garage or service station.)
2. For a rake or hoe, just slide a couple of 4-inch sections of the hose over the wooden handle. It should fit snugly; if it doesn't, secure it with duct tape. Position the hose sections to match your natural hand grips. You'll find raking and hoeing more comfortable, particularly if you also wear work gloves.

Tool storage

1. Keep tools organized: Frame a sheet of perforated hardboard with 1 x 2's and screw it to the garage or workshop wall. Then position your tools and put hooks or pegs of the appropriate sizes in place. Paint a white outline of each tool on the hardboard so that everyone can put it back where it belongs.
2. Lay an aluminum broiler pan in a drawer to store files and chisels—its corrugated bottom makes a cradle for each tool. Or glue lengths of half-round molding on the bottom of a drawer to make divisions.
3. To separate small items, groove the sides of an open-ended wooden box and slide in muffin tins to serve as storage drawers for nails, screws, washers, bolts, hangers, and other small items.
4. To prevent the engine of your power mower from rusting during off-season storage, rid the tank and fuel lines of gasoline by running the engine until it stops. Brush off any debris, then coat bare metal parts with motor oil. Remove the spark plug and pour in a spoonful of motor oil. Hand-crank the engine to get oil into the cylinder. Cover, but do not seal, the engine.

Toothache

1. Saturate a small piece of sterile cotton with oil of cloves or make a paste of powdered cloves and water; pack the cotton or paste in the sore tooth's cavity or place it on the surface. Be warned: the cloves may do more than just numb your toothache; they may also sting your lips and tongue.

2. If your tooth has only begun to ache, drink hot liquids. For an on-going ache, suck on ice.

3. Gargle hourly with warm salt water and take aspirin or an aspirin substitute (p. 12) every 4 hours.

4. Try trigger-point pressure: with your index finger, press gently all over your face, neck, and head; when you find an especially sensitive area, press hard for 10 seconds and release.

5. Massage the web of skin between your thumb and index finger with an ice cube. Rubbing that part of the right hand will affect the right side of your mouth; the left hand, the left side. (This may sound strange, but it works.)

Toothbrush

No toothbrush? Use a clean cotton ball, a bit of towel, or your finger; rub in the toothpaste or baking soda with your tongue.

Tooth filling

1. For a temporary replacement for a lost filling, make a stiff paste of eugenol and powdered zinc oxide (both are available at drugstores). Pack the paste in the hole, then bite down hard to press it in and shape it.

2. If you lose a filling in a front tooth and you're worried about how it will look, use white bread or melted white candle wax.

Caution: All these measures are strictly temporary; go to a dentist as soon as possible.

Tooth stains

1. Lighten stains by rubbing with baking soda; rinse thoroughly.

2. If your teeth stain easily, avoid tea, coffee, cola, red wine, grape juice, blueberries, curried foods, and cigarettes.

› Tornadoes

THE WATCH

1. Look for rotating funnel-shaped clouds or a rotating haze of dust and debris pulled up from the ground and roaring like a jet plane. Report them to the nearest office of the National Weather Service or your local police department.

2. Listen to local radio or television stations for information; do not use the telephone.

THE WARNING

1. The safest place to go is a storm shelter or a basement. Lacking those, head for an interior room, such as a bathroom, hallway, or closet, with as many walls as possible between you and the tornado. Lie under something sturdy, such as a table, to protect yourself from falling debris.

2. If outside, don't try to outrun a tornado in a car. Get out of the car and move away from the tornado's path at a right angle or drop face-down in a ditch or depression and cover your head with your arms.

Towel racks

1. If the bar of your towel rack is broken or missing, use an adjustable curtain rod as a substitute.

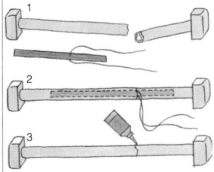

2. If the bar is hollow, try this: Find a piece of wooden dowel wide enough to almost fill the hollow of the broken bar. Cut it slightly shorter than the longer piece of broken bar. Drill a hole in the middle and hang a length of thread through it (1). Put the long piece of the bar in its holder and slip the dowel in-

---

side. Then put the other piece of the bar in place and pull on the thread, sliding the dowel over to bridge the break (2). Pull the thread out and apply glue to the broken bar ends (3). Let dry for 24 hours.

Toys

Tired of buying expensive toys?

1. Most school-aged children love playing with magnifying glasses, flashlights, magnets, bells, wooden beads, and other such items. Preschoolers enjoy empty cardboard boxes or tents made by throwing a sheet over a table.

2. Make a "tunnel" by lining up two rows of straight-backed dining room chairs and covering them with sheets or blankets. Or sew a piece of canvas all the way around the edge of a beach umbrella to convert it into a special hideaway for your youngsters and their friends.

3. Don't throw away a once-used Halloween costume—make a life-size doll to wear the outfit. To make the pattern for the doll, have your child lie on a large piece of paper while you draw her outline on it. Cut out the pattern on a double layer of fabric. Sew the fabric together, and stuff; draw a face or appliqué features onto the doll and then dress it in the costume.

4. If plastic toys become misshapen, dunk them in hot water for several minutes, then work them back to their original form.

5. Vacuum stuffed toys; use the upholstery-brush attachment. If they're really dirty and can't be machine-washed, put them in a large paper bag with plenty of cornmeal; shake vigorously, remove the toys, and gently brush off the cornmeal.

6. To extend the life of cardboard games, coat them with shellac.

7. To prevent rust and keep colors bright, coat metal toys or painted toys with clear varnish or shellac.

Transplant shock

Transplanting damages the fine root hairs that take up a plant's water and nutrients. Give them time to recover by moving trees and shrubs when the plants don't need much water—before the leaves appear in spring or after they drop in autumn.

If the soil is dry, water the yet-to-be-transplanted tree or shrub thoroughly several days ahead of time; the moisture will help keep the earth intact around the roots. After replanting, spray evergreen foliage with an antitranspirant (available at most garden stores). This gluey liquid plugs the leaf pores temporarily, retarding dehydration.

To help flower and vegetable seedlings survive transplanting, slip the plants from their containers upside down, keeping the soil intact around the roots, and dip the stems and leaves in a bucket of antitranspirant before planting.

Spray newly laid sod with antitranspirant, too, to keep the grass from browning before it can send roots down into the soil.

Trash compactors

1. Eliminate the need for frequent compactor cleaning: wrap wet food waste, such as fruit pulp, in a couple of layers of newspaper before compacting.

2. Load rigid items, such as cans and bottles, in the center of the drawer, preferably in a cushion of paper, for the best compaction.

3. To make sure that trash is prop-erly compacted, wait until the drawer is at least one-third full before running the appliance.

4. Do not put the following items into the compactor: clothing; cans with a residue of gasoline, paint, or thinner; or any aerosol cans or containers that held insecticides, hair spray, engine-starting fluid, or any other poisonous or explosive product (see *Hazardous waste,* p. 104).

Travel for the elderly

1. The good news about growing old: you get terrific financial breaks when you travel. Many hotel chains, airlines, bus companies, and local transportation systems offer substantial discounts; ask when you make your reservations or pay your fare to make sure you're getting the full benefits due your years. Don't forget to inquire about restrictions—travel discounts are often limited to certain hours or days of the week.

2. A number of associations for older people, including the American Association of Retired Persons and the National Council of Senior Citizens, provide travel discounts for their members. Elderhostel offers inexpensive learning vacations for senior citizens on college campuses all over the world. Many local senior centers and church groups organize short bargain tours designed for older people.

TAKING CARE OF YOURSELF

1. Careful preparation can ensure that age does not hinder the fun of traveling. Carry extra sets of glasses and dentures and copies of your prescriptions (written with generic names) to remedy the occasional breakage or loss. Pack all medications in carry-on luggage and take them on the plane with you.

2. A complete physical checkup is a wise precaution before a long journey, since even minor ailments can ground an otherwise happy senior traveler. Ask your doctor to recommend emergency medical facilities in the areas you'll be visiting. (See also *Illness away from home*, p.114.)

3. Designate at least one contact at home: a trusted friend, a colleague, or a relative. Give him your itinerary and the numbers on your traveler's checks; ask him to cancel lost or stolen documents, transfer funds, or notify your family in case of an emergency.

4. Avoid overtaxing yourself; schedule meals, naps, and bedtime as close to normal as possible. A leisurely pace and occasional rest stops increase endurance while touring; plan short outings rather than long day trips.

Traveling abroad

1. Research before making reservations. Get information about foreign destinations from the public library, a travel agent, or a country's tourist board (located in major cities like New York and Los Angeles); buy or rent a travel video to preview a country's sights.

2. Buy a good guidebook and a foreign dictionary or phrase book (see *Foreign phrases*, p.91).

3. Arrange for a passport (p.151) and round-trip transportation. Check with a country's consulate, its embassy, or your travel agent about applying for a visa or tourist card. If you plan to drive, get an international driver's license from your automobile association.

4. Make a hotel reservation (p.173) for your first night and confirm it before departure; take any confirmation letters with you.

5. If you're going to Europe, consider buying a Eurail pass; it gives you discount railroad transportation across most of Europe. You can buy one only in this country, so get yours before you depart.

6. Pack lightly; make a list of everything in your suitcase and carry it with your passport. Such a list is handy when making a claim for lost luggage (p.129).

7. If you're taking any electrical appliances, carry a current converter. Take a plug adaptor, too; many foreign countries use round-prong plugs rather than the flat prongs found in the U.S.

8. Before visiting a country that has an unstable political climate, check with the State Department.

9. Try to fit unobtrusively into any country's culture. Smile and show appreciation or enthusiasm; don't make negative comparisons.

10. Find out what is taboo for picture-taking; always ask permission before photographing anyone.

11. Keep the receipts for your purchases to show customs (p.60) and to reclaim any value-added tax when you leave the country.

12. If you plan to stay in any country longer than a month, register on arrival with the nearest American consulate. In any case, carry the address and phone number of the local American diplomatic office; if you have any trouble, contact officials there.

13. Remember, however, that while in another country you are subject to its laws. Learn the local laws and obey them.

14. Reconfirm your return transportation at least 72 hours before departure. (See also *Exchanging currency*, p.73; *Illness away from home*, p.114.)

Traveling alone

1. Before leaving on a trip, read about your destination and map out a tentative itinerary; without plans you might have too much time on your hands and get lonely.

2. Always carry full identification; don't forget to include the name and phone number of a friend or family member and the address of your hotel.

3. To discourage unwanted advances, wear a decorative ring on the third finger of your left hand so that you can slip it around to resemble a wedding band.

4. Before tipping the bellhop, be sure your hotel room is suitable—in a safe location (preferably near the elevator) and with functional locks on door and windows.

5. Always double-bolt your door locks. If there is a peephole, use it before opening the door. Never sleep with balcony doors open. The *Do Not Disturb* sign may discourage prowlers, but it will also keep the maid from entering your room.

6. When you arrive at your destination, take a city tour to acclimate yourself and get the opportunity to meet friendly people who may be looking for companionship.

7. If you want company, look for a Meet the People program; contact local chapters of any professional, fraternal, or social organizations you belong to; or stay at a bed-and-breakfast where you'll be likely to meet congenial people.

DINING ALONE

1. Make sure the hotel you stay in has a dining room. If you get cold feet about going out alone at night, at least you won't have to eat in your room. On the other hand, it's always a good idea to bring along an immersible water heater and tea bags or instant coffee so that you can economize with an occasional takeout meal in your room. You might even carry a few packets of freeze-dried meals, available in camping supply stores.

2. If you want to eat at a popular restaurant but fear rejection, make a reservation for before or after peak time. If you're still given a tiny table near the kitchen, firmly ask for a better location or use your hideaway as a vantage point for observing the local scene.

CHILDREN ALONE

Most forms of transportation have provisions for unaccompanied children over 5 years old but usually charge the adult fare. Children younger than 5 are generally not allowed to travel alone; check with your travel agent.

Airlines must always be advised ahead of time when a child will be traveling alone. The child should board the plane early and be escorted from it by airline personnel; someone must be present to meet her on arrival. Whatever the mode of travel, don't leave the terminal until you've seen the bus, train, or plane depart with the child aboard.

Traveling with children

1. Always carry a kit with snacks, drinking straws, a night light, paper towels, towelettes, and first-aid supplies.
2. Give each older child a backpack and let him carry whatever he needs to amuse himself: books, paper and crayons, games, and so forth.
3. Avoid highly salted foods—they make children drink more, necessitating more pit stops.
4. Ask restaurants to bring young children's dinners out as soon as they're ready. The kids will stay occupied, and you'll probably have their food cut up by the time your meal arrives.
5. Instead of expensive souvenirs, encourage children to collect shells or stones. Arrange them in a nice display when you get home.
6. Childproof your hotel or motel room as soon as you arrive: tape bathroom locks open, remove any breakables or hazards, and lock dangerous windows. Don't leave children alone in a hotel room.
7. American consulates in most foreign countries have lists of local babysitters.

BY AIRPLANE

1. If you are flying with an infant, call the airline ahead of time; it may provide a bassinet and assign you a bulkhead seat with room to put it at your feet. Ask to board early.
2. Always try to book night flights; children are more likely to sleep.
3. Give your infant a bottle or pacifier just before the plane takes off and lands; the sucking will ease the pressure in the baby's ears. Give older children gum or hard candy.
4. If your child has a cold, consult your doctor before flying—the pressure of takeoff and landing can damage eardrums.

BY CAR

1. Tie toys to your child's car seat so that they don't fall to the floor.
2. If your toddler is teething, tie a bagel to a string and put it around her neck. It will keep her occupied, and perhaps she won't put other things in her mouth.

3. On a long car trip, take an extra map and a colored pencil and let the kids mark your progress. Then they won't ask about it every few minutes.
4. Take a tape recorder and cassettes with favorite stories or songs. Include blank tapes so that the children can make up their own plays.
5. Try these car games:
Dog catcher. One player counts all of the dogs on the left side of the road; the other counts dogs on the right. Spotting a white horse doubles your score. If you spot a graveyard on your opponent's side, he loses all his points.
License plates. With pen and pencil jot down the different state license plates and the motto beneath the numbers.
Special cars. Have younger children look for yellow moving vans, horse trailers, cement mixers, and so on. Award 1 point to the first child who spots a special car.

Traveling without children

Before you go away, even on a short trip, leaving your small child behind, take steps to ease his anxiety:
1. Include the child in discussions about the trip so that he understands why it is necessary.
2. Act out the departure and the return home: Stage a little drama in which everyone says good-bye with hugs and kisses and smiles. Then go out the door with a suitcase, wait a while, ring the bell, open the door, and cry, "I'm home!" Again, hugs, kisses, and smiles.
3. Prepare a travelogue in advance, using illustrations cut from magazines (let the child help) to show where you'll be, how you'll get there, and what you'll do. Make the trip sound interesting and safe.
4. Mark the calendar to show when you'll leave and when you'll return. Let the child mark off the days. Leave an envelope for each day you'll be gone, with stories, little love notes, jokes, riddles, and gifts. Or record tapes of songs you and the child sing together.

Treasury securities

To avoid paying a substantial fee to a brokerage firm or bank, buy your own Treasury security (bill, note, or bond) in person or by mail from a Federal Reserve bank or from the Treasury Department in Washington, D.C. (There's a $10,000 minimum required for bills; $5,000 for 2- and 3-year notes; and $1,000 for 4- to 10-year notes and all bonds.)
1. Simply fill out a tender form or write a letter; include your name and address, Social Security number, bank account number, and the nine-digit identification number of your bank (it precedes your account number on your checks).
2. Submit a *noncompetitive* bid; this guarantees that your bid will be accepted at the average rate of accepted competitive bids.
3. Include a certified check for the face value of the security in an envelope marked "Tender for Treasury

Security." The Treasury will then deposit refunds, interest, and principal payments directly into your account and send you a statement.
4. For more information, contact the Bureau of the Public Debt, Washington, DC 20239.
5. If you're in the market for "used" securities or if it's unlikely that you'll hold the security until its maturity, use a bank or a broker.

Tree blights

ELM

There's not much you can do to halt *Dutch elm disease* once it's taken hold, but you can protect disease-free elms with injections of the fungicide methyl-2-benzimidazolecarbamate-phosphate, available from your local tree surgeon or through the nonprofit Elm Research Institute (Harrisville, NH 03450). The institute also works with Boy Scout troops throughout the country to distribute seedlings of a disease-resistant elm called Liberty; contact a local troop or call the institute at 1-800-FOR-ELMS.

A similar disease is *elm yellows,* distinguishable from Dutch elm disease by the way it usually yellows all the tree's foliage at once and discolors the inner bark. It's too late to save a tree once the symptoms have appeared, but you can protect a healthy elm by having a tree surgeon treat it with tetracycline. Elm leafhoppers carry the disease, so regular spraying with an insecticide such as Malathion also helps.

ASH

Sluggish growth, a premature display of fall color, or the appearance of "witches'-brooms" (tightly clustered bunches of leaves) are signs of *ash yellows.* There is no cure for this fatal disease, which occurs in northeastern states. To help healthy specimens resist infection, water deeply during droughts and feed annually with a balanced tree fertilizer in late fall or early spring.

DOGWOOD

Feed and water dogwoods as you do ash trees to help protect them from *anthracnose.* The fungus begins by killing twigs; it then infects the lower branches and goes on to consume the entire tree. Prune off infected branches to slow the blight's progress, being sure to disinfect the pruning shears in alcohol between cuts. In autumn bag and discard the leaves from infected trees; don't add them to the compost heap, where they may spread the disease's spores. Clip water sprouts from the trunk or main branches to help reduce infection.

MAPLE

Maple decline attacks red, Norway, and sugar maples. Reduced twig growth, sparse foliage, dead branches in the upper canopy, and early fall coloration are brought on by environmental stress, principally by the roots' exposure to de-icing salts, the attacks of leaf-chewing insects, and road and sidewalk construction. If caught in its early stages, the decline can often be reversed through feeding and watering, removing dead branches, and ringing the tree with a berm, or curb, to divert salt-laden runoff.

Tripod

To keep your photographs from blurring, use a beanbag as a substitute tripod. It molds itself perfectly to rocks, tree branches, or

the rim of a car window while the camera or a long lens rests firmly on top. Use it for timed exposures, low-light shots, and ground-level close-ups of flowers.

Make or buy a beanbag about 10 x 12 inches with a zipper or Velcro closure on one end. Carry it empty and fill it with beans, corn, rice, or pebbles when needed.

Tulips

1. To keep cut tulips from drooping, add a few drops of vodka to the water in the vase.
2. When dividing your tulip bulbs, plant the smallest ones in an out-of-the-way place; they'll take a few years to flower.
3. Spotted petals and foliage are signs of a fungus called tulip fire *(Botrytis tulipae).* Destroy all diseased plants; lift the remaining bulbs from the soil and dust with the fungicide PCNB, available at most garden centers.

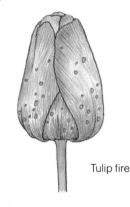

Tulip fire

Turkey

1. To select a tender, juicy bird, look for a USDA grade A stamp. The younger and fleshier the turkey, the better its texture and taste.
2. What weight should you buy? Allow at least 1 pound per person unstuffed, 1¼ pounds stuffed.
3. You can store a frozen turkey for up to a year at 0°F or below. But a fresh turkey should be cooked within a day of purchase.
4. Frozen birds that weigh 12 pounds or less can be thawed, still

wrapped, in the refrigerator. Allow 1 to 2 days. Do not defrost a larger turkey in the refrigerator—the process takes too long, and bacteria can develop.

5. To defrost a large turkey, submerge it completely in a pot of cold water. This method is also good in an emergency for smaller birds. Check that the wrapping has no tears and change the water often. Allow 4 to 5 hours for an 8- to 12-pound bird; 11 to 12 hours for a 20- to 24-pounder.

6. Cooking a turkey on a rotisserie is a nice alternative to roasting. Be sure to truss the bird compactly so that it doesn't slip on the spit.

7. Before cooking a turkey in an oven bag, put a tablespoon of flour into the bag and shake it around; this will keep the bag from bursting. And follow the manufacturer's directions to the letter.

Tweezers

1. If it hurts to tweeze your eyebrows, numb the area by pinching it for 15 seconds or by rubbing it with an ice cube.

2. When your tweezers don't grip properly, you can tighten the legs by putting a pencil between them and bending the tips together. Or just twist a small rubber band around the tips.

3. For household emergencies, use needle-nose pliers, tongs, binder clips, or the metal clasps on manila envelopes in place of tweezers.

Twine

Need to tie something in a hurry and there's no twine around?

1. Knot your shoe or sneaker laces together and you'll have about 4 feet of cord.

2. Use heavy leather laces or a leather belt to tie up a car's tail pipe or muffler until you can get to a garage. Or, if your car has a 6- or 8-cylinder engine, remove a long spark plug wire (the engine will still run) and use it as an emergency cord.

Twins & triplets

Here are some ways to encourage a healthy sense of individuality in matching sets of children:

1. Give them very different names (Ann and Rachel, for example, rather than Karen and Corinne). Refer to them by name, not as "the twins" or "the triplets."

2. Avoid dressing them alike past their first birthday. If they're given matching outfits, don't use them on the same day. If they *want* to dress alike, however, don't prevent them from doing so, but provide each with a varied wardrobe and a separate place to keep it.

3. Give each child her own toys.

4. Spend some special time alone with each child every day.

5. For their birthday, bake two (or three) cakes and sing "Happy Birthday" twice (or thrice).

Ulcers

Try some of these ways to make your restricted diet tastier and more interesting:

1. Mix fresh-pressed cabbage juice, often prescribed for peptic ulcers, with carrot or celery juice; it's more palatable that way.

2. Purée ½ cup of fresh, frozen, or canned vegetables and blend the

result with a cup of thin white sauce to make a tasty soup.

3. Use a little freshly ground lean meat (broiled or baked but not fried) in casseroles or soufflés to tempt the appetite.

4. Don't avoid dinner at a friend's house because you're on a restricted diet. Ask if you can bring your own precooked meal for reheating.

5. Coffee and tea may be taboo, but well-diluted fruit juices are permitted. Mix and match grapefruit, orange, and prune juices. You can also make soothing milk-based drinks from milk and canned fruit or fruit juice; just sweeten with honey and whirl in a blender.

6. Even the blandest bill of fare can be improved by making it *look* better. Serve small portions on pretty plates. Dress it up with bright bits of pimiento, parsley sprigs, and showy condiments. Use your best china, napkins, and place mats.

Umbrellas

1. To repair a broken rib, tape a small piece of wire coat hanger across the broken part with masking or duct tape.

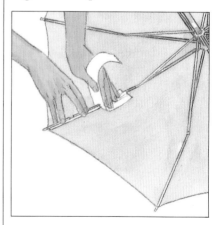

2. Has the fabric come loose from the tip of a rib? You can fix it in an emergency by inserting a paper clip or safety pin through the cloth and then through the hole in the tip. When you get home, whipstitch the cloth to the hole.

3. Is a rib bent? Bend it back very

Real men don't carry umbrellas

□ The Egyptian pharaohs sat under ceremonial umbrellas, which were said to bring them power from heaven.

□ In ancient Greece and China, parasols were used in religious ceremonies. And in Japan, the emperor was followed by an attendant with a red sunshade, symbolizing absolute power.

□ In Europe, however, umbrellas were used only by women until some 300 years ago. Men wore hats and got drenched.

□ Robert Louis Stevenson felt that an umbrella displayed a lack of character—too much concern about getting wet.

□ Carrying an umbrella also betrayed a lack of social status; it suggested you did not own a carriage. Another good reason not to carry one was that the early models weighed some 10 pounds. Furthermore, the oil-soaked cotton wasn't very waterproof.

□ It wasn't until the 16th century, when the pope decided that the umbrella was a symbol of honor, that bumbershoots gained favor in European society. Even so, the first Englishman to tote a rain shield, one Jonas Hanway, suffered public ridicule. And coachmen steered through puddles in order to splash him with mud.

□ When the fashionable "Beau" MacDonald began carrying a silk umbrella in 1778, his sister refused to be seen with him. Nevertheless, he persisted, and others soon followed suit. Men had finally figured out that one umbrella costs a lot less than catching a cab every rainy day.

gradually so that you don't break it. And don't straighten it too much—it's supposed to be curved.

4. To fix a loose handle, remove it and apply epoxy glue to the shaft. Quickly replace the handle; let dry for at least 24 hours.

5. When buying an umbrella, check for sturdiness by pressing on the ribs—they shouldn't give.

Unwanted visitors

1. Don't be afraid of telling the truth. If someone arrives unexpectedly and you are tired or busy, say so and suggest that you get together at a more convenient time.

2. If, however, you don't enjoy the person's company, don't feel obliged to encourage another visit—cutting the relationship short will save wear and tear on both parties in the long run.

3. What about dinner guests who linger too long? Since considerate people would be embarrassed to overstay their welcome, the nicest thing is to say, "I wish I weren't so tired so we could talk more." If that doesn't work, you can always resort to doing the dishes or making an important phone call.

4. How do you discourage coworkers from dropping in? Put a few books and papers on the chairs in your office so that there will be no place to sit; they won't stay as long.

Upholstery

1. Don't let zippers on chair and sofa cushions fool you—the fabric will probably shrink unless it's cleaned in place. If the fabric is washable, you can scrub it with a solution of mild detergent, warm water, and a dash of white vinegar or chlorine bleach. Work on one section at a time, removing the suds with a wet rough cloth.

2. Repair a cigarette burn by darning it with matching yarn.

3. Mend a rip by placing adhesive or iron-on tape on the underside of the fabric, sticky side up. Press the edges closed; trim off stray threads.

4. If new upholstery isn't in the budget, drape your chair with fabric, quilting, a tablecloth, or a bedspread. Secure it to the underside of the frame with upholstery tacks. (See also *Slipcovers*, p.188.)

5. Cover worn spots with crocheted doilies, lacy handkerchiefs, or matching pieces of suede or leather. Just tack them down with a few quick stitches.

6. To prevent soiled and worn spots, have matching covers made for the back and armrests that can be removed and laundered.

7. Is your wooden chair uncomfortable? Pad the arms and the slats on the back by wrapping with polyurethane foam; then cover with fabric. For trim, sew on strips of contrasting fabric or ribbon.

8. Plump a matted-down cushion by tumbling it in a clothes dryer for 5 minutes on *Air Fluff*. Include a few bath towels for proper balance.

9. Keep seat pads in place by sewing ties onto the back corners. Or use Velcro.

10. Make your own seat pad by cutting a piece of 1½-inch-thick polyurethane foam to size and covering it with fabric.

11. Before stuffing a cushion with shredded foam rubber, put the material in an old pillowcase. Then stuff the whole thing into the cushion cover.

Vacation pet care

Traveling is stressful for pets, but sometimes it can't be avoided. Here are some tips:

SHIPPING PETS

1. Many animals escape from carrying cases—even "locked" ones. Fasten the doors with twist ties for extra insurance, then wrap bungee cords around the case from front to back and side to side. Don't ship your pet in a wicker or cardboard case; neither is sturdy enough.
2. In cold weather put a blanket in the case—one with your scent on it. For long trips the polyester fur fabric sold in pet stores is an especially good insulator.
3. If the top can be removed from the case, let your pet use it as a bed for a few days before traveling. The animal won't feel as threatened.

LEAVING THE PET BEHIND

1. If you're leaving an animal with friends or in a kennel, supply its regular bedding, toys, and dishes. Your pet will feel more secure.

2. In case of emergency, give the caretaker the name of your vet.
3. Cats usually do best in their own homes with someone coming in to feed them. Be sure to keep the cat locked up while you're packing. They often panic and run away.

4. If a cat is destructive and you must leave it with friends, save wear and tear on both. Buy a cage large enough for the cat and its dishes, bed, and litter box.
5. Large cages also work well for dogs that bark or destroy furniture. A nervous dog perceives most sounds and smells as threatening; the cage makes it feel more secure.
6. If you plan to leave a pet in a kennel, make sure well ahead of time that it has all its vaccinations or it may not be accepted.

TRAVELING WITH YOUR PET

1. Wicker pet carriers are drafty. In cold weather line the bottom and sides with newspaper.
2. If your pet is unaccustomed to being in the car, take it on short drives before you leave.
3. If your pet is a particularly anxious traveler, ask your vet to prescribe a tranquilizer.
4. Check before taking your pet on any kind of public transportation—some lines will allow an animal in a case; some won't. In hot weather put a cool, damp cloth on top of the case. (See also *Parked cars*, p. 115.)

Vacation plant care

1. Safeguard your indoor greenery while you're on vacation by constructing a temporary greenhouse. Line the inside of your bathtub with a plastic drop cloth and cover with several layers of newspaper, the thicker the better. Set your houseplants (except succulents, African violets, and similar fuzzy-leaved plants) on the paper and spray with cold water just long enough to wet all the leaves, soil, and newspaper. Fasten another transparent drop cloth to the wall behind the tub with duct tape and drape it over the shower curtain rod to create a tent. Leave the bathroom lights on; your plants should survive a week or two, even a month, in the humid atmosphere.
2. Since African violets, other fuzzy-leaved plants, and succu-

lents would rot in your homemade greenhouse, furnish them with reservoirs instead. With a pencil, force a length of pantyhose up through each pot's drainage hole and into the soil. Fill a plastic margarine tub with water, cover it, and punch a hole in its lid. Set the plant on top, threading the dangling strip of hose down through the hole and into the water. Like a wick, the nylon will draw water up into the soil around the plant's roots.

Pantyhose

Vacuum cleaners

1. If your vacuum isn't picking up dirt as well as it used to, see if the hose or wand is clogged. Look through both ends; if you can't reach the clog with your hand, use a yardstick or the end of a straightened wire clothes hanger.

2. Never pick up cigarette butts with your vacuum. Not only could they clog the machine, but a smoldering one could be dangerous.

3. Before replacing the dust-bag jacket on an upright vacuum, try to repair it with iron-on patches.

4. If the hose attachments stick when you're pulling them apart, rub the joints with wax paper.

5. The rule of thumb for vacuuming: pass over the rug three times for light cleaning and seven times for heavy cleaning.

Valuables

1. Hire a professional appraiser to set the worth of all jewelry, antiques, and rare objects; then make sure that your insurance covers the full value of what you own.

2. To enable you to identify your property if it's ever stolen, mark it indelibly with a code such as your Social Security number or driver's license number. Use waterproof paint on the bottom of ceramic or wooden pieces, an etching pencil or carbide-tip scriber (available at hardware and art supply stores or at your local police department) on metal or glass.

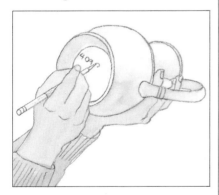

MAKING A HOUSEHOLD INVENTORY

1. Compile a complete written inventory of your most valuable household belongings; keep one copy at home, another in your safe-deposit box, and a third with your insurance agent. Although making the inventory may be tedious, it will be extremely valuable if you're ever the victim of theft, fire, flood, or other disaster.

2. Catalog each room; open every drawer and cupboard and carefully list anything of value. Write a description of each piece (including its serial number and brand name), the date you bought it, and its price. Keep receipts and appraisals for very valuable items.

3. If you wish, you can also photograph or videotape each room to supplement your written inventory and prove ownership. But pictures don't replace lists because small items may be overlooked and details like carving may not show up. (See also *Homeowners insurance,* p.109; *Insurance claims,* p.117; *Safe-deposit boxes,* p.176.)

Varicose veins

1. Exercise your legs regularly: jog, walk, cycle, or swim.

2. Don't sit or stand for long periods of time. When you do sit, avoid crossing your legs at the thighs.

3. Avoid wearing overly tight boots, girdles, socks, or pantyhose. Wear support stockings and sturdy-soled shoes with 1-inch heels; no sneakers, flats, high heels, or thin soles.

4. If your legs feel especially tired, give them a gentle, soothing massage, starting at the ankles.

5. Keep your weight down; eat a high-fiber, low-sodium diet (p.130).

6. Ask your doctor about nonsurgical removal of varicose veins. One method involves lasers; another, chemical injections into the veins.

Vases

1. If there's a whitish film on the inside of your vase, soak it in vinegar or a mild solution of chlorine bleach and water.

2. To remove water rings, rub them with salt. If the vase is narrow and you can't reach them, fill it with a strong saltwater solution and shake until clean; then wash.

3. Coat the inside of a leaky vase with hot paraffin and let harden. Or, if the vase is opaque, put a glass inside it to hold water.

4. Many household items make pretty vases. Teapots, wine carafes, copper kettles, and pitchers are es- pecially nice. Put single stems in a wineglass or goblet. Let wildflowers or daisies spill out of a basket (first put them in a small waterproof container that won't show). For dinner parties use small bottles and put a tiny bunch of violets or lilies of the valley at each place setting.

5. If your vase has a wide mouth, crisscross the opening with transparent tape—it will hold your arrangement in place.

VCR's

Most VCR care is simply preventive maintenance; once a problem occurs, there are no do-it-yourself remedies—take the unit to an authorized service center.

1. Record on high-quality videotapes only. Cheap tapes harm the recording heads—as will *any* tape after about 100 hours of use.

2. Cover your VCR when not in use to keep dust and debris out of the vents and to prevent children from putting things in the cassette slot.

3. Moisture can ruin a VCR. Don't rest a container of coffee, soda, or any other liquid on the machine and don't use liquid cleaning products on its exterior. If you live in a humid area, buy small packages of silica from an electronics supply store and put them on top of the VCR to absorb moisture. When the packages are soaked, bake them dry in the oven and reuse.

4. If your picture is snowy and the sound is fuzzy, it's time to clean the tape heads; follow the manufacturer's instructions. If you use many rented tapes, you may need to clean the heads fairly often. (See also *Televisions,* p.207.)

Vegetable peelers

1. For peak efficiency, push the blade away from you when using a peeler with a swivel blade; pull it toward you if the blade is rigid.

2. Use a vegetable peeler to make neat chocolate curls to garnish desserts. Using tongs, hold an ounce of unwrapped baking chocolate over a steaming kettle to soften it slightly. Or place it on a plate in the microwave on 50 percent power for 15 to 20 seconds. Dip your peeler in hot water and draw it across the edge or bottom of the chocolate.

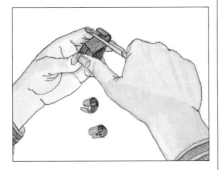

Vegetable steamers

1. For a make-do steamer, use an electric frying pan with an inch of water in it. Place the food on a heat-proof plate and balance it on some kind of platform—a canning jar ring, perhaps, or an empty tuna can with both ends removed. Then cover, leaving a small air vent so that condensed steam doesn't drip onto the food.

2. Or make a steamer from two thicknesses of foil and set it over an inch or two of water in a saucepan. Jab small holes in the foil with a sharp pencil and tightly crimp the edges over the rim of the pan. Place the food inside, cover, and steam.

Vegetable varieties

If your homegrown vegetables aren't up to snuff, you may be planting the wrong varieties. Believe it or not, the names on seed packets *do* make a difference. Look for those few varieties that are best suited to your conditions: fungus-resistant if you live in a humid zone, wilt-resistant if soil-borne diseases are a problem in your area (see *Tomato plants,* p.212).

1. Note whether the variety is specified as *early, midseason,* or *late* and how many days are specified to maturity. If your growing season is short, choose early varieties that can be harvested before the first frost puts an end to the season.

2. If you want to save seeds for next season, choose *standard* (sometimes listed as *open-pollinated)* varieties instead of hybrids; vegetables grown from hybrid seeds lose their desirable qualities after the first generation.

3. Beware of commercial varieties, tailored to the needs of large-scale growers and packers. Their characteristics, such as tough skin and long shelf life, are pointless in the home garden and usually take precedence over taste and texture. Choose varieties that are described as "for the home garden" or look for clues that the variety is intended for commercial growers: "excellent for shipping" and "suitable for processing" are warnings to stay away.

4. To put old-fashioned flavor back into your garden, plant *heirloom* varieties. A 19th-century tomato like Ponderosa offers a balanced acid-sugar ratio that still sets the standard for flavor; New Englanders swear that only Jacob's Cattle beans can give baked beans an authentic Yankee taste; and the Blue Flint corn that southwestern Indians have grown since before the Spaniards arrived has proved to be richer in protein than modern types. Plant Finders of America (532 Beaumont Court, Fort Wright, KY 41011) can help you locate mail-order sources of these and other varieties for a small fee.

Videotaping

1. For knock-'em-dead home movies, take a few minutes to plan your shots. Better yet, jot down a rough shooting script. Have it tell a story; show preparations for a trip, for example, and then the departure. After filming vacation highlights, attach an ending—perhaps something humorous about arriving home exhausted.

2. When shooting, do what the pros do: Hold the camera as steady as possible. Pan slowly and smoothly.

3. Don't overdo zooms; too many are visually disturbing. Use them to emphasize something important, like a close-up of a child's face blowing out birthday candles.

4. Don't make scenes interminably long; linger on one angle for only 8 to 10 seconds before you switch to another view.

Vines

Afraid you'll plant a vine in the wrong place? Learn how it grows and you'll know how best to use it in your garden.

TWINING TYPES

Wisteria, bittersweet, morning glory, honeysuckle, glory bower, Carolina jessamine, and silver-lace vines wrap their stems around their host. Because they can choke a tree, confine them to a trellis, arbor, or fence.

TENDRIL TYPES

Passionflower, Mexican ivy, coral vines, and perennial sweet peas pull themselves aloft with delicate tendrils. They clamber up a tree or shrub harmlessly if thinned by periodic pruning and provide the host with a bonus period of bloom or a colorful fall foliage display.

HOLDFAST TYPES

Masonry-climbing vines such as English ivy, Boston ivy, trumpet creeper, Virginia creeper, star jasmine, and climbing hydrangea literally glue themselves to a wall with resinous holdfasts. Contrary to popular belief, they won't damage the mortar; instead, they protect it by insulating the masonry from heat and frost.

Vision loss

1. Look for large-print books and periodicals; they're available in most public libraries, senior centers, and retirement communities, as well as from mail-order catalogs and some bookstores. Or try audiocassettes of recorded books, movies, and periodicals.

2. Investigate the many household items that are now designed with large print: watches, telephone buttons and dials, thermometers, clocks, typewriter keys, even software for personal computers. In addition, there are many new magnifying devices, ranging from a simple 2x glass with a light attached, to a closed-circuit television that enlarges up to 60x. (See also *Magnifying glass,* p.131.)

3. Seek out a low-vision specialist to teach you how to make the best of your impaired eyesight. Contact the National Association for Visually Handicapped in New York City to find a specialist near you.

Volunteering

Want to work with a volunteer group but don't know where to start?

1. Check the town library, where civic groups often leave pamphlets describing their activities.

2. Scan the classified pages of the newspaper for small display ads placed by nonprofit organizations.

3. Call the mayor's office; the superintendent of schools; or a local hospital, church, or synagogue. Say you're interested in volunteer work and ask if they can give you a lead.

Vomiting

1. To prevent dehydration after a bout of vomiting, drink as much fluid as you can keep down. Avoid drinks that contain caffeine; it may irritate your stomach. Once the liquids stay down, ease back into eating solid foods, beginning with dry toast, clear soup, gelatin, applesauce, and tapioca.

2. Support a child's body and forehead while he vomits, then wipe his face with a cool moist cloth and help him rinse his mouth and brush his teeth. If he's frightened, explain that his stomach is just getting rid of something it dislikes.

3. Call a doctor if there is abdominal pain, bloating, or constipation or if vomiting persists for more than a day—or 12 hours in a baby. (See also *Airsickness,* p.9; *Hangovers,* p.104.)

Walkers

1. To make carrying odds and ends easier, attach a small wicker bicycle basket to the front of the walker. Run an elastic loop or a sturdy rubber band through the wicker to hold a glass of liquid firmly inside. (For maximum safety, use a covered container or a cyclist's plastic water bottle.)

2. Tie a plastic supermarket bag to one side of the frame to hold tissues and other light items; a second one on the other side can serve as a wastebasket.

3. Door-closing problems? Run a cord from the knob to a screw eye on the hinge side; then just pull the cord to close the door behind you.

4. If something is out of reach, use a pair of long tongs; suspend them from the walker frame with string.

5. For comfort and to prevent your hands from slipping, wrap the top bar of the walker with friction tape.

Wallboard

1. To repair wallboard tape that has pulled away from the wall, wet the back slightly to make it flexible. Then squeeze on a little white glue and spread it with a toothpick. Press the tape to the wall, hold a sheet of wax paper over it, and apply pressure with a hardcover book or board for 3 or 4 minutes.

2. Hammer a popped wallboard nail back into the wall stud and drive another nail an inch or so above or below it. Fill nailhead dimples with spackle; when dry, sand lightly and repaint. Or pull popped nails and replace with drywall screws.

DID YOU KNOW . . . ?

Volunteer firemen: hometown heroes

☐ Most volunteer fire companies are in rural communities that can't afford a paid fire department. But they began in the cities. Boston had the first in 1717; in 1736 Ben Franklin organized the Union Fire Company in Philadelphia with 20 volunteers and 40 buckets.

☐ By the 19th century, volunteer fire companies were an urban institution. Prestige (and often money) went to the first company to reach a fire, and engines sometimes ran over pedestrians in their haste. The rivalries generated huge street brawls. After one such donnybrook, Cincinnati decided to pay their firemen salaries. Other cities followed suit.

☐ The first fire trucks were pulled by hand. But by the early 19th century horses were being used. Today's volunteer firefighters have hook-and-ladder trucks, high-volume pumpers, oxygen masks, two-way radios, and other state-of-the-art equipment. Since the cost of a new fire truck runs into six figures, the volunteers often must spend as much of their time raising money as they do fighting fires.

☐ Today roughly 85 percent of the nation's firefighters are volunteers. Sadly, many communities are having trouble finding enough volunteers. The job can require as much as 110 hours of training, and many working parents are just too busy. However, for the men and women who volunteer, the rewards are many—camaraderie, pride in doing a job well, and, above all, satisfaction in helping to save their neighbors' property and lives.

Wallflowers

1. Ask the shy guest to help you serve the hors d'oeuvres or the drinks—you'll get a helping hand and he'll have a good reason to circulate among the other guests.

2. Introduce the timid soul to another person who looks lost; be sure to give them both some useful information about each other so that they can start a conversation: "Dick, I'd like you to meet John Smith, visiting from Boston, where he practices law. John, this is our neighbor Dick Jones, who teaches at the high school."

3. If you are having a small party, take the trouble to brief your guests ahead of time on who else is coming. It will help break the ice. If one person isn't participating, ask her something she knows a lot about so that she can have the spotlight for a while.

4. You can do a lot to keep people mingling by arranging the room properly: place the drinks at one end, the food at the other. And don't provide too many chairs; if potential wallflowers have to stand, they'll be more likely to move around and chat with other guests. (See also *Party guests*, p.151.)

Wallpaper

1. To keep the wallpaper around a baby's crib clean, staple clear non-adhesive vinyl over it.

2. To dust papered walls, tie a dust-cloth over your broom and work from the top down.

3. To remove pencil marks and other nongreasy spots from non-washable papers, use an art-gum eraser or a slice of fresh rye bread.

4. To remove greasy spots, crayon marks, and food stains, apply a paste of cleaning fluid and fuller's earth, cornstarch, or whiting. Let dry and brush off. Repeat the treatment until the spot is gone.

5. Wipe off fingerprints with a damp cloth, then sprinkle the moist area with fuller's earth; let it dry and then brush it off.

6. To prevent splash marks when you're washing baseboards or other woodwork, mask wallpaper with a wide ruler, venetian blind slat, or piece of rigid plastic.

7. When you save scraps of wallpaper for patching, tack them to a wall in the attic or closet. When you use them for repairs, they won't look so brand-new.

8. Patches that have cut edges tend to show, so don't *cut* the paper—tear it instead. The feathered edges won't be so noticeable.

9. If you don't have any wallpaper left for making patches, just touch up the damaged spots with some matching paints.

HANGING WALLPAPER

1. Make a resting place for the sticky paste brush by slipping a length of coat hanger through the bail eyes on your pail. Then set the bristles on the wire and the handle on the side of the pail.

2. To smooth out air bubbles under freshly applied paper, use a paint roller.

3. If you're papering over old wallpaper, cover any grease spots with clear shellac so that they won't bleed through.

4. Use leftover wallpaper for wrapping paper, book covers, or drawer liners (see *Wallpaper*, p.333).

Wallpaper removal

1. To make wallpaper easier to remove, first slash it diagonally with a single-edge razor blade or a utility knife every 12 inches. Then mix a 50-50 solution of vinegar and warm water in a spray bottle and squirt it behind the cut edges. Let the glue soften for a few minutes, then scrape off the paper with a 6- or 8-inch putty knife or metal spatula. (Tape the tool to a broom handle to scrape near the ceiling.)

2. To strip a small area of stubborn paper, cover it with a clean cloth and press with a steam iron to soften the glue. If your iron won't produce steam when held vertically, wet the cloth before ironing.

Warm-up & cool-down exercises

If you exercise strenuously without warming up, you can injure muscles. If you stop exercising without cooling down, your blood pressure can drop suddenly and cause dizziness, nausea, and irregular heartbeat; this can be life-threatening to someone with a heart problem. Check with your doctor before starting any exercise regime.

1. The first step in warming up is to raise your body temperature and increase your muscle flexibility. Jogging in place and slow aerobic activities are both good. So is a fast

Warming up

walk: Step out briskly, heel first; swing your arms and shake them vigorously as you walk to stimulate circulation. Lengthen your stride and increase your speed as you warm up.

2. Once your muscles have gotten somewhat warm, do at least 5 minutes of stretching exercises (p. 199). If you're warming up to run, choose exercises that will stretch the groin, hamstrings, calves, and quadriceps. If you're preparing to lift weights, concentrate on the muscles of your upper body, particularly those of your shoulders. A good book on your sport should include some specific suggestions for stretching exercises.

3. After a workout, the best way to cool down is to stay in motion while gradually reducing your effort; walk briskly or jog slowly for 5 to 15 min-

utes in order to stabilize your blood pressure and steadily slow your heart rate.

Cooling down

Warped wood

1. To prevent a board from warping or cupping, saw two ¼-inch-deep kerfs along the board's length in the bottom or back surface. Space the kerfs a couple of inches apart; they act as stress-release gaps and allow the board to expand and contract without warping.

2. If warpage causes a board to pull its nails free, replace them with screws; clamp the board back in place before driving the screws.

3. For even greater holding power, bore holes through the board and bolt it down.

4. To correct a warped board, place it, concave side up, on a stack of wet towels near (but not on) a radiator or other source of heat. Put heavy weights on each end of the board and let it sit for several days, rewetting the towels as necessary. (If the board is sealed with a finish, sand it off so that the board will absorb moisture.)

Warts & moles

Although they may look similar, warts and moles are unrelated skin conditions. To be sure which you have, consult your doctor before attempting any self-treatment.

Warts vary in size, shape, roughness, and color and grow mainly on the face, neck, hands, forearms, legs, and feet; almost always harmless, they may disappear all by themselves within 6 to 24 months. To treat a wart that has been so diagnosed, soften it overnight with a bandage moistened with a 30 percent salicylic acid solution; then soak the wart for 30 minutes in Epsom salts and hot water and file it gently with an emery board or a pumice stone. Or squeeze the con-

---

LOOK BEFORE YOU LEAP

The hazards of exercising

Exercise is not always a good thing. Too much too soon can cause injuries.

☐ Running injuries are most frequent in people who log more than 30 miles a week. Sports medicine experts say 20 to 25 miles is quite enough to keep you in top condition.

☐ No pain, no gain—right? Wrong! Strenuous exercise may cause some discomfort, but pain is a warning to back off before you injure yourself.

☐ Never take salt tablets before exercising—they can cause nausea and vomiting. To counter salt loss, drink salty liquids or add a little extra table salt to your food.

☐ Many people are seriously injured working out on weight machines because they don't use them properly. Get instructions first and be sure they come from a qualified instructor.

☐ The myth that you shouldn't drink water while exercising is not only wrong but dangerous. Working out when you're dehydrated puts extra strain on your heart and muscles. Drink a glass of water before you start and have more if you feel thirsty.

☐ Don't proceed as usual in very hot, humid weather—you could get heatstroke. Ask your doctor for guidelines for your age and fitness level.

☐ If you haven't played a sport in a long time, don't start up at your former intensity. Start slowly to build up strength and endurance.

☐ Exercise can be addictive. Beware if you continue to exercise despite injuries, if you find it hard to sleep even though you're exhausted, if exercise is interfering with your work or social life, or if you feel guilty or out of control when you miss a workout.

tents of a gelatin capsule of vitamin A and one of fish oil onto the wart twice a day for 2 to 5 months.

Moles, small dark spots, can occur anywhere on the body. If you are subject to moles, examine your skin monthly with a hand-held and full-length mirror. Look for growths larger than a pencil eraser and those that have an irregular raised surface, an asymmetrical outline, and a mottled color; also look for color changes, scaliness, oozing, bleeding, itching, tenderness, and a bump or nodule. If you spot any of these features or if after 35 you begin to develop dark, smooth spots, see a dermatologist immediately.

Water conservation

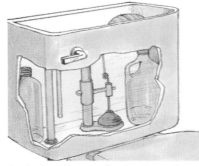

1. At 7 gallons a flush, the toilet is your household's worst water waster; to save as much as a gallon a flush, displace some water in the tank with rocks, a brick, or a plastic jug of sand. Don't overdo it or you'll cause an incomplete flush.

2. Take shallow baths and short showers; install a flow restrictor in your shower head to cut the flow from 8 to 2 gallons per minute.

3. Rinse dirty dishes in a pan instead of under running water.

4. Collect rainwater for irrigation (see *Barrel,* p.339).

5. Keep your flowers and shrubs alive with "gray water," the waste that would otherwise go down the drain. Use water from the washing machine or the bathtub only, and only if you've used bar soap or soap flakes (no detergents, bleach, borax, or water softeners).

Run a hose from the drain to a plastic garbage can; carry the water to your plants in a bucket.

Caution: Don't use gray water on food crops and don't use water in which you've washed diapers. Cover the storage container outdoors so that the water doesn't become a breeding ground for mosquitoes.

Water heaters

Take these steps if you must drain the water from a heater:

1. Shut off the water, electricity, and gas.

2. Shut the cold-water supply valve.

3. Open a hot-water faucet nearby and let it run dry.

4. Attach one end of a garden hose to the drain valve near the base of the heater; run it outdoors or into a drain or sink that's on a lower level. Then open the valve.

5. When the emergency is over, open the cold-water supply valve and refill the tank until water flows from an open faucet before turning the heater back on. Never operate a water heater when it's empty.

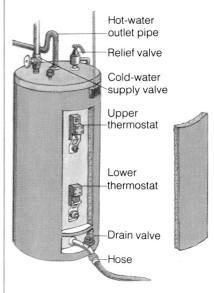

❯ Water leaks

Your first step in any leaking-water emergency should be to cut off the water supply at your home's main shutoff valve so that the flood won't get worse while you look for the trouble spot. If you use city water, your main shutoff valve is the one nearest the meter. If you have your own well, the main valve is near the water storage tank.

Once you've located the source of

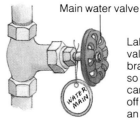

Main water valve

Label the main valve and the branch lines so that anyone can quickly shut off the water in an emergency.

the leak, look for a shutoff valve for the branch line to that part of the house (it's usually located where it branches off the main line) and shut it. Most sinks, toilets, showers, and bathtubs have their own shutoff valves for both the hot and cold water. As soon as you isolate the problem area, you can restore the water supply to the rest of the house while making your repair or waiting for the plumber. (See also *Pipes*, p.157.)

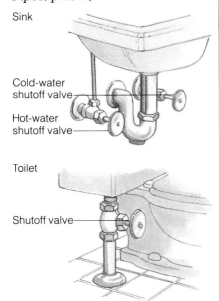

Sink

Cold-water shutoff valve

Hot-water shutoff valve

Toilet

Shutoff valve

Water purification

1. To purify water, first filter it. Fill a clean sock with successive 1-inch layers of fine gravel, crushed charcoal, and sand. Pour water into the sock and let it drain into a cup. Then boil the water for 5 minutes (1 minute longer for each 1,000 feet in elevation).
2. If you use purification tablets, allow 1 hour for them to take effect. Follow the directions on the bottle carefully; dosage can vary significantly with temperature.

SOLAR STILL

At a campsite you can make a solar still that produces 1 to 3 pints of pure water a day.
1. Dig a bowl-shaped hole 40 inches in diameter and 20 inches deep.

2. Set a clean bucket or bowl in the center of the hole.
3. Secure a large piece of clear plastic over the hole with earth or rocks. Then place a rock in the middle of the plastic so that the sheet's lowest point is directly above the container. Solar heat will penetrate the plastic and bake moisture out of the soil. The water will condense on the lower side of the plastic and run down to drip into the container; night cuts accumulation in half.
4. Delay collection as long as possible; opening the still lets out moisture-laden air, which takes some 30 minutes to resaturate.
5. When the soil is baked dry, rebuild the still in another spot. Hollows and dry washes are likely to have wetter soil than high ground.
6. You can use the same method to purify salty or polluted water, even urine, or to extract moisture from plant materials. Just put the water source off-center in the hole and let the sun work its wonders.

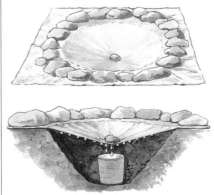

Water retention

If bloating and swelling are recurring problems for you, consult your doctor to see if there is cause for concern. If not, consider taking the following measures:
1. Decrease your salt intake; avoid all canned and processed foods, from soup and salami to salted nuts and potato chips (see *Low-sodium diet*, p.130). It may help to cut back on sugar and caffeine as well.
2. Eat foods that are natural diure-

tics: cucumbers, parsley, beets, watercress, asparagus, dandelion greens, strawberries, apples, and grapes, for example.
3. Exercise regularly—swim, bicycle, jog, walk briskly—to improve your circulation.
4. Wear support stockings.
5. Elevate your feet for 20 minutes during the day and an hour or two before going to bed.
6. Avoid extreme stress (p.198); it can sometimes activate a water-retaining hormone.
7. If your doctor prescribes diuretics, use them with caution; they can cause potassium deficiency. Instead (believe it or not), drink lots of water; it won't add to the bloat but rather will make your kidneys work harder. (See also *Puffiness*, p.164.)

Water softener

1. Today's built-in water softeners are not for everyone; they add sodium to the water. So if you're on a no-sodium diet, don't use one. If on a low-sodium diet, check with your physician and take into account the original hardness of the water.
2. Eliminate "telltale gray" from your laundry by using a heavy-duty liquid detergent and adding ½ cup borax or washing soda to the wash water. A quart of white vinegar in the final rinse water will help remove the last traces of soap scum. Don't do this too often, however; the enamel in washer tubs is not acid-resistant.
3. To rid your your clothes washer of hard-water buildup, fill it with water, add 1 cup white vinegar, and let it run—without laundry—through a complete cycle.

Water stains

1. If the fabric is nonwashable, gently scratch off the stain (which is made up of mineral deposits) with your fingernail. Still there? Hold the spot over a steaming teakettle until well dampened. As it dries, rub the stain, working from its outer edges toward the center.

2. Remove hard-water stains from glasses and bottles by rubbing with steel wool dipped in vinegar.

3. Cover hard-water stains on bathroom fixtures with a paste of baking soda and vinegar. Then drape with a terry-cloth towel and let stand for about an hour; wipe off, rinse, and dry.

4. Keep the toilet bowl ring-free by pouring a half-gallon of white vinegar in it once a month. Let it soak overnight before flushing.

Water testing

1. If the odor, taste, or color of your water suddenly seems strange to you, call your municipal water company for a free test.

2. If you have your own well, you must pay for all tests; they run from a few dollars for coliform bacteria and nitrate tests to over $1,000 for a screening of more than 100 different contaminants. To find a reliable water-testing service, call a local real estate agent, the board of health, or a state-certified testing laboratory (check "Laboratories—Testing" or "Water quality" in the Yellow Pages).

3. There is danger of contaminating the pipes *anytime* you break into the plumbing system. Test your water for coliform bacteria immediately after doing so.

4. It's a good idea to test your water every 9 to 15 months to get an idea of its varying quality in different seasons. Regular testing also gives you a baseline so that you can see immediately if there are any changes in water quality.

Weatherstripping

1. Through-the-wall air conditioners are notorious for inadequate weatherstripping. To seal, wad up aluminum foil and, using a ruler or putty knife, pack it around the unit, especially the gap underneath. Then seal with duct tape.

2. Wipe rubber weatherstripping with a thin film of household oil from time to time. This will keep it flexible longer. It also keeps the weatherstripping from sticking to the door or window on hot days. (See also *Insulation*, p.116.)

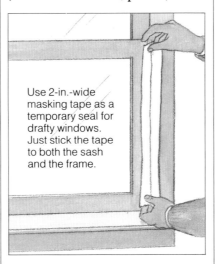

Use 2-in.-wide masking tape as a temporary seal for drafty windows. Just stick the tape to both the sash and the frame.

Weddings

If you're planning a wedding and are worried about the price tag, relax. Here are some ways to cut costs and still have a day to remember:

1. A beautiful location doesn't have to be expensive. You could have the ceremony on the beach, aboard a ferryboat, in a park, in a garden, at a historic site, or, of course, in a church or synagogue.

2. Instead of renting a room, hold the reception at home. Make a festive—if not waterproof—tent by sewing strips of brightly colored fabric or parachute silk together. Then tie it to the trees. Or lash tent flies or canopies to poles and set them up in clusters or against the side of the house. For an evening wedding why not string the backyard with a gala canopy of tiny white lights?

3. Ask a music student to play at the ceremony. For the reception hire a local deejay or make your own dance tapes.

4. Rather than serving a sit-down meal, plan an afternoon wedding and serve high tea or cocktails and hors d'oeuvres. Champagne punch

costs less than champagne, and domestic brands less than the imports. Look for someone who makes wedding cakes at home; the cake will probably cost less than one from a bakery and should taste just as good—maybe a lot better.

5. Hire a professional photographer to take formal shots, but ask friends who are photo buffs to take the candid shots at the reception. Develop and print the film yourself.

6. Make your own floral arrangements and bouquets with blossoms from your garden or with wildflowers. (Pick wildflowers the same day you want to use them; they wilt quickly.)

7. Scout antique shops for the wedding dress. You can often find beautiful gowns that are relatively inexpensive that way.

8. Instead of engraved invitations, ask someone who does calligraphy to write them by hand. Or ask an artistic friend to design an invitation that reflects the personalities or interests of the couple. (See also *Love & Marriage*, p.267.)

Weeds

1. Want to get rid of weeds without using herbicides? Rototill and fertilize the soil in early spring, then cover it with a sheet of black plastic. The plastic will absorb sunlight to warm the soil; when weed seeds germinate, it will smother the unwelcome seedlings. Some 6 to 8 weeks later, the bed will be ready to uncover and plant with flowers or vegetables.

2. Make sure you don't sow weeds in your garden. Compost horse and cow manure before adding it to your soil (p.54); in the process you'll destroy any seeds the animal may have ingested. Because fresh hay is full of weed seeds, mulch with salt hay instead; the weeds it hosts can't compete on dry land.

3. Weed on a 10-day schedule. Till the soil 10 days before planting and hoe out any seedlings that appear in the interval before you sow your crops. Cultivate again 10 days after planting, when the weeds are still small and easy to uproot. Ten days later work the soil yet again. For fast-growing and late-season crops, this should be all the weeding you'll need to do.

Wheelchair access

1. Make a ramp from 2 x 4's covered with ¾-inch plywood. Store it in the garage and use it to cover stairs, rough terrain, or sand when you need wheelchair access.

2. To make it easy for a wheelchair to pass through narrow interior doorways, pop the hinge pins and remove the door. Keep the area behind other doors clear of wastebaskets, furniture, and other items that might impede easy opening.

3. Tape down the latches on doorknobs so that doors can be pushed open and closed.

4. Tie short lengths of rope to the handles of sliding doors and refrigerators so that they can be pulled open without difficulty.

5. Take up all area rugs and hallway carpet runners to provide a smooth floor surface. (See also *Walkers*, p.223.)

Whipped cream

1. For a substitute, whip a cup of nonfat dry milk powder in a cup of ice water for 5 minutes. Use it quickly, before the "cream" collapses.

2. Overwhipped cream can some-

times be salvaged by whipping in 1 or 2 tablespoons of half-and-half or evaporated milk. Or you can keep whipping, and pretty soon you'll have some sweet butter; drain off the liquid before using.

Wicker

1. Remove dust from wicker by vacuuming with the dust-brush attachment. To remove grime, wash with a solution of 2 tablespoons ammonia per gallon of water; use a paintbrush or a toothbrush to get at hard-to-reach places. Rinse well; air-dry in the shade.

2. To prevent wicker from drying out, wet it down at least once a year. Don't leave it outdoors when not in use—sunshine dehydrates wicker; water rots it.

3. Never strip paint from wicker or it will get brittle. Repaint instead, using spray paint.

4. For a smooth finish, remove any whiskerlike fibers from wicker by singeing them off with a propane torch before painting. Keep the flame moving so that you don't burn the reed.

5. If paint is caked on the weave, remove it with an ice pick or awl.

Widowhood

Adjusting to the loss of a spouse takes time, no matter how well you manage the first few days or weeks or how much help you get. Not only must you absorb your grief, but you must learn what it is like to be single again.

1. Give yourself permission to mourn. Filling each day with activity will only delay and perhaps compound the grief.

2. Don't panic if you think you're losing your mind; grief can cause erratic behavior and many unusual feelings. If you weren't mentally ill before, you're not likely to become so now.

3. Beware of the temptation to rely on tranquilizers or alcohol to numb the pain; they will only postpone it and make matters worse.

4. Avoid making irreversible decisions during the first year; if you are contemplating a change, try it out first. Instead of quitting your job, ask for a leave of absence; consider renting your house rather than selling it.

5. Since stress may weaken your immune system, be extra careful: eat balanced meals, exercise regularly, and report any physical problems to your doctor immediately.

6. It may help to talk to others who have felt what you are feeling now. If you don't know any widowed people, get in touch with the American Association of Retired Persons' Widowed Persons Service in Washington, D.C., for help.

7. If you feel that your children aren't doing enough for you, it may be that they need more parenting than they did before. This is a difficult time for everyone; it helps to share your feelings.

Wigs & hairpieces

1. When the time comes to cut your long hair, why not save it for a perfectly matched hairpiece? Braid your hair, cut the braid off, then restyle your hair. Or cut your hair first, secure one end of the cuttings with a rubber band, and make a braid. When you want long hair, attach the braid to the underside of your own hair with bobby pins and a small comb.

2. To get a wig of the right style, buy one with long hair and take it to a salon to have it custom-cut.

3. Need a wig stand? Use a soda bottle with a roll of toilet paper over its neck.

4. If you have a wobbly wig stand, glue the bottom to an unwanted long-playing record.

5. The easiest way to hide baldness is with a hairpiece. Ask a friend who has one that looks good where he got it or consult a hair stylist or dermatologist. Most people need at least two so that one can be worn while the other is being cleaned and restored.

6. If you've lost hair because of illness or medical treatment, you may be entitled to reimbursement for your hairpiece under your health insurance plan. You'll need a refillable prescription for a "medical hair prosthesis" from your doctor; be sure to use that terminology on insurance forms rather than writing "wig" or "hairpiece."

Wilderness sanitation

1. Don't bury leftover food at your campsite, particularly in areas where bears are common. The animals will just dig it up and perhaps bother the next camper in the vicinity. Carry out cans, bottles, and food wastes when you leave.

2. Bury human feces 4 to 12 inches deep. Save overlying sod to hide the hole. In areas of little soil, follow local recommendations for shallow burial and cover waste with whatever soil is available.

3. For a latrine that will be used by more than one person and have to decompose more waste, lengthen rather than deepen the hole.

4. Be sure toilet areas are at least 100 feet from watercourses, trails, and campsites.

5. Use biodegradable toilet paper, often sold by recreational vehicle dealers. It decomposes much faster than grocery store brands. Or burn toilet paper after use.

6. Improvise a toothbrush by chewing the end of a green twig. Baking soda, salt, or soap can all serve as substitutes for toothpaste.

Wilderness survival

1. To learn which way is south, look for anthills; they're built on the warm south sides of trees and rocks. (See also *Compass direction,* p.54.)

2. When you're walking to safety, your first 5 to 7 minutes of rest do more good than the next 15 minutes. So several short rest stops are better than one long one.

3. Save strength when climbing a steep slope by zigzagging back and forth rather than charging straight up. Go around barriers; don't just barrel through thickets and bogs.

4. Snow is an excellent insulator, but don't sit or sleep directly on it. It will melt, wetting your clothes. Even a thin piece of plastic or some bark will increase your comfort.

5. Insect repellent from a bottle (*not* from an aerosol can) may provide heat if you try burning it in a small, flat container. Use a matchstick or large splinter as a wick.

6. If your hands and feet are cold, put on a hat. If you keep your head from losing heat, more warming blood will flow to extremities.

7. Dressing too warmly in cold weather can make you colder if you sweat. Loose or open clothes allow water vapor to escape and may be warmer than tight garments.

Winch

Come-along

1. If the weight of whatever you want to haul (plus the friction) is less than 4,000 pounds, a relatively inexpensive come-along could do the job, though slowly. Wrap a chain around a sturdy tree and join its links with one hook of the come-along. Secure another chain to the object you want to pull and run its length to the other hook of the come-along. Then operate the lever to pull the weighty object toward you, reposition the hook, and do it again.

2. To haul a car out of a ditch or an outboard runabout onto dry land, fix a block and tackle to a hefty tree trunk and the hauling end to the car or boat. Get some help if you can't pull it alone.

Windows

1. To keep windows from frosting over during winter, sponge them with salt water and wipe dry.

2. If your windows tend to fog up, wipe them with bar soap rubbed on a moist cloth; rinse and dry, then go over them with a glycerin-dampened cloth.

3. Hold a cracked pane together temporarily with adhesive tape.

4. For more privacy in a room, try frosting the window: Brush it with a solution of 1 tablespoon Epsom salts in 1 cup beer. "Defrost" with concentrated ammonia.

5. To loosen sticky windows, lubricate the channels with silicone spray, a bar of soap, or a candle.

6. When painting or varnishing windows, leave the metal channels and fittings alone. When dry, slide

the windows up and down a few times or open and shut the casements to make sure nothing sticks.
7. To break a paint seal, force the blade of a putty knife between the sash and the frame; slide the blade up and down the length of the window and across the top and bottom as necessary.

Window shades

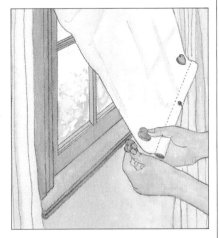

1. If a window shade tends to curl up at the bottom, you can usually weight it with matched pairs of refrigerator magnets.
2. A towel can make an adequate temporary shade; secure it to the frame with pushpins or thumbtacks. Dark-colored towels do the best job of blocking the sun's rays; lightweight white ones give a translucent glow.
3. Resurface worn shades with new fabric affixed with rubber cement or spray-on adhesive. Bed sheets, cut to fit, are ideal for the purpose. Be careful to smooth on the new fabric so that there are no air bubbles, or the shade will wrinkle when it rolls up.
4. To remove stains and smudges from a window shade, lay it on a flat surface and clean the blemishes with an art-gum eraser or a dough-type wallpaper cleaner.
5. If a shade won't stay down, easing the tension usually helps. Roll the shade up, remove it from its brackets, and unroll it by hand;

then replace it in the brackets and roll it up again.
6. To put a windowshade in a frame that is rounded or odd-shaped at the top, install the brackets at the base and a small pulley at the top; then run a cord through the pulley to raise and lower the shade.

Window treatment

1. Festoon fabric across the top of a frame, hanging it from knobs or tiebacks mounted at the corners. Then drape it in deep pleats down the sides. If the window is wide, loop or tack the fabric around a decorative rod or wooden pole to make swags.
2. For total seclusion, make folding screens of light plywood. Cover them with fabric or wallpaper and hinge them to the inside of the window frames.
3. Make "stained glass" windows with glass paints and leading, available at many crafts stores. After painting your design on the window pane, outline its elements by squeezing strips of leading directly from the tube.
4. In winter have your kids decorate their windows with paper snowflakes. Take a square sheet of paper, fold it in half lengthwise and then up into quarters. Fold again into thirds, as shown below, and trim off the irregular corners at the bottom. To create the snowflake pattern, make cuts in one of the folded edges—the closer you cut to the opposite edge, the more delicate the design will be. Unfold and tape to the window.

Windshields

1. Keep a box of table salt in your glove compartment all winter; it will melt the ice on your windshield.
2. Foggy windshield? A blackboard eraser works better than cloth.
3. To prevent fogging, use a soft cloth to apply a solution of 1 tablespoon silicone liquid emulsion in 3 cups water.

Windshield wipers

Are your wipers doing a lousy job? Before buying new squeegees, clean both the glass and blades thoroughly. If you've had your car cleaned at the car wash, you may have to use a mild household abrasive cleaner to remove any silicone wax. If that doesn't do the trick, try the following:
1. Water beads are the result of grease or silicone buildup. Clean the windshield with the solvent used for removing grease or silicone from bodywork.
2. To end smearing, add antifreeze (the kind made for the washer, not the engine) to the washer solution in winter, solvent in summer.
3. If the wipers are smearing in only one direction or if they chatter, the squeegees may be frozen. Warm them between your hands or use a hair dryer; if that doesn't help, dip them in warm water.
4. Chattering may also be caused by a bent wiper arm. In this case, stop the wipers in midstroke to see if they are parallel to the windshield. If an arm is bent, straighten it with two pairs of pliers until it remains parallel to the glass when

released. If the tip of the arm is bent, remove the blade before you straighten the arm. The problem may also be corroded joints. Free them up with penetrating solvent.

5. Streaking may occur when the nozzle of the windshield sprayer is blocked; insert a needle to clear it. Or the washer fluid may not be spraying in the wiper's path; straighten the nozzle with needle-nose pliers or a screwdriver and keep checking until the spray pattern is on target. Some nozzles aren't adjustable; don't force them.

6. If the squeegee on the driver's side isn't working, switch it with the one on the passenger's side.

7. Before driving in the rain, rub your wiper blades with baking soda—you'll see better.

Wine

1. To decide how many bottles you'll need for a dinner, follow this rule: a standard bottle is generally ample for three people, a half-bottle for two.

2. If you're serving two dinner wines, remember this simple protocol: white before red, young wine before old. And a dry wine always precedes a sweet one; the sweet taste will linger. Save your sweet wines to serve with dessert.

3. Uncork red wines an hour before drinking so that they can "breathe" and develop flavor; then serve at room temperature. Chill whites and rosés but don't uncork them until you're ready to serve.

4. Don't throw out wine left in the bottle. Recorked, it will keep in the refrigerator for a few days.

5. Even if you don't have a cellar, any dark corner with some humidity and no vibration can be turned into a wine storage area. A dark closet, a fireplace with a blocked-off chimney, or a corner of a well-insulated garage will all do. Keep the temperature as close to 50°F as possible. Store the bottles horizontally so that the corks remain moist.

6. If you don't have a wine rack,

use empty cardboard liquor cases with dividers; liquor stores are usually happy to give them away.

Wine stains

1. If you spill wine on your clothing or a tablecloth, blot it up immediately with an absorbent cloth, then sponge with club soda or cool water. If the fabric is washable, stretch the stained area over a pot (hold it in place with a heavy rubber band), put salt on it, and pour boiling water through from 1 foot above. (If boiling water would harm the fabric, just cover the stain with moistened salt.) Wash normally with detergent.

2. On nonwashable fabrics, cover the stain with a pad moistened with a mixture of detergent, water, and a few drops of vinegar; then rinse. Dry-clean as soon as possible.

3. If red wine is spilled on your carpet, sponge it with club soda. Or cover the stain with salt and let it absorb the wine; vacuum the residue. If a stain remains, wipe gently with a solution of detergent, water, and a few drops of white vinegar.

Winter clothing

1. There's no need to buy the latest in ski pants if you're heading off on an impromptu ski trip. Spray your old jeans with a water repellent and wear them. The jeans won't keep you very warm, so don't forget your long johns! (Long underwear made of wool or polypropylene is especially good; it wicks perspiration away from your body.)

2. If your jacket isn't windproof, you can, in a pinch, use a large plastic garbage bag as a windbreaker. Cut head and arm holes and wear it under your coat. Small bags over your socks and gloves will also keep out wind. (However, plastic will permit moisture to build up, so be careful.) If you don't have plastic bags, put newspaper or foam under your coat or shirt and inside your boots. Wear a shower cap under your hat for insulation.

3. If your child gets a rash from his

---

wool or synthetic winter hat, attach a cotton liner or tie a large cotton handkerchief around his head before putting on the cap.

› Winter storms

1. During winter in snow country, stay posted on weather conditions at all times—a warning of even a few hours can be a lifesaver.
2. Keep some extra blankets and an emergency heat source (enough to make at least one room livable) always at the ready.
3. Stock a battery-operated radio; candles, lanterns, or flashlights; and extra batteries.
4. Store a week's supply of food and water and, if your range is electric, a camp stove or burner with fuel. (See also *Power outage,* p.162; *Snowed-in car,* p.191; *Winter clothing,* p.232.)

Wire cutter

1. One blow of a hammer on a cold chisel over a vise anvil will sever ordinary electrical wire. Cutting cable the same way will take two or three strikes.
2. No cold chisel at hand? Wrap the wire over the corner of a metal file and saw through it.
3. Slice wire with the spinning edge of an abrasive wheel in an electric drill. Wear eye protection.
4. Remember the wire-cutting bite on your pliers. It's designed to cut thin wire.
5. In a pinch, pruning shears will do the job on thin wire, but the edge will be damaged. Be sure to resharpen the shears before using them on your roses or other shrubs.

Wires

1. Anticipate and avoid electrical wires that are drilled through studs before driving any nails into walls. The wires are usually 12 to 24 inches from the floor.
2. Straighten kinks in thin electrical wire by drawing it between your thumb and a screwdriver handle as though you were combing long hair.

After a few passes, the wire will have a long, uniform curve that makes it easy to roll into coils.

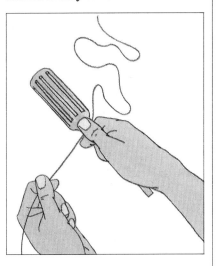

Withered plants

1. Foliage wilting in the garden? It's not necessarily a sign of dry soil; it may just be a reaction to hot summer wind. If the plant revives at sunset, everything's fine. But if the foliage still droops in the morning, water at once. Don't flood the garden; sprinkle only until the soil is moist to a depth of 5 to 6 inches. Then stretch some water-soaked burlap between stakes to shade the wilted plant until it revives.

2. To revive a wilted houseplant, plunge its pot into a bucket of tepid water. Let it soak until bubbles stop rising from the soil. Drain the

excess water and set the plant in a humid spot like a bathroom or greenhouse. Or cover the plant with a transparent plastic bag, supporting the plastic with a frame of stakes or coat hanger wire so that it doesn't touch the plant. Secure the bag to the pot's rim with twine or a large rubber band. Keep the plant out of direct sunlight while it recovers.

Witnessing a crime

1. When you see—or suspect you see—a crime being committed, call the police at once; don't assume someone else already has. And don't feel intimidated—there's no need to give your name or address when describing what you've seen over the telephone.
2. Don't linger near the scene of a crime. Wait for the arrival of the police at a safe distance.
3. If you see a street crime from indoors, call the police, then open a window and shout that the police are on their way. (Move away fast; there may be danger.)
4. To help the police, write down a description of the criminal or criminals while your memory is still fresh (height? build? hair and skin color? clothing?) and the make, model, color, and license number of the vehicle if you know them. Jot down exactly what happened from beginning to end, then double-check yourself by going over the story backward, from the end to the beginning.
5. If you hear screams or other loud or unusual noises coming from a neighbor's home, telephone the police. Don't try to investigate or interfere yourself.

Wobbly furniture

1. First, check to see that all screws and bolts are tight.
2. For a quick fix on a glued joint like that of a chair rung, pull the dowel out of the socket as far as you can (take care not to break another joint). Soften the old glue (p.98) and scrape it from both the dowel

and its socket. Apply carpenter's glue all around the dowel, shove it back into the socket, and wiggle it to spread the glue. Wipe off any excess with a damp cloth and apply a tourniquet clamp (p.47) until the glue is dry.

3. If a screw or dowel is loose because the wood has dried out and the hole is too big, push glue-dipped flat toothpicks in beside it to tighten the fit. Or wrap the end with a paper shim before pushing it into the joint. Or cut two strips of cloth a bit narrower than the dowel's tip and hold them over it before inserting in the glue-primed hole; use a razor to trim off any visible cloth.

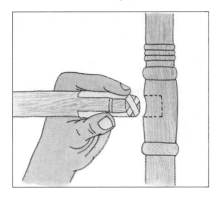

4. If a table or chair leg is shorter than the others, force it into a glob of wood putty placed on a piece of wax paper. When it's even with the other legs (check with a spirit level), use a utility knife to scrape away excess putty. Then let the putty dry, sand it smooth, and finish as you wish.

Wood filler

1. Save the sawdust when you're doing heavy sanding on a woodworking project. Mixed with white glue, it makes a good-as-store-bought crack filler.

2. If you do buy filler, choose one containing silex (finely powdered quartz). Because it packs the wood grain more tightly, it's better than the liquid kind.

3. If you're going to stain your woodwork, buy a wood filler in a natural tone and tint it with oil pigments until it matches the stain you plan to use.

Wood floors

1. On waxed floors remove food or dried milk stains with a damp cloth, water stains with superfine (No. 00) steel wool, and heel marks with steel wool dipped in floor cleaner or mineral spirits. For alcohol spots use boiled linseed oil, silver polish, or a cloth dampened with ammonia. Harden crayon marks, chewing gum, or candle wax with an ice cube in a plastic bag, then scrape off with a dull knife or your fingernail. Or pour cleaning fluid around the spot to loosen it. In all cases, after the floor has dried, rewax if necessary and polish.

2. Fill wide cracks between floorboards with a paste of shellac and fine sawdust stained to match.

Workbench

To make a reasonable standby for a workbench, nail a sheet of ¼-inch hardboard on top of a 3- x 8-foot slab of ¾-inch plywood, then nail the boards over two sawhorses.

To prevent the work surface from swaying (while you plane lengthwise, for example), fasten the underside of the plywood to wall studs with at least two steel angle braces.

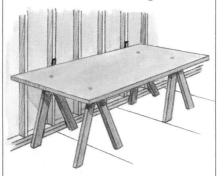

Wrapping packages

1. Want that package tied really tight? Moisten the twine before tying; it will dry snug.

2. Don't use string if you're mailing a package — it can snag on automatic sorting equipment. Use nylon filament or waterproof or pressure-sensitive tape. Avoid transparent and masking tape.

3. If you have papers to mail that you don't want to fold, wrap them around the cardboard tube from a box of aluminum foil. Cover with paper or foil, place back in the aluminum foil box, wrap, and mail.

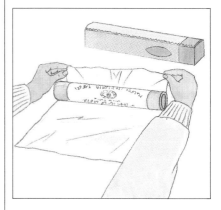

4. To get some brown wrapping paper for a package, just cut up a large grocery bag.

5. Not sure how much paper you'll need? Wind a piece of twine around the package and add 2 inches. Measure the length the same way.

6. To cushion an object in its packing box, use balled-up newspaper, yarn, old clothes, or popcorn.

Wrench

1. When possible, pull rather than push a wrench handle; it's easier and more efficient.

2. The longer a wrench handle, the more leverage it gives. To add muscle, slip a piece of pipe over it. (But use common sense—too much pipe breaks tools.)

3. A series of sharp tugs works better than an extended pull in loosening a balky nut. For a really hard case, tap the wrench handle with a mallet or piece of 2 x 4.

4. To protect the finish of plumbing fixtures, cover the teeth of a pipe wrench with several layers of electrician's, duct, or cloth tape.

5. If a wrench isn't handy, try a set

of locking-grip pliers. The next alternative is offset pliers, then standard slip-joint pliers. (See also *Belts*, p.289.)

6. To turn a large nut or secure a bolt head, try a C-clamp.

7. If nothing seems to work and the work is portable, lock the nut in a vise and turn the work.

Wrinkles

1. To slow the wrinkling process, apply a sunscreen (p.201) whenever you go out, even during winter. Put sunscreen on children, too.

2. Prevent your skin from becoming weatherbeaten—protect it from harsh winds, intense cold, and biting salt sprays.

3. Don't make faces: don't frown, squint, scowl, grimace, or purse your lips. To prevent overusing facial muscles, stick cellophane tape on areas prone to wrinkling.

4. To prevent temporarily creasing your face, make a special effort to sleep on your back.

5. Make a short-term antiwrinkle mask: apply a beaten egg white to your face for 10 minutes, then rinse off. Your face should look smoother for a few hours afterward.

6. Apply a cloth soaked in witch hazel to frown lines for 5 minutes at a time.

7. Rub a light eye cream on outer-eye lines. Then open your eyes wide, press the heels of your hands against the areas, and hold for a minute; repeat daily. (See also *Dry skin*, p.68.)

Xeriscaping

Low-water-use landscaping, or xeriscaping, is almost a necessity for homeowners in the arid western states, and it's becoming important to the rest of the country, too. By redesigning your yard accord-

ing to a few basic rules, you can reduce your water usage by as much as two-thirds.

1. Divide the yard into zones. The area closest to the house is the most used, so plan to water it well to create an oasis of green. Just beyond lies the area you may use only for an occasional game of volleyball or football; plant it with rough grass that you have to water only occasionally. Plant the outer perimeter with drought-tolerant shrubs or wildflowers so that you won't have to supplement the rainfall.

2. Group plants with similar needs together. You'll make it easier to give them only the water they need.

3. Ask your local nursery for plants that thrive without constant watering. Those that are native to the region are likely to be good choices. Sagebrush, for example, with its silver foliage and purple flowers, is ornamental and withstands hot southwestern summers with ease.

4. Keep as little lawn as possible. Though you may want some grass in the front of the house, substitute a patio or deck in the back. Plant hardy ground covers, such as blackfoot daisy, in little-traveled parts of the yard. Lay down pine bark or white gravel mulch, which conserves water by shielding soil from the sun.

5. Water in early morning or late evening to reduce evaporation. Install a drip irrigation system, available at garden centers; it delivers water far more efficiently than sprinklers and eliminates runoff. (See also *Barrel*, p.339; *Water conservation*, p.226.)

Xerophytes

If you live in an arid zone and your garden plants suffer from water restrictions, grow species that need hardly any water at all. Growing such drought-tolerant plants, or xerophytes, can cut outdoor water consumption by 50 to 75 percent. Because many are desert natives, they give the garden an exotic look

and make good substitutes for thirsty flowers.

Among the best and most colorful xerophytes are liatris (*Liatris* species), toadflax (*Linaria vulgaris*), desert four-o'clock (*Mirabilis multiflora*), two perennial flaxes (*Linim perenne lewisii* and *L.p. alpinum*), and three native penstemons (*Penstemon rydbergii, P. strictus,* and *P. whippleanus*).

X-rays

X-rays are invaluable in the early detection and diagnosis of many diseases, but too much exposure to them can be harmful. Here are some tips to help you make wise decisions involving this vital aspect of your health care:

1. Get smart about your own X-rays. Ask the doctor to show you the results and to explain them.

2. The most important aspect of X-rays is their interpretation. If you have any doubts about what your doctor has told you, show your X-rays to another doctor and get a second opinion.

3. If you have a health problem that requires periodic X-rays, don't put them off. Find out what the accepted guidelines are and follow them.

4. You have a right to your own X-rays. In some cases the originals will be given to you; in others you may be asked to pay for copies. Clarify this point ahead of time.

REDUCING RADIATION EXPOSURE

About 90 percent of the manmade radiation to which you're exposed probably comes from medical and dental X-rays. However, there are no national standards for maximum exposure, nor are there national requirements for equipment inspection or operator training. Although states inspect radiation equipment, only about a third of them require that the operator be trained. So it pays to be alert when X-rays are taken. Here are some tips to reduce exposure:

1. Make sure there's a real need for

X-rays before they are taken. Ask your doctor or dentist whether a less hazardous test would yield similar information or whether an old set of X-rays could be used.

2. If you have any reason to be suspicious, check when your doctor's X-ray equipment was last inspected. (It should be done yearly and the date should be posted on or near the machine.)

3. Find out whether the operator is formally trained and licensed.

4. Ask the operator to be sure that the collimator is properly adjusted. If she doesn't know what a collimator is, go elsewhere. (It focuses the beam on a specific area—a wide-open collimator scatters X-rays all over your body.)

5. Make sure that a lead shield is provided to cover your reproductive organs while the X-ray is being taken.

6. Keep a record of all your X-rays (if possible, keep copies on file). Note the date, the type, and the name of the doctor who has the films. Take copies of recent X-rays with you when you visit a doctor or dentist for the first time.

Xylophone

Make a nifty substitute for a xylophone with eight kitchen glasses filled with water:

Line up the glasses and fill the first one nearly to the top; tap the rim with a pencil and think of the note produced as *Do*. Put a little less water in the next glass and adjust the level until a tap produces *Re*. Continue in this fashion, putting a little less water in each glass, until you've created a complete scale: *Do-Re-Mi-Fa-Sol-La-Ti-Do*. Then use these tunes to get started playing (the low *Do* is 1):

Mary Had a Little Lamb:
3-2-1-2-3-3-3; 2-2-2; 3-5-5;
3-2-1-2-3-3-3; 3-2-2-3-2-1.

Row, Row, Row Your Boat:
1-1-1-2-3; 3-2-3-4-5; 8-8-8-
5-5-5-3-3-3-1-1-1; 5-4-3-2-1.

Yellowjackets

1. To minimize the risk of a sting, don't wear perfume or brightly colored clothing.

2. Don't try swatting a yellowjacket if it lands on you; simply blow on it instead.

3. Wear loose-fitting clothing to reduce the chances of penetration by the insect's ¼-inch-long stinger.

4. At a picnic take along box traps, sold at camping supply stores. Then release the insects when the picnic's over or drown them by immersing the traps in a bucket of soapy water.

5. If several yellowjackets attack you at once, you've probably disturbed their nest; run indoors if possible. Or run into the woods—it's harder for the insects to follow you there than in an open area.

6. If an insect flies in a car window, slow down, open all the windows, and let it find its way out.

Yogurt

Try one of these methods to incubate homemade yogurt (p.423):

1. Wrap the just-filled canning jar in a wool blanket, down jacket, or sheet of bubble plastic.

2. Put it in a box along with a hot-water bottle and pack crumpled newspapers loosely around both.

3. Turn an electric heating pad to its lowest setting and wrap it around the jar.

4. Set the jar in a metal box with a glowing Christmas tree bulb.

5. Put it in a gas oven with only the heat from the pilot light.

6. Turn on the TV and set the yogurt jar on top.

Zippers

1. To make a zipper work smoothly, run a candle up and down the teeth. If it's really sticky, use wax paper or a lead pencil.

2. If you've lost or broken the pull tab of your zipper, use a safety pin or a paper clip.

3. Has your zipper pulled apart at the bottom? Carefully undo the stitching, remove the stop, and separate the zipper completely. Put the sides back into the pull and zip it up. Then run a zigzag stitch across the bottom of the zipper, creating a new stop.

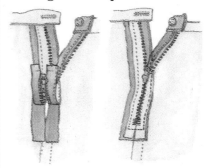

4. Before replacing a zipper, remove the old stitches from the fabric but *don't* press the fabric until you've tacked the new zipper in place—you might lose track of the folds and seam allowances.

5. Before installing a zipper, press the underside of the tape to smooth out the folds; if the teeth are plastic, be careful not to iron over them.

6. Preshrink any tape that is not 100 percent polyester by submerging the zipper in hot water for 3 minutes; then let the tape dry before pressing it flat.

Zucchini

1. To keep squash borers from damaging your crop, soak zucchini seeds in kerosene overnight before planting. This trick also works for yellow squash, winter squash, and cantaloupe.

2. By the end of the growing season, when you're likely to have more zucchini than you know what to do with, cull the crop by making a meal of the buds just before they open into blossoms; they're delicious sautéed in butter or tossed raw into crisp green salads. (See also *Zucchini bread*, p.423.)

2.CHARTS & CHECKLISTS

*DO YOU WANT TO GET ORGANIZED?
STAY HEALTHY? PREPARE FOR A
PLEASANT RETIREMENT? IF SO, THE
NEXT 46 PAGES—FILLED WITH MORE
THAN 80 CHARTS, CHECKLISTS,
AND QUIZZES ON THESE AND MANY
OTHER SUBJECTS—CAN BE
IMPORTANT TO YOU. HERE YOU'LL
FIND FACTS AT A GLANCE ON
EVERYTHING FROM TIPPING TO
TOOLS, BUYING A HOME TO SELLING
ONE, STRETCHING A BUDGET TO
STRETCHING A RECIPE.*

The paper chase

Organizing important papers

	Personal file	Safe-deposit box	Fireproof strongbox	
Financial documents	Stocks	Bonds	Bank book	Canceled checks	Income tax returns
Insurance policies	Life	Health	Homeowners	Car	Valuables
Certificates	Birth & adoption	Marriage	Divorce	Citizenship	Death
Numbers	Social Security	Credit cards	Driver's license	Employee & student ID's	Bank accounts
Legal documents	Will (copy)*	Power of attorney	Contracts	Deeds	Mortgages
Personal documents	Military discharge papers	Pension plans	Academic diplomas	Passports	Personal property inventory

*Leave original with your lawyer.

A foolproof filing system

☐ For your own files, an alphabetical system will suffice. For a family file, use a color-coded system. Or you can combine the two.

☐ Gather all the papers to be filed and make a list of general categories, such as receipts, contracts, correspondence, and insurance.

☐ Make a separate folder for each category and label it. File each document in its appropriate folder.

☐ If an item falls under more than one category, make copies. Or note its location on index cards for other relevant folders.

☐ If any misfits remain that don't deserve their own folders, store them in a *Miscellaneous* file.

☐ Within each folder, place items in chronological order, with the most recent item in front.

☐ Review the contents of a folder periodically; toss obsolete material into the "round file" (wastebasket).

☐ Staple material together—paper clips snag and rubber bands snap.

☐ If you don't have time to file regularly, keep items in a *To file* folder so that they aren't lost.

☐ If you remove material for an extended period, leave a note in its folder to remind you where it is.

☐ File business cards separately in a handy business card holder.

☐ Establish a weekly and monthly *Tickler* file to remind you of important deadlines.

Cures for the chronic procrastinator

☐ Break the chronic procrastinator's habit: whenever you catch yourself thinking "I can do it later," stop and make a point of doing it now.

☐ Tell others about your goals so that you'll have extra motivation to accomplish them.

☐ Eliminate distractions, even if it means locking the door or taking the phone off the hook.

☐ Make plans that require you to complete your chores by a certain date.

☐ If a project is large or complex, break it down into smaller, more manageable parts.

☐ Take time out to ask yourself: "Is there an easier way to do this?"

☐ Don't wait until you have time to finish the entire task. Do as much as you can whenever you can.

☐ Set firm but realistic deadlines for yourself.

Protecting personal time

☐ Ask friends, relatives, or co-workers to call before they drop by.

☐ Post a list of where everything in the house is stored, and train family members to help themselves.

☐ Teach children that a closed door means "Do Not Disturb." If necessary, post the message on the door.

☐ Invest in a telephone answering machine.

☐ Interruptions provide a good excuse to avoid work; resist the temptation to extend them by prolonging a conversation.

☐ If you don't want to cut a telephone conversation short, keep small, mindless projects nearby and complete them while you're talking.

☐ If you can't concentrate at home, take your work to the library, and don't tell anyone where you're going.

☐ If you don't have a receptionist at work, ask a willing coworker to take your calls, and offer to return the favor when she's busy.

☐ Start with the simplest or the most enjoyable part of a job, even if it's not the first logical step. The rest will be easier once you have gained momentum.

☐ Or try the opposite strategy: tackle the toughest part of the project first so that you can coast if your energy or enthusiasm runs out later on.

☐ Deal with smaller projects or problems as soon as possible, but in order of priority.

☐ Make a list of everything you have to do, and don't stop until you've checked off every item.

☐ Don't be a perfectionist; you can polish your work as much as you wish after you've made some headway.

☐ Don't interrupt yourself by starting another task before you've completed the first one.

☐ Remember that buckling down to a task, although it seems hard at first, really makes your life easier in the long run.

☐ Treat yourself to a small reward for each deadline you meet.

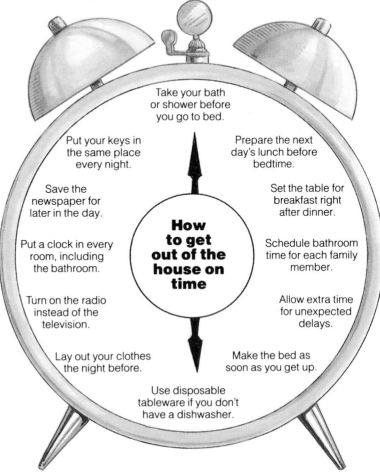

How to get out of the house on time

Take your bath or shower before you go to bed.

Prepare the next day's lunch before bedtime.

Set the table for breakfast right after dinner.

Schedule bathroom time for each family member.

Allow extra time for unexpected delays.

Make the bed as soon as you get up.

Use disposable tableware if you don't have a dishwasher.

Lay out your clothes the night before.

Turn on the radio instead of the television.

Put a clock in every room, including the bathroom.

Save the newspaper for later in the day.

Put your keys in the same place every night.

Type	Explanation	Sources	Advantages	Disadvantages
Annuity	Provides interest on your money and income for retirement	Life insurance companies; brokerage firms	Tax-deferred interest; lifetime income; low risk; can be collateral	Sales charges; low yield & interest rates; sometimes taxable
Certificate of deposit	Money deposited for specified period and interest rate	Commercial and savings banks; credit unions; brokers	Low risk; federally insured; higher yield than savings account	Substantial penalty for early withdrawal (except with brokers)
Common stock	Shares owned in a corporation	Brokerage firms; financial services companies	Potentially high profits; losses are tax-deductible	High risk; not insured; value fluctuates daily; brokerage fees
Individual retirement account	Long-term savings for retirement	Mutual funds; banks; insurance companies; credit unions; brokers	Interest untaxed until retirement; contributions may be tax-deductible	Penalty for withdrawal before retirement
Keogh plan	Retirement plan for self-employed people and their employees	Mutual funds; banks; insurance companies; credit unions; brokers	Taxes deferred until withdrawal; contributions tax-deductible	Penalty for withdrawal before retirement
Money market fund	Funds pooled, invested in interest-bearing short-term securities	Mutual fund companies; banks; brokers; insurance companies	High short-term interest; liquid; diverse investments	Often not insured; interest rates can decline
Municipal bond	Municipal debt obligation, to build and repair public facilities	Commercial banks; brokers; mutual funds; insurance companies	Low risk; interest exempt from federal tax; can be insured	Interest fluctuates; long maturities common; broker required
Mutual fund	Pooled funds invested in various common stocks or bonds	Mutual fund companies; brokerage firms; insurance companies	Low risk; diverse securities at low cost; many types of funds	Not insured; values fluctuate; management and sales fees
Preferred stock	Shares in a corporation that yield a fixed dividend	Brokers; financial services companies, including bank subsidiaries	Low risk; dividends stable, paid before those of common stock	Lower appreciation potential than common stock
Real estate	Investment in land or buildings	Owner of deed; real estate broker; brokerage firms	Tangible asset; value often appreciates; can yield income	Not liquid; long-term investment; high buying and selling costs
U.S. savings bond	Nonmarketable security of the U.S. Treasury Department	Savings, commercial, or Federal Reserve banks; Treasury Department	Guaranteed interest exempt from state tax; easily replaced or redeemed	Low interest rate; must be held 5 years for maximum yield
Treasury bill/bond	Short- and long-term securities of the U.S. Treasury Department	Federal Reserve and commercial banks; U.S. Treasury Department; brokerage firms	Low risk; interest exempt from state tax; $1,000 minimum (bonds), short maturities (bills)	Bond interest variable; service charge with banks, brokers; $10,000 minimum (bills)

Investing in your future

Although the national economy and market conditions fluctuate, financial experts still agree on two basic rules: Never buy medium- or high-risk securities before you have put aside the equivalent of at least 6 months' income in safe, liquid assets. When you can set aside money for investment, aim for diversity.

Your annual budget planner

INCOME

Your take-home pay _____

Spouse's take-home pay _____

Bonuses _____

Part-time work _____

Interest _____

Dividends _____

Tenant's rent _____

Other _____

TOTAL INCOME $ _____

EXPENSES

Housing

☐ Rent _____

☐ Mortgage _____

☐ Maintenance _____

☐ Repair _____

☐ Improvement _____

Utilities

☐ Telephone _____

☐ Gas _____

☐ Water _____

☐ Fuel _____

☐ Electricity _____

Taxes (not withheld)

☐ Federal & FICA _____

☐ State _____

☐ Local _____

☐ Property _____

Car

☐ Maintenance, repairs _____

☐ Gasoline _____

Insurance

☐ Life _____

☐ Homeowners _____

☐ Auto _____

☐ Health _____

☐ Disability _____

Medical (not reimbursed)

☐ Doctor _____

☐ Dentist _____

☐ Prescription drugs _____

☐ Eyeglasses _____

Clothing

☐ New garments _____

☐ Laundry, dry cleaning _____

Transportation

☐ Commuting _____

☐ Garage _____

☐ Taxi _____

☐ Public transportation _____

Recreation

☐ Dining out _____

☐ Books & magazines _____

☐ Movies, theater _____

☐ Vacations _____

☐ Hobbies _____

Gifts

☐ Birthday _____

☐ Anniversary _____

☐ Seasonal _____

☐ Wedding _____

Tuition _____

Furnishings, appliances _____

Food & beverages _____

Loan payments _____

Contributions _____

Dues _____

Regular savings _____

Other _____

TOTAL EXPENSES $ _____

Total income minus total expenses = $ to save or invest

QUIZ ?

Are you an overspender?

Do you spend money on the assumption that your income will rise?

Do you fail to keep an accurate record of your purchases?

Do you hide your purchases from your family?

Do you often fail to pay your monthly bills on time?

Do you own more than five credit cards?

Does having several credit cards make you feel richer?

Do you spend more than 20 percent of your income on credit card bills?

Do you tend to make only the minimum payment on your credit card bills?

Do you take cash advances on one credit card to pay the balance on another?

Do you often pay for groceries with a credit card?

When you eat in a restaurant, do you collect cash from friends and then pay the bill with your credit card?

Do you have trouble imagining how you would survive without credit?

If you answered yes to 4 or fewer questions, you're probably not an overspender.

If you answered yes to 5–8 questions, it's time to pay off your debts and follow a strict budget.

If you answered yes to 9 or more questions, consult a credit counselor or financial planner for help in changing your spending habits.

Income tax countdown

What could be more satisfying than to have your tax return completely organized, filled out, and signed well before the dreaded April 15 deadline? What feels worse than hunting around for missing records at the last minute, being greeted by an angry glare from a frazzled tax preparer on April 13, or even finding out that you owe more taxes than you expected to pay? You can make things easier on yourself and your accountant by taking these simple steps during the year.

DECEMBER

☐ Using payroll records, checkbook stubs, and receipts, estimate your taxable income and deductions.

☐ Roughly calculate your federal, state, and local taxes. If you owe a large sum, you can pay certain expenses early (such as a January mortgage or interest payment) to gain the deduction for the current year. Or defer some income until January 1. If you have underpaid estimated taxes, file a revised W-4 form with your employer to avoid having to pay a penalty.

JANUARY

☐ Start keeping records (p.172) for the current year's expenses.

☐ If tax forms don't arrive in the mail, pick them up at a local bank or post office. Or call the IRS at 1-800-424-FORM.

☐ Make an appointment with your accountant or tax preparer.

☐ If you are preparing your own return, consult a current-year tax guide.

FEBRUARY

☐ If you have dependents 2 years old or older who don't have Social Security numbers, fill out Form SS-5 at your local Social Security office.

☐ If you were exempt from withholding from wages last year, file a new W-4 form with your employer to continue your exemption this year.

☐ If you have not received a W-2 form from your employer or 1099 forms from your bank, broker, and so forth, report the oversight to them.

☐ Review your payroll records, check stubs, and receipts; list itemized deductions.

☐ List your sources of income, including salary, interest, dividends, capital gains, professional fees, and pensions.

MARCH

☐ Provide your tax preparer with all necessary records and information.

APRIL

☐ Review completed tax forms for errors and omissions. (See also *Income tax returns*, p.114.)

☐ Sign the forms and write your Social Security number on them. Your spouse should sign a joint return. Make photocopies for your files and keep them for at least 3 years.

☐ Make out checks for the amounts due, if any. Send forms via certified mail by midnight, April 15.

☐ For a 4-month extension, complete Form 4868. You must still pay what you owe. Make out a check for the estimated amount (or a little more) and mail it with Form 4868 to the IRS by midnight on April 15.

☐ Consult your accountant about changes in the tax laws, especially deductions, for the coming year. Adjust your spending, investments, and your files accordingly.

Where to complain

1. Salesperson or supervisor. Talk calmly; avoid anger.

2. Company's 800 hot line (p. 71). State problem clearly; note name of the person you talk to.

RESOURCES
Product label may include company address, phone number.
AT&T Toll-Free 800 Directory, Consumer Edition. (To order, call 1-800-426-8686.)
Before You Sue, by Fletcher Knebel and Gerald Clay (William Morrow).

3. Owner (small business) or regional manager or president (large company). Send letter by certified mail, return receipt requested.

	Your address
	Date
Name of manager	
Company name	
Company address	
Dear ———:	
☐ Purchase/date/make & model	
☐ Problem/steps taken so far	
☐ Resolution wanted	
☐ Expect a reply by ———	
	Very truly yours,

RESOURCE
Standard & Poor's Register of Corporations, Directors, and Executives. Available in most libraries.

4. Local Better Business Bureau. Register complaint; ask about mediation programs, small claims court, regulatory agencies.

5. Consumer advocates. Contact local newspapers, radio, TV.

RESOURCE
Consumer Adviser, Revised Edition, Reader's Digest, Pleasantville, NY 10570. Covers mediation programs, consumer advocate groups.

10 consumer caveats

Do . . . patronize local businesses; transient dealers can disappear if something goes wrong.

. . . read all fine print on the front and back of a contract. Get a full explanation of any clause unclear to you.

. . . keep and file your copy of any contract, warranty, or large bill; keep your canceled checks.

. . . check a vendor's reputation with the Better Business Bureau. Ask the appropriate city or state board whether the person or business is licensed or has a record of complaints.

. . . remember that the FTC's cooling-off rule lets you cancel a contract, in writing, within 3 days in most circumstances.

Don't . . . pay cash. Write a check payable to the company, not the salesperson.

. . . forget to shop around for prices and financing terms; ask about extra delivery or installation charges.

. . . accept oral promises; get everything in writing.

. . . sign a contract with blank spaces in it; have them all filled in.

. . . be pressured into hasty decisions. If "this great offer expires in 24 hours," let it.

6. Professional organization (doctors, lawyers); trade association (movers, dry cleaners, et al.); or consumer advocate group should get copy of certified letter.

RESOURCES
Directory of State and Local Consumer Groups, Consumer Federation of America, 1424 16th St. NW, Washington, DC 20036; also available in libraries.
Encyclopedia of Associations, Gale Research Company. Available in libraries. Lists trade and professional groups by interest and area.

7. Small claims court (p. 189).

8. State licensing and regulatory agencies (monitor patterns of complaints; may prosecute a company with a history of fraud).

RESOURCES
State consumer affairs department (in Blue Pages of phone book) for appropriate state agency.
Consumer Resource Handbook. Free. Lists state agencies, trade associations, and other helpful data (see *Free information,* p. 91).

9. Federal agencies (act only on large numbers of complaints).

10. Private attorney to file suit in civil court (for money amounts larger than small claims court handles).

RESOURCES
Consumer Adviser, rev. ed. Addresses of state attorneys general and federal agencies.
Encyclopedia of Associations.
How to Choose and Use a Lawyer. American Bar Association, 750 N. Lake Shore Dr., Chicago, IL 60611.

Are you a workaholic?

Does your life revolve around your job to the exclusion of family concerns, social pleasures, and other interests? If so, you may be a workaholic. To find out, ask yourself the following questions:

1. Does your family complain that you're never home?

2. Do you lose sleep over work worries?

3. Do you get anxious about delegating work to your staff?

4. Has starting your workday early and ending it late become a habit?

5. Do you gobble your lunch while working at your desk?

6. Are you angry when coworkers don't work as hard as you do?

7. Is your work the only thing you find enjoyable?

8. Do interruptions in your workday annoy you?

9. When you have more work than you can handle, does it make you feel inadequate?

10. Are social events a waste of time?

11. Do you often work weekends?

12. Do you feel guilty when you take time off?

13. Can you leave work on your desk for the following day?

14. Do you always say yes to more work?

15. Do you go to work when you're not feeling well?

16. Are you able to enjoy doing nothing?

17. Do hobbies interest you?

18. Do you get restless while on vacation?

19. If your doctor told you to slow down, could you?

If you answered yes to most of the first 15 questions and no to some of the questions between 16 and 19, you may be a workaholic. Do not be alarmed. This is not necessarily unhealthy if work gives you real satisfaction. But it can be as dangerous as any addiction if it takes you unawares and if you derive pleasure from nothing but work. If this is the case, try to slow down or look for a less demanding job.

Is your job right for you?

☐ Are your coworkers warm, friendly, and courteous?

☐ Is your job so enjoyable that you do extra work?

☐ Does your work challenge your imagination?

☐ If you inherited a large sum of money, would you keep your job?

☐ Are your efforts appreciated?

☐ Are you fairly paid?

☐ Does your day go by quickly?

☐ Is your job conveniently located?

☐ Are you allowed to take time off when personal emergencies arise?

☐ Are people promoted from within your organization?

☐ Is your work area pleasant?

☐ Are your special talents and skills utilized?

☐ Is your boss helpful, capable, and encouraging?

☐ Does the benefits package match your needs?

☐ Could you transfer to another department if it made sense to do so?

☐ Is your company concerned about the health and well-being of its employees?

☐ Is your routine varied enough to forestall boredom?

☐ Are your work hours right for you and your family?

☐ Does your work make a difference to the company?

If you answered yes to 15 or more of these questions, chances are you are well suited to the career you have chosen. If you didn't, you might consider changing careers, returning to school, or retiring early. A good place to start is a career planning course, which may put you on a new path of personal growth and satisfaction.

Writing résumés

A résumé advertises you. It should be convincing and present your achievements honestly. Here are some points to remember when writing yours.

Use simple, clear language. Be brief—one page is enough.

Place your name, address, and telephone number at the top.

Relate your résumé to the job being offered.

List former employers and the cities or towns in which they are located.

Give the dates of job changes and promotions. Describe the activities performed for each position.

Stress your achievements. Explain them with such action verbs as *managed, taught, appointed.*

Cite the schools you attended, graduation dates, and degrees or diplomas earned.

Include your photograph and reveal your age, height, and weight only if you are seeking work in the glamour, entertainment, or certain sales professions.

Divulge your marital status if you want to.

Define your job objective in your résumé or in a covering letter.

State special interests if they relate to the job you want.

Spell correctly and be careful to avoid grammatical errors.

Supply references upon request.

Forget gimmicky résumés—ones printed on colored paper or delivered with flowers. They're generally inappropriate.

Eliminate music and chatty language from your home telephone answering machine.

Evaluating a company's benefits package

Give careful thought to your needs and those of your family. Do you need a medical plan that covers dependents or day care for children? Is vacation time important? Does your spouse's benefits package fill missing gaps in yours? Are you concerned about a pension? Remember, there's no point in opting for benefits you won't use. Here are some questions to ask.

MEDICAL BENEFITS

☐ Are you offered a group health insurance plan, or membership in a health maintenance organization (HMO) or preferred provider organization (PPO)?

☐ Is major medical insurance for catastrophic illness included?

☐ How about dental coverage? Does it cover orthodontics and dentures?

☐ Are mental health costs paid for?

☐ At what age do dependents cease to be covered?

☐ What out-of-pocket expenses are not reimbursed? Is there a deductible? How much is the premium?

☐ Will a preexisting illness preclude you from coverage?

☐ What doesn't the plan cover?

VACATION

☐ How much paid annual vacation will you receive?

☐ Can it be taken any time during the year? Do you have to take it all at once?

☐ Are there paid holidays?

DISABILITY BENEFITS

☐ What percentage of your earnings, if any, would you receive if you became disabled, and for how long would you receive benefits?

☐ How much of the disability insurance premium must you pay?

EDUCATION

☐ Are education expenses reimbursed?

☐ Is there on-the-job training, or are work-related seminars provided?

CHILD CARE

☐ Do child care facilities exist on the premises, or is there a referral service?

☐ Are any child care costs reimbursed?

HEALTH MAINTENANCE PROGRAMS

☐ Are exercise facilities available?

☐ Is the cost of sports and health club activities reimbursed?

☐ Are there stop smoking, weight loss, and stress management programs?

FINANCIAL SAVINGS PLANS

☐ Is there group life insurance?

☐ Does the employer pay the premium?

☐ Is there a profit-sharing plan?

☐ Can you purchase company stock?

☐ Is the company a member of a consumers union?

FLEXIBLE BENEFITS

☐ Can you tailor your own benefits package by, for example, taking cash instead of time off or choosing from a selection of medical plans?

PENSION PLANS

☐ Is there a pension plan, and can you make contributions to it?

☐ How long must you be employed before becoming vested?

☐ Is there a 401(k) plan?

☐ At what age can you start receiving your pension?

☐ If you retire early, what percentage of your pension will you receive, and when will payments begin?

☐ Will your pension include cost-of-living increases?

☐ Will you have lifetime medical coverage for yourself and your spouse?

☐ If your spouse outlives you, how much of your pension will he receive?

☐ Under what circumstances could you lose your pension?

Planning your retirement

Like a second career, a rewarding retirement requires advance planning and some important choices. But this time *you're* the boss. There are no right or wrong answers in the following checklist. It's designed to help you decide which issues are most important to you.

1. For my continued well-being, I'll
☐ Follow a nutritious diet.
☐ Exercise a little every day.
☐ Develop activities and hobbies.

2. My savings program can most use
☐ Diversification.
☐ Regular contributions.
☐ Professional advice.

3. If I remain in my home, I'll
☐ Replace old appliances now.
☐ Fix dim lighting, frayed rugs.
☐ Rent part of it for income.

4. For retirement living, I'd enjoy
☐ The city/country/small town.
☐ Nonstop sunshine/four seasons.
☐ The seashore/the mountains.

5. After I retire, I plan to get around
☐ By public transportation.
☐ Driving the family car.
☐ With the help of the children and neighbors.

6. The most important legal documents I'll need will be
☐ A contract to buy/sell my home.
☐ An up-to-date, valid will.
☐ Power of attorney for myself and my spouse.

7. If I leave my community, I'll
☐ Travel for a while.
☐ Sell my house and move for good.
☐ Rent for 6 months or so before I decide to move permanently.

8. Other than my spouse, the relationships that matter most will be
☐ The children.
☐ Old friends and neighbors.
☐ A new and different social circle.

9. When I take a trip, I'll opt for
☐ Independent travel/group tours.
☐ Europe/Mexico/the U.S.A.
☐ Cruises/going by car/camping.

10. If I volunteer my time, I may want to work for
☐ The elderly/children/minorities.
☐ My favorite political causes.
☐ My church or synagogue.

11. I'll work until I'm 65 because
☐ I want full pension benefits.
☐ I enjoy working.
☐ I don't want to stay home all day.

12. I want to retire early because
☐ I don't like my job.
☐ My spouse wants us to move.
☐ I have lots of other things to do.

Building your nest egg

According to most financial experts, after retirement the average American family can live comfortably on about 85% of their preretirement budget. But inflation can play cruel tricks with this formula. For example, if you're 65 and plan to retire soon on a budget of $15,000 a year, you probably expect to spend roughly $300,000 over a 20-year retirement. But given a 6% annual inflation rate, the same lifestyle will cost some $510,000! By the same token, a 58-year-old planning to retire in 7 years on $20,000 (in today's terms) will need not $400,000 ($20,000 x 20 years) to maintain the same standard of living, but $1,050,000. Fortunately, your assets can grow at roughly the same—or an even faster—rate.

To make a rough projection of your retirement income, add the pension and Social Security income you expect to receive to any income from your investments and savings. Deduct 25% (or whatever figure

If you are now	Cost of a 20-year retirement				
	Projected annual expenses beginning at age 65				
	$10,000	**$15,000**	**$20,000**	**$25,000**	**$30,000**
48	$935,000	$1,402,000	$1,870,000	$2,337,000	$2,805,000
53	$700,000	$1,050,000	$1,400,000	$1,750,000	$2,100,000
58	$525,000	$785,000	$1,050,000	$1,310,000	$1,575,000
65	$370,000	$510,000	$740,000	$880,000	$1,110,000

most closely approximates your tax bracket). If the result is about 85% of what you now spend and you can handle some annual inflation, you are financially prepared to retire.

If your nest egg is smaller than you would like it to be, remember that you may be adding to it by selling your home and that many families are able to live on their capital in carefully planned annual installments. If there is a substantial gap between your projected income and your anticipated needs, here are some things that you can do about it now.

☐ Plan to retire later.
☐ Save more money now.
☐ Try for a higher return on your present investments. (For example, could you move money from a savings account yielding 5.5% interest into tax-free bonds that pay 7%?)
☐ If you rent, make every effort to buy a house. The money you're spending on rent could go toward paying off a mortgage on property that is likely to appreciate in value.
☐ Consider a second job; or perhaps your nonworking spouse can get a full- or part-time job and earmark the income for a retirement fund.

Enjoying your time

Once you stop working, you may be surprised at how much leisure you have. What are you going to do with all that time?

In a Cornell University survey, most retirees cited watching TV as their number-one activity, yet it ranked nearly last on their list of things they enjoyed doing. People who reported the highest degree of satisfaction in retirement had developed both balance and variety in their daily routine.

Before you retire, make a list of all the activities—hobbies, volunteer work, travel, club membership, recreation, social gatherings, and the like—that you enjoy or that you'd like to try for the first time. Ask the following questions about each activity and give it one point for every "yes" answer.

☐ Is it healthy?

☐ Is it mentally stimulating?

☐ Is it meaningful and gratifying?

☐ Is it relaxing, refreshing, fun?

Not only do the scores on your list tell you which activities are apt to be the most (and least) rewarding, but they also show you whether all four important aspects of retirement living have been included in your plans.

Retirement housing options

Type	Advantages	Pitfalls	Precautions
Trailer	Low cost, mobile	Small space. Noisy parks. Depreciation	Check construction quality. Visit site
Manufactured home (mobile home)	Must meet HUD building code. Most parks have recreational facilities	Can't be moved without special equipment. Banned in some places	Factor installation, lot rental, into cost. Check rules on resales
Apartment (rental)	Can move relatively easily. Landlord does maintenance	Rents go up. Possible surcharges for fuel, cable TV	Negotiate written lease carefully. Check appliances, air conditioning
Condominium	Can be willed, like house. Outside maintenance done by association	Common charges escalate. Loopholes in contracts. Shoddy or unfinished construction	Have lawyer specializing in real estate check deed. Builder should post bond for completion
Cooperative	Buyers screened. Most repairs financed by all members	Not as easily sold or willed as condos. Board can levy special assessments	Read minutes of co-op board meetings for planned repairs. Check building construction
Purchase land, build home	Privacy, custom features, extra space	Land swindles. Dishonest contractors. Maintenance costs. Ties up capital	Check credit of owner and builder. Be sure owner has clear title. Investigate water rights, local zoning laws
Retirement community	Services for retirees. Some have medical facilities	May have high initial cost or be too far from family	Check credit and reputation of owners

Considering a move?

Reasons to stay . . .

☐ The crime rate in your community is not as bad as in others.

☐ You enjoy the climate where you presently live.

☐ You enjoy the friends and neighbors you have now.

☐ The cost of living is affordable where you are.

☐ You like your current doctor and hospital.

☐ The children and grandchildren can visit you.

☐ A trip now and then will satisfy any need to see new places.

Reasons to go . . .

☐ Taxes and prices are lower in another place that attracts you.

☐ Your doctor recommends a different climate.

☐ You fear that your neighborhood is deteriorating.

☐ You want to move closer to your children.

☐ You'd like a new lifestyle, new friends.

☐ You want to be closer to modern health facilities.

☐ Another area has more chances for part-time work in your field.

QUIZ ?

How long will you live?

The average life expectancy for men and women in the United States is at best a very general statistic. Individual life spans vary greatly; the reasons are sometimes genetic, but some are under a person's control.

To get a more precise idea of how long you may expect to live —and what you can do about it— find the average life expectancy for someone your age in the chart at right, then answer the lifestyle questions below.

Average life expectancy		
AGE	MEN	WOMEN
25	73	79
35	74	80
45	75	80
55	76	81
65	80	84

1. For every 5 years that your father lived past 70, add 1 year. Add 1 year for every 5 years your mother lived past 78. _____

2. If you are single, deduct 1 year for each decade you are unmarried after age 25. _____

3. If you are married, add 5 years. If there is an unusual amount of family strife, subtract 2 years. _____

4. If you live in a city, subtract 2 years. If you live in a small town or on a farm, add 2 years. _____

5. If you have been either poor or wealthy most of your life, subtract 3 years. _____

6. If you're over 40, subtract a year for every 5 pounds above your best weight (p.252). Men only: Deduct 2 years per inch that your waist measurement exceeds your chest measurement. _____

7. If you exercise moderately but regularly, add 3 years. If you regularly do vigorous exercise, add 5 years. _____

8. If you think you have a hard-driving, competitive personality or are often tense, deduct 5 years. Add 5 years if you're usually cheerful and easygoing. _____

9. If you drink heavily, subtract 5 years; very heavily, 10 years. If you take recreational drugs, subtract 5 years. _____

10. If you smoke ½ to 1 pack of cigarettes daily, subtract 3 years. If you smoke 1 to 1½ packs, subtract 5 years; 2 packs, 10 years. _____

11. If you have regular medical and dental checkups, add 3 years. If you're often ill, subtract 2 years. _____

12. If your diet is high in fats, salt, and sweets, deduct 4 years. If you eat a balanced diet with plenty of fruit, vegetables, and low-fat proteins, add 4 years. _____

Your life expectancy _____

Stress in your life

Scientists rank the causes of stress by severity in Life Change Units (LCU's). Although some stress (up to 150 LCU's) is normal, too much can lower your body's resistance to infection, aggravate allergies, and raise your blood pressure, increasing your risk of heart disease or stroke. More than 300 LCU's in a given year is considered a threat to health. (For ways to cope with stress, see *Stress*, p.198.)

Christmas 12
Vacation 13
Trouble with in-laws 29   Child leaving home
31   Mortgage over $10,000
35   Career change
36   Death of a close friend
37   Change in finances
Sexual dysfunction 39 Birth of a child
Pregnancy 40
Retirement 45
Loss of your job 47
Marriage 50
Personal injury or illness 53
Death of a family member 63
Marital separation 65
Divorce 73
Death of a spouse 100

The well-stocked medicine cabinet

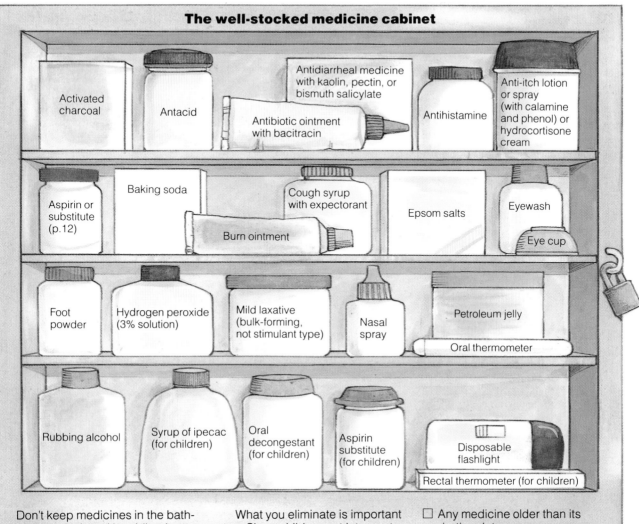

- Activated charcoal
- Antacid
- Antibiotic ointment with bacitracin
- Antidiarrheal medicine with kaolin, pectin, or bismuth salicylate
- Antihistamine
- Anti-itch lotion or spray (with calamine and phenol) or hydrocortisone cream
- Aspirin or substitute (p.12)
- Baking soda
- Burn ointment
- Cough syrup with expectorant
- Epsom salts
- Eyewash
- Eye cup
- Foot powder
- Hydrogen peroxide (3% solution)
- Mild laxative (bulk-forming, not stimulant type)
- Nasal spray
- Petroleum jelly
- Oral thermometer
- Rubbing alcohol
- Syrup of ipecac (for children)
- Oral decongestant (for children)
- Aspirin substitute (for children)
- Disposable flashlight
- Rectal thermometer (for children)

Don't keep medicines in the bathroom; warmth and humidity shorten their life. And you don't want to reach for nose drops in the night and use mouthwash or something even more harmful by mistake.

What you eliminate is important too. Since children get into wastebaskets, flush these things away:
- ☐ Aspirin that smells vinegary.
- ☐ Prescription medicines from a former illness.

- ☐ Any medicine older than its expiration date.
- ☐ Over-the-counter medicines you no longer need.
- ☐ Any medicine without a label or not in its original container.

Health records to keep

For yourself and your spouse

- ☐ Any negative reaction to a prescription or over-the-counter drug.
- ☐ Allergies. Blood type.
- ☐ Medications you take regularly.
- ☐ Date and diagnosis of any illness requiring a doctor's attention.
- ☐ Frequent or chronic illnesses.
- ☐ Date of last eye examination.
- ☐ Date and reasons for any hospitalization or surgery.
- ☐ Last pap smear, mammogram.
- ☐ Dates of any immunizations
- ☐ Date, nature, location of X-rays for last 3 years.
- ☐ Appointments for next physical and dental checkups.

For each child

- ☐ Birth date and weight.
- ☐ Birth defects, if any. Blood type.
- ☐ Allergies and any adverse reactions to medications.
- ☐ Types of immunizations given, with dates.
- ☐ Dates of childhood illnesses, such as measles and chicken pox.
- ☐ Types of infections (such as ear, eye); efficacy of medications.
- ☐ Any serious injury or accident.
- ☐ Next appointments with pediatrician, dentist, ophthalmologist.
- ☐ Reports of school physicals.

Dealing with common ailments

Problem	Home care	Call the doctor for
Fever	Shake oral thermometer, leave under tongue 3 minutes No extra clothing or blankets, even if body is chilly Lukewarm sponge baths to lower body temperature 1 cup fluid (nonalcoholic) every 2 hours	Dehydration: dry, tight skin; lightheadedness; dry mouth; extreme thirst; dark or frequent urine Rash, headache, stiff neck, with irritability or confusion Severe abdominal pain or back pain. Listless behavior Fever over 101°F or lasting 3 days or more. Vomiting or seizures Fever after new medication. Respiratory distress Cough with brown or green sputum. Earache or ear drainage
Back pain	For prevention and self-help, see p.14	Pain resulting from injury, especially at work Abdominal pain; painful or bloody urination Pain that travels down leg; weakness or numbness in legs or feet No improvement in 3–7 days. Fever over 101°F Any severe pain during pregnancy
Headaches	Aspirin, massage, cold compresses for muscle-tension headache Decongestant, hot showers for sinus headache (hurts more when chin is lowered to chest)	Fever over 102°F or neck stiffness. Pain worse in morning Recent head injury, slurred speech, visual disturbance, numbness, weakness in arms or legs. Vomiting or convulsions Recurrent, unusually intense, or persistent (3 days or more) pain
Heartburn, indigestion	Elevate head of bed No aspirin, caffeine, smoking, irritating foods Take antacid	Severe chest pain; shortness of breath; pain felt through to back; heavy perspiration; sharp pains in arms and shoulders Bloody, black vomit or black stool Severe abdominal pain Abdominal pain that increases or is worse after meals Symptoms lasting more than 3 days; not relieved by antacids
Sprains	Elevate limb. Apply ice once an hour for 15 minutes, up to 24 hours Aspirin for pain as needed Apply heat for soreness after 24 hours While limb heals, use elastic bandage	Unsteady, misshapen, cold, blue, or numb limb Sprain that resulted from serious accident, such as car crash or high fall Tenderness in particular area of bone (possible fracture) Pain lasting more than 4 days or requiring large doses of painkiller
Cuts	Control bleeding by pressure (10–15 minutes) Soap and water cleansing; rinse thoroughly. Clean again with sterile gauze wet with antiseptic solution or spray Butterfly bandage (p.17), then adhesive strip. Change dressing in 24 hours	Uncontrolled bleeding; unclosable wound Cut more than skin deep, more than 1 inch long; deep cut on torso Loss of motion or numbness of digits. No tetanus shot in 5 years Infection (pus, streaks, swelling, fever, redness) Cut not healed within 3 weeks. Persistent numbness
Cough, stuffy nose	Fluids; steam (see *Laryngitis,* p.123) Don't smoke. Suck cough drops. Try nasal spray or antihistamine Family members should wash hands often	Fever over 102°F for more than 2 days Chest pain, wheezing, or shortness of breath Brown, green, bloody, or purulent mucus Cough that lasts 10 days. Nasal congestion for 2 weeks
Vomiting, diarrhea	Flat ginger ale or water; suck ice chips No aspirin products No antidiarrheal product for 5–6 hours after onset (let bacteria flush out) After nausea subsides, slowly begin bland diet	Vomiting after head injury or accompanied by severe headache Yellow cast to skin or whites of eyes Abdominal pain, tenderness, or distension; fever Dehydration (see *Fever,* above). Liquids not retained after 12 hours Stools that are black, bloody, or have "coffee grounds" look Symptoms that last 3 days or recur
Sore throat	Drink fluids. Don't smoke. Limit talking Saltwater gargle or over-the-counter anesthetic solution Lozenges or hard candy	Exposure to someone with strep throat Fever of 101°F or more, with no other cold symptoms Breathing difficulty; almost impossible to swallow Concurrent earache, chest pain. Skin rash Severe headache; difficulty bending head White spots on tonsils or large, ulcerated tonsils Hoarseness. Swollen lymph nodes on neck for longer than 3 weeks

Finding the right hospital

It's wise to familiarize yourself with hospitals in your community before you need one. A good hospital is also a resource to use if you're looking for a family doctor or specialist.

☐ Visit two or three hospitals convenient to you. Is there a 24-hour emergency room? Is a physician (perhaps a pediatrician or cardiologist, depending on your priorities) always there? Someone "on call" may take 40 minutes to arrive.

☐ Is the hospital accredited by the Joint Commission on Accreditation of Healthcare Organizations? A certificate should be posted. If not, telephone the commission in Chicago at (312) 642-6061.

☐ A community hospital can give you good care for less money than a teaching hospital if your illness does not require a large medical team and high technology. (Open-heart surgery, organ transplants do.)

☐ A teaching hospital or specialized medical center should evaluate you and initiate treatment for a complex problem (such as some cancers or kidney or liver disease). Your doctor can follow through closer to home.

☐ If you have children, ask your pediatrician which hospital has the best pediatric facilities. It may not be the same one that serves your needs.

☐ The Government Printing Office and some libraries have copies of *Medicare Hospital Mortality Information*, a survey of 6,000 U.S. hospitals. Ask your doctor to explain any figures that concern you.

☐ Ask members of the local nurses association about a hospital's nurse-patient ratio and peer review committee.

☐ Ask members of the emergency rescue service where they send their own families.

Questions to ask before surgery

Here are 11 of the most commonly performed surgical procedures in the United States, along with possible alternatives. If you're told that you need an operation, it's worth finding out what choices you have—perhaps a less major operation or another form of treatment. If you want a second opinion (many insurance companies now require one), check column 2 for the medical professionals who act as consultants in a particular field.

The information on these pages is intended as a helpful home reference guide and was compiled with the help of medical authorities. But it is not meant to be a substitute for your physician's advice.

Procedure	Health professional	Surgery alternative	Other therapies
Back surgery	Chiropractor Neurologist Neurosurgeon Orthopedist Physiatrist	Cortisone injections	Anti-inflammatory medications Exercise program Heat applications Rest
Carotid artery surgery	Neurologist Neurosurgeon Vascular surgeon		Anticoagulants Aspirin therapy
Cataract surgery	Ophthalmologist	Intraocular lens implant	Corrective glasses Wait-and-see approach, if vision not badly impaired
Coronary bypass	Cardiologist Cardiothoracic surgeon	Angioplasty	Medications Diet Exercise program
Gallbladder removal	Gastroenterologist General surgeon	Shock wave therapy	Dissolution therapy (with medication)
Hemorrhoid-ectomy	Colorectal surgeon Gastroenterologist General surgeon	Laser surgery Rubber-banding Cauterization	Creams; local care Stool softeners Bulk diet
Hysterectomy	Gynecologist Oncologist	D&C Myomectomy	Hormonal therapy Wait-and-see approach
Joint surgery	Orthopedist Physiatrist	Arthroscopy	Magnetic resonance imaging for specific diagnosis
Pacemaker implant	Cardiologist specializing in arrhythmia		Medications
Prostate surgery	Oncologist Urologist	Orchiectomy Needle biopsy Open, trans-urethral, or radical prostatectomy	Chemotherapy Hormone therapy Radiation
Removal of varicose veins	Internist Vascular surgeon	Injection therapy	Support stockings Diet Exercise

What should you weigh?

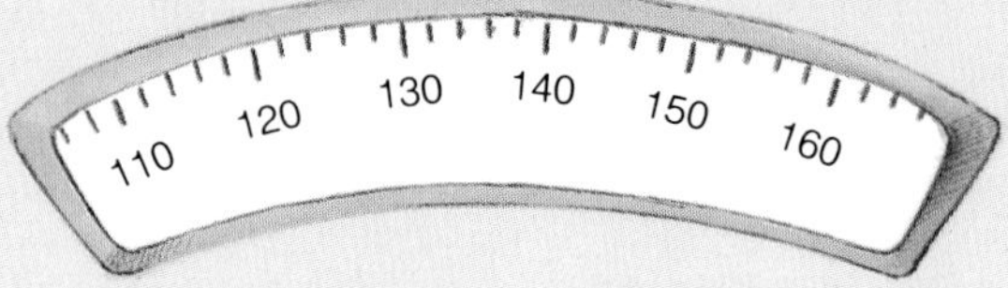

110 120 130 140 150 160

WOMEN

Height	Small frame	Medium frame	Large frame
4' 10"	102–111	109–121	118–131
4' 11"	103–113	111–123	120–134
5' 0"	104–115	113–126	122–137
5' 1"	106–118	115–129	125–140
5' 2"	108–121	118–132	128–143
5' 3"	111–124	121–135	131–147
5' 4"	114–127	124–138	134–151
5' 5"	117–130	127–141	137–155
5' 6"	120–133	130–144	140–159
5' 7"	123–136	133–147	143–163
5' 8"	126–139	136–150	146–167
5' 9"	129–142	139–153	149–170
5' 10"	132–145	142–156	152–173
5' 11"	135–148	145–159	155–176
6' 0"	138–151	148–162	158–179

MEN

Height	Small frame	Medium frame	Large frame
5' 2"	128–134	131–141	138–150
5' 3"	130–136	133–143	140–153
5' 4"	132–138	135–145	142–156
5' 5"	134–140	137–148	144–160
5' 6"	136–142	139–151	146–164
5' 7"	138–145	142–154	149–168
5' 8"	140–148	145–157	152–172
5' 9"	142–151	148–160	155–176
5' 10"	144–154	151–163	158–180
5' 11"	146–157	154–166	161–184
6' 0"	149–160	157–170	164–188
6' 1"	152–164	160–174	168–192
6' 2"	155–168	164–178	172–197
6' 3"	158–172	167–182	176–202
6' 4"	162–176	171–187	181–207

To determine whether you have a small, medium, or large frame, bend your elbow to form a 90° angle and have a friend measure from the inside to the outside of the bone. For women: 2¾ inches or more is a large frame; 2¼–2¾ inches is medium; less than 2¼ inches, small. For men: Over 3¼ inches is a large frame; 2½–3¼ inches is medium; less than 2½ inches, small. The weights above allow for 3 pounds of indoor clothing.

The benefits of exercise

The chart at the right tells you how seven medical experts on the President's Council on Physical Fitness and Sports rated 14 popular forms of exercise on a scale of 0 to 3 in terms of their benefits in four categories. The highest possible score in any one category is 21.

Bear in mind, however, that strenuous exercises, such as handball and squash, can be downright dangerous for anyone who has been sedentary and is out of shape. Be sure to check with your doctor before you begin any exercise program. (See also *Endurance building*, p.72.)

Exercise	Weight control	Muscle tone	Digestion	Sleep	Total score
Jogging	21	14	13	16	64
Bicycling	20	15	12	15	62
Swimming	15	14	13	16	58
Ice skating, roller skating	17	14	11	15	57
Cross-country skiing	17	12	12	15	56
Handball, squash	19	11	13	12	55
Basketball	19	13	10	12	54
Calisthenics	12	18	11	12	53
Tennis	16	13	12	11	52
Downhill skiing	15	14	9	12	50
Walking	13	11	11	14	49
Softball	7	5	8	7	27
Golf	6	6	7	6	25
Bowling	5	5	7	6	23

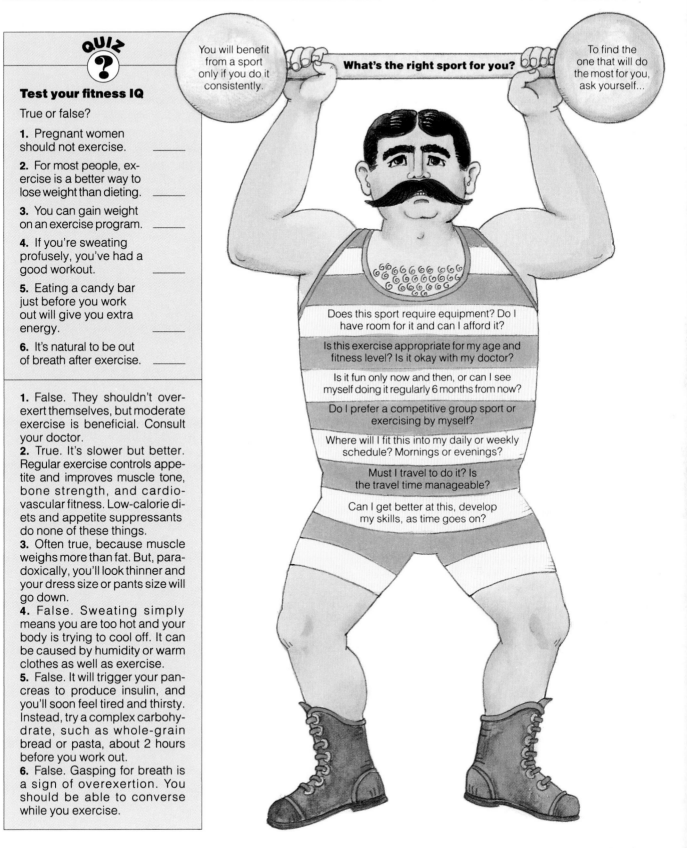

QUIZ ?

Test your fitness IQ

True or false?

1. Pregnant women should not exercise. _____

2. For most people, exercise is a better way to lose weight than dieting. _____

3. You can gain weight on an exercise program. _____

4. If you're sweating profusely, you've had a good workout. _____

5. Eating a candy bar just before you work out will give you extra energy. _____

6. It's natural to be out of breath after exercise. _____

1. False. They shouldn't overexert themselves, but moderate exercise is beneficial. Consult your doctor.
2. True. It's slower but better. Regular exercise controls appetite and improves muscle tone, bone strength, and cardiovascular fitness. Low-calorie diets and appetite suppressants do none of these things.
3. Often true, because muscle weighs more than fat. But, paradoxically, you'll look thinner and your dress size or pants size will go down.
4. False. Sweating simply means you are too hot and your body is trying to cool off. It can be caused by humidity or warm clothes as well as exercise.
5. False. It will trigger your pancreas to produce insulin, and you'll soon feel tired and thirsty. Instead, try a complex carbohydrate, such as whole-grain bread or pasta, about 2 hours before you work out.
6. False. Gasping for breath is a sign of overexertion. You should be able to converse while you exercise.

You will benefit from a sport only if you do it consistently.

What's the right sport for you?

To find the one that will do the most for you, ask yourself...

Does this sport require equipment? Do I have room for it and can I afford it?

Is this exercise appropriate for my age and fitness level? Is it okay with my doctor?

Is it fun only now and then, or can I see myself doing it regularly 6 months from now?

Do I prefer a competitive group sport or exercising by myself?

Where will I fit this into my daily or weekly schedule? Mornings or evenings?

Must I travel to do it? Is the travel time manageable?

Can I get better at this, develop my skills, as time goes on?

Nutritional values of foods

For optimum health, your body requires some 40 nutrients, but you don't have to live with a calculator to keep track of them all if your daily meals include servings from each of the four basic food groups (see *Counting calories*, p.31). Check labels at the supermarket for food values (processed foods may contain extra sugar, sodium, or fat). The chart below lists nutrients in many foods that are sold without labels.

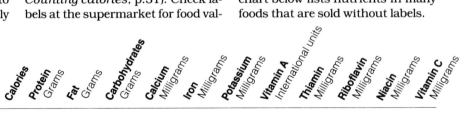

Food	Calories	Protein Grams	Fat Grams	Carbohydrates Grams	Calcium Milligrams	Iron Milligrams	Potassium Milligrams	Vitamin A International units	Thiamin Milligrams	Riboflavin Milligrams	Niacin Milligrams	Vitamin C Milligrams
Fruits & Vegetables												
Apple, 3¼" dia.	125	*	1	32	15	0.4	244	110	0.04	0.03	0.2	12
Apricots, 3 fresh	50	1	*	12	15	0.6	314	2,770	0.03	0.04	0.6	11
Avocado, Florida, 3½" dia.	340	5	27	27	33	1.6	1,484	1,860	0.33	0.37	5.8	24
Banana, medium size	105	1	1	27	7	0.4	451	90	0.05	0.11	0.6	10
Cantaloupe, ½	95	2	1	22	29	0.6	825	8,610	0.10	0.06	1.5	113
Grapefruit, ½	40	1	*	10	14	0.1	167	10	0.04	0.02	0.3	41
Grapes, 10	35	*	*	9	6	0.1	93	40	0.05	0.03	0.2	5
Orange, 2⅝" dia.	60	1	*	15	52	0.1	237	270	0.11	0.05	0.4	70
Peach, 2½" dia.	35	1	*	10	4	0.1	171	470	0.01	0.04	0.9	6
Pear, Bartlett, 2½" dia.	100	1	1	25	18	0.4	208	30	0.03	0.07	0.2	7
Pineapple, 1 cup diced	75	1	1	19	11	0.6	175	40	0.14	0.06	0.7	24
Prunes, 5	115	1	*	31	25	1.2	365	970	0.04	0.08	1	2
Asparagus, 4 spears	15	2	*	3	14	0.4	186	500	0.06	0.07	0.6	16
Beets, cooked, 2 2" dia.	30	1	*	7	11	0.6	312	10	0.03	0.01	0.3	6
Broccoli, cooked, medium stalk	50	5	1	10	205	2.1	293	2,540	0.15	0.37	1.4	113
Brussels sprouts, cooked, 7–8	60	4	1	13	56	1.9	491	1,110	0.17	0.12	0.9	96
Cabbage, raw, 1 cup chopped	15	1	*	4	33	0.4	172	90	0.04	0.02	0.2	33
Carrot, 7½" x 1⅛"	30	1	*	7	19	0.4	233	20,250	0.07	0.04	0.7	7
Cauliflower, 1 cup florets	25	2	*	5	29	0.6	355	20	0.08	0.06	0.6	72
Celery, 8" stalk	5	*	*	1	14	0.2	114	50	0.01	0.01	0.1	3
Corn, 5" ear	85	3	1	19	2	0.5	192	170	0.17	0.06	1.2	5
Cucumber, 8 ⅛" slices	5	*	*	1	4	0.1	42	10	0.01	0.01	0.1	1
Kale, cooked, 1 cup	40	2	1	7	94	1.2	296	9,620	0.07	0.09	0.7	53
Lettuce, Boston, 5" head	20	2	*	4	52	0.5	419	1,580	0.10	0.10	0.5	13
Lettuce, iceberg, 6" head	70	5	1	11	102	2.7	852	1,780	0.25	0.16	1	21
Mushrooms, 1 cup chopped	20	1	*	3	4	0.9	259	0	0.07	0.31	2.9	2
Okra, cooked, 8 3" pods	25	2	*	6	54	0.4	274	490	0.11	0.05	0.7	14
Onions, white, raw, 1 cup chopped	55	2	*	12	40	0.6	248	0	0.10	0.02	0.2	13
Peas, 1 cup	65	5	*	11	67	3.2	384	210	0.20	0.12	0.9	77
Peppers (5 per lb.), 1 pod	20	1	*	4	4	0.9	144	390	0.06	0.04	0.4	95
Potato, baked, 8 oz.	220	5	*	51	20	2.7	844	0	0.22	0.07	3.3	26
Radishes, 4	5	*	*	1	4	0.01	42	*	*	0.01	0.1	4
Spinach, fresh, 1 cup chopped	10	2	*	2	54	1.5	307	3,690	0.04	0.10	0.4	15
Squash, summer, cooked, 1 cup	35	2	1	8	49	0.6	346	520	0.08	0.07	0.9	10
Sweet potato, baked, 5" x 2"	115	2	*	28	32	0.5	397	24,880	0.08	0.14	0.7	28
Tomato, 2½" dia.	25	1	*	5	9	0.6	255	1,390	0.07	0.06	0.7	22
Breads, Cereals & Grains												
Biscuit, homemade, 2" dia.	100	2	5	13	47	0.7	32	10	0.08	0.08	0.8	*
Bread crumbs, 1 cup	390	13	5	73	122	4.1	152	0	0.35	0.35	4.8	0
Cereal, oatmeal, 1 cup cooked	145	6	2	25	19	1.6	131	40	0.26	0.05	0.3	0
Cupcake, devil's food, chocolate icing	120	2	4	20	21	0.7	46	50	0.04	0.05	0.3	*
Macaroni, cooked, 1 cup	190	7	1	39	14	2.1	103	0	0.23	0.13	1.8	0
Muffin, bran, 2½" dia.	125	3	6	19	60	1.4	99	230	0.11	0.13	1.3	3
Noodles, cooked, 1 cup	200	7	2	37	16	2.6	70	110	0.22	0.13	1.9	0
Pie, 9" dia., 1 slice												
Apple	405	3	18	60	13	1.6	126	50	0.17	0.13	1.6	2

Food	Calories	Protein Grams	Fat Grams	Carbohydrates Grams	Calcium Milligrams	Iron Milligrams	Potassium Milligrams	Vitamin A International units	Thiamin Milligrams	Riboflavin Milligrams	Niacin Milligrams	Vitamin C Milligrams
Pie (*continued*)												
Banana cream	455	3	23	59	46	1.1	133	210	0.06	0.15	1.1	0
Lemon meringue	355	5	14	53	20	1.4	70	240	0.10	0.14	0.8	4
Pumpkin	320	6	17	37	78	1.4	243	3,750	0.14	0.21	1.2	0
Popcorn, plain, 1 cup	30	1	*	6	1	0.2	20	10	0.03	0.01	0.2	0
Dairy Products												
Milk, whole, 1 cup	150	8	8	11	291	0.1	370	310	0.09	0.40	0.2	2
Milk, skim, 1 cup	85	8	*	12	302	0.1	406	500	0.09	0.34	0.2	2
Cheese, blue, 1 oz.	100	6	8	1	150	0.1	73	200	0.01	0.11	0.3	0
Cheese, Cheddar, 1″ piece	70	4	6	*	123	0.1	17	180	*	0.06	*	0
Cheese, Swiss, 1 oz.	105	8	8	1	272	31.0	240	0.01	0.10	*	0	
Yogurt, plain, 1 cup	145	12	4	16	415	0.2	531	150	0.10	0.49	0.3	2
Fish, Poultry, Meat, Eggs, Legumes, Nuts & Seeds												
Bluefish, baked in butter, 3 oz.	135	22	4	0	25	0.6	0	40	0.09	0.08	1.6	0
Clams, raw, 3 oz.	65	11	1	2	59	2.6	154	90	0.09	0.15	1.1	9
Crabmeat, canned, 1 cup	135	23	3	1	61	1.1	149	50	0.11	0.11	2.6	0
Haddock, breaded & fried, 3 oz.	175	17	9	7	34	1.0	270	70	0.06	0.10	2.9	0
Ocean perch, fried, 1 fillet	185	16	11	7	31	1.2	241	70	0.10	0.11	2.0	0
Oysters, raw, 13–19 medium	160	20	4	8	226	15.6	290	740	0.34	0.43	6.0	24
Shrimp, canned, 3 oz.	100	21	1	1	98	1.4	104	50	0.01	0.03	1.5	0
Chicken												
½ breast, fried	220	31	9	2	16	1.2	254	50	0.08	0.13	13.5	0
drumstick, fried, 2.9 oz.	120	13	7	1	6	0.7	112	40	0.04	0.11	3.0	0
½ breast, roasted	140	27	3	0	13	0.9	220	20	0.06	0.10	11.8	0
Turkey, roasted												
dark meat, 4 slices, 2½″ x 1⅝″	160	24	6	0	27	2.0	246	0	0.05	0.21	3.1	0
light meat, 2 slices, 4″ x 2″	135	25	3	0	16	1.1	259	0	0.05	0.11	5.8	0
Beef, trimmed, cooked												
3 oz. (lean & fat)	220	25	13	0	5	2.8	248	*	0.06	0.21	3.3	0
Lamb, cooked												
3-oz. rib chop	315	18	26	0	19	1.4	224	*	0.08	0.18	5.5	0
3-oz. piece leg	205	22	13	0	8	1.7	273	*	0.09	0.24	5.5	0
2.2-oz. piece shoulder	220	20	15	0	16	1.5	195	*	0.04	0.16	4.4	0
Liver, beef, 6½″ x 2⅜″ slice, fried	185	23	7	7	9	5.3	309	30,690	0.18	3.52	12.3	23
Pork, fresh, cooked												
2½-oz. lean chop	165	23	8	0	4	0.7	302	10	0.83	0.22	4.0	*
3-oz. piece roast	270	21	20	0	9	0.8	313	10	0.50	0.24	4.2	*
Veal, cooked												
3-oz. cutlet	185	23	9	0	9	0.8	258	*	0.06	0.21	4.6	0
Egg, large												
Hard-boiled or poached	80	6	6	1	28	1.0	65	260	0.04	0.14	*	0
Fried or scrambled in butter	95	6	7	1	29	1.1	66	320	0.04	0.14	*	0
Almonds, shelled, 1 cup	795	27	70	28	359	4.9	988	0	0.28	1.05	4.5	1
Brazil nuts, shelled, 1 oz.	185	4	19	4	50	1.0	170	*	0.28	0.03	0.5	*
Lentils, cooked, 1 cup	215	16	1	38	50	4.2	498	40	0.14	0.12	1.2	0
Lima beans, cooked, 1 cup	260	16	1	49	55	5.9	1,163	0	0.25	0.11	1.3	0
Navy (pea) beans, cooked, 1 cup	225	15	1	40	95	5.1	790	0	0.27	0.13	1.3	0
Peanuts, roasted in oil, 1 cup	840	39	71	27	125	2.8	1,019	0	0.42	0.15	21.5	0
Peas, dry split, cooked, 1 cup	230	16	1	42	22	3.4	592	80	0.30	0.18	1.8	0
Sunflower seeds, hulled, 1 oz.	160	6	14	5	33	1.9	195	10	0.65	0.07	1.3	*
Walnuts, black, 1 cup chopped	760	30	71	15	73	3.8	655	370	0.27	0.14	0.9	*

Asterisk (*) indicates that only traces of a nutrient are present.

Getting more for your food dollar

Do you get nervous at the supermarket as you watch your receipt flowing from the cash register? Are you always wondering how you managed to spend so much money on so little? Here are some simple ways to stretch your food budget without sacrificing quality.

Make a list to prevent impulse buying.

Buy sale items only when needed and if you have ample storage space.

Shop in stores that discount your favorite products.

Buy unwrapped seasonal fruits and vegetables.

Leave the kids at home whenever you can. They may prompt you to buy items you don't want.

Clip and use coupons wisely. The money saved can purchase something special.

Don't go shopping on an empty stomach. You'll buy more than you meant to.

Bone chicken and cut up or grind less expensive cuts of beef, lamb, and pork for stews and patties.

Don't be fooled. Foods displayed at the ends of aisles are seldom good buys.

Check unit pricing.

Try store brands and generic products.

Make tasty meals from leftovers instead of tossing them out.

Think small. Buy only what you will use. Throwing out food and unused household products is throwing out money.

Be creative with substitutes. Use powdered instead of whole milk, and lentils, dried peas, or beans instead of meat occasionally.

Season your own rice, make your own sauces, bake your own cakes, and steam your own fresh vegetables.

Food-borne illness

Food poisoning is unpleasant at best and can be life-threatening. Here are some tips to help you eliminate the risk of illness.

☐ Discard any food that smells or looks spoiled.

☐ Keep food hot or cold. Bacteria thrive at room temperature.

☐ Scrub your hands with soap and warm water before preparing food and after handling raw fish, meat, or poultry.

☐ Wash utensils and cutting boards after each use.

☐ Replace sponges, washcloths, and kitchen towels as soon as they look or smell musty.

☐ If you're going to sneeze or cough, turn away from food. Cover your mouth, then wash your hands.

☐ If you have broken skin on your hands or an infection, wear thin rubber or plastic gloves in the kitchen.

☐ Don't eat very rare meat, fish, or poultry. Test for doneness with a meat thermometer.

☐ Don't let food stand on a counter to defrost. Thaw it in a microwave oven, the refrigerator, or cold water. Cook immediately.

☐ Discard bulging or leaking cans.

☐ Cool leftovers in the refrigerator. Reheat solids thoroughly and boil sauces and gravies.

☐ Refrigerate perishables as soon as possible.

☐ Freeze food in small, shallow, closed containers. Never refreeze frozen food that has thawed.

☐ Take the "use by" date on packaged food seriously.

☐ Keep pets away from food and off the table.

Microwave do's and don'ts

☐ Use ceramic and glass ovenware. If you buy new cookware, check that it's labeled "microwave safe."

☐ Never cook in metal containers. Aluminum foil is safe in some ovens but not others. Check your owner's manual.

☐ Be sure that your microwave cookware is tall enough to accommodate boiling foods.

☐ To avoid explosions, loosen the lids of frozen food containers, slit plastic food pouches, and pierce food with skin so that steam can escape during cooking.

☐ Do not deep-fry.

☐ Center food in the oven and have the thicker, denser parts facing outward, toward oven walls.

☐ Follow the recipe and let food stand after you take it out of the oven; it's still cooking.

☐ Keep oven turned off when not in use (don't leave the oven rack inside). The door should close tightly.

Perishable food storage

Freezer 0°F or lower		Items	Refrigerator 34° to 40°F	
Months Cooked	Months Uncooked		Days Cooked	Days Uncooked
		Meat and poultry		
2–3	1–3	Bacon (opened package)	3–4	5–7
1	2–9	Chicken, whole/pieces	2–4	1–2
–	–	Eggs	–	7–35
–	1–2	Cold cuts	–	3–5
		Beef		
4–6	6–12	Roast	4–5	3–4
2–3	4–6	Ground	3–4	1–2
2–3	12	Steak	3–5	2–3
2–3	1–2	Frankfurters	3–4	3–5
		Lamb		
4–6	6–9	Roast	3–4	2–3
2–3	6–9	Chops	3–4	2–3
		Pork		
4–6	4–8	Roast	3–4	2–3
2–3	3–4	Chops	3–4	2–3
2–3	1–2	Ground	3–4	1–2
2–3	1–2	Sausage	3–4	1–2
2–3	2–6	Turkey, whole/pieces	2–4	1–2
6–9	4–8	Veal roast	3–4	2–3
		Fish		
		Lean white fish		
1–2	4–6	Cod, flounder, sole	2–3	1–2
		Oily fish		
1–2	2–3	Mackerel, bluefish	2–3	1–2
3	3–6	Shrimp	2–3	1
		Dairy products		
–	6–9	Butter	–	7–14
–	6	Cheese, hard	–	90–180
–	–	Cheese, soft	–	14
–	–	Cream, light & heavy	–	10
–	–	Half & half	–	10
–	1	Milk	–	3–5

The chart above lists the temperatures and times at which commonly used perishable foods can be stored for optimum safety, good taste, and nutrition.

Handy helpers when supplies run short

Food	Substitutes	Stretchers
Acorn squash	Butternut squash, pumpkin	Stuffing of leftover meat, rice
Baking powder 1 tsp.	¼ tsp. baking soda plus ½ tsp. cream of tartar	——
Beer	——	Ginger ale, lemon-ade, tonic water
Bread crumbs	Cracker crumbs, wheat germ, cereal	——
Cake	——	Ice cream, fruit top-ping; mix broken pieces with custard
Cake flour 1 cup	1 cup less 2 tbsp. sifted all-purpose flour	——
Champagne	White or rosé wine	Fruit juices, seltzer
Chicken	Veal, turkey	Onion, celery, rice
Chili	——	Bulgur, beans, rice, spaghetti, corn
Coffee	——	Roasted chicory or dandelion root
Cornstarch 1 tbsp. (as thickener)	2 tbsp. all-purpose flour	——
Cream, light 1 cup	¾ cup milk plus ¼ cup melted butter	——
Creamed corn	——	Milk and onion (for soup)
Egg 1 whole	2 egg yolks	Omelet with vegeta-bles, cheese, poultry
Egg salad	——	Celery, potatoes, tofu
Fish	——	Cut up, stir-fry with vegetables
Fruit juice, fruit punch	——	Club soda, ginger ale, tea
Gravy	Cream of mush-room soup with bouillon	Puréed vegetables, ketchup, mush-rooms
Green pepper	Red pepper, yellow pepper	Stuffing of rice, leftovers
Ground beef	Ground pork, veal, or lamb	Shredded squash or pumpkin, rice, pas-ta, wheat germ, un-sweetened cereal, onion, green pepper

Food	Substitutes	Stretchers
Honey 1 cup	1¼ cups sugar plus ⅓ cup water	——
Ice cream	Frozen yogurt, sherbet, ice milk, pudding	Fruit, sauce, cereal topping
Iced tea	——	Fruit juice, herb teas
Ketchup or chili sauce ½ cup	½ cup tomato sauce plus 2 tbsp. sugar	——
Lemon juice 1 tsp.	½ tsp. vinegar; lime juice	——
Meat loaf	——	Crackers, rice, rolled oats, shredded car-rots, hard-boiled eggs, wheat germ
Milk, whole 1 cup	1 cup skim milk plus 2 tsp. melted butter	Instant dried milk
Noodles	——	Leftover vegeta-bles, diced meats
Pudding	——	Vanilla wafers, sliced bananas, cubes of stale cake
Salad	——	Meat, fish, legumes, vegetables, avocado
Soups	——	Vegetables, pasta, legumes, tofu, sour cream, barley, yogurt
Sour cream	Plain yogurt	——
Spaghetti sauce	——	Extra meat, shell-fish, vegetables
Steak	——	Cut up and stir-fry with vegetables or grill on skewer
Stews	——	Creamed corn, shredded wheat
Tartar sauce ½ cup	6 tbsp. mayonnaise plus 2 tbsp. sweet pickle relish	——
Tomato sauce 2 cups	¾ cup tomato paste plus 1 cup water	Carrots, broccoli, green pepper
Tuna salad	White-meat chicken salad	Olives, relish, cel-ery, pasta, eggs
Vegetables	——	Aspic, pasta, rice
Wine	——	Seltzer, fruit juice
Yogurt	Buttermilk	Fruit, nuts, wheat germ

Spices & seasonings

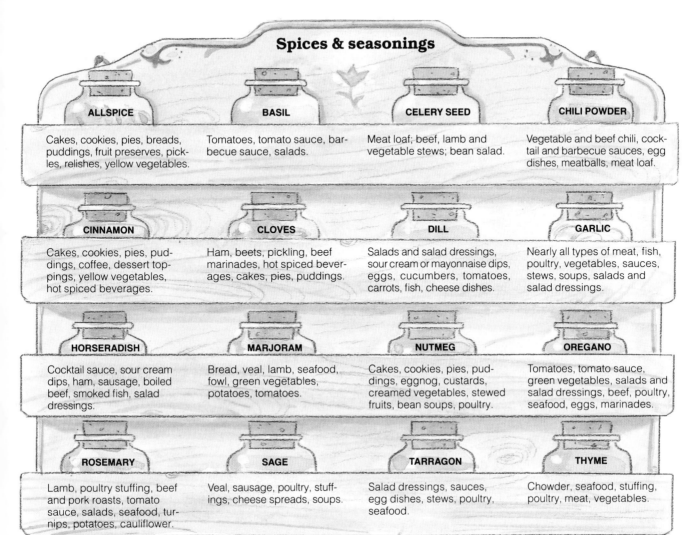

ALLSPICE
Cakes, cookies, pies, breads, puddings, fruit preserves, pickles, relishes, yellow vegetables.

BASIL
Tomatoes, tomato sauce, barbecue sauce, salads.

CELERY SEED
Meat loaf; beef, lamb and vegetable stews; bean salad.

CHILI POWDER
Vegetable and beef chili, cocktail and barbecue sauces, egg dishes, meatballs, meat loaf.

CINNAMON
Cakes, cookies, pies, puddings, coffee, dessert toppings, yellow vegetables, hot spiced beverages.

CLOVES
Ham, beets, pickling, beef marinades, hot spiced beverages, cakes, pies, puddings.

DILL
Salads and salad dressings, sour cream or mayonnaise dips, eggs, cucumbers, tomatoes, carrots, fish, cheese dishes.

GARLIC
Nearly all types of meat, fish, poultry, vegetables, sauces, stews, soups, salads and salad dressings.

HORSERADISH
Cocktail sauce, sour cream dips, ham, sausage, boiled beef, smoked fish, salad dressings.

MARJORAM
Bread, veal, lamb, seafood, fowl, green vegetables, potatoes, tomatoes.

NUTMEG
Cakes, cookies, pies, puddings, eggnog, custards, creamed vegetables, stewed fruits, bean soups, poultry.

OREGANO
Tomatoes, tomato sauce, green vegetables, salads and salad dressings, beef, poultry, seafood, eggs, marinades.

ROSEMARY
Lamb, poultry stuffing, beef and pork roasts, tomato sauce, salads, seafood, turnips, potatoes, cauliflower.

SAGE
Veal, sausage, poultry, stuffings, cheese spreads, soups.

TARRAGON
Salad dressings, sauces, egg dishes, stews, poultry, seafood.

THYME
Chowder, seafood, stuffing, poultry, meat, vegetables.

Equivalents for common cooking ingredients

1 lb.	**Apples**	3 or 4 medium
1 lb.	**Bananas**	3 or 4 medium
1 lb.	**Beans, dried**	5–6 cups cooked
1 quart	**Berries**	3½ cups
1 slice	**Bread**	½ cup crumbs
¼ lb.	**Cheese, grated**	1 cup
1 oz.	**Chocolate, 1 square**	1 tbsp. melted
½ pint	**Cream**	1 cup
1 cup	**Cream, heavy**	2 cups whipped
1 lb.	**Flour, all-purpose**	4 cups sifted
1 envelope	**Gelatin**	1 tbsp.
1 tsp.	**Herbs, dried**	1 tbsp. fresh
2–3 tbsp. juice	**Lemon**	1½ tsp. grated rind
1 cup dry	**Macaroni**	2¼ cups cooked
1 lb.	**Meat, diced**	2 cups
1 lb.	**Mushrooms**	5–6 cups sliced
¼ lb.	**Nuts, shelled**	I cup chopped
1 medium	**Onion**	½ cup chopped
6 – 8 tbsp. juice	**Orange**	⅓–½ cup pulp
3 medium	**Potatoes**	1¾–2 cups mashed
1 cup uncooked	**Rice**	3 cups cooked
½ lb.	**Spaghetti**	3½–4 cups cooked
1 lb.	**Sugar, confectioners**	4½ cups unsifted
1 lb.	**Sugar, granulated**	2 cups
1 lb.	**Tomatoes**	3 or 4 medium
1 lb.	**Walnuts, in shell**	1¾ cups chopped

PARTY CHECKLIST

Four to three weeks before
- [ ] Decide on type of party.
- [ ] Set budget.
- [ ] Draw up guest list. Mail or telephone invitations.
- [ ] Hire help if needed.
- [ ] Rent equipment.
- [ ] Arrange entertainment.

Two weeks before
- [ ] Decide on food and drink.
- [ ] Plan setup: bar, buffet, decorations.
- [ ] Choose utensils, dishes, glassware, table linens, napkins, candles, and other supplies.

One week before
- [ ] Shop for nonperishable food, drinks, and supplies.
- [ ] Order flowers.
- [ ] Prepare those dishes that can be frozen.

Five to two days before
- [ ] Polish silver.
- [ ] Clean house.
- [ ] Make or buy ice.
- [ ] Arrange seating plan and write out place cards.
- [ ] Clean, press party attire.
- [ ] Choose music (if there's no entertainment).

One day before
- [ ] Buy perishable food.
- [ ] Set up bar and buffet table.
- [ ] Put out ashtrays and matches.
- [ ] Check bathroom supplies.
- [ ] Determine area for coats.

Day of party
- [ ] Arrange decorations.
- [ ] Set out uncooked foods.
- [ ] Prepare cooked foods.
- [ ] Set table (if a dinner party).
- [ ] Chill white wine.
- [ ] Do last-minute tidying up.
- [ ] One hour before: put ice, water, garnishes at bar. Open red wine.

How much do you need?

It's a nuisance to run out of supplies during a party or to cope with too many leftovers afterward. The amounts given here are meant for 20 guests. If you are having more or fewer people, simply divide or multiply by the appropriate number.

DRINKS
1 liter each vodka, gin, scotch, and bourbon
2 cases beer
5 bottles white wine
3 bottles red wine
4 quarts seltzer
1 quart each club soda, tonic, orange juice, tomato juice, cola, diet soda, ginger ale
3 limes, 1 lemon
20 pounds ice cubes

HORS D'OEUVRES
2 pounds cheese
3 loaves bread
3 bags chips
1 pound crackers
3 cups dip
2 pounds nuts
5 pounds raw vegetables or 150 finger foods (tiny sandwiches, frankfurters, shrimp, and so forth)

DINNER
(Choose from among the following.)
10 pounds meat with bone
5 pounds boneless meat
10 pounds poultry
5 pounds fish fillets
1 pound pasta
5 cups rice
5 pounds any vegetable
4 heads lettuce
5 pounds fruit
2 cakes or 3 pies
60 cookies
3 quarts ice cream

Setting a place at your table

Nowadays people are having fewer formal dinner parties. The diagram below illustrates where all the elements in a rather informal place setting go. You may want to eliminate a soupspoon or a wineglass from the arrangement, depending on the menu you've selected.

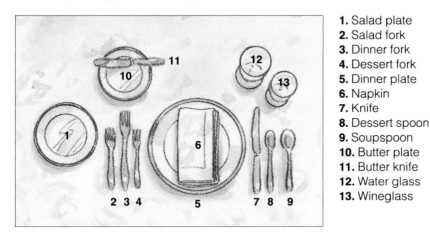

1. Salad plate
2. Salad fork
3. Dinner fork
4. Dessert fork
5. Dinner plate
6. Napkin
7. Knife
8. Dessert spoon
9. Soupspoon
10. Butter plate
11. Butter knife
12. Water glass
13. Wineglass

Cheese choices

Easy to store and serve, cheese is an excellent protein food to have on hand when people are drinking alcohol. It works equally well as an hors d'oeuvre or a dessert.

☐ If you want to try before you buy, go to a store that sells cheese in bulk, rather than packaged, and ask for a sample to taste.

☐ Store cheeses in the door or vegetable compartment of the refrigerator. Rewrap leftover pieces tightly in plastic or aluminum foil.

☐ Remove cheese from the refrigerator at least an hour before serving (except for cottage, pot, or cream cheese).

☐ For dessert, combine apples and pears with Brie, Gorgonzola, Cheddar, Colby, Monterey Jack, Muenster, or Port du Salut.

Oranges or tangerines go well with Stilton, cream cheese, or Neufchâtel. Peaches complement the flavor of Bel Paese, blue cheese, or Camembert.

☐ A red Bordeaux or a good white dessert wine, such as a sauterne, complements most cheese and fruit combinations. Save Burgundy for strong cheeses.

☐ To satisfy everyone's taste, serve a varied selection, with an assortment of crackers and dark bread.

SOFT AND SEMISOFT CHEESES
Bel Paese, Boursin, Brie, Camembert, feta, Muenster, Neufchâtel, Pont l'Evêque, and Weisslacker.

FIRM AND SEMIFIRM CHEESES
Cantal, Edam, Emmentaler, Esrom, Fontina, Gouda, Gruyère, Jarlsberg, and Swiss.

☐ Serve at least one pungent cheese for your adventurous guests: Danish blue, Roquefort, Stilton, Liederkranz, or Limburger.

☐ Aromatic cheeses should be served on a separate board with their own serving knife so that they don't overwhelm milder cheeses.

☐ Use a wire cutter for blue cheeses to keep them from falling apart.

Tips on tippling

No one wants an inebriated guest, especially since many states now hold hosts legally liable in cases of a guest's drunk driving.

IF YOU'RE THE HOST
Never urge drinks on guests.

Keep a good supply of ice on hand and put plenty of ice into drinks.

When you make the cocktails for your guests, measure the alcohol exactly with a jigger.

Have plenty of nonalcoholic beverages available.

Set out high-protein food, such as cubes of meat or fish, near the bar.

If you think a guest is getting tipsy, stop serving him liquor.

If someone is obviously drunk, either call a cab or drive her home yourself. Take a guest's car keys if necessary.

IF YOU'RE A GUEST
Drink milk or have a snack before you go to a party; eat when you get there as well.

Sip your drinks slowly. Keep replenishing the ice in your drink.

Ask for diluted drinks.

Drink nonalcoholic beverages (but not carbonated drinks, which enhance the effects of alcohol) part of the time. Make every other drink fruit juice or water.

Are you in love?

☐ Do you think about her every day? Sometimes call just to ask her what she's doing?

☐ Do you have pretty much the same standards, laugh at the same things, have fun together?

☐ How about the way he looks? What others consider a flaw—that gap between his teeth, for example—do you think it's cute?

☐ Do you buy things you think she'd like, even give her something dear to you, such as an heirloom?

☐ Are you intensely curious about his family background, interests, and work, and do you want to show him things you've accomplished?

☐ Do you want to discuss everything important with her?

☐ Does he always seem to be involved in your plans for the future?

☐ Do you want to become a better person for her sake?

☐ Do you go to the theater because he loves it, even though you don't?

☐ Do you feel a strong emotional and mental attraction to her? Do you enjoy being affectionate?

☐ Do you find it easy to resist attractions to other people?

☐ Do you feel young, buoyant, glad to be alive? Do people keep asking you why you're so happy?

If you've answered yes to all or most of these questions, it may be time to move on to the *Wedding checklist.*

10 tips for a happy marriage

1. Fight, but within limits. Express your feelings, but don't explode. Encourage your partner to tell you when something's wrong. As tactfully as you can, try to get to the root of problems and resolve them.

2. Have your own interests. If your life is totally focused on your spouse, you'll place a burden on him and limits on yourself. Keep in touch with your friends, pursue activities you enjoy, join organizations and take classes that interest you. Your mate is apt to find such a multifaceted person intriguing.

3. Support your partner. If she's worried about a speech she has to give, let her know that you care, even if you can't really help. Be proud of her achievements; remember that she's not your rival — her accomplishments can only reflect well on you.

4. Be affectionate. Don't stifle an urge to hold hands or take his arm. Let him know that he's still attractive to you. And don't forget to say "I love you"—perhaps the sweetest words in the English language. He won't get tired of hearing them.

5. Make time for each other. No matter how busy you are, find time to be alone with your mate—whether you set aside a couple of hours on Sunday afternoon or go away for the weekend. Make "dates" with each other if you need to, and keep them.

6. Appreciate your spouse. Do you thank her when she does you a favor? Do you treat him as considerately as you would a friend? Do you compliment her enough? Sometimes we forget the basic courtesies when we live with someone.

7. Keep the good times in mind. When you're going through a hard period, bring up wonderful memories; sharing them will reinforce the bond between you and remind you of the things that made you love each other in the first place.

8. Forgive and forget. Don't keep replaying the same fight. If your spouse has apologized for something, try not to bring it up again unless it seems helpful. If it keeps bothering you, ask yourself why. If you can't break destructive patterns, see a counselor. If your spouse refuses, go by yourself.

9. Communicate your feelings. If you say, "When you do that, I feel hurt (humiliated, angry)," you're explaining your own reactions rather than accusing your spouse. And if you remember to say, "I love it when you do that," it will encourage behavior that makes you both happy.

10. Give in sometimes. Go to that movie just because he wants to. Eat Italian just because she wants to. Chances are that your compromises will even out in the long run—and besides, no one should be counting.

Your wedding checklist

Planning a formal wedding can test the fortitude of even the most organized mind. Here's a chronological checklist to minimize any last-minute crises on the happy day.

The wedding day
- [ ] Best man gives minister a fee.
- [ ] Relax, take a bath, eat something.
- [ ] Get to the wedding on time!

Two weeks before
- [ ] Make date with hairdresser. Have wedding pictures taken.
- [ ] Call people who haven't answered their invitations.
- [ ] Tell caterer final number of guests. Schedule wedding rehearsal.
- [ ] Arrange your own wedding-day transportation.
- [ ] Recheck honeymoon reservations, blood tests, marriage license.

Two months before
- [ ] Plan reception seating, bar, menu, decor.
- [ ] Mail invitations. Arrange rehearsal dinner.
- [ ] Arrange transportation for wedding party.
- [ ] Select and order gifts for attendants.

One month before
- [ ] Arrange lodging for out-of-town guests.
- [ ] Final fitting for bride's, bridesmaids' dresses.
- [ ] Address announcements. Assign person to mail them after the wedding. Order wedding cake.

Six months before
- [ ] Decide date, time, and place for ceremony and reception.
- [ ] Set a budget.
- [ ] Determine number of guests and make invitation list.
- [ ] Choose a caterer.
- [ ] Discuss ceremony plans with the person who will officiate.

- [ ] Select wedding attendants.
- [ ] Bride orders wedding dress, accessories, and attire for bridesmaids.
- [ ] Register china, crystal, silver, and linen preferences at stores.
- [ ] Order stationery for invitations, announcements, thank-you notes.
- [ ] Choose wedding rings.
- [ ] Hire musicians and photographer.

Three months before
- [ ] Order flowers for wedding, reception.
- [ ] Arrange honeymoon travel, hotel.
- [ ] Groom orders his wedding attire.
- [ ] Mothers select their dresses.
- [ ] Announce engagement in papers.
- [ ] Call state agency about requirements for marriage license.
- [ ] Plan recording, display of gifts.

A wedding in a week

Six days before
- [ ] Arrange time, place (maybe city hall or friend's home).
- [ ] Find a minister or judge to officiate.
- [ ] Telephone people you want to invite (not too many).
- [ ] Ascertain state's requirements for marriage license.

Five days before
- [ ] If you want reception at friend's home, get consent.
- [ ] Have blood tests if needed. Get marriage license.

Four days before
- [ ] Decide on wedding attire. Order flowers if desired.

Three days before
- [ ] Buy the rings.

Two days before
- [ ] Buy food, liquor, any decorations for the reception.

One day before
- [ ] Final details: shine shoes, borrow Mom's pearls.

The day
- [ ] Get married.

Why a baby cries

Cause	Indications	What to do
Hunger	Two hours since last feeding, or small feeding. Baby may make sucking motions.	Give milk or formula.
Thirst	Hot day; baby perspiring.	Give water or diluted fruit juice.
Illness	Change in color or appearance. Cold symptoms. Diarrhea.	Consult medical book or pediatrician.
Fatigue	Baby missed nap or has had more stimulation than usual (e.g., company). Baby may yawn or put hands to eyes.	Put to bed. If baby can't sleep, rock or walk her.
Discomfort	Soiled diaper. Cold or hot room. Bathwater too hot or cold. Clothes tight or stiff.	Check for and change source of discomfort.
Gas/colic	Baby may pull up legs, scream, pass wind.	Burp baby. Lay him on his stomach and rub back. Carry, rock, or take for a drive.
Needs contact	Stops crying when picked up.	Hold baby or put in carrier. Or position older baby so that she can see you.

A babysitter checklist

What the sitter needs to know
☐ Time you'll be home
☐ Children's bedtimes
☐ What TV shows and snacks are allowed
☐ Whether to answer the door
☐ How to answer the phone (it may be wise not to say that you're out)
☐ Special instructions for infants or sick children
☐ Where things are: diapers, toys, food, books, fire extinguishers, flashlight, phone, first-aid supplies, fire exits, children's rooms
☐ How to lock and unlock windows and doors

Telephone numbers
☐ Where you can be reached:
☐ Neighbor:
☐ Doctor:
☐ Police:
☐ Fire:
☐ Ambulance:
☐ Poison control:

Provisions for the sitter
☐ Soft drinks, snacks
☐ Magazines, pillow

Finding the right day care

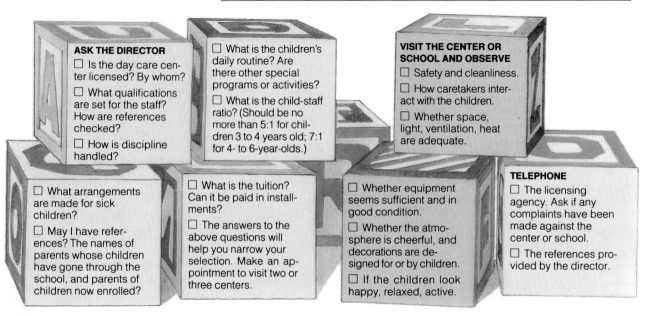

ASK THE DIRECTOR
☐ Is the day care center licensed? By whom?
☐ What qualifications are set for the staff? How are references checked?
☐ How is discipline handled?
☐ What arrangements are made for sick children?
☐ May I have references? The names of parents whose children have gone through the school, and parents of children now enrolled?

☐ What is the children's daily routine? Are there other special programs or activities?
☐ What is the child-staff ratio? (Should be no more than 5:1 for children 3 to 4 years old; 7:1 for 4- to 6-year-olds.)
☐ What is the tuition? Can it be paid in installments?
☐ The answers to the above questions will help you narrow your selection. Make an appointment to visit two or three centers.

VISIT THE CENTER OR SCHOOL AND OBSERVE
☐ Safety and cleanliness.
☐ How caretakers interact with the children.
☐ Whether space, light, ventilation, heat are adequate.
☐ Whether equipment seems sufficient and in good condition.
☐ Whether the atmosphere is cheerful, and decorations are designed for or by children.
☐ If the children look happy, relaxed, active.

TELEPHONE
☐ The licensing agency. Ask if any complaints have been made against the center or school.
☐ The references provided by the director.

Games for a rainy day

☐ Cut out pictures from magazines and glue them onto construction paper to make greeting cards for a child's friends or relatives.

☐ You can create a picture storybook on pages of colored paper in the same way.

☐ If you have childproof musical instruments, such as maracas or tambourines, put on a record and let them play along.

☐ Invent your own instruments. Give children a lidded coffee can or shoebox as a drum; chopsticks become drumsticks. Staple beans or buttons inside two aluminum pie plates for a tambourine.

☐ Have a cooking class: make some simple recipes together. The family can enjoy them at dinner.

☐ Act out a familiar fairy tale, or start making up your own story and let each child add a section in turn.

☐ Make necklaces by painting spools or pasta with acrylic or tempera paints. String them together with yarn or cord. You might intersperse a few leftover buttons.

☐ Put together a gift box for a favorite friend or relative; it can include the child's photo, poems, or stories.

☐ Make costumes for next Halloween (see *Halloween costumes*, p.103).

You and your teenager

☐ Try not to overreact to a teenager's emotional highs and lows. They're to be expected at this age.

☐ If your child isn't as willing to talk as he once was, or wants to be alone, don't take it personally. Respect his privacy.

☐ Listen seriously to your child's opinions. If you disagree, refute an argument with the same logic and courtesy you would employ with an adult at a party or the office.

☐ Give her total responsibility in appropriate areas—for example, her appearance or room. She needs to learn to make decisions and to live with the consequences, good or bad.

☐ Avoid comparing him to yourself at his age.

☐ When conflicts arise, try not to blame or attack. Stick to your basic standards, but be open to negotiation and compromise on less important points.

☐ Remember to praise good behavior and admire her achievements.

☐ It's natural for a teenager to want acceptance by his peers. Try not to criticize his friends or, conversely, to compare him unfavorably to them.

☐ Make sure she receives accurate information about alcohol, drugs, and sex. Encourage her to come to you or another trusted adult if she needs to talk.

☐ If you're not sure how to deal with a problem your teenager has, or if there are difficult family problems, talk to the school counselor or seek other professional help.

Seasonal home checkups

In the spring

OUTSIDE

☐ Label and store removable storm windows (p.198) and storm door.

☐ Wash windows. Put up screens; patch any with holes.

☐ Check roof. Repair leaks; replace damaged shingles.

☐ Check for termites; call exterminator if needed.

☐ Clean out gutters and downspouts. If gutters sag, replace supports or add extra supports.

☐ Examine exterior paint. Repaint where needed.

☐ Check siding. If nails have popped, add new ones.

☐ If brickwork is damaged, add mortar where needed.

☐ Caulk any leaks or cracks in basement walls.

☐ See that all doors close properly.

INSIDE

☐ Open basement and attic windows to ventilate.

☐ Have qualified inspector check any stains, bulges on ceilings and walls. Wash walls, woodwork if needed.

☐ Get out outdoor furniture, barbecue grill. Check that any play equipment for children is still sturdy.

☐ Check all household drains; clean out if sluggish.

☐ Clean or replace filters in room air conditioners. Vacuum units and install them if they were stored.

☐ Have chimney cleaned.

In the fall

OUTSIDE

☐ Check mounting straps, screws, bolts for TV antenna.

☐ Inspect chimney for cracks or loose mortar. If flashing is loose, secure and add roof cement.

☐ Clean downspouts and gutters; install wire strainers.

☐ Prune any tree branches that rub against house.

☐ Check weatherstripping; caulk around windows if needed.

☐ Rake lawn (save twigs for fireplace). Store lawn equipment.

☐ Clean and store outdoor furniture, barbecue grill.

☐ Wash and put up storm windows, storm door. Check fit and add weatherstripping where needed.

☐ Turn off, drain outside faucets.

INSIDE

☐ Close off any unused rooms, such as the attic (turn off heat; be sure door closes tightly).

☐ Store air conditioners if possible; cover and seal remaining units.

☐ If you have humidifiers, clean filters and reservoirs.

☐ Check that electrical outlets don't have too many plugs; replace any worn wires.

☐ Inspect weatherstripping at door to unheated garage.

☐ Check furnace and remove any debris or flammable objects (such as cardboard boxes) from the vicinity.

☐ Bleed air from radiators if needed (p.168).

☐ If you have a boiler, bleed if necessary.

☐ Make sure that smoke detectors work.

Selecting and working with contractors

☐ First, make a clear set of plans for your project. Unethical contractors will "low ball" a bid, knowing that they will more than make up the difference in price on the extras or changes that occur when a contract is not clear.

☐ For small jobs of 1 or 2 days, have a list of specific materials, colors, textures, and finishes. For medium-size work (3—5 days), add drawings and detailed measurements.

☐ For work that will take more than 15 days to complete, have detailed drawings done by a certified draftsman or architect.

☐ Never hire a contractor who "happens to be in the neighborhood" and offers you a bargain price because he wants to keep his people busy or for some other reason. Good contractors don't have to solicit new business.

☐ Find work that you like in your community and ask the homeowner who did it. Ask your friends for recommendations too.

☐ Other good sources of information on a contractor's reputation are local realtors, architects, and lumberyards, as well as his bank and the Better Business Bureau.

☐ Solicit three or four written bids. (An estimate is a guess. A bid is a legal document.) Make sure all bids are for the same brands, grades, and specifications you listed.

☐ The work you want done will often require building permits. Be sure your contractor obtains them. Otherwise you, not he, will be liable for any code violations.

☐ The contract you sign should spell out everything the contractor is to do (including weights, sizes, and grades of materials; brand names and model numbers of appliances); the time in which he is to do it; and penalties for late completion.

☐ Include a provision limiting the cost overrun you'll accept. A maxi-

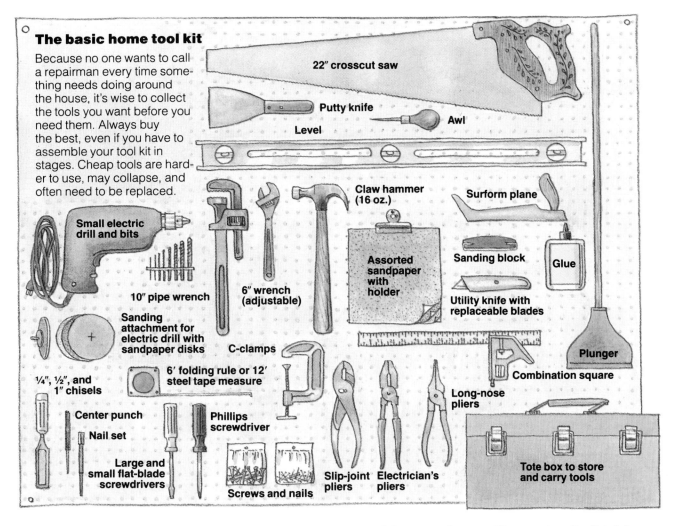

The basic home tool kit

Because no one wants to call a repairman every time something needs doing around the house, it's wise to collect the tools you want before you need them. Always buy the best, even if you have to assemble your tool kit in stages. Cheap tools are harder to use, may collapse, and often need to be replaced.

22" crosscut saw

Putty knife

Level

Awl

Claw hammer (16 oz.)

Surform plane

Small electric drill and bits

Assorted sandpaper with holder

Sanding block

Glue

10" pipe wrench

6" wrench (adjustable)

Utility knife with replaceable blades

Sanding attachment for electric drill with sandpaper disks

C-clamps

Plunger

Combination square

¼", ½", and 1" chisels

6' folding rule or 12' steel tape measure

Long-nose pliers

Center punch

Nail set

Phillips screwdriver

Large and small flat-blade screwdrivers

Screws and nails

Slip-joint pliers

Electrician's pliers

Tote box to store and carry tools

---

mum of 10 percent will encourage bidders to give you a realistic price.

☐ Your contract should specify who does the cleaning up, where things may be stored, and whether you want old appliances and lumber saved or thrown out.

☐ The contractor must agree in writing to install warranted items according to the manufacturers' instructions. All warranties should be in writing and include the addresses of whoever is to honor them.

☐ An insurance company will issue a certificate of insurance, with your name on it, for property damage, worker's compensation, and personal liability. Do not accept a copy of the original.

☐ At the outset get a list of the contractor's subcontractors or suppliers. If he doesn't pay them, they can put a lien on your home. You may be able to put a "release of lien" clause in your contract or to put your payments in escrow until you have seen receipts showing that the contractor has paid these bills.

☐ Avoid changing your mind in the middle of a project. If you must do so, submit a written change order to the contractor, not a workman, and get his price in writing.

☐ For small jobs, pay a maximum of 10 percent at the time of agreement and the balance on completion. For medium-size jobs, 10 percent upon agreement, 25 percent when work

begins, 25 percent on the third day, and the balance on completion. If you have complaints, withhold 15 percent of the balance until the problems have been corrected.

☐ For large jobs, pay 10 percent at the time of agreement. After that, schedule 10 percent progress payments on a weekly or monthly basis —for completed work only. At no point should you or the contractor have more or less than 10 percent between what is completed and what is paid for.

☐ Withhold the final 10 percent until at least 10 to 15 days after the job is finished and, if permits were required, the local building inspector has approved it.

Safety tips for your home

Most accidents and fires that occur in the home are preventable (see *Fire safety,* p.82). Here are many of the danger spots in the average American home. Note that safety tips in one room may apply in other rooms as well.

Bedroom

Keep bulb wattage to that of lamp, light fixtures. If not known, limit to 60 watts.

Keep electric blankets smooth and flat. Don't tuck them under the mattress. Don't place on baby or anyone who can't tell you that blanket is too hot.

Space heaters are dangerous. Keep them away from paper items, draperies, rugs, furniture, traffic paths. Keep children, pets away. Check stability, UL label.

Have lamp and phone accessible from bed.

Avoid clutter on floor near bed.

Hallways, stairs, and landings

Ensure good lighting with switch at ground floor and each landing.

Have smoke detector on each floor, one near bedrooms.

Keep clear of clutter or of furniture with sharp or protruding parts.

Treads should have nonskid surfaces. For visibility, use 2-inch white tape on edges.

Never leave anything on the stairs.

Install safety gates across bottom of stairs and at each landing if you have small children.

Living room

Compare wattage on cords to that on appliances, lamps. Overloaded extension cords or outlets cause fires.

Install cover plates on all outlets and switches. Call electrician if any outlet or plate is warm to the touch.

Provide wide-rimmed ashtrays; don't empty them into wastebaskets.

Shield fireplace with screen or heat-tempered glass doors. (Keep area clear of newspapers.) Keep chimney clean; check often with flashlight for cracks.

Leave air space around TV and stereo to prevent overheating.

Keep fire, police, poison control numbers near the phone.

Don't run electrical cords under rugs or furniture or in traffic areas. Replace frayed, cracked, or pinched cords.

Tack carpeting down.

Make sure railing is sturdy.

Tack down carpets; back rugs with slip-resistant coating or pads. Use nonslip polish on waxed floors.

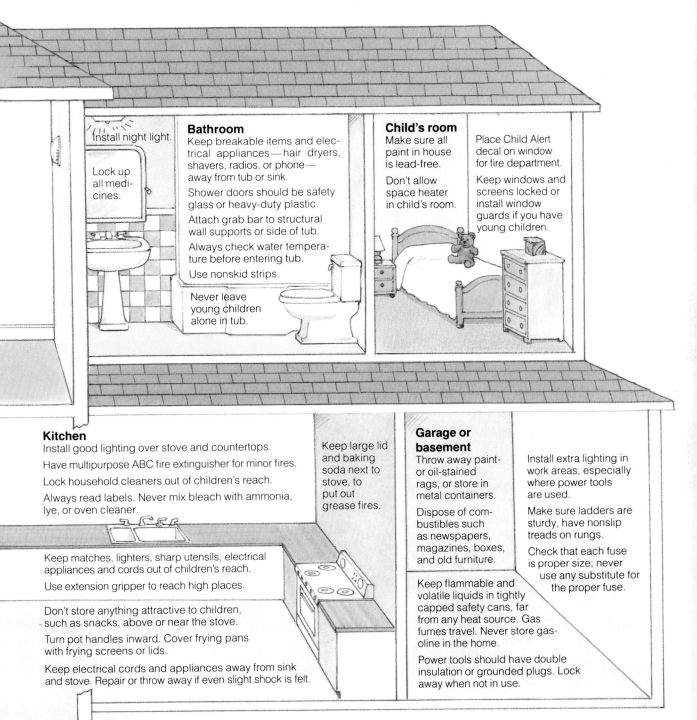

Install night light.

Lock up all medicines.

Bathroom
Keep breakable items and electrical appliances—hair dryers, shavers, radios, or phone—away from tub or sink.

Shower doors should be safety glass or heavy-duty plastic.

Attach grab bar to structural wall supports or side of tub.

Always check water temperature before entering tub.

Use nonskid strips.

Never leave young children alone in tub.

Child's room
Make sure all paint in house is lead-free.

Don't allow space heater in child's room.

Place Child Alert decal on window for fire department.

Keep windows and screens locked or install window guards if you have young children.

Kitchen
Install good lighting over stove and countertops.

Have multipurpose ABC fire extinguisher for minor fires.

Lock household cleaners out of children's reach.

Always read labels. Never mix bleach with ammonia, lye, or oven cleaner.

Keep matches, lighters, sharp utensils, electrical appliances and cords out of children's reach.

Use extension gripper to reach high places.

Don't store anything attractive to children, such as snacks, above or near the stove.

Turn pot handles inward. Cover frying pans with frying screens or lids.

Keep electrical cords and appliances away from sink and stove. Repair or throw away if even slight shock is felt.

Keep large lid and baking soda next to stove, to put out grease fires.

Garage or basement
Throw away paint- or oil-stained rags, or store in metal containers.

Dispose of combustibles such as newspapers, magazines, boxes, and old furniture.

Keep flammable and volatile liquids in tightly capped safety cans, far from any heat source. Gas fumes travel. Never store gasoline in the home.

Power tools should have double insulation or grounded plugs. Lock away when not in use.

Install extra lighting in work areas, especially where power tools are used.

Make sure ladders are sturdy, have nonslip treads on rungs.

Check that each fuse is proper size; never use any substitute for the proper fuse.

When cooking, tie back long hair and avoid loose sleeves.

Keep paper items, curtains, dish towels, pot holders, plastic utensils away from stove.

If you smell gas, family should leave house immediately; don't use phone, flashlight, or candles. Call fire department from neighbor's house.

Protecting your home

One of the most effective ways to protect your home is with an alarm system. You can install some systems yourself; others are best left to professionals. Ask the crime-prevention officer of your police department for information. Here are some other ways to safeguard your home.

Windows

Stick alarm-system decals, adhesive-backed foil tape (window alarm tape), or beware-of-dog signs on windows—whether or not you have an alarm system or a dog.

Have timers turn certain lights and the radio on and off at staggered times when you're away at night.

Leave radio on during day when you're out.

To substitute for a lock, drill holes at a slightly downward angle through inside sash about three-quarters of the way into outside sash at top corners of lower window. Insert eyebolts or nails into holes.

Install key locks on windows.

Close curtains or blinds and lock all the windows if you're going out.

Place TV's, VCR's, and the like with illuminated parts facing away from window.

Fasten air conditioner securely to window frame or sill so that it can't be pulled out.

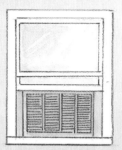

Doors

Solid wood or metal doors should fit snugly into frames.

Give a set of keys to trusted neighbors. Don't hide or hang them outside.

Mount dead-bolt locks securely to doorframes. Cover tumblers with plates.

Replace glass or lightweight panels in doors or install double-cylinder locks with both inside and outside keys. Or cover glass panels with grillwork.

If you have no alarm system, hang battery-operated doorknob alarms on inside doorknobs.

Install lights over doorways. Have house number lit and visible from street.

Ground-floor windows

Consider shatterproof glass for ground-floor windows, or safety gates allowed by fire department.

120

Install wide-angle peephole and chain lock. Have second peephole for children.

Never leave notes on door that indicate you're absent.

Don't install a pet door; a thief may have a child accomplice.

Shrubs and trees

Don't grow trees where they obscure windows or doors.

Keep shrub height below windows and use prickly plants, such as cacti, roses, and holly.

Basement windows

Install steel bar securely midway across basement windows so that intruders can't get through opening. Or install gate or metal grating.

Mailbox

Use only last name on mailbox if you live alone.

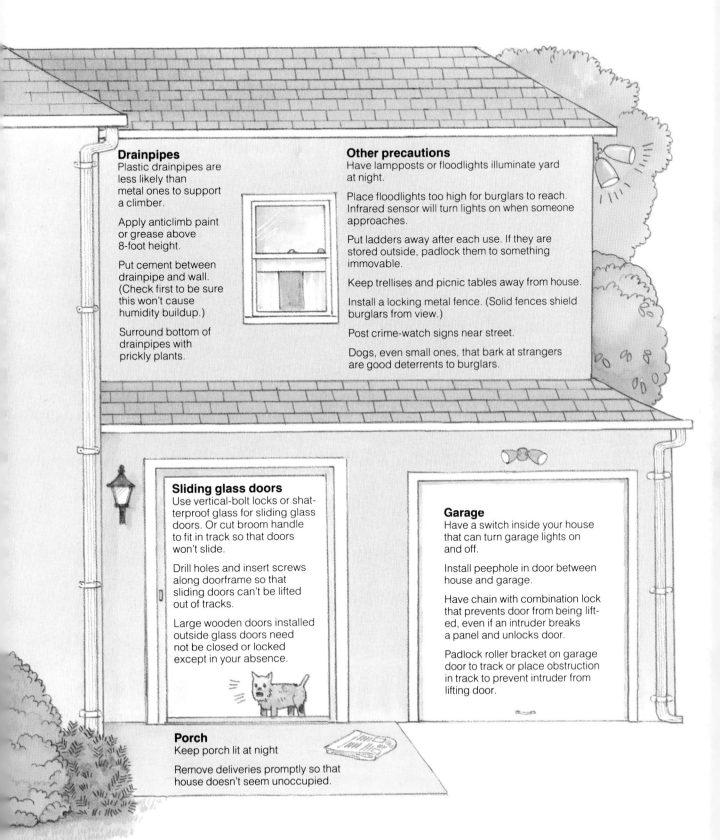

Drainpipes

Plastic drainpipes are less likely than metal ones to support a climber.

Apply anticlimb paint or grease above 8-foot height.

Put cement between drainpipe and wall. (Check first to be sure this won't cause humidity buildup.)

Surround bottom of drainpipes with prickly plants.

Other precautions

Have lampposts or floodlights illuminate yard at night.

Place floodlights too high for burglars to reach. Infrared sensor will turn lights on when someone approaches.

Put ladders away after each use. If they are stored outside, padlock them to something immovable.

Keep trellises and picnic tables away from house.

Install a locking metal fence. (Solid fences shield burglars from view.)

Post crime-watch signs near street.

Dogs, even small ones, that bark at strangers are good deterrents to burglars.

Sliding glass doors

Use vertical-bolt locks or shatterproof glass for sliding glass doors. Or cut broom handle to fit in track so that doors won't slide.

Drill holes and insert screws along doorframe so that sliding doors can't be lifted out of tracks.

Large wooden doors installed outside glass doors need not be closed or locked except in your absence.

Garage

Have a switch inside your house that can turn garage lights on and off.

Install peephole in door between house and garage.

Have chain with combination lock that prevents door from being lifted, even if an intruder breaks a panel and unlocks door.

Padlock roller bracket on garage door to track or place obstruction in track to prevent intruder from lifting door.

Porch

Keep porch lit at night

Remove deliveries promptly so that house doesn't seem unoccupied.

Plant	Light and care	Plant	Light and care
African violet Delicate flowers (white, blue, pink, purple, bicolor) in rosette of leaves.	Diffused light. Add peat moss to soil. Keep pot on wet pebbles. Keep soil moist, not soggy. Clean leaves with lukewarm water; let dry in shade.	**Philodendron, split-leaf** Sectioned glossy leaves are toxic.	Diffused light. Use soil containing humus. Keep soil moist, not soggy. Mist leaves regularly. In spring and summer, feed every month.
Aloe Juice in thin, long, succulent leaves soothes burns but is toxic if ingested.	Maximum light. Use desert-cactus soil mix. Water when soil dries completely, once or twice weekly in summer, once or twice a month in winter.	**Pothos, golden** Heart-shaped, waxy leaves, mottled with yellow. Poisonous if eaten.	Diffused light. Water when soil is nearly dry.
Amaryllis Large flowers (white, pink to red) on stalk with long, thin leaves. Bulb is poisonous.	Maximum or moderate light. Water only during active growth period (midwinter to fall), when soil dries. Feed monthly during this time.	**Rubber plant** Broad oval leaves on tall stalk.	Maximum to diffused light. Keep soil moist, not soggy. Give all-purpose plant food every 6 months. Spray or wash leaves.
Asparagus fern Needlelike leaves on thin, graceful stems.	Moderate light. Keep soil moist, not soggy. In spring and summer, give all-purpose foliage plant food monthly.	**Schefflera** (umbrella tree) Whorls of compound leaves on long stalk.	Moderate or diffused light. Water thoroughly when soil is nearly dry.
Begonia, wax Shiny foliage on fleshy stems. Numerous white, pink, or red flowers.	Maximum to moderate light. Allow soil to become slightly dry between thorough waterings. Feed monthly.	**Snake plant** Long, knife-shaped, leathery leaves grow vertically from the soil.	Maximum to minimum light. Water after soil is nearly dry. Give all-purpose plant food occasionally in spring and summer.
Boston fern Cascading, lush. Various types include those with ruffled and lacy leaflets.	Moderate light in winter, diffused in summer. Use soil containing humus. Keep pot on wet pebbles. Keep soil moist, not soggy.	**Spider plant** Slender leaves, green with white stripes, cascading from rosette; spidery plantlets sprout along shoots.	Diffused light. Keep soil moist, not soggy. Give foliage plant food every 2 months. Plantlets can be cut and rooted.
Coleus Green leaves variously marked with pink, red, orange, and yellow.	Maximum light in winter, moderate in summer. Keep soil moist, not soggy. In spring and summer, give foliage plant food every 2 weeks.	**Thanksgiving cactus** Drooping jointed branches with clawlike notches bear showy pink blooms.	Maximum light, but diffused in summer. Use porous soil. In dormant period, water when soil is dry. During flowering, water after surface soil dries.
Grape ivy Shiny, three-part leaves on climbing vine.	Moderate or diffused light. Keep soil moist, not soggy. Give all-purpose plant food every 2 to 3 months.	**Velvet plant** (purple passion plant) Purple hairs on jagged leaves give fuzzy texture.	Maximum light. Use soil containing humus; keep it moist, not soggy. Give foliage plant food once monthly.
Jade plant Fleshy leaves on branching stems; sometimes has pink or white flowers.	Maximum light. Use desert-cactus soil mix. Water after soil is nearly dry.	**Wandering Jew** Cascading oval leaves are green and silver on top, purple underneath.	Diffused light. Keep soil moist, not soggy. In spring and summer, give foliage plant food once monthly.

Caring for your houseplants

The chart above lists the needs of some of the most popular houseplants. In the *Light and care* column, *maximum* means direct sunlight, as from an unblocked eastern or southern exposure; *moderate* describes sunlight from a western or a blocked eastern or southern exposure; *diffused* light comes from a northern exposure; *minimum* means very low light or shade.

Weapons for weed-haters

☐ When buying grass seed, it's worth paying a higher price for brands with the lowest percentage of weeds. Check labels.

☐ Feed and top-dress your lawn regularly to aid grass growth.

☐ To deny weeds the light they need and to keep grass roots competitive, don't mow until grass has reached a height of 2 to 3 inches.

☐ Douse weeds that grow in the cracks of your walks with boiling water to which you've added salt.

☐ If moss grows in your yard, it's a clue that your lawn needs better drainage, more frequent fertilization, and the addition of lime.

☐ Find out which of your weeds are annual, biennial, and perennial. *Biennials* will die if you pull out the tops. (This is also true of *annuals* in the summer and fall.) *Perennials* must be completely eradicated.

☐ Pull out difficult weeds with pliers; extract small patches with the forked end of a claw hammer.

☐ Where you must weed by hand, wait until just after a rain.

☐ Avoid using weed-killing chemicals where they may also affect ornamental plants. Use your hoe or rake.

☐ If you must use chemicals, wait for a windless day and follow instructions carefully.

☐ Adding lime to the soil discourages such weeds as red sorrel.

☐ Poison ivy clumps can be destroyed with boiling water. Pull out large amounts with a rake. Wash the rake and your hands thoroughly when you're finished.

☐ Some weeds, such as young dandelion greens, lamb's quarters, and purslane, make a tasty salad.

☐ If you own weedy land near your yard, make sure it's mowed at least twice a year. Goats and sheep love weeds but, if not fenced off, will also devour your favorite flowers.

☐ Clover, English daisies, Queen Anne's lace, and other flowering weeds can be decorative. You may not need to rid the entire lawn of them; some gardeners restrict them to a limited area and add them to flower arrangements indoors.

Safety tips for power mowers

Every year thousands of people are injured in lawn mower accidents. To make sure you're not one of them, take the following precautions.

☐ Carefully read and follow safety instructions in your owner's manual. (Some may be printed on the mower.)

☐ Periodically check the machine. Make sure nuts, bolts, and screws are tight, and remove grass, debris, and excessive grease from the engine.

☐ Fill gas tank outdoors while the engine is cold. Stay away from all heat sources (including cigarettes). Immediately wipe up any spills. Replace gas cap securely.

☐ Before mowing, clear the yard of stones, wire, sticks, and other objects that could be picked up and spun out by the blades. Set the blade height for at least 2 to 3 inches. Never run a mower over gravel.

☐ Never wear sneakers or sandals when using a power mower. Safety shoes are best. Avoid loose clothing and jewelry. Tie back long hair.

☐ Make sure the machine is on level ground when you start it. Stand clear of the blades.

☐ Mow only when grass is dry; wet grass can make you fall and can clog the machine.

☐ Allow no one, especially children and animals, in the area where you're working. If someone should approach you, turn off the engine.

☐ Mow across, rather than up or down, a slope. You'll have better control, and if you should slip, you'll be less likely to fall toward the mower. Never make a sharp turn on a slope.

☐ Frequently remove debris from the blades with a stick. First, turn the engine off and wait for the blades to stop. Unplug an electric mower. With a gasoline-powered mower, disconnect the spark plug.

☐ Turn the engine off if you need to leave the mower unattended, even for a few minutes.

☐ Always put the mower away after you use it. Let the engine cool off first.

WALK-BEHIND POWER MOWERS

☐ Buy a mower that has the Outdoor Power Equipment Institute (OPEI) stamp near the chute; this shows that the machine has met certain safety standards.

☐ Once it's running, never raise or tilt the mower.

RIDING MOWERS

☐ Buy a mower certified to meet the 1986 revisions to the American National Standards Institute (ANSI) B71.1 Standard.

☐ Never carry passengers. Look behind you before you back up, to be sure no one has strayed into the area.

☐ Mow slowly and avoid holes and sudden drops, which could cause the machine to overturn.

☐ Be sure the blade is disengaged and the transmission is in *Park* before putting your foot on the ground.

Before you look for a house

DETERMINE YOUR PRICE RANGE

☐ Shop for financing first. The amount of your loan will determine which houses you can consider.

CONSIDER THE NEIGHBORHOOD

☐ Do local zoning laws prohibit any changes you might wish to make? Do they permit commercial development you might not want to live close to?
☐ Are schools, transportation, shopping nearby?
☐ What are the local property, school taxes?

INTERVIEW ATTORNEYS, REALTORS

☐ Is the attorney experienced in handling local real estate transactions?
☐ What services will he provide?
☐ What is his hourly or flat rate?
☐ Will there be additional costs?
☐ Is the real estate agent a realtor? Does she subscribe to the Ethics of the National Association of Realtors? Will she give references?
☐ Remember that the realtor represents the seller; however, she owes the buyer honest disclosure of all known facts about a property.

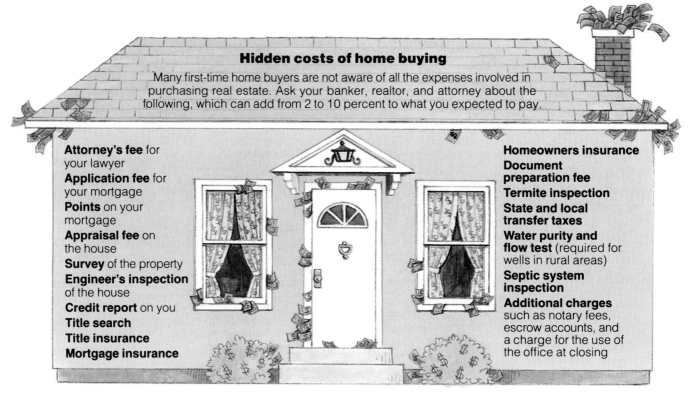

Hidden costs of home buying

Many first-time home buyers are not aware of all the expenses involved in purchasing real estate. Ask your banker, realtor, and attorney about the following, which can add from 2 to 10 percent to what you expected to pay.

Attorney's fee for your lawyer
Application fee for your mortgage
Points on your mortgage
Appraisal fee on the house
Survey of the property
Engineer's inspection of the house
Credit report on you
Title search
Title insurance
Mortgage insurance

Homeowners insurance
Document preparation fee
Termite inspection
State and local transfer taxes
Water purity and flow test (required for wells in rural areas)
Septic system inspection
Additional charges such as notary fees, escrow accounts, and a charge for the use of the office at closing

Paying for your house

Shopping for a mortgage is the most crucial step in the home-buying process. Talk to several banks, and take the list of hidden costs (above) with you. Ask which of them the bank will charge. Generally, each 1 percent of closing costs is equivalent to adding ⅛ percent to the interest rate on your mortgage. As the chart illustrates, even such a "small" increase can add substantially to your monthly payments and leave you with less money to offer for the house you want. (See also *Down payments,* p.66.)

Monthly payments on a fixed 30-year mortgage

Interest rate	$70,000	$80,000	$90,000	$100,000	$110,000	$120,000
16%	941	1,076	1,210	1,345	1,479	1,614
15%	885	1,012	1,138	1,264	1,391	1,517
14%	829	948	1,066	1,185	1,303	1,422
13%	774	885	996	1,106	1,217	1,327
12%	720	823	926	1,029	1,131	1,234
11%	667	762	857	952	1,047	1,143
10%	614	702	790	878	966	1,053
9%	563	644	734	805	885	966
8%	514	587	660	733	807	881

Evaluating a house

Once you know what you can afford and have found a neighborhood you like, you can narrow the field to two or three houses.

☐ Ask yourself, Do I want a house this new (or this old)?

☐ Determine that the house meets your basic space requirements—for example, if you plan a family or want a downstairs bedroom for an elderly parent.

☐ Have a licensed inspector or engineer check the structural soundness of the house and the heating and plumbing systems.

☐ Ask to see the owner's utility bills for the last 12 months.

☐ Ask to see owner's real estate and school tax bills.

☐ Have a termite inspection done if the owner has not.

☐ In rural areas have a plumber inspect the septic system. Have the well water tested for quality and for flow.

☐ Before negotiating the price, find out how much comparable houses in the neighborhood have fetched recently.

If you put your house up

FOR SALE

☐ First decide whether you want to do the work of selling the house yourself or whether you'd rather pay a broker to screen buyers and advertise and show your home.

☐ If you interview a broker, ask: Is she licensed? How does she plan to advertise your house? Will she give you a multiple listing? What price does she suggest for your home?

☐ Your contract with your broker should specifiy your asking price, her fee, and a time limit (often 90 days) for finding a qualified buyer.

☐ You or a professional appraiser must determine what the market is doing and set the right price for your house.

☐ You or your realtor should check with a local lawyer and banks on types of available financing so that you can advise potential buyers.

☐ Have your attorney or realtor prepare a contract that can be offered to a serious buyer on request.

☐ Even after you accept an offer, go on showing your house until the buyer gets financing and signs a contract. If your deal falls through, you'll have other buyers waiting.

Sprucing up

After you decide to sell your house, make it as attractive as possible to potential buyers. Avoid expensive or unusual renovations. Your goal is to make your house look bright, neat, cheerful, and problem-free.

OUTDOORS
☐ Get rid of any clutter in yard.

☐ Mow lawn, weed flower beds, prune shrubs, sweep walks.

☐ Spend about $100 to plant colorful flowers or shrubs where they can be seen from the street.

☐ See that outdoor lighting works.

☐ Have gates, fences painted and in good repair.

☐ Touch up exterior paint where needed. Give special attention to front door, garage door, and woodwork around windows.

☐ See that roof is in good condition.

INDOORS
☐ Put away any clutter. Storing extra furniture makes rooms look more spacious.

☐ Arrange storage areas and closets neatly.

☐ Fix leaky faucets. Remove water or rust stains from sinks and tubs.

☐ Be sure furnace, air conditioning are working smoothly.

☐ Have a spring cleaning: shampoo rugs, wax floors, wash walls and windows, wipe away fingerprints, smudges, dust, mildew.

☐ Replace burned-out or dim bulbs with higher-wattage light bulbs.

☐ Replace tired-looking shower curtains or kitchen curtains.

☐ Glue down any loose wallpaper.

☐ In the kitchen, clear off countertops, wax cabinets, and clean the oven. Replace flooring if it's in very bad condition.

☐ Give your house the "sniff test." To get rid of food odors and pet odors, bake an apple or sprinkle vanilla in a warm oven on days when you're expecting buyers.

Shopping for a used car

Because depreciation is less, used cars cost about 25.5¢ per mile to operate, on average, as opposed to 48.5¢ for a new car. Here are some tips to help you tell the bargains from the lemons.

Shop

for your car loan first. You will save time by knowing which cars you can afford.

Check

the *NADA Used Car Guide*, available at libraries and banks, for the going prices of cars you like. Check frequency-of-repair records in *Consumer Reports*.

The visual inspection

☐ Always wait for a sunny day.

☐ Suspect any cosmetic paint job (check trim, rubber around doors for signs of overpainting).

☐ Reject a car that's rusting badly. Check wheel wells, edges of doors, window trim.

☐ See whether mileage on the odometer matches that on service stickers on the door post.

☐ Examine underside for rust, broken frame, fluid leaks, new welding.

☐ Push down hard on fenders, then let go. If car bounces up and down repeatedly, shocks are worn. Strut-type shocks are costly to replace.

☐ Uneven wear on tires or spare tire may mean wheels need alignment or may indicate serious front-end problems or bad ball joints.

☐ Be sure that windows and doors open and close properly.

☐ Water stains in trunk, around windows, on carpet indicate leaks.

☐ Beware of cars with cracked windshields or headlights; they may not pass state inspections.

☐ Open hood. Check engine block for cracks, oil leaks. Repaired wiring shows previous electrical problem.

☐ Check belts, hoses, cables for wear. Powdery residues on hoses indicate leaks.

☐ Engine oil dipstick should read *Full*. Milky color or flakes in oil indicate serious engine problems.

☐ Open the radiator cap; look at the coolant. If it is rusty or strawberry colored, radiator is corroded.

☐ Turn the ignition on. Do all dashboard lights go on at once? Oil light should go off soon after engine starts if there is good oil pressure.

☐ Check accessories. Do headlights work on both high and low beams? Is parking light OK? Do windshield wipers and turn signals function?

☐ Start the engine; if it clanks when you start it or grinds or knocks when you rev it, reject the car. Blue or black exhaust smoke means the engine burns too much oil.

☐ With the engine warm and idling, pull the automatic transmission dipstick; it should read *Full*. Fluid should be red; if it's dark or smells burned, the car may need costly valve-train repair.

Test-driving a used car

☐ While car is stationary, push the brake pedal briefly. If it sinks to the floor, there may be a leak in the hydraulic system. Don't drive the car.

☐ Map out a route that includes a city street, a parking lot, a bumpy road, a hill, and a freeway.

☐ On a street with little traffic, accelerate to 35 m.p.h. If the gears stick, grind, or jerk, reject the car.

☐ Brake gently and slow down to about 8 m.p.h. Car should not pull to either side; brakes should not squeak or grind.

☐ When no driver is behind you, speed up to 15 m.p.h and brake hard. The car should stop at once without swerving; the brakes shouldn't squeal.

☐ In an empty parking lot, test the transmission by shifting into *Reverse*, braking to a stop, shifting into *First*, braking at about 4 m.p.h., and shifting into *Reverse* again. Car should run smoothly.

☐ Make some sharp right, left, and U turns. A car that doesn't handle well may have a faulty front suspension or steering linkage.

Don't

onfine your shopping to used-car lots. Check trade-ins at new-car dealers as well as owners' ads, especially those from affluent suburbs.

Best buys

are usually cars 3 years old or newer that have been driven no more than 10,000 to 15,000 miles annually.

Avoid

convertibles and luxury cars, which won't be bargains. Small and medium sedans are easier to maintain and repair.

☐ At 20 m.p.h. remove hands from the wheel; after a minute, brake smoothly. If car didn't keep a steady course, have mechanic check the front end.

☐ On a bumpy road, notice if the car sways, bounces, or shimmies and shakes. If it does, don't buy it.

☐ At a hill, accelerate to 40 m.p.h. to see if the engine labors, indicating a faulty automatic transmission.

☐ Stop halfway down a hill, shift into *Neutral*, and set the parking brake. Does the parking brake hold when you remove your foot?

☐ At a freeway, wait till way is clear, then pull on rapidly. If the engine doesn't accelerate smoothly to 55 m.p.h. in about 15 seconds, or if smoke comes from the tailpipe, the car may need expensive repairs.

☐ Make sure you can pass other cars easily.

☐ At the end of the test drive, let the engine idle a few minutes before shutting it off. Raise the hood and look for leaks or seepage.

☐ Examine the ground under the car. There should be no fluid drips except from the air conditioning, which normally drips clear water.

Before you make an offer

If a car has passed your visual inspection and test drive and you want to make an offer, here are some final steps to take.

☐ Get the name of a reliable diagnostic center, service station, or mechanic from friends or the American Automobile Association. The mechanic should do the following:

1. Perform a compression test and a cylinder power-balance test.

2. See that the exhaust passes state standards for emissions. (Otherwise you may have to spend hundreds of dollars refitting it.)

3. Tell you if the car is missing any parts and estimate the cost of any needed repairs. (Deduct repair costs from the asking price of the car.)

☐ If you're buying a car that costs $2,000 or more from a dealer, get a drivetrain guarantee that covers all parts and labor and runs for at least 30 days.

☐ If buying from a private owner, ask a dealer whether a technical service bulletin has ever been issued for that car model. (Such bulletins are the next step to a recall.)

☐ Call the National Highway Traffic Safety Administration hot line (1-800-424-9393) and ask if the car model was ever the subject of a recall. If so, ask owner or dealer for proof that the recall work was done.

☐ Remember to check that the car's ID numbers and engine number match those on its papers. If you suspect the seller, ask the police to run a stolen car check. A stolen car can be reclaimed by its owner.

Coping with car noises

Sound	Possible problem	Solution	Sound	Possible problem	Solution
Backfiring	Incorrect ignition timing; faulty ignition parts or valves	Have a mechanic check ignition and valve timing	Hiss	Leak in tires, hoses, or exhaust system	Check tires or see a mechanic
Buzz	Loose dashboard or heater components	Tighten accessible clamps or screws	Moan when steering	Power steering fluid level is too low	Check fluid level; add fluid if needed
Clatter from engine	Insufficient oil level. Defective valves or lifters	Check oil level or see a mechanic	Rattle when engine accelerates	Wrong grade of fuel or engine needs tuning	Try higher octane gas or get a tune-up
Clatter under car with rear-wheel drive	Faulty U-joints	See a mechanic	Roar as car accelerates	Rusted-out muffler or exhaust pipes	Have exhaust system inspected without delay
Clicking under hood	Fan blade may be striking radiator	Check fan and radiator for damage	Screech when braking	Worn or defective brake parts	Have brakes checked
Clicking from wheels	Loose hubcap or stone under hubcap. Bad wheel bearing	Check for stones. If none, see a mechanic	Squealing as car accelerates	An engine accessory drive belt is loose	Tighten or replace drive belt
			Squealing as wheels turn	Power steering drive belt is loose	Tighten or replace drive belt

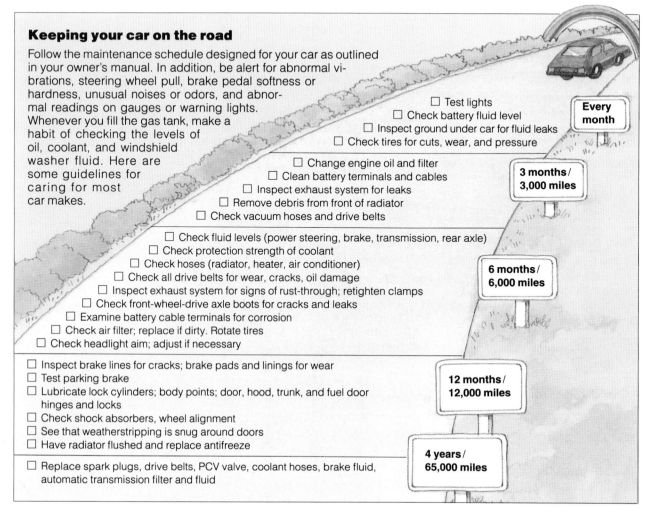

Keeping your car on the road

Follow the maintenance schedule designed for your car as outlined in your owner's manual. In addition, be alert for abnormal vibrations, steering wheel pull, brake pedal softness or hardness, unusual noises or odors, and abnormal readings on gauges or warning lights. Whenever you fill the gas tank, make a habit of checking the levels of oil, coolant, and windshield washer fluid. Here are some guidelines for caring for most car makes.

☐ Test lights
☐ Check battery fluid level
☐ Inspect ground under car for fluid leaks
☐ Check tires for cuts, wear, and pressure

Every month

☐ Change engine oil and filter
☐ Clean battery terminals and cables
☐ Inspect exhaust system for leaks
☐ Remove debris from front of radiator
☐ Check vacuum hoses and drive belts

3 months / 3,000 miles

☐ Check fluid levels (power steering, brake, transmission, rear axle)
☐ Check protection strength of coolant
☐ Check hoses (radiator, heater, air conditioner)
☐ Check all drive belts for wear, cracks, oil damage
☐ Inspect exhaust system for signs of rust-through; retighten clamps
☐ Check front-wheel-drive axle boots for cracks and leaks
☐ Examine battery cable terminals for corrosion
☐ Check air filter; replace if dirty. Rotate tires
☐ Check headlight aim; adjust if necessary

6 months / 6,000 miles

☐ Inspect brake lines for cracks; brake pads and linings for wear
☐ Test parking brake
☐ Lubricate lock cylinders; body points; door, hood, trunk, and fuel door hinges and locks
☐ Check shock absorbers, wheel alignment
☐ See that weatherstripping is snug around doors
☐ Have radiator flushed and replace antifreeze

12 months / 12,000 miles

☐ Replace spark plugs, drive belts, PCV valve, coolant hoses, brake fluid, automatic transmission filter and fluid

4 years / 65,000 miles

If you're in an accident

1. Stop as soon as you safely can. Check for injuries to yourself and to any passengers or pedestrians.

2. Call the police; request an ambulance if someone is hurt.

3. Write down the names, addresses, and telephone numbers of all those involved, including passengers and witnesses. Note if anyone was injured.

4. In addition, get the other car's license plate number, the driver's license number, the name and address of his insurance company, and his policy number.

5. Make a note of the time, weather, and road conditions.

6. Take snapshots or make a diagram of the accident scene. Be sure to show the automobiles involved, the directions in which they were moving, any skid marks, and nearby road signs or traffic lights.

7. When a police officer arrives, get his name and badge number. Make every effort to cooperate, but try to limit your remarks about how the accident occurred. Ask for a copy of the accident report.

8. Don't sign any statements.

9. If you are taken to a hospital, write down its name and the names of all the doctors who treat you, in addition to their diagnoses. Even if you don't think you're hurt, consider going to your own doctor to get an evaluation.

10. Write down your impressions of the event as soon as you get home. Keep a journal afterward to note any additional recollections or medical symptoms in case you ever need to testify.

11. Notify your insurance company as soon as possible; ask how to proceed, and especially how to fill out an accident report.

Don't get taken for a ride

☐ Shop around for a reliable local mechanic and repair facility *before* you have an emergency.

☐ Ask your friends and neighbors (especially those with older cars that run well) for recommendations.

☐ Ask local used-car dealers which garages they use.

☐ Having small problems taken care of before they become big problems is a good practice and helps you assess the general reliability of a shop.

☐ Make a written list of your car's symptoms and give it to the service writer or, preferably, directly to the mechanic. (Keep a copy for your own reference.)

☐ Don't ask for a specific repair unless you're absolutely sure about the nature of the problem. You may end up paying for a repair you didn't need.

☐ If you don't feel that you can accurately describe what's wrong, ask the mechanic to go with you for a test drive.

☐ Insist on a detailed written estimate and the guarantee that no additional work will be done without your permission. Leave a phone number where you can be reached.

☐ When you pick up the repaired car, it's a good idea to test-drive it before you take it home.

☐ Request an itemized bill and a receipt in case the problem wasn't solved and you have to return the car for further adjustment.

☐ When possible, pay for repairs with a credit card.

☐ Should a problem develop that can't be resolved by negotiation, refuse to pay that amount on the credit card bill.

☐ Promptly write to your credit card company. Tell them that the amount is in dispute and give them details explaining the situation.

Packing light

Want to avoid long waits at the baggage counter or, worse yet, lost luggage? Try to pack everything into carry-on bags. (Women can also fit some items into a large handbag.) Wear your heaviest clothes; wear layers unless it's too hot. Here's a checklist to help you choose which items you really need.

CLOTHES
- ☐ Walking shoes
- ☐ Dress shoes
- ☐ Sweater
- ☐ Waterproof jacket or raincoat
- ☐ Socks (can double as slippers)
- ☐ Nightwear that can double as robe
- ☐ Two skirts, preferably reversible
- ☐ Jeans or shorts
- ☐ Three shirts or blouses (T-shirt can double as undershirt and beach covering)
- ☐ Bathing suit, reversible if possible
- ☐ Underwear

TOILETRIES AND OTHER ITEMS
- ☐ Medications and prescriptions
- ☐ Extra eyeglasses or a prescription
- ☐ Sunglasses
- ☐ Folding umbrella
- ☐ First-aid items
- ☐ Toothpaste and toothbrush
- ☐ Dental floss
- ☐ Shampoo, soap, deodorant, cosmetics, sunscreen in small plastic travel containers

OPTIONAL
- ☐ Laundry detergent in travel-size packets
- ☐ Paperbacks
- ☐ Magazines
- ☐ Camera and film
- ☐ Travel alarm
- ☐ Small cassette player or radio
- ☐ Travel-size hair dryer

A car survival kit

Keep the following items on hand to ensure that you and your family are safe and comfortable on automobile trips.

IN THE GLOVE COMPARTMENT
- ☐ Owner's manual
- ☐ Registration
- ☐ Insurance card
- ☐ Auto club ID
- ☐ Emergency phone numbers
- ☐ Coins for tolls and telephone
- ☐ Paper and pen
- ☐ Maps

FOR YOUR COMFORT
- ☐ Tissues
- ☐ Trash bag
- ☐ Bottle opener
- ☐ Sunglasses
- ☐ Air cushion

FOR REPAIRS AND CLEANUPS
- ☐ Jumper cables
- ☐ Spare tire
- ☐ Jack and lug wrench
- ☐ Tire pressure gauge
- ☐ Instant tire inflator
- ☐ Small fire extinguisher (UL approved)
- ☐ Tool kit—including pocketknife, pliers, magnetic screwdrivers, adjustable wrench
- ☐ Duct or electrical tape
- ☐ Flares
- ☐ Reflective warning triangle
- ☐ Waterproof flashlight
- ☐ Gallon of water
- ☐ Paper towels, rags

IN WINTER
- ☐ Blankets
- ☐ Nonperishable snack
- ☐ Ice scraper
- ☐ Can of de-icer

- ☐ Windshield washer fluid
- ☐ Shovel
- ☐ Bag of sand or road salt
- ☐ Snow chains or traction clamps
- ☐ Rugs or traction mats
- ☐ Empty gasoline can
- ☐ Portable CB radio

FOR TRIPS IN REMOTE AREAS
- ☐ Brake fluid
- ☐ Motor oil
- ☐ Power steering fluid
- ☐ Transmission fluid
- ☐ Drive belt
- ☐ Fuses, fuse puller
- ☐ Fuel filter
- ☐ Tire pump
- ☐ Tire repair kit
- ☐ Flexible copper electrical wire
- ☐ Gallon of drinking water
- ☐ Nonperishable foods (candy bars, dried fruit, nuts)
- ☐ First-aid kit

Traveling on a budget

Transportation costs and hotel bills are not the only major expenses an average traveler encounters. Here are a few ideas for saving money on your next trip.

☐ Try the tourist information office for package deals and discount tickets to various events.

☐ Movie theaters often sell tickets at a discount on certain days and at certain hours; so do many museums that require admission.

☐ Peruse local newspapers to find free or inexpensive museums, concerts, walking tours, and other attractions. Local events are also an enjoyable way to meet people.

☐ Avoid restaurant bills by preparing delicious picnics. Explore local markets and buy bread, cheese, vegetables, fruit, and regional delicacies. Then have a lovely meal in your room or in a park.

☐ Pack an immersion heater for making soups and hot drinks.

☐ When you do eat at a restaurant, make lunch your main meal—it's usually cheaper than dinner. Have a snack or picnic for supper.

☐ Department stores often have inexpensive lunch counters.

☐ Look for popular neighborhood cafés rather than dining at hotel restaurants, which tend to be more expensive and duller.

☐ Avoid making many telephone calls from your hotel, which will often add exorbitant surcharges. Whenever possible, call only to give your number and have the person call you back.

☐ When shopping abroad, it is often appropriate—even expected—to haggle with a vendor. If you're unsure, offer to pay about half the stated price and observe how the vendor reacts.

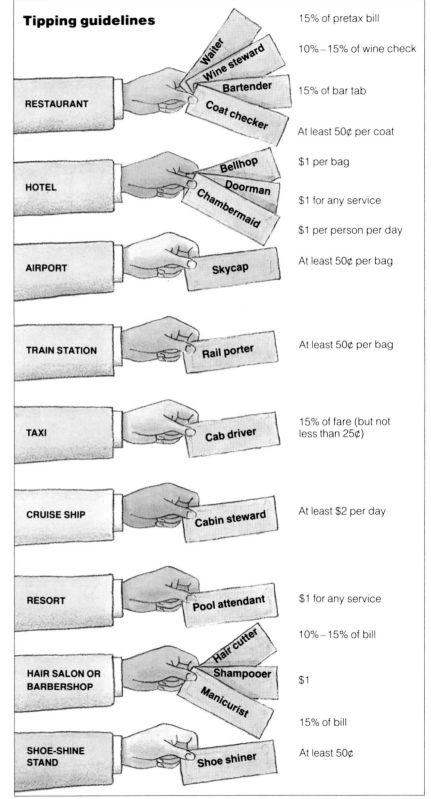

Tipping guidelines

RESTAURANT — Waiter	15% of pretax bill
Wine steward	10%–15% of wine check
Bartender	15% of bar tab
Coat checker	At least 50¢ per coat
HOTEL — Bellhop	$1 per bag
Doorman	$1 for any service
Chambermaid	$1 per person per day
AIRPORT — Skycap	At least 50¢ per bag
TRAIN STATION — Rail porter	At least 50¢ per bag
TAXI — Cab driver	15% of fare (but not less than 25¢)
CRUISE SHIP — Cabin steward	At least $2 per day
RESORT — Pool attendant	$1 for any service
HAIR SALON OR BARBERSHOP — Hair cutter	10%–15% of bill
Shampooer	$1
Manicurist	15% of bill
SHOE-SHINE STAND — Shoe shiner	At least 50¢

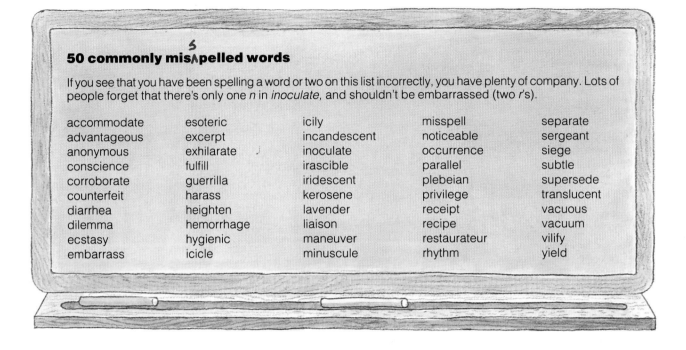

50 commonly misspelled words

If you see that you have been spelling a word or two on this list incorrectly, you have plenty of company. Lots of people forget that there's only one *n* in *inoculate,* and shouldn't be embarrassed (two *r*'s).

accommodate	esoteric	icily	misspell	separate
advantageous	excerpt	incandescent	noticeable	sergeant
anonymous	exhilarate	inoculate	occurrence	siege
conscience	fulfill	irascible	parallel	subtle
corroborate	guerrilla	iridescent	plebeian	supersede
counterfeit	harass	kerosene	privilege	translucent
diarrhea	heighten	lavender	receipt	vacuous
dilemma	hemorrhage	liaison	recipe	vacuum
ecstasy	hygienic	maneuver	restaurateur	vilify
embarrass	icicle	minuscule	rhythm	yield

Misused words and phrases

Some words are easy to confuse with others, often because of similar spellings or pronunciations. The following may help you to use *le mot juste* (see *Foreign flavors,* opposite).

All right is the correct form, not *alright.*

All together, altogether. *All together* means all at the same time. *Altogether* means entirely.

Between you and me. Never "between you and I." The preposition *between* requires an object—hence, *me.*

Canvas, canvass. Canvas is the heavy fabric; to solicit something, such as votes, is to canvass.

Cement, concrete. Cement is powdered rock and clay; mixed with water and gravel, it forms concrete.

Climactic, climatic. *Climactic* refers to a climax. If you're talking about the weather, it's *climatic.*

Cohort. A cohort is a band of people; the word is often misused to mean an individual companion.

Comptroller, controller. A comptroller is usually a governmental financial officer; a controller is a business financial officer. They're pronounced the same way— "controller."

Could care less. Often used erroneously. To express a total lack of concern, use *couldn't care less.*

Differ from, differ with. One thing differs from another. Two people who disagree about something differ with each other.

Disinterested, uninterested. A disinterested person is unbiased, impartial. An uninterested person is unconcerned, bored.

Faze, phase. *Faze,* meaning to disrupt or bother, should not be confused with *phase,* which is a stage.

Gibe, jibe. To gibe is to ridicule. To jibe is to move a sail or boom to the other side of the boat, to change the direction of a boat, or, more commonly, to agree ("The numbers don't jibe").

Incredible, incredulous. Something that's incredible is not believable; a person who's incredulous is disbelieving or skeptical.

Jail, prison. A jail confines those awaiting trial or sentencing and those convicted of misdemeanors and civil offenses. A prison confines those convicted of felonies.

Noisome, noisy. *Noisome* means offensive; it has nothing to do with the words *noisy* or *loud.*

Prone, supine. If you're lying down with your face up, you're supine, but if your face is down, you're prone.

Tortuous, torturous. *Tortuous* means winding, like a tortuous road. *Torturous* means painful, like torture.

Troop, troupe. A troop is a group; a troupe is a company, usually referring to actors ("troupers").

Foreign flavors

An advantage of living in the American "melting pot" is that foreign words flavor our conversations and writings like exotic spices. At the left are some examples from German, French, Latin, and Yiddish; can you match them with their English definitions?

1. pièce de résistance ___
2. crème de la crème ___
3. modus operandi ___
4. je ne sais quoi ___
5. mise-en-scène ___
6. caveat emptor ___
7. chef d'oeuvre ___
8. comme il faut ___
9. coup de grâce ___
10. fait accompli ___
11. wunderkind ___
12. tour de force ___
13. trompe l'oeil ___
14. raison d'être ___
15. roman à clef ___
16. cri de coeur ___
17. pied-à-terre ___
18. au courant ___
19. succès fou ___
20. bon vivant ___
21. pro forma ___
22. mot juste ___
23. idée fixe ___
24. mensch ___
25. tant pis ___
26. de trop ___

A. The blow bringing death to one who is mortally wounded; any finishing stroke

B. An illusion created so that the viewer may think the representation is reality, such as a window painted on a brick wall

C. Something already done and probably irreversible

D. Chief dish at a meal; most outstanding item in a group or series, especially in art

E. An obsession, a firmly lodged idea not subject to modification

F. The word or phrase that is precisely correct

G. Up-to-date, aware of current events

H. A person who enjoys living well

I. Appropriate or proper; applies especially to behavior or dress

J. A heartfelt plea or protest

K. Excessive, superfluous

L. Hard to define or describe

M. Arrangement of actors in a play or film; an environment

N. Method of doing something; in police jargon, known as a criminal's M.O.

O. An honorable, responsible person

P. According to or as a matter of form

Q. The purpose of a thing or action

R. A novel with real persons or events thinly disguised

S. A second or temporary home

T. An exceptionally skillful act

U. Let the buyer beware

V. An unusual, total success

W. So much the worse

X. The best of its kind

Y. Child prodigy

Z. Masterpiece

Key
1-D, 2-X, 3-N, 4-L, 5-M, 6-U, 7-Z, 8-I, 9-A, 10-C, 11-Y, 12-T, 13-B, 14-Q, 15-R, 16-J, 17-S, 18-G, 19-V, 20-H, 21-P, 22-F, 23-E, 24-O, 25-W, 26-K

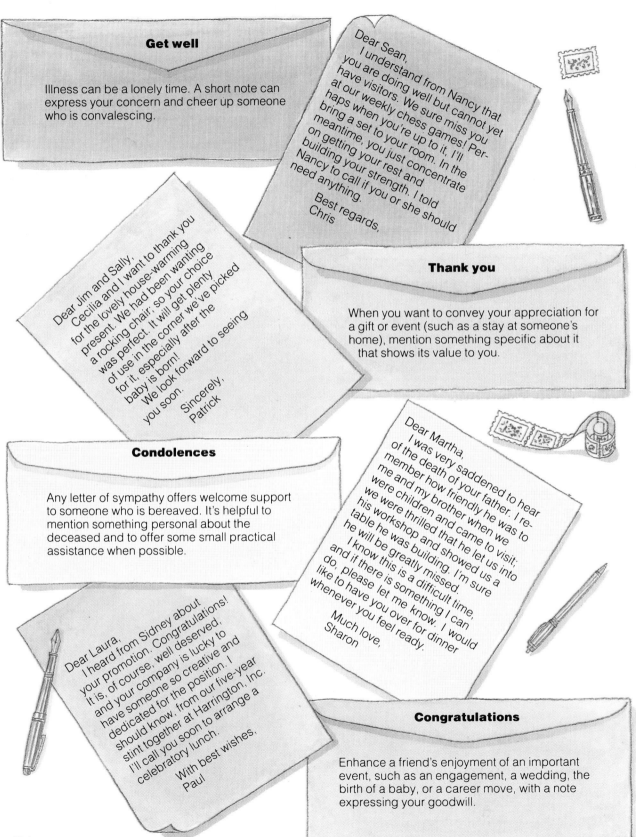

Get well

Illness can be a lonely time. A short note can express your concern and cheer up someone who is convalescing.

Dear Sean,
I understand from Nancy that you are doing well but cannot yet have visitors. We sure miss you at our weekly chess games! Perhaps when you're up to it, I'll bring a set to your room. In the meantime, you just concentrate on getting your rest and building your strength. I told Nancy to call if you or she should need anything.
Best regards,
Chris

Dear Jim and Sally,
Cecilia and I want to thank you for the lovely house-warming present. We had been wanting a rocking chair; so your choice was perfect. It will get plenty of use in the corner we've picked for it, especially after the baby is born! We look forward to seeing you soon.
Sincerely,
Patrick

Thank you

When you want to convey your appreciation for a gift or event (such as a stay at someone's home), mention something specific about it that shows its value to you.

Condolences

Any letter of sympathy offers welcome support to someone who is bereaved. It's helpful to mention something personal about the deceased and to offer some small practical assistance when possible.

Dear Martha,
I was very saddened to hear of the death of your father. I remember how friendly he was to me and my brother when we were children and came to visit; we were thrilled that he let us into his workshop and showed us a table he was building. I'm sure he will be greatly missed. I know this is a difficult time, and if there is something I can do, please let me know. I would like to have you over for dinner whenever you feel ready.
Much love,
Sharon

Dear Laura,
I heard from Sidney about your promotion. Congratulations! It is, of course, well deserved; and your company is lucky to have someone so creative and dedicated for the position. I should know, from our five-year stint together at Harrington, Inc. I'll call you soon to arrange a celebratory lunch.
With best wishes,
Paul

Congratulations

Enhance a friend's enjoyment of an important event, such as an engagement, a wedding, the birth of a baby, or a career move, with a note expressing your goodwill.

284

3. COMMON THINGS WITH UNCOMMON USES

IF YOU HATE TO THROW THINGS AWAY, IF YOU DELIGHT IN DREAMING UP NEW WAYS TO USE ORDINARY HOUSEHOLD ITEMS, YOU'LL WELCOME THE SUGGESTIONS IN THIS SECTION. AND YOU'LL BE AMAZED AT THE PROBLEMS YOU CAN SOLVE AT THE SAME TIME. OUR LIST IS BY NO MEANS COMPLETE. SO LOOK AROUND YOUR HOME AND SEE HOW MANY CLEVER USES YOU CAN DEVISE FOR OBJECTS THAT YOU ONCE DISMISSED AS USELESS.

Air compressors

1. Broom. Use blasts of air to clear dirt and leaves from the garage floor, driveway, and sidewalks.

2. Film cleaner. Rather than scratch a slide or negative with a cloth or brush, blow dust off the surface.

3. Air pump. With an adapter, you can blow up balloons and inflatable toys, rafts, and lounges.

4. Spark plug cleaner. To prevent dirt from getting into cylinders, blow air around spark plug holes before you remove the plugs. As a precautionary measure, wear safety goggles and a face mask while working.

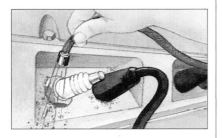

5. Dust and dirt remover. Blow out dust and crumbs from hard-to-reach places. (Place a wet towel behind to catch the dust.)

6. Pesticide sprayer. Use the paint sprayer attachment to apply insecticide or herbicide to plants. Clean all parts thoroughly right after use.

7. Workshop cleaner. Blow sawdust around the workshop into an easily swept-up pile. As a precautionary measure, wear safety goggles and a face mask while working.

Alcohol

1. Pepper neutralizer. If your hands burn and sting after handling hot peppers, pour rubbing alcohol over them.

2. Windowsill cleaner. If your wooden windowsills are rain spotted or discolored, refresh them by wiping them with a little diluted rubbing alcohol on a soft cloth.

3. Bathroom cleaner. Keep a bottle of rubbing alcohol handy to shine chrome fixtures and to remove hair spray from the mirrors.

4. Knickknack polish. Carefully clean crystal and porcelain ornaments with a cloth dampened with rubbing alcohol.

Aluminum foil

1. Sun box. Remove the top and one side from a cardboard box; line the other three sides with aluminum foil. Place plants in the box and set it near a window—the foil will reflect light, helping the stems to grow straight instead of bent toward the sun.

2. Heat reflector. Conserve energy by taping heavy-duty foil to insulation board and placing it behind radiators and baseboard convectors.

3. Foot warmer. Cover heated stones with foil, wrap them in a towel, and place them at the bottom of your sleeping bag to warm your feet while camping in cold weather.

4. Funnel. Roll a double thickness of heavy-duty foil into a cone shape.

5. Wallpaper. Cut foil into 1-foot squares; coat one side with wallpaper paste and apply in a haphazard, overlapping fashion.

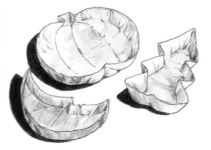

6. Specialty cake pans. Make a teddy bear birthday cake, Valentine heart cake, Christmas tree cake, or whatever shape cake you wish by forming a double thickness of heavy-duty foil into the desired contour within a large cake pan.

7. Fishing lure. Wrap foil around a hook or safety pin. Fringe the foil so that it covers the hook and wiggles as the line is reeled in.

8. Reflector. Glue foil to a mat board or heavy cardboard to make a reflector for photography. Make three identical panels and hinge or tape them together so that the reflector stands upright and is easy to carry.

9. Platter. Make a convenient disposable dish for picnics by covering a piece of cardboard with heavy-duty aluminum foil.

10. Decorating tube. Instead of a pastry bag, use a tube of heavy-duty foil filled with free-flowing frosting.

11. Paint masking. Crimp around doorknobs and wall phones before beginning to paint; remove when the walls are dry.

Ammonia

1. Furniture renewer. If an old piece of furniture is heavily stained, rub it with a cloth dampened with full-strength ammonia; when the cloth gets dirty, rinse it in water and reuse.

2. Wax remover. Before waxing a very dirty resilient floor, remove the old polish with a solution of 1 cup ammonia in 1 gallon water.

3. Jewelry cleaner. Soak gold jewelry in equal parts ammonia and lukewarm water for 10 minutes; rub with a soft brush and let dry without rinsing.

4. Silverware polish. Here's a quick way to a brighter shine: combine ammonia with paste polish and apply with a soft cloth to your silver-plated and stainless-steel cutlery.

5. Brass beautifier. Remove tarnish from solid brass by scrubbing it lightly with a soft brush dampened with a little ammonia.

6. Oil remover. When laundering sheets, towels, and clothes, remove absorbed body oils by adding 1 cup ammonia to the usual amount of granular detergent. (Do not use ammonia with chlorine bleach.)

Aprons

1. Bib. Tie an apron around your youngster's neck for an instant bib.

2. Portable cash box. Turn up the bottom of an apron and stitch five pockets so that you can wear your cash box around your waist during your garage sale, keeping your coins

and bills separated and safe from theft. Or sew some extra pockets into a carpenter's apron.

3. Ladder tool pocket. An efficient way to hold your tools while working on a ladder is to tack or staple a carpenter's apron to the top step.

Ashes

1. Fertilizer. Don't discard wood ashes; sprinkle them onto the compost pile or work them into your soil in the spring—but not around acid-loving plants, such as rhododendrons and azaleas. (Store ashes in a covered metal container, well away from buildings and flammable material; even long-dead ashes harbor hot embers that sometimes burst into flame.)

2. Glare reducer. Cut the glare and ultraviolet radiation reflected behind your sunglasses—moisten your fingertip with oil, dip it in ashes, and apply a dark line under your eyes.

3. Halloween makeup. For that ghoulish look, rub ashes all over the face and arms.

4. Pewter prettifier. Moisten sifted ashes with water and rub on pewter with a soft cloth.

5. Grease cutter. When camping or barbecuing, soak greasy pans and utensils in ashes mixed with water or make a thick ash-and-water paste for scrubbing.

6. Pest repellent. To discourage slugs and snails, build low ridges of wood ash around plants and between row crops.

Aspirin tins

1. Sewing box organizer. A neat way to store snaps, sequins, buttons, and beads is in individual aspirin tins in your sewing box. Label the lids or glue on a sample of the contents for easy identification.

2. Stamp saver. Prevent stamps from sticking together by storing them in an aspirin tin.

3. Emergency sewing kit. Keep a tin fitted with needle and thread in your purse or pocket for on-the-spot repairs.

4. Birthday keepsake. Decorate the outside of a tin, line it with felt or silk, and insert a penny from the birth year of your friend.

5. Broken-jewelry box. Keep all the little pieces safe and together in an aspirin tin.

6. Tangle preventer. Keep necklaces separate and untangled in their own individual tins.

7. Workshop helper. The tins are great for storing brads, glazing points, setscrews, lock washers, and other small items.

8. Earring keeper. Prevent pairs of small earrings from straying; store them together in aspirin tins.

9. Mini safe. Hide the keys to desks and lockboxes—it's unlikely that a thief will suspect an innocent-looking aspirin tin in your medicine chest.

10. Fuse cache. You'll always know where your spare car fuses are if you store them in an aspirin tin in the glove compartment.

Baking pans

1. Dustpan. Cut out one side of an old cake pan with a coping saw. If you want a handle, drill two holes through the opposite side and bolt onto an old broomstick.

2. Utility tray. Here's a good way to store nuts, bolts, nails, screws, and other workshop materials: bolt a heavy-duty muffin tin to the underside of a bench or shelf by one corner, using a washer as a spacer, so that the pan can be swung out as needed. Or attach cleats under your workbench or shelf to serve as runners for the rim of the muffin tin.

3. Serving tray. Avoid spills—use a muffin tin to carry cold drinks.

4. Corn catcher. Rest the stem end of an ear of corn in the center of a tube pan; as you slide your knife down the cob, the kernels will fall into the pan.

5. Plant holder. Place a tube pan in the center of your umbrella table and use it to hold cut flowers or decorative shade plants.

6. Water bowl. Does your dog make a habit of overturning its backyard water bowl? Drive a stake into the ground through the center hole of a tube pan to keep it upright.

Baking soda

1. Dishwasher deodorant. If you use your dishwasher less than once a day, toss a handful of baking soda into the bottom between washes.

2. Wallpaper washer. Remove resistant smudges from wallpaper by rubbing them with a thick baking powder paste. (Test first in an inconspicuous corner.)

3. Furniture blancher. To spruce up white painted furniture, wash it with a solution of 1 tablespoon baking soda in 1 quart warm water.

4. Grill scourer. To remove grease and encrusted food from the rack, soak it in a solution of ¼ cup baking soda per quart of warm water. For tough stains, put baking soda on a damp sponge and scrub.

5. Dog shampoo. To add softness and luster to your pet's coat, put 2 tablespoons baking soda in its bathwater. Baking soda also works well as a dry shampoo for your dog.

6. Sting salve. A paste of baking soda and water will ease the discomfort of bee stings.

7. Battery saver. Eliminate acid build-up on car battery terminals—apply a paste of 3 parts baking soda and 1 part water with a toothbrush; rinse with water and wipe dry. Wear safety goggles and rubber gloves to protect eyes and hands.

8. Skin emollient. For softer, smoother skin, add ½ cup baking soda to your bathwater.

Balloons

1. Party invitations. Inflate brightly colored balloons, then write out your invitations—very carefully—with a contrasting felt-tip pen. Deflate the balloons, put them in envelopes, seal, and mail to your guests; in order to read your message, they'll have to re-inflate them.

2. Mold. Use a balloon as a mold for a papier-mâché piñata or mask.

Banana peels

1. Fertilizer. Bury peels no more than 1 inch deep around rosebushes. If you have any more, add them to your garden's compost pile; they are an excellent source of phosphorus and potassium.

2. Wildlife food. Place banana peels in an empty birdbath in winter as forage for deer.

3. Emergency shoe shine. For a spur-of-the-moment job, rub your leather shoes with the inside of the peel; then clean and buff with a paper towel or napkin.

Banks

1. Paperweight. Fill with pennies and place atop papers to keep them from flying away.

2. Doorstop. A coin-filled bank in front of a door will prevent it from blowing shut.

3. String dispenser. Place a small ball of string inside the bank and slip its tail through the slot.

Bar stools

1. Work stand. For access to all sides when painting or working with clay, set the piece on a swiveling bar stool.

2. High chair. A stool with a back can serve as a toddler's high chair; use a belt to secure the child.

3. Side table. Drape a circular tablecloth over a backless bar stool; top with a sheet of glass.

4. Plant stand. Paint a wooden stool and place a vining plant on top.

5. Barber chair. Seat your child on a bar stool to cut his hair.

6. Tomato cage. Remove the seat; push the legs into the soil and wrap them with strong twine to support small tomato plants.

7. Lazy susan. Place small serving bowls filled with snacks, appetizers, or condiments on a revolving bar stool at a buffet.

8. Jack rest. Remove the seat and keep it in the trunk to use as a jack rest when your car is on soft ground.

Beer

1. Setting lotion. Comb some through your hair before styling it.

2. Insect lure. When entertaining outdoors, set open beer containers around the perimeter of the yard; stinging insects, such as yellow jackets, will be attracted to the beer rather than to you and your guests.

3. Marinade. To increase flavor and tenderness, marinate inexpensive cuts of meat in beer for an hour or so before cooking.

Belts

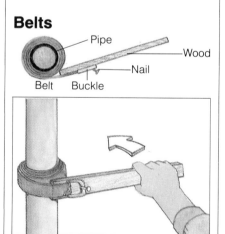

Pipe · Wood · Nail · Belt · Buckle

1. Strap wrench. Wrap a belt around a pipe or handle as shown and pull it tight; hook the belt buckle on a nail driven into a 1 x 2 or a 2 x 3, then exert leverage with the wood.

2. Luggage guard. Wrap an old belt around a suitcase and through its handle; buckle it to protect against rough handling or faulty latches.

3. Laundry carrier. Sort the laundry and bundle each load with a belt for carrying to the launderette.

4. Strop. Keep a leather belt in the kitchen for sharpening knives.

5. Book strap. An old belt can lash books together and provide a carrying handle as well; punch new holes if necessary.

6. Organizer. Nail a belt to the wall in several places, leaving loops large enough to hold tools or utensils.

7. Sling. Run a belt through a sturdy jacket sleeve, pull the sleeve on over the splinted forearm, run the belt around the back of the victim's neck, and buckle on the side.

8. Pet collar. Cut a belt to the correct length, punch new holes as needed, and add a metal ring to the buckle to attach identification and license tags.

Berry baskets

1. Orchid planter. Line a plastic mesh basket with sphagnum moss, add a little potting soil, plant an orchid, and hang with monofilament or yarn.

2. Plant protector. Invert a basket and secure it firmly over small seedlings and plants to protect them from rabbits and squirrels.

3. Bulb cage. To foil rodents, set a mesh basket in a garden bed at the correct depth, place bulbs inside, and cover with soil.

4. Easter basket. Attach a pipe cleaner for a handle and fill with shredded paper "grass."

5. Bow saver. When mailing a gift, protect the bow with an inverted basket.

6. String dispenser. Place twine inside two baskets, tie them together, and pull the twine through a hole.

7. Breadbasket. Cover the inside with aluminum foil or a napkin and serve bread or rolls in it.

8. Bubble maker. Dip the basket into a soap bubble solution and wave it in the air to make clouds of bubbles.

9. Colander. Drain pasta or wash fruits and vegetables under cold running water in the basket.

10. Frog. Turn a basket upside down in a bowl to hold flower stems in place.

11. Dishwasher basket. Put baby bottle caps and nipples in a mesh basket; using rubber bands, secure another one upside down on top. Place in the upper rack of the dishwasher.

12. Party favors. Weave decorative ribbons through baskets to make party favors or candy dishes.

13. Portable cage. Tape two together to carry small pets (mice, toads, turtles, and so forth) to school for show-and-tell.

14. Mobile. Suspend one upside down over an infant's crib and tie bells, scraps of ribbon, or colorful fabric to it.

15. Seed starter. About 2 to 3 weeks before outdoor planting time, line baskets with newspaper, fill with potting mix, and sow four or five cucumber, squash, or melon seeds in each; thin later to three plants. Outdoors, plant one basket per hill, making sure soil is mounded over the basket.

Bicycle wheels

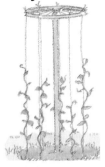

1. Trellis. Mount a bicycle wheel horizontally atop a tall pole, then run strings from the rim or spokes to pegs planted firmly in the ground; train pea or bean vines on the strings.

2. Tool hanger. Suspend a bicycle wheel horizontally and hang tools or utensils from the spokes and rim with S-hooks.

3. Mobile. Hang a bicycle wheel horizontally and suspend brightly colored paper cutouts from it.

4. Drying rack. Dry your hand laundry by hanging it from a bicycle wheel suspended from the ceiling.

5. Christmas wreath. Cover a bicycle tire with chicken wire, then weave pieces of evergreen boughs through it; attach a brightly colored ribbon.

Blankets

1. Poncho. Fold a blanket in half, then cut and hem a slit in the center to go over the head.

2. Insulation. Insert pieces of blanket inside pot holders, hot pads, and place mats.

3. Hammock. Hang an old blanket between two backyard trees.

4. Curtain padding. Sew a blanket between the curtain fabric and lining for fullness and insulation.

5. Quilt. Insert batting between two blankets and stitch together.

6. Pet stretcher. Place an injured pet in the center of a blanket; ask someone to lift two corners at one end while you lift the other two.

7. Mattress pad. Cut the blanket to the desired size, then sew on a strip of 1-inch-wide elastic across each corner to secure the pad to the mattress.

Blue jeans

1. Draft dodger. Cut each leg in half lengthwise. Stitch all four halves into tubes and fill with rags or fiberfill; stitch closed and use to block winter drafts at windows and doors.

2. Sneaker bag. Cut 18 inches off one leg; close one end with stitches and make a casing for a drawstring at the other (or simply cut holes to thread cord through).

3. Patches. Save pieces of tattered jeans so that you have ready patches for a pair that's still worth saving.

4. Pillow. Cut off one leg, hem the raw edges, and tie one end tightly with decorative cord. Stuff the leg with old pantyhose or other filler, then close the other end with a cord.

5. Easel case. Stitch the legs closed, insert a drawstring at the waist, and sew a carrying strap between one cuff and the waist. Put the easel's legs into the jean legs, supplies in the pockets, canvases in the trunk.

6. Tripod holder. Cut off a leg and stitch the bottom closed. (See also *Blue jeans,* p.342.)

Boards

1. Garden edging. Cut three boards 10, 12, and 14 inches high and sink them 6 inches into the ground; repeat the sequence for an undulating border.

2. Lock. Jam one end of a board under the doorknob and the other end tight against a carpeted floor.

3. Seesaw. Make a child's teeter-totter by placing the center of a long 8-inch-wide board across a barrel or other firm support; sand and paint with enamel to prevent splinters.

Bobby pins

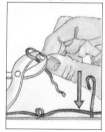

1. Wire router. Secure speaker or phone wires to the baseboard or molding. Clip the ends off the bobby pins so that they slide easily into the cracks.

2. Necklace. String pins with colored beads and knots of ribbon between them.

3. Ornament hanger. Slip through the ornament loop, then clip to the tree branch.

4. Apple bobbing. Let your guests bob for apples without getting wet. Insert bobby pins in the tops of a dozen apples; leave part of each pin exposed and thread a string through it. Hang the apples from a broomstick suspended between two chairs.

5. Zipper pull. Replace a broken one with a bobby pin.

6. Cuff links. Insert a bobby pin through both cuff-link holes; secure by twisting it or, if you wish, bending the ends into the shape of your initials with long-nose pliers.

7. Bookmark. Use a bobby pin to mark your place in a book.

8. Peg. When propagating plants by layering, hold their stems down with bobby pins.

9. Paper clip. Hold several pieces of paper together with a bobby pin.

10. Nail holder. Spare your fingers— use a bobby pin to grip a nail when hammering in tight spaces.

11. Invisible tie clip. Run the rear apron of your necktie through the loop on the back of the front apron, then clip it to your shirt with a bobby pin.

Book jackets

1. Place mat. Old book jackets make eye-catching table settings for informal dinner parties.

2. Party hat. Fold into a cone or other hat shape and punch two holes for a string or an elastic.

3. Blotter. Protect your youngster's working area by using a book jacket as a desk blotter.

4. Container cover. Coordinate a room's decor by covering canisters, pencil holders, and wastebaskets with book jackets.

5. Wallpaper. Paper one or several walls in the den or family room with colorful book jackets.

6. Notepaper. Take notes about the book you're reading on the inside of its jacket. Or, in a pinch, use the jacket as stationery.

Books

1. Coffee-table base. Place a thick sheet of glass with finished edges atop several stacks of unwanted coffee-table books.

2. Insulation. Put book-filled shelves on exterior walls to help keep the heat in and the cold out and on the walls between rooms to muffle sound.

3. Bookend. Glue together three or four old books to make an extra-heavy bookend.

4. Story wall. Rather than discard a book, cut pages from it, apply wallpaper paste, and use as a wainscotlike panel at the 3-foot level of a bedroom or study wall.

5. Clamp. Hold just-glued surfaces together by weighting them down with a couple of books.

6. Doorstop. Glue together three or four unwanted old books to hold a stubborn door open.

Boots

1. Umbrella stand. Weight the bottom of an attractive old leather boot (a riding boot perhaps) or a tall rubber boot with pebbles or marbles and place near your home's front or back door.

2. Birdhouse. Take an old boot outdoors and hang it upside down. It probably won't be long before wrens, swallows, or chickadees build a nest in the toe area.

3. Doorstop. Fill a boot with golf balls or pebbles.

4. Fish bucket. Keep your just-caught fish fresh: bring them home from the river in a water-filled boot.

Borax

1. Fertilizer. Fill a shaker with borax and sprinkle on the soil all around beet plants.

2. Diaper freshener. Add ½ cup borax along with the recommended amount of soap or detergent to a hotwater wash to eliminate odors and stains and make diapers absorbent.

3. China shiner. For an especially brilliant shine, rinse your fine china in a sinkful of warm water with ½ cup borax added; rinse again in clear water.

4. Flower preserver. Place a 1-inch layer of 1 part borax and 2 parts cornmeal in an airtight container; put in one or two flowers and leave in a cool dry place. After 7 to 10 days, pour off the mixture and dust the flowers with a soft artist's brush.

5. Cat litter deodorizer. Blend 6 parts cat litter with 1 part borax to reduce odor in the litter box.

Bottle caps

1. Christmas decorations. Paint caps gold, drill a hole in each one, and hang on the Christmas tree with string or a hook. Or knot each on a string to make a garland.

2. Fish scaler. Nail caps, fluted side up, onto a 3- x 4-inch block of wood. Run the block up and down a fish to rid it of scales.

3. Mini paint can. Mix small amounts of touch-up paint in a bottle cap.

4. Bird chaser. String caps together and hang them in the garden. Birds will be frightened by the reflection.

5. Kids' cola beads. Paint bottle caps, punch a hole in the center of each, and string them together on a piece of thin elastic or ribbon.

6. Trap. Fill with ant or roach bait and set out where pests congregate.

7. Mud scraper. For a "doormat" that will scrape off even the stubbornest mud, glue or nail bottle caps side by side, smooth side down, on a piece of plywood.

Bottles

1. Mole and rabbit repellent. When set in the ground near molehills with ½ inch of their necks exposed, bottles will whistle in the wind and scare off moles. Half-filled bottles placed throughout the garden will do the same for rabbits.

2. Rolling pin. Fill a bottle with water, cap it, and roll out the dough.

3. Cruets. Use perfume, hair-tonic, or other exotically shaped bottles as oil and vinegar cruets.

4. Drill holster. To hold an electric drill or screw gun, cut the neck off a plastic bottle, then cut the bottle about halfway on the diagonal. Screw to the wall above your workbench or cut slits in the bottle so that you can put it on a belt.

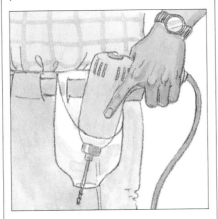

5. Bud vase. Remove the atomizer from an empty perfume bottle, wash thoroughly, and display a few small flowers in it.

6. Boot trees. Insert large soda-pop bottles into your boots to help them keep their shape.

7. Bowling pins. Paint the numbers 1 through 10 on clean plastic bottles and use an old rubber ball to bowl at home on a rainy day.

8. Bellows. When cleaned, a squeezable plastic detergent or ketchup bottle with a hole in its spout can serve as a bellows for encouraging a slow charcoal or fireplace fire.

9. Rodent deterrent. Wrap a glass bottle in a heavy cloth and smash it; carefully stuff the shards into steel wool and stick in the openings around your pipes.

10. Newspaper saver. Cut off a large plastic bottle on the diagonal about a third of the way from the bottom. Tie a piece of string around the neck of the bottle and attach the other end of the string to your delivery box. Ask your newsperson to put the bottle over the open end of the box after putting in the paper on a rainy day.

Bread

1. Bread bowl. Scoop out the center of a round, crusty loaf and fill with an appetizer or a dip.

2. Fat sopper. A piece of bread in a broiler pan will soak up any fat dripping from the meat and reduce the chance of smoke and fire.

3. Cake preserver. Fasten two slices of bread with toothpicks to the open faces of a cut cake to prevent drying out.

4. Edible place markers. Attach name tags to toothpicks and insert into rolls; place one at each setting.

5. Pipe wick. Before soldering a copper pipe, push a wad of white bread as deeply as possible into it to absorb any remaining moisture. When the water pressure is restored, the bread will dissolve and wash out.

6. Hand saver. Pick up broken glass with a piece of bread.

7. Flower cleaner. A good way to clean velvet flowers is to brush them with a shaving brush, rub them lightly with fresh rye bread, then rebrush.

Bricks

1. Desk organizer. Glue felt to the bottom of a brick and stick pencils and scissors in the holes.

2. Grill base. Place an old oven rack over four even stacks of bricks.

3. Bookend. Cover with fabric or heavy wallpaper.

4. Garden border. Recess bricks to outline garden beds or to help prevent water runoff around trees.

Broom handles

1. Window washer. To reach upper windows without a ladder, attach a large sponge or a squeegee to the end of a broom handle.

2. Garden stake. Support a tall, top-heavy plant, such as a tomato, on a broom handle; sharpen one end for easy insertion into the ground.

3. Paintbrush stretcher. Attach a broom handle to a paintbrush with duct tape.

4. Rolling pin. Cut to the size you need to roll out pie and cookie dough.

5. Reach extender. Attach a screw hook to a broom handle to lengthen your reach so that you can get hold of those socks behind the washer or the basket on the highest shelf.

6. Closet rod. Screw large screw hooks into beams in the closet ceiling and rest a broom handle on them. Hang out-of-season clothing on broom handles attached to the basement ceiling joists with screw hooks.

7. Curtain rod. Cut a broomstick to the desired length and drill holes at both ends. Hang it from L-hooks fitted through the holes or finishing nails driven into the window molding and bent upward with pliers.

8. Bird caller. Insert a screw eye into the end of a short length of broom handle; remove it and sprinkle rosin into the hole. Then turn the screw back and forth in it to attract birds.

9. Paint can holder. Slide a broom handle into the rung of an aluminum extension ladder. Notch each end of the pole to keep the can from sliding off.

10. Stoopless scoop. Prevent a backache—pick up leaves and refuse with a stoopless scoop, made from two broom handles and a plastic planter tray cut in half.

Pivot bolt

11. Wall-hanging support. Thread a handle through the top of a macramé hanging to display it on the wall.

Brooms

1. Edger. When coating a driveway with tar emulsion, use an old broom as an edger in spots where your squeegee won't fit.

2. Textured paintbrush. Dip an old broom in paint to create special effects and unusual textures on a canvas or a wall.

3. Bird guide. If birds fly in through open doors or windows, use a broom to assist them out so that they don't batter themselves against any glass windows.

4. Oiler. For those hard-to-reach places, dip a broom straw in oil and work it around the squeaky part.

5. Dolly. Tip the heavy object so that one edge rests on the broom bristles. Ask someone to push the object while you pull the broom.

Bubble pack

1. Pillow. Stuff rectangular sheets of bubble pack into a pillowcase.

2. Mattress. Several layers of bubble pack can serve as a temporary guest bed on the floor.

3. Insulation. Glue to the inside walls of the doghouse to keep Rover warm on chilly nights.

4. Halloween costume. Turn your youngster into a spaceman or Mr. Bubble by wrapping bubble pack around her arms, legs, and trunk.

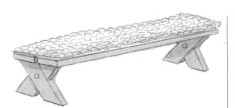

5. Picnic table cushion. For pleasanter picnicking, stretch a length of bubble pack along the benches.

6. Bleacher upholstery. Soften those hard stadium benches; take a layer or two of bubble pack to the game with you.

7. Table pad. When repairing glass or china, prevent breakage by covering the work surface with bubble pack.

8. Worry beads. Pop the bubbles to relieve tension.

Buckets

1. Mini stilts. Make working on a ceiling easier by attaching a pair of old work shoes to two sturdy buckets without handles. Drive screws through the shoe soles and into wood blocks inside the buckets. Or punch holes in the bucket bottoms and strap or tie the shoes down.

2. Christmas tree stand. Fill a bucket with wet sand or gravel and stand the tree in it.

3. Lobster cooker. If you don't have a large kettle, boil lobster in an old metal bucket.

4. Shower. A perforated bucket makes an excellent campsite shower.

5. Paint tray. Use the lids from 5-gallon joint-compound buckets as trays for 1-gallon cans of paint. The lids serve as platforms for the paint cans and are also large enough to hold a paintbrush.

Buckles

1. Scarf clasp. Pass a scarf through a pretty buckle and wear at the neck of a plain sweater or dress.

2. Curtain ornament. Attach to a tieback as an added decoration.

Buttons

1. Dollhouse decorations. Use buttons for sconces, plates, and wall hangings in your child's dollhouse.

2. Poker chips. For an impromptu game, use buttons as chips, with each color carrying a different value.

3. Beanbag filler. Instead of dried beans, use small buttons.

4. Game pieces. Substitute buttons for lost backgammon, bingo, or Parcheesi pieces. Or use them for a game of tiddledywinks.

5. Christmas tree garland. Knot buttons on a sturdy length of string to give your Christmas tree an old-fashioned look.

6. Necklace. String attractive buttons, alternating large and small, on two strands of heavy-duty thread.

C

Calendars

1. Drawer liners. Take apart an old calendar and use its pages to line your desk drawers.

2. Jigsaw puzzle. Glue a favorite calendar page onto a heavy piece of cardboard, then cut it into pieces.

3. Place mats. Use the pages from beautifully illustrated calendars as place mats when setting the table for a special party.

4. Collage. Glue the pages of a calendar on ¼-inch plywood to make a collage of memories.

5. Greeting card. Glue a favorite old calendar picture on thin poster board for an inexpensive but attractive greeting card.

6. Wallpaper. Use calendar art to paper a powder room; protect and "antique" it with a coat of shellac.

7. New Year's tablecloth. Pull apart the outgoing year's calendar and glue the months randomly to a large piece of freezer paper for a New Year's retrospective.

Candles

1. Envelope sealer. Reseal an envelope with a few drops of melted wax from a lighted candle.

2. Egg decorator. Drip melted wax onto hard-boiled Easter eggs and then dye. Peel off the wax to reveal an intricate pattern.

3. Candle holder. Drip melted wax into the socket of a candlestick to hold wobbly candles in place.

4. Fire starter. Toss a couple of candle stubs into the kindling and light.

5. Shovel lubricant. The snow will slide right off your shovel if you rub it down with a candle stub before using.

Can openers

1. Grout remover. Use the tip of a beer can opener to gouge old grout from between ceramic tiles.

2. Plumb bob. Suspend one from a string so that it hangs freely with its point down.

3. Screwdriver. Use a can opener sideways to turn a large-slotted faucet screw.

Cans

1. Outdoor candle holder. Remove the label from an empty can, punch holes in the sides, place a candle in the bottom, and light. To help control bugs, use citronella candles.

2. Floor patch. Nail can lids to a wooden floor to plug knotholes and thwart rodent entry.

3. Plant protector. Remove both ends and push the can into the earth as a collar to protect young garden plants from cutworms.

4. Pans. Different-size cans will nestle together compactly to provide cheap, disposable pans when camping; handle with pliers when hot.

5. Amplifier. There's no need to open the door of the baby's room repeatedly to check on him. Hold the open end of an empty can against the door to amplify any noises from inside.

6. Table lock. For large dinner parties, lock card tables together by setting adjacent pairs of legs into cans.

7. Egg poacher. Remove the top and bottom of a tuna can; place in a skillet of simmering water and crack an egg into it.

8. Bird feeder. Wedge a small can filled with suet between tree branches or posts.

9. Seeder. Perforate the bottom of a can, fill it with grass seed, and shake over the lawn.

10. Rain gauge. Set open coffee cans around the garden. A 1-inch accumulation means an inch of water fell onto the soil.

11. Reflectors. Remove the bottom of an empty can; with tin snips, cut the can in half lengthwise. You've just made two reflectors for campsite or backyard lights.

12. Pedestal. Fill several wide cans with rocks or sand, glue together, then screw a piece of wood into the bottom of the top can before attaching it to the others. Place a plant, lamp, or statue on top.

13. Miniature golf markers. Arrange cans with both ends removed so that the ball must go through them, go up a ramp into them, or ricochet off a 2 x 4 through them.

14. "Basket tennis." Play basketball with a tennis ball. Nail a coffee can above the garage door, bottom open and top flipped up as a backboard.

15. Bread pan. Bake or steam bread in clean coffee cans.

16. Ash spreader. Punch holes in the bottom of a coffee can. Fill with wood ashes and shake over garden soil.

17. Pigeonholes. Glue half a dozen or more cans together, paint them with bright enamel, and store silverware, office supplies, nails, or other odds and ends in them.

Cardboard boxes

1. Sled. Pull a small child (or a load of firewood) over the snow in a large cardboard box.

2. Dust cover. Keep dirt out of a small appliance, power tool, or typewriter— cut off the flaps of a box, put decorative adhesive plastic, such as Con-Tact, on the sides and top, and use as a cover.

3. Table guard. Cut a large flat piece to protect work surfaces from ink, paint, glue, or knife and scissor nicks.

4. Mechanic's helper. Keep a piece under your car's engine in the garage or carport. Not only will it keep the floor clean by catching drips, but the color and location of the leaked fluids on the cardboard will help a mechanic identify potential problems.

5. Gift of suspense. Place a friend's gift inside a series of increasingly bigger cardboard boxes, each one specially wrapped.

6. Bed tray. Remove the top flaps and cut lap-wide arches from the two long sides; cover the top with attractive adhesive plastic, such as Con-Tact.

7. In box. Cut off the top and one large panel from a cereal box; slice the short sides at an angle.

8. Puppet theater. Stand a large cardboard box on end; cut a big hole in the back for puppeteers to crouch in and a smaller one high up in the front for the stage.

9. Magazine holder. Remove the top of a detergent box, then cut the box at an angle, from the top of one side to the bottom third of the other.

10. Place mats. Cut several 12- x 18-inch pieces of cardboard and cover them with colorful adhesive plastic, such as Con-Tact. (See also *Liquor cartons,* p.311.)

Cardboard tubes

1. Megaphone. When you need to amplify your voice, talk through a cardboard tube.

2. Boot trees. Stick tubes into boots to hold their shape.

3. Knitting-needle case. Prevent bending and breaking—store plastic needles in an empty cardboard tube.

4. Fluorescent light storage. Prevent breakage by keeping unused fluorescent lamps in cardboard tubes.

5. Light detangler. For trouble-free decorating next year, wrap Christmas tree lights around a tube and secure with tape or a rubber band.

6. Document holder. Before storing diplomas, marriage licenses, and other certificates, roll them tightly and insert them in paper towel tubes. This prevents creases and keeps documents clean and dry.

7. Play logs. Notch the ends with a utility knife and construct "log" cabins, fences, and other toys.

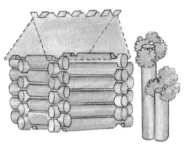

8. Linen press. After laundering tablecloths and napkins, roll them around tubes so that they won't show creases where they were folded.

9. Fabric keeper. Store leftover fabric scraps, tightly rolled, inside a tube. For easy identification, staple a sample of each fabric on the outside.

10. Kazoo. Cut three finger holes in the middle of a paper towel tube and attach wax paper with a rubber band to one end. Hum into the other end, plugging different holes to alter the pitch.

11. Plant guard. Prevent accidental scarring when cutting down weeds—cut a tube lengthwise and put it around the trunks of young trees or plants; slip off afterward for use elsewhere.

Car jacks

1. Post puller. Rather than use a shovel, wrap a chain around the post, fastening the ends with a bolt or strong clamp. Lap the chain over the hook of a bumper jack and hoist the post out of the ground.

2. Emergency accident repair. You can often pry a bent fender away from a tire by placing a scissors or bottle jack between the fender and frame, then forcing the fender outward.

3. Mini crane. To raise a sagging deck for repair or to lift a grand piano for fixing a leg or straightening a rug, use a scissor-type car jack.

Car mirrors

1. Monitor. Mount a car mirror on the side of the house so that you can simultaneously watch youngsters in the front and back yards.

2. Organist's friend. A car mirror attached to a wood block will enable an organist to keep an eye on the congregation or choir director while reading her music.

3. Signal. To signal fellow hikers atop distant heights, carry a sturdy car mirror in your backpack. (See also *Lost in the woods,* p.129.)

Carpet scraps

1. Insulation. Cover the walls of a room with carpet scraps for sound-proofing and temperature control.

2. Clatter killer. Cut pieces of carpet to fit under typewriters and sewing machines, on cabinet shelves, and in toolboxes.

3. Bed bumper. Pad the corners of a sharp bed frame to prevent scraping or gouging the walls.

4. Foot warmers. Trace your feet on a piece of paper and use as a pattern to fit thin carpeting inside your boots, rubbers, or work shoes.

5. Dolly. Set a heavy item atop a piece of carpet and pull it by one of the corners.

6. Drop cloth. When doing messy repairs, protect the floor with old carpeting; if you're using a stepladder, make sure the piece is wide enough so that all four legs rest securely on it.

7. Exercise mat. Cut a piece of old carpet 3 feet wide and as long as you are tall. Roll it up when not in use.

8. Knee pad. Cut two pieces of carpeting 10 inches square; cut two slits or holes in each. Run old neckties or scarves through the slits to tie the pads to your knees.

9. Buffer. Glue an old piece of carpet to a block of wood; use it to clean window screens, buff shoes, or erase blackboards.

Car seats

1. Dog bed. Cut the foam-rubber padding from a car seat to the right size for your dog. (Ticks don't seem to like foam rubber.)

2. Furniture. Use old car seats as cheap rec room or dorm furniture.

3. Porch swing. Hang an old back seat from four strong, well-secured ropes or chains.

Castor oil

1. Eye cream. Before going to bed, rub odorless castor oil all around the eye area.

2. Mole repellent. Drench molehills with a mixture of ½ cup castor oil and 2 gallons water.

3. Lubricant. Use it instead of petroleum oil on kitchen scissors and other utensils that touch food.

Cat litter

1. Drying agent. Preserve flowers by placing them on a bed of cat litter in an airtight container for 7 to 10 days. (See also *Flower drying*, p.87.)

2. Deodorizer. To remove unpleasant odors, sprinkle cat litter in garbage cans, in the fireplace, or on the floors of musty rooms; before packing a suitcase or a trunk, leave a litter-filled can inside overnight.

3. Oil absorber. Sprinkle onto oil puddles and other spills on the garage floor. After the fluids have been absorbed, sweep it up.

4. Filler. Use to stuff dolls, toys, and beanbags.

Caulk

1. Gasket. If the seal is torn on your refrigerator or dishwasher, repair it with caulk.

2. Shoe gum. Temporarily fill a hole in your sole with a dab of caulk; let dry before walking on it.

Chalk

1. Rust preventer. Place several pieces of chalk in the toolbox to eliminate moisture and prevent rust.

2. Marble polish. Wipe clean marble with a damp soft cloth dipped in powdered chalk; rinse with clear water and dry thoroughly.

3. Grease remover. Rub chalk on a grease spot on clothing or table linens, let it absorb the oil, then brush off. If the stain lingers, rub chalk into it again just before laundering.

4. Metal polish. Wipe metal with chalk dust on a damp cloth.

5. Repellent. Scatter powdered chalk around garden plants to repel ants and slugs.

Chamois

1. Photographer's helper. Wipe dusty photographs and camera lenses with a clean chamois.

2. Glove patch. Using hide glue, attach pieces of chamois to worn areas on work gloves.

Cheesecloth

1. Food tents. Protect your food from dirt and insects at outdoor parties—wrap a piece of cheesecloth around an old wire umbrella form and place over serving plates.

2. Paint strainer. Remove the clots from an old can of paint by straining it through cheesecloth.

3. Pressing cloth. When ironing delicate fabrics, press over a damp piece of cheesecloth—it leaves no lint and won't overwet your clothes.

4. Minnow catcher. Cheesecloth makes a good bait net.

5. Dry cleaner. To remove oil and dirt from your hair, cover your brush with cheesecloth.

6. Digital drape. If the light from your digital clock keeps you awake at night, cover it with a piece of cheesecloth—you'll still be able to see the numbers, but they won't be so bright.

7. Landscape cloth. To protect newly sown grass seed from wind and birds, cover with a layer of coarse-mesh cheesecloth weighted with rocks.

8. Shade. Drape over stakes to partly shade vegetable transplants.

9. Butterfly net. Glue or staple cheesecloth to a hoop formed from a wire coat hanger.

10. Tea strainer. Strain freshly brewed tea into a cup or mug through a piece of cheesecloth.

11. Jelly strainer. When making berry jelly, pour the cooked fruit through three layers of cheesecloth to strain out seeds and skins.

12. Fat remover. To skim fat from soups or stews, wrap ice in cheesecloth and draw across the surface.

13. Vacuum attachment. Instead of removing the contents of a drawer to dust it, cover the nozzle of your vacuum with cheesecloth so that small objects aren't sucked into it.

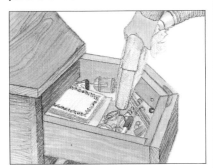

Chewing gum

1. Valuables retriever. To recover a coin or piece of jewelry that's fallen down the drain, stick just-chewed gum to the bottom of a fishing weight; dangle it from a string in the weight's hole, let it take hold, then pull up.

2. Crab lure. Chew a stick briefly; when it's soft but still has flavor, attach it to a crab line. Lower the line and wait for the crabs to go for the gum.

3. Filler. Fill a crack in a wall or a clay flowerpot with well-chewed gum.

4. Window putty. Hold a loose pane of glass temporarily with a wad of chewing gum.

5. Hose sealer. Chewed gum will seal punctures in garden hoses.

Chicken wire

1. Deer repellent. Stake chicken wire flat around the perimeter of your garden—deer won't walk on it.

2. Rust-out repair. Push wire into a cleaned-out rust-out on your car; it will form a backing for the body filler.

3. Bulb protectors. To prevent rodent damage, line the bottom of a prepared bed with wire, plant the bulbs, and cover with soil.

4. Frog. Squish wire together and place in the bottom of a vase to hold cut flowers.

5. Fence setter. To hold a fence post more securely, before setting it in concrete, wrap the base with chicken wire and nail it in place.

6. Insulation holder. After placing fiberglass batting between the roof and floor joists, staple chicken wire to the joists' edges to secure it.

Chlorine bleach

1. Bacteria zapper. When refilling your humidifier, add 1 or 2 drops chlorine bleach per gallon of water to prevent bacteria growth.

2. Deodorizer. Remove odors from coolers and other closed containers with diluted chlorine bleach.

3. Mold exterminator. Apply bleach directly to the tub and shower to rid them of mold and mildew.

Christmas trees

1. Dog repellent. Boughs positioned vertically around tree trunks may help discourage neighborhood dogs.

2. Bean pole. Drive a 6-foot metal fence post into the ground. Cut the branches off a Christmas tree, leaving short stubs, and attach it to the fence post with string or twist ties. (Collect extra trees from your friends and neighbors or get unsold ones from local markets the day after Christmas.)

3. Fishing habitat. If you drop a Christmas tree into your favorite fishing hole, the fish will very likely gather around it, and you'll know just where to catch them.

4. Bird shelter. Make a winter shelter for neighborhood birds by piling several trees in the backyard. They'll be especially grateful if the trees were decorated with popcorn or cranberry garlands.

5. Holiday trimming. Insert the branches trimmed from a Christmas tree into a chicken-wire wreath or wire them together into evergreen swags to decorate mantles or railings.

6. Bathroom freshener. Tie a bow on a freshly cut branch and hang in the bathroom for an evergreen scent. Mist frequently.

7. Animal deterrent. Cut off the branches and mulch flower beds and shrubs with them; they'll also serve to ward off animals.

8. Fire starter. Use dried-out sprigs to ignite kindling in a fireplace. Don't overdo it—they burn furiously.

Citrus rinds

1. Suet bowl. Place a suet-bird-seed mixture in an empty orange or grapefruit half; suspend with string from a backyard tree.

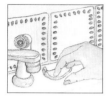

2. Nail groomer. Press nail tips into the pithy side of a lemon rind to clean them after doing dirty chores.

3. Pan cleaner. To clean a blackened aluminum pan, boil citrus rinds in it. If any discoloration remains, rub with a steel-wool pad.

4. Tea flavoring. Add citrus peel to tea leaves while they're brewing or put several small strips in a cup of just-boiled water with a teabag.

5. Potpourri. Add rinds to simmering cinnamon and cloves to fill your home with a wonderful aroma.

6. Cutting board freshener. Rub a lemon rind over your cutting board to clean and deodorize it.

7. Fireplace freshener. Add some dried citrus rinds to the fire for a spicy fragrance.

8. Deodorizer. Put small mesh bags filled with orange or lemon peels in drawers and closets.

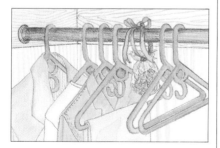

Clamshells

1. Gravel. Crushed clamshells make an excellent pathway.

2. Paint palette. Use as disposable paint containers for small projects.

3. Garden trowel. A large clamshell is an ideal tool for transplanting.

4. Jewelry holder. Glue small shells onto a large shell and use as a decorative container for pins, chains, and earrings.

5. Plant drain. Crush shells and use the fragments for drainage when repotting a houseplant.

6. Seafood casserole. Cook and serve miniature seafood casseroles or deviled crab in them.

7. Wind chimes. Punch holes in shells, then run monofilament through them, knotting it to keep them evenly spaced; attach several strings of shells to a small piece of wood and hang.

Clipboards

1. Pants hanger. Suspend a clipboard from a hook inside the closet or on the bedroom door; hang trousers overnight by clipping the cuffs.

2. Place mat holder. Hang a clipboard inside a kitchen cabinet door and use the clamp for convenient place mat storage.

3. Recipe retainer. For easy reading of recipes cut from magazines and newspapers, attach a clipboard on the kitchen wall at eye level.

4. Travel aid. Before starting on a long trip, fold the map to the area in which you plan to travel; attach it to a clipboard and keep it nearby to check at rest stops.

5. Music holder. To keep flimsy pages upright, in place, and invulnerable to drafts, attach sheet music to a clipboard.

Clothespins

1. Clamps. When gluing a thin object, position spring clothespins around it until the glue sets.

2. Clipboard. Make a rack for small tools, toothbrushes, or kitchen utensils by screwing several clothespins onto a piece of wood.

3. Cord holder. To keep the vacuum cleaner cord from retracting while in use, clip a clothespin to it after pulling it to the desired length.

4. Fastener. Close up packages of crackers, snacks, cereal, or seeds.

5. Paper clips. A spring clothespin holds more than a paper clip does and is handier.

6. Bag holder. Nail two to your backyard fence to support a plastic leaf bag for easy filling.

7. Boot organizer. In crowded closets and coat rooms, clip your right and left boots together.

8. Note holder. Glue or screw to a surface to hold recipe cards near the food preparation area or messages on bedroom doors.

9. Spark plug reminder. Number clothespins and attach to spark plug cables before disconnecting them. Number from the front of the engine, adding D if it's on the driver's side, P for the passenger's side.

10. Christmas decorations. Make angels or toy soldiers by decorating clothespins; use the clips as legs.

11. Paintbrush. Clamp a clothespin over a small square of foam rubber and use for painting touch-ups.

12. Paintbrush saver. Keep your paintbrush from sinking into the solvent residue when you clean it; clamp it to the container with a clothespin.

Spacer stick

1" minimum

13. Hem pins. There's no need to baste; while pressing the new hemline in place, hold it with clothespins.

14. Memory jogger. Clip a note on the sun visor or the steering wheel of your car as a reminder to turn off the headlights or take a package out of the trunk.

15. Toothpaste stretcher. Catch the bottom of a toothpaste tube with a pin and roll up.

Club soda

1. Soft drink. Add to fruit juice for a healthful and inexpensive beverage.

2. Rust remover. Pour over rusty nuts and bolts to loosen them.

3. Cleanser. Clean and shine porcelain fixtures by pouring club soda over them; no soap or rinsing is necessary, and it won't mar the finish.

4. Tummy tamer. Cold club soda with a dash of bitters works wonders on an upset stomach due to indigestion or a hangover.

Coffee

1. Fertilizer. Work coffee grounds into the topsoil in your garden.

2. Dye. An inexpensive way to color fabric brown is to soak it in strong black coffee—without sugar.

3. Bait carrier. Going fishing? Take your worms in a can or paper cup of moist coffee grounds; they'll be easier to pull out.

Combs

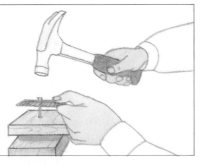

1. Nail holder. Avoid hammering your fingers—hold a small nail in place between the teeth of a comb.

2. Music maker. Fold a piece of wax paper over the teeth, hold it up to your lips, and hum.

3. Wallet guard. To make your wallet less accessible to a pickpocket, put a small comb, tines up, in your pocket; the tines will catch on the pocket edges and help secure the wallet.

4. Vacuum cleaner cleaner. Save old combs to clean vacuum brushes.

5. Washboard. After immersing a stained fabric in soap and water, rub it across the teeth of a comb.

6. Back scratcher. Clip a comb to the end of a ruler with paper clips or spring clamps.

Concrete blocks

1. Anchor. Tie with a rope or chain and use to hold a rowboat in place.

2. Traction. Place in the trunk of your car to provide extra weight in winter.

3. Flower box. Make a planter that drains well and is guaranteed not to tip over—fill the holes of a concrete block with soil and add flowers.

Cooking spray

1. Shovel slicker. Keep snow from sticking to the shovel by applying cooking spray beforehand.

2. Grease repellent. To speed cleaning, spritz tools and barbecue grills with cooking spray before use.

3. Debugger. Spray the car radiator with cooking spray before driving in the bug-infested summer months. Simply hose off the crushed critters; respray when the radiator dries.

Corks

1. Jewelry. Punch holes through the centers of several corks and string together; for variety, use different sizes and paint them.

2. Pincushion. Store needles in corks so that they won't stick you or get lost so easily.

3. Makeup. Burn the end and use the ashes as makeup on Halloween.

4. Trivet. Glue wine bottle corks together for a hot pad to protect the table.

5. Key ring. Attach your boat key to a large painted cork; if it falls overboard, it will stay afloat and be visible.

6. Tugboat. Glue corks together to entertain a toddler in the bath.

7. Stamp. Draw a design in the end, cut away the material outside the outline, and ink the cork on a pad.

8. Safety marker. String large corks on a yellow polypropylene line to define a special swimming area for small children.

9. Knife cleaner. Dip a dampened cork in scouring powder and pass it along the edges of a carbon-steel kitchen knife.

10. Scratch guard. Attach thin slices of cork to the bottoms of ashtrays, vases, and lamps.

11. Recipe holder. Cut a slit in a cork and glue it to the lid of a recipe file box; place a card upright in it so that you can easily refer to it while cooking.

12. Rust preventer. Rub kitchen utensils and garden tools with a cork dipped in cooking oil.

13. Rocker guard. To help prevent tipping, glue corks under both ends of each rocker.

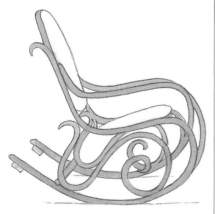

Cornstarch

1. Window cleaner. For a nice polish on your windows, mix a little cornstarch with ammonia and water.

2. Roach killer. Mix with plaster of paris (half and half) and sprinkle behind appliances or cupboards. The pests will "petrify" once they ingest the concoction.

3. Knot detangler. To help untie a stubborn knot, sprinkle it with a little cornstarch.

4. Glove skid. Sprinkle cornstarch inside your rubber gloves—they'll be much easier to put on and take off.

5. Pastry aid. Before rolling out pastry dough, sprinkle the board and rolling pin with cornstarch—it's tasteless and cleans up easily.

6. Pet shampoo. To remove dirt and add fluff without bathing, rub cornstarch into your pet's coat, then comb and brush out.

7. Baby powder. Apply sparingly when diapering a baby.

Cotton

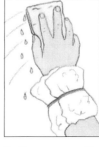

1. Arm guard. To keep water from running down your arms when washing walls, wrap a strip of cotton batting around your wrists and secure it loosely with rubber bands.

2. Summer refresher. Dab cotton balls in your favorite cologne, seal in a plastic bag, and store in the freezer. When you need a lift on a blistering summer day, remove one of the balls and dab your wrists and neck.

3. Deodorizer. To eliminate a sour odor in your refrigerator, dampen a handful of cotton with vanilla extract and place it on the middle shelf.

4. Glove extender. Push bits of cotton into the fingertips of rubber gloves so that your nails don't poke through.

5. Stuffing. Use as filler for dolls, toys, pillows, and so forth.

6. Swab. Wrap cotton around a matchstick or toothpick; use to remove grit from filigree and carvings.

7. Air freshener. Saturate a ball with cologne and place in the bag of your vacuum cleaner to sweeten the air.

Cotton swabs

1. Paint swab. Do touch-up paint jobs around the house and on the car. Swabs also make good paintbrushes for kids; they can use one for each color and throw them all away at the end of the painting session.

2. Tape cleaner. Dip cotton swabs in head cleaner (available at electronics supply stores) to clean the heads on tape recorders and VCR's.

3. Crevice cleaner. Clean between blender and phone buttons, in sewing machine and camera crevices, in shower door runners, and in other tight spots.

4. Makeup applicator. A sanitary cotton swab is ideal for applying eyeshadow and removing mascara globs.

5. Insect flicker. Knock insects from houseplants with an alcohol-moistened cotton swab.

Crayon stubs

1. Candle dye. Save stubs to melt with paraffin for making colored candles.

2. Sealing wax. Melt the remnants and use to seal envelopes.

Credit cards

1. Scraper. When nothing else is handy, use a credit card to scrape frost from your windshield.

2. Door key. If you accidentally lock yourself out, press the latch into the door by sliding an old credit card between the door and the frame. If the bevel faces the other way, cut the card into an L-shape, insert, and pull toward you.

3. Guitar pick. Can't find your pick? Use a corner of a credit card instead.

4. Manicure tool. Clean your fingernails with a credit card.

Cup hooks

1. Place mat hangers. Place a series of hooks inside a cabinet door or behind the dining room door.

2. Supports. Hang tools and utensils from cup hooks.

3. Miscellany haven. Use magnetic cup hooks in your kitchen, bathroom, or car as temporary places to hang your keys, glasses, or other items.

Curtain rods

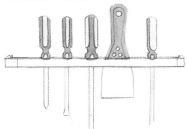

1. Workshop organizer. Fasten a short length to mounts on the wall. Store screwdrivers, chisels, and other tools with handles, blade down, between the rod and the wall.

2. Garden stakes. Use old curtain rods to support vegetable plants in the garden.

3. Drying rack. Suspend on ropes over the washer and dryer.

4. Pointer. Use when calling children to attention.

D

Dandelions

1. Beverage. Clean and dry the roots, roast in a warm oven until they turn dark brown, grind, and brew into a coffeelike drink; perk like coffee, using 1 teaspoon per cup of water. (This beverage is said to be diuretic.)
Caution: Do not use dandelions that have been treated with herbicides.

2. Salad greens. Use tender young shoots for vitamin-rich salads or steam as a potherb. After flowers form, the greens are too bitter to eat.
Caution: Do not use dandelions that have been treated with herbicides.

3. Dye. Boil the flowers for a yellow dye, the roots for magenta.

4. Tonic. Steep 2 teaspoons dried leaves in 1 cup boiling water; strain and use as an appetite stimulant.
Caution: Do not use dandelions that have been treated with herbicides.

5. Timepiece-barometer. If dandelion flowers are wide open, it's morning; if they're closed, however, it's late afternoon (or it's going to rain).

Dental floss

1. Umbrella salvager. Retie an umbrella to its ribs with dental floss—it's stronger than thread.

2. Cooking aid. Use unwaxed floss to truss poultry or to tie a rolled roast.

3. Jewelry string. Use in an emergency to restring beads and pearls.

4. Cake knife. Split a cake layer horizontally with floss instead of thread or a knife.

5. Picture wire. Hang lightweight pictures with dental floss—it's nearly invisible on white walls.

6. Moccasin saver. Replace worn stitching on your moccasins with dental floss (use a large needle); to match the color of the shoes, touch up the floss with a felt-tip marker.

7. Ornament hanger. Use with or without hooks to hang Christmas tree ornaments.

8. Photo separator. When two photographs are stuck together, work a piece of dental floss between them and gently pull both ends from the top to the bottom.

Diapers

1. Bed pad. Sew several together for a thick, absorbent mattress pad.

2. Compress. Use diapers as hot or cold compresses for aching muscles or bruised limbs.

3. Cover. Wrap a hot-water bottle in a diaper to protect your skin.

4. Car waxer. Use one to apply and buff auto wax and polish.

5. Drip catcher. If your roof has sprung a leak, put disposable diapers under it; they're an absorbent and quiet alternative to pans. Or put one in a pan; it will absorb the sound while the pan holds the excess water.

Dishpans

1. Closet organizer. Store toys, clothing, towels, sheets, and pillowcases in square plastic dishpans; label the contents on the sides.

2. Seed-starting flat. Spread a layer of moist vermiculite on the bottom, sow seeds, and cover with clear plastic wrap.

3. Oil pan. Place a dishpan beneath the drain plug when changing your car's oil; make sure the container is large enough to hold at least 6 quarts.

4. Baby's bathtub. Fill with an inch or two of lukewarm water and lower the baby gently into the water, supporting his head and shoulders.

5. Birdbath. Set on or into the ground and surround with rocks and foliage.

Dishwashing detergent

1. Shampoo. A mild dishwashing detergent cleans hair as well as many shampoos.

2. Flea exterminator. Place a bowl of water and dishwashing detergent a few inches below a light bulb; the heat will attract the fleas, which will fall off the bulb into the water and drown.

3. Auto cleaner. Fill a nearly empty detergent bottle with water and keep in the glove compartment for emergency treatment of spills.

4. Puncture finder. Mix with a little warm water and brush on a leaky tire or tube; the bubbles will indicate the exact location of the puncture.

5. Bubble solution. Dilute the concentrate slightly and dip a bubble blower in it. For longer-lasting bubbles, add a few drops of glycerin to the solution.

Doors

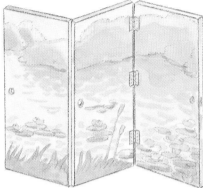

1. Folding screen. Hinge three together; decorate with paint or wallpaper if desired.

2. Bench. Place a solid door on concrete blocks.

3. Desktop. Flat, solid doors provide a sturdy surface for computers, typewriters, and other large or bulky equipment. (Buy wooden or steel legs at your local home center or use file cabinets of matching height.)

4. Work surface. Place a solid door across a pair of sawhorses.

5. Table extender. Enlarge a small dining table by placing a flat door on top. Put a pair of thin rubber gloves on the table first to keep the door from sliding. Toss a tablecloth over the door and no one will be the wiser.

6. Raft. Attach two large pieces of plastic foam to a door.

7. Ramp. Use a flat solid wood or steel door as a ramp when wheeling furniture or other heavy objects up a step or an incline.

8. Walkway. After a heavy rainstorm, lay old doors over soggy ground for easy walking.

Dowels

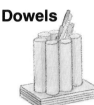

1. Pencil holder. Drill ¼-inch holes close together in a board, then glue and insert dowels.

2. Shelf extender. Nail ½-inch dowels along the edge of a shelf to contain rolling toys such as miniature cars and marbles.

Drawers

1. Shadow box. Paint or paper the interior of a drawer and hang it on the wall to display trailing plants and favorite knickknacks.

2. Rolling storage container. Fit old mismatched drawers with casters and slide under your workbench or bed for extra storage.

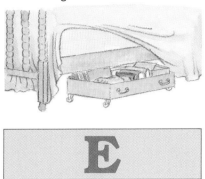

E

Eating utensils

1. Nail holder. Don't hammer your fingers; hold the nail between the tines of a fork.

2. Multipurpose tool. Use an old table knife as a spare screwdriver, a saw for cardboard, a putty knife, or a file for odd jobs.

3. Message bearer. Anchor a fork in a pebble-filled soup can and use to hold recipes or telephone messages.

4. Houseplant hoe. Bend the tines of an old fork at a right angle and use to aerate the soil of your potted plants.

5. Cabinet handles. Bend the handle of a spoon; drill holes in the handle and in the center of the bowl and screw to the cabinet door.

6. Egg run. At the starting line, give each contestant a raw egg in a tablespoon; the first person to cross the finish line with an intact egg in the spoon is the winner.

Egg cartons

1. Desk organizer. Remove the top and place the carton inside a desk drawer to hold paper clips, rubber bands, and other small items.

2. Coin toss. Write a different number in each section and let your children compete for a high score by tossing pennies.

3. Jewelry box. Store rings, earrings, chains, and cuff links in the individual cups.

4. Fire starter. Place several cardboard egg cartons under the kindling wood in the fireplace.

5. Toy "centipede." Cut the compartments out and string them together; make legs and antennae from pipe cleaners.

6. Christmas storage. Store small Christmas tree bulbs and fragile ornaments in empty egg cartons.

7. Seed starter. Punch a hole in the bottom of each cup, fill with potting soil, water, then drain overnight. Sow one or two seeds per cup and cover with plastic wrap; uncover when the seeds begin to sprout.

8. Palette. Children can mix paints neatly in an empty plastic egg carton.

9. Game storage. Keep track of the small items in your children's games: use one carton per game, label it with the name of the game, and keep it closed with a sturdy rubber band.

10. Ice cube tray. When you need extra ice for parties, fill plastic egg cartons with water.

Eggshells

1. Mini funnel. Poke a hole in half an eggshell, then pour the liquid through it into a container.

2. Planter. Punch a tiny hole, add soil, moisten, and plant a seed. Support the eggshell in an egg carton cup.

3. Decoration. Poke a small hole in both ends of an egg; blow out the contents. Let the shell dry, then paint and decorate with scraps of jewelry and rickrack. To hang, glue ribbon or string to one end.

4. Fertilizer. Sprinkle crushed shells around garden plants to discourage slugs. Toss any extra eggshells into the compost heap.

5. Pot scrubber. When cleaning pots and pans while camping, a good substitute for steel wool is a handful of broken eggshells.

6. Mosaic. Paint the inside and outside of eggshells a variety of colors, then crush them in a paper bag. Draw a picture on cloth or paper and spread slightly diluted white glue over it; sprinkle appropriately colored shells over the glue and protect with several coats of acrylic sealer.

7. Garden aid. Sprinkle rows of freshly planted seeds with crushed eggshells to keep birds away and to mark the rows.

Emery boards

1. Glass restorer. File rough edges on glassware with the fine-grit side of a damp emery board.

2. Pencil pointer. Glue an emery board under your workbench or desk to put a needle-sharp point on pencils.

Erasers

1. Key cleaner. Remove finger marks from piano keys with a rubber eraser; choose a size that fits easily between the black keys and gets into all the corners. For extra-tough spots, wrap the eraser with a cloth soaked in cleaning fluid.

2. Table stabilizer. Cut rubber erasers to fit the bottoms of table legs; fasten with adhesive or countersunk common nails.

3. Window cleaner. Give just-washed windows extra sparkle; wipe them with a clean blackboard eraser.

4. Wall saver. Glue rubber erasers to the bottom edge of the back of a frame; the frame will hang straighter, and it won't damage the wall.

5. De-skidder. Glue thin slices of a rubber eraser to the underside of a woven mat or sisal throw rug at its corners to keep it from slipping.

6. Household cleaner. Rub scuff marks from floors and fingerprints from woodwork with a rubber or an art-gum eraser.

7. Blade protector. Protect your utility knife—and yourself—by storing the tip in an eraser.

8. Rubber stamp. Draw a design on the flat side of a soft pink eraser, then outline it with the tip of a utility knife to a depth of about ¼ inch. Carve away the waste, leaving the design.

9. Golf ball cleaner. On your next golf outing, take a rubber eraser with you to clean the ball at holes where there's no bucket.

10. Pincushion. Keep safety pins from drifting to the bottom of the dresser drawer; stick the points into an eraser.

11. Upholstery cleaner. Rub lightly soiled cotton upholstery with an art-gum eraser.

12. Bit cushion. Store small drill bits, point first, in a large eraser.

Eyedroppers

1. Egg decorator. Apply dye to Easter eggs with eyedroppers.

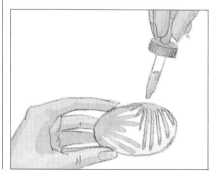

2. Glue dispenser. If the top of the glue container is clogged, use an eyedropper to dispense the glue.

3. Quicksilver catcher. Use an eyedropper to slurp up the mercury from a broken thermometer.

Eyeglass cases

1. Fishing companion. Keep hooks and lures in a safe, convenient place—slit open an old eyeglass case and fasten them to the liner.

2. Pocket protector. Prevent pens and pencils from damaging your clothing by keeping them in an empty eyeglass case in your pocket.

F

Fabric softener sheets

1. Screen cleaner. Save used sheets of fabric softener to remove dust and static from TV and computer screens.

2. Deodorizer. Line drawers and closet shelves with fresh sheets.

3. Car freshener. Place several under the front seat to freshen stale air.

4. Shoe shiner. Buff shoes to a high gloss with a fabric softener sheet.

5. Static cutter. To reduce static electricity in your hair, rub a sheet over your hairbrush.

6. Eyeglass cleaner. Wipe lenses with a fabric softener sheet to clean them and prevent fogging.

7. Sewing aid. To help prevent tangling, run your threaded needle through a sheet before sewing.

Fat

1. Cleanser. If your hands need heavy-duty cleaning after gardening or working on the car or in the shop, rub in shortening before using soap.

2. Bird food. Combine melted kitchen fat, bread crumbs, and sunflower seeds in a paper cup. When the mixture hardens, peel away the cup and hang the contents from a tree in a mesh bag.

3. Ink remover. Rub away ballpoint pen stains with vegetable shortening.

File cabinets

1. Crib. When a baby comes to visit the office, empty the bottom drawer of a file cabinet and pack in several pillows or jackets.

2. Desk base. Place a couple of two-drawer file cabinets under a sturdy flat door for a desk.

Film canisters

1. Toolbox. Store small nails, screws, nuts, or bolts inside.

2. Paperweight. Fill with sand and decorate.

3. Dry box. On camping and boating trips, film canisters will keep your paper money dry.

4. Shakers. Drill holes in the lids of metal film canisters and fill with salt, pepper, or spices. Now you have disposable dispensers for camping and picnicking.

5. Pillbox. Keep aspirin, pills, and vitamins in separate canisters when traveling; label with masking tape.

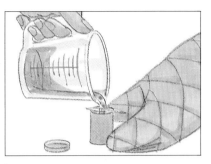

6. Candle mold. Tape a wick to the bottom of the canister and tie it to a toothpick across the top. Pour in hot paraffin and let harden overnight.

7. Organizer. Put paper clips, rubber bands, and safety pins in individual canisters and label.

8. Coin holder. Use to hold change for telephones, buses, tolls, parking meters, or laundry.

9. Jewelry box. Store earrings and rings in a canister; put chains in individual canisters to keep them tangle-free.

10. Swimmer's helper. Carry your earplugs to the beach in a film canister. Then make a swap—put earrings and other small jewelry inside the canister so that they'll be protected from moisture and sand.

11. Battery holder. Use as a container for AA and AAA batteries.

12. Stamp saver. Keep stamps unstuck and all in one place.

13. "Dry" ice cubes. Partially fill with water, freeze, then cap tightly. Place several in a pitcher of iced tea, lemonade, or martinis to chill the beverage without diluting it.

14. Sewing kit. Put two needles, black and white thread wrapped around a piece of toothpick, a couple of buttons, and several safety pins in a canister and pack in your suitcase for emergency repairs.

Flowers

1. Wreath. Dry your garden's prettiest flowers (p.87), wrap clusters of three to five stems with wire, and attach to a straw wreath.

2. Potpourri. Dry garden flowers (p.87); place in an airtight container along with a few crushed fragrant leaves and spices and a drop or two of aromatic oil.

3. Salad makings. Put pansies, nasturtiums, violets, and the leaves of peonies, yuccas, and carnations in your salads.

4. Cake decorations. Dip fresh violet or rose petals in egg white, then place in a saucer of confectioner's sugar; let dry on a wire rack, then arrange decoratively on your cake icing.

Freezer paper

1. Tracing. Because the paper is so translucent, it's ideal for tracing patterns and drawings.

2. Finger painting. There's no need to go to the art supply store to buy special paper—just use the waxy side of freezer paper. (If you don't have finger paints, mix dry wallpaper paste with liquid poster paint).

3. Shelf paper. Line closet and cabinet shelves with this less expensive alternative.

4. Chopping board. Dice, mince, and chop vegetables on the waxy side of this sanitary paper.

5. Wrapping paper. Wrap packages for mailing with freezer paper.

6. Pastry bag. Form paper into a cone, waxy side in, and fill with soft foods such as icing, whipped cream, or mashed potatoes.

Frisbees

1. Cookie tray. Turn upside down and fill with cookies for your child's birthday party.

2. Plate holder. To stabilize a paper plate at picnics, fit it into a Frisbee.

3. Pet dish. When you're out roughing it with your dog, a Frisbee works well as a food or water dish.

4. Birdbath. Punch through the Frisbee's edge at three points, insert wire plant hangers, and hang from a tree.

Furniture polish

1. Tile saver. To prevent water spots and soap scum on shower walls, coat them with furniture polish.

2. Lubricating oil. In a pinch, use furniture polish to oil a squeaky door.

Fusible iron-on tape

1. Decal. Let kids cut and iron their own designs onto sweatshirts.

2. Camping aid. Patch tears in a tent or tarpaulin with iron-on tape.

3. Patch. Use the tape to repair work clothes or children's play clothes.

4. Identification. Cut out player numbers and letters for the name of the team and press them onto baseball, soccer, or baseball shirts.

5. Decoration. Make hatbands from tape or adorn T-shirts with cut-out and pressed-on flowers.

Garbage bags

1. Disposable apron. Cut holes for your head and arms and wear to protect clothes while doing grubby chores; throw the bag out when finished.

2. Barbecue cover. When it's not in use, protect your outdoor grill with a big plastic garbage bag.

3. Summer storage. Add a few mothballs to a bag filled with your winter woolens; squeeze out the excess air and seal with a twist tie.

4. Clothing protector. In case of a roadside emergency, keep several large garbage bags in your trunk to spread on the ground and keep you clean while you work under the car.

5. Ground cloth. When camping, place your sleeping bag on several large garbage bags to prevent moisture from seeping in.

6. Windshield de-icer. Before leaving the car on an icy day, cut open a heavy-duty garbage bag and place it over the windshield, covering the wipers; close the car doors on the bag's edges to hold it in place. When you return, sweep off any snow, then peel off the plastic.

7. Solar shower. Fill a heavy-duty garbage bag with water and tie it to a solid tree branch. After allowing time for the sun to heat the water, strip down, soap up, and poke a small hole in the bag to rinse off.

8. Floor cover. Place under a potted plant or Christmas tree to protect the floor from spilled water.

Garden hoses

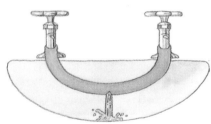

1. Water mixer. To get just the right water temperature when you have old-fashioned double faucets, slip a short section of hose over both faucets, then make a V-shaped cut in the bottom middle of the tubing.

2. Tine guard. Cut an old hose into sections and slip them over the tines of your rototiller when not in use so that they won't bang your shins.

3. Bucket handle. For more comfortable carrying, slit a 4-inch length of old garden hose and slip it over the handle of the bucket.

4. Scary snake. Paint splotches on a short length of hose and leave it coiled in the garden to scare off animal intruders. Or twine it in the branches of a berry bush to frighten birds when the berries ripen.

5. Car door protector. Nail lengths of slit hose to the garage wall where the car door usually makes contact with the wall.

6. Blade guard. Slit a section of an old hose and slip it over the blade of an ax or a saw to protect the cutting edge and prevent injuries.

7. Tree protector. Slit through one side of an old hose, then slip a section of it around the trunk of a very young tree to protect it from support ropes. Or put the hose around the ropes instead of the tree.

Gloves

1. Toy antlers. Stuff and use them on Halloween costumes or Christmas decorations.

2. Hand insulation. Keep one of your old gloves handy for unscrewing hot light bulbs.

3. Finger puppets. Create a face by sewing on buttons, yarn, and rickrack, or just paint one on. Insert your fingers to animate.

4. Tool holder. Cut off one side to the knuckles, fold over the other side, and stitch a tunnel to slip onto your belt.

5. Salvage. Cut up old leather gloves to make elbow patches or to re-cover leather buttons.

6. Venetian blind cleaner. Wearing soft cotton gloves sprayed with furniture polish, wipe each slat with one long stroke.

Greeting cards

1. Recipe tag. When sending home-baked goodies as a gift, write the recipe on the back of an old greeting card illustration.

2. Picture frame. Cut out a rectangle, oval, or circle ¼ inch smaller on all sides than your picture; tape the picture inside and close.

3. Place mat. Glue greeting card pictures onto a 12- x 18-inch piece of cardboard; coat with clear acrylic.

4. Christmas ornament. Punch a tiny hole in the top, then insert an ornament hanger.

Hair dryers

1. Wax remover. If candle wax drips onto a table, scrape off as much as possible with a dull knife blade, soften the remainder with warm air from a hair dryer, then lift it with a paper towel.

2. Invisible ink dryer. After writing a message on a piece of paper with lemon or onion juice, make it invisible by drying it on *Low*.

3. Invisible ink revealer. If you're the recipient of the secret message, make the writing visible again with a dryer set on *Hot*.

4. Traveler's aid. Hang just-washed garments on a towel rack or shower curtain rod and blow-dry.

5. Mirror defogger. If a hot shower fogs up your bathroom mirror, clear it with warm air from your dryer.

6. Bandage remover. Ease a bandage off a wound by blowing hot air on the adhesive.

7. Heat leak detector. While someone holds a lit candle just inside a window, go outside with a hair dryer and blow air around the frame; if the flame wavers, the window is leaking heat. Repeat this procedure around every exterior door and window.

8. Fire starter. Fan the charcoal briquettes in an outdoor grill.

9. Duster. Blow dust off a high shelf or out from under an appliance.

10. Sneaker dryer. If the toes of your sneakers never seem to dry, aim the nozzle of a dryer, set on *Low*, into each shoe for about 5 minutes.

Hair spray

1. Insecticide. Stop insects in their tracks with a shot of hair spray.
Caution: Do not use hair spray near an open flame.

2. Fabric saver. If hair coloring drips onto your clothing, spritz it with hair spray, then sop it up with a towel.

3. Artist's fixative. Protect a child's pastel artworks and pencil drawings with hair spray.

4. Run stopper. If you get a run in your stocking, spray it immediately to prevent it from getting any longer.

5. Tarnish preventive. Spray it on freshly polished pieces of brass to retard tarnishing.

6. Flower extender. For longer-lasting cut flowers, give them a dash of hair spray; stand a foot away and direct it at the undersides of the leaves and petals.

7. Needle threader. Stiffen the end of the thread with hair spray.

Hammocks

1. Garden canopy. Make a simple frame and attach a flattened hammock to the top.

2. Utility tarp. Cover roof racks or truckloads with an old hammock. Or gather brush and leaves in it.

3. Storage. Tie one up high in the basement to hold sleeping bags, out-of-season clothes, and other lightweight items.

Handbags

1. Needlework tote. Keep your craft project in an old handbag (make sure it's clean); store needles, thread, scissors, and other supplies in its compartments.

2. Clothespin holder. Clip or slip the bag's handle over the line to keep your clothespins close at hand.

3. Tool carrier. Keep a handbag filled with emergency tools in the trunk of your car; the bag is light, rattleproof, and easy to carry.

Handkerchiefs

1. Evening bag. Put your evening essentials in the center of one and tie the corners diagonally.

2. Emergency sun hat. Tie knots in all four corners of a large handkerchief or bandanna and cover your head.

3. Smoke mask. If you're ever caught in a burning building, soak a handkerchief with water and tie it around your nose and mouth to filter out smoke and gas.

4. Bouquet garni. Tie herbs and spices in a handkerchief and put in soup or stew while cooking; remove from the dish before serving.

Hangers

1. Plant marker. At the end of each row of seedlings, insert a straightened hanger tagged with the plant's name and the planting date.

2. Green box. To convert a window box into a mini greenhouse, bend three or four small pieces of hanger into U's and place the ends into the soil; punch small holes in a dry-cleaner bag, wrap around the box, and place in bright light.

3. Caulking tube stopper. Here's a way to prevent oozing from the tube once a job is done: cut a 3-inch piece of hanger; insert one end into the tube after shaping the other into a hook so that you can easily pull out the stopper as needed.

4. Christmas trim. Cut and bend into star and angel shapes, spray-paint, and hang on the tree.

5. Bubble maker. To make extra-big bubbles, shape a hanger into a hoop with a handle, dip into the solution (p.419), and wave through the air.

6. Arm extender. If a utensil has fallen behind the refrigerator or you want to reach a cup or pitcher (preferably plastic) on a high shelf, straighten a hanger completely, except for the hook at the end.

7. Wicket. Replace a lost wicket in your croquet set with one made out of a coat hanger.

8. Boot dryer. To speed the drying of boots and other footwear, form two loops in a hanger, and hang with the boots inverted.

9. Soldering iron rest. Prevent a hot soldering iron from rolling away by placing it in a coat hanger rest as shown.

10. Plant hanger. Wrap a straightened hanger around a 6- to 8-inch pot just below the lip; twist it back on itself to secure it, then hang.

11. Wings. Use for making wings on Halloween and Christmas costumes.

Hatpins

1. Tack. Use them instead of pushpins or thumbtacks.

2. Stickpin. File down the point and attach to your lapel.

3. Ironing aid. Hold a difficult-to-press garment on the ironing board with several of them.

4. Upholstery securer. Keep upholstery covers from slipping off sofa arms with hatpins.

Hydrogen peroxide

1. Rust remover. Make a paste of cream of tartar and hydrogen peroxide and rub on rust stains in sinks and bathtubs.

2. Scorch eraser. Remove (or at least lighten) ugly scorch marks by saturating them with peroxide.

3. Bleach. When whitening or brightening fabrics, substitute hydrogen peroxide for liquid oxygen bleach.

Ice

1. Plant waterer. Put several ice cubes on houseplant soil so that the moisture seeps in gradually. But don't let the ice touch the foliage.

2. Flavor negater. Before your child takes an unpleasant-tasting medicine, have him suck on an ice cube for a few minutes so that his taste buds are numbed.

3. Indentation inflater. Put an ice cube in each dent left in carpeting by furniture legs—the moisture will plump up the fibers.

Ice cream scoops

1. Beach toy. Give one to your child for making castles in the sand (or the sandbox).

2. Trowel. When transplanting seedlings, use a scoop to make same-size planting holes quickly and easily.

3. Soil scoop. For mess-free repotting, use an ice cream scoop to add soil to the container.

4. Server. Scoop equal portions of rice or mashed potatoes onto the family's dinner plates.

5. Melon scoop. Use an ice cream scoop to make large melon balls.

Ice cream sticks

1. Stirrer. An ice cream stick neatly mixes small amounts of paint, putty, and glue—and you can throw it away afterward without feeling guilty.

2. Ruler. In a pinch, draw a straight line with one.

3. Trivet. Glue a summer's worth of sticks together to form a square.

4. Index file marker. Cut to size if necessary, tape to an index card, and letter the top with a marker pen.

5. Splint. In an emergency, secure a stick to an injured finger with tape or strips of cloth.

6. Garden marker. Write the name of the plant and the date with indelible ink and insert it into the soil.

7. Shim. Glue to the bottom corners or legs of a piece of furniture so that it stands level on the floor.

8. Insulator. If you have to check for the spark from a plug wire, hold it with two sticks; if the wire is leaking high-voltage current, you won't get shocked.

9. File. Glue sandpaper to one end and use for sanding.

10. Caulking trowel. Use a wet stick to spread caulk evenly around window and door frames.

Ice scrapers

1. Paint remover. Scrape paint splatters off acrylic bathtubs or other nonmetallic surfaces that would be marred by a razor blade.

2. Spackle knife. A smooth scraper is great for small spackling jobs.

3. Freezer cleaner. Scrape away the frost without damaging your freezer.

4. Wax remover. Take the old wax off ski bottoms with one.

5. Counter cleaner. Scrape up sticky bits of bread or pastry dough from a counter or breadboard.

Iodine

1. Furniture renewer. Dab some over scratches in mahogany furniture.

2. Water purifier. When camping in areas without a safe water supply, stir in 6 to 8 drops of iodine per quart of drinking water; wait 20 minutes before consuming it.

Jar lids

1. Reflectors. Cover with reflective paint and place along walkways and driveways.

2. Cookie cutter. Dip the lid in flour, then press it into the dough.

3. Food saver. To keep the remaining half of an apple or orange fresh for a day or so, place it facedown on a lid and refrigerate. To save a partially consumed glass of milk, cover it with a large lid and refrigerate. Cover leftover canned soup or fruit with a jar lid and refrigerate.

4. Coaster. Glue felt or cork inside a lid, then rest your cold drink in it.

5. Candle holder. On a camp-out, use them to hold candles.

6. Frame. Paint the lid or cover it with a fabric remnant; cut a photograph to fit and glue it inside.

7. Paint palette. For quick touch-ups, pour paint into a lid and dip into it with an artist's brush.

Jars

1. Terrarium. Place a 1-inch layer of pebbles and charcoal chips and 3 inches of sterilized potting mix in a large jar. After planting, moisten slightly and place in a bright spot, uncovered, for a day, then cover.

2. Cocktail shaker. Use for mixing daiquiris, margaritas, and other such liquid concoctions.

3. Bank. Cut a slit in the lid with an old screwdriver or chisel.

4. Mitten dryer. Pull a wet mitten over the bottom of a small jar; stand the open end on a radiator for quick drying.

5. Glue pot. Drill a hole through a canning jar lid to fit the handle of a disposable foam paintbrush. To let the brush hang in the pot, rest the lid on top of the screw-on ring. Wipe off excess glue on the ring.

6. Shop storage. Nail lids to a rafter or the underside of a shelf in the workshop and screw in jars filled with nails, screws, nuts, and bolts.

7. Washer. Put small hand-washables in a large jar and add detergent and water. Shake the jar 1 minute, let soak for 3 minutes, then shake again; rinse and air-dry.

8. Boat storage. Keep paper money or matches dry by storing them in a screw-top jar; screw the lid to the underside of one of the seats.

Keys

1. Fishing sinker. With their pre-drilled holes, unidentified keys make great weights for fishing lines.

2. Drapery weight. To keep draperies hanging properly, slip old keys in the hems.

Knife holders

1. Fishing lure organizer. There's no need to poke around in your tackle box for lures—mount a magnetic knife holder inside to keep them all together.

2. Tool holder. Mount one on the workshop wall and attach screwdrivers, pliers, and other small tools.

3. Sewing box organizer. Reduce the risk of injury—keep a magnetic knife holder inside your sewing box to hold scissors and loose needles and pins in one place.

4. Medicine chest neatener. Use a magnetic knife holder to keep nail clippers, scissors, and tweezers close at hand.

Ladders

1. Planting guide. Place a ladder flat on the soil and press down; repeat to make a series of parallel rows.

2. Sawhorse. Just lay an open stepladder on its side.

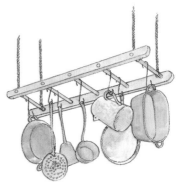

3. Utensil holder. Hang a section of ladder from the ceiling with ropes and suspend pots and pans from it.

4. Loading ramp. Place a ladder against the doorstep or the trunk of the car and put boards on top.

5. Trellis. Use an old ladder (preferably one with rounded rungs) to support climbing vines. Stand two facing each other and span a third across the top to make an arbor.

6. Scaffolding. Place planks across the rungs of two ladders; adjust the height by using higher or lower rungs.

7. Clothing rack. Hang out-of-season clothing in the basement or attic by extending a long pole across the top rungs of two stepladders.

Laundry basket

1. Toy box. Store children's toys in brightly colored laundry baskets.

2. Sled. Use a laundry basket for spur-of-the-moment play on snow-covered hills.

3. Carrier. Keep a spare one handy at the top and the bottom of the stairs for transporting odds and ends from one floor to the other.

Leaves

1. Insulation. Rake leaves up around your home's foundation and hold them in place with a weighted tarp.

2. Doily. When entertaining guests, serve cheeses, hors d'oeuvres, or individual pastries on plates covered with shiny clean leaves.

3. Place mat. Dry and press several leaves and arrange them between two sheets of clear adhesive plastic.

Lemon juice

1. Fingernail treatment. Soak fingertips for 5 minutes in 1 cup warm water and the juice of half a lemon. After pushing back the cuticles, rub lemon peel back and forth against the nail.

2. Hair lightener. Comb lemon juice evenly through hair, then let it dry in the sun; repeat once a day for at least a week.

3. Bathroom cleanser. Rub stained enamel fixtures with a cut lemon; for stubborn stains, use a paste of lemon juice and borax.

4. Lettuce crisper. Soak soggy lettuce in a bowl of cold water to which you've added the juice of half a lemon; refrigerate for 1 hour.

5. Blemish healer. Dab a pimple with lemon juice several times a day.

6. Pore cleanser. Combine 1 quart boiling water, the juice of one-half lemon, and 1 to 2 tablespoons dried thyme or mint. Steam your face 12 inches above the mixture for 15 minutes, then rinse with very cold water.

7. Sponge renewer. To salvage a soured sponge, saturate it with lemon juice, then rinse it thoroughly.

8. Apple preservative. Keep sliced apples from turning brown by coating the cut surfaces with lemon juice.

9. Piano prettifier. Rub a paste of 2 parts salt and 1 part lemon juice on piano keys; wipe off with a damp cloth, then buff with a dry one.

10. Air freshener. If the odor of fish lingers long after you've cooked it, place a pierced lemon in a 300°F oven for 15 minutes, leaving the oven door slightly open.

11. Hand deodorizer. Can't get rid of that fishy smell on your hands? Sprinkle powdered mustard on them, then add enough lemon juice to make a paste; rub in well, then wash with soap and water.

Lint

1. Tinder. Dispose of the lint from your dryer by using it under kindling.

2. Filler. Use dryer lint to stuff a small toy or pincushion—it's very clean.

Lip balm

1. Moisturizer. Rub it on your face to protect the skin while skiing.

2. Face saver. Dab some on a shaving nick to stop bleeding.

3. Zipper lubricant. Run it up and down the teeth to ease a balky zipper.

4. Wax. Use it to groom mustaches or eyebrows.

Liquid starch

1. Piñata. Blow up a balloon and cover it with strips of newspaper soaked in starch.

2. Threader. Dampen the end of the thread with a bit of liquid starch before threading your sewing machine.

Liquor cartons

1. "Ski ball." Place a carton at an angle and erect a small ramp in front (a rubber mat over a pile of books will do). Assign numbered values to each section of the carton and roll golf or tennis balls up the ramp and into the box.

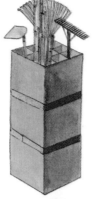

2. Tool keeper. Put a topless box on the garage floor; cut off the tops and bottoms of two others. Stack the cartons so that the dividers match up and attach them to one another with duct tape. Store a long-handled garden tool in each divider.

3. Art preserver. A clean liquor carton with its partitions intact is a great place to store rolled-up drawing papers and canvases.

4. Ornament storage. Wrap Christmas ornaments individually with newspaper, then place several in each of the carton's segments.

5. Workshop organizer. A sectioned carton is a great place to store dowels, moldings, furring strips, weatherstripping, 2 x 2's, and metal rods.

6. Glass protector. Keep fine crystal glassware or light bulbs, sorted by wattage, in one.

7. Sports caddy. Keep one in your child's room for neat storage of tennis rackets, baseball bats, fishing poles, and such. Decorate with adhesive plastic, such as Con-Tact. (See also *Cardboard boxes*, p.295.)

M

Magazines

1. Stadium cushion. Wrap several thick magazines in a heavy-duty plastic bag and place between you and cold, hard bleacher seats.

2. Funnel. Roll a large magazine into a cone, tape it, and use it to funnel dry substances.

3. Boot trees. Roll magazines inside boots to keep them in shape.

Magnets

1. Gas-cap holder. Attach a magnet near the opening to your car's gas tank to hold the cap while you're filling up.

2. Drawer organizer. Place a magnet in your catch-all drawer to keep pins and paper clips together.

3. Picker upper. Use a magnet to pick up spilled pins, needles, tacks, and staples.

Mailboxes

1. Train tunnel. Cut out both ends and run the tracks of an electric train set through it.

2. Garden caddy. Place one in a convenient spot in the garden to hold seeds and often-used tools.

3. Birdhouse. Set one in a tree or on a pole with the door open.

4. Breadbox. Clean and decorate a mailbox thoroughly, then use it to hold bread or snacks in the kitchen.

Margarine tubs

1. Paint can. Pour paint into an empty margarine tub for small touch-up jobs around the house.

2. Mold. Make individual molded salads or desserts in them.

3. Pet dish. Take several of these lightweight and disposable containers along when you're traveling with your pet.

4. Baby bowl. Store leftover baby food in them. Or use them for feeding the baby away from home—you can even carry the food in them.

5. Bank. Cut a slit in the lid.

6. Starter pot. Poke holes in the bottom, add potting mix, then sow seeds as recommended on the packet.

7. Storage bin. Clean and use to store odds and ends in the kitchen, garage, workshop, or kids' rooms.

Mattresses

1. Gym pad. Hang one on the wall behind a basketball hoop to prevent injuries to players.

2. Party chairs. A mattress is better than chairs at children's parties.

3. Crash pad. Place one under a child's jungle gym to prevent injuries.

4. Trundle bed. Keep an old mattress under the bed. When unexpected guests spend the night, pull it out and make it up—it will be much more comfortable than the floor.

5. Bumper saver. Nail one to the back wall of your garage, just in case.

6. Door protector. Nail a mattress to the side of the garage where the car door usually hits.

7. Trampoline. Keep an old one in the basement for small children to bounce on.

Mayonnaise

1. Ring loosener. Smear some on your finger and slide a tight ring off.

2. Furniture cleaner. Cover a water mark on finished wooden furniture with mayonnaise, then sprinkle with salt; using a clean cloth, rub the mixture in until the stain disappears, then buff until dry. Rewax if necessary.

Mesh bags

1. Salad spinner. Place washed lettuce leaves in a mesh bag, then twirl it around outdoors for several minutes.

2. Frog. Crumple one up and stuff it in a vase before arranging flowers.

3. Shoe scraper. In winter and during mud season, put a mesh bag over your doormat to give it a rough surface.

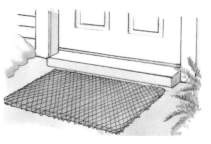

4. Fish stringer. Put the fish in a bag and hang it in the water until you're ready to go home.

5. Bird feeder. Combine melted fat with birdseed, let harden, then place in a mesh bag and hang from a branch; the holes make the food visible and give bird beaks easy access.

6. Lingerie bag. Place delicate underwear in a mesh bag so that it doesn't tangle with other clothes in the washer.

7. Dishwasher basket. Put baby bottle caps and nipples in a mesh bag to prevent them from flying all over the dishwasher when it's running.

8. Soap on a string. On camping trips, carry your bar of soap in a mesh bag. Use the soap right in the bag, then hang the bag on a tree to dry.

9. Drain filter. To prevent clogging the drain, place a mesh bag over the shower drain to catch hair.

10. Harvester. String a heavy cord along the top of a bag and put just-picked vegetables in it; hose dirt off the produce while it's still in the bag.

11. Fish net. Bend a wire hanger into a ring as large as the bag's mouth and stitch the open edge of the bag to it.

12. Scrub pad. Place a sponge inside a mesh bag, dampen, and use as a gentle but effective scrub pad for your car, grill, or pots and pans. If you can't find a sponge, simply bunch up the bag and scrub.

13. Soap holder. Fold a small plastic mesh bag and put it in the bottom of the kitchen soap dish; it will keep the soap dry and also serve as an emergency pot scrubber.

14. Beach bag. Before leaving the beach, put all the children's toys in a mesh bag and dip it in the water so that you don't transport sand back home.

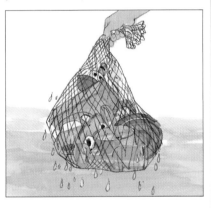

Microwave ovens

1. Ironing aid. Sprinkle clothes lightly with water, place in a plastic bag, and microwave on *High* for 1 minute or until warm to the touch; iron immediately. **Caution:** Make sure clothes have no metal parts.

2. Raisin rejuvenator. Place ½ cup dry raisins and 1 teaspoon water in a glass measuring cup; cover with plastic wrap and microwave on *High* 30 seconds; stir, then let stand 1 minute.

3. Crisper. To freshen soggy potato chips, pretzels, or crackers, microwave them on *High* for 30 to 60 seconds; let stand 2 minutes.

4. Squash splitter. To cut acorn squash easily, pierce the skin of an uncut squash with a fork, cook on *High* for 1 to 2 minutes, then cut it into halves, quarters, or slices.

5. Compress warmer. Microwave a plastic-wrapped dampened washcloth on *High* for 15 to 30 seconds or until it's warm to the touch.

Milk cartons

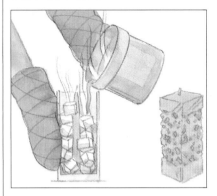

1. Candle mold. Coat the inside of a carton with cooking spray, put a taper candle in the center, anchoring it with a base of melted wax, then fill with ice cubes. Pour in hot wax; when the wax cools, peel off the carton and a delicate, lacy candle will appear.

2. Holding tank. Fill a clean half-gallon carton with water to hold your fish while you're cleaning their aquarium.

3. Bunny air conditioner. During hot, humid weather fill empty milk cartons with water, freeze, and place in the hutch to keep pet rabbits comfortable. The same idea can work in a doghouse as well.

4. Garbage sorter. Keep an empty carton next to the kitchen sink so that you can easily dispose of the wet garbage. Throw all dry refuse in the trash can.

5. Weight. To keep a tarpaulin from blowing off, half-fill milk cartons with sand or stones. Punch a hole in the top of each and loop a string through to tie to the grommets at the edge of the tarpaulin.

6. Toe guard. When camping, help prevent stubbing your toes on tent pegs in the dark; put cut-off carton tops over the pegs.

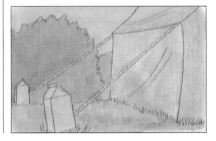

7. Bird feeder. Combine melted suet and birdseed, pour into a carton, and insert a loop of string into the mixture. After it hardens, tear away the carton and hang from a branch.

8. Paint can. Pour paint into the bottom half of a cut-off carton; discard when the job is finished.

9. Seed starter. Cut the top off a carton, punch holes in the bottom, fill with potting mix, and sow seeds according to the packet's instructions.

10. Cooler. Put a glass container of vodka, punch, or lemonade inside one, fill with water, and freeze. Peel off the carton; to pour the beverage, wrap the icy bottle in a towel.

11. Vegetable collar. Cut off the top and bottom and push into the ground around tomatoes and peppers to discourage grubs and cutworms.

12. Block. Remove the spout end of a well-washed carton and cut slits at each corner to make four flaps. Fold the flaps, tape in place, and decorate.

13. Dustpan. Cut off the front and bottom of a carton, then slice the sides at an angle to sweep dirt in easily.

Mirrors

1. Handkerchief presser. Stick a just-washed cotton handkerchief onto the bathroom mirror; as it dries in place, it will press itself.

2. Reflector. Place mirrors along walkways and driveways.

3. Tray. Use epoxy to glue a mirror to a piece of fiberboard.

4. Shelf. Put them on the bottom and back of your china cabinet to make your glassware sparkle.

5. Signal mirror. Using long and short flashes, send messages via Morse code.

6. Compact. Fit a small rectangular mirror (perhaps a piece of a broken one) inside the lid of an aspirin tin.

7. Basement detective. If your basement seems damp, attach a mirror to one wall. Check it the next day; if it's moist or fogged over, the problem is condensation; if it's dry and the wall is damp, the problem is seepage.

8. Flush enhancer. Check under the rim of your toilet bowl with a small mirror; if the openings appear clogged, ream them out with a wire hanger.

Modeling clay

1. Anchor. When repairing broken china or pottery, hold the pieces together on a bed of modeling clay until the glue sets; when dry, remove the clay.

2. Book cleaner. To clean a book's soiled edges, press a lump of modeling clay over the dirt, kneading it frequently to get a fresh surface. Clean one small area at a time, being careful not to rub.

Monofilament

1. Necklace cord. Restring beads or pearls without a needle.

2. Chandelier hanger. If the hook for a chandelier pendant is broken or lost, rehang it with monofilament.

3. Heavy-duty thread. Sew or repair dog leashes, pack straps, nylon mesh lawn furniture, or window screens with monofilament. (Don't use it on anything that needs ironing—it may melt.)

4. Invisible trellis. Attach monofilament to the garage and to pegs set in the ground.

5. Picture wire. Use it to hang pictures, wind chimes, mobiles, and Christmas ornaments.

Mothballs

1. Summerizer. When washing woolens you're about to store, dissolve a few mothballs in the final rinse water.

2. Rust preventer. Place some in the toolbox to absorb moisture.

3. Trash can deodorant. Put a couple of mothballs between the trash can and the plastic garbage bag—at least you won't smell garbage!

4. Pest deterrent. Place mothballs around holes and vents or in trash cans to discourage squirrels, raccoons, and other animal invaders.

5. Tarnish inhibitor. Place some in the silverware drawer or chest to help prevent discoloration.

Motor oil

1. Tool cleaner. Add used motor oil to a bucket of sand, then thrust the metal parts of garden tools into the mixture to clean them after use and help keep them rust-free.

2. Brush saver. After cleaning paintbrushes with mineral spirits, squeeze a little clean oil onto the bristles and wrap tightly with aluminum foil. Before using a brush again, rinse with a little more mineral spirits.

3. Body protector. To prevent corrosion from salted roads in winter, spray the underside of your car with used motor oil.

4. Concrete lubricant. To prevent sticking, brush onto wooden forms before pouring concrete.

Mousetraps

1. Wall clamp. Fasten a spring trap to your workshop or kitchen wall to hold frequently used but easily misplaced items, such as gloves, cloths, or recipes.

2. Paperweight. Keep several spring mousetraps on your desk for organizing bills, receipts, business cards, and other loose papers.

3. Glue clamp. If you're short a spring clamp or two, a mousetrap or rattrap will do the trick.

Mugs

1. Utensil container. Keep spoons, spatulas, and other kitchen utensils in an attractive mug that has cracked and can't hold fluids anymore.

2. Planter. Even if it's chipped, a mug still makes a terrific container for small plants on the kitchen windowsill.

3. Pencil holder. Keep pens or pencils handy for telephone messages.

Nail polish

1. Personalizer. Print names or initials on cups or glasses with bright nail polish.

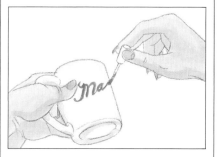

2. Ornament paint. Decorate or touch up Christmas ornaments with a bit of nail polish.

3. Run stopper. Dab clear nail polish on a stocking or pantyhose run to prevent it from growing.

4. Sealing wax. Seal letters with a dab of fingernail polish—it doesn't need warming in a flame, and it sticks just as well as wax.

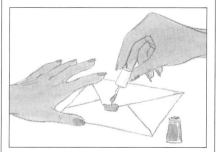

5. Measure marker. Make the ounce indicators on baby bottles or measuring cups easier to read by marking them with bright red nail polish.

6. Brand. Paint your initials on wooden tool handles with nail polish. Before it dries, set a match to it and the polish will burn, leaving your brand in the wood.

7. Sealant. Keep a bottle or jar from leaking while you're traveling; apply a light coat of nail polish around the base of the cap.

Nails

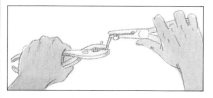

1. S-hook. Hold a thin nail with pliers and bend it into an S with a second pair; clamp a larger nail in a vise and hammer it into shape.

2. Weight. Use nails of various sizes as weights for a balance scale.

3. Potato baker. To shorten baking time, insert clean 10d nails into potatoes before putting them into a conventional oven. Remember to remove them before serving!

4. Post setter. For a stronger hold, hammer a few long or bent nails partway into the base of a fence post before setting it in concrete.

Neckties

1. Skirt. Remove the stitching and press about a dozen ties flat; sew them together at their edges, starting at the wide end. Make a waistband out of a solid-color tie.

2. Belt. Instead of the self-belt, wrap a tie around the waistline of a solid-color outfit.

3. Crazy quilt. Remove the stitching and press ties flat. Arrange on a flat surface to determine the right design, then sew together. (Not enough ties? You can usually get a good buy on them at garage sales.)

4. Ribbon. Use to tie packages.

5. Serpent. Stuff the opening of an old necktie; add buttons for eyes and a felt forked tongue.

Newspapers

1. Fire starter. Overlap two or three sheets of newspaper to form a tight roll, then make an overhand knot. Half a dozen of these will start the most stubborn logs. (See also *Firewood*, p.82.)

2. Oven cleaner. Use crumpled-up balls of newspaper to remove heavy grease, then wipe with a damp cloth or sponge.

3. Penny roll. Lay coins diagonally across a piece of paper and, while holding the pennies still, bring a corner over them and carefully start to roll. As you continue to roll, tuck in the corners at each end; when done, tape the end of the paper to the roll.

4. Glass cleaner. After washing windows or mirrors with soap and water, crumple up newspaper and wipe the glass dry—it will sparkle and be streak-free.

5. Duster. For reaching those hard-to-dust places, roll a sheet of newspaper into a tube and fringe one end.

6. Cat litter. In a pinch, shred newspaper for the litter box.

7. Draft blocker. Keep out the cold by stuffing newspaper under doors and in the cracks of windows that won't close all the way.

8. Boot dryer. Stuff crumpled newspapers in wet boots or shoes and let dry overnight.

9. Deodorizer. Stuff wads of newspaper into shoes or boots to remove unpleasant odors overnight.

10. Window repair. Glue newspaper to both sides of a cracked pane of glass. When dry, chip away the putty, and the pane will come out without splintering.

11. Plastic container sweetener. A piece of crumpled printed (no colors) newspaper sealed in a container overnight will remove most foul odors.

12. Luggage freshener. If trunks and suitcases haven't been used in a while, stuff crumpled newspapers inside and leave for a couple of weeks.

13. Moplets. For cleaning up grease or sopping up paint remover, keep a supply of newspapers on hand in your workshop. Pile them up an inch or so thick, then cut them into quarters with a sharp knife. Stack the papers and drill a hole in one corner with an electric drill. Run a wire through the hole and hang from a convenient hook.

14. Tablecloth. For messy meals, set the table with newspapers.

15. Raccoon deterrent. Crumple up newspapers between rows of corn in the evening when ears are ripe.

16. Carpet padding. Place several thicknesses of newspaper under rugs and carpets.

17. Moth deterrent. Since moths appear to hate newsprint, try packing out-of-season clothing in newspaper; roll papers inside rugs before storing.

18. Mulch. Spread papers out flat or tear them into strips and place around plants. Water thoroughly to hold in place; if necessary, secure the papers with a few rocks.

Olive oil

1. Chamois revitalizer. To renew an old piece of chamois, soak it for 15 minutes in a bucket of warm water to which you've added 1 teaspoon olive oil; be sure to agitate the bucket every few minutes.

2. Eye makeup remover. Moisten a cotton ball with olive oil, dab onto the eye area, and tissue off.

3. Leather softener. Rub it into dry leather with a soft, clean cloth; tissue off the excess.

4. Paint remover. If you get paint in your hair, dip a piece of cotton in olive oil and rub it gently over the unwanted coloring.

5. Body insulator. If you don't want to wear bulky clothes while exercising outdoors, cover your exposed skin with olive oil to stay warm.

6. Dry hair repair. Heat oil until warm, then apply liberally to hair. Cover with a plastic bag, then wrap in a towel; leave on for 45 minutes, then shampoo and rinse thoroughly.

7. Hand softener. To treat hands, immerse them in a bowl of warm olive oil for about 10 minutes, then wipe off the excess.

8. Table ring remover. Rub a paste of equal parts olive oil and salt gently onto the mark with your finger; wipe it off with a dry cloth after 2 hours. Rewax if necessary.

9. Overflow inhibitor. Before boiling water, pour in a little olive oil.

Onions

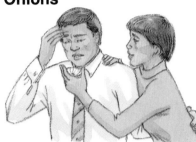

1. Smelling salts. Hold a cut onion under the nose of a person who is feeling faint.

2. Deodorizer. To remove the smell of paint from a cabinet, leave a sliced onion inside for several hours.

3. Dye. Boil red onion skins to make red dye, yellow skins for yellow dye.

4. Eyewinker remover. Something in your eye? Chop up an onion and let your tears wash the foreign body out. (See also *Eyewinker,* p.76.)

5. Knife renewer. Plunge a rusty knife into an onion two or three times.

6. Windshield defogger. Rub a cut onion on the inside of your windshield to prevent it from fogging up.

7. Athlete's foot soother. To relieve the itch, rub onion juice on the affected area.

8. Wart remover. Rub a stubborn wart with a raw onion dipped in salt; repeat until the wart disappears. (See also *Warts and moles,* p.225.)

Oven mitts

1. Beverage cozy. If you're called away, put your mug of tea, coffee, or bouillon inside an oven mitt to keep it warm until you return.

2. Bulb changer. There's no need to wait to replace a burned-out light bulb—protect your hand from the heat in an oven mitt.

3. Duster. Use one side of the mitt for applying wax, the other for buffing.

4. Egg warmer. Keep boiled eggs warm for half an hour inside one.

Paintbrushes

1. Puppet. Paint the base and handle, then draw on a face; add a bow tie for the Mr., a collar for the Ms.

2. Glazer. Brush pie crusts with milk or egg white for a shiny golden finish.

3. Toaster cleaner. Use a fine sash brush to get into the more inaccessible crevices.

4. Duster. Wipe houseplant leaves clean with a moistened paintbrush.

5. Baster. Brush a marinade or pan juices over poultry or meat.

Pantyhose

1. Onion dryer. Push an onion into the foot and tie; continue knotting onions in the leg, then hang to dry. When you need one, simply cut it off.

2. Stuffing. For sturdy, washable filler for pillows, quilts, and toys, cut up old pantyhose.

3. Paint saver. To get rid of the lumps, strain old paint through pantyhose tied over the top of a receptacle.

4. Rubber band. Cut off the two legs, then slice them into segments about 1½ inches wide. Use to hold boxes closed or to tie newspapers together.

5. Deer repellent. Fill with fresh human or dog hair clippings and hang from bushes; renew regularly.

6. Scrub pad. Moisten scrunched-up pantyhose with warm water and a few drops of dishwashing detergent to clean nonstick cookware.

7. Photo enhancer. To add a misty, soft-focus quality to a photograph, fasten a piece of pantyhose over the camera lens with a rubber band.

Paper bags

1. Lantern. Light up your walkway when company is coming. Fill a bag halfway with sand and insert a candle.

2. Corn saver. Protect ripening corn from light frost, birds, and raccoons by placing bags over the ears.

3. Fish cooker. Prevent fish from drying out—bake it partially, then place it in a greased bag and finish cooking in the oven.

4. Mailing paper. Instead of buying craft paper, cut up old grocery bags.

Paper clamps

1. Music holder. Keep sheet music in place, songbooks open to the correct page.

2. Workshop hanger. Clamp paintbrushes, gloves, or safety goggles and hang on a hook or nail.

3. Hair clip. Use to section off hair for cutting or styling.

4. Exerciser. Squeeze a large one again and again to strengthen your grip and release tension.

Paper clips

1. Ornament hanger. Shape a paper clip into an S and carefully hook one looped end through the ball's opening; hang the other loop on the tree.

2. Money clip. Fold your bills in half, then hold them together with a jumbo paper clip.

3. Brad holder. Avoid banging your fingers when hammering a small brad. Wedge the brad between the legs of a paper clip.

4. Watch setter. Use the tip of a straightened paper clip to press the tiny time-setting controls on your digital watch.

5. Bra strap repair. If the adjustable buckle breaks, substitute a paper clip.

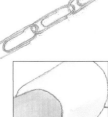

6. Garland. Hook 100 or more clips together for glittery Christmas tree trim.

7. Cuff links. Partially straighten a paper clip and insert a looped end into each of the two cuff holes; then reshape the paper clip.

8. Bookmark. Finding your place in a book is easy when the page has been clipped.

9. Tie clip. Fasten both aprons to the shirt's front placket with a paper clip.

10. Soap bubble frame. Shape a big paper clip into an S, then, with needle-nose pliers, pinch the larger loop to make a closed circle.

11. Collar stay. If you lose a stay, replace it with a paper clip; it will keep the tip of your shirt collar neatly in place. (Remove before laundering.)

12. Unclogger. Clean the clogged holes of a shower head, a saltshaker, or an aerosol nozzle with the clip's tip.

13. Chip clip. Keep bags of potato chips and other snacks fresh by closing them with a large paper clip.

14. Coin retriever. Reach coins that have fallen between the windshield and dashboard with a large paper clip reshaped into a hook.

15. Pipe cleaner. Cover a straightened large paper clip with a strip of facial tissue or paper towel and run it through the length of the pipe stem.

Paper cups

1. Ice mold. Freeze water in cups, then peel the paper off.

2. Funnel. Poke a hole near the edge in the bottom.

3. Pouring cup. Crimp the rim to create a spout.

4. Tomato protector. Fend off cutworms and other pests by removing the bottoms of paper cups and sinking them into the soil around young plants.

5. Oil funnel. Remove the bottom of a small (3- to 5-ounce) paper cup. Crimp the small end if necessary to fit it into your car's oil filler and pour oil into the large end.

6. Wind vane. Remove the bottom and suspend the cup from a string so that it hangs horizontally; the wide end will tend to face into the wind.

Paper towels

1. Desilker. Shuck an ear of corn, then wipe it down from tip to base with a dampened paper towel—the silk will come off in a single stroke.

2. Wax remover. Place a paper towel over melted wax on the carpet, then iron—the wax will melt into the towel.

3. Tea strainer. Did the bag break in your tea? Layer two paper towels over another cup and carefully pour the tea through—the leaves will stay on top.

Paraffin

1. Thread strengthener. Pull a threaded needle over a piece of paraffin before sewing on a button.

2. Drawer glider. Remove a sticky drawer and rub a cake of paraffin up and down the edges and sides, especially where they appear rough from rubbing against the frame.

3. Lubricant. Rub paraffin on the shaft of a nail or screw for easier insertion into wood.

4. Window aid. Rub paraffin on window sash tracks to prevent sticking. Also rub it on rods so that curtain rings or drapery hooks slide easily.

5. Rainproofer. After writing identifying details on garden markers, dip them in a pan of melted paraffin.

Peanut butter

1. Residue remover. Rub away the remains of price tags on pots, pans, and other metal or plastic items with a dab of peanut butter.

2. Wildlife bait. To lure a wild bird or small mammal into camera range, smear peanut butter on the spot where you want it to perch, making sure you keep the spread slightly out of view of the camera. Focus on that spot—your subject can't run off with the peanut butter as it can with nuts or seeds.

3. Tar remover. To rid your car or your shoes of messy road tar, rub with peanut butter.

Pencils

1. Play logs. Slice off the eraser and tapered ends of a lot of old pencils. Glue them together to build a miniature cabin; cut up a disposable aluminum pan to make a tin roof.

2. Plant stake. To keep a small plant upright, insert a pencil into the soil next to it and tie them together with soft string.

3. Page turner. Use the eraser end for turning the pages of catalogs or phone books.

4. Moth repellent. Most pencils are made of cedar. Put the shavings from a pencil sharpener in lightweight bags to make sachets for your closets and bureau drawers.

5. Diviner. Insert a pencil eraser into a houseplant's soil; if it comes out dry, get out your watering can.

6. Calculator puncher. The eraser end is ideal for pushing the small buttons of a pocket calculator.

Petroleum jelly

1. Squeeze easer. To prevent the cap on a tube of glue from becoming permanently stuck, put a thin layer of petroleum jelly on the threads before recapping it.

2. Cuticle softener. Massage it in each morning and night.

3. Easy wheeler. To ease rolling and eliminate squeaking, lubricate the axles of TV-stand, wagon, and roller-skate wheels with petroleum jelly.

4. Glider. Apply a thin coat of jelly to window sash tracks. Dab jelly on the track of a balky bureau drawer so that it slides in and out easily.

5. Paint masker. Cover hardware or windowpanes with a thin film of jelly when painting; if you overbrush, you'll be able to wipe the paint off easily.

6. Rust preventer. Protect the metal parts on tools, fishing rods, cooking utensils, skates, skis, and exterior trim by lubricating them with jelly.

7. Dancer's gleam. For special occasions, give yourself an extra glow—apply a thin film of petroleum jelly to your face and shoulders, then dust lightly with colored glitter.

8. Santa brows. Apply a light coat of jelly to eyebrows, then dust with cornstarch or flour.

9. Paw protector. Apply a thin coating to animal paws to prevent irritation from rock salt in winter.

10. Fake bait. Use small pieces of sponge coated with petroleum jelly to simulate fish-egg bait.

11. Ring budger. Slide a tight ring off with the help of petroleum jelly.

12. Mitt softener. Keep your baseball mitt pliable by rubbing it regularly with petroleum jelly.

Photographs

1. Paperweight. Make a cube out of a milk carton (p.314) and fill it with sand for weight; tape pictures on all sides, then protect them with acrylic spray.

2. Wall hanging. Mount an assortment of various-size prints on a clean window shade with rubber cement.

3. Mobile. Glue photographs back to back on cardboard, then darken the edges with a marker. Suspend with monofilament from three pieces of wire hanger.

4. Headboard. Enlarge a simple photograph and mount it on a semicircle of ¾-inch plywood the same width as the bed.

Pillowcases

1. Sheets. Use standard-size pillowcases as sheets for baby's bassinet.

2. Defroster. Cover short tomato plants with old pillowcases whenever frost threatens.

3. Sweater saver. To help prevent pilling when washing sweaters, put them inside a pillowcase and tie with string before placing in the machine. (This also works well when machine-washing lingerie.)

4. Strainer. When making jelly, separate the fruit juices from the seeds and pulp by pouring through a pillowcase.

Pipe cleaners

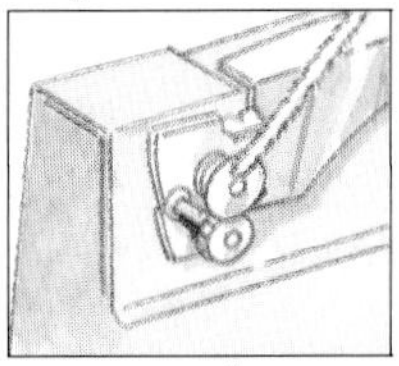

1. Mini scrubber. Remove the dirt from the wheel of a can opener or clean the bobbin area of a sewing machine.

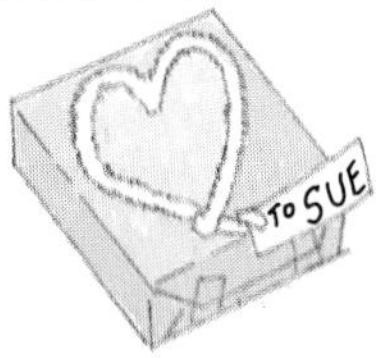

2. Gift decorator. Shape into a bow or a heart or whatever is appropriate, poke one end through a hole in the name tag, and affix to the package with transparent tape or a dab of glue.

3. Twist tie. Use a pipe cleaner to seal the top of a trash bag.

4. Unclogger. Open and clean the ports in gas ranges, steam irons, and aerosol containers.

5. Napkin ring. Shape them into circles, squares, or hearts.

6. Plant tie. Secure small plants to stakes or vines to trellises or other supports.

Plastic bags

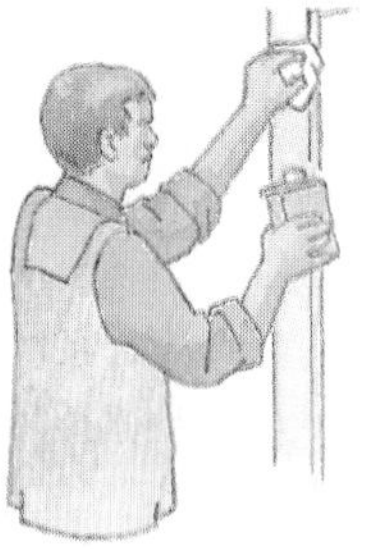

1. Shop apron. Cut 1 inch off the bottom of a plastic trash bag with handles and put it over your head, slipping your arms through the handles.

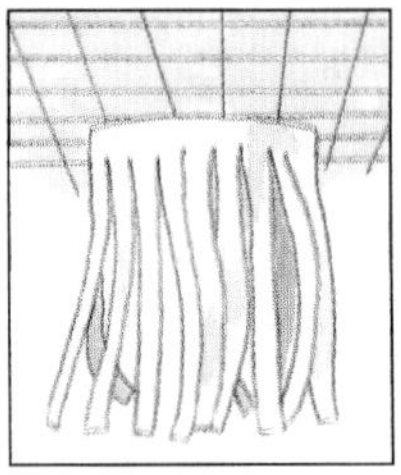

2. Streamers. Here's an easy way to hang party streamers—cut a bag into strips, starting from the open end and stopping short of the bottom.

3. Paintbrush protector. If you're interrupted while painting, prevent the brush from drying out by slipping it into a plastic bag and tying it closed.

4. Liner. Tape pieces of plastic bags into the bottoms of picnic baskets, paint trays, or boots.

5. Pastry bag. Fill a small plastic bag with icing or whipped cream, snip a corner, and squeeze.

6. Plant ties. Cut into 1-inch strips to secure plants to a pole or trellis.

7. Filler. Cut bags into strips and use to stuff outdoor cushions, bathtub toys, and other items likely to get wet.

Plastic jugs

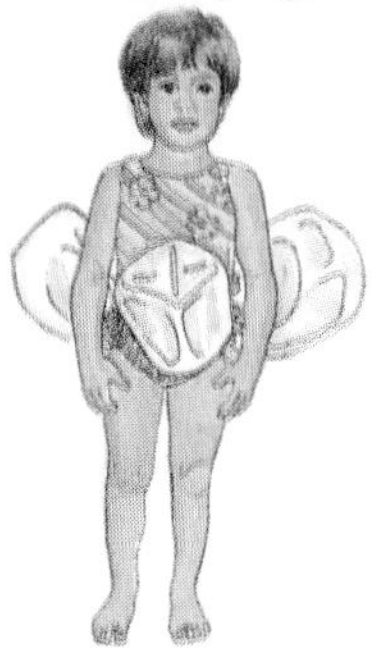

1. Water wings. Knot a sturdy rope through the handles of four empty, tightly capped 1-gallon jugs and tie them around the child's waist.
Caution: Do not leave the child unattended.

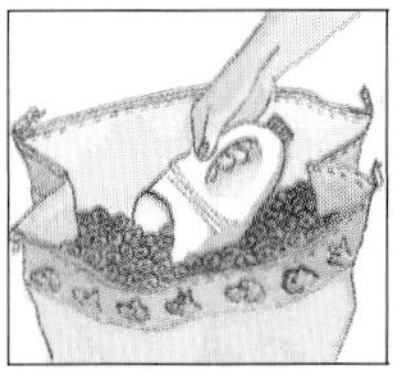

2. Scoop. Cut diagonally across the bottom of a plastic jug and use it to scoop up dog food, sand, or fertilizer.

3. Hip bucket. Keep your hands free for harvesting. Cut a large hole from the side opposite the jug's handle and string your belt through it.

4. Boat bailer. Cut off the bottom half of a large plastic bleach bottle diagonally. Don't forget to keep the cap on so that the water doesn't just slosh through.

5. Funnel. Cut a jug in half; remove the cap and turn upside down to use as an emergency funnel for motor oil, antifreeze, or just about anything.

6. Buoy. Cap several jugs tightly and string them together to define swimming and boating areas.

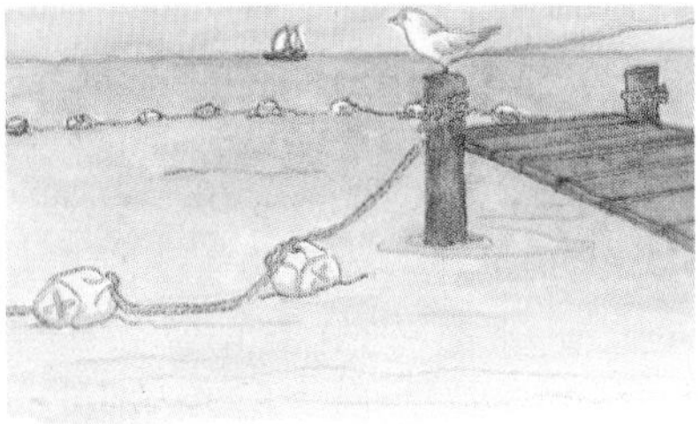

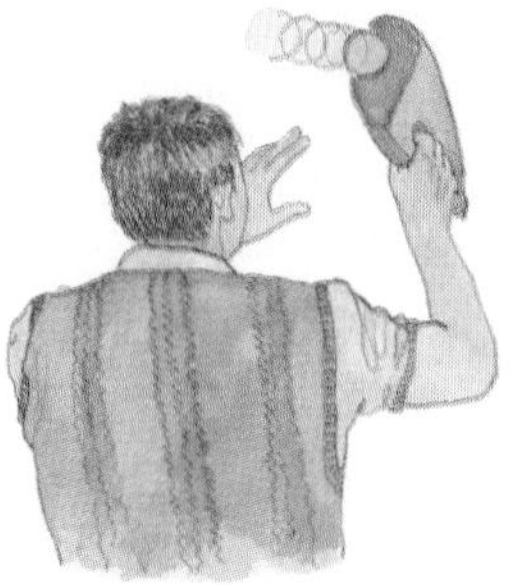

7. Toss-and-catch game. Cut a plastic bleach bottle as shown. Using a tennis ball, toss and catch alone or, with two containers, play with a friend.

8. Clothespin holder. Cut off the top of a plastic jug, punch holes in the bottom to let out rainwater, and hang by its handle from the clothesline.

9. Weight. Fill 2-quart or 1-gallon jugs three-quarters full of water and tie to the grommets in a tarp or pool cover to hold it down on windy days.

Plastic lids

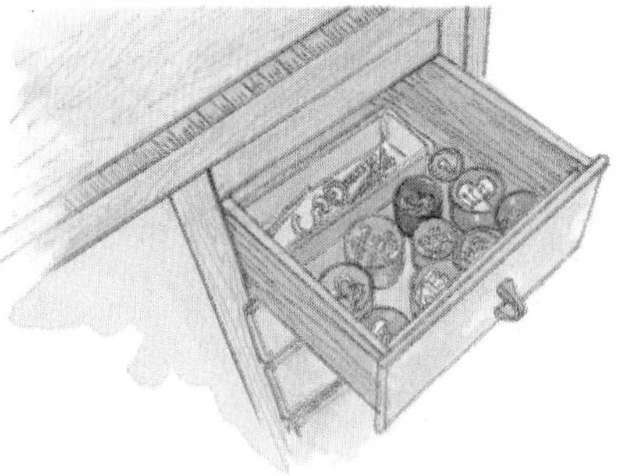

1. Drawer organizer. Store small nails, screws, and other supplies in the tops of aerosol cans; attach them with contact cement to hardboard cut to fit your workshop drawers.

2. Sink stopper. Place a plastic lid, its rim facing down, over the drain.

3. Scraper. Cut a lid in half and use the straight edge to scrape batter from bowls or leftovers from plates.

4. Lens cap. Keep your eyes open for plastic lids that are just the right size to fit snugly over camera, binocular, or telescope lenses.

5. Water tray. Place under plants to protect tabletops.

6. Frisbee. Toss a large lid with a flip of the wrist. (See also *Frisbees,* p.306.)

7. Hair clip. To keep your hair out of your face while cooking or cleaning, cut a large X in the center of a plastic lid and poke your hair through it.

8. Hand shield. To keep paint from dripping onto your hand, slit an X in the center of a lid and slide the paintbrush handle through it.

9. Dust buster. When making holes in drywall or plaster ceilings, drill through a plastic lid. Although the lid won't catch all the dust, it will protect your eyes and reduce cleanup.

10. Coaster. Protect tables on hot, humid days by placing plastic lids under icy drinks.

11. Stencil. Cut out numbers, letters, or shapes for tracing.

Plastic tablecloths

1. Game board. Use checkered tablecloths to play checkers or chess.

2. Shower curtain. Punch holes 6 inches apart and ½ inch from one edge of a hemmed tablecloth. Insert shower curtain rings or loop strings through the holes and loosely tie to the curtain rod.

3. Floor cover. Spread a plastic tablecloth beneath the baby's high chair to save on floor cleaning.

4. Leaf collector. Rake leaves onto an old plastic tablecloth, then grab the corners and drag it out to the curb for roadside pickup.

5. Window shade. Remove the roller and slat from an old shade. Cut a tablecloth to the size of the shade; hem one end of the cloth to hold the slat and glue or staple the other end to the roller.

6. Drop cloth. Use them to protect rugs and floors when doing touch-up paint jobs or other messy chores.

Plastic trays

1. Plate. Save the plastic foam trays from packages of meat and other foods to use as camp dishes.

2. Plant saucer. Place trays under plants to catch runoff water.

3. Palette. Use them for mixing small amounts of paint.

4. Padding. Slip foam trays between plates or around other breakables when packing.

Plastic wrap

1. Book cover. Protect a dust jacket with a sheet of plastic wrap.

2. Seal. Place a scrap of wrap between the neck and the screw top before closing a bottle of soda pop.

3. Window repair. Tape plastic wrap over a small hole to temporarily block out wind or rain.

4. Paint saver. To prevent a skin from forming, place a layer of plastic wrap over a paint can before tapping its lid back in place.

5. Screw setter. To hold a screw in position, push its threads through a piece of plastic wrap. Then fit the screwdriver into the slot in the head and wrap the plastic back over the blade of the screwdriver.

Plungers

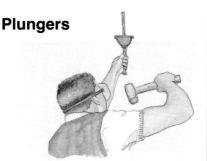

1. Chip catcher. When using a star drill overhead, catch falling chunks of plaster, cement, or brick by placing a plunger cup over the shank. Cut a small-enough hole through the rubber to make a tight, slipproof fit over the drill handle.

2. Dent remover. Try pulling out a shallow dent in a car door, trunk, or hood by pushing a wet plunger over the dent and pulling out sharply.

3. Outdoor candle holder. Insert the handle into the ground and put a citronella candle into the cup.

Potatoes

1. Shoe restorer. If your badly scuffed shoes do not take polish, rub them with a raw potato, then polish.

2. Stain remover. Rub away vegetable stains from your hands with a slice of raw potato.

3. Black paint. Bake potatoes until they're totally dried out and black. Grind thoroughly with a mortar and pestle; add enough linseed oil to make a paintlike consistency.

4. Itch reliever. Rub a thin slice of salted raw potato on hives or insect bites.

5. Blackhead remover. Put warm mashed potatoes inside a cheesecloth pouch and apply to a stubborn blackhead several times a day to soften it for easy removal.

6. Hair darkener. Dip a comb in water in which potatoes have been boiled and run it through blond or brown hair several times. To speed up the darkening and help set the color, dry hair in the sun.

7. Compress. Potatoes retain heat or cold well. Boil one to use as a warm compress or refrigerate a cooked one for a cold compress.

Pots & pans

1. Oil catcher. Place an old 5-quart (or larger) pot beneath the drain plug when you change your car's oil.

2. Birdbath. Set an old pan atop a flower pot in the garden and keep it filled with water.

3. Caddy. Leave those 50-pound sacks of fertilizer or grass seed in the garden shed and use a pot to carry what you need to the place you're tending.

4. Grill. Build your charcoal fire in a large discarded pot and cook on a wire cake rack placed over it. After you're finished, put the pot's cover on to choke out the fire and save the charcoal for another cookout.

5. Scoop. A pot with a handle works well as a boat bailer, dog food dipper, or compost shovel.

Quills

1. Pen. Cut the horny, hollow barrel of a feather into a point and dip into ink.

2. Duster. Use a large stiff feather to clean delicate bric-a-brac.

Quilts

1. Rug. Use sturdy movers' quilts as floor coverings in the family room.

2. Lining. Cut a piece to fit the inside of your silverware drawer—it will sound-proof and scratchproof the interior.

3. Place mat. Use an old mat as a pattern, then trim the edges with bias tape.

4. Dish separators. Cut pieces the size of your good china with pinking shears and place between the stacked plates for protection.

Quivers

1. Holster. Carry a rolled canvas or an umbrella in one.

2. Camping aid. Transport beverage cans, tent poles, or pegs to the camping site.

Quoits

1. Furniture bumper. Before you begin to vacuum, put these flat plastic or wooden rings around furniture legs to protect them.

2. Coaster. Cut a piece of cork to fit inside one.

Razor blades

1. Scraper. Remove paint, decals, or stickers from windows with a single-edge blade set in a holder or a double-edge blade set in a paper clamp.

2. Stencil. Use the design of the cut-out in a double-edge blade to decorate small boxes or plaques. Tape the edges of the blade for safety's sake and apply the pattern with a felt-tip marker or a stiff-bristled brush, using a small amount of paint or ink.

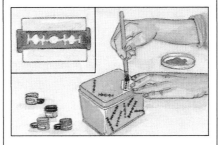

Refrigerators

1. Dryer. Suspend an old refrigerator rack from the garage ceiling with a rope and hang laundry on it to dry.

2. Tool chest. Remove the door and store tools and other shop equipment inside it.

3. Root cellar. Remove the door from an old refrigerator. In a well-drained part of the backyard, dig a deep hole large enough to hold the refrigerator box horizontally; line the hole with rocks, then lower the appliance into the ground. Alternate layers of sand or hay with root vegetables. Cover the opening with plywood. Use concrete blocks to hold the plywood in place.

Rubber bands

1. Table stabilizer. Fasten two or more card tables together to form one long table by placing sturdy rubber bands around adjacent legs.

2. Garter. Use them to hold up socks or protect sleeves. But make sure they're loose enough not to cut off your circulation.

3. Clamp. When gluing something small, hold the parts together with a rubber band.

4. Gripper. Wrap around doorknobs, jar lids, or tools to get a better handle on them.

5. Roll guard. Wrap one or more rubber bands around a flashlight or screwdriver handle to prevent it from rolling.

Rubber gloves

1. Hand warmer. When doing wet work on cold days, put rubber gloves over your garden gloves to keep your hands dry and warm.

2. Broom stabilizer. Slip a finger from an old glove over the end of a broom so that it won't fall down when propped against a wall.

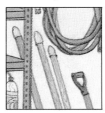

3. Pliers guard. To prevent ugly marks, cover the pliers' jaws with fingers from a ripped glove.

4. Pastry bag. Tie off all but one finger of a clean unlined rubber glove; fill it with icing, snip the tip, and squeeze.

5. Jar grip. Put on dry rubber gloves, hold the container in one hand, and twist the stubborn lid counterclockwise with the other.

6. Ice pack. Fill with ice, then tie the cuff to prevent leakage.

Rubber jar rings

1. Bathtub mat. Lash rings together with strong thread or monofilament.

2. Skid guard. Sew one or more on each corner of a throw rug.

3. Quoits. For a rainy-day indoor game, let preschoolers compete at tossing rubber jar rings over an upright post (perhaps the leg of an upside-down stool).

4. Table protector. Place under vases and lamps to protect the surface of furniture from scratches.

5. Party game. Warm and stretch a rubber ring to make it supple, then step into it and work it up your body and over your head without breaking it.

Safety pins

1. Stitch counter. When knitting, use them to mark or hold stitches.

2. Embroidery. Add sparkle to pockets, blue jeans, or the backs of jackets by "stitching" designs on them with large safety pins.

3. Chain. Hook them together to replace a broken pull chain until you can get a new one.

4. Missing link. Use a small safety pin to replace a broken clasp or link on a necklace.

5. Rivet. If a rivet connecting a rib and a stretcher on your umbrella has broken, remove the stub with pliers or wire cutters and substitute a safety pin.

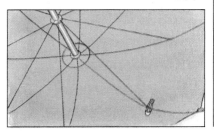

Salt

1. Stain remover. Combined with lemon juice, salt removes fruit stains from your hands.

2. Flower cleaner. Clean artificial flowers by shaking them in a large paper bag with ½ cup salt.

3. Dripproofer. To prevent wax dripping onto the candlestick or the table, soak candles in salt water. Use 2 tablespoons salt for each candle and just enough water to cover.

4. Suds controller. If detergent is overflowing the washer, sprinkle salt on the excess suds to tame them.

5. Spill container. Cover fresh oven spills with salt, let stand for 15 to 20 minutes, and wipe up. (Follow the same procedure when you drop grease or a raw egg on the floor.)

6. Herbicide. Kill poison ivy by spraying it with salt water.

Scarves

1. Belt. Make a solid-colored dress look sensational or an old outfit look like new by twisting a scarf of a contrasting color around your waist.

2. Sarong. Wrap a 45- or 54-inch-square scarf under your arms, at your waist, or low on your hips; pull the fabric taut, then knot the top ends where you want the opening to fall.

3. Handbag. Place your makeup, coin purse, and other miscellany in the center of a square scarf and tie the four corners diagonally. (Make a tote bag from a larger scarf.)

4. Bag sling. If your grocery bag starts to give way, take off your scarf and loop it under the bottom of the bag to support it.

5. Necklace. Fold a 24-inch-square scarf in thirds on the bias and knot several times.

6. Robe. Wrap a scarf around your shoulders and use it as a cover-up when traveling or on the beach.

Seeds

1. Artwork. On heavy paper, "paint" your design with white glue, then drop seeds onto the glue and let dry. Use different types of seeds for color and texture.

2. Jewelry. String fresh seeds with monofilament and a heavy-duty needle; let dry.

3. Snack. Coat fresh sunflower, melon, squash, or pumpkin seeds with oil, spread in a shallow pan, season, and bake in a 200°F oven for an hour or until they're dry.

Shampoo

1. Shaving cream. In a pinch, apply a small amount of shampoo to your wet skin and work up a lather.

2. Detergent. If you've run out of a gentle soap for hand-washables, use shampoo instead.

Shaving cream

1. Lubricant. Spray both sides of the joint of a squeaky hinge with foamy shaving cream.

2. Upholstery cleaner. Rub a fresh stain on upholstered furniture with shaving cream, wipe with a damp cloth, then dry. (Test first in an inconspicuous corner.)

3. Defogger. To prevent your bathroom mirror from fogging up during cold weather, spread a little shaving cream on the mirror and wipe it off with a tissue.

Sheet music

1. Lampshade. Attach sheet music to an old lampshade, then brush with linseed oil and let dry thoroughly before turning on the light. (Be sure to use a low-wattage bulb.)

2. Wrapping paper. Wrap up a music lover's birthday gift with sheet music.

3. Book cover. If you've lost the jacket to a book, cover it with some sheet music.

4. Wallpaper. Paper a small room with sheet music, using mildew-resistant wallpaper paste.

Sheets

1. Bull's-eye. Hang an old sheet on the wall and draw a target on it; let youngsters try to score bull's-eyes with beanbags.

2. Tablecloth. Convert a patterned sheet into an attractive table covering.

3. Deer repellent. Circle the garden with a cord about 3 feet above the ground, then tie strips of *white* sheets to it every 2 feet; a tail-height flash of white is a danger signal to deer.

4. Leaf scoop. Rake leaves onto an old sheet, gather the four corners together, and haul to the curb or compost pile.

5. Drop cloth. Place old sheets over the furniture before painting a room or under the table when having a children's party.

6. Banner. Advertise your garage sale or wish a neighbor "Happy Birthday" by painting the message on an old white sheet.

7. Christmas wrap-up. After removing holiday decorations, wrap an old sheet around the tree so that you can carry or pull it out of the house without leaving a trail of pine needles.

Shoe bags

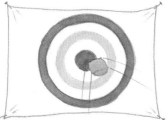

1. Magazine rack. Hang one from a hook on the bathroom door to hold magazines, paperbacks, and other types of reading material.

2. Toy bag. Hang a shoe bag over the car window or attach it to the back of the front seat to provide storage space for traveling toys and games, as well as books and snacks.

3. Kitchen caddy. Fasten a shoe bag to the back of the kitchen door to keep cleaning supplies all in one place.

Shoe boxes

1. Play bricks. Kids can use them to build play houses and forts.

2. Whelping box. To reduce the risk of the mother rolling onto a newborn and smothering it, place one or several puppies or kittens in a towel-lined shoe box while the others are being born.

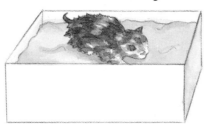

3. Safe. Store keepsakes, canceled checks, and other valuable items in one or more labeled shoe boxes.

4. Seed starter. Punch holes in the bottom of a box, cover with 2 inches of moist vermiculite, then plant.

5. Gift box. They're the perfect size for loaves of homemade bread, but you can also pack cookies in them.

6. Lunchbox. Paint a sturdy old box, then seal it with acrylic; keep it closed with twine or a belt.

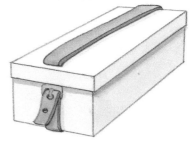

Shoe polish

1. Wood stain. Mix two or more colors together to get just the right shade and apply with a dry cloth.

2. Paint. Touch up scratches and picture hook holes on walls.

Shower caps

1. Plant saucer. If a hanging plant doesn't have an adequate saucer, put a shower cap over the container's bottom while you water it.

2. Ice bag. Fill one with ice cubes and apply to the injury.

3. Hair helper. Wear one when you paint the ceiling or deep-condition your hair.

4. Bowl cover. Use a clean one to cover leftovers in the refrigerator.

Shower curtain hangers

1. Closet organizers. Slip several of them over the end of your closet rod to hang purses, umbrellas, and belts.

2. Key ring. Keep rarely used keys in one place.

Shower curtains

1. Apron. Cut an old shower curtain into a cobbler's apron with pinking shears and attach ties at the top and the middle; wear it when doing extra-messy jobs around the house.

2. Ground cover. Place an old shower curtain under a tent or sleeping bag.

3. Poncho. Fold in half, snip an opening for your head, then trim the length as necessary.

4. Mulch. When landscaping with gravel or bark chips, place old shower curtains beneath the material to prevent weeds from growing through.

5. Raincoat. Toss them over the barbecue grill and outdoor furniture during sudden summer storms.

6. Babyproofer. Cut a 36- to 48-inch square to protect the floor beneath the high chair; use leftover scraps to make bibs.

7. Tablecloth. Use one to cover the picnic table.

8. Tarp. Throw a shower curtain over your wood pile to protect it from rain, snow, and dew.

9. Defroster. On wintry nights cover your windshield with a plastic liner with magnetic hem.

10. Drop cloth. Since paint can't seep through, plastic shower curtains are better than sheets for covering floors and furniture.

Silly Putty

1. Exercise equipment. Knead it to strengthen your hands and forearms.

2. Caulking. Use to temporarily plug cracks around windows.

3. Tranquilizer. Play with it to calm your nerves—especially useful when you've just given up smoking.

4. All-purpose cleaner. Remove lint from clothes, erase pencil marks, and clean computer keys.

Skateboards

1. Laundry cart. Keep a basket atop a skateboard directly below the chute. When you're ready to do the laundry, simply roll the load over to the washer.

2. Decorative shelf. Support an old skateboard (or just its deck) with two shelf brackets in a child's room.

3. Paintmobile. Prevent backaches—when painting baseboards and lower walls, sit cross-legged on a skateboard and roll along with your paintbrush and can.

Skirt hangers

1. Mat keeper. Hang place mats from a skirt (or slacks) hanger on the inside of a kitchen cabinet door.

2. Place keeper. When working from printed plans, hold the page in place with a skirt hanger; hang it from a nail or wire.

3. Dryer. Use them to dry your children's artwork.

Soap

1. Pomander. Place soap scraps in drawers or luggage to keep their contents smelling fresh.

2. Deer deterrent. To keep deer away, drill a hole through a wrapped bar of soap (preferably deodorant or perfumed), put a string through it, then hang it from a tree at browsing height.

3. Candle extender. To make your candles smokeless and long-lasting, soak them in thick soapsuds, being careful not to wet the wick; let them dry before lighting.

4. Magnetic hammer. When driving carpet tacks, rub the face of your hammer over a bar of soap, and your tacks will cling to it.

5. Soap mitt. Collect soap remnants in a cotton sock; tie with elastic or string and use when bathing.

6. Pincushion. Stick pins and needles into a wrapped bar of soap to keep them all in one place with their points lubricated.

7. Tailor's chalk. Store a few dry slivers of soap in your sewing box and use them to mark darts and hems on washable apparel.

8. Bubble bath. Shave or grate to make flakes; store in a container by the tub.

9. Collar-ring remover. Put odd bits of soap in a mesh bag and use to scrub collar stains.

10. Screw smoother. Scrape screws across a bar of soap before driving them into hardwoods.

Socks

1. Pet bandage. If your dog or cat has a wound on its leg, pull a clean old sock over the dressing to help hold it in place.

2. Scratch preventer. Before moving a piece of heavy furniture, slip socks onto the legs. Do the same on ladder tops so that you won't scratch the paint or siding.

3. Cozy. When interrupted, slip a thick sock over a baby bottle or a mug of coffee, tea, or cocoa to help keep the contents warm.

4. Shoe keeper. Pull a pair of socks over your shoes while painting; remove them before leaving the room.

5. Bath fragrance. Put potpourri into a cotton sock and toss it into the tub while the water is running; remove the mixture before you get in and dry it for reuse.

6. Buffer. Use them to apply wax and to polish shoes or cars.

7. Arm bib. Cut the feet off old socks and use the leg portions as sleeve protectors for messy little eaters.

Sponges

1. Sound soother. Insert dry sponges between large appliances and walls to reduce vibrations and eliminate rattling sounds.

2. Sealer. Before mailing a lot of greeting cards, "lick" the envelopes and stamps by whisking them over a damp sponge in a jar lid filled with water.

3. Soaper. Make a sudsy scrubber for bathing or cleaning by slitting a sponge and inserting soap scraps.

4. Pincushion. Push pins and needles into a dry sponge.

5. Paint applicator. Use a sponge to add an unusual texture to walls and other surfaces (p.369).

6. Produce preserver. Put a few water-soaked sponges in the vegetable drawer of your refrigerator to keep fruits and vegetables fresher longer.

7. Critter repellent. If raccoons and other pests won't leave your property alone, soak old sponges in diluted household ammonia and place them around their usual hangouts.

8. Knee pad. Sew pockets onto the knees of old pants and slip in small soft sponges.

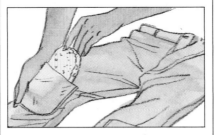

9. Blocks. Cut into wedges and squares and let your kids use them as building blocks.

Spray bottles

1. Mister. Fill a trigger spray bottle with tepid water and treat houseplants to a good misting.

2. Glass cleaner. Mix 2 tablespoons vinegar with 1 cup water in a trigger spray bottle.

3. Clothes dampener. Fill a trigger spray bottle with water and keep with your ironing supplies.

4. Athlete cooler. During the hot summer months, bring a trigger spray bottle of water to children's ball games. Spray any overheated athletes during the time-outs.

Squeeze bottles

1. Water gun. Fill and use for backyard "combat."

2. Fire controller. Use a water-filled squeeze bottle to damp down flames when barbecuing outdoors.

3. Ice pack. Fill an empty bottle three-quarters full of water and freeze.

4. Spotter. Put liquid laundry detergent in a squeeze bottle to pretreat grimy collars, cuffs, and stains.

5. Condiment carrier. Clean small squeeze bottles and use to transport salad dressing, mayonnaise, and other condiments that are not available in squeeze bottles.

Steel wool

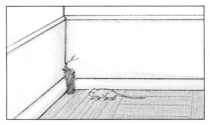

1. Pest control. Plug small cracks and holes with steel wool to help keep out rats and mice.

2. Screw tightener. Wind strands of steel wool around the threads of a screw before you reinsert it into the old hole.

3. Sneaker cleaner. A soapy steel-wool pad and a little elbow grease will make those dirty sneakers presentable again.

4. Clog preventer. When washing a dog in the tub or shower, put a ball of steel wool in the drain opening to catch stray hairs.

Straws

1. Stem stretcher. If you want to arrange short-stemmed flowers in a tall (preferably opaque) vase, slip the ends of the stems into drinking straws before placing them in the container.

2. Unclogger. Insert a straw into a ketchup bottle to break the surface tension and get the contents flowing.

3. Bubble mold. Shape into circles, squares, and triangles, dip into bubble solution, and wave through the air.

4. Spout extension. When lubricating hard-to-reach spots, put a plastic straw into the end of the spout of the oil can.

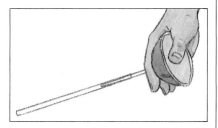

5. Dropper. Insert into liquid, then place your finger over the open end—the liquid will stay put until you let go.

String

1. Slam-no-more. Loop a piece of string around both doorknobs, avoiding the latch, so that the door won't bang shut.

2. Schedule anchor. Punch a hole at the top of the weekly TV schedule, loop a string through the hole, then tape the string to the TV set or hang it over the dial.

3. Clothesline. When traveling, make it a habit to carry a length of string so that you can hang hand-washables over the tub to dry.

4. Leak silencer. Stop the tom-tom effect of a dripping faucet by tying a string around the nozzle and dropping the end into the drain—the water will slide down the string and into the drain (silently).

Stuffed animals

1. Draft resister. In the winter, line them up along the bottoms of windows and doors for decorative insulation.

2. Scarecrow. Mount in gardens or on rooftops to scare off birds.

3. Safe. Cut open the underside, remove a small amount of stuffing, and insert small valuables.

4. Hand puppet. Open the bottom and remove all the stuffing so that your thumb and fingers can reach the head and limbs; ring the opening with elastic.

5. Bookend. Slit the back or underside of a pair of stuffed animals; remove some of the stuffing and fill with marbles or lead sinkers. Sew up the slit and glue a piece of an old rubber glove to the bottom to prevent the animals from slipping.

Tape

1. Pedal light. For safer nighttime bicycling, attach reflective tape to your pedals' edges.

2. Lock de-icer. When there's a forecast for a winter storm, cover your car's locks with masking tape. (This is also a good idea before going through a car wash in winter.)

3. Label. Cut masking tape to the desired length, stick it on, and write the information with a ballpoint pen.

4. Ant exterminator. Pick up an advancing line of ants with tape.

5. Comb cleaner. Press adhesive or transparent tape along the teeth, then lift it off and dip the comb in an alcohol or ammonia solution.

6. Court marker. Tape off your driveway or walkway for outdoor games.

7. Boot insulation. Put duct tape, silver side up, inside your boots to help keep your feet warm.

8. Gripper. Wrap duct, masking, or electrician's tape around a knife or tool handle until it's fat enough for a good grip.

9. Key finder. Put reflective tape on the tops of car or house keys so that you can distinguish them in the dark.

10. Sign letters. Make block letters or numbers; use reflective tape if you want the sign seen at night.

11. Nail caddy. Place nails or tacks between layers of tape so that they'll be instantly ready to use.

12. Hat shrinker. If your hat feels loose after a haircut, wrap adhesive tape around the sweatband.

13. Caster cover. To prevent marks on flooring, wrap caster wheels with adhesive tape.

14. Tube hanger. To store sticky tubes of household cement or caulk, cut a strip of adhesive or duct tape several inches long and fold it over the bottom of the tube, leaving a flap at the end. Punch a hole in the flap and hang the tube on a nail or hook.

15. Garage saver. To help you aim the car down the center of the garage, stick reflective tape on the rear wall. Also put some on anything that seems to be in your way at night.

16. Crayon extender. Wrap masking tape around crayons to prevent their breakage.

17. Hand protector. To remove a broken window without cutting yourself, crisscross it on both sides with adhesive or masking tape, then gently tap the inside edges with an 8-ounce hammer until the pane breaks free. Peel off the tape to remove any shards.

Tea

1. Facial. Don't throw out that used herbal tea bag. Empty its contents into a pot of boiling water, lean over it with a towel over your head, and enjoy a scented herbal facial sauna.

2. Eye lift. If your eyes are tired or swollen, place moist tea bags over them for at least 15 minutes.

3. Hair brightener. For golden highlights, rinse red or brown hair with orange pekoe tea.

4. Plant invigorator. Help ferns and other houseplants to thrive by watering them once a week with a weak solution of tepid tea.

5. Pet soother. If your dog has hot spots (wet, red skin eruptions), put cold wet tea bags on them, then see a veterinarian.

6. Poultice. Apply wet tea bags or loose tea leaves (preferably chamomile) directly on a burn; cover with gauze to secure them.

7. Lacquer lusterizer. Wash black lacquer pieces with strong tea, then wipe dry with a soft cloth.

8. Dust damper. To keep the dust from rising when you clean the fireplace, sprinkle moist tea leaves over the ashes first.

9. Dental aid. To help stop a gum from bleeding after an extraction, press a cool moist tea bag against it with your finger.

Telephone books

1. Origami. Cut pages into squares and fold into original pieces of art.

2. Confetti. Cut through several pages at once or run them through the office shredder.

3. Insulation. Lay them side by side over the floor of your young camper's backyard tent or over the bottom of the doghouse.

4. Towel. Use the pages of an old phone book to remove the first layer of grime from your hands.

5. Booster seat. Slipcover an outdated phone book so that your youngster can reach the table.

Tennis balls

1. Garden border. Spray-paint halves, then lay them side by side, keeping them in place with wire hangers cut and bent into small stakes.

2. Cultivator guard. As a safety measure when storing garden cultivators or other sharp-pointed tools, push old tennis balls onto their tips.

3. Massager. Put several in a tube sock, tie at the end, and use as a back massager.

4. Safe. Make a 2-inch slit along one seam, then place jewelry and spare cash inside; store with other sports equipment to prevent detection.

5. Chair feet. Slit tennis balls and put them over the feet of a deck chair so that it doesn't fall through the spaces between the boards.

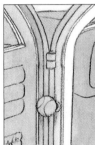

6. Battery saver. When keeping your car door open for an extended period of time, wedge a tennis ball into the door jamb so that it depresses the interior light switch.

7. Drip catcher. Before beginning a paint job, split a tennis ball and make a slit in the top of one of the halves; slip it onto the brush handle, concave side up, to prevent paint from dripping onto your hand.

8. Christmas wreath. Paint balls green; when dry, drill holes through each one and string onto a hanger shaped into a circle. Fill in with greenery and attach a bow.

9. Maraca. Punch a hole in a ball and put in some rice or beans; insert a dowel in the opening for a handle.

10. Doorstop. Cut one in half, then nail or screw it into the wall behind a swinging door.

11. Gas barrier. To keep sewer gas from entering your home through dry floor drains, drop a tennis ball into the drain basin. In the event of an emergency, the ball will float and allow water to escape.

12. Bumper. Attach to a string and hang from the garage ceiling so that the ball hits the windshield when the car is the proper distance from the back wall.

Timers

1. Prod. Use one to remind you to make a telephone call or to call again if you get a busy signal on your first try.

2. Organizer. When working in blocks of time, let a timer cue you to move on to the next task.

3. Memory jogger. Set one to remember to turn off the sprinkler or to turn on the TV for a special program.

4. Mediator. When youngsters can't resolve whose turn it is to play with a toy, give each one 15 minutes with the plaything. When the buzzer sounds, the turn is over.

Tires

1. Wading pool. Drape a shower curtain over the center of a large truck tire and fill with water.

2. Doormat. Cut tires into short strips with a hacksaw and wire together.

3. Planter. Plant tomatoes, potatoes, eggplants, and peppers inside tires laid on the ground—they'll protect the plants from the wind, and the dark rubber will warm the surrounding soil.

4. Greenhouse. Lay one on its side, plant seedlings, and cover with plastic wrap; ventilate and keep out of the sun.

5. Skid preventer. Glue or nail tire strips to ramps, docks, and stairways.

6. Fish environment. Weight down with rocks and toss in the pond to make a pleasant residential neighborhood for local fish.

7. Rolling cylinder. Bolt several tires of the same size together and use for practicing your balancing act, or make several and hold races.

8. Swing. Drill holes in a tire (so that rainwater can escape), paint it white (so it won't get hot in summer), bolt two chains to it, and hang from a tree.

9. Safety stand. For easy splitting, place logs close together and on end in an old tire.

10. Buoy. Drill holes in a tire (for drainage), paint white, then anchor with a concrete block.

11. Bumper barrier. Nail tire sections to the garage wall at the level of your car's bumper.

12. Retaining wall. Fill with dirt and embed along a hillside; grow ground cover in between.

Tissue paper

1. Cookie keeper. Crush tissue paper and put it in the bottom of the cookie jar to keep baked goods fresh.

2. Glass protector. When storing panes of glass in the workshop, separate them with sheets of tissue paper—the panes will be safer to pick up, and the paper will reduce the possibility of breakage.

3. Candle stabilizer. Prevent wobbling by stuffing several 1½-inch rounds of tissue into the holder around the candle.

4. Sound effects. Taping a happening or a playlet? Depending on how you crunch it near the microphone, tissue paper can sound like wind in the trees, a breaking wave, or footsteps in a leafy forest.

5. Tracing paper. Tape it tightly over the drawing and work under a good light or on a sheet of glass placed over a light source.

Tongue depressors

1. Shim. Place one or several under the short leg of a piece of furniture to keep it steady.

2. Sander. Glue sandpaper to one end and use it to file small objects.

3. Stirrer. Mix a small quantity of paint or glue with one.

4. Splint. Secure one to an injured finger with adhesive tape.

5. Condiment spreader. Put one in each container of mustard, relish, and other sauces at picnics and buffets.

Toothbrushes

1. Mini scrubber. Unblock small-appliance vents and get at grungy tile grout, grimy combs, and dirty typewriter keys.

2. Crevice cleaner. Use with silver polish to remove tarnish from filigreed pieces or with furniture polish to remove dust in carved wood.

3. Manicure implement. Clean fingernails and toenails with a soft toothbrush and soapy water.

4. Motor cleaner. A toothbrush dipped in kerosene is great for getting oily gunk out of hard-to-reach nooks and crannies.

Toothpaste

1. Blemish remover. Cover unsightly pimples with nonfluoridated toothpaste while you sleep; repeat nightly until the blemish disappears.

2. Surface restorer. Cover a stain or scratch on acrylic or plastic with toothpaste, let dry, then rub with a soft cloth.

3. Jewelry cleaner. Work it into jewelry grooves with a toothbrush, then rinse well and polish dry with a soft cloth.

4. Christmas decoration. Write holiday messages or draw festive pictures on your window with toothpaste. Afterward, use it to clean the window—first with a wet cloth, then a dry one.

Toothpicks

1. Bookmark. Save your place in a book or magazine.

2. Glue applicator. Dip one end into glue or epoxy to apply just a drop for small jobs.

3. Plug. Dip the end of a toothpick into glue, then force it into thumbtack holes, brad marks, or other tiny holes in wood; trim flush with a single-edge razor blade, sand the area smooth, and refinish the wood.

4. Sausage cooker. To facilitate frying, thread two or three sausages at a time onto pairs of wooden toothpicks; they'll be easier to turn, and they'll brown more evenly.

Towel rack

1. Leaf storage. Keep extra table leaves behind a towel rack screwed to a closet wall or some other out-of-the-way place.

2. Spread hanger. Attach a sturdy towel rack to the back of a solid-wood bedroom door to store the bedspread overnight.

3. Garage organizer. Mount one on a garage wall to store rags, trash bags, or drop cloths.

4. Reading rack. Place one on the wall alongside the toilet to hold newspapers and magazines.

Towels

1. Beach dress. Stitch the long sides of two bath towels together, allowing for armholes at one end, then sew up one of the short sides, leaving room for your head. (See also *Beach towel,* p.340.)

2. Neck support pillow. Roll up a towel, wrap it with a scarf, and tie the ends with ribbon or yarn.

3. Antilocking device. Drape a towel over the top of the bathroom door to prevent small children from locking themselves in.

4. Sink cushion. Line the bottom of your kitchen sink with terry-cloth toweling to protect delicate crystal and china when you wash them.

Trash can lids

1. Birdbath. Place a lid upside down on a somewhat smaller trash can and fill with water.

2. Toy shield. Make your child a gladiator's costume for Halloween, complete with trash-can-lid shield.

3. Bag holder. Cut out the center of a plastic lid, leaving a 2-inch-wide rim. Place a garbage bag in the can, stretch it over the rim, and press the lid down over it. Fill the bag through the cutout.

4. Sled. One with handles on the sides makes an excellent sledding disc.

5. Cymbal. Let your youngsters use pairs of metal lids as cymbals.

6. Jack rest. When using a car jack on soft ground, rest it on an inverted lid.

7. Leak pan. If your car is leaking oil or another fluid, put an upside-down plastic lid under the engine overnight. In the morning you'll see how much you lost—and of what.

T-shirts

1. Rope. Remove the hem, then cut a 1-inch continuous strip until you get to the sleeves; use to tie packages. Or knit with it (p.122).

2. Dustcloth. They're soft and washable, and dust clings to them.

3. Filler. Cut T-shirts into strips and use them to stuff pillows, beanbags, and toys.

4. First aid. Use clean shirts as compresses to control heavy bleeding or as padding for splints.

5. Plant tie. Cut old T-shirts into strips and tie vines and top-heavy plants to garden stakes.

Twist ties

1. Shoelace. If your child's shoelace breaks, keep her shoe on by putting twist ties in the eyelets.

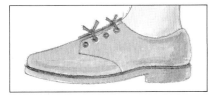

2. Key coder. Using different colors, knot twist ties through the holes in keys so that you can pick out the one you want in a hurry.

3. Cuff links. Pull the tie through so that the twist is inside the cuff.

4. Plant tie. Secure a drooping plant stem to a stake or hold vines to a trellis. Don't twist the ties too tight or you'll injure the stem and restrict its growth.

5. Craft aid. Use them as stitch markers or to hold knit or crocheted projects in place while you sew them together.

6. Binder. Hold sheets of loose-leaf paper together by inserting twist ties in the holes.

7. Auto router. To prevent electrical wires from making contact with (and being damaged by) hot engine parts, use twist ties to direct their paths under the hood.

8. Ornament hanger. Use them to secure balls and other ornaments to the Christmas tree.

9. Reminder. Tie one around your finger if you're out of string.

Umbrellas

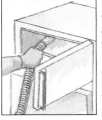

1. Drying rack. Remove the fabric from the umbrella frame and hang upside down.

2. Seedling shield. An old open umbrella, with its handle removed, will protect seedlings from an unexpected spring frost.

3. Wall saver. Hold an open umbrella behind your houseplants while you spray them.

4. Stake. Use the ribs from a broken umbrella as supports for top-heavy plants.

5. Picnic cover. Keep flies off your food by removing the handle from an old umbrella and using the open frame to shield the dishes.

6. Trellis. Remove the fabric from an umbrella, insert the handle in the ground, and use to support ivy or morning glories.

Vacuum cleaners

1. Defroster. Reverse the airflow on a canister vacuum and direct the stream of warm air to help eliminate the frost in your freezer.

2. Air broom. Reverse the airflow to a utility vacuum hose and blow leaves and dirt from the garage, driveway, or sidewalks.

3. Quicker picker-upper. Try vacuuming your shedding cat or dog with the brush, upholstery, or shag-rug attachment. (Before you attempt this, make sure that your pet isn't frightened by the machine's noise.)

Vegetable oil

1. Egg preserver. Store leftover egg yolks for up to 4 days in the refrigerator by placing them in a bowl and covering them with a film of flavorless vegetable oil.

2. Splinter easer. Soak the wounded area in vegetable oil for a few minutes before trying to remove the splinter. (See also *Splinters,* p.194.)

3. Defroster. Prevent car doors from freezing up in bad weather—before the cold strikes, rub down the gaskets with vegetable oil.

4. Conditioner. Massage lukewarm vegetable oil into dry hair; cover with plastic wrap for 30 minutes, then shampoo and rinse thoroughly.

5. Lubricant. Give your shovel a heavy coating of vegetable oil to prevent snow from sticking to it and weighing it down.

6. Skin smoother. Massage a generous quantity of oil into your skin; after 15 minutes remove the excess with a paper towel and take a hot-water bath. Be extra careful when you step out of the tub, since this luxurious bath is also slippery.

7. Cholesterol reducer. Mix equal parts melted butter and polyunsaturated vegetable oil and refrigerate to make a healthier substitute spread.

Venetian blinds

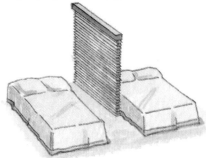

1. Room divider. Hang a row of blinds from a board attached to the ceiling to set off a dining area or den in your living room. Or, if your youngsters share a bedroom, use the blinds to partition a private area for each one.

2. Carpet protector. When painting a carpeted room, spread out a drop cloth and slide disassembled slats under the baseboard and over the edges of the cloth—they're just broad enough to catch errant drips.

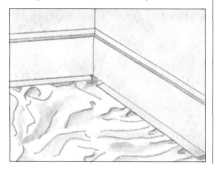

Vinegar

1. Pain reliever. If ice doesn't seem to ease the discomfort of a strain or sprain within 24 hours, apply hot vinegar compresses. (See also *Strains & sprains,* p.198.)

2. Hand deodorant. Remove the smell of onions or fish on your hands by rinsing them with vinegar.

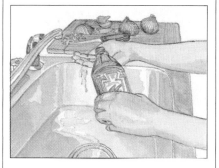

3. Kettle cleaner. Lime deposits in your teakettle? Fill it with equal parts vinegar and water; bring to a boil and allow to stand overnight.

4. Decal detacher. Give decals an extra-heavy dose of vinegar and let it sink in. Then peel them off.

5. Prespotter. Rub a paste of vinegar and baking soda into collar grime. Saturate perspiration stains with vinegar before laundering.

6. Brush softener. Revive old paintbrushes in a distilled white vinegar and water solution, then wash them in heavy-duty detergent.

7. Ironing aid. Remove mineral deposits from an old steam iron by filling it with a solution of equal parts white vinegar and water and letting it steam until dry; rinse the tank with plain water, then refill it and shake the water out through the steam holes.

8. Rust remover. Soak a corroded bolt in a small container of vinegar for several days or until the rust begins to dissolve.

9. Bath additive. To relieve aching muscles or itching skin, pour 1 cup cider vinegar into a tub of warm water and soak in it for 15 minutes.

10. Egg container. To poach an egg without having the white spread out too far, add 1 tablespoon vinegar to the water.

11. Laundry rinse. To brighten white clothes and get rid of detergent residue, soak them in 1 gallon warm water with 1 cup white vinegar; follow with a clear-water rinse.

12. Hair treatment. Make dark hair extra shiny by rinsing it with a mixture of 2 cups water and 1 cup vinegar; follow with clear water.

13. Crease setter. Mix equal parts of white vinegar and water and apply to creases before pressing them in place. (Test first to see if the solution stains the fabric.)

14. Window washer. Clean windows with a solution of 2 tablespoons vinegar in 1 quart warm water. Wash from top to bottom on the inside and from side to side on the outside, so that you can tell where there are streaks.

Vodka

1. Astringent. Apply some with a cotton ball to close your pores and give your face a fresh, clean feeling.

2. Teething remedy. Rub cold vodka on a teething baby's gums.

3. Pipe cleaner. Soak a pipe cleaner in vodka to clean and freshen the interior of a pipe stem. (Do not use it on the bowl or exterior of the pipe.)

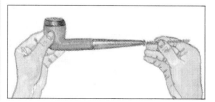

Wading pools

1. TV lounge. To prevent spills on the carpet, let snacking children sit in an empty wading pool while watching TV.

2. Storage bin. Put toys, craft items, and out-of-season clothing in a plastic wading pool and slide it under a bed.

3. Cooler. Chill beverages for an outdoor party in a wading pool half-filled with ice.

Wallpaper

1. Jigsaw puzzle. Cover a piece of cardboard with a scrap of wallpaper and cut it into intricate shapes.

2. Liner. Use wallpaper strips in drawers or on shelves.

3. Place mat. Cut into a rectangle or an oval and spray with acrylic.

4. Screen. Customize a folding screen by covering it with wallpaper.

5. Book cover. Protect schoolbooks with leftover wallpaper.

6. Room coordinator. Use leftovers from covering the walls as delightful accents on canisters, planters, wastebaskets, and shutters.

7. Wrapping paper. For an elegant-looking gift, cut wallpaper to fit the package.

Washers

1. Surface protector. When drilling holes into a finished surface, slip a rubber washer over the bit to protect the finish if the bit breaks.

2. Weight. Sew them into the hems of draperies.

3. Jewelry. Knot graduated sizes on monofilament.

4. Pull. Put one on the end of a string to turn a ceiling light on and off.

5. Sinker. Loop one or more metal washers to the end of your fishing line; change the weight depending on the current and depth of the water.

Wastebaskets

1. Umbrella stand. Line a tall wastebasket with a plastic bag and keep it near the front or back door.

2. Sports equipment. Remove the bottom and attach the basket high on the family room wall. Using wadded paper or foam balls, play a game of indoor basketball.

3. Plant holder. Display a big plant in an attractive wastebasket.

4. Magazine rack. Keep reading material in one.

5. Vase. Use an attractive wastebasket to hold tall dried-flower or cattail arrangements.

Wax paper

1. Stamp saver. In humid weather keep stamps between sheets of wax paper to prevent them from sticking together.

2. Floor keeper. Clean and shine a floor between waxings by putting wax paper under the mop head.

3. Leaf preserver. Assemble colorful autumn leaves in a pleasing pattern on wax paper, cover with another sheet, then iron to seal; trim the paper around the leaves to any desired shape.

4. Super sealer. Place a piece over the opening of a jar before closing it.

5. Cheese easer. Fold a sheet of wax paper over a dull knife to cut cheese cleanly and easily.

6. Kitchen buffer. For a nice shine, rub appliance exteriors and other surfaces with wax paper.

Weatherstripping

1. Gripper. Wrap flat weatherstripping around tool handles for a better and more comfortable grip.

2. Cleats. Glue felt weatherstripping to rubber boots to improve traction on slippery surfaces.

3. Scratch guard. Attach to the bottoms of rockers, chair legs, or sofa feet to prevent marking the floor.

4. Skid preventer. Attach strips to the bottoms of telephones and other lightweight appliances to keep them from sliding off tables and desktops.

5. Leak fixer. Use slivers of household weatherstripping to shim up dented or sagging automotive weatherstripping and prevent wind whistles and water leaks around the car's doors and trunk.

Window screens

1. Seed saver. Lay a screen over re-seeded patches so that seeds don't blow away and birds don't eat them.

2. Drying rack. Cover a screen with a clean sheet and support it on two crates or stools.

3. Strainer. Put a section over the drain to collect hair and other debris.

4. Sieve. Use an old window screen to separate debris from play sand or fine topsoil.

Window shades

1. Play mat. Put one down for kids to play on—it will protect the floor and give them a boundary for their activities. When playtime is over, roll up the shade for easy storage.

2. Canvas. Use an unrolled shade for a watercolor or pastel painting. Roll up to store your artwork neatly.

3. Crafts cloth. Cover the table with one to protect the surface.

4. Projection screen. View your movies or slides on a shade pulled down over the window or hung from a wall.

5. Room divider. Hang shades from joists above a basement workshop so that they surround the workbench. Pull down the shades to keep sawdust from flying all over or when working on a surprise project for the family.

6. Ground cloth. Keep an old window shade in the trunk of your car. Unroll it when doing emergency work under the car to protect your clothes.

7. Dust cover. Drape one over your drawing table or workbench.

8. Disappearing door. Conceal clutter by hanging shades in cupboards and closets.

Wood scraps

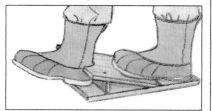

1. Boot jack. Assemble with nails or screws as shown. Hold the baseboard flat on the floor with one foot and pull the other back into the semicircular cut until the overshoe hooks; pull up.

2. Chessboard. Cut a 16-inch square, paint black and white squares on it, then coat with shellac.

3. Kitchen aid. Turn clean pieces into bread, cheese, or pastry boards.

4. Jigsaw puzzle. Glue a photograph onto a piece of ¼-inch plywood and cut it into a puzzle with a jigsaw.

5. Shim. Place pieces of old shingles under cabinets, tables, and appliances on uneven floors; use two overlapping shingles for bad dips.

6. Cleat. Screw 4- to 6-inch strips of wood to the backs and/or undersides of chests, desks, and other heavy furniture. These "handles" will make the furniture easier to move when cleaning.

Yarn

1. Pom-pom. Wrap yarn at least 20 times around a small piece of cardboard, a rolled-up magazine, or other mold; tie the loops together at one end, then remove the mold and cut through the loops at the other end.

2. Ribbon. Use it to tie birthday or Christmas packages.

Yogurt

1. Facial toner. Spread a thick coating of plain yogurt all over your face; wait at least 15 minutes before removing it with lots of warm water.

2. Cleanser. Take off your makeup with plain yogurt and facial tissues.

Yo-yos

1. Exercise equipment. Use them to strengthen your arms.

2. Stress reliever. To feel more relaxed, try "walking the dog" and "rocking the cradle."

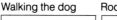

Walking the dog	Rocking the cradle

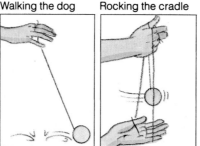

3. Mobile. Hang different colored and shaped yo-yos at varying lengths from sections of a straightened wire hanger; suspend from the ceiling with monofilament.

4. Clothesline. In an emergency, tie the two ends of the string to towel racks or lamp poles and hang underwear or light clothing on the line.

Zippers

1. Valuables securer. Sew a zipper across the inside pocket of a coat or jacket to keep your passport, traveler's checks, and other valuables safe.

2. Puppet mouth. Make a puppet out of an old sock by sewing on buttons for the eyes and nose and a small zipper for the mouth.

3. Convertible jeans. Make cutoffs by carefully removing most of the legs from a pair of blue jeans, then reattach them with zippers. Wear the cutoffs when you go hiking or biking on a hot day; zip on the legs in the evening or when it gets chilly.

Zucchini

1. Rolling pin. In a pinch, roll out biscuit dough with a large zucchini.

2. Exercise equipment. Use the big ones as hand weights when doing arm exercises.

3. Juggling object. Try to keep two or three continuously in motion in the air.

4. RECYCLING & RENEWING

INSTEAD OF CONTRIBUTING TO THE EVER-GROWING MOUNTAIN OF TRASH, WHY NOT RECYCLE? WITHOUT MUCH TROUBLE AT ALL, YOU CAN MAKE GOOD USE OF VIRTUALLY ANYTHING—FROM A REFRIGERATOR CARTON TO AN OLD ROAD MAP TO AN EXTRA PICTURE FRAME. ALONG WITH THE RECYCLING PROJECTS, YOU'LL FIND OTHER WAYS TO GIVE YOUR BELONGINGS NEW LIFE—THROUGH SIMPLE RENEWAL TECHNIQUES FOR EVERYTHING FROM CARD TABLES TO LAMPSHADES, AND MUCH MORE.

Aquarium / Herb garden

A dusty old fish tank, cleaned and shined, becomes a striking indoor herb garden in a few easy steps. Rich black earth shows through the glass walls and becomes a feature unto itself; above it, the plants form a forest of green and look more natural than they would in individual pots.

Herbs are a practical choice for this window garden, but the idea works just as well for ornamental purposes. Consider planting crocuses or tulips, flowering cacti, or even tufts of ornamental grass. Or sow some annuals for an unexpected show of color in winter.

To start, fill the tank with water to check for leaks. If you find one, seal it with epoxy sealant or use transparent plastic weatherproof tape. (Plan to turn that side of the finished garden to the window so that the repair won't show.) Wash with warm soapy water and rinse several times. Buff away fingerprints with a dry cloth (*don't* use window cleaner on the inside). If you plan to keep the garden on a wood table, line the bottom of the tank with felt to protect the finish.

If the tank still has its gravel, recycle it to use as a drainage base for the soil; just be sure to wash it well to remove slime and chemicals. Or buy new gravel or stones and spread a 1-inch layer over the bottom of the tank. Then top with a 1-inch layer of charcoal chips.

Fill the tank to within about 5 inches of the top with sterilized potting soil. Transplant some healthy herbs from your local nursery and place the garden on a table or portable TV cart next to a sunny window. Keep the soil moist but don't overwater.

Auto tire / Storm sandals

Use an old tire to make a pair of high-traction sandals you can wear over your shoes. Keep them in the trunk of your car in case you have to negotiate a slippery stretch of ice or mud on foot. Or hang them on the garage wall to wear when you have to carry your garbage cans down a slick driveway.

To start, cut two sections from a tire tread (don't use a steel-belted radial—it's almost impossible to cut). Then nail them flat to a board or piece of plywood, tread side down, and outline your shoes on them with chalk, adding about 1 inch all around. Then draw a 1-inch-square wing on each side at the back of the heel.

Detach the tire and cut out the sandal. A table saw will do the job, though slowly. A quicker way is to drill ⅛-inch holes along the outline, then redrill them with a ¼-inch bit. A table saw or utility knife will now easily finish the job.

Now use the drill and knife to cut a slit in each of the wings at the heel for a heel-and-ankle strap.

An old ¾-inch-wide leather belt makes a good strap; you can trim a wider belt fairly easily with a craft or utility knife, but you'll have to buy a buckle to fit. Cut the belt 5 inches from the buckle end and thread it down through the slit in one of the heel wings—the right-hand wing for the right sandal, the left-hand one for the left sandal.

Cut about 12 inches from the other end of the belt (hold it over your ankle first to measure) and thread it through the other wing in the same way. Now cut a third piece long enough to fit around your heel with your shoe on. Use a leather punch to make corresponding holes in all three straps, then join all three with copper rivet sets, sold at hardware stores.

For the toe straps, drill two holes near the front of the sandal; then thread a leather thong through each hole and knot it at the side with two half hitches. Be sure the thongs are long enough to be tied securely over the top of your shoe.

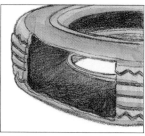

1. Use a heavy utility knife or table saw to cut a flat 12- x 18-in. piece of tire tread. Scrub the treads clean.

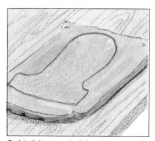

2. Nail it tread side down and chalk an outline of your shoe 1 in. larger all around, adding wings at the heel. Cut it out.

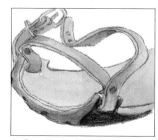

3. Cut slits in the wings and thread belt sections through. To hold them together, punch holes and install rivet sets.

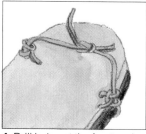

4. Drill holes at the front and thread leather thongs through them; knot with two half hitches at the sides.

Baby blankets / Bath mat

You can turn a few old baby blankets into a superabsorbent bath mat with the aid of an easy-to-make loom. Use five or six flannel or knit blankets and don't worry about coordinating their colors—a rag rug look is what you're after.

First, put together a simple loom of 1 x 3 clear pine—cut two 33-inch lengths and two 23-inch ones. Use lap joints at the corners, making sure they're square; glue and secure the pieces with ¾-inch nails driven from both sides.

On the face of the frame, trace a pencil line along the center of each board. Then drive 6d finishing nails about ½ inch deep along the lines, spacing them 1 inch apart on the long sides of the frame and 1 ½ inches apart on the short sides. Make sure that the nails align with those on the opposite side and that they're secure enough to hold the strips of fabric you'll be weaving.

Now cut the baby blankets into 3-inch-wide strips and sew several strips together end to end. Have a sewing machine or needle and thread handy so that you can sew on more strips as you weave. Use your least stretchy blankets for the warp strips (the ones that you'll be attaching first, running lengthwise on the loom) because they'll form the base through which the other strips are woven.

Begin by folding the end of your continuous strip in half lengthwise (unfinished seams inward) and knotting it to the second nail on a 23-inch side of the loom (ignore the corner nails; you won't use them). Now stretch it to the nail on the opposite side, creasing the strip down the center as you go. Loop it around and back to the next nail on the other side. Continue in this way, keeping the fabric tight and sewing on more strips as you need them, until you've reached the end. Tie off the strip on the last nail (be sure to knot tightly).

Now start weaving. Use strips cut

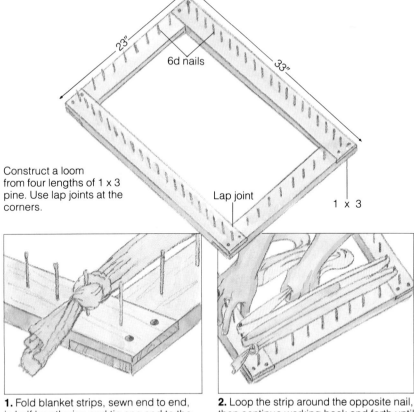

Construct a loom from four lengths of 1 x 3 pine. Use lap joints at the corners.

6d nails

23"

33"

Lap joint

1 x 3

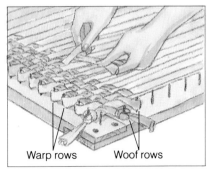

1. Fold blanket strips, sewn end to end, in half lengthwise and tie one end to the second nail on the long side of the loom.

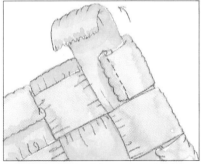

2. Loop the strip around the opposite nail, then continue working back and forth until you tie off on the last nail.

Warp rows   Woof rows

3. Weave the woof rows over and under the warp rows, using strips from stretchy blankets to make the job easier.

4. Untie the knots at the corner of the rug and trim the excess fabric. Hand-stitch the edges onto the underside of the rug.

from stretchy blankets—they'll be easier to work through the warp. As before, fold the strip in half lengthwise; this time, knot it to the second nail on the 33-inch side. Weave it through the warp strips to the nail on the opposite side, creasing it as you go. Loop it around and start back, adding more strips as you need them.

As you work, push the strips as

snugly as possible against one another. If the last few rows are hard to weave, use the end of a spoon to help push and pull them through. Knot the strip to the last nail.

Remove the rug from the loom by gently working it off the nails. Turn the rug over and untie the knots at the corners, trimming the excess fabric and hand-stitching the cut edges onto the underside of the rug.

Balusters / Table base

Replacing the banister on your stairs? Save four of the balusters to make a handsome base for an occasional table. You can use plywood, lumber, or even the inverted saucer of a flowerpot as a footing; likewise, use whatever you like as a tabletop—a large metal tray, a marble slab, the discarded top of a small desk, or a cut-to-order wooden top that you finish yourself.

Most balusters are 24 inches long; occasional tables should stand 17 to 22 inches high. Cut the balusters to size, then paint, strip, or stain them as you like.

An easily made footing is a circle of ¾-inch plywood. Use a saber saw to cut it about 12 inches in diameter. Stain or paint the footing to match the balusters and then finish the edge with a matching adhesive veneer tape.

Cut an 8-inch square of ¼-inch plywood to support the tabletop and draw a 4½-inch square in the center. Draw another 4½-inch square in the center of the footing. Then drill and countersink for No. 12 screws at each corner of both squares. Use 4-inch screws to attach the footing and 2-inch screws to attach the support.

For the sake of stability, don't choose a tabletop longer or wider than about 28 inches. Center it on the support and attach it with brass carriage bolts, lag bolts, or epoxy glue, depending on the material.

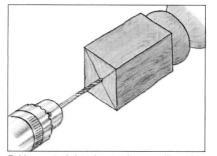

1. Saw the balusters to 15 to 20 in.—about 2 in. shorter than the desired height of your table.

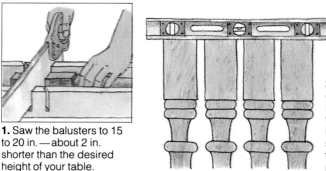

2. After sawing, check with a spirit level to make sure that the four balusters are the same height and the cuts are perfectly even.

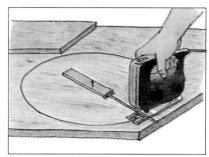

3. Cut an 8-in. square from a piece of ¼-in. plywood. With the aid of an edge guide, cut a 12-in. circle from ¾-in. plywood.

4. Draw a 4½-in. square in the center of both pieces; drill and countersink at each corner for No. 12 screws.

5. Use a straightedge to draw an X on the bottom and top of each baluster and drill a pilot hole exactly in the center.

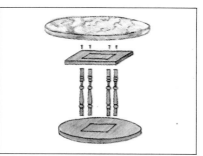

6. To assemble, drive No. 12 flathead screws through the plywood pieces and into the balusters. Then attach the top.

Barn siding / Wainscoting

Wainscoting made from beautifully weathered barn siding can give a room a warm country feeling.

You'll have to nail the siding to three 1 x 4 stringers. But rather than attaching the stringers directly to the wall surface, strip the wallboard down to the studs in the area where the wainscoting will go; otherwise it may protrude beyond adjoining doorframes and window casings. Then nail the stringers across the studs.

For a baseboard, rip a few of the boards to 3-inch widths, with square edges on both sides. For a cap rail, rip the beveled edges ½ inch wider than the thickness of the siding.

1. Cut the most attractive boards to the desired height of the wainscoting; 30 to 32 in. is traditional.

2. Rip straight edges from other boards to use as a baseboard. Then rip the beveled edges for a cap rail.

Barrel / Garden irrigator

You can cut down on utility bills and help ensure plenty of water for your garden with an old barrel and a few brass plumbing fixtures.

In addition to the barrel, you'll need two ½-inch brass shoulder nipples at least 1½ inches long, a ½-inch brass pipe elbow, and a ½-inch sill cock or shutoff hose bib.

Use a ¾-inch wood bit to drill two holes in the barrel, one 4 inches from the top and the other an equal distance from the bottom. Then install the nipples; if the seals aren't watertight, caulk with silicone.

Set the barrel next to a downspout, elevating it on concrete blocks to increase the water pressure. Cut the downspout just above barrel level and affix one or two aluminum elbows, sold at roofing supply companies, to position the end over the lid. Cut a hole in the lid to admit the downspout, making sure the seal is tight so that mosquitoes won't be able to breed in the stored water.

Now run a hose from the sill cock to the garden, connecting it to a soaker hose (p.359) set between rows of plants. After rainwater has collected, just turn on the tap when you want to water your plants.

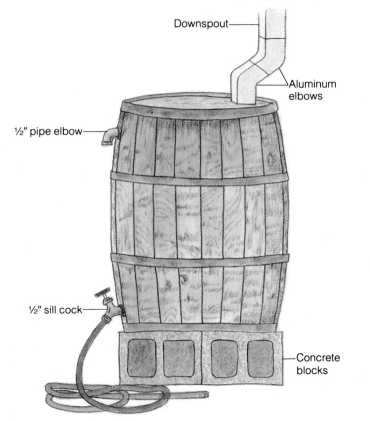

Downspout
Aluminum elbows
½" pipe elbow
½" sill cock
Concrete blocks

1. Drill ¾-in. holes near the top and bottom of the barrel. Install a brass shoulder nipple in each, making sure they're watertight.

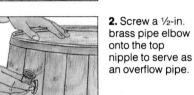

2. Screw a ½-in. brass pipe elbow onto the top nipple to serve as an overflow pipe.

3. Screw a ½-in. sill cock onto the bottom nipple, adding a rubber washer for a watertight seal.

4. With a saber saw, cut a square in the lid just large enough to admit the end of the downspout.

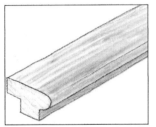

3. Rabbet the square edge of the cap rail sections deep enough to fit over the top of the wainscoting—about ½ in.

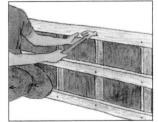

4. Remove part of the plaster or wallboard from the section to be wainscoted and nail 1 x 4 stringers to the studs.

5. Nail boards to stringers with 8d finishing nails. Place top and bottom nails to be hidden by baseboard and cap rail.

6. Nail the baseboard sections to the bottom. Install the cap rail on top, nailing at an angle into each wall stud.

Beach towel / Wrap

With a few strips of Velcro, you can turn a beach towel into a terrycloth wrap to wear over your bathing suit.

Any large towel—from a solid color to the gaudy map-of-Hawaii type—will do, although thin ones work better than plush.

To get the proper fit, wrap the towel around you so that it's snug under the arms and it overlaps in front. With a felt-tip pen, mark three 4-inch strips as shown along both top edges. Then cut three pairs of 4-inch strips from 1-inch Velcro and stitch them onto the marks—and your beach wrap is ready to wear. Add a cinch belt or brightly colored fabric sash, if you like, to give it the look of a dress.

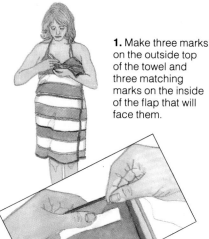

1. Make three marks on the outside top of the towel and three matching marks on the inside of the flap that will face them.

2. Sew the Velcro over the marks, making sure to match a "loop" (soft) strip with a "hook" (scratchy) strip.

3. The three pairs of Velcro strips should now line up and hold the towel securely in place as a wrap.

Bedspread / Wall hanging

Don't toss out that old, worn bedspread. An undamaged section with a complete design can be mounted on plywood as a wall hanging (like the project shown here) or backed and stuffed as a throw pillow. If the spread is a complete loss, store it in the garage to use as a painting drop cloth or a furniture pad for moving.

All you'll need for the wall hanging are some ½-inch plywood, a few thumbtacks, a stapler, and screw eyes and picture wire for hanging. Use thumbtacks to make sure the fabric stays straight as you staple it to the back of the plywood. Staple one side first, then the opposite side, then the other two ends. Do the corners last, pulling them tight and folding neatly in place before stapling them down.

1. Measure off a section of bedspread that contains the complete picture or design that you want to mount and display; add 3½ in. to all four sides and cut the section out.

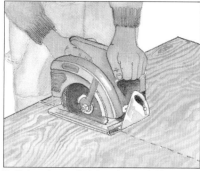

2. Cut a piece of ½-in. plywood 6 in. shorter and narrower than the cut-out fabric. Make sure all corners are square.

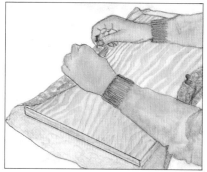

3. Lay the fabric facedown, center the plywood on it, pull it taut over the edges, and secure with a thumbtack at each side.

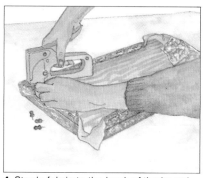

4. Staple fabric to the back of the board, leaving the corners open. Pull the corners tight, fold so that they lie flat, and staple.

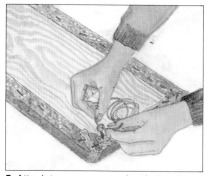

5. Attach two screw eyes just below the top edge of the fabric, then thread with picture wire for hanging.

Bicycle / Exercise bike

If you have an old 1-speed bicycle or the 3- or 5-speed kind that has the gears inside the rear hub, you can turn it into an exercise bike with this simple stand.

The base is a 5½- x 20-inch rectangle of ¾-inch plywood. The sides are two 15-inch equilateral triangles of the same material. To assemble you'll need four 3-inch inside corner braces; two 6-inch mending plates (the thickest you can find); and 20 ³⁄₁₆-inch stove bolts, 1 inch long, with nuts. Enlarge the top hole in the mending plates to accept your bike's axle.

To provide resistance as you pedal, make a tension rod from two screen door springs, an 8-inch length of ⅛-inch threaded rod with two nuts, and a large wooden spool. You'll also need two ¼-inch eye bolts and a pair of S-hooks to secure the spring.

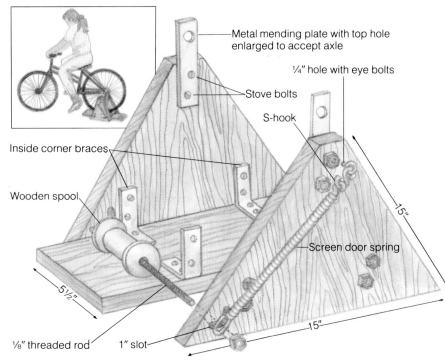

Metal mending plate with top hole enlarged to accept axle

¼" hole with eye bolts

Stove bolts

S-hook

Inside corner braces

Wooden spool

Screen door spring

15"

5½"

⅛" threaded rod   1" slot   15"

1. Cut the rectangle with the grain running the long way. Saw 1 in. off the top of each triangle. Clamp the pieces together with the grain of the triangles running straight up from the base. Position the hardware and mark the holes for drilling; place the mending plates so that the axle holes are ¼ in. higher than the distance from your bike's axle to the ground.

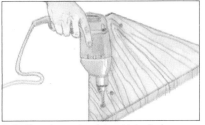

2. Drill and countersink a ¼-in. hole near the top of each triangle as shown; at the opposite corner, cut a 1-in. slot for the tension rod (exact position depends on the size of the bike tire). To cut the slots, drill two ¼-in. holes and saw between them with a saber saw.

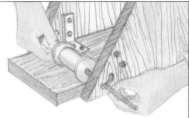

3. Drill ³⁄₁₆-in. holes and assemble the stand with stove bolts. Put an eye bolt in each ¼-in. hole. Run the threaded rod through the 1-in. slots with the spool in the middle (you may need two smaller spools or two nuts to keep it positioned in the center of the rod).

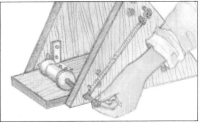

4. Use S-hooks to attach screen door springs to the eye bolts, then slip the springs over the ends of the threaded rod and secure with washers and nuts. If more tension is needed, shorten the top end of the spring with wire cutters and loop it around the S-hook two or three times.

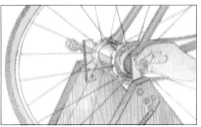

5. To place the bike on the stand, remove the rear wheel axle nuts. Loosen one set of bolts on one of the triangles so that you can fit the axle into the holes in the mending plates; retighten. Replace the axle nuts on the wheel, this time on the outside of the mending plates.

Birdhouse / Clock

Once the wrens have abandoned your birdhouse, bring it indoors and convert it into a unique wall clock. For best effect, don't paint or stain it—weathered wood is part of the charm.

For the clock mechanism, buy an inexpensive mini-quartz type from a craft store or hobby shop. They run on AA or C batteries and are easy to install.

The kind of birdhouse that's designed to be nailed to a tree trunk is easiest to convert. If you have the two-sided hanging type, you can make two clocks from it—just saw it in half and mount each half on a board cut to size. If the birdhouse doesn't have a removable roof, hinge the back or bottom so that you can install the clock mechanism and change the battery.

To mark the hour positions, make a paper template as shown. Trace around the rim of a glass; make a mark at the 12, 3, 6, and 9 positions, then place two equidistant marks between each pair of numbers. On the clock itself, shiny copper rivets can be glued in place to mark the hours, as shown here. To avoid drilling, use upholstery tacks or paint dots or numbers on the wood. As a finishing touch, why not glue a colorful carved bird to the perch?

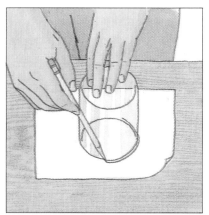

1. Draw a perfect circle on a piece of paper as a template for your clock face. Mark the hour positions.

2. Center the template on the birdhouse and use a nail set to mark the positions of the center hole and each hour.

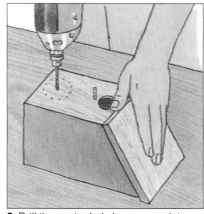

3. Drill the center hole large enough to accept the clock shaft, the others the size of the rivets being used as hour markers.

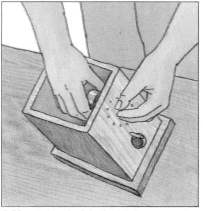

4. Mount the clock in the birdhouse and glue the rivets in place. Insert a battery and hang the clock on the wall.

Blue jeans / Bag

When the legs of your jeans wear out but the top part still has strong seams, transform the pants into a handy denim bag. Just cut off the legs and stitch the holes closed. Then add the kind of handle or straps that will turn the bag into a clothespin or nail sack, sewing bag, shoulder bag, or child's backpack. (See also *Blue jeans*, p.290.)

1. Turn the jeans inside out and mark them for cutting about 2 in. below the crotch. Cut off the legs on the mark.

2. Sew the leg openings closed with two or three lines of straight stitches. Turn the jeans right side out and press.

3. For a handle, cut a 3-in.-wide strip from one of the jeans legs. Crease, stitch on the wrong side, and turn inside out.

4. Sew ½ in. of the handle to the inside of the waistband at both sides. Use a cross-stitch for extra strength.

SEWING BAG
Keep yarn, thread, and pincushions inside; needles and thimbles fit in the pockets. Run a measuring tape through the belt loops as a drawstring.

SHOULDER BAG
Use a strip of colorful fabric, heavy ribbon, or cording for the handle. Make the drawstring from the same material.

CHILD'S BACKPACK
Attach the straps as shown and make an easy-to-operate drawstring with cord and a piece of leather.

Book / Jewelry safe

Foil thieves by turning a book into a small safe and lining it up with the other books on your shelf.

Choose a hardcover book at least 1½ inches thick. Glue all but the first few pages together with a mixture of 3 parts white glue to 1 part water. Insert a sheet of wax paper between the first glued page and the loose ones; insert another between the last page and the back cover. Close the book, weight it down with several heavy volumes or some concrete blocks (don't skimp on the weight or the pages may wrinkle), and let dry overnight.

When the glue is dry, scribe the section to be cut; leave at least a 1-inch margin at the edges. Drill starter holes in the corners and use a coping saw to remove the section. Glue the back cover in place and weight the book down again. For a finishing touch, line the cutout with satin or felt.

1. With a wide brush, apply glue sparingly to all pages except the first few.

2. Leave a margin of at least 1 in. all around when you scribe the section to be cut out.

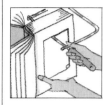

3. Drill starter holes in the corner and cut out the book section with a coping saw.

4. Glue down the back cover, then use white glue to line the cutout with satin or felt.

To turn the bag into a child's backpack, first measure for straps. Hold the bag to the child's back and loop your measuring tape from the top of the bag, over the shoulders, and back to the bottom of the bag. Allow an extra 3 inches so that you can cross-stitch the straps to the inside of the waistband and the bottom of the back pockets. Rip open a few stitches in the bottom of the pockets and tuck the straps inside, then sew them in place.

To make a drawstring that even a little one can operate, cut a 1-inch square of heavy leather and drill or punch a ⅛-inch hole in each corner. Run a long piece of strong cord through the belt loops in the backpack, then through the top set of holes in the leather. Cross the cords to make an X, then thread them through the bottom holes. Knot the cord ends. Just pull on the cords to close the bag; to open it, hold the leather patch and tug at the part of the cord that runs through the belt loops.

Brake drum / Forge

For light metalwork—making your own fireplace tools or other wrought-iron implements—you can build a blacksmithing forge from the old brake drum of a truck.

You'll also need the lid of an oil drum, three 3-foot lengths of ¾-inch threaded steel pipe to use as legs, and three ¾-inch flanges to hold them. For the blower assembly you'll need a length of 2-inch threaded pipe and matching flange, T-coupling, pipe cap, and two brass nipples.

Assemble the parts as shown. Connect the blower pipe to a motor-driven blower or an old-fashioned bellows.

Because the grate is made from the thin steel of an oil drum, you'll have to replace it occasionally. Other than that, your only maintenance will be removing the cap from the bottom of the center pipe to clean out ashes.

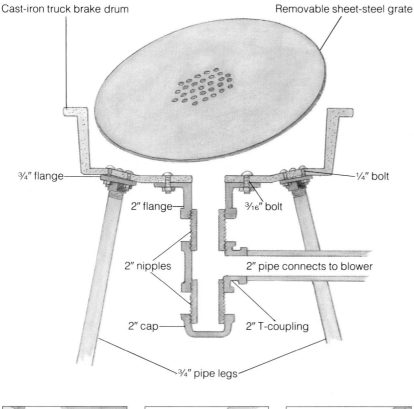

Cast-iron truck brake drum

Removable sheet-steel grate

¾″ flange

¼″ bolt

2″ flange

³⁄₁₆″ bolt

2″ nipples

2″ pipe connects to blower

2″ cap

2″ T-coupling

¾″ pipe legs

1. Drill holes and bolt three ¾-in. flanges to the bottom of the brake drum to hold the threaded pipes that will be used as legs.

2. Use tin snips to cut the lid of an oil drum to fit inside the brake drum. Drill a few ⅛-in. holes in the center to let in air.

3. Attach a 2-in. flange to the bottom with ³⁄₁₆-in. bolts. You should be able to bolt through the existing holes in the drum.

Cable spools / Child's table

The big wooden spools that hold cable or rope can make nifty furniture for kids. Turn a 24-inch spool and two 12-inch ones into a table and stools.

If the spool ends are secured with protruding dome-head screws, countersink them. Then attach three rubber feet to the bottom of each spool to keep it steady.

Paint the spools ends in a bright

1. Lightly sand the spool ends and paint with alkyd semi-gloss. Apply an extra coat to the tabletop.

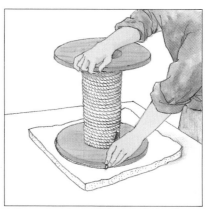

3. Trace the shape of the small spool ends on a sheet of foam rubber and cut out one piece for each seat.

color and decorate the reels with thin rope as shown. Just spread white glue randomly around the reel, nail down the end of the rope at the inside base of the reel, and wrap, pushing each coil down tightly against the previous one. If you find you have to use more than one piece of rope, secure the ends with tacks and remove them when the glue has dried.

For comfort, fit the two small spools with padded seats of foam rubber and fabric. If you want to cover the two or three holes in the center of the tabletop (used for mounting the spools on rods), cut a piece of hardboard or plastic laminate the size of the tabletop and glue it down.

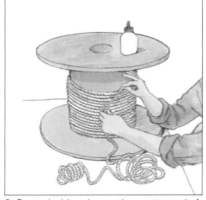

2. Spread white glue on the center reel of each spool and wrap rope around, securing the ends with tacks.

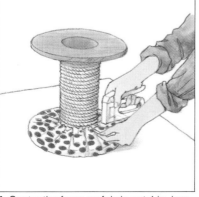

4. Center the foam on fabric cut 4 in. larger all around, place the spools on top, and staple the fabric down.

Candles/Luminaria

Save candle stubs to melt down, remold, and turn into your own luminaria—decorative lanterns to place along your walkway for the holidays.

Melt the candle stubs in a double boiler and use a slotted spoon to skim off the wicks that float to the surface. If you need more wax, buy some taper wax from a craft store or hobby shop and add it to the stubs.

Use old clean milk cartons for the molds. For each lantern you'll need a 47-ounce juice can or a large coffee can with the label removed. With a nail set or chisel, punch the holes for the candlelight to shine through.

If you like, place a few luminaria in rock gardens or flower beds as well as on the front walk.

1. Melt the candle stubs in a pan set in a larger pan filled with at least 2 in. of simmering water. Cut quart- or pint-size milk cartons down to 3 in.

2. Pour ¼ in. of wax into the bottom of each carton. Then hold a 3-in. candle stub upright in the middle until it stands by itself. Fill the carton to the top.

3. With the aid of a compass and straightedge, draw a series of geometric dot patterns on a piece of paper and tape the paper all the way around the can.

4. Clamp the end of a scrap of 2 x 4 in a vise and slip the can over it. Use a nail set and hammer to punch out the design on all sides of the can.

5. Peel the milk cartons from the candles, place a candle in each decorated can, and line up the cans at the edge of the walkway to your front door.

Cardboard boxes / Table

Glued together, several sheets of corrugated cardboard are strong enough to make a lightweight piece of furniture that even children can move from place to place.

The carton that a refrigerator comes in, plus a smaller box or two,

yields enough material to build the project shown here. Cut out matching sections with a utility knife and straightedge and use white glue to sandwich them together in fours, making sure that you stack the sheets so that their corruga-

tions run in alternating directions.

Your table can be any size or shape. Shown here is an occasional table 24 inches high by 30 inches across. The corners are trimmed for a decorative effect.

When you cut the slits in two of

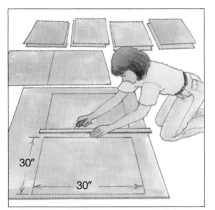

1. Draw four 30-in. squares and eight 20- x 24-in. rectangles on the cardboard and cut them out with a utility knife.

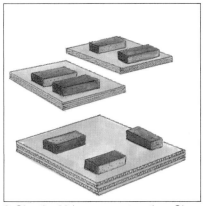

2. Glue the 30-in. squares together. Glue the rectangles together in two groups of four each. Weight down.

3. Cut a 12-in. slit in each rectangle just wide enough to enable the two parts to be fitted together to form a stand.

Cardboard boxes / RENEWAL

With the help of adhesive plastic, such as Con-Tact, you can turn a plain cardboard box into an attractive storage container.

The material comes in 18-inch-wide rolls. To determine how many you'll need, measure the five sides of the box you're covering (six if you're covering the lid) and add them together. Then double the amount so that you can cover the inside, too.

Cover the inside bottom of the box first, cutting the paper an extra ¼ inch all around. (To release the paper from its backing, roll a corner back and forth between your fingers.) Miter the corners of the plastic by making a cut from the corner of the box outward, then a second cut at a 45° angle.

Next, use a single sheet to cover the outside bottom and both sides of both ends. Cut the plastic to the exact length and add 2 inches to the width so that you'll

have an edge to fold over on each side. Fold the sheet in half and crease it across the middle so that you can find the center when you align the paper on the box.

Peel off two-thirds of the backing and lay the plastic down, adhesive side up. Center the box on the crease and press down; then smooth the plastic up one end, slit the extra inch at each side, and smooth it down the inside. Peel off the remaining backing and repeat the process on the other end. Press down the overlaps.

Cover the other two sides of the box in the same way (the bottom will have another thickness of paper for extra strength), but don't add any extra width; you won't need to fold over edges this time.

Always smooth the plastic from the center. If the surface still has air bubbles, just puncture them with a straight pin and flatten the bumps with your fingers.

1. Cover the inside bottom, cutting the plastic with an extra ¼ in. all the way around. Miter the corners.

2. Cut a sheet to cover the outside bottom and two ends, inside and out, as shown. Add 2 in. to the width.

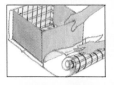

3. Peel most of the backing, center box on plastic, and cover one end. Peel the rest and cover other end.

4. Slit the corners and fold the edges over. Cut a second sheet and cover the remaining two sides.

the sections to fit them together as a stand, make sure the slits are the same length; otherwise the table will rock. And make them exactly as wide as the thickness of the glued cardboard. Four strips of a single thickness of cardboard, folded lengthwise and glued to the top edges of the stand, will enable you to attach the tabletop.

Cover the tabletop and stand with an adhesive plastic, such as Con-Tact, in any pattern you like. Instead of going for imitation wood grain, why not try stripes, a solid bright color, or a floral print? Another idea is to glue a collage of your own design onto the surface. Or, if the table is for children, use their crayon drawings and finger paintings for the collage.

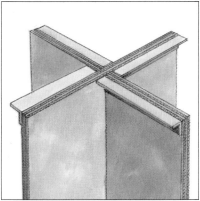

4. Cut four 8½- x 3-in. strips of cardboard, score lengthwise, and bend in half. Glue to the stand and weight down.

5. Cut narrow strips of adhesive plastic to cover the edges of the cardboard, then cut pieces to cover the surfaces.

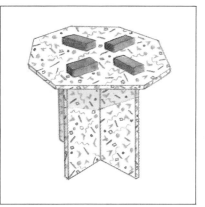

6. Apply glue to the cardboard strips on the stand, center the tabletop, and weight it down until completely dry.

Ceramic tiles / Trivet

Glue some leftover tiles to a piece of ½-inch plywood and you have a trivet that looks as good as the expensive ones sold in kitchen stores. This one is made of four square ceramic tiles, four corner pieces, and eight curved edging tiles. To ensure even joints, use ⅛-inch plastic spacers between the tiles as you cement them down; then remove them and apply grout.

Bevel the top edge of the plywood so that the curved edging tiles will fit. Then attach four rubber feet to the bottom—they'll keep the piece from sliding around as you apply adhesive to the surface. Cut the edging tiles to size; if the edges are rough, smooth them with a grinding wheel.

Before you apply tile adhesive to the top of the plywood base, position the tiles to check for fit. Once you've glued down the tiles and finished grouting, turn the trivet upside down and fill the gaps at the edges with more adhesive.

1. Insert spacers between two tiles and upside-down edging tiles. Measure the inside.

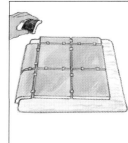

2. Cut the plywood ¼ in. larger all around and use an orbital sander to bevel the top edge.

3. Mark and cut the edging tiles: score the glaze with a hacksaw, then break with a hammer.

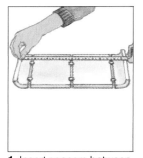

4. Drive a nail into the center point of the base. Use a notched trowel to cover the surface with adhesive.

5. Place the tiles around the nail. Remove the nail and insert ¹⁄₁₆-in. plastic spacers between tiles.

6. Remove spacers and grout the joints, wiping away excess with a wet sponge. Buff when dry.

Chair / Rocker

Slot two hardwood rockers into the legs of an old straight chair to create a whole new piece of furniture.

First, enlarge the rocker pattern shown here, using 1-inch grid paper for an average chair (12 to 14 inches between the front and back legs). Then transfer it to a length of ½-inch hardwood for cutting.

Cut both rockers at the same time so that they will be identical. Clamp both pieces of wood together before rough cutting, then reclamp for si-multaneous trimming and sanding.

Before you slot the chair legs for the rockers, make sure the chair will tilt at a comfortable angle by cutting about ½ inch off the back legs. Experiment with the angle by trimming the legs a little at a time.

The easiest way to cut the slots in the chair legs is with a dado head on your table saw. Position the rip fence so that the slots will be centered in the legs. Extend the fence to guide both legs by clamping a board to it (this will ensure that both legs are slotted at exactly the same angle). Make several passes, raising the dado in small increments. Remember that the slots must align exactly with the rockers, which, in turn, must be vertical. If the chair legs you are cutting are slanted, make the slots aligned and vertical by raising the opposite pair of legs with a board as you work.

If you cut the slots by hand, use a backsaw or hacksaw and a chisel.

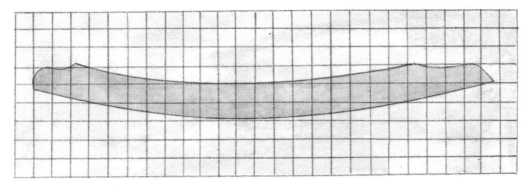

To make the wooden rockers for an average-size chair whose front legs are 12 to 14 in. from the back legs, transfer this rocker pattern to 1-in. grid paper (use a straightedge and ruler to draw the grid yourself). For larger chairs, use a 1¼-in. grid; for smaller ones, use a ¾-in. grid.

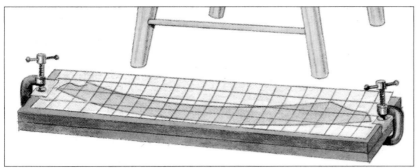

1. Firmly clamp two pieces of ½-in. hardwood together. Tape two sheets of carbon paper to the top piece, tape the rocker pattern over them, and transfer the pattern to the wood. Then rough-cut both pieces of wood at once.

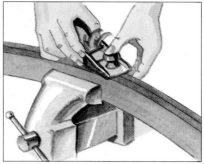

2. Reclamp the rough-cut rockers and shape them, using a drawknife or spokeshave, plane, and sandpaper.

3. Cut slots for the rockers in all four legs. Make them the exact width of a rocker and about ¾ in. deep.

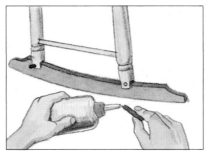

4. Place the rockers in the leg slots as shown and drill a ¼-in. hole through each leg to receive a dowel pin.

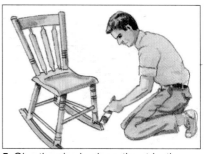

5. Glue the pins in place, then trim them flush when the glue dries. Paint or stain the rockers to match the chair.

Chest of drawers / Bookcase

Have an old chest of drawers that's missing a drawer or two? Remove the back, insert some pine shelves, paint or refinish, and you have a free-standing, two-sided bookcase that makes an attractive room divider.

If the vertical space between the drawer supports is less than 8 inches, you'll have to pry out every other support to make the shelves tall enough for books. Leave one or two of the smaller spaces for magazines or oversize books that can be laid on their sides.

Use wood filler on any holes, then finish the back of the chest and the shelves to match the front. Or paint the whole thing and stencil on a design (see below).

1. Remove the drawers and carefully pry the backing from the chest.

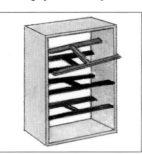

2. If necessary, remove every second support. Pry out the center drawer rail.

3. Measure the inside for width and depth and cut shelves of ¾-in. pine to size.

4. Drill and countersink for No. 8 screws and secure the shelves to the supports.

Stenciling / TECHNIQUE

Imperfect tables, chairs, and chests, with their scratches and nicks, are the best candidates for stenciling. Painted in mat white or ivory and wiped down with a thin stain to accentuate age marks, they become instant "antiques" onto which you can transfer any design you choose, from traditional Pennsylvania Dutch motifs to whimsical hearts and flowers.

Although ready-made stencils are sold at craft stores, you can make your own by tracing a design and enlarging it as shown. Just be sure to incorporate enough uncut sections, or "ties," to hold the stencil together.

Cut your stencils from nonabsorbent cardboard or waxed stencil paper. For paint, use a quick-drying acrylic. And your work will look more professional if you buy a stenciling brush— round with stiff bristles.

If you're grouping several designs together, first work out your overall pattern on a piece of paper cut to the same size as your work surface. Then use it as a visual guide to position the stencils when you're ready to paint.

1. Choose a simple design from a pattern book or magazine. Use a sheet of carbon paper to trace the design on another piece of paper. Then draw an evenly spaced grid on top of the tracing.

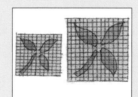

2. To enlarge your design to the desired size, use a ruler to draw a larger grid on a separate piece of paper and draw the design on it by carefully duplicating the pattern in each square of the smaller grid.

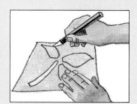

3. Using a sheet of carbon paper, transfer the design to the stencil board. Then cut out the design with a sharp craft knife, being sure to leave ties of at least ⅛ in. Trim any ragged edges of the cutouts.

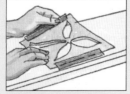

4. Position the stencil on the work surface and tape down the outside edges with masking tape. If you plan to use more than one color, use more tape to cover the cutouts that will be painted later.

5. Dip your brush in the paint and blot it on a paper towel. Dab paint into each cutout with a quick up-and-down motion, working from the sides to the center. Apply two light coats instead of one thick one.

6. Lift the stencil carefully and wipe any wet paint from the back before reusing it. When the stenciling is complete, allow the paint to dry overnight before applying a finishing coat of varnish or polyurethane.

Christmas cards / Decorations

Recycle your Christmas cards as seasonal decorations. Make little paper baskets, fill them with greenery or small ornaments, and hang them on the tree. Or create colorful place mats for the holiday table.

PAPER BASKETS

These colorful baskets make unusual Christmas tree ornaments. When you glue the paper strips together, first fold each strip in half, unfold, and use the crease as a center mark so that the top of the basket will be even. And make sure the handle is long enough to fit around the end of a tree branch.

1. For each basket, mark off the fronts of the cards with a ruler and cut them into nine ½- x 8-in. strips. Then cut one ½- x 11-in. strip for a handle.

2. Use white glue to join the centers of eight of the 8-in. strips. Stack them color side down, forming the spokes of a wheel; weight down until the glue dries.

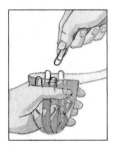

3. Cup the strips in your hand to make a basket. Glue the remaining 8-in. strip around the top and secure each strip with a paper clip until the glue dries.

4. Attach the 11-in. strip as a handle and let the glue dry. Then fill the basket with holly sprigs or a bouquet of baby's breath before hanging on the tree.

PLACE MATS

Twenty to 25 cards are enough to make one 13- x 18-inch oval place mat with scalloped edges.

1. Use a compass or glass to trace 28 circles, each about 3½ in. across, on the fronts of the cards. Cut them out.

2. Overlap 16 to 18 cutouts to form an oval on the sticky side of a 13- x 18-in. sheet of adhesive plastic, such as Con-Tact. Fill in the center with the remaining cutouts.

3. Place clear adhesive plastic on top of the cards, sticky side down, and smooth from the middle to the edges.

4. With sharp scissors, trim away the excess adhesive plastic—both backing and top sheet—to finish the place mat.

Clothing / Rag rug

Instead of using old clothes as rags, cut them into strips and create a one-of-a-kind rug. Any lightweight fabric will do, from old shirts, skirts, and shorts to neckties, ribbons, and shoelaces—even string.

Besides the fabric strips, you'll need a 3-count rug canvas, a latch hook to knot the strips onto the canvas, and some 2-inch binding to finish off the edges.

Start by cutting the canvas to the desired size of your rug, adding an extra inch all around. Then press masking tape over the edges to keep them from fraying as you work.

Cut your fabric into ½-inch strips 5 inches long (don't cut on the bias or the strips will tend to fray). Then use the latch hook to knot them onto the rug canvas as shown, mixing the colors, textures, and patterns for the most interesting effect.

When you've finished the rug, remove the masking tape, crease the binding over the extra inch of canvas, and sew it on as close to the knots as possible.

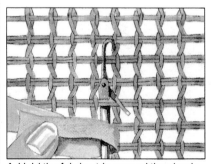

1. Hold the fabric strip around the shank of the latch hook and slip the tip under a strand of canvas. Flip the latch back.

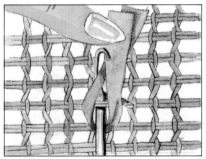

2. Still holding the fabric strip, and with the latch open, bring the ends of the strip up and into the open hook as shown.

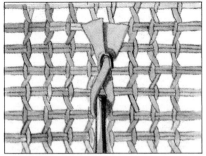

3. Carefully pull the hook across and under the strand. When the latch closes, release the fabric strip.

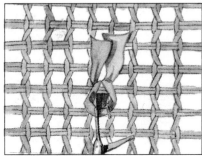

4. Continue to pull the hook across and under. The ends of the fabric strip will be pulled with the hook to form the knot.

5. Tug on the ends of the fabric strip to tighten the knot and to bring both ends even with each other.

Concrete block / Birdhouse

Chisel a hole in a concrete block to create an instant house for bluebirds. Just be sure not to make the hole larger than 1½ inches or you'll attract starlings instead. And chisel slowly and carefully to keep the hole neat and round.

Use an 8-inch-square hollow concrete block, which is smooth on four sides. Use a piece of pipe or a stout wooden pole as a stake to support the block 4 to 5 feet off the ground. Or try a shapely tree branch or a piece of driftwood for a more ornamental effect. Implant the stake at least 2 feet deep so that it won't blow over in the wind.

Position the birdhouse on the base with the hole facing east. After each family of birds leaves the nest, lift it up and clean it out to attract others.

1. Use a felt-tip pen to draw a quarter-size (1-in.) circle centered about 2 in. from the top of the concrete block. Make punch marks all the way around the circle with a sharp center punch or large masonry nail.

2. Slowly drill all the way through the punch marks with a ³⁄₁₆-in. masonry bit. Then use the center punch or nail and a hammer to carefully chisel out and enlarge the hole to a diameter of no more than 1½ in.

3. Cut two 9-in. squares from a piece of ¼-in. plywood. Use epoxy to glue one to the top of the block as a roof. Firmly secure the other square to the top of the stake.

Deck chairs / RENEWAL

Deck chairs that have suffered from exposure to rain and sun can look like new with a little stain or paint and some bright new fabric.

Be careful as you pry out the staples when stripping the old fabric from the frames; gloves and protective eyewear are both good ideas. Then sand the wood with medium sandpaper, paying special attention to any dark or rusty marks left by metal hardware. Paint or stain the frames as you prefer. If you use the chairs outdoors, finish with a coat of exterior polyurethane.

Choose heavy canvas or awning cloth (don't use synthetic fabric—it deteriorates in the sun). When you cut the fabric, allow a few inches extra to wrap around the back rails and seat frame; trim it to the exact size just before hemming and stapling. And pull the fabric as tight as you can when you staple.

1. Remove the old fabric by loosening the staples with a screwdriver, then pulling them out with pliers.

2. Wipe the wood with mineral spirits. If necessary, sand and refinish with paint or stain and polyurethane.

3. Use the old fabric as a pattern for the new canvas. Or measure between rails and add 4 in. for stapling.

4. Hem the rough edges. With a heavy-duty stapler, secure the new seat and back panel to the frame.

Desk / Workbench

1. Measure the desktop and cut two pieces of ¾-in. plywood and one piece of ¼-in. hardboard to its exact dimensions. Cut four 2 x 4's to the width of these panels and two more to the desired length of the cross braces.

An old desk is a perfect base for a workbench, complete with storage drawers. Instead of blocking it up to raise the work surface to a comfortable level, build a new top of ¾-inch plywood and 2 x 4's and cover it with a sheet of ¼-inch hardboard. The hardboard should fit snugly into a recess at the top so that it doesn't need to be nailed down and can easily be replaced.

Trim the edges all around with pine stock, making it ¼ inch higher than the plywood surface to create a recess for the hardboard. Two pieces of 1 x 6 stock the same length as the plywood top will yield material for the front and back trim. Two lengths of 1 x 8 stock 1½ inches longer than the width of the plywood provide the side trim (end pieces).

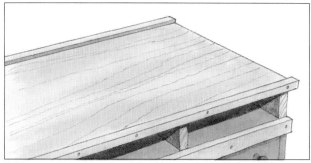

4. Rip two 1-in. widths from the other 1 x 6 for the front and back top trim. Glue and nail them to the edges of the plywood so that they extend ¼ in. above the surface, creating a recess for the hardboard work surface.

Doilies / Bowls

You can turn crocheted doilies into delicate, lacy bowls by simply stiffening them with a sugar-and-water solution. Use the smallest bowls as candy dishes or for potpourri; larger ones make good fruit bowls and centerpiece holders.

This recipe is enough to convert one 9-inch doily. Mix fresh solution for each bowl.

As you dip a doily into the solution, squeeze it gently with your fingertips for even distribution; repeat two or three times and squeeze out the excess. For a mold, place a bowl of the desired size upside down on a heavy towel.

When you want to restore the doily to its original form, just knead it under warm running water until it's no longer sticky, then wash with a mild detergent.

1. To make the stiffening solution, place ½ cup sugar in a large bowl and stir in ¼ cup boiling water. Stir for 3 min. or until the mixture is almost opaque.

2. Dip a dry doily into the solution until it's thoroughly soaked. Squeeze out the excess and stretch it over the mold. Pin the edges to the towel with rustproof pins.

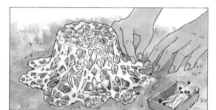

3. Let the doily dry for at least 6 hr. Then unpin it. Loosen it by wedging your fingers between the mold and the doily and working slowly around the perimeter.

4. Gently pull the loosened doily and the mold apart. To prevent small objects from falling through the holes in the bowl, line it with plastic wrap.

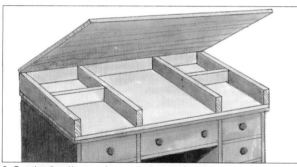

2. Set the 2 x 4's on edge and glue and nail them to one of the plywood panels as shown—four vertically and two horizontally. Then glue and nail the other panel on top so that the 2 x 4's are sandwiched between the plywood panels.

3. Cut two lengths of 1 x 6 stock the same length as the desktop. Rip one in half as bottom trim for the plywood. Hold the front piece in place before nailing to make sure that it doesn't interfere with opening the drawers; trim if necessary.

5. For end pieces, cut two lengths of 1 x 8 stock equal to the width of the plywood plus the trim. Glue and nail them in place so that they extend ¼ in. above the top. The bottoms should overlap the existing desk by about 2¼ in.

6. Rip a 1½-in. width from the remainder of the 1 x 6 and use it to trim the exposed ends of the 2 x 4's so that they are flush with the rest of the trim. Insert the hardboard top in the recess and attach a vise to the corner of the plywood top.

Doorknob / Ashtray

An old doorknob and a discarded pot lid make an unusual ashtray, complete with a center post for stubbing out cigarettes or knocking the ashes from a pipe. Or, if you're a nonsmoker, you can use the tray as a candy or nut dish.

Any kind of knob will do—brass, ceramic, or glass. Choose a pot lid of anodized aluminum or other heat-resistant metal; a copper-colored finish looks best.

For the base, use a square of hardwood. Cut a hole in the center for the inverted pot lid to rest in. Once you've sanded

Doorknob
Setscrew
Spindle
Washer
Pot lid
Washer
Hose clamp
Hardwood base
Brass drawer pulls

and finished it, attach feet—brass drawer pulls make good ones—so that the knob spindle will clear the surface the ashtray is sitting on.

Assemble the pieces as shown after removing the handle from the lid and enlarging the hole to about ½ inch. Secure the spindle to the lid with a hose clamp—standard nuts won't fit. If the knob wobbles after assembly, use epoxy to glue it and its washer to the lid.

To make cigarette rests, use pliers to bend the lid flange in four places. Tape the jaws of the pliers to protect the metal.

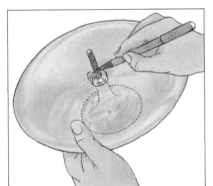

1. Drill a ½-in. hole in the center of the lid and assemble the pieces to mark the spindle for cutting. Cut, reassemble, and apply epoxy if the doorknob wobbles.

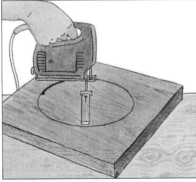

2. Measure the diameter of the lid, add 2 in., and cut a square of hardwood this size. Then use a saber saw to cut a hole about 1 in. smaller than the lid.

3. With a rasp or saber saw, bevel the inside edges of the hardwood base at a 30° angle. Then round off the corners and sand the edges smooth.

4. Stain the base and apply two coats of polyurethane. When it is dry, attach screw-in brass drawer pulls as feet and put the inverted pot lid in place.

Doors / Folding screen

Hinge two or three old doors together for a folding screen that can divide a room or conceal a corner. Then try your hand at marbleizing (p.355) or stenciling (p.349) to turn your screen into a true original.

Buy double-action hinges the proper width for the doors. You'll also need some wood filler to level the old hinge mortises.

If the tops of the doors are out of alignment, place the unfolded screen across some sawhorses. Clamp a board all the way across the top, flush with the lowest door, as a fence. Then trim the protruding tops with a circular saw.

1. Sand or strip the doors. Remove the old hinges and level the mortises by applying wood filler slightly higher than the surface. After it has set, sand it smooth.

2. Align the doors at the bottom and install double-action hinges 6 in. from the top and bottom. If the doors are heavy, install a third hinge in the middle.

Marbleizing / TECHNIQUE

Give walls, woodwork, or furniture the look of fine marble with this simple painting technique.

First, select six complementary shades of acrylic paint: one base color, two "drift" colors, two "vein" colors, and black or another color that contrasts strongly with the others. At the same time, buy extender and thickener. Then sand your work surface smooth and clean it with a tack cloth. Apply two coats of the base color, then spray on a clear mat acrylic sealer.

Use four nonabsorbent paper plates as palettes—one for each phase of the painting.

1. Squeeze the two drift colors onto a paper plate with an even circular motion, then repeat the process with the extender and thickener. Tilt the plate back and forth until all of the ingredients run together but are not fully mixed. Wet a sponge with water, wring it out, and dip it into the paints. To paint, dab the surface gently but firmly, turning the sponge to make drifts as shown.

2. When the drift colors are completely dry, pour a small puddle of each vein color onto another paper plate and mix each color with extender and thickener. Then dip a fine brush into the paint; holding it loosely, choose a few of the drifts to outline with a combination of jagged and smooth strokes. Begin at the top end of a drift and move quickly down and around it.

3. To create a speckled effect over the drifts and veins of your marbleized surface, dip an old toothbrush into the contrasting color. Then flick a knife or your thumb across the bristles. Be careful not to overdo it—a few well-placed splatters should be enough. When the paint is completely dry, apply a couple of coats of mat-finish polyurethane to seal and protect the surface.

Drain tile / Uplight

A lamp that shines up from the floor creates a dramatic effect of light and shadow, especially if it's placed indoors among potted plants. For an uplight that's as attractive as it is simple, you can easily convert a round clay drain tile.

All you need besides the drain tile is a piece of ½-inch plywood and a lamp kit (sold at lighting stores) that contains a socket, a threaded brass nipple, nuts and washers, and a lamp cord with the plug attached.

Cut a plywood disc to fit inside the tile, attach the lamp parts, and screw in a bulb. Turn the lamp on by simply plugging it in, or, if you prefer, install a line switch.

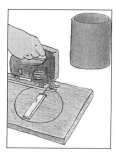

1. Measure the inside diameter of the drain tile and cut a circle of ½-in. plywood about ¹⁄₁₆ in. smaller.

2. Drill a ⅜-in. hole in the center of the plywood. Then drill a hole near the bottom of the tile with a ¼-in. masonry bit.

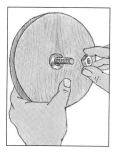

3. Insert a 1½-in. brass nipple into the hole in the plywood and secure it with a washer and nut on each side.

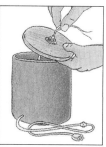

4. From the outside, thread the bare end of the lamp cord through the hole in the tile, then up through the nipple.

5. Wrap the two wires clockwise around the terminal screws of the socket. Screw the socket onto the nipple.

6. Turn the plywood disc on edge and wedge it into the bottom of the tile. Screw in a bulb and plug in the lamp.

Drying rack / Tie rack

The top of an old drying rack makes a space-saving tie holder for your closet door. All you need are a couple of brass hinges and lightweight chains to put it in place. Then add a screw eye and hook to keep it up out of the way. Just make sure the rack is wide enough to attach to the stiles or side panels of your door; the center section is too flimsy to support the hardware.

Start by removing the rack from the legs. Measure between the arms of the rack and cut a section of leg to size to use as an end piece. Cut the ends of the arms square if they are rounded or notched, then screw the end piece in place or join it with dowel pins. Sand and paint the rack or finish it to match the door.

Once you've screwed brass hinges into the end piece, attach a chain near the end of each arm of the rack and mount the rack at eye level on

the back of the closet door. Fold the rack up and mark the positions of the chains on the door; then level the rack, hold the chains to the marks, and and cut them to the appropriate length. Fix the chains to the door with screws.

Put a screw eye in the center of the front dowel, then fold the rack flush with the door to position the hook.

1. Free the top section of the drying rack from the accordion legs by removing the small brads or prying out the nails that hold it in place.

3. Attach hinges about 1 in. from each end of the end piece. Then secure chains near the other ends of the arms with No. 4 screws.

5. Fold the rack against the door and mark the position of the chains. Then, using a spirit level, level the rack and cut the chains to the correct length.

2. Cut a section from one of the rack legs. Drill and countersink for No. 8 screws to attach it to the end of the arms as an end piece.

4. Install a screw eye in the front dowel. Scribe a level line on the closet door and mount the rack on it, screwing the hinges into the stiles or side panels.

6. Fold the rack flat against the door to mark the position for a screw hook. Then install it so that it engages the screw eye on the rack.

Eating utensils / Wind chime

For a charming wind chime with a surprisingly musical tone, turn to your old flatware. Use only silver-plated forks, spoons, or knives; stainless-steel utensils don't have an appealing ring, and sterling silver is obviously too valuable for this kind of recycling.

Use a rubber mallet or a cloth-covered hammer to flatten the utensils on a block of wood. Then polish them so that the silver will glint in the sun. And be sure to have some extra forks on hand;

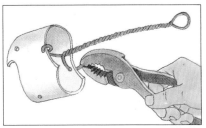

1. Cut a 4-in. section of PVC pipe and notch the edges. Drill two ⅛-in. holes exactly opposite each other about ½ in. from the top of the cylinder. At the other end, drill four equidistant holes.

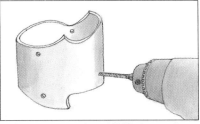

3. Remove the pipe. Thread the ends of the wires through the two top holes in the PVC cylinder, working from the inside, and use pliers to bend them over the top to secure.

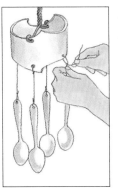

5. Drill a ⅛-in. hole ¼ in. from the end of each utensil handle. Knot a 12-in. length of fishing line onto the end of each utensil, then hang the four spoons from the holes drilled in the PVC pipe.

bending the tines is tricky, and you'll probably break a few before you get the hang of it.

Besides the utensils, you'll need a 4-inch section of 3- or 4-inch PVC pipe, some heavy-gauge copper wire, a small cylinder to use as a mandrel in shaping a hanging loop (½-inch pipe works fine), and some 4-pound or stronger fishing line.

When cutting the PVC pipe, notch the lower edge or cut it in an irregular shape so that it will catch the wind and keep the chimes tinkling.

2. Cut a 40-in. piece of 12-gauge copper wire and fold it in half around a ½-in. pipe. Clamp the pipe in a vise and grip the wires 5 in. from the ends with locking-grip pliers. Twist until the wires are intertwined.

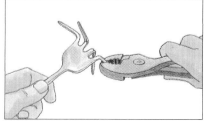

4. Flatten four spoons and a fork. With pliers, bend one of the middle tines of the fork to 90°; bend another in the opposite direction. Then bend the outer tines upward and sideways as shown.

6. Hang the fork from the crotch of the copper wire hanger, positioning it so that its tines strike the bowls of the spoons. Trim the excess fishing line from the knots and hang the chime to catch the wind.

Fabric scraps / Napkins & gift decorations

Use the leftover fabric from sewing projects to decorate jars of homemade preserves and other goodies. Your scraps can also be turned into small sacks to dress up the bottles of spirits or liqueur you're giving for Christmas. And several squares can be cut out of larger scraps with pinking shears—and left unhemmed—to make pretty fabric napkins for parties and gifts. All three projects are easy enough for children to do.

JAR LID COVERS

These handmade fabric tops give your jars of homemade relishes and preserves the professional finish of those sold in specialty stores. Use traditional checked gingham for a country look or choose a solid color and trim it with lace or rickrack. If you're passing out the jars as gifts, why not combine them in a basket with a few napkins that match the lid covers?

NAPKINS

Use these to complement your gifts of homemade treats. Or make several from different fabrics to use at a party or buffet. Although left unhemmed, the napkins will stand up to four or five trips through the washing machine if you use pinking shears to help keep the edges from fraying.

BOTTLE SACK

With a sewing machine, you can make one of these clever little gift sacks in less than 5 minutes. Use a running stitch on the wrong side of the fabric and turn the piece inside out so that the seam won't show.

Your finished product doesn't have to be used just for a bottle of Christmas cheer. Make sacks of different sizes for other gifts—toys for a child's birthday or assorted kitchen gadgets for a bride-to-be. Decorate, if you like, by gluing on a few felt cutouts or sequins, or use felt letters to form a name or greeting. Tie with a bow of ribbon or yarn.

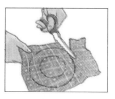

1. Trace the jar lid on the wrong side of the fabric, add 2 in. all around, and cut out with pinking shears.

2. Use white glue to affix the trim. Secure the cover on the lid with a rubber band, then tie with ribbon.

Cut out a 10-in. square of cardboard and use chalk to trace around it on the wrong side of the fabric. Cut out with pinking shears and fold.

1. Cut a 13- x 15-in. piece of fabric, lay it face-down, and hem a short side by folding over ½ in. of material.

2. Fold in half lengthwise, wrong side out. Press, then sew the long side and bottom with a running stitch.

3. Turn right side out and press the seam flat. Put the bottle inside and tie at the neck with ribbon or yarn.

357

Fence / Headboard

To give your plain bed the look of a handsome antique, attach a section of decorative iron fence to the frame as a headboard. Two gates can be bolted together to serve the purpose as well.

A hacksaw will probably be strong enough to cut the fencing to size; be sure to have several coarse blades (18 teeth per inch) on hand—they'll dull quickly. If the metal is too heavy to cut, take the fence to a body shop and have it trimmed with a cutting torch.

If your bed frame is already equipped with flanges for mounting a headboard, all you'll need are flat metal mending plates and some heavy stove bolts. For a bed frame without the flanges, substitute inside corner braces (angle brackets) for the front mending plates.

1. Choose an attractive section of fence and cut it to the width of your bed frame with a hacksaw equipped with a coarse blade; replace blades as necessary.

Folding table & chairs / RENEWAL

Give your bridge set a face-lift by painting the metal frames. Then re-cover the seats and tabletop with padding and a bright waterproof or vinylized fabric, and they'll look like new.

To start the job, turn the set over and remove the screws or metal tabs that hold the seats and tabletop in place (bend metal tabs straight with pliers for easy removal). Prepare the metal as shown, wipe down with mineral spirits, and spray-paint in a well-ventilated place. Prevent drip marks by applying two light coats instead of one heavy one.

If the seats are cardboard, use a standard office stapler to staple the foam padding and fabric to them; if they're wood, use a heavy-duty stapler. A glue gun will work, too.

Let the paint dry overnight. Then reassemble the table and chairs and finish them up with new rubber leg tips, available at hardware stores.

1. Scrub the metal frames with a wire brush and sand any rust spots with fine sandpaper. Then spray the spots with a metal primer.

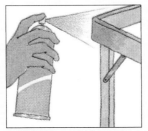

2. Place the table frame and chairs in a well-ventilated place and clean with mineral spirits. Spray-paint with two light coats.

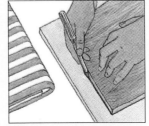

3. Cut ⅛-in. foam padding to the size of the tabletop and chair seats. Cut fabric 2 in. larger all around and place it facedown.

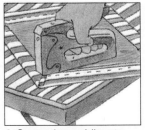

4. Center the padding, tabletop, and seats on top of the fabric. Pull the fabric tight and staple it down. Reassemble table and chairs.

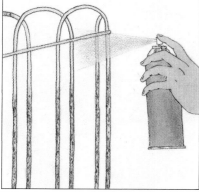

2. Scrub the fence headboard with a wire brush, wipe down with mineral spirits, and prime with metal primer. Spray-paint to match the decor of your bedroom.

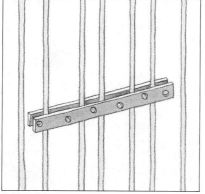

3. Use 1-in. stove bolts to clamp two flat mending plates together across three rods at both sides of the fence at the level of the bed frame; tighten well.

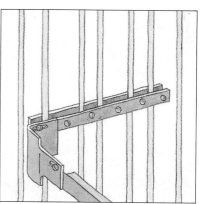

4. Use more stove bolts to attach the mending plates to the headboard brackets at the end of the frame; the brackets are slotted to allow for adjustment.

Food storage container /Night light

You can turn a translucent plastic food storage container and an old lamp base into a decorative night light for a child's room or hallway. All you have to do is dismantle the base and cut down the spindle, reattach the socket and lamp cord, and secure the upside-down container on top with a nut and washer.

Best to use is a simply designed lamp base with a flat top at least 3 inches across. To dismantle it, remove the cardboard socket cover, disconnect the wires from the socket, and unscrew the socket from the spindle. Then unscrew the spindle from the base, setting the nuts and washers aside, and pull the electric cord out.

If your lamp spindle doesn't have a threaded section at least 4 inches

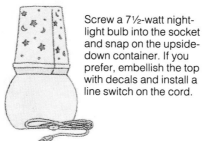

Screw a 7½-watt night-light bulb into the socket and snap on the upside-down container. If you prefer, embellish the top with decals and install a line switch on the cord.

long, buy a threaded brass nipple at the hardware store, along with two nuts and washers to fit it.

Choose a food storage container that has a snap-on or screw-lock lid. If you'd rather not have to take the container off to reach the switch, install a line switch on the cord. Once the night light is assembled, knot the cord just inside the base so that an accidental tug on the cord won't disconnect the wires from the socket.

Be sure to drill vent holes in the the plastic container and its lid. A 7½-watt night-light bulb should provide enough illumination, but you can also use a 40-watt appliance bulb; just be sure it doesn't come too close to the top of the container, which will melt easily.

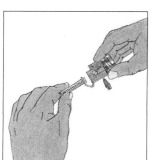

1. With a hacksaw, cut a 4-in. length from the threaded part of the spindle. Screw it into the hole in the metal arm attached to the socket, leaving enough room for the wires that will pass through.

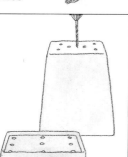

2. Drill a ⅜-in. hole in the center of the lid of the food storage container, then drill four or five smaller vent holes around the edges. Drill five or six ¼-in. vent holes in the bottom of the container.

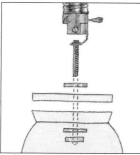

3. To assemble, push the bottom of the spindle through a 1-in. washer, the upside-down lid of the food storage container, the base of the lamp, and another washer. Secure with a nut.

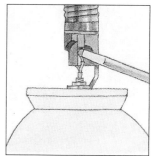

4. Push the stripped end of the electric cord through the bottom of the spindle and out the top, then connect the wires to the screws on the socket. Pull the wire taut and replace the socket cover.

Freezer door / Dolly

By law, you have to remove the door before you dispose of an old refrigerator or freezer. Instead of carting it to the dump, put the door to good use: attach wheels and turn it into a dolly for moving heavy objects. Once you've removed the plastic shelf panel and rubber gasket from the door, all you have to do is screw on a sheet of plywood and attach four revolving casters and a rope. Then use it for moving air conditioners and other heavy appliances or for ferrying several garbage cans to the curb at once.

1. Remove the door handle. Unscrew and remove the rubber gasket and panel of shelves to expose the layer of insulating material and the metal frame that holds it in place.

2. Cut a piece of ¾-in. plywood the same size as the door. Position a caster 3 in. from each corner of the plywood and mark for drilling. Drill holes and bolt on the casters.

3. Place the plywood on the insulation side of the door, casters up, and drill holes around the edge and into the metal frame. Fasten the wood to the frame with 1½-in. screws.

4. Drill ¼-in. holes all the way through the plywood and door between the two front casters. Turn the dolly right side up, put ¼-in. eye bolts in the holes, and tie a pull cord to the bolts.

Garden hose / Soaker hose

That leaky old garden hose can be a boon to your garden. Just drill more holes in it and use it as a soaker hose. It waters more deeply and gently than the usual spray or sprinkler—and more efficiently, as less water is lost to evaporation.

Place the hose next to plants—or, for an invisible watering system, bury it in a trench alongside. If you plan to use it to water shrubs or trees, save still more water by drilling holes only in the sections adjacent to the plants; the ground between will remain dry.

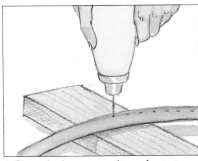

1. Place the hose on a piece of scrap wood and drill ¹⁄₁₆-in. holes all the way through, spacing them about 1 in. apart.

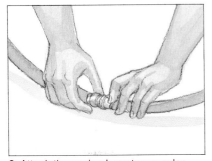

2. Attach the soaker hose to a regular hose with a brass or plastic coupling that has two female receptors.

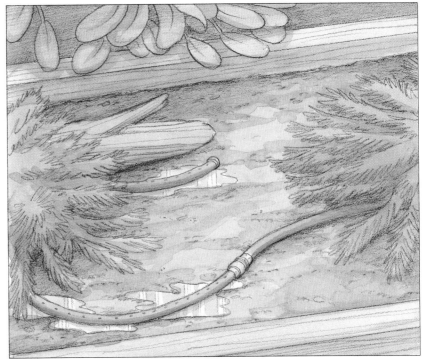

3. Seal off the end of the soaker hose with a plastic end cap. Place the hose next to the plants you want to water or bury it in a trench alongside (take care not to damage roots when you dig). Adjust the water to a trickle and leave it on for 30 to 40 min.

Hangers / RENEWAL

Old wooden hangers—the kind with a single bar—can be transformed into luxurious and colorful padded ones with a scrap of quilt batting and an easy-to-sew cover.

The puckered sleeve that fits over the hanger is usually made from silk. Sew three pieces of fabric together to make it, gathering two of them to form the decorative puckers. Finish off the hanger with a ribbon bow in a contrasting color at the hook; you might want to tie on a small sachet as well, which will lightly perfume the whole closet.

The directions given here are for one standard 16-inch hanger.

1. Cut the quilt batting to 10 x 18 in. Cut an opening in the center, stick the hanger hook through, and wrap the batting around the hanger. Secure with a basting stitch.

2. Cut fabric into three 5-in.-wide strips—two 12-in.-long top pieces and a 19-in.-long bottom piece. Sew a gathering stitch along the long sides of the top pieces.

3. Lay the top pieces on the bottom piece, wrong side out. Arrange the puckers until the pieces fit together. Sew one of the top pieces to the bottom piece.

4. Sew the second top piece to the bottom, leaving most of one side open so that you can fit it over the hanger. Then turn this fabric sleeve right side out.

5. Gently pull the sleeve over both ends of the hanger. Hand-stitch the open side of the sleeve together. Stitch the top pieces together at the hook.

6. Tie a ribbon bow of a contrasting color to the hook to decorate the hanger. Or, if you like, attach a small lightly scented sachet with ribbon.

Ice cream tubs / Storage unit

Collect 10 containers from your local ice cream parlor after a busy weekend and you'll have the materials for an ingenious wall storage unit. Just cover the tubs with an adhesive plastic, such as Con-Tact, and attach them to a triangular piece of plywood. Then mount the unit on the wall and use it for storing clothes or toys. Most ice cream tubs measure 9½ inches in diameter. If your tubs are a different size, adjust the plywood base to fit.

1. Mark a 40-in. equilateral triangle on a piece of ½-in. plywood and cut it out. Stain or paint it if you like.

2. Draw a second triangle 3 in. inside the plywood base as a guideline; drill a pilot hole at the top.

3. Drill a hole in the exact center of the bottom of an ice cream tub and align it with the pilot hole.

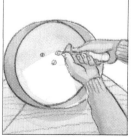

4. Attach it to the plywood with a screw and washer; place two more screws toward the point of the triangle.

5. Position two more tubs on the guideline, fitting snugly against the first. Attach them the same way.

6. Attach another row of three tubs and a bottom row of four. Mount the unit to a wall stud with 2½-in. screws.

Lampshade / RENEWAL

If an old lampshade has grown discolored and splotched, give it a face-lift with a new fabric cover.

Don't remove the old fabric or paper from the shade—sew the new cover directly on top. To determine the amount of fabric you'll need, measure the bottom diameter of the shade and multiply by 3½ to get the length, then measure the height of the shade and add 2¼ inches to get the width.

Cut the fabric, sew it end to end, then pleat and stitch it as shown. To trim the top and bottom of the new shade, use double-fold bias tape, ribbon, or braid.

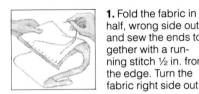

1. Fold the fabric in half, wrong side out, and sew the ends together with a running stitch ½ in. from the edge. Turn the fabric right side out.

3. Remove the cover from the shade and stitch the pleats closed with a continuous running stitch 1 in. from the top edge. Remove the straight pins.

5. Again replace the cover, align the stitches with the edges of the shade, and use an overcast stitch to sew the cover to the shade. Cut off excess fabric.

2. Place the cover over the shade and fold the top edge into pleats, securing each pleat with a straight pin. Be sure to tuck the seam into a pleat.

4. Pin the cover to the shade with clothespins, aligning the top stitch with the top edge. Then pleat the bottom. Remove and stitch 1 in. from the bottom edge.

6. To trim the shade and cover and conceal the stitches around the top and bottom edges, affix double-fold bias tape, ribbon, or braid with white glue.

Lattice / Window cover

Screen an unsightly view or filter bright sunlight with a piece of left-over wooden lattice. Edged with a wooden frame and painted to match the decor of your room, it makes an appealing change of pace from curtains or blinds.

Make the frame from pine 1 x 2, then lock the lattice panel inside with ½-inch strips ripped from lattice stock. If the cover doesn't fit snugly in the window frame, keep it in place with a couple of hooks on top and matching screw eyes on the window frame; this makes it easy to remove when you want to clean or open the window.

1. Measure the inside of the window and use 1 x 2 to build a wooden frame to fit inside. Cut the lattice panel to size.

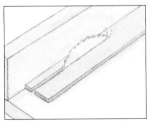

2. Rip eight ½-in. widths of ¼-in. lattice stock to make the groove for holding the lattice in the frame.

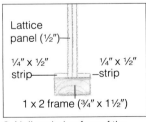

Lattice panel (½")

¼" x ½" strip

¼" x ½" strip

1 x 2 frame (¾" x 1½")

3. Nail and glue four of the strips inside the frame as shown. Insert the lattice panel and install the remaining strips.

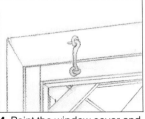

4. Paint the window cover and attach two hooks to the top. Install matching screw eyes on the window frame.

Oil drum / Wood stove

An oil drum fitted with a simple conversion kit from the hardware store becomes a wood-burning stove that can provide cheap heat for a large studio, loft, or country cabin—even a barn.

The conversion kit you'll need includes a cast-iron fire door with adjustable draft shutter, a collar for the stovepipe, two double leg sets, and assembly instructions. Buy some furnace cement, as well, to seal the seams between the parts; a high-temperature RTV sealant works best.

No welding is required for this project. But it's necessary to take a few precautions before you start: First, see that the stove will have its own flue; don't connect it to your furnace chimney. Second, choose a 30- or 55-gallon drum that has never contained flammable or toxic substances and steam-clean it thoroughly. Before you install the stove, check with a building inspector for approved clearances and in-

spect and clean your chimney before connecting the stovepipe. And once the stove is in use, check it regularly for signs of deterioration. With plenty of use, the barrel will probably burn out within 2 or 3 years, but you can extend its life by lining the inside with fire brick (no mortar is necessary).

For a more ambitious project, connect a second oil drum on top with an extra section of stovepipe and a collar; brace it to the first barrel with a set of legs. This double-barrel version is a more efficient heater, since the top drum traps and radiates heat that is otherwise lost. You can also install a Dutch oven in the top drum—a consideration if your stove is going to be used in a vacation cabin. (The oven should be made of steel—at least 24 gauge— and have flanges that can be attached to the drum with sheet metal screws.) Even the one-drum stove shown here can be used for stovetop cooking; just fasten a wire rack on top.

Attach the stove to a vented stovepipe before placing wood inside for burning.

Stovepipe collar

Oil drum

Fire door

Air shutter

1. Stand the barrel on end, center the fire door on top, and draw an outline for the door and draft shutter. Mark the positions for the bolts.

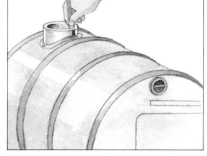

2. Turn the barrel on its side with the door outline upright. Trace the collar opening at the opposite end and mark positions for the bolts.

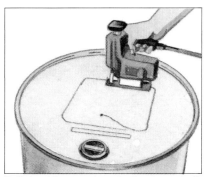

3. Cut out the openings for the door, draft shutter, and stovepipe with a saber saw, then file off the sharp edges. Drill holes for the bolts.

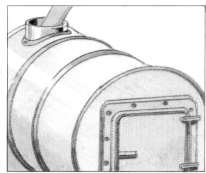

4. Bolt down the fire door assembly and fill the gaps with high-temperature RTV sealant. Put the stovepipe collar in place and bolt it down.

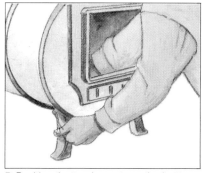

5. Position the two leg sets on the bottom side of the barrel and mark the holes for drilling. Bolt the legs on by reaching in through the fire door.

Packing crate / Table

A rough, weather-beaten crate makes an interesting end table that fits perfectly with country-style decor. If weathered wood is not to your taste, sand and prime the crate; then paint it. Another alternative is bleaching the wood (below).

Set the crate on its side to work on it. Drive in any loose nails and pull out rusty ones and replace them. Then cut a piece of ½-inch plywood to fit the top of the crate and nail four small plywood blocks to the underside to keep the top from shifting (place them just close enough to the edge to fit inside the crate).

Use a piece of burlap to make a no-sew throw to complement your rustic table. Then, depending on its height and shape, top the table with a lamp and use it as an end table or place it in front of a couch as a coffee table with an arrangement of dried flowers.

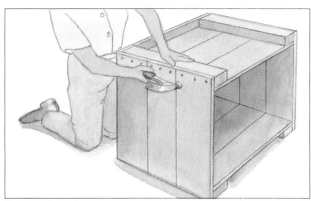

1. Hose down the crate; if necessary, use a scrub brush to remove dirt or peeling paint. Pound raised nailheads into the wood and sand any rough corners that might snag carpeting.

Wood bleaching / TECHNIQUE

Stripping a piece of furniture will lighten it, but bleaching will make the wood look still fresher. This simple technique can transform a chair, picture frame, or an entire room of paneling.

Wood bleaching kits containing sodium hydroxide or hydrogen peroxide are sold at hardware stores and home centers. Some bleaching solutions are self-neutralizing, while others need an application of vinegar and water. Whatever kind you choose, read the instructions carefully and wear rubber gloves and old clothing when you brush it on.

The key to a good bleaching job is removing all the old finish. To test, wet the wood with water after you've stripped it. If it darkens evenly, it will bleach to a uniform color; any areas that remain light must be stripped again.

Once the wood dries after the first application, it should be lighter. To make it lighter still, apply the solution two or three more times. But don't overdo it—after four or five applications the wood may start to look gray and lifeless. If this happens, improve its appearance by wiping on a light stain to highlight the grain.

1. Protect the work area with newspapers covered with plastic garbage bags. Use an old brush to apply an even coat of wood bleach to the wood.

2. Let the wood dry for 3 hr. before you decide whether it needs another application. Use spot applications to touch up areas where the color is uneven.

3. Let the wood dry overnight (or as long as the directions recommend). Then sand twice, first with medium sandpaper, then with a finer grit.

4. Protect the wood with a wipe-on oil finish. If the wood is overbleached and lifeless, apply a light stain to highlight the grain and apply the oil after it dries.

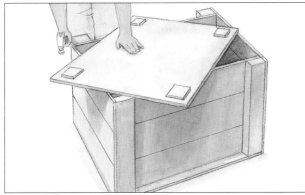

3. Cut a piece of burlap or country-print heavy cotton fabric to fit the top. For a still more rustic look, pull several threads off the edges of the fabric to create a fringe on all four sides. Place the burlap over the table at an angle for best effect.

2. Cut a piece of ½-in. plywood to fit the outside dimensions of the top of the crate. Then glue and nail small plywood blocks to the underside of the top.

Paper towel tubes / Napkin rings

For some terrific-looking napkin rings, cut up paper towel tubes and cover them with fabric, bias tape, or yarn. Children love to make the simpler ones, embellishing them with discarded costume jewelry or dried flowers. When you cut the tubes, take care not to mash the cylinder out of shape.

GATHERED FABRIC

Gather or pleat the fabric as you stitch little sleeves. These are sewn on only one end; if you prefer, you can cut the fabric in half lengthwise and stitch both ends.

1. Cut a 4- x 9-in. piece of fabric, fold it in half lengthwise, and press with an iron.

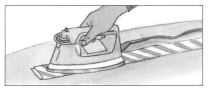

2. Cut a 1½-in. section of paper towel tube with a single-edge razor blade and insert it into the fold.

3. Sew the cut edges of the fabric, gathering it as you go. Knot the last stitch and trim off the excess fabric.

BIAS TAPE

For a party, wrap each section of paper towel tube with a different bright color. This method is so simple that children can churn out rings by the dozen.

1. Glue a 50-in. strip of bias tape inside the cylinder at a slight angle.

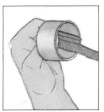

2. Wind the tape around the cylinder, slanting it slightly and overlapping half of each previous turn as you go.

3. Secure the last turn with a few stitches and attach a bauble to cover the thread.

YARN OR STRING

To make a slender row of knots at one edge of these napkin rings, wind to the left and tuck to the right (or vice versa). Use a 50-in. length of doubled yarn or string.

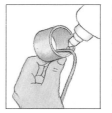

1. Glue the end of the doubled yarn to the inside of the cylinder and let the glue set. Begin winding over the top and up again.

2. At each top turn, tuck the yarn under the previous loop and pull it out all the way. Continue winding to the left and tucking to the right.

3. When you've covered the whole cylinder, sew down the last few loops with several stitches. Then decorate the ring with a bit of jewelry.

Phonograph records / Planter

Have some old 45 rpm records gathering dust in the attic? Turn them into a novel reminder of the fifties with this blast-from-the-past planter.

You can also adapt these instructions to LPs to build a larger version. In either case, you'll need 11 records, but be sure to have plenty of extras on hand—the plastic breaks easily when drilled. Save the most nostalgic (or bizarre) titles for the four visible uprights; this project is meant to be a conversation piece, after all.

Seven records—the top three of them slotted to accept the uprights—are glued together to form the base of the planter. To make the job look as neat as possible, use RTV silicone glue, sold in hardware and auto parts stores; it dries black.

Use a drill to cut the slots, moving the bit sideways along the top edge of your masking-tape template. As you drill, the bit will heat up and collect plastic; push the residue off with a putty knife before it hardens.

To cut a flat edge on the uprights, first scribe a deep line. Then bend the edge back and forth with flat-jaw pliers until the plastic breaks. When you cut the notches, use the side of your drill bit, cutting through the plastic as if you were using a knife.

To bend the edges of the uprights, scribe deep lines exactly 5¾ inches apart. Preheat an electric curling iron for 5 minutes and place it against the outside of a line for 30 seconds. Then quickly align the line with the edge of a board and bend the record to a 90° angle.

Let the glue dry for at least 24 hours. Then place a saucer inside and add a potted houseplant.

1. Cut a 5¾-in. square of cardboard, center it exactly on a record, and scribe a centered 2-in. line onto the record at each edge of the cardboard. Mark each line with a 2-in. strip of masking tape.

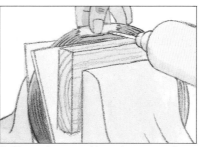

2. Clamp the record in a vise, protecting it with pieces of cardboard. Slowly drill along the inside edges of the tape strips with a ⅟₁₆-in. bit, using a piece of 1 x 4 as a brace and guide. Remove the tape.

3. Tape the record to two more, clamp them in the vise, and drill slots all the way through, using the slotted record as your guide. Smooth the inside edges of the slots with a nail file.

4. Glue all three records together, taking care to see that the slots are exactly aligned. After the glue has dried for at least 8 hr., glue four more records to the bottom; let dry.

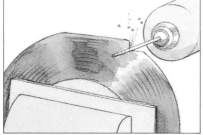

5. Select four more records and cut ³⁄₁₆ in. off the bottom of each. Then cut a notch, about ¼ in. deep, at each end of all the flat bottoms to create flanges that will fit into the slots in the base.

6. Glue two records into facing slots in the base. When the glue is dry, score the edges of the two remaining records and bend them to a 90° angle with an electric curling iron; then glue them in place.

Picket fence / Garden trellis

When you replace an old picket fence, save a section or two to use as a garden trellis. Lashed together to form an A-frame, two sections provide climbing space—and in hot climates, welcome shade—for beans, peas, tomatoes, and cucumbers. Or you can attach one horizontal section to a planter box and use it on a patio or deck for climbing roses or jasmine.

A-FRAME TRELLIS

Use two equal sections of fencing to construct this simple trellis. If you don't want to bolt them together, try securing them with wire.

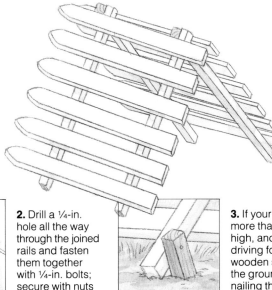

1. Cut two sections of fence (from 4 to 8 ft.), so that the rails extend about 2 in. beyond the pickets at each end. Then position the two sections to form an A-frame, positioning them so that the rails are flush against each other.

2. Drill a ¼-in. hole all the way through the joined rails and fasten them together with ¼-in. bolts; secure with nuts and washers.

3. If your trellis is more than 6 ft. high, anchor it by driving four wooden stakes in the ground and nailing the four rails to them.

PLANTER BOX TRELLIS

Use an existing planter box or make your own from any 1 x 12 stock (waterproof the wood first). Just be sure that the box is slightly longer than the section of fence you plan to use for the trellis.

1. Cut a section of fence and pry off the bottom two pickets. For a uniform look, saw the pointed ends off. Sand rough areas and paint with several coats of exterior paint.

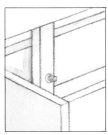

2. Position the exposed rails at the back of the box and drill ¼-in. holes. Attach the fence with ¼-in. bolts and fill the box with soil to keep it from tipping over.

Sanding / TECHNIQUE

Having trouble sanding the curves and crevices on a piece of furniture? Some common household items can become simple sanding aids.

TAPE

To make a sanding strip, cut a strip of duct, electrical, or masking tape 6 in. longer than the sandpaper and center it on the back of the paper along one edge. Fold the extra tape over the grit side as handles, then cut the sandpaper to the width of the tape.

PLAYING CARDS

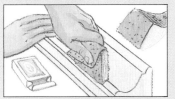

For hard-to-reach grooves or drawer tracks, use a deck of playing cards as a sanding block. Wrap the sandpaper around the deck, then push the edge of the deck against the irregular object you want to sand; your playing card "block" will take on the shape.

BLACKBOARD ERASER

Wrap sandpaper around a blackboard eraser when you sand large flat areas. Use the hard top side for rough sanding, the soft side for fine sanding.

Picture frame / Serving tray

Old picture frames can become elegant and unusual trays. Convert a large one to accommodate an entire coffee service. Or turn smaller frames into individual hors d'oeuvre and dessert trays.

A piece of hardboard makes a sturdy bottom for your tray; top it with a thin sheet of cork. Or, for a more decorative (and easier to clean) tray, cover the hardboard with fabric and then with the original glass. Protect against seepage by running a bead of latex caulk around the inside of the frame before putting the glass in place.

Use 1-inch brads to hold the hardboard in the frame. When you squeeze the brads in place, protect the frame with a piece of cardboard. Finally, line the bottom of the tray with felt or another sheet of cork so that it won't scratch the surface of your table.

1. Remove the picture, glass, and cardboard backing. Then cut a piece of ¼-in. hardboard the same size as the backing. Or measure the interior length and width of the rabbet in the frame.

2. Glue a slightly larger sheet of ¹⁄₁₆-in. cork to the top of the hardboard. Then, when the glue is completely dry, use a sharp utility knife to trim the edges of the cork flush with the hardboard.

3. Mount the hardboard in the frame, cork side toward the front, and use locking-grip pliers to squeeze 1-in. brads into the frame at a slight angle. Put cardboard in the pliers' jaws to protect the frame.

4. Use a small hammer to tap down the protruding parts of the brads so that they hold the hardboard in place. Then line the bottom of the tray with a piece of felt or cork to prevent scratches.

Pill bottles / Spice rack

Save your glass or plastic pill bottles, especially the brown-tinted ones; they make perfect containers for dried herbs and spices. The ones shown here are apothecary-type bottles, 2 inches across, like those that many vitamins come in. The rack, custom-built to hold eight of them, is made of pine 1 x 6; if your carpentry skills are sufficient, you could use maple, ash, or another hardwood. Stain or paint the rack as you like, or simply apply a wipe-on oil finish to the sanded wood. Or give the rack an interesting stippled look with a sponging technique (p.369).

Adjust the size and placement of the holes to accommodate the size of your bottles. The ones in the project shown here measure 2⅛ inches in diameter and are centered exactly 1⁹⁄₁₆ inches from the sides and 1⁹⁄₁₆ inches and 4⅛ inches from the ends of the top board. The holes are easily cut with an inexpensive hole saw fitted to your electric drill.

Wash the pill bottles thoroughly and make sure they're completely dry before you fill them with spices. Label each bottle with an adhesive file label, lettering it decoratively, or use one of the preprinted spice labels sold in gourmet shops and most stationery stores.

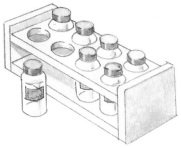

1. To construct the rack, cut two 10⅞-in. lengths and two 4¼-in. lengths of 1 x 6 pine stock or a hardwood such as maple, oak, or ash.

2. Mark the exact centers for eight holes on one of the 10⅞-in. boards, taking care to space the holes evenly from the ends and sides.

3. Clamp the board down on a piece of scrap wood. Use a hole saw to bore holes ⅛ in. larger than the diameter of your pill bottles.

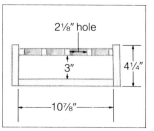

4. Assemble the rack with glue and 4d finishing nails, taking care to see that the nails do not protrude into the holes. Finish the wood as desired.

Quilt / Place mats

When an old quilt is worn beyond repair, cut out the undamaged sections and use them as place mats and pot holders. It's as simple as stitching extra-wide double-band bias tape around the edges.

For a set of place mats, you'll need quilted sections about 12 x 18 inches. To determine the length of bias tape you need for the edging, measure the perimeter of the piece and add 3 inches. Make pot holders 10 inches square; add 8 inches to the tape so that you'll have enough to make a hanger hook.

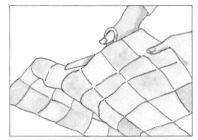

1. Cut out an undamaged section of quilt and measure the perimeter. Cut extra-wide double-band bias tape to the measurement, adding 3 in. for a place mat and 8 in. for a pot holder.

2. Unfold the bias tape at one end and stitch a ½-in. hem. Align the outside edge of the unfolded tape with the edge of the fabric and pin it down. Stitch the tape to the fabric along the first crease.

3. Pin and stitch the tape to the other three sides, one side at a time. Miter the corners as you go. Then fold the end of the tape under and stitch a ½-in. hem. Remove the straight pins.

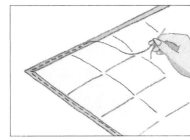

4. Fold the tape over the edge of the fabric so that there is a double fold of tape on the back side of the place mat. Sew it to the back side with a running stitch down the middle of the fold.

Sponging / TECHNIQUE

All it takes is a sponge (natural—*not* synthetic) and acrylic paints to give an attractive stippled pattern to anything from a wooden spice rack (left) to a living room wall. (Remember that dishes are off-limits, however, unless you intend only to display them in a cupboard or on the wall.)

Start by choosing two or three colors that look good together—one for the base coat and another one or two for the sponged-on glaze. The base coat should be the lightest.

To keep the stipples neat and uniform, thin the glaze by mixing 1 part paint with 2 parts paint thinner or solvent. The more thinner you use, the lighter the glaze will be.

1. Choose a color for the base coat that is lighter than the glaze. Paint it on and let it dry thoroughly.

2. Cut a sponge into 2- x 2-in. pieces. Drench a piece with the thinned glaze and squeeze out the excess.

3. Lightly dab the glaze onto the surface, rewetting the sponge often. After each application, dab the paint with a dry sponge.

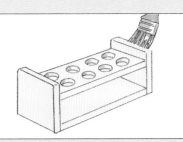

4. When the paint is dry, spray it with a clear glaze or paint with mat-finish polyurethane to seal the surface.

Ribbons / Purse

Weave some old ribbons together to create a piece of silky material. Then, after lining the back, turn it into a one-of-a-kind clutch purse.

Hardly any sewing is involved; instead, weave the ribbons directly on top of a 12- x 19-inch piece of fusible interfacing, pinning the ends as you go. Then press with a hot iron. The work will go even more smoothly if you place the interfacing on a padded surface, such as a folded towel or a clean throw rug.

Once you've lined the material and folded it into a purse, attach a snap, catch, or button and loop to keep it closed.

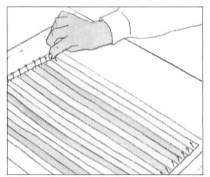

1. Cut enough 18-in. lengths of ribbon to measure 11 in. across when placed side by side. Pin both ends to the interfacing.

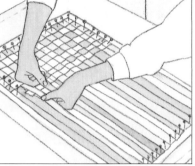

2. Cut several 11-in. ribbons and weave them through, pushing them tight and pinning each end as you go.

3. Remove the pins and fuse the ribbons to the interfacing with a hot iron. Then trim the material to 10 x 17 in.

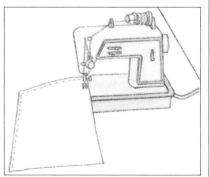

4. Turn the piece ribbon side down on a 10¾- x 17¾-in. piece of lining fabric. Stitch around three sides as shown.

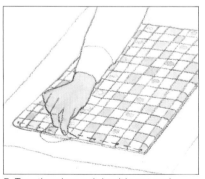

5. Turn the pieces right side out and stitch the fourth side by turning down the edge with a ¼-in. seam.

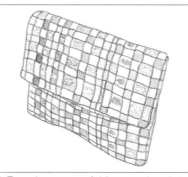

6. To make a purse, fold one end up 5½ in. and stitch the edges to the lining. Fold the top flap over and sew on a catch.

Road maps / Paper trim

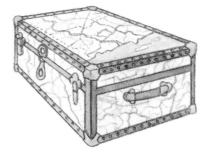

The most eye-catching paper for covering boxes, trunks, or small wall areas may already be stashed away in your closet — old road maps! Once you've bought some vinyl paste and sizing for wallpaper, you'll find the paper is almost as easy to apply as the adhesive plastic sold in stores, especially if you

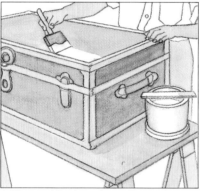

1. Thoroughly clean the surface to be covered and use a wide brush to prime it with wallpaper sizing. Let the sizing dry for at least 3 hr.

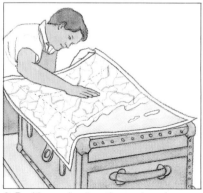

3. Position a sheet on the work surface, paste side down, and use your hands to slowly smooth it from the center toward the edges to prevent air bubbles.

let it lie flat for a while and press out the creases with a warm iron.

Road maps aren't the only material you can use for this decorative technique. Be imaginative and try navigation charts, vintage magazine covers—even sheet music. Remember, however, that some paper is so thin that even a new razor blade can't trim it without fraying the edges. If this is the case, paste the paper down and let it dry before trimming (before the paste dries, use your fingernail to make an outline of the area to be cut).

If the surface you're covering has a bold pattern that might show through, give it a coat of white paint and let it dry before priming with the sizing.

2. Spread vinyl paste onto the back of the paper with a small roller or paste brush. Temporarily fold the pasted sides of large sheets together until you need them.

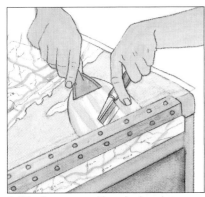

4. Trim the paper with a single-edge razor blade, using a wide putty knife as a guide. If the paper tears easily, wait until it is dry before trimming.

Cloth painting / TECHNIQUE

Fabric paints, sold at craft stores and hobby shops, enable you to give new life to old sweatshirts, jeans, or sneakers you might otherwise throw away. Paint colorful designs or emblazon the clothes with your name. Or use the paints to give your own touch to the ribbons you use for a hand-made clutch purse (p.370) or a table runner and napkins (p.374).

These steps show you how to paint a piece of clothing. To decorate canvas sneakers, make cardboard patterns of your designs and trace them onto the shoes with a pencil. Then fill in the designs with the fabric paints.

1. Insert a stiff piece of cardboard beneath the area to be painted and pin the corners to the cloth. Leave the cardboard in as you sketch and paint your design.

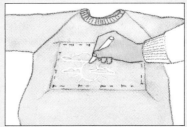

2. Use a piece of chalk to sketch out your design—white chalk for dark fabrics and colored chalk for lighter colors and whites. Erase mistakes by rubbing lightly with a damp cloth.

3. Paint your design with the fabric paints, using brushes of several different sizes for variety in strokes and shapes. Apply the paint sparingly and let it dry for at least 12 hr.

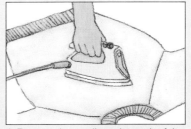

4. Remove the cardboard, turn the fabric wrong side out, and place a towel under the painted area. Press the wrong side of the painting with an iron set at the hottest setting for the fabric.

Rolling pin / Key keeper

What to do with an old, battered rolling pin? Make a bracket of scrap wood and create a revolving bulletin board, of course. Mounted on the wall and adorned with a few cup hooks, paper clamps, and gator clips, it makes an ingenious catchall for your various keys, business cards, and messages.

The bracket consists of a baseboard and two arms with 1-inch holes for the rolling pin handles. Use any scrap wood you have on hand and make it as decorative as you like: bevel the front edges of the arms with a rasp or a saw and incorporate a few scrolls and turns—or even some hand carving—into the entire piece. Drill and countersink for four screws to hold the pieces together.

Another idea is to saw kerfs into the rolling pin itself. With your table saw set at 30°, the kerfs will be angled downward to hold business or calling cards. Regular kerfs, sawn both horizontally and vertically on the pin, can form a decorative pattern of squares in which you can center the cup hooks and other holders. But be sure to use a fence to ensure that the kerfs are as straight as possible.

Before you assemble the unit, stain or paint the bracket—and the rolling pin if you like (be aware, however, that the stains are not likely to match)—and apply two light coats of mat-finish polyurethane. Or try pickling the rolling pin and the bracket (p.373) for a still more interesting look.

Use No. 10 screws to mount the unit to wall studs in a place where it will be seen often—near the back door or next to the kitchen phone.

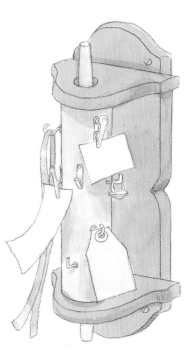

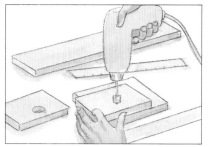

1. From a piece of ¾-in. pine, cut a baseboard about 4 x 16 in. (or 1 in. longer than the length of your rolling pin). From the same stock, cut two 4- x 5-in. arms and drill a 1-in. hole centered about 1½ in. from the long edge of each.

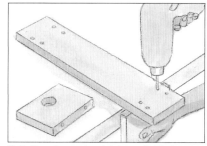

2. Drill and countersink two pilot holes at each end of the baseboard for the No. 4 screws that will attach the unit to a wall. Position the arms and drill two pilot holes for No. 4 screws through the baseboard into each arm.

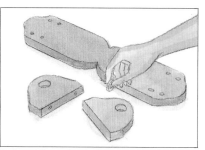

3. Bevel the edges of the wood; shape and decorate as you like. Sand and stain, then apply two coats of polyurethane, sanding lightly between coats. Glue a fiber washer to the hole in the lower arm so that the rolling pin will rotate more easily.

4. Predrill several holes for cup hooks and No. 2 screws on all sides of the rolling pin. Screw in the cup hooks and screws and hang paper clamps from the protruding screw heads. Attach gator jaws with smaller screws.

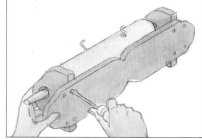

5. Attach the upper arm to the base from behind with flathead No. 4 screws. Insert the top handle of the rolling pin through the hole, then place the lower arm over the bottom handle and attach with screws as shown.

6. Choose a spot in the kitchen or near the back door. Hold the unit against the wall at eye level and mark the positions of the holes on the wall, then drill for No. 10 screws. Mount the unit and fill it with keys, cards, and messages.

Salad bowls / Bird feeder

Glass or wooden salad bowls of two different sizes make a clever bird feeder that has the added advantage of thwarting squirrels. No feeder is entirely squirrel-proof, of course, but the slippery roof of this one makes it harder for the furry thieves to reach the seed.

The two bowls, one of them upside down, are joined with a threaded rod and secured with nuts and washers. (For glass bowls, drill with a carbon-tipped glass or masonry bit.) To hang the feeder, bend the top of the rod into a hook (allow a few inches for the hook when you put the first nut in place) or attach a lamp hook with a nut.

The kinds of birds you attract depend on the positions of the bowls. Leave plenty of space between the bowls to attract large birds, or place them close together to limit the feed to smaller visitors.

1. Choose a large bowl as a roof and another about half the size as a feeder. Drill a ¼-in. hole through the center of each, using scrap wood as a backing.

2. Place a nut near the end of a threaded rod, add a flat washer, and insert the rod through the inside of the large bowl. Secure with another washer and nut on top.

3. Place another nut and washer at the other end of the rod and secure the small bowl so that the insides of the two bowls face each other.

4. Bend the rod above the large bowl to form a hanging hook. Or attach a lamp hook with a nut. Then fill the small bowl with birdseed and hang the feeder outdoors.

Wood pickling / TECHNIQUE

Of all the methods for giving bare wood an appealing washed, "pickled" look, this is the simplest. All that's involved is brushing on some oil-base paint and immediately wiping it off with a burlap rag.

Choose an off-white paint. Brush it onto a small area at a time and wipe it off with a smooth, even stroke. Depending on the color of the wood and the effect you want, you may need to make more than one application after letting the previous one dry. Lightly sand the surface between coats. Then finish the wood with a light coat of satin-finish polyurethane to seal and protect.

1. Remove the old finish. If you want a smooth surface, apply a coat of sealer to fill the pores of the wood; let it dry completely.

2. Use a wide brush to apply an off-white oil-base paint to a small area of the wood. Then wipe it off with a burlap rag.

3. If you need to apply a second coat, sand the surface lightly beforehand. Then finish with a coat of satin polyurethane.

Tablecloth / Runner & napkins

Don't consign a stained or torn tablecloth to the rag bin. Instead, cut out an unmarred panel and hem it for use as a table runner; then cut out some smaller sections to turn into matching place mats or napkins. If the cloth is lint-free linen, you can make dish towels from it, too. You're limited only by your imagination and the size of the tablecloth.

First cut your runner to a width of 15 inches. Cut place mats to 15 x 18 inches and napkins in 16-inch squares (use colored chalk as your marker for a white tablecloth, white chalk for dark fabric). After hemming, this will yield a 14-inch runner, 14- x 17-inch place mats, and 15-inch-square napkins. As you stitch the hems, miter all corners as shown.

1. Cut a clean section of cloth. Fold the right side over ½ in. on all four sides and press with an iron.

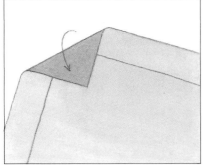

2. To miter a corner, first fold the point back on itself and press with an iron to make a crease.

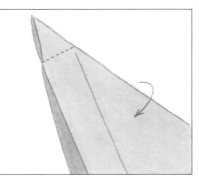

3. Unfold the corner, place the unfolded hem flaps together wrong side out, and stitch along the diagonal crease.

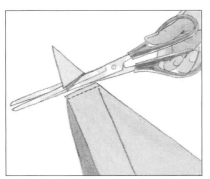

4. Trim the fabric just above the stitch. Turn the hem flaps right side out and straighten to form a neat corner.

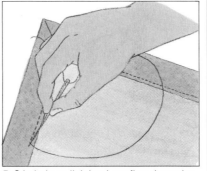

5. Stitch the adjoining hem flap down the edge and miter the next corner when you come to it.

Tin cans / Containers

Here's the simplest recycling project of all: Save tin cans and spiff them up with a coat of spray paint. Then use them as attractive containers for fudge, candy, and other holiday handouts. Or convert the kinds with snap-on plastic lids into coin banks—a simple and entertaining project for children. You can even glue a few painted cans together to make a desk organizer for your odds and ends.

For an interesting look, try using a fleck-type spray paint. Like the automobile trunk paint sold at auto parts stores, it gives a splatter finish in two colors that dries to a hard, bumpy texture. Unlike trunk paint, however, it comes in bright primary colors.

DESK ORGANIZER

Choose cans of different sizes and shapes. Spray-paint the cans as at right, then put them together in any design you choose. Use a glue gun to attach the cans to one another with hot glue. Fill your catchall with pens, paper clips, and such.

COIN BANK

Use a can that has a snap-on plastic lid. Spray-paint as at right; then, with a sharp utility knife, cut a ⅛-inch slit in the center of the lid. Let your child decorate the bank with stickers once the paint is dry—either placing a few figures in a ring around the can or covering most of the surface with a colorful collage.

GIFT CANS

Use cans with snap-on plastic lids. Or make your own cover by cutting a piece of fabric with pinking shears and securing it with colored string or yarn. Even plastic wrap is fine, especially if you dress it up with stick-on stars or other designs.

To make your gift cans look even neater, leave the metal rims unpainted (do the same with the desk organizer and coin bank if you like). Just mask the rims with masking tape. As a bonus, the bottom circle of tape will keep the can lifted off the surface and make painting easier.

1. To give your paint job a professional finish, protect the shiny metal rims with masking tape, then paint with a fleck-type spray paint or auto trunk paint.

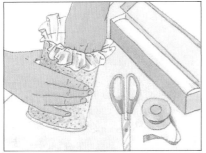

2. When the paint is dry, line the inside of the can with plastic wrap. Once you've filled it, snap on the lid or secure a cover on top with a piece of yarn.

Spray-painting / TECHNIQUE

Spray-painting small objects like drawer knobs, wooden cutouts, and doll house furniture isn't easy. Just keeping them still in the force of the spray is usually a challenge. And if you place the objects on a flat, solid surface, you'll find that the overspray will bounce back onto whatever you're painting and cause drips. A cloud of overspray also tends to dull a high-gloss finish.

Here are some ways to solve the problem using a few common items that you probably already have around the house.

BED OF NAILS

Tap finishing nails into a ceiling tile to act as little poles to support small objects. If the bottom of an object already has a recess—as a drawer knob has—it will stay atop the head of the nail without a problem. If there's no recess, you'll need to reverse the position of the nail (drive it

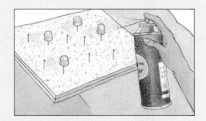

through the tile, pointed end up) and stick the sharp point far enough into the underside to keep the object from moving around in the force of the spray. Either way, supporting the object on a nail allows you to spray all sides and most of the underside at the same time.

HARDWARE CLOTH PLATFORM

Bend a rectangular piece of large-mesh hardware cloth—or even chicken wire—into a rough box shape. The raised wire mesh makes a handy platform for spraying flat objects such as wooden and cardboard cutouts without having them stick to the surface. Spray-paint lightly; when one side

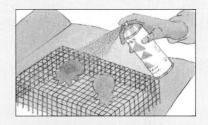

is almost dry, turn the objects over and spray them on the other side.

To make the platform, choose a piece of hardware cloth 1 to 2 feet long. Cut 4-inch squares from each corner, then bend the edges over to form sides. The wire is stiff enough to hold its shape by itself.

CARDBOARD SPRAYING BOOTH

Make a nifty little spraying booth from an old cardboard box, a wooden dowel, and some clothespins. The booth enables you to spray small objects from several angles and also neatens the job by containing all the overspray.

Use a sharp utility knife to cut the box as shown. Cut two notches for

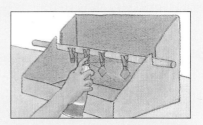

the dowel near the top of the box, then glue the top ends of the clothespins (the ends that you pinch) to the dowel with epoxy. Clamp small objects in the clothespins and spray (don't overdo it; a couple of light coats will look neater than one heavy one). To spray the other side, simply pick up the dowel and turn it around. When the objects are dry, reclamp them upside down in the clothespins and spray again.

Tree branch / Post & door handle

Recycle some of Mother Nature's castoffs—fallen tree branches—as rustic signposts, mailbox supports, or door handles.

When you go to a wooded area to find your material, choose a branch that's a little heavier than you think you'll need. Be sure to check it thoroughly to see that it shows no signs of decay or insect damage.

For a signpost, look for a large, straight branch and a couple of smaller ones to form a right-angle arm. An irregular board sawed from another branch can provide the sign that you'll hang from the post.

For a support for an old-style rural mailbox, choose a heavy branch with a natural crook at the top. The crook should fit within the bottom of your mailbox.

For a door handle, use a sharply curved or kinked branch small enough to fit in your hand. If you plan to leave the bark on, make sure it is smooth enough to be comfortable to the touch.

Use galvanized nails or brass screws for all three of these projects. And lengthen the life of the posts by treating the bottoms with wood preservative before you place them in the ground.

SIGNPOST

Choose a sturdy branch 5 or 6 feet long, then pick out two smaller branches to construct the arm that your sign will hang from. Drill a 1- to 2-inch hole near the top of the post and whittle the end of one straight small branch to fit snugly into the hole. Then brace the joint with a branch that has a natural curve; hold it in place with large brass screws and reinforce with a loop of rope. Attach two small chains to hang your sign.

MAILBOX SUPPORT

Cut a piece of 1 x 8 to the size of the recess in the bottom of your mailbox. Then take it along when you search for a branch with a natural crook that will fit within the length of the board. Cut the crook to size.

Once you've implanted the branch in the ground and the concrete is dry, nail or screw the board to the two arms of the crook, place the box on top, and secure with galvanized nails driven into the holes in the flange.

DOOR HANDLE

Find a branch you can get one of your hands around and cut out a nicely curved 18-inch section. Saw or plane the back side to make a flat surface

for mounting the branch on a door. You can leave the bark as it is or strip it off; either way, the branch will eventually develop a nice patina from being handled.

Predrill two holes about 2 inches from each end. Position the branch on the door and mark for drilling, then attach with brass screws.

INSTALLING THE POST

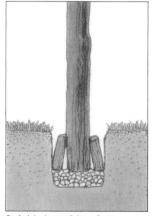

1. Choose a fairly straight, heavy tree branch and measure the diameter. Multiply the diameter by 3 and dig a hole to at least that depth.

2. Add about 2 in. of stones to the hole and insert the post. Use two or three smaller pieces of wood to plumb it up and hold it in position.

3. Prepare a small bag of dry-mix concrete and fill the hole with it, forcing it around the pieces of wood and packing it just above ground level.

4. Using a trowel, smooth the concrete around the base of the post so that it tapers to the ground at an angle to shed rainwater.

Wicker furniture / RENEWAL

Don't retire wicker furniture to the attic just because a few spokes and strands are broken or unraveling. They're easily renewed.

Wicker is made from pliable plant fibers. Cane, reed, and rattan are the most common—all are sold in craft stores. When you need to replace a piece, snip off a sample and take it to the store so that you can buy a replacement of exactly the same size.

You'll need binding cane, which is flat on one side, to replace the unraveling cane on chair legs. To replace broken spokes in chair seats, arms, and backs, buy reed spline. You'll also need a hammer, a pair of tin snips, some ½-inch wire brads, white glue, masking tape, and a bucket of warm water.

Before you start, use a soft brush to scrub the piece of furniture with a mild detergent-and-water solution. Rinse with a fine mist from a garden hose, using as little water as possible, then wipe dry. Another way to remove dust without damaging the wicker is to blow it away with an air hose.

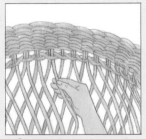

1. Soak replacement reeds in warm water for 10–20 min. Cut their tips to a point and weave them into place.

2. To rewrap a chair leg, turn the piece upside down and secure binding cane to the top with a ½-in. wire brad.

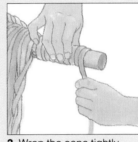

3. Wrap the cane tightly around the leg toward the bottom. Trim it with a knife when you reach the end.

4. Apply white glue to the end of the cane and tack down with a ½-in. brad. Secure with masking tape until dry.

Wine bottle / Lamp

A plain wine bottle makes a simple lamp base with clean lines. All you need to convert it is a bottle adapter lamp kit (sold at hardware and lighting stores) and a shade.

Because the lamp cord runs from the socket instead of being concealed in the base, this lamp is best used in an informal setting, such as a weekend house or a recreation room. If you decide you want to conceal the cord, drill the bottle with a carbon-tipped glass or masonry bit and follow the instructions in *Food storage container/Night light* (p.359).

Your kit should include drilled corks in three different sizes, a spindle, harp, socket with cover, lamp cord with plug, and nuts and washers to put them all together. If the bottle is tall and slender (as some commemorative or decorative containers are), it may need ballast. In that case, fill it with small stones, shells, or sand. If the bottle glass is clear, you might want to use the colored fish-tank gravel sold at pet shops.

Another way to make a tall bottle more stable is to detach the harp from the socket assembly and use a shade that snaps directly over the light bulb. This will lower the center of gravity.

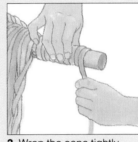

1. Select the drilled cork that fits your bottle. Insert the spindle and secure washers and knurled nuts on both ends. Then twist the cork into the bottle.

2. Place the harp cradle over the spindle. Screw the socket base over the spindle and tighten the setscrew. Insert the cord through the socket base and strip the ends.

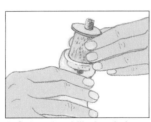

3. Attach the wire ends to the socket connections, wrapping clockwise before tightening the terminal screws. Install the socket cover and snap the assembly into the socket base.

4. Unscrew the finial on the harp, place a shade over the spindle, and replace the finial. Or, if the bottle is tall, remove the harp and use a shade that snaps over the bulb.

Wok lid / Hanging lamp

The shiny aluminum lid of a Chinese wok makes a contemporary shade for a hanging lamp. All you have to do is drill a hole in the center and rig up one of the hanging lamp socket sets sold at hardware and lighting stores. The sets usually come with a frosted round bulb and a long cord complete with switch and plug.

Or you can simply use a standard lamp kit (see *Drain tile/Uplight*, p.355). In this case, you'll need to drill a hole only ¾ inch in diameter.

1. Remove the handle and place the inverted lid on a piece of scrap wood. Drill a 1¾-in. hole in the center with a hole saw attached to your electric drill.

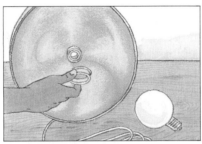

2. Insert the light socket into the hole and make sure that it is exactly centered. Then tighten the trim ring to lock it securely in place.

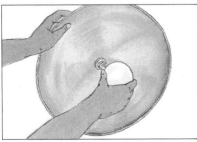

3. Screw a globe-shaped bulb into the socket. Install a hook in the ceiling where you want the fixture to hang and another hook in the ceiling above an outlet.

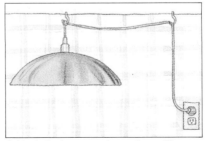

4. Hook the lamp cord over the ceiling hook and adjust the lamp to the desired height. Lead the cord to the second hook and then down to the outlet.

Potato printing / TECHNIQUE

Carve a design on a cut potato, dip it in paint, and use it as a print block. Your prints will have an attractive imperfection, reminiscent of stenciling and other early American crafts.

Potato prints are great for customizing gift wrap (use ordinary white shelf paper and decorate it as you like), but don't confine them to paper. Print the designs on painted furniture (a chair back or the top of a wooden chest, for example) or on smaller wooden items like the candle holders shown on p.379; then protect the design with a polyurethane finish.

If you're printing a row of the same design, cut a notch in the potato skin at the top of the design so that you can keep the prints aligned.

1. Cut a large potato in half and use a pencil to sketch your design on the surface. With a paring knife or artist's knife, carve ¼ in. deep into the pulp to remove the sections that are not part of the design.

2. Saturate an ink pad with ink and press the potato onto it. Clean up your design by trimming any rough edges that you see. Press the potato onto the surface you're printing, reinking each time.

Wood scraps / Art board & candle holders

The leftover wood on your workshop floor doesn't have to end up as fireplace kindling. Instead, turn some of the end scraps into interesting little candle holders; just cut them to various heights, bore holes in the ends, and glue them together in any design you choose. Or use a piece of shelving stock and some elastic belting to craft an art board for a child. Both projects are easy to make, and both make terrific gifts.

ART BOARD

This child's art board, complete with handle, has room for four colored markers. The drawing pad is secured by stapling the cardboard backing onto the board (use heavy-duty staples to make sure the pad stays in place).

When you staple down the strips of elastic belting to hold the markers, pull them tight before you shoot the second staple, then neatly trim away the excess.

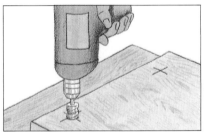

1. Cut a scrap of 1 x 12 pine to a length of 18 in. Drill a 1-in. hole centered 3 in. from one edge and 1½ in. from the top.

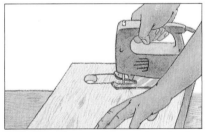

3. Use a coping or saber saw to cut out the area between the holes to make a handle. Sand and apply a wipe-on finish.

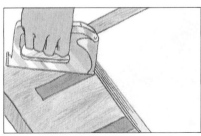

5. Staple the end of a piece of elastic belting just beneath the pad. Place a marker next to the staple.

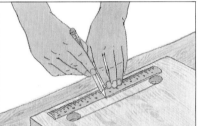

2. Drill another 1-in. hole in the same position at the opposite side, then draw horizontal lines to connect the holes.

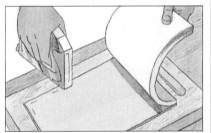

4. When the finish dries, center an 8- x 11-in. drawing pad below the handle and staple down the cardboard back.

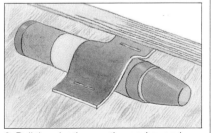

6. Pull the elastic over the marker and staple it to the other side. Make holders for three more markers in the same way.

CANDLE HOLDERS

The project shown here uses 2 x 2 pieces of wood, but you can use scraps of any shape. Half the fun is coming up with your own design.

Caution: These are best used for decoration only. If you burn candles in them, don't leave them unattended; a sputtering flame can ignite the wood.

1. Rip 2 x 4 pine scraps in half. Then cut these fairly square pieces into 3-in., 5-in., and 7-in. lengths.

2. Check the diameter of the candles you plan to use and bore a hole the same size in the end of each piece of wood.

3. Sand the pieces smooth and use white glue to attach them to each other, side by side. Clamp together until the glue dries.

4. Stain with a one-step wipe-on finish or paint as you like. Or, if you choose, leave the wood unfinished. Insert candles.

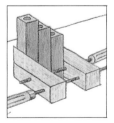

379

Wooden ladder / Toy box

To make handy storage for toys or other bulky objects, mount an old ladder horizontally on a wall and hang some brightly colored canvas tote bags from its rungs. You'll need little more than screws, bolts, and a couple of wooden supports.

A short section of ladder—five or six rungs—should be adequate, but the unit can be as long as you like. Clear pine ⁵⁄₄ stock, ripped to a width of 2¼ inches, makes the best supports, since it most nearly matches the dimensions of most ladder rails. Make sure that the supports are no taller than 18 inches

so that the toy-filled bags will be within easy reach of children.

Sand the ladder to remove splinters. Then use 3-inch screws to attach it to each wall stud it spans. If the unit is longer than 4 feet, add a third support in the center.

Canvas tote bags that measure about 16 x 22 inches are big enough to fill the spaces between the rungs. Secure them at each corner with a screw and washer, then screw each side to the center of a rung. You can either remove the handles of the bags or drape them over the sides.

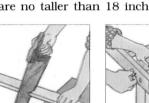

1. To make the supports for the ladder, saw two pieces of ⁵⁄₄ clear pine stock to a width of 2¼ in. and a length of 18 in.

2. Attach the supports near both ends of the ladder rail, using a ⁵⁄₁₆- x 2¼-in. carriage bolt and a washer to secure each one.

3. Position the unit on the wall and drill for No. 10 screws at each wall stud. Then attach it with 3-in. screws or longer.

4. Hold a canvas tote bag between each set of rungs and drill ⅛-in. pilot holes in the corners and at the center of both rungs.

5. Secure each canvas bag with ¾-in. No. 8 roundhead screws and washers at all four corners and at the center of the rungs.

6. If the bags lose their shape when filled with toys or other items, cut a piece of ¼-in. plywood to fit into each as a solid bottom.

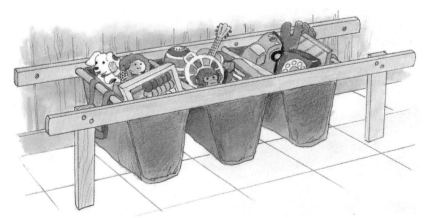

Wrought iron / RENEWAL

Renewing wrought-iron patio furniture, porch supports, and handrails isn't as simple as just covering up the flaws with a coat of paint. First you have to remove rust spots and corrosion and fill the pitted areas.

When you buy your paints, make sure the primer and the top coat are manufactured by the same company. That way, you can be sure they'll be compatible.

1. Scrub the wrought iron with a wire brush, wetting it often. Use a beer can opener to remove rust and paint from small crevices.

2. Use your fingers or a putty knife to fill pits and dents with a polyester-base wood filler or an automotive body filler. Sand smooth when dry.

3. Paint with a rust-inhibiting primer. The next day, apply a top coat of oil- or alkyd-base enamel. A high-gloss finish withstands weather best.

5. FORMULAS & RECIPES

*WHY PAY MORE THAN YOU HAVE TO?
WHY PAY FOR FANCY PACKAGES,
DISTRIBUTION COSTS, AND
MIDDLEMEN'S PROFITS WHEN YOU
CAN DO IT YOURSELF WITH THESE
FOOLPROOF FORMULAS AND
RECIPES INSTEAD? THEY'RE EASY
AND FUN TO MAKE, THEY'RE JUST
AS GOOD OR BETTER THAN THEIR
COMMERCIAL COUNTERPARTS—AND
THEY'LL SAVE YOU MONEY TOO.
FROM AFRICAN VIOLET POTTING
SOIL TO ZUCCHINI BREAD, ALL 250
FORMULAS AND RECIPES HAVE BEEN
CAREFULLY TESTED.*

African violet potting soil

Also suitable for gesneriads, fibrous begonias, caladiums, and most ferns.

3 parts peat moss

2 parts vermiculite

1 part perlite

5 tablespoons crushed egg-shells (or 5 teaspoons dolomitic lime) per quart of mixture

Mix all the ingredients in a bucket. When repotting African violets, do not give the roots too much space—unless the roots thoroughly penetrate the soil, it will remain wet and the plant will rot. As a rule, the diameter of the pot should be one-third that of the plant.

After-bath splash

A refreshing citrus-scented lotion.

½ cup rubbing alcohol

3 teaspoons lemon extract

Juice of 1 lime

In a small bowl, combine the alcohol, lemon extract, and lime juice. Shake well, then transfer to a covered jar and store in the refrigerator. Yield: 5 ounces.

After-shave

To soothe your skin and leave it smelling fresh.

2 cups rubbing alcohol

1 tablespoon glycerin

1 tablespoon dried lavender

1 teaspoon dried rosemary

1 teaspoon ground cloves

Combine all the ingredients in a medium-size bowl. Transfer to a lidded jar and refrigerate for 3 to 4 days, shaking occasionally to mix the ingredients. Strain before using. Will keep 1 to 2 months tightly covered and refrigerated. Yield: about 2 cups.

Air freshener

A spicy fragrance that will overpower even such strong odors as onion.

¼ cup dried sage

½ cup crushed bay leaves

1 cup witch hazel

In a large jar, mix all the ingredients well. Cover and let sit, unrefrigerated, for 3 days. Strain out the herbs and pour the remaining liquid into a spray bottle. Use as necessary. Yield: 1 cup.

All-purpose cleaner

For heavy-duty help when removing tough stains from countertops, woodwork, or tile.

½ cup household ammonia

½ cup washing soda

7 cups warm water

1. In a ½-gallon plastic jug, combine the ammonia, washing soda, and 1 cup of the warm water. Cap the jug, shake briskly, then add the remaining warm water; label.
2. To use, in a bucket, mix ½ cup cleaner with about 1½ gallons hot water. Before using on delicate surfaces, such as wallpaper, test on a small, inconspicuous area. Yield: ½ gallon concentrated cleaner.

Almond butter

Tired of plain old PB and J? Here's a nice change of pace.

2 cups blanched almonds, whole or slivered

2 tablespoons vegetable oil

½ teaspoon salt

1. Preheat the oven to 300°F. On an ungreased cookie sheet, roast the nuts about 20 minutes or until they are lightly browned. Let cool and transfer to a blender or food processor. (For a chunkier spread, coarsely chop ⅓ cup nuts and set aside.)

2. Add the oil and salt and blend until creamy, working in batches if necessary. (if chopped nuts were set aside, stir them in.) Transfer to a covered container. Will keep 1 month tightly covered and refrigerated. Yield: 1 cup.

Aluminum cleaner

Removes tarnish and greasy film from cookware.

½ cup cream of tartar

½ cup baking soda

½ cup white vinegar

¼ cup soap flakes

Combine the cream of tartar and the baking soda in a medium-size bowl. Add the vinegar and mix until the ingredients form a soft paste. Add the soap flakes and transfer to a jar or bottle with a secure lid; label. To use, apply with a steel wool pad, then rinse off. Store out of the reach of children. Should keep 1 to 2 years. Yield: 1½ cups.

Antiperspirant

A rose-scented spray meant to keep you fresh and dry.

1 cup water

1 cup rubbing alcohol

2 tablespoons alum

*3 tablespoons
rose water (p.416)*

In a small bowl, mix together the water, alcohol, alum, and rose water. Transfer the mixture to a plastic spray bottle and use as needed. Yield: 1 pint.

Ant traps

Give the tiny black intruders a fatal but unchemical case of indigestion.

⅓ cup molasses

6 tablespoons sugar

6 tablespoons active dry yeast

Stir all the ingredients together in a small bowl until they form a smooth paste. Coat strips of cardboard with the mixture or pour it in individual bottle caps, then place in and around infested areas.

Apple butter

A spicy low-sugar spread. The apples are cooked uncored and with their skins on because their pectin adds body to the butter.

*4 pounds assorted apples
(Cortland, MacIntosh,
Northern Spy), quartered*

2 cups apple cider

1 vanilla bean, split

2 cinnamon sticks

4 whole cloves

1. Put the apples in a large Dutch oven, cover, and cook over low heat about 50 minutes or until they are soft. (The apples should contain enough moisture to keep them from burning; if not, add a few tablespoons of water).
2. Force the apples through a food mill into a large saucepan; discard the solids. Add the cider, vanilla bean, cinnamon sticks, and cloves; cook the mixture, uncovered, stirring frequently, over low heat about 1 hour 15 minutes or until very thick.
3. Let cool slightly, then remove the vanilla bean, cinnamon, and cloves. While still warm, transfer the apple butter to hot, sterilized ½-pint preserving jars and cover. Will keep 1 month refrigerated. Yield: 2½ cups.

Astringent

Tightens pores and helps remove excess oil from your skin.

½ lemon, sliced thin

½ orange, sliced thin

¾ cup ethanol alcohol

Place the lemon and orange slices in a blender, add the ethanol alcohol, and blend until the fruits are well pulverized—about 1 minute. Using a small strainer or cheesecloth, strain into a jar. Will keep 6 months refrigerated. Yield: ¾ cup.

Baby powder

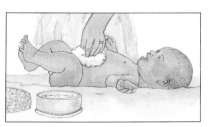

Keep tender skin soft and dry.

*2 tablespoons crumbled dried
chamomile flowers*

¼ cup cornstarch

1 tablespoon orrisroot

½ teaspoon alum

In a small bowl, mix all the ingredients together. Store in flour shakers or old dusting powder boxes. Do not use on a baby's diaper rash. Yield: ½ cup.

Barbecue sauce

A delicious sauce good with beef, chicken, or pork. And none of the preservatives found in most store-bought brands.

*1 medium onion,
peeled and finely chopped*

¼ cup vegetable oil

1 cup ketchup

¾ cup water

*2 tablespoons
Worcestershire sauce*

2 tablespoons sugar

¼ cup cider vinegar

*2 tablespoons
prepared mustard*

1 teaspoon salt

½ teaspoon black pepper

Combine all the ingredients in a medium-size saucepan. Simmer over low heat, uncovered, for 20 minutes; let cool. Will keep several days refrigerated in a clean glass jar with a tight-fitting lid or 6 months in a freezer container at 0°F. Yield: about 2½ cups.

Bath oil

Soothing and a great skin softener.

1 cup honey

2 cups milk

1 cup sea salt or plain salt

¼ cup baking soda

½ cup baby oil

In a large bowl, combine the honey, milk, sea salt, and baking soda; stir well. Pour the mixture into a tub filled with warm water, add the baby oil, and mix well.

Bath salts

To revitalize your tired muscles.

1 cup sea salt

1 cup baking soda

1 cup inexpensive shampoo

Fill a bathtub half full of warm water. Pour the ingredients into the tub, then add more water, swirling it around with your hand to spread out the bubbles.

Bird treats

Keep the backyard birds atwitter in the winter.

¾ pound lard

1 cup sesame seeds

1 cup hulled sunflower seeds

1 cup crushed crackers

⅓ cup raisins

¼ cup peanut butter

Using a double boiler, melt the lard over low heat. Let cool, then transfer to a medium-size bowl. Mix in the sesame and sunflower seeds, crackers, and raisins. Add the peanut butter; stir until combined. Let the mixture harden by refrigerating overnight. Put in a bird feeder or hang in netting coarse enough to allow birds to penetrate it with their beaks. Yield: 1½ cups.

Biscuit mix

Also use it to whip up biscuits, pancakes, or waffles in a flash.

6 cups all-purpose flour (or 3 cups all-purpose flour and 3 cups whole wheat flour)

3½ tablespoons baking powder

1 cup instant nonfat dry milk

1 tablespoon salt

1 cup solid vegetable shortening

In a large bowl, combine the flour, baking powder, dry milk, and salt. Mix well. With a pastry blender, cut in the shortening until the mixture resembles coarse meal. Will keep 6 weeks in a closed container at room temperature. Yield: about 8 cups. (See also *Biscuits*, below; *Pancakes*, p.411; *Waffles*, p.421.)

Biscuits

So quick to prepare and good to eat, you'll want to make them often.

2 cups biscuit mix (above)

½ cup water or milk

1. Preheat the oven to 450°F. In a medium-size bowl, stir the biscuit mix and water with a fork until just blended.
2. On a lightly floured surface, gently knead the dough 10 times; roll out to a ½-inch thickness. Cut into 2½-inch rounds. Bake on an ungreased cookie sheet for 10 to 12 minutes or until golden. Serve hot. Yield: 10 biscuits.

Bloody Mary mix

Eliminate guesswork; now you'll make a perfect drink every time.

4 cups tomato juice

2 tablespoons lime or lemon juice

2 tablespoons Worcestershire sauce

2 teaspoons prepared horseradish

1 teaspoon salt

¼ to ½ teaspoon hot red pepper sauce

In a pitcher, mix all the ingredients; refrigerate. To use, stir well. Fill a balloon wineglass with ice, add a jigger of vodka, and fill to the brim with the drink mix. Add a wedge of lemon or lime and a celery stalk for a stirrer. Will keep 4 days refrigerated. Yield: about 4¼ cups or enough for 6 Bloody Marys.

Blueberry syrup

Delicious on strawberry, blueberry, or plain pancakes and waffles.

4 cups blueberries

2 thin strips lemon peel, 1 x 3 inches each

3 cups water

3 cups sugar

1 tablespoon lemon juice

1. In a large saucepan, crush the berries with a wooden spoon. Add the peel and 1 cup water. Bring to a simmer over moderate heat. Reduce heat to low; cook, uncovered, for 5 minutes without simmering.
2. Put the berries in a cheesecloth-lined strainer and squeeze out all the juice—about 2 cups. Set the juice aside and discard the pulp.

3. Boil the remaining 2 cups water and the sugar in a large saucepan, stirring constantly until the sugar dissolves and the solution is clear. With a pastry brush, wash down the sides of the pan. Keep boiling, without stirring, until a candy thermometer reads 260°F.

4. Add the blueberry mixture; boil, uncovered, 1 minute. Let cool. Add the lemon juice. Will keep 1 month refrigerated. Yield: about 3½ cups.

Brass ager

Gives new brass an antique patina.

*Lacquer thinner or
paint remover*

½ ounce liver of sulfur

2 ounces copper sulfate

2 gallons warm water

1. Strip the brass piece in the lacquer thinner.

2. Mix the liver of sulfur and half the water in a medium-size bucket. In another medium-size bucket, mix the copper sulfate and the remaining water. Use caution—copper sulfate is poisonous.

3. Using a hook to hold the brass and gloves to protect your hands, quickly dip the piece in each solution in turn. Do not rinse between dippings. Repeat as much as desired; rinse in clear water. Let dry. Scrub with extra-fine (No. 000) steel wool to enhance the antique effect.

Brass & copper cleaner

Tough enough for black, cooked-on grease and food particles.

½ cup all-purpose flour

½ cup salt

½ cup powdered detergent

¾ cup white vinegar

¼ cup lemon juice

½ cup very warm water

1. In a large glass bowl, mix the flour, salt, and detergent well. Pour in the remaining ingredients and stir. Transfer the mixture to a glass quart jar, close tightly, and label. Store out of the reach of children.

2. To use, shake briskly, then pour some of the cleaner on cookware and rub gently with a dishcloth. For tough spots, scrub with an old toothbrush or a plastic scouring pad (test first on an inconspicuous area). Rinse with clear water, dry, and polish with a soft cloth.

Breakfast cereal

A quick meal that's high in protein and complex carbohydrates.

2 cups 1-minute oatmeal

*1 cup whole wheat flakes
or coarsely crumbled
shredded wheat*

1 cup bran or bran cereal

1 cup wheat germ

*1 cup any
combination unsalted walnuts, almonds, pecans, or cashews, coarsely chopped*

½ cup chopped pitted dates

*1 cup any combination chopped
dried prunes, apricots, pears,
apples, or bananas*

1 cup light or dark raisins

1 cup instant nonfat dry milk

In a large bowl, combine the oatmeal, wheat flakes, bran, wheat germ, and nuts. Add the dates and dried fruit and toss to coat with the oatmeal mixture. Add the raisins and dry milk and mix thoroughly. Will keep 2 months refrigerated in tightly sealed canisters. Yield: about 9½ cups.

Brown-and-serve rolls

For hot homemade bread in minutes, make a supply of these ahead of time.

1 envelope active dry yeast

2 tablespoons lukewarm water

*2 tablespoons
light brown sugar*

*½ cup (1 stick)
unsalted butter or margarine,
at room temperature*

*1 cup milk, scalded and
cooled to lukewarm*

2 large eggs, beaten

4 cups sifted all-purpose flour

1 teaspoon salt

*¼ cup (½ stick) lightly salted
butter or margarine, melted
(optional)*

1. In a small bowl, stir together the yeast, water, and 1 tablespoon of the sugar and let stand until bubbly—about 5 minutes. Stir until the ingredients are dissolved.

2. In a food processor or an electric mixer fitted with a dough hook, cream the unsalted butter and the remaining tablespoon of sugar until light and fluffy (about 3 minutes in the mixer, 30 seconds in the food processor). Add the milk, eggs, and yeast; continue beating until very light (about 1 minute in the mixer, 15 seconds in the processor). Sift in the flour and salt and mix until smooth (2 minutes in the mixer, 30 seconds in the processor).

3. This dough is too soft to knead. Transfer to a large, lightly greased bowl, turning the dough to coat it, and cover with plastic wrap. Let the dough rise in a warm, draft-free place until doubled in bulk—about 1 hour 15 minutes.

4. Punch the dough down and, on a lightly floured board, roll out to ⅓ inch thick. Cut into 3-inch rounds. Brush each round with the melted butter, if desired, and top with a second round. Place 2 inches apart on ungreased baking sheets.

5. Preheat the oven to 400°F and, if desired, brush the top of each roll with the remaining melted butter.

Cover with plastic wrap and let rise in a warm, draft-free place until doubled in bulk—about 25 minutes. Bake about 5 minutes or until the rolls begin to brown.

6. Let cool to room temperature, wrap in aluminum foil, label, and freeze for up to 3 months at 0°F.

7. To serve, preheat the oven to 400°F. Remove the aluminum foil and place the rolls on an ungreased baking sheet. Bake 10 to 12 minutes or until the rolls are golden brown. They taste best when eaten hot. Yield: 2 dozen.

Brownie mix

It's cheaper and better than store-bought—and no preservatives.

3½ cups sugar

2½ cups all-purpose flour

1½ cups unsweetened cocoa

2 teaspoons baking powder

1½ teaspoons salt

*2 cups
solid vegetable shortening*

In a large bowl, mix together the sugar, flour, cocoa, baking powder,

and salt. With a pastry blender or 2 knives, cut in the shortening until the brownie mix resembles coarse meal, working in batches if neces-

sary. Will keep 6 weeks refrigerated in tightly covered canisters; 6 months at 0°F in freezer containers. Yield: 9 cups or enough for 3 batches of 16 brownies.

Brownies

For a delicious twist, make them with peanut butter chips.

3 cups brownie mix (above)

2 large eggs

1 teaspoon vanilla extract

*½ cup semisweet chocolate
or peanut butter chips*

1. Preheat the oven to 350°F. Place all the ingredients in a medium-size bowl and mix thoroughly. Pour into a greased 8-inch-square pan, smooth the surface, and bake for 30 minutes or until a knife inserted in the center comes out clean.

2. Place the pan upright on a wire

rack and let cool to room temperature. Then cut into squares and serve. Yield: 16 brownies.

Brown ink

Here's how to make your own with ordinary tea bags.

½ cup boiling water

5 tea bags

1 teaspoon gum arabic

In a medium-size bowl, pour the water over the tea bags. Stir in the gum arabic and let steep until cool. Squeeze the tea bags to get all the tannic acid out. Use with a paintbrush or quill pen or any other type of writing utensil. Yield: ⅓ cup. (See also *Ink*, p.404.)

Bubble bath

A long soak will leave your skin sweet-smelling and soft.

2 cups liquid soap (p.406)

*2 cups inexpensive shampoo
or dishwashing detergent*

¼ cup glycerin

*Few drops of scented oil
or perfume*

In a small bowl, mix the soap with the shampoo, glycerin, and scented oil. Transfer the bubbly mixture to a quart container, cover, and store in the bathroom. Add about 1 cup per bath. Yield: 1 quart.

Buttermilk dressing

Adds a new twist to Caesar, chef, and bean salads.

*10 tablespoons buttermilk
dressing mix (below)*

1 cup warm water

¼ cup cider vinegar

2 tablespoons sour cream

In a small mixing bowl, combine all the ingredients. Let the mixture sit for about 1 hour at room temperature, then stir before using. Yield: about 2 cups.

Buttermilk dressing mix

A great do-ahead and good for you.

4½ cups buttermilk powder

1½ cups freeze-dried chives

½ cup dill weed

½ cup sugar

¼ cup dry mustard

Put all the ingredients in a large bowl and mix thoroughly. Will keep about 1 month refrigerated in a 2-quart jar with a tight-fitting lid. Yield: about 7 cups.

Butterscotch sauce

Pour it over ice cream, pound cake, or apple pie.

*1 cup firmly packed
dark brown sugar*

¼ teaspoon salt

1 cup light corn syrup

*½ cup half-and-half
or evaporated milk*

*2 tablespoons
butter or margarine*

2 teaspoons vanilla extract

1. In a medium-size saucepan, combine the sugar, salt, corn syr-

up, and half-and-half. Bring to a boil over moderate heat, stirring constantly. Then boil briskly for 5 minutes, stirring occasionally. Remove from the heat and stir in the butter and vanilla extract.

2. Serve immediately. Or let cool slightly and pour into hot, clean glass jars; then let cool to room temperature and cover. Will keep 1 month refrigerated.

3. To reheat, place in the top of a double boiler over hot (not boiling) water. Yield: 1½ cups.

Cantaloupe ice

Light, refreshing, and only 136 calories in each ½ cup serving.

1 envelope unflavored gelatin

3 tablespoons cold water

*1 cantaloupe
(2½ pounds), peeled, seeded,
and coarsely chopped*

*¼ cup each
orange juice and honey*

1 tablespoon lemon juice

*2 teaspoons
finely grated orange rind*

1. In a small saucepan, soften the gelatin in the cold water for about 5 minutes. Set over low heat and stir until dissolved—about 3 minutes.

2. In a food processor or blender, purée the melon in batches and transfer to a medium-size bowl. Stir in the gelatin, orange juice, honey, lemon juice, and orange rind until well mixed. Pour the mixture into a nonaluminum 9-inch baking dish, cover tightly with plastic wrap, and freeze until firm—2 to 4 hours.

3. In a food processor or blender, purée the cantaloupe ice in batches until smooth but not liquefied; refreeze. Will keep up to 3 days at 0°F. Yield: about 1 pint.

Watermelon variation: Follow the directions above, but eliminate the orange rind and orange juice and substitute the flesh of a 3-pound

watermelon, seeded and coarsely chopped, for the cantaloupe; use ½ cup light corn syrup (or to taste) instead of the honey and increase the lemon juice to 2 tablespoons. Store as directed for cantaloupe ice.

Canvas waterproofing

Paint on the surfaces of tents, awnings, and car and boat covers to help prevent rot from setting in.

1 cup soybean oil

½ cup turpentine

In a medium-size bowl, mix together the soybean oil and turpentine. Store in a cool place, out of the reach of small children and pets.

Caramel corn

Make this on a dry day. The sugar may crystallize in high humidity.

*5 quarts unseasoned popped
corn (about 1½ cups kernels)*

1 cup light corn syrup

¼ teaspoon salt

½ cup (1 stick) unsalted butter

2 teaspoons cider vinegar

*1½ cups firmly packed
light brown sugar*

1 teaspoon vanilla extract

½ teaspoon baking soda

1. In a large roasting pan or bowl or two 13- x 9- x 2-inch pans, spread the popped corn; set aside.

2. In a medium-size saucepan, mix the corn syrup, salt, butter, vinegar, and sugar. Cook over moderate heat, stirring occasionally, until the butter melts and the sugar dissolves; use a pastry brush to wipe down the pan sides.

3. Increase the heat slightly and place a candy thermometer in the syrup. Cook, without stirring, until the mixture reaches the hard ball stage (250°F).

4. Remove the pan from the heat and stir in the vanilla and baking soda. Pour the syrup over the popcorn and mix in with a wooden spoon. Let stand on wax paper or shape the warm popcorn into tennis-ball-size clusters; let cool. Yield: about 24 popcorn balls.

Caraway cheese sticks

A tasty snack or hors d'oeuvre. You can make the dough ahead of time and bake them fresh as needed.

*1 cup (2 sticks) unsalted
butter or margarine,
at room temperature*

*½ pound shredded Cheddar
cheese (2 cups)*

¼ teaspoon cayenne pepper

2 cups sifted all-purpose flour

½ teaspoon salt

2 tablespoons caraway seed

1½ teaspoons dry mustard

*1 egg beaten with
1 tablespoon water*

*1 ounce grated Parmesan
cheese (about 2 tablespoons)*

1. In a large bowl, cream the butter and Cheddar cheese with an electric mixer. Beat in the cayenne pepper, flour, salt, caraway seed, and dry mustard. Shape the dough into a flat patty, cover with plastic wrap

or aluminum foil, and chill for 2 hours. (At this point the dough can be kept 1 week refrigerated, 6 months at 0°F.)

2. Preheat the oven to 350°F. On a lightly floured surface, roll out the dough ¼ inch thick. Using a sharp knife, cut into 5- x ½-inch strips. On an ungreased baking sheet, place the strips ½ inch apart. Brush each strip with the egg wash, then sprinkle with the grated Parmesan cheese.

3. Bake 10 to 12 minutes or until golden brown and crisp. Let the sticks cool 1 minute, then transfer to a wire rack. Will keep 2 days in an airtight container. Yield: 6 dozen sticks. (See also *Cheese crackers*, p.389.)

Car wash concentrate

Cleans and shines.

*1 cup liquid
dishwashing detergent*

*¾ cup powdered
laundry detergent*

3 gallons water

Mix the 2 detergents in a bottle. To use, combine ½ cup of the concentrate with the water. If a stronger solution is desired, slightly reduce the amount of water.

Car wax

To avoid overdrying, wax your car one section at a time.

½ cup melted ceresin wax

*2 tablespoons melted yellow
beeswax*

2 cups turpentine

1 tablespoon pine oil

In a double boiler, heat the ceresin wax and beeswax. Stir, then allow to cool just until the mixture starts to harden. Stir in the turpentine and pine oil. To use, apply with a rag; polish with a soft cloth.

Cat food

A balanced supplement that fulfills the feline minimum daily requirement for all vitamins and trace minerals.

1 pound ground beef, cooked

*¼ pound beef or pork liver,
cooked and diced*

*1 cup cooked rice
(without added salt)*

1 teaspoon vegetable oil

*1 teaspoon calcium carbonate
(crushed antacid tablets)*

Combine the ingredients in a medium-size bowl and mix thoroughly. Yield: 1¾ pounds.

Chamomile astringent

Especially good for oily skin.

4 cups water

*½ cup chopped fresh mint
or 2 tablespoons dried mint*

*2 tablespoons dried chamomile
flowers, crumbled*

Place all the ingredients in a medium-size saucepan and boil for 10 minutes. Remove from the heat and let steep for 5 minutes, then strain into a jar and screw on the lid. Will keep 2 weeks refrigerated. Apply with cotton balls.

Chamomile tea

A relaxing beverage to help you get a good night's sleep.

*2 tablespoons dried mint,
crumbled*

*2 tablespoons dried
chamomile flowers, crumbled*

1½ cups water

1 teaspoon honey

1 teaspoon lemon juice

In a small saucepan, boil the herbs in the water for 5 minutes. Then remove from the heat and let steep for 5 minutes. Drain and add the honey and lemon juice. If desired, reheat without boiling.

Cheese & walnut balls

A tasty change of pace from plain cheese. For parties, you can make them ahead and freeze them.

*1 package (3 ounces)
cream cheese*

*4 ounces gorgonzola
or blue cheese*

⅔ cup finely chopped walnuts

1. In a small mixing bowl, blend the cream and blue cheeses. Roll the mixture into 1-inch balls with your hands (use about 1 teaspoon for each one).

2. On a sheet of wax paper, roll the balls in the chopped walnuts. Will keep 1 week refrigerated on a plate covered with plastic wrap. To freeze, place the balls in a single layer on a plate and cover tightly with aluminum foil. When frozen,

transfer to double plastic bags (one inside the other) and freeze at 0°F; will keep 1 month. Yield: about 24.

Cheesecake

Simply scrumptious, right down to the last crumb.

CRUMB CRUST

*1½ cups vanilla wafer or
graham cracker crumbs (make
in a blender or food processor)*

¼ cup sugar

⅓ cup butter, melted

FILLING

*5 packages (8 ounces each)
cream cheese, at
room temperature*

1¾ cups sugar

3 tablespoons all-purpose flour

¼ teaspoon vanilla extract

*1½ teaspoons
grated lemon rind*

*1½ teaspoons
grated orange rind*

5 eggs plus 1 egg yolk

¼ cup heavy cream

1. To make the crumb crust: In a small bowl, mix the crumbs, sugar, and butter. Stir well to moisten all the crumbs. Press the mixture over the bottom and up the sides of a 9-inch springform pan, to ½ inch from the top. Chill 10 minutes in the freezer to set the crust.

2. To make the filling: In a large

bowl, cream the cheese with an electric mixer. Add the sugar, flour, vanilla extract, and lemon and orange rinds; beat well. Add the eggs and the egg yolk, one at a time, beating lightly after each addition and scraping down the sides of the bowl. Add the heavy cream, beat lightly, and pour the filling into the prepared pan.

3. Bake for 10 minutes at 500°F. Lower the temperature to 250°F and continue baking 1 hour 20 minutes. Place the cake in the pan on a wire rack and let cool to room temperature. Cover and refrigerate at least 4 hours.

4. With a narrow spatula or knife, loosen the crumb crust from the sides of the pan. Remove the sides but not the bottom of the pan. Slice and serve. Will keep 2 days refrigerated; replace the sides of the pan and cover tightly. Will keep 1 month at 0°F; remove the sides of the pan but not the bottom and wrap tightly. Yield: 12 servings.

Cheese crackers

A flavorful snack to keep on hand for unexpected guests.

*1 cup (2 sticks)
unsalted butter or margarine,
at room temperature*

*½ pound shredded
Cheddar cheese (2 cups)*

2 cups sifted all-purpose flour

½ teaspoon salt

¼ teaspoon cayenne pepper

*1 egg beaten with
1 tablespoon water*

1. In a large bowl, cream the butter and cheese with an electric mixer. Beat in the flour, salt, and cayenne pepper. Shape the dough into a flat patty, cover with plastic wrap, and chill for 2 hours. (At this point the dough can be kept 3 or 4 days refrigerated, 6 months at 0°F.)

2. Preheat the oven to 350°F. On a lightly floured surface, roll out the dough ¼ inch thick. Cut into any desired shape (a 2½-inch biscuit cutter works well). Or use Christmas cookie cutters. Place on ungreased baking sheets and brush each cracker with the egg wash.

3. Bake 10 to 12 minutes or until the crackers are crisp and golden. Let the crackers cool for 1 minute on the baking sheet, then transfer to a rack. Will keep up to 2 weeks in an airtight container. Yield: 4½ dozen 2½-inch crackers.

Chili sauce

Packs more punch than ketchup.

1 can (1 pound) tomatoes

1 can (1 pound 12 ounces) tomato purée

1 large yellow onion, grated

2 cloves garlic, minced

¼ cup cider vinegar

1 tablespoon chili powder

2 teaspoons salt

2 teaspoons sugar

⅛ teaspoon crushed red pepper flakes

⅛ teaspoon ground allspice

2 tablespoons cornstarch

2 tablespoons cold water

1. Purée the tomatoes in a blender or food processor, transfer to a large saucepan, and set over moderate heat. Add all the remaining ingredients except the cornstarch and water and mix well.

2. Heat until bubbling, then stir the cornstarch into the water and add to the mixture. Cook for 2 to 3 minutes, stirring constantly. Reduce the heat to *low* and simmer, uncovered, for 20 minutes.

3. Let cool to room temperature, then transfer to 1-pint freezer containers, leaving ½ inch space at the top, and cover. Will keep 1 week refrigerated in a covered jar. Yield: 5½ cups.

Chocolate sauce

A special blend of rich chocolates.

2 tablespoons Dutch processed cocoa

3 tablespoons cold water

½ cup (1 stick) unsalted butter

6 ounces Swiss dark chocolate

4 ounces semisweet chocolate

1 cup boiling water

1 cup firmly packed light brown sugar

¾ cup granulated sugar

½ cup light corn syrup

¼ teaspoon salt

1 teaspoon vanilla extract

1. Dissolve the cocoa in the water. Melt the butter in a double boiler set over low heat. Add the cocoa and the dark and semisweet chocolate, then stir in the boiling water, brown sugar, granulated sugar, corn syrup, and salt.

2. Set the top half of the double boiler over moderate heat and boil the mixture, uncovered, for 5 minutes (7 minutes for a thicker sauce that will harden the moment it hits ice cream). Remove from the heat and let cool to room temperature, then stir in the vanilla extract. Yield: about 2½ cups.

Christmas snow

Paint on Christmas tree branches and have a white Christmas even where it's 102°F outside.

⅔ cup liquid starch

2 cups soap flakes or detergent granules

2 to 4 tablespoons water

Blue food coloring

In a medium-size bowl, mix together the liquid starch and soap flakes, then add the water. Beat with a rotary egg beater until the mixture becomes very thick. With an eyedropper, add the food coloring, beating until the "snow" has an icy-white color. After painting the snow on your Christmas tree, add white glitter to give it a crystalline appearance.

Christmas tree fireproofer

Makes evergreens flame-resistant.

½ gallon water

½ cup ammonium sulfate

¼ cup boric acid

1 tablespoon borax

Combine all the ingredients in a medium-size bucket. Then use a spray bottle to spritz the tree with the formula; pour the remainder into the tree stand.

Chutney

Quick to make and delicious with beef or curried lamb or chicken.

*1 jar (12 ounces)
apricot or peach preserves*

½ teaspoon garlic powder

½ teaspoon ground ginger

½ teaspoon dry mustard

½ teaspoon salt

¼ teaspoon ground coriander

1 tablespoon cider vinegar

*¼ cup light or
dark raisins (optional)*

Mix all the ingredients in a small bowl. Store in a covered container. Will keep 6 months refrigerated. Yield: 1½ cups.

Cinnamon tea

Good for relieving nausea.

*1 tablespoon dried
chamomile flowers*

*1 teaspoon whole cloves or
½ teaspoon ground cloves*

1 cup boiling water

*1 tablespoon
ground cinnamon*

1 teaspoon ground nutmeg

In a small pan, steep the chamomile flowers and whole cloves in the water for 15 minutes. (If you use ground cloves, do not add at this time.) Strain the flowers from the water with a tea strainer. Add the

cinnamon and nutmeg (and the ground cloves if using) and stir. Reheat in a mug in the microwave or in a small pan on the stove. Make fresh every time. Call your doctor if condition persists more than a couple of days.

Cockroach exterminator

Get rid of the pests with this easy-to-make insecticide.

2 tablespoons borax

1 tablespoon flour

1½ teaspoons cocoa powder

Mix all the ingredients in a small bowl. Set out in bottle caps or other small, unsealed containers in areas where the roaches congregate. **Caution:** Keep out of the reach of pets and small children.

Cocktail sauce

Adds zest to seafood. For a hotter sauce, add more horseradish or hot red pepper sauce.

*1 cup ketchup (p.405) or
chili sauce (p.390)*

*1 tablespoon
prepared horseradish*

1 tablespoon lemon juice

*½ teaspoon
Worcestershire sauce*

*⅛ teaspoon
hot red pepper sauce*

Combine all the ingredients in a small bowl. Cover and chill for 1 hour before serving. Will keep 1 month tightly covered and refrigerated. Yield: about 1 cup.

Coffee cake

Whip it up the night before and pop it in the oven in the morning.

CAKE

2 cups sifted all-purpose flour

1 teaspoon baking powder

1 teaspoon baking soda

1 teaspoon ground cardamom

¼ teaspoon salt

*½ cup (1 stick) butter or
margarine, at room
temperature*

1 cup sugar

2 eggs

¾ cup sour cream

½ cup light brown sugar

*½ cup
chopped walnuts or pecans*

*¼ teaspoon each
ground allspice and cinnamon*

GLAZE

½ cup confectioners sugar

2 teaspoons lemon juice

*½ teaspoon vanilla extract
or water*

1. On wax paper, sift together the flour, baking powder, baking soda, cardamom, and salt.
2. In a large bowl, cream the butter with the sugar until fluffy. Add the eggs and beat for 1 minute or until well mixed. Then spoon in the sour cream and beat again thoroughly. Combine with the sifted ingredients. Pour the batter into a 9- x 9- x 2-inch baking pan that has been lightly greased and floured.
3. Combine the brown sugar, walnuts, allspice, and cinnamon and sprinkle evenly over the batter. Cover with plastic wrap and refrigerate overnight.
4. Preheat the oven to 350°F. Bake for 50 minutes or until a toothpick inserted in the center comes out clean. (If the cake browns too quickly, cover it loosely with alumi-

num foil.) Let cool for 10 minutes.
5. Meanwhile, in a small mixing bowl, make the glaze by combining the sugar, lemon juice, and vanilla. Drizzle over the cake after it has cooled for 10 minutes. Serve warm or at room temperature. Will keep 3 days refrigerated and tightly covered; 1 month at 0°F. Yield: 8 to 12 servings.

Coffee liqueur

Cheap and easy to make. Serve with ice cream or as an after-dinner drink.

1½ cups instant coffee powder

3 cups boiling water

6 cups sugar

1 vanilla bean

1 bottle (750 milliliters) vodka

In a large saucepan, dissolve the instant coffee in the water. Add the sugar and vanilla bean and set over low heat, stirring with a wooden spoon until the mixture becomes syrupy. Remove from the heat, let cool, and stir in the vodka. Pour the mixture into a glass or earthenware gallon jug, cap tightly, and let stand for at least 30 days before serving. Yield: about 2 quarts.

Cold cream

A good, inexpensive moisturizer.

1 egg yolk, beaten

2 tablespoons lemon juice

½ cup olive oil

½ cup vegetable oil

Combine the egg yolk and lemon juice in a small mixing bowl. Stirring constantly with a wire whisk,

gradually add both oils until the mixture thickens. If too thick, add more lemon juice.

Cologne

A lovely, light scent at a fraction of the cost of most commercial brands.

1 cup rubbing alcohol

½ cup dried lavender flowers

1 tablespoon olive oil

1 cup distilled water

3 drops oil of bergamot

Pour the alcohol into a jar and add the lavender and olive oil. Cover tightly for 2 days, shaking occasionally. Discard the lavender flowers, then add the water and oil of bergamot. Cap tightly.

Comb & brush cleaner

Removes oily residue.

½ cup household ammonia

1 quart water

½ teaspoon shampoo or mild detergent

Mix all the ingredients in a bowl. Add the comb and brush and let them soak in the formula for 5 to 10

minutes. Then remove from the solution, clean the comb with the brush, and vice versa. Rinse the brush and comb with water and let dry before using.

Cornbread

For a Tex-Mex accent, add to the batter 2 ounces (½ cup) shredded Monterey Jack cheese and a 4-ounce can of jalapeño peppers, drained and chopped.

2½ cups cornbread mix (below)

3 eggs, lightly beaten

1 cup water

Preheat the oven to 425°F. Place all the ingredients in a large mixing bowl and mix well. Pour into a greased 8- x 8- x 2-inch pan. Bake about 17 minutes or until a knife inserted in the center comes out clean. Cut into squares and serve hot with butter. To store, cover the pan tightly with aluminum foil. Will keep 3 days refrigerated, 2 months at 0°F. Yield: 8 servings.

Cornbread mix

A real time-saver. You can have piping-hot muffins on the table in minutes.

3 cups sifted all-purpose flour

3 cups yellow cornmeal

1½ cups instant nonfat dry milk

3 tablespoons sugar (optional)

3½ tablespoons baking powder

2½ teaspoons salt

¾ cup solid vegetable shortening

Mix together all the dry ingredients in a large bowl. Using 2 knives or a pastry blender, cut in the shortening until the mixture resembles coarse crumbs. Will keep 6 weeks refrigerated in covered containers. Yield: about 8 cups.

Cough drops

An old-fashioned alternative to sweet candy-counter confections.

1 quart
horehound leaves and stems,
washed and chopped

2 cups water

3 cups sugar

¼ cup (½ stick) butter

In a medium-size saucepan, boil the horehound leaves in the water for 30 minutes. Strain and discard the leaves. Add the sugar. Place a candy thermometer in the mixture and boil to the hard crack stage (300°–310°F). Stir in the butter, remove from the heat, and transfer to a buttered shallow pan. When cool, crack into pieces. Wrap the pieces individually in wax paper, twisting the paper at the ends, and store in a tightly covered jar.

Cough syrup

Simple and effective for soothing a nagging cough.

3 tablespoons lemon juice

1 cup honey

¼ cup warm water

In a medium-size bowl, combine the lemon juice and honey and slowly stir in the water. Store in the refrigerator until needed; take 1 or 2 tablespoons once every 3 hours to relieve coughing.

Cradle cap remedy

For baby's irritated scalp.

2 ounces dried
comfrey root, cut up

1 quart water

1. Place the comfrey root in the water in a medium-size saucepan. Cover, bring to a boil, and simmer for 20 minutes. Strain and discard the comfrey root. Let the remaining liquid cool until tepid.
2. With a washcloth, gently work the rinse into the baby's scalp or use after a shampoo. Let it dry naturally on the scalp. Repeat the process nightly until the irritated area clears up. Will keep 4 days refrigerated; heat to skin temperature before using. Yield: 4 rinses.

Caution: If condition persists more than 7 days, call your doctor.

Cranberry-orange relish

Both tart and sweet, this is a superb accompaniment to roast chicken, turkey, or pork. A nice holiday gift.

⅔ cup pecan halves

1½ cups sugar

⅓ cup fresh orange juice

1 cinnamon stick

1 vanilla bean, split,
or 1 teaspoon vanilla extract

1 orange, peeled and diced
into ½-inch chunks
(about 1⅔ cups)

2 bags (12 ounces each)
fresh or solidly frozen
cranberrries, picked over

¾ cup golden raisins

1. Preheat the oven to 350°F. In a small baking pan, roast the pecans about 7 minutes or until lightly fragrant and crispy. Let cool, then coarsely chop or halve.
2. Combine the sugar, orange juice, cinnamon stick, and vanilla bean in a large heavy saucepan (if using vanilla extract, do not add now). Set over moderate heat and cook, uncovered, stirring occasionally, until the sugar melts and begins to color—about 7 minutes.
3. Add the orange chunks to the mixture and cook, stirring often, until they soften slightly—about 4 minutes. Add the cranberries and cook 8 to 10 minutes longer or until all the berries pop. Let cool to room temperature. Scrape the vanilla bean seeds into the mixture, then discard the vanilla bean and cinnamon stick. (If using vanilla extract, add it now.) Stir in the pecans and raisins. Cover and refrigerate until serving time. Will keep 2 months refrigerated. Yield: 6 cups.

Crème de menthe

Surprisingly easy to make.

2 cups vodka

1 cup light corn syrup

½ teaspoon
peppermint extract

40 drops green food coloring

Pour the vodka into a sterilized quart jar. Add the remaining ingredients, cover, and shake to mix. Serve as an after-dinner drink, add to chocolate sauces, or pour over ice cream. Yield: 3 cups.

Crème fraîche

Spoon over fresh berries or use as called for in recipes.

1 cup heavy cream

2 tablespoons
sour cream, plain
yogurt, or buttermilk

Stir the heavy cream and sour cream together in a medium-size jar and cover loosely with plastic wrap. Let stand at room temperature overnight or until thickened. Stir again and cover tightly. Refrigerate 2 hours before serving. Will keep 1 week refrigerated. Yield: 1 cup.

Crumb-coated chicken

Low in fat and very tasty.

¼ cup vegetable oil

1 broiling or frying chicken (about 3 pounds), cut into 8 pieces

½ cup crumb coating (below)

Preheat the oven to 350°F. Brush some of the vegetable oil on a baking pan large enough to hold all the chicken pieces. Then brush each piece of chicken with oil. Place the crumb coating in a paper bag, add 2 chicken pieces, and shake until both pieces are evenly coated. Repeat. Place the chicken pieces in the greased pan and bake, uncovered, until the chicken is no longer pink on the inside—about 1 hour; dark pieces may take an extra 5 to 10 minutes. Yield: 4 servings.

Crumb-coated fish

Easy to make and holds in moisture.

¼ cup vegetable oil or melted butter

2 pounds fish fillets or steaks

6 tablespoons crumb coating for fish (below)

Preheat the oven to 375°F. Grease a baking sheet with some of the oil and then brush oil on both sides of each piece of fish. Spread the crumb coating on a sheet of wax paper and dredge the fish until well coated; shake off any excess. Arrange the fish on the greased baking sheet and bake until it flakes easily—10 to 20 minutes depending on the thickness of each piece. Yields: 4 servings.

Crumb-coated pork chops

Great taste without any additives.

¼ cup vegetable oil

4 pork chops, trimmed

6 tablespoons crumb coating (below)

Preheat the oven to 350°F. Brush some of the vegetable oil onto a baking pan large enough to hold all the chops. Brush each chop with oil. Put the crumb coating in a paper bag and shake each chop in the mixture until evenly coated. Place the chops in the greased pan and bake until they are no longer pink on the inside—45 to 75 minutes, depending on the thickness of the chops. Yield: 4 servings.

Crumb coating

Cheaper than store-bought and lower in sodium. Good with chicken or pork. Use the variation for fish.

2 cups sifted all-purpose flour

1 tablespoon paprika

2 teaspoons each dried marjoram and thyme, crumbled

4 teaspoons onion powder

1 teaspoon dried rosemary, crumbled

1 teaspoon salt

Put all the ingredients in a plastic or paper bag. Close it and shake to mix. Pour the mixture into a jar and cover tightly. Will keep 6 months in a cool, dark place. Yield: enough to coat 20 pork chops or 4 chickens (about 3 pounds each).

Fish variation: To 2 cups all-purpose flour, add 2 teaspoons dried tarragon, 1 tablespoon dill weed, 2 teaspoons black pepper, 2 teaspoons parsley flakes, 2 teaspoons salt, 2 teaspoons onion powder, and 1 teaspoon paprika. Proceed as directed above. Will keep 6 months in a cool, dark place. Yield: enough to coat 30 fish fillets or steaks.

Currant jelly sauce

Turns plain roasted chicken or game hens into company fare.

½ cup red currant jelly

1 tablespoon lemon juice

1 teaspoon Dijon mustard

¼ teaspoon paprika

In a medium-size saucepan, warm the jelly over moderate heat until it begins to melt. Stir in the lemon juice, then add the mustard and paprika. When heated, transfer the sauce to a medium-size bowl and serve immediately.

Curry powder

Try this basic recipe. Then vary the ingredients to suit your own taste.

¼ cup ground coriander

2 tablespoons ground turmeric

2 teaspoons each ground cumin, ginger, and allspice

1 teaspoon each ground cinnamon, celery seed, and black pepper

¼ teaspoon cayenne pepper

Thoroughly mix all the ingredients in a medium-size bowl. Will keep 6 months in a glass jar at room temperature. Yield: ½ cup.

Cuticle cream

Softens cuticles and cures hangnails.

3 tablespoons paraffin

½ cup mineral oil

1 tablespoon coconut oil

1 tablespoon glycerin

1. In a double boiler, slowly heat the paraffin with the mineral and coconut oils until blended. Stir in the glycerin, remove from the heat, and let cool.

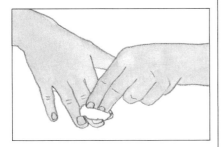

2. To use, apply directly to the cuticles with cotton balls. Or soak fingertips in the cream for about 5 minutes. Store in the refrigerator, where it will thicken.

Dandruff rinse

Combats itching and flaking.

1 cup witch hazel

1 tablespoon dried rosemary

1 tablespoon dried lavender

1 tablespoon ground comfrey root

Combine the witch hazel and the herbs in a medium-size bowl and let steep for 2 days. Strain the herbs and discard. To use, massage the rinse into the scalp and let dry. Then shampoo your hair. Store refrigerated in a covered jar.

Date & nut balls

Only minutes to make—and no baking required.

2 eggs, lightly beaten

1 cup finely chopped pitted dates

¾ cup sugar

1 cup finely chopped pecans or walnuts

2 cups toasted rice cereal

1½ cups coconut flakes

1. Place the eggs, dates, and sugar in a medium-size saucepan and cook over moderately low heat, stirring constantly, until the mixture thickens—about 5 minutes. Let cool 5 minutes, then stir in the pecans and cereal; let cool for 10 minutes longer.
2. Meanwhile, spread the coconut on a sheet of wax paper. Roll the cooled candy mixture in the coconut, a teaspoonful at a time, until well covered and shaped into balls. Will keep 2 weeks refrigerated in airtight containers. Yield: 3 dozen.

Delicate-washables soak

Save on dry-cleaning expenses and keep fine fabrics looking new longer.

½ cup soap flakes or grated soap ends

2 cups soft water

½ cup borax

Mix all the ingredients in a saucepan. Simmer and stir until the solution develops an even consistency. Strain into a jar or jug, cover, and store. To clean, use enough soap and hot water to make good suds. Use cold water for wool.

Deodorant

Stay dry all day without the chemicals or perfume of commercial products.

4 teaspoons alum

2 teaspoons baking soda

1 cup rubbing alcohol

In a small mixing bowl, stir the ingredients together. Transfer to a spray bottle and apply to the skin right after showering.

Diaper rash ointment

Ease baby's skin problems.

1 tablespoon dried chickweed

1 tablespoon dried marshmallow root

1 tablespoon dried comfrey root

⅛ teaspoon goldenseal powder

1 cup sweet almond oil

2 ounces beeswax

Combine all the ingredients except the beeswax in a medium-size saucepan. Cook over moderately low heat until soft, 5 to 10 minutes. Add the beeswax and keep cooking until the beeswax melts completely. Then strain through cheesecloth into a small glass jar;

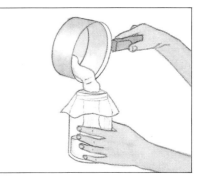

seal tightly and refrigerate until solid. Apply when changing a diaper. Will keep 2 months in a cool place. Yield: 20 applications.

Caution: If the rash doesn't disappear after 3 or 4 applications, call your doctor and ask whether or not to continue the treatment.

Diet cat food

A healthy regimen for cats.

*2½ pounds
beef liver or chicken liver,
cooked and ground*

2 cups cooked rice

2 teaspoons vegetable oil

*2 teaspoons calcium carbon-
ate (crushed antacid tablets)*

Put all the ingredients in a medium-size bowl and mix well. Feed a 5-pound cat ¼ pound daily, a 7- to 8-pound cat ⅓ pound daily, and one that weighs 10 or more pounds ½ pound daily. The cat food will keep 5 days tightly covered and refrigerated; 3 months in a tightly covered freezer container at 0°F. Yield: 3½ pounds.

Diet dog food

Contains all the vitamins and minerals your pet needs.

½ pound lean ground beef

*1 cup low-fat or fat-free
cottage cheese*

4 cups cooked sliced carrots

4 cups cooked green beans

*3 teaspoons bonemeal
(nutritional)*

Broil the beef until no longer pink. Drain off the fat and let the meat cool. Combine with the remaining ingredients in a medium-size bowl. Feed a 5-pound dog ⅓ pound daily, a 10-pound dog ⅔ pound, a 20-pound dog 1 pound, a 40-pound dog 1¾ pounds, a 60-pound dog 2½ pounds, and a dog that weighs 80 or more pounds 3 pounds. Will keep 5 days tightly covered and refrigerated; 3 months at 0°F. Yield: 3½ pounds.

Disinfectant

Use on countertops and floors.

*4 cups powdered
laundry detergent*

12 cups hot water

4 cups pine oil

1. Mix the laundry detergent and water in a bucket and stir slowly until all the detergent dissolves. If foam surfaces, stop stirring and skim off the bubbles or wait until they melt. Gradually add the pine oil; mix well.
2. To use, dilute the disinfectant with water, except when cleaning areas such as toilet bowls where bacteria flourish. Store in a jar with a tight-fitting lid, out of the reach of small children.

Dog biscuits

Tasty treats for your pup—and you know what's in them.

1¾ cups dog food (below)

1 cup unprocessed bran

1 cup old-fashioned oatmeal

½ cup vegetable oil

1. Preheat the oven to 250°F. Mash the dog food in a medium-size bowl to remove all lumps, then mix in the bran and oatmeal. Slowly add the oil, mixing to a consistency that is easy to mold into patties or bone shapes. (You may find it necessary to use more or less oil than the recipe calls for.)
2. Bake for 3½ hours. Let cool and

store in a covered can. Will keep 1 month refrigerated. Yield: 16 medium-size biscuits.

Dog food

A well-balanced diet for your pet.

*1 pound
ground beef (not lean)*

2 eggs, hard-cooked

4 cups cooked rice

6 slices white bread, crumbled

*2 teaspoons calcium carbon-
ate (crushed antacid tablets)*

Cook the meat in a covered skillet until no longer pink, retaining the fat. Then mix it thoroughly with the remaining ingredients in a medium-size bowl. This mixture tends to be dry; to improve palatability, add water (not milk). Feed a 5-pound dog about ¼ pound, a 10-pound dog ⅓ pound, a 20-pound dog ⅔ pound, a 40-pound dog 1½ pounds, a 60-pound dog 2 pounds, and a dog that weighs 80 or more pounds 2¾ pounds. Yield: 3 pounds.

Drain cleaner

Deodorizes drains and fights buildup in traps.

1 cup baking soda

1 cup salt

¼ cup cream of tartar

1. Place all the ingredients in a covered jar and shake well to mix.
2. To use, pour ¼ cup directly down the drain, followed by 2 cups

boiling water. After 1 minute, flush out with cool tap water. Repeat weekly. Store in a dry place in a tightly sealed container.

Dry carpet cleaner

Brightens rugs and adds a fresh scent.

2 cups baking soda

½ cup cornstarch

5 bay leaves, crumbled, and 1 teaspoon ground cloves or 1 cup potpourri (p.414)

1. In a covered container, mix all the ingredients well. Store in a safe place, away from children.
2. To use, shake well and sprinkle generously on the carpet. Leave for several hours (overnight if possible), keeping children and pets off the carpet. Vacuum thoroughly.

Dry shampoo

To avoid staining the rug, apply over the sink or bathtub.

2 tablespoons cornmeal

1 tablespoon ground almonds

1½ tablespoons orrisroot

Combine all the ingredients in a small mixing bowl. Massage 1 teaspoon into the scalp, then brush through the hair. Repeat the process if necessary.

Ebonizer

Blackens any wood that contains tannin, such as mahogany, walnut, cherry, or oak.

1 fine steel-wool pad

2 cups cider vinegar

1. Put the steel-wool pad in a small plastic or glass bowl; add the vinegar and let sit for several days or until the steel wool dissolves.
Caution: Do not cover the bowl; gas from the reaction between the vine-

gar and the steel wool could possibly cause it to explode.
2. To use, sponge the solution evenly onto a sanded wood surface.

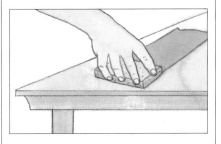

If a second coat is desired, wet the wood liberally but evenly with tap water and let it sit at least 1 hour before restaining. Allow to dry overnight before applying a finish.

Egg facial mask

Smooth your face and moisten dry skin.

1 egg

½ cup coconut oil

1 tablespoon honey

1. Beat the egg well in a small bowl. Slowly add the coconut oil and honey, beating until the mixture is the consistency of mayonnaise. Set an empty toilet paper roll upright in a bowl and pack the mask into it with a spoon. Freeze overnight.
2. To use, peel away some of the cardboard and rub the frozen stick over your face. After 5 or 10 minutes, rinse off with warm water. After using, cover the exposed end of the stick with plastic wrap and return to the freezer.

Facial mask

Cleans and revitalizes.

1 tablespoon instant nonfat dry milk

½ cucumber, peeled

1 teaspoon plain yogurt

Purée the ingredients until smooth in a blender. Apply to your face, avoiding the area around the eyes, and let dry for about 20 minutes. Rinse off. It's best to mix a fresh batch for each use, but if a large quantity is desired, freeze at 0°F in an ice cube tray; thaw for each use.

Facial scrub

Apply over the kitchen sink to avoid a clogged bathroom drain.

⅓ cup cornmeal

2 tablespoons honey

1 tablespoon ground almonds or walnuts

Combine the ingredients in a small bowl, adding a little water if the mixture is too dry to apply easily. To use, pack onto your face and leave at least 5 minutes. Remove with warm water and a washcloth.

Fertilizer

General nutrition for most nonflowering houseplants with foliage.

1 tablespoon Epsom salts

1 teaspoon baking soda

½ teaspoon saltpeter

¼ teaspoon household ammonia

1 gallon warm water

Combine the Epsom salts, baking soda, saltpeter, and ammonia in a small bowl. Dissolve the mixture in the warm water in a bucket. To use, apply once a month instead of regular watering. For an acid-loving plant, add 4 drops white vinegar or 5 tablespoons black coffee per gallon of fertilizer.

Fig bars

Tastier than store-bought brands.

3 cups sifted all-purpose flour

½ teaspoon salt

½ teaspoon ground cinnamon

⅔ cup butter or margarine

*½ cup firmly packed
light brown sugar*

*½ cup firmly packed
dark brown sugar*

2 egg whites

1 teaspoon vanilla extract

*1¾ cups finely chopped
dried golden figs
(about 11 figs)*

1 cup water

*2 tablespoons
granulated sugar*

2 tablespoons lemon juice

1. Combine the flour, salt, and cinnamon in a small bowl; set aside.

2. In a large mixing bowl, cream the butter and light and dark brown sugar until fluffy. Beat in the egg whites and vanilla extract, then slowly beat in the flour mixture. Shape the dough into a ball. Cover with plastic wrap and refrigerate 2 to 3 hours.
3. Place the figs, water, granulated sugar, and lemon juice in a medi-

um-size saucepan. Cook over moderate heat, stirring constantly, until the mixture is thick—about 7 minutes. Let cool but don't chill.
4. Preheat the oven to 350°F. Place one-fourth of the dough between sheets of wax paper and roll to a thickness of ⅛ inch. Cut the dough into 2½- x 3-inch pieces.
5. At the narrow end of each strip, place 2 level teaspoons of the filling. Roll the dough into bars and place 1 inch apart on 2 ungreased baking sheets. With a spatula, flatten them to a ½-inch thickness.
6. Bake in the center of the oven for 12 to 14 minutes or until the bars are lightly browned. Transfer to a rack to cool. Will keep 1 week in an airtight container at room temperature, 3 months at 0°F. Yield: about 30 fig bars.

Finger paints

A colorful diversion to keep children occupied.

1¼ cups all-purpose flour

1 cup water

3 tablespoons glycerin

Assorted food colorings

Mix the flour and water in a medium-size bowl. Divide the mixture equally among 3 small bowls. Stirring constantly, add 1 tablespoon glycerin to each batch, along with food coloring. Make fresh as needed.

Fire extinguisher

More effective than plain water; especially useful when leaving a campsite.

4 teaspoons baking soda

4 teaspoons salt

2 quarts water

Place the baking soda and salt in a spray bottle. Add the water and combine thoroughly. To put out fires, aim the mixture at the base of the flames.

Fireplace cleaner

Removes heavy-duty soot and grime.

*2 bars (6½ ounces each)
naphtha soap*

3 quarts hot water

1½ pounds powdered pumice

1½ cups household ammonia

1. Shave the naphtha soap into a Dutch oven or stockpot. Pour in the water and heat until the soap dissolves. Remove from the heat and let cool. Then stir in the pumice and the ammonia until the mixture is thoroughly combined.
2. To use, brush the cleaner on sooty areas with a paintbrush and let stand for about 1 hour. Then scrub the mixture off with a stiff brush and soap or liquid detergent. Rinse with a sponge and clear water.

Florida water

A toilet water with a sweet citrus scent.

1 teaspoon lavender oil

1 teaspoon lemon oil

2 teaspoons jasmine oil

3 teaspoons bergamot oil

*4 drops each clove, cinnamon,
and neroli oils*

2 teaspoons tincture of musk

2⅔ cups vodka

*¼ cup plus 4 teaspoons
rose water (p.416)*

Mix the oils and tincture of musk with ½ cup of the vodka. Gradually add the remaining vodka and the rose water, stirring constantly. Transfer the liquid to a bottle with a secure lid. Let stand 1 to 2 months to mature, shaking every few days. If the mixture gets cloudy, strain it through a coffee filter until clear. Store in a tightly covered bottle out of the reach of small children.

Flypaper

Easy to make and effective.

¼ cup maple syrup

*1 tablespoon
light or dark brown sugar*

1 tablespoon granulated sugar

Combine the ingredients in a small bowl. Pour over strips of brown paper and let soak overnight. To use, poke a hole in one end of a strip, insert a string, and hang.

French toast

You can make this the night before and just pop it in the oven the next morning.

3 eggs

1½ cups milk

*2 tablespoons unsalted
butter or margarine, melted*

*3 tablespoons
light or dark brown sugar*

*½ teaspoon
finely grated lemon rind*

*⅛ teaspoon each
ground nutmeg and cinnamon*

*14 slices French bread
(about ¾ inch thick)*

*1 tablespoon
confectioners sugar*

1. In a medium-size bowl, beat the eggs, milk, butter, brown sugar, lemon rind, nutmeg, and cinnamon. Pour half the mixture into a greased 17- x 11½- x 3-inch baking dish. Lay the bread slices on top in a single layer, pressing them as close together as possible. Pour the remaining mixture over the bread slices and cover the pan with aluminum foil. Refrigerate overnight or at least 2 hours.

2. Preheat the oven to 350°F. Bake, uncovered, until the toast is puffy and golden brown—50 to 60 minutes. Sprinkle with the confectioners sugar. Serve piping hot with maple or blueberry syrup, honey, or fresh fruit, nuts, and yogurt. Yield: 4 servings.

Fruit compote

Keep dried fruit on hand and whip up a delicious dessert in no time.

*1¼ cups (6 ounces)
dried pitted prunes*

*⅔ cup (4 ounces)
golden raisins*

½ cup (3 ounces) dried figs

*½ cup (3 ounces)
dried apricots*

1½ cups orange juice

⅓ cup water

¼ cup sugar

1 cinnamon stick, broken

¼ teaspoon ground ginger

⅛ teaspoon ground cloves

Pinch black pepper

*¾ teaspoon vanilla extract
(optional)*

1. Place all the ingredients except the vanilla in a medium-size enamel or stainless-steel saucepan. Set over high heat and bring to a boil; then reduce the heat to low, cover, and simmer for 25 to 30 minutes or until the fruit is tender.

2. Remove from the heat. Take out the cinnamon stick and discard. Let cool to room temperature and add the vanilla, if desired. Chill. Serve with heavy cream or crème fraîche (p.393). Will keep 3 days tightly covered and refrigerated. Yield: 6 servings.

Fruit gelatin

More nutritious than commercial brands. Vary the sugar according to the sweetness of the juice.

2 envelopes unflavored gelatin

6 to 8 tablespoons sugar

*2 cups grape, cranberry,
prune, apple, or orange juice*

*1 cup chopped fresh fruit
(optional)*

Mix the gelatin with the sugar in a small saucepan and slowly stir in ½ cup of the juice. Let stand for 5 minutes. Cook over moderately low heat, stirring, until the sugar and gelatin dissolve. Remove from the heat and stir in the remaining juice. Pour into a mold or bowl, let cool, cover, and refrigerate. When the gelatin is syrupy, add the fresh fruit if desired. Chill until firmly set—about 3 hours. Will keep 2 days refrigerated. Yield: 4 servings.

Furniture cleaner

Removes surface dirt and grime from finished wood.

1 cup boiled linseed oil

⅔ cup turpentine

⅓ cup white vinegar

Thoroughly mix all the ingredients in a large bowl. Apply to wood surfaces with a soft cloth, rubbing to remove dirt and excess polish. For badly caked-on dirt, use superfine (No. 0000) steel wool. Store in a tightly covered jar out of the reach of children.

Garden insect repellent

To help protect flowers, vegetables, and shrubs from insect attacks.

½ cup dead insects

2 cups water

When insects infest flowers, vegetables, or shrubs, identify the pest and collect ½ cupful. Place in an old blender—not your kitchen appliance—with the water; liquefy. Strain this "bug juice" through a piece of cheesecloth or a fine sieve and dilute at a rate of ¼ cup to 1 cup water. Transfer to a garden sprayer and apply to plants. Will keep 1 year stored in a tightly covered container at 0°F.

Gargle

Soothes a sore throat.

1 cup warm water

3 tablespoons cider vinegar

2 drops hot red pepper sauce

Pinch salt

Pour the water into a glass and add the remaining ingredients. Gargle as much as necessary. If the mixture is too spicy, add another tablespoon water. Make only as much as needed at one time. If sore throat persists, consult a physician.

Gentian root tonic

Perks up a declining appetite.

*2 to 4 teaspoons
chopped dried gentian root*

2 cups water

*2 teaspoons dried
peppermint (optional)*

In a small saucepan, bring the gentian root and water to a boil; reduce the heat and simmer for 15 minutes. Remove from the heat and add the peppermint if desired. Cover and let steep for 5 minutes.

Transfer to a cup. Let cool until lukewarm. Will keep 2 days tightly covered and refrigerated.

Gesso

A primer coat to be used on raw wood before applying gold leaf.

¼ cup rabbitskin glue

1½ cups water

*3 to 4 cups gilders whiting,
sifted*

1. In a glue pot or the top of a double boiler (stainless steel is easiest to clean), mix the rabbitskin glue with 1 cup of the water. Let sit until it swells and softens—about 5 minutes. Heat until the glue melts and runs clear—about 15 minutes. **2.** Meanwhile, mix the gilders whiting with the remaining ½ cup water in a large jar. Add about 3 ounces of the heated glue and stir thoroughly. The gesso should have the consistency of heavy cream. If too thick, add more glue. Use as needed. Will keep 2 days tightly covered and refrigerated.

Bole variation: If more glue is added, the result will be a very thin gesso called bole. Use this variation for the last coat to form a perfectly smooth ground on which to apply the gold leaf.

Ginseng tea

An ancient Chinese remedy said to increase energy and relieve stress.

1 cup water

2 tablespoons ginseng extract

1 teaspoon honey

Bring the water to a boil in a small saucepan, then add the ginseng and the honey. (For a sweeter tea, add more honey.) The ginseng tea may be reheated, although its flavor will decrease each time. It is preferable to make it fresh as desired. Do not drink for more than 10 consecutive days.

Glair

A light finish for raw wood that adds a soft sheen without changing the color while it repels moisture, dirt, and oil. Nontoxic, it is ideal for children's wooden toys.

1 cup egg whites

1 cup water

Pinch sugar

Gum arabic

Mix the egg whites and water in a medium-size bowl, then add the sugar. To use, brush on and let dry overnight, then sand. Apply 2 more coats, letting each dry overnight. Because glair tends to be very thin and seeps into wood easily, you might want to thicken it with gum arabic. You may have to recoat occasionally, as this is not a very durable finish. Will keep 1 week tightly covered and refrigerated.

Glass cleaner

The alcohol lets you clean windows in temperatures below 0°F.

½ cup rubbing alcohol

½ cup household ammonia

7½ cups warm water

Pour the alcohol and ammonia into a bucket, then add the water and mix well. To use, transfer the cleaner to a spray bottle. Spritz the window with the cleaner and let it sit

for 30 seconds, then wipe the glass with newspaper, making sure to turn it frequently. Store tightly covered, out of reach of children.

Glue

A waterproof binding mixture, good on most fabrics and paper.

6 tablespoons water

2 envelopes unflavored gelatin

2 tablespoons white vinegar

2 teaspoons glycerin

1. Bring the water to a boil in a small saucepan. Remove from the heat and stir in the gelatin until it dissolves. Pour in the vinegar and glycerin; stir well. Let cool, then transfer to a jar and cover tightly.

2. Apply the glue while warm. Will keep many months in a tightly sealed jar but will gel after a few days. Heat the jar in hot water before reusing.

Graham crackers

You'll never want to buy them again.

1 cup all-purpose flour

1¼ cups whole wheat flour

5 tablespoons sugar

*½ teaspoon each
salt and baking soda*

1 teaspoon baking powder

¼ teaspoon ground cinnamon

3 tablespoons chilled butter or margarine, in small pieces

*¼ cup
solid vegetable shortening*

2 tablespoons honey

1 tablespoon molasses

¼ cup water

1 teaspoon vanilla extract

1. In a medium-size bowl, combine the all-purpose and whole wheat flours, sugar, salt, baking soda, baking powder, and cinnamon. Work in the butter and shortening

with a pastry blender or your fingertips until the mixture has the consistency of coarse crumbs.

2. In a small bowl, mix the honey, molasses, water, and vanilla extract. Sprinkle slowly over the dry ingredients, then toss with a fork until well blended. Form the dough into a ball (it may be crumbly, but don't add water). Cover with plastic wrap and chill for several hours.

3. Preheat the oven to 350°F. Cut the dough in half and let it sit for 15 minutes at room temperature.

4. Lightly sprinkle a piece of wax paper with whole wheat flour. Put a piece of the dough on top and flatten it with a rolling pin. Sprinkle the dough with more whole wheat flour and cover with another sheet of wax paper. Roll out to form a rectangle measuring roughly 7 x 15 inches. If the dough breaks, pinch the pieces together with your fingers and continue rolling.

5. Peel off the top piece of wax paper, then use a fork to prick the dough at ½- to 1-inch intervals. Cut into 2½-inch squares. With a spatula, transfer to a large, ungreased baking sheet, placing the squares close together.

6. Repeat the process with the remaining piece of dough, then reroll and cut the scraps. Bake the crackers on the center rack of the oven for 15 minutes or until lightly browned on the edges.

7. Let the crackers cool on a rack. Will keep 1 month in an airtight canister at room temperature or 6 months in a tightly covered freezer container at 0°F. Store at least 24 hours before serving. Yield: 24 to 28 crackers.

Grease solvent

Removes stubborn oil stains from your skin.

*2 tablespoons
liquid soap gel (p.406)*

3 tablespoons cornmeal

1 teaspoon glycerin

Combine the ingredients in a small bowl. Pour the mixture onto your hands and scrub until stains disappear; rinse off.

Gum arabic adhesive

Use to mend broken dishes and crockery.

3 tablespoons gum arabic

1 tablespoon glycerin

½ teaspoon water

In a small mixing bowl, thoroughly combine the ingredients. To use, apply a thin coating to each surface, fit the pieces together, and hold firmly in place until the glue dries—about 1 hour. Let dry at least 24 hours before washing or using the piece. The glue will keep 1 year in an airtight jar.

Hair conditioner

Softens dry hair and helps prevent split ends.

⅓ cup olive oil

⅓ cup vegetable oil

⅓ cup honey

Place all the ingredients in a small saucepan and set over low heat until just boiling. Remove from the heat and let cool for 5 minutes. Transfer to a 1-pint plastic spray bottle. Spray on hair and rub in thoroughly. Wet a towel with warm water and wrap around head for 1 hour. Shampoo to remove, then wash and style hair as usual. Store in a cool, dry place.

Ham & cheese bread

A meal in itself. Make it ahead of time for box lunches or breakfast toast.

2 cups
unsifted all-purpose flour

½ cup yellow cornmeal

2¼ teaspoons baking powder

½ teaspoon salt

¼ teaspoon black pepper

¾ cup (4 ounces)
coarsely chopped ham

1 cup plus 2 tablespoons
grated Parmesan cheese
(about 3½ ounces)

¾ cup milk

⅓ cup olive oil

2 eggs

1. Preheat the oven to 375°F. In a large mixing bowl, sift together the flour, cornmeal, baking powder, salt, and pepper. Stir in the chopped ham and 1 cup of the grated Parmesan cheese.

2. In a small bowl, whisk together the milk, olive oil, and eggs. Add to the flour mixture and stir until just combined. Pour the batter into a greased 9- x 5- x 3-inch loaf pan. Sprinkle the remaining cheese on top and bake until a toothpick inserted in the center comes out clean—45 to 50 minutes. Set the pan on a wire rack and let cool for 20 minutes, then turn out. Serve warm or at room temperature. Will keep 1 week covered with aluminum foil and refrigerated; 3 months wrapped tightly in aluminum foil and stored at 0°F. Yield: 1 loaf.

Hand treatment

Moisturizes and softens chapped hands.

3 tablespoons almond meal

2 tablespoons
dried comfrey root

1 tablespoon chopped parsley

1 egg

1 tablespoon honey

1 tablespoon glycerin

Mix the almond meal, comfrey root, and parsley in a small bowl and set aside. In another bowl, combine the egg, honey, and glycerin. Stir in 3 tablespoons of the almond mixture. Dip your hands in the concoction and gently massage it in, giving special attention to the area around the nails. Let it penetrate for about 30 minutes; rinse off with warm water. Will keep 5 days refrigerated.

Herbal face mask

Cleans skin and tightens pores.

1 tablespoon honey

1 egg

1 teaspoon dried
chamomile flowers, crumbled

1 teaspoon finely chopped
fresh mint

Mix all the ingredients together in a small bowl. To use, apply the mixture to your face and neck. Let dry and rinse off with warm water.

Herbal ice cubes

For an upset stomach. The peppermint and bitters are soothing, and the ice cubes are easier to keep down than liquids.

1 cup water

1 peppermint tea bag

2 cups cranberry-apple juice

1 teaspoon angostura bitters

1. Bring the water to a boil in a small saucepan. Add the tea bag, turn off the heat, and let steep for 10 minutes.
2. Discard the tea bag. Let the tea cool for 5 minutes, then stir in the remaining ingredients.
3. Transfer the mixture to an ice cube tray and place in the freezer until solidly frozen.
4. To use, suck or chew up to 3 ice cubes each hour or rub a little bit on your lips.
Caution: Call your doctor if vomiting lasts more than 24 hours or if it's unusually severe.

Herbal shampoo

Makes oily hair shiny and manageable. If hair needs conditioning, add the egg and milk.

2 tablespoons
dried peppermint

2 tablespoons
dried spearmint

1 tablespoon dried sage

1 cup water

⅓ cup baby shampoo

1 egg, beaten (optional)

⅓ cup milk (optional)

Place the herbs in a small saucepan, add the water, and bring to a full boil. Remove from the heat and let steep for 20 minutes. Strain and discard the herbs. In a jar, mix the baby shampoo with ¼ cup of the herbal water. Shampoo as usual.
Variation for dry hair: Substitute 1 tablespoon dried comfrey root, 1

tablespoon dried rosemary, and 1 tablespoon dried chamomile for the peppermint, spearmint, and sage; proceed as directed.

Herb butters

Freeze them and enjoy the delicate flavor of fresh herbs all year long.

*½ cup (1 stick) butter
or margarine,
at room temperature*

*¼ cup minced dill or
2 tablespoons minced tarragon
or 3 tablespoons
minced chives or
1 to 3 cloves garlic, minced*

¼ teaspoon salt

Combine the butter with the herb or garlic and the salt in a small bowl. Refrigerate until firm enough to handle. Shape into a stick and cover with plastic wrap and aluminum foil. Or place 2 to 3 tablespoons in each section of an ice cube tray, cover with aluminum foil, and freeze. Will keep 5 days refrigerated, 4 months at 0°F. The dill butter is particularly good on broiled fish or vegetables; the tarragon butter, on steaks or poultry; the chive butter, on baked potatoes, scrambled eggs, or fresh vegetables; the garlic butter, on hamburgers, steaks, lamb chops, or bread. Yield: 8 servings.

Herb dressing

For a stronger flavor, add ½ teaspoon more herb dressing mix.

*2 tablespoons
herb dressing mix (below)*

1½ cups warm water

2 tablespoons olive oil

*5 tablespoons white vinegar or
tarragon vinegar*

2 cloves garlic, crushed

Mix the herb dressing mix with the warm water, olive oil, vinegar, and

garlic in a small bowl. Whisk the ingredients together and let the dressing sit at room temperature for 30 minutes before using. Whisk again, then pour the desired amount over your salad. Will keep 1 week tightly covered and refrigerated. Yield: 2 cups.

Herb dressing mix

Fresh taste and no preservatives.

½ cup parsley flakes

*¼ cup each
dried oregano, basil, and
marjoram, crumbled*

¼ cup sugar

*2 tablespoons
fennel seed, crushed*

2 tablespoons dry mustard

1 tablespoon black pepper

Place all the ingredients in a quart-size glass jar. Cover the jar and shake thoroughly until well blended. The dressing mix will keep 6 weeks in a cool, dark, dry place. Yield: 2 cups.

Herbed cheese spread

As good as the imported brands and less costly.

*2 packages (3 ounces each)
cream cheese, softened*

1 teaspoon minced parsley

¼ teaspoon minced garlic

¼ teaspoon salt

¼ teaspoon black pepper

¼ teaspoon lemon juice

Mix all the ingredients in a small bowl, cover, and refrigerate at least 2 hours to allow the flavors to blend. Will keep 7 days refrigerated in a tightly sealed container. To freeze, shape the cheese spread into a log and cover with plastic wrap, then aluminum foil. Will keep 3 months at 0°F.

Herbed rice

Contains less salt than packaged mixes and takes just minutes to make.

2⅔ cups water

*4 tablespoons
herbed rice mix (below)*

*1⅓ cups
raw white or brown rice*

*2 tablespoons
unsalted butter or margarine*

Bring the water to a boil in a large saucepan. Pour in the herbed rice mix and stir to combine. Add the rice and lower the heat until the water just simmers. Cover and cook white rice for 25 minutes or until tender; brown rice as directed on the package. Stir in the butter and serve hot. Yield: 6 servings.

Herbed rice mix

Use with either white or brown rice.

*2½ tablespoons
dried onion flakes*

1¼ teaspoons salt

1 bay leaf

*¾ teaspoon
dried basil, crumbled*

¾ teaspoon celery flakes

½ teaspoon sweet paprika

½ teaspoon garlic powder

⅛ teaspoon ground lemon peel

Place all the ingredients in a plastic bag and shake to combine. Store in a tightly covered jar or canister. Yield: ¼ cup.

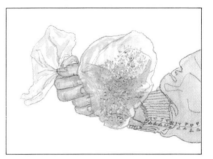

Hot dog relish

Exceptionally quick and easy.

*1 large yellow, Bermuda,
or Spanish onion,
finely chopped*

2 tablespoons cider vinegar

2 tablespoons sugar

¼ teaspoon salt

*1 jar (4 ounces) pimientos,
drained and chopped*

Mix all the ingredients in a medium-size bowl. Let stand at room temperature for 30 minutes before serving. Will keep 1 week covered and refrigerated. Yield: 1 cup.

Hot pepper jelly

Serve with cold ham or pork.

*2 medium-size sweet red
peppers, cored, seeded,
and chopped (about 1 cup)*

*3 jalapeño peppers, cored,
seeded, and finely chopped*

2 cups cider vinegar

6½ cups sugar

*2 pouches (3 ounces each)
liquid pectin*

1. In a food processor or blender, process the peppers with 1 cup of the vinegar until finely minced.
Caution: Don't touch your eyes until you have thoroughly washed your hands.
2. Transfer the mixture to a large stainless-steel saucepan and add the sugar and remaining vinegar. Set over high heat and bring to a rolling boil. Then stir.
3. Remove the pan from the heat and skim the surface.
4. Stir in the pectin. Return the pan to the heat and bring to a boil for 1 minute. Repeat step 3.
5. Pour the jelly into hot, sterilized ½-pint preserving jars. Wipe the jar rims and seal. Will keep 6 months. Yield: 8 ½-pint jars.

Houseplant insecticide

Death to aphids, mealybugs, and thrips.

*Handful of tobacco
(pipe or cigarette)*

1 gallon water

*4 teaspoons
liquid soap (p.406)*

Steep the tobacco overnight in the water. Strain and discard the tobacco. Add the liquid soap to the water and mix well. To use, pour into spray bottles and thoroughly spray infested plants, wetting both the tops and bottoms of leaves.

This treatment is most effective in warm weather. Do not apply to petunias, nicotiana, tomatoes, or other plants that are susceptible to tobacco mosaic virus.
Caution: Test any new insecticide on a few small leaves before a full-scale application.

Hyssop cough syrup

Soothes an irritated throat and has a pleasant licorice taste.

1 cup honey

¼ cup water

*2 tablespoons dried
flowering hyssop tops or ⅓ cup
chopped fresh hyssop flowers*

1 teaspoon aniseed

Place the honey in a small heavy saucepan and add the water 1 table-spoon at a time, stirring until the mixture has the consistency of pancake syrup. Over medium heat, gradually bring the mixture to a boil, skimming off any scum that surfaces. Use 1 or 2 tablespoons water to moisten the dried hyssop, then crush the aniseed with a spoon. Add both ingredients to the honey and stir. Cover and simmer over low heat for 30 minutes. Uncover and let cool; while the mixture is still slightly warm, strain it into a jar with a screw-on lid. Let cool to room temperature and cover tightly. Will keep for 1 week.

Ink

Buy lamp black in a tube or make it by holding a plate over a lit candle.

1 egg yolk

1 teaspoon gum arabic

½ cup honey

½ teaspoon lamp black

Water

Mix the egg yolk, gum arabic, and honey in a small bowl. Add the lamp black and thin with a little water if necessary.

Insecticide

For shrubs, flowers, and vegetables.

*3 hot green peppers
(canned or fresh)*

2 or 3 cloves garlic

*¾ teaspoon
liquid soap (p.406)*

3 cups water

Purée the peppers and garlic cloves in a blender. Transfer to a spray bottle and add the liquid soap and water. Let stand 24 hours, strain, and spray onto infested plants.
Caution: Always test any new insecticide on a few small leaves before embarking on a full-scale application.

Insect repellent

Discourage mosquitoes, gnats, and other biting pests.

¼ cup denatured alcohol

1½ teaspoons camphor

*1½ teaspoons
calcium chloride*

Place all the ingredients in a small bowl and stir until dissolved. To use, rub on exposed areas of skin before going outdoors.
Caution: Be careful not to use near the eyes. Discontinue if you notice a rash or other allergic reaction.

Jewelry cleaner

Cheaper than commercial brands.

*1 tablespoon
dishwashing detergent*

*1 tablespoon washing soda
(sodium carbonate)*

*1 tablespoon
household ammonia*

3 cups warm water

1. Combine the ingredients in a medium-size bowl and pour into a glass jar. Label, cover, and store out of children's reach.
2. To use, soak the jewelry in the solution for 1 to 10 minutes depending on how heavily tarnished it is. If a piece has an intricate pattern or several cracks or crevices, use agitation (swish it through

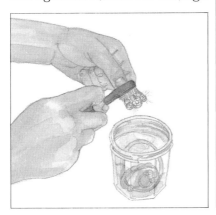

the liquid). A toothbrush with soft bristles works especially well for cleaning large items. Wash an old mascara brush and use it to clean small, hard-to-reach spaces. Rinse and dry with a soft clean cloth.
3. Don't soak pearls; rub them gently with a soft chamois cloth dampened in the solution.
Caution: Do not combine the cleaner with any substance containing chlorine bleach; together they produce hazardous fumes.

Ketchup

Much fresher-tasting than commercial brands. A nice gift. To prevent the ketchup from splattering as it cooks, put a wire mesh splatter shield over the pot.

*2 cans (1 pound 12 ounces
each) tomato purée*

2 bay leaves

1 teaspoon celery seed

1 teaspoon mustard seed

1 teaspoon whole allspice

1 stick cinnamon

½ teaspoon peppercorns

1½ teaspoons salt

1 cup white vinegar

1 cup sugar

1. In a large, deep saucepan set over moderate heat, cook the tomato purée, uncovered, at a slow boil for 1½ hours, stirring occasionally. Tie the bay leaves, seeds, and spices in a piece of cheesecloth and add to the saucepan, then add the salt. Set the lid askew, reduce the heat to low, and simmer 30 minutes longer.
2. Remove the spice bag and add the vinegar and sugar. Increase the heat to moderate and cook, uncovered, at a slow boil, stirring often, until very thick—about 1½ hours. At the end of the cooking time, you may have to stir constantly to prevent scorching.
3. Ladle the hot ketchup into 2 hot, sterilized 1-pint preserving jars,

leaving ⅛-inch head space. Wipe the rims and seal. Will keep 1 month refrigerated. Yield: 2 pints.

Laundry presoak

Penetrates heavily soiled spots.

¼ cup household ammonia

2 tablespoons baking soda

1 tablespoon liquid detergent

1 quart water

1. Combine the ingredients in a jar and shake thoroughly. Transfer a part of the mixture to a spray bottle. Store the remaining portion in a clean ½-gallon jug. Label and store out of the reach of children and pets.
2. To use, spray soiled areas and let sit for 5 to 10 minutes; launder as usual. It may be necessary to repeat the process more than once.

Lawn fertilizer

A quick and easy springtime feeding.

1 cup Epsom salts

1 cup household ammonia

Water

Combine the Epsom salts and ammonia in a clean jar. To use, mix 2 tablespoons of the mixture with 2 gallons water in a watering can and sprinkle over 150 to 200 square feet of turf. Or for use with a hose sprayer, mix the entire batch with

enough water to equal 1 quart total volume and pour into the sprayer container. A quart of diluted fertilizer will cover 2,500 square feet.

Lawn fertilizer for fall

Help grass roots get a jump on spring.

2 cups Epsom salts

3 tablespoons baking powder

Water

Mix the Epsom salts with the baking powder in a clean jar. To use, dissolve 2 tablespoons of the mixture with 1 gallon water in a watering can and sprinkle over 100 square feet of turf. Or for application with a hose sprayer, mix the entire batch with enough water to equal 1 quart total volume and pour into the sprayer container; will cover 1,500 square feet of lawn.

Laxative

One glass should ease minor constipation in just a few hours. It's nutritious, too.

2 cups tomato or vegetable juice

1 cup sauerkraut juice

½ cup carrot juice

Combine all the ingredients in a small pitcher. Drink half of the mixture; store the remainder in the refrigerator. Yield: 28 ounces.

Lemonade mix

For pink lemonade, add ¾ cup grenadine syrup. For limeade, substitute lime juice for the lemon juice.

1 quart fresh lemon juice (about 24 large lemons)

1 cup sugar

2 cups light corn syrup

Stir all the ingredients together in a large bowl until the sugar dis-

solves. Pour into a screw-top jar, cover, and store in the refrigerator. For each serving, shake well and add ¼ cup of the mix to ¾ cup water or club soda and stir well. Add ice if desired. Will keep 2 weeks refrigerated. Yield: 24 servings.

Lemon curd

A versatile spread. Serve it in tart shells, as a filling for sponge cake, or on toast. (For variety, substitute lime juice for the lemon juice.) Also makes a nice gift.

½ cup (1 stick) butter or margarine

2 cups sugar

⅔ cup fresh lemon juice (about 4 large lemons)

Grated rind of 2 lemons

4 large eggs, lightly beaten

Pinch salt

1. Melt the butter in a small saucepan over low heat. Remove from the heat and add the sugar, lemon juice, lemon rind, eggs, and salt. Mix thoroughly. Cook over moderate heat, stirring constantly, until the mixture thickens—about 8 minutes. Do not let it boil.

2. Strain the mixture through a sieve into a bowl and discard the solids. Let cool for 5 minutes, then spoon the lemon curd into a clean jar and let cool to room temperature; cover. Will keep 1 month refrigerated. Yield: 2½ cups.

Lip balm

An inexpensive way to keep your lips soft in all kinds of weather.

1 tablespoon olive oil

1 teaspoon glycerin

2 tablespoons honey

Mix all the ingredients in a small bowl. To use, apply to chapped lips with your finger or a cotton ball. Use as often as necessary for chapped lips until condition improves. Store refrigerated in a tightly covered jar.

Liquid soap

Turn leftover bits of bar soap into a versatile cleaning agent.

2 cups soap flakes or grated soap

1 gallon water

2 tablespoons glycerin

Mix the ingredients together in a stockpot or Dutch oven and set over low heat, stirring occasionally, until the soap has dissolved. Transfer to a storage container, cover tightly, and store out of the reach of children. Use as a hand soap or for general household cleaning chores.

Gel variation: For a thicker, more gelatinous soap, use only ½ gallon of water.

Low-fat coffee cake

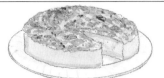

A scrumptious light, spongy cake.

⅓ cup firmly packed
dark or light brown sugar

1½ teaspoons
ground cinnamon

¼ teaspoon ground nutmeg

¼ cup chopped
pecans or walnuts

¼ cup (½ stick) margarine

1 cup granulated sugar

2 cups sifted all-purpose flour

2 teaspoons baking powder

½ teaspoon salt

¾ cup skim milk

1 teaspoon vanilla extract

3 egg whites, stiffly beaten

1. To make the topping, combine the brown sugar, cinnamon, nutmeg, and pecans in a small bowl and set aside.
2. Preheat the oven to 375°F. Cream the margarine in a large bowl, then slowly add the sugar, beating until light and fluffy.
3. Sift the flour, baking powder, and salt onto a sheet of wax paper. Add the flour mixture, ½ cup at a time, to the butter mixture, alternating with ¼ cup milk at a time; beat well after each addition. Beat in the vanilla extract, then fold in the egg whites.
4. Pour the batter into a greased 8- x 8- x 2-inch baking pan; sprinkle with the topping. Bake until a toothpick inserted in the center of the cake comes out clean—about 35 minutes. Let cool in the pan on a wire rack. Serve warm or at room temperature. Will keep 2 days covered with aluminum foil and refrigerated; 2 months at 0°F. Yield: 8 to 10 servings.

Low-sodium mustard

Tasty without added salt.

⅓ cup mustard seed

⅓ cup dry white wine

½ cup white vinegar

½ cup water

2 tablespoons honey

¼ teaspoon ground allspice

⅛ teaspoon each
ground cinnamon and ginger

1. Mix the mustard seed, white wine, and vinegar in a medium-size bowl and let stand 3 hours at room temperature. Transfer to a food processor or blender and add the water, honey, allspice, cinnamon, and ginger. Process until fairly smooth.

2. Place the mixture in the top of a double boiler over simmering water and cook, stirring occasionally, until thickened—10 to 12 minutes. Pour into a hot, clean canning jar and let cool to room temperature, then cover tightly. This low-sodium mustard will keep 1 year refrigerated. Yield: 2 cups. (See also *Mustard*, p.409.)

Makeup remover

An excellent way to moisturize skin.

½ cup melted paraffin
(about 1 bar)

1 cup mineral oil

½ cup water

2 tablespoons alum

Warm the paraffin in a small saucepan set over low heat, then stir in

the mineral oil. In a separate small saucepan, heat the water until simmering, then dissolve the alum in it. Let cool and add to the warm mineral oil and paraffin. As the mixture cools, the wax will rise to the top. Drain off the water and use the residue to remove makeup. Store in a covered jar. Yield: 2 cups.

Marble cleaner

A good nonabrasive cleaning agent.

¾ cup sodium sulfate

¼ cup sodium sulfite

Mix both ingredients in a small bowl. To use, sprinkle on marble and rub with a damp sponge, then wipe clean. Store in a tightly covered jar out of the reach of children. Yield: 2 cups.

Marshmallow cough syrup

The orange juice helps to keep the syrup from crystallizing. For a tangier syrup, substitute the juice of 1 lemon for the orange juice.

1½ to 2½ teaspoons
chopped dried
marshmallow root

2 cups water

2 cups sugar

¼ cup orange juice

In a small saucepan, stir the marshmallow root into the water; bring to a boil over moderately high heat. Reduce the heat to low and simmer 20 minutes. Strain the decoction into another saucepan (you should have about 1 cup). Over low heat, slowly stir in the sugar, so that a thick syrup forms. Simmer another 5 minutes, making sure the grains dissolve completely. If the mixture gets too thick, stir in a little more water. Let cool slightly, then gradually add the orange juice and mix. Transfer to a container with a lid; cover when cool. Yield: about 3 cups.

Wild cherry variation: Decoct 1 teaspoon wild cherry bark with the marshmallow root, omit the orange juice, and add a scant ½ teaspoon cream of tartar to the sugar.

Milk paint

Because milk paint is almost impossible to remove except with lye, you will have to repaint over it. Do not use on antiques.

1 pound hydrated lime

1 gallon skim milk

1 cup linseed oil

5 pounds whiting

In a large tub, mix the hydrated lime with some of the skim milk until it reaches the consistency of heavy cream. Gradually stir in the linseed oil, the remaining milk, and the whiting. Add powdered pigment for color, if desired. Will keep 2 to 3 days refrigerated. Yield: about 5 quarts.

Mock mayonnaise

Only 18 calories per tablespoon and no cholesterol in this creamy spread. For a little spice, add a tablespoon of ketchup or hot red pepper sauce.

2 cups cold water

2 tablespoons cornstarch

¼ cup olive oil

¼ cup white vinegar

¼ cup plain low-fat yogurt

*2 teaspoons
prepared yellow mustard*

*1 teaspoon
prepared horseradish*

1. Whisk together the water and cornstarch in a small saucepan. Set over moderate heat and cook, stirring continuously, until the mixture comes to a boil. Boil for 1 or 2 minutes or until the mixture is

clear. Transfer to a small bowl.

2. Whisk in the remaining ingredients in the order listed. Will keep 2 weeks tightly covered and refrigerated. Yield: about 2 cups.

Mock sour cream

Just 11 calories per tablespoon and no saturated fat. A delicious topping for fruit, soups, and vegetables, but do not use in cooking.

1 cup milk

*4 teaspoons
buttermilk powder (available
in health food stores)*

*½ teaspoon
unflavored gelatin*

½ cup plain low-fat yogurt

1. Combine the milk and buttermilk powder in a medium-size saucepan. Sprinkle the gelatin on top and let stand until the gelatin softens—about 5 minutes.

2. Set the pan over low heat and cook, uncovered, stirring occasionally, for 5 minutes or until the gelatin dissolves. Remove from the heat and whisk in the yogurt.

3. Transfer the mixture to a medium-size bowl, cover, and refrigerate for 1 hour or until thickened. Will keep 5 days tightly covered and refrigerated. Yield: 1½ cups.

Moisturizer

Softens skin and removes makeup.

1 tablespoon olive oil

1 tablespoon coconut oil

1 tablespoon vegetable oil

*2 tablespoons
mashed strawberries*

*1 or 2 drops
vitamin E oil (optional)*

Mix together the olive, coconut, and vegetable oils in a small bowl, then stir in the strawberries. If desired, add the vitamin E oil. Store in the refrigerator in a covered jar.

Mosquito repellent

Smells better than most commercial brands and doesn't leave a heavy, greasy feeling on your skin.

3 cups rubbing alcohol

*1½ cups
red cedar wood shavings*

½ cup eucalyptus leaves

Mix all the ingredients in a large jar or bowl. Cover and let stand 5 days. Strain the solid ingredients out and save the alcohol. Apply to skin to repel mosquitoes. Store tightly sealed. Yield: 2 cups.

Mouthwash

If mint is not to your liking, substitute other spices until you find the taste you like best.

2 cups water

*3 teaspoons
fresh or dried parsley*

2 teaspoons whole cloves

2 teaspoons ground cinnamon

*2 teaspoons
peppermint extract*

Boil the water in a small saucepan, then remove from the heat. Add the remaining ingredients and let steep. Strain. Will keep 2 weeks tightly covered and refrigerated.

Mushroom barley soup

For heartier soup, add sautéed mushrooms or leftover meat or chicken.

5 cups water

*1 recipe mushroom barley
soup mix (below)*

*1 can (14½ ounces) whole
peeled tomatoes with juice*

*1 small carrot, peeled, halved
lengthwise, and thinly sliced*

Bring the water to a boil over moderately high heat in a medium-size saucepan. Add the mix, tomatoes

(breaking them up with a spoon), and carrot. When the mixture returns to a boil, turn the heat to low and let simmer, covered, until the barley is tender—about 30 minutes. Remove from the heat and let sit, covered, at room temperature for 10 minutes. Remove the bay leaf and serve. Yield: 4 servings (1½ cups each).

Mushroom barley soup mix

Great to have on hand. Polish mushrooms can be found near the canned mushrooms in most supermarkets.

*2 containers (½ ounce each)
dried Polish mushrooms*

½ cup dried pearl barley

*2 tablespoons
dried minced onion*

*1 tablespoon
dried green pepper flakes*

1 teaspoon ground sage

*1 teaspoon dried
marjoram, crumbled*

1 small bay leaf

1 teaspoon salt

½ teaspoon garlic powder

¼ teaspoon black pepper

Rub the mushrooms with paper towels to remove any surface dirt, then break into small pieces, discarding any tough stems. Place in a plastic bag or small container, add the remaining ingredients, seal tightly, and shake to mix. Will keep 6 months in a tightly covered container at room temperature. Yield: 4 servings soup (1½ cups each).

Mustard

Hot and spicy. Good with cold meats or on sandwiches or hot dogs.

⅓ cup mustard seed

3 tablespoons dry mustard

½ cup cider vinegar

½ cup dark beer

2 cloves garlic, finely chopped

*¼ cup firmly packed
light brown sugar*

¾ teaspoon salt

½ teaspoon ground ginger

¼ teaspoon ground allspice

1. Mix the mustard seed, dry mustard, and vinegar in a small bowl. Cover with plastic wrap and let sit 3 hours at room temperature.
2. Place the remaining ingredients in a small saucepan, add the mustard mixture, and stir well. Bring to a boil over moderate heat, then reduce the heat to low and let simmer 5 minutes, stirring occasionally. Remove from the heat and transfer to a clean, hot preserving jar. Seal tightly and cool to room temperature. Will keep 1 month tightly covered and refrigerated. Yield: 1 cup.

Mustard plaster

A folk remedy for relieving chest congestion due to colds.

1 tablespoon dry mustard

*¼ cup flour (for adults) or 6
tablespoons flour (for children)*

Lukewarm water

1. Sift together the mustard and flour in a medium-size bowl. Slowly add just enough water to make a paste. Spread the plaster on a piece of muslin big enough to cover the chest area. Place another piece of muslin on top.
2. To use, make sure the skin is dry, then place the mustard plaster on the chest. Check frequently and, when the skin begins turning red, usually after 10 to 20 minutes, remove the plaster. (Do not use for more than 30 minutes at a time.) Rub the area with petroleum jelly to hold in the heat. Use the plaster twice a day until the congestion clears up.
Caution: Discontinue use immediately in case of allergic reaction.

Newspaper preservative

Clippings won't yellow so long as they're kept out of direct sunlight.

*2 quarts club soda,
at room temperature*

2 milk of magnesia tablets

Pour the club soda into a medium-size bowl and add the milk of magnesia tablets. Let them dissolve overnight, then pour ¼ inch of preservative into a baking pan. Lay the clippings out flat in the solution until saturated, then remove. Let dry on a flat surface. Yield: 2 quarts preserving solution.

No-fry chicken

Crusty, moist meat without all the mess and calories of deep fat. For a less spicy dish, omit the ginger and hot red pepper sauce.

¼ teaspoon dried oregano

¼ teaspoon ground ginger

½ teaspoon dried basil

1 clove garlic, minced

2 tablespoons all-purpose flour

½ teaspoon salt

2 whole skinless boneless chicken breasts (about 12 ounces each), separated into 4 halves

2 tablespoons milk

⅛ teaspoon hot red pepper sauce

1 cup bran flakes or corn flakes, coarsely crumbled

1. Preheat the oven to 350°F. Put the oregano, ginger, basil, garlic, flour, and salt into a paper bag and shake to mix. Place the chicken in the bag and shake until coated evenly with the mixture.
2. In a pie pan, combine the milk and pepper sauce. Place the cereal crumbs on a plate. Dip each breast in the milk mixture, then roll in the crumbs until coated all over.

3. Spray a cake rack with nonstick cooking spray or oil (below). Place the chicken on top and set the rack on a cookie sheet. Bake, uncovered, until the breasts are no longer pink on the inside—about 15 minutes. Serve hot or at room temperature. Yield: 4 servings.

Nonstick cooking oil

Cheaper than the commercial sprays.

¼ cup liquid lecithin

2 tablespoons vegetable oil

Mix the lecithin with the oil in a small jar and stir well. Brush the mixture on pans before heating. Do not use on any surface, such as pancake griddles or waffle irons, that must be preheated over high heat or the nonstick will burn. Will keep 6 months at room temperature in a tightly covered jar. Stir before using if necessary. Yield: ¼ cup.

Nose drops

Relieves stuffed nasal passages. If you don't have distilled water, let tap water stand overnight in a shallow pan to allow the chlorine to escape.

1 teaspoon salt

2 cups distilled water

Mix the salt with the water. Transfer to an atomizer and spray into your nose. Or place a tablespoon in the palm of your hand and inhale. Use alone or before using decongestant drops such as ephedrine.

Onion cough syrup

A soothing and aromatic remedy.

2 medium onions, thinly sliced

1 cup honey

½ cup warm water

1 jigger vodka (optional)

Juice of 1 lemon

Place the onions in a medium-size bowl. Pour the honey, water, and vodka (if desired) over them and let sit overnight in the refrigerator. Strain the liquid, discarding the onions, and transfer to a bottle; cover tightly. Will keep 1 week refrigerated. Take 2 teaspoons every 3 to 4 hours. Yield: 1½ cups.

Oven cleaner

Works well on outdoor barbecues too.

2 tablespoons liquid soap (p.406) or powdered detergent

2 teaspoons borax

1½ cups warm water

¼ cup household ammonia

Nonchlorine scouring powder

1. Pour the soap and borax into a 1-pint spray bottle. Shake and let stand until all the crystals dissolve so that they won't clog the sprayer.
2. To use, put old newspapers on the floor in front of the oven. Make sure your work area is well ventilated. Put on protective glasses and gloves, then spray the liquid onto the oven surface.

3. Let sit about 10 minutes. Then spread some scouring powder on an area and use a wet piece of fine steel wool to scrub. It may be necessary to use more cleaner, water, and scouring powder. For tough spots, rub with pumice or scrape with a razor blade; first test on an inconspicuous area for scratching. Wipe clean with water and sponges or paper towels and dry.
Caution: Before using, check the instruction manual for your oven to find out if it is safe to use a cleaner on it. Do not use on continuous-clean or self-cleaning ovens.

Pancakes

For variety, add ½ cup strawberries, blueberries, or sliced bananas to the batter, then proceed as directed.

2 cups biscuit mix (p.384)

2 large eggs, lightly beaten

1 cup water or milk

Place the biscuit mix in a large bowl and stir in the eggs and milk until just blended; do not overmix. (The batter should be slightly lumpy.) Heat a well-oiled griddle or large skillet over moderate heat until hot but not smoking. Spoon about ¼ cup batter per pancake onto the griddle and cook until bubbles form across the top—about 2 minutes. Turn the pancakes and cook 2 minutes longer. Serve immediately with butter and honey, maple syrup, or blueberry syrup (p.384). Yield: 10 to 12 pancakes.

Papier-mâché

A good way to make inexpensive birthday and holiday gifts.

1 cup flour

⅔ cup water

*Newspaper strips
(about 1½ inches wide)*

1. Mix the flour and water in a medium-size bowl. It should be the consistency of thick glue. If a thicker mixture is desired, add more flour.
2. Dip each strip separately in the paste and gently pull it through your fingers to remove any excess.

Then apply to a surface you want to cover (clay, cartons, bottles, or any disposable container makes a good base). Repeat until well covered.
3. When dry, decorate with poster paint. For a longer-lasting and harder surface, coat with shellac after the paint dries.

Paste

An all-purpose paste, excellent for papier-mâché projects.

1½ cups all-purpose flour

½ cup sugar

1 cup cold water

2 cups boiling water

1 tablespoon alum

1 teaspoon oil of cinnamon

Combine the flour and sugar in a large saucepan and slowly stir in the cold water. Add the boiling water gradually, then bring the mixture to a boil, stirring constantly. When the mixture is stiff, remove from the heat and stir in the alum and oil of cinnamon. Store in a tightly sealed container. Thin, if necessary, with boiling water.

Peach jam

Natural fruit juices are the primary sweetener in this low-sugar preserve. It's best made when peaches are in season and bursting with flavor.

2½ pounds ripe peaches or frozen dry-pack peaches

*3 strips orange peel,
½ x 2 inches each*

⅔ cup fresh orange juice

*⅔ cup unsweetened
white grape juice*

*⅔ cup firmly packed
light brown sugar*

1 tablespoon fresh lemon juice

¼ teaspoon ground ginger

1. If using fresh peaches, bring a large saucepan of water to a boil

over moderate heat. Drop the peaches in, 2 or 3 at a time, and boil for 30 seconds. Remove with a slotted spoon and rinse with cold water to cool. Peel off the skins, remove the pits, and coarsely chop. If using dry-pack peaches, thaw and chop them.

2. Transfer the peaches to a large saucepan, add the remaining ingredients, and set over moderate heat. Let the mixture boil slowly, stirring frequently, until it thickens and reaches 220°F on a candy thermometer—about 30 minutes.
3. Discard the orange rind and transfer the jam to hot, sterilized half-pint preserving jars. Cover and let cool to room temperature. Will keep 2 months refrigerated. Yield: 3 cups.

Peanut butter

Pure, delicious, and easy to make.

*2 cups salted
dry-roasted peanuts*

*1 tablespoon plus 1 teaspoon
vegetable oil*

1. For creamy peanut butter, process the peanuts with the oil in a food processor or blender until creamy, working in batches if necessary. Stop the machine occasionally and scrape down the sides.
2. To make chunky peanut butter, coarsely chop about ⅓ cup of the peanuts in a blender or food processor and set aside. Process the remaining peanuts with the oil until creamy, then stir in the coarsely chopped peanuts. Will keep for 1 month refrigerated in a covered jar. Yield: 1 cup.

Peanut butter bars

A protein-packed snack. For extra crunch, add the unsalted peanuts.

½ cup sugar

1 cup light corn syrup

*1 jar (12 ounces)
crunchy peanut butter*

4 cups toasted rice cereal

*1 cup coarsely chopped
unsalted peanuts (optional)*

In a very large saucepan over moderate heat, bring the sugar, syrup, and peanut butter to a boil, stirring constantly. (Watch carefully to make sure the mixture does not burn on the bottom of the pan.) Remove from the heat and mix in the remaining ingredients. Press into a well-greased 13- x 9- x 2-inch baking pan and let cool to room temperature. Cut into 1- x 2-inch bars and serve. Store in tightly covered container. Will keep 1 week at room temperature, 2 weeks refrigerated, and up to 3 months at 0°F in freezer containers. Yield: 54 bars (1 x 2 inches each).

Peppermint lotion

Relieves itching. Oil of eucalyptus or oil of cade can be substituted for the peppermint oil.

½ cup water

½ cup rubbing alcohol

3 to 4 drops peppermint oil

Pour the water and alcohol into a bottle, then add the oil. Cap tightly and shake well. Apply with a clean cloth. Test your skin's sensitivity before using; dab a little on the inside of your wrist and wait a few hours to see if it causes a reaction. If not, use as needed.

Peppermint tea

Ease a stuffy nose or stimulate a sluggish digestive system.

⅓ cup dried peppermint

1 cup water

*1 tablespoon grated
lemon and orange rind*

*2 teaspoons
crème de menthe liqueur*

1 teaspoon honey

Put the peppermint leaves in the water and bring to a boil in a small saucepan; remove pan from the heat and let the tea steep for 10 minutes. Strain the liquid and add more hot water, if needed, to make 1 cup. Add the grated lemon rind, grated orange rind, crème de menthe, and honey. Make the tea fresh every time.

Perfume

A nice spicy scent at a bargain price.

½ cup rubbing alcohol

¼ cup whole cloves

1 teaspoon orrisroot

Mix the alcohol and cloves in a small jar; add the orrisroot. Cap the jar and shake; let sit for 2 days, stirring occasionally. Strain the liquid, discarding the solids, and transfer it to a jar; cover tightly. To use, dab on behind your ears or on wrists. Store out of the reach of small children.

Pesto

An easy-to-prepare sauce that is great on pasta or potatoes. Or mix it with mayonnaise to make a dip for raw vegetables. It freezes well too.

*2 cups loosely packed fresh
basil leaves, washed and
patted dry with paper towels*

½ cup olive oil

2 cloves garlic, minced

*3 tablespoons pine nuts
(pignoli) or chopped almonds*

½ teaspoon salt

*½ cup
grated Parmesan cheese*

Put all the ingredients except the cheese in a blender or a food processor and purée until smooth; if using a blender, stop frequently and push the mixture down with a rubber spatula. Stir in the cheese (the mixture will be very thick). Stir in 2 or 3 tablespoons water and serve. Will keep 1 week refrigerated or 6 months at 0°F in freezer containers with ½ inch of space at the top. Yield: about 1 cup or enough for 1 pound of pasta.

Parsley variation: For a lighter sauce, omit the pine nuts and substitute 1 cup fresh Italian parsley for 1 cup of the basil.

Pine potpourri

Bring the scent of the forest indoors.

½ cup bayberry leaves

*½ cup
snipped balsam needles*

½ cup miniature pine cones

½ cup rose hips

2 teaspoons orrisroot

2 drops pine-scented fixative

Mix the bayberry, balsam, pine cones, and rose hips in a large bowl. Add the orrisroot and fixative and stir well. Transfer to a decorative container.

Pizza

A quick low-calorie, low-fat version of the old favorite. For variety, top with sautéed mushrooms, cooked crumbled sausage, or steamed spinach.

DOUGH

½ cup all-purpose flour
or ¼ cup all-purpose flour and
¼ cup whole wheat flour

⅛ teaspoon salt

1½ teaspoons baking powder

3 to 4 tablespoons water

TOPPING

⅓ cup low-salt marinara sauce

¼ cup shredded skim-milk mozzarella cheese

½ large green pepper, seeded and sliced

1 tablespoon chopped basil (optional)

1. Combine the flour, salt, and baking powder in a small bowl. Add the water and stir with a fork until the dough comes together, adding a few teaspoons more water if necessary. Knead the dough until smooth—about 2 minutes. Shape it into a ball, cover with a towel, and let rest 5 minutes.
2. Roll the dough into a 10-inch circle, using flour as needed to prevent it from sticking.

3. Preheat the broiler. Brush a medium-size nonstick skillet lightly with vegetable oil and set over moderate heat until very hot—about 1 minute. Add the dough and cook until the underside is dry and flecked with brown spots—2 to 3 minutes. (The dough will puff up in spots, but the sauce will cover them up.)
4. Transfer to an ungreased cookie sheet and spread the sauce evenly over the crust. Sprinkle with the cheese and top with the green pepper rings.
5. Broil 4 inches from the heat until the sauce is bubbling and the cheese has melted—2 to 3 minutes. Before serving, sprinkle with the basil if desired. Serve immediately. Yield: 4 slices.

Play clay

A good modeling dough for children. It can also be used to make Christmas tree decorations.

½ cup table salt
(do not use rock or sea salt)

½ cup hot water

½ cup cold water

½ cup cornstarch

2 drops food coloring
(optional)

1. Mix the salt and hot water in a large saucepan and bring to a boil over high heat.
2. Place the cold water in a small bowl and stir in the cornstarch; mix well. Add the food coloring if desired.
3. Add the cornstarch mixture to the boiling salt water and stir vigorously to keep it from lumping up. Cook over low heat, stirring constantly, until the mixture is stiff.
4. Remove from the heat and, using a large spoon, carefully turn the mixture onto a bread board. Let cool, then knead until smooth. Use immediately or wrap in plastic wrap and store in an airtight container. If desired, clay models can be preserved by air-drying at room temperature for 3 days or by baking for 2 hours at 200°F.
5. To make Christmas tree decorations, roll out the dough ¼ inch thick, then use cookie cutters to make a variety of shapes. Using a toothpick, make a hole at the top of each one where a string or wire can be inserted. Bake at 200°F for 2 hours. Decorate as desired.

Pomander

Gives a fresh fruity scent to closets and drawers.

6 ounces whole cloves

1 apple, lemon, lime, or orange

2 tablespoons orrisroot

2 tablespoons ground cinnamon

Push the cloves into the fruit you've chosen, placing them so close together that none of the skin is exposed. In a medium-size bowl, mix the orrisroot and cinnamon; roll the clove-studded fruit in this mixture until it is completely coated. Wrap in cheesecloth or netting. Hang in the closet or wrap in tissue paper and put in a drawer.

Porcelain cleaner

Use to remove heavy-duty stains from figurines and dishes.

2 bars (6½ ounces each) naphtha soap

4 gallons hot water

1 cup mineral spirits

Cut the soap into shavings with a knife. Place the water, soap and mineral spirits in a large bowl and stir until the soap dissolves. Using a brush, spread the cleaner on the stains; rinse off.

Potato sausage

A delicious way to stretch meat and much less fatty than most sausage.

*1½ pounds all-purpose
potatoes, peeled and sliced*

*2 large yellow onions,
finely chopped (2 cups)*

*2 medium-size tart apples
(such as Granny Smith),
peeled, cored, and
finely chopped*

3 cloves garlic, finely chopped

2 tablespoons olive oil

1 pound ground veal

1 pound ground pork

*1½ tablespoons
prepared mustard*

4 teaspoons salt

1½ teaspoons black pepper

1½ teaspoons ground sage

1 teaspoon ground allspice

¼ teaspoon ground nutmeg

1½ tablespoons vegetable oil

1. Bring a large saucepan of salted water to a boil over moderate heat and cook the potatoes until tender—about 20 minutes. Let cool, then mash the potatoes until smooth; set aside.

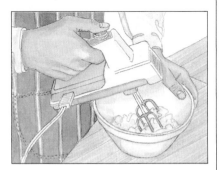

2. In a large skillet, heat the olive oil over moderate heat, then add the onions, apple, and garlic. Cook, stirring occasionally, until soft—15 to 20 minutes.
3. Combine the remaining ingredients except the vegetable oil in a large mixing bowl. Add the mashed potatoes and the onion mixture; mix well. Using a pastry bag, stuff the mixture into casings to form link sausages. Or add 3 eggs to the mixture and form into 2- x 3-inch patties.
4. To cook, warm the vegetable oil in a large skillet over moderate heat. Add the sausage and cook until lightly browned and cooked through—about 15 minutes for link sausage, 4 minutes on each side for the patties. Add more oil if necessary. Will keep 3 months at 0°F (thaw before cooking). Yield: 4 pounds.

Potpourri

Bring the wonderful aroma of garden flowers inside your home.

10 marigold blossoms

6 geranium leaves

5 rose blossoms

2 teaspoons dried lavender

2 teaspoons orrisroot

2 drops rose fixative

Combine all the ingredients in a medium-size bowl. Then set out in bathrooms, living room, or bedrooms for a sweet flowery scent.

Potting soil

Use to plant or repot houseplants.

*10⅔ quarts
sterilized garden soil*

10⅔ quarts peat moss

10⅔ quarts perlite

*½ cup dolomitic limestone or
1½ cups crushed eggshells*

3 tablespoons superphosphate

*1 tablespoon
10-10-10 fertilizer*

Sift all the ingredients through a sieve made from ¼-inch hardware cloth to eliminate pebbles and twigs. Store in a covered container. (See also *African violet soil*, p.382; *Soilless potting mix*, p.419.)

Poultice

Fades bruises and relieves the pain and inflammation.

1 ounce comfrey root

*1 ounce
dried wintergreen leaves*

1 quart water

1. In a medium-size saucepan, combine the herbs and water and bring to a boil over high heat. Reduce the heat to low and simmer 5 minutes. Drain off the water, reserving the herbs.
2. Dampen a 12-inch-square towel in warm water and place the herbs in the center. Fold the towel over the herbs and place the poultice on the bruise. Leave on until the herbs have cooled. Reheat and use once a day until symptoms subside.

Pretzels

These soft pretzels are a delicious change from the packaged variety. Serve as a snack or with soup.

1¼ cups warm water

4 teaspoons sugar

1 envelope active dry yeast

1 teaspoon salt

¾ cup gluten or bread flour

2½ cups all-purpose flour

*1 quart water, at
room temperature*

3 tablespoons baking soda

*1 tablespoon coarse salt or
1 teaspoon table salt*

1. In a small bowl, combine ½ cup of the warm water with 1 teaspoon of the sugar and the yeast. Let sit until bubbly—about 10 minutes.
2. Put the remaining ¾ cup warm water in the bowl of an electric mixer or food processor along with the salt, gluten flour, and 1 cup of the all-purpose flour. Beat on medium-low speed until well blended—about 1 minute. Add the yeast mix-

ture and beat 4 to 5 minutes longer. Then stir in the remaining flour.

3. On a floured surface, knead the dough until very smooth—about 5 minutes. Add more flour if the dough is too sticky. Form into a ball, place in an ungreased bowl, and cover with a dish towel. Let the dough rise until doubled in bulk—45 minutes to 1 hour.

4. Preheat the oven to 425°F. Punch the dough down, cut into 12 equal pieces, and cover with a dish towel. Roll each piece, stretching it as you do so, into a rope about 20 inches long. Twist each rope into a pretzel shape, then lay on a lightly floured surface. Cover them all and let rise until not quite doubled—about 20 minutes.

5. In a medium-size enameled or stainless-steel skillet, combine the remaining 1 quart water, the baking soda, and the remaining 3 teaspoons sugar. Bring to a simmer over moderately low heat. Place 3 pretzels in the water and cook for 20 seconds on each side, flipping them gently with a large slotted spoon. As you remove each pretzel, let it drain over the pan for a few seconds, then place on a dish towel. Repeat until all the pretzels have been cooked and drained, then transfer them, top side up, onto baking sheets coated with nonstick cooking spray and sprinkle with the salt.

6. Bake in the center of the oven until nicely browned—about 15 minutes. Serve warm or at room temperature. Yield: 12 pretzels.

Pudding

For vanilla, add a few grains of nutmeg along with the milk. For chocolate, add 3 tablespoons cocoa to the pudding mix and proceed as directed.

1 cup pudding mix (below)

1 cup milk

1 cup water

2 teaspoons vanilla extract

1 egg, lightly beaten

1 tablespoon butter or margarine, cut into small pieces

1. Place the pudding mix in a medium-size heavy saucepan and gradually whisk in the milk and water. Cook, stirring constantly, over moderate heat until the mixture thickens—3 to 5 minutes. Cook, still stirring, 1½ minutes more.

2. Remove from the heat. In a small bowl, stir the vanilla into the egg. Whisk in about ½ cup of the hot mixture, stir, then whisk in another ½ cup. Pour the egg mixture into the saucepan and whisk until combined. Whisk in the butter.

3. Strain the pudding into a bowl, cool a few minutes, then spoon into dessert dishes. Cover with plastic wrap and refrigerate for several hours before serving. Will keep 2 days refrigerated. Yield: 4 servings.

Pudding mix

Better tasting than store-bought and takes only minutes to make. Keep it on hand for emergencies.

3 cups instant nonfat dry milk

1½ cups sugar

1½ cups cornstarch, measured without packing

1½ teaspoons salt

Using a whisk, combine all the ingredients in a large bowl. Store in a closed container or canister. Will keep 3 months refrigerated. Yield: 6 cups or 24 servings.

Puffed pancake

Impressive looking and easy.

2 large eggs

½ cup sifted all-purpose flour

½ cup milk

¼ teaspoon ground nutmeg

½ teaspoon salt

¼ cup butter or margarine, melted

1 tablespoon confectioners sugar (optional)

½ teaspoon ground cinnamon (optional)

Preheat the oven to 400°F. Lightly beat the eggs in a medium-size bowl, then beat in the flour, milk, nutmeg, and salt until just blended. Do not overbeat. Cover the bottom of a 13- x 9- x 2-inch baking dish with the melted butter, then pour in the batter. Place in the center of the oven and bake until puffed and golden brown—about 20 minutes. If desired, mix the sugar and cinnamon together and sprinkle over the pancake just before serving. Cut into 2 or 4 equal pieces and serve with honey or syrup and a small pitcher of melted butter if desired. Yield: 2 servings.

Raspberry liqueur

Intensely flavored, with a rich, red hue—delicious over ices or ice cream.

¾ cup sugar

½ cup water

2 cups fresh raspberries or 1 package (12 ounces) frozen dry-pack berries

3 strips lemon peel, ½ x 2 inches each

½ vanilla bean, split

1 teaspoon lemon juice

1½ cups vodka

1. Combine the sugar and water in a medium-size heavy saucepan.

415

Add the raspberries, lemon peel, and vanilla bean, and cook over low heat until the sugar dissolves.

2. Raise the heat to medium-low and boil 3 minutes, then cover. Let sit 30 minutes. Strain through a cheesecloth-lined sieve (you should get about 1½ cups liquid). Discard the lemon peel and vanilla bean.

3. Stir in the lemon juice and vodka, pour into a bottle or other container, and cover tightly; let cool. The liqueur may be served immediately. Will keep 1 month refrigerated. Serve chilled or at room temperature. Yield: 3 cups.

Refrigerator deodorizers

Work better and quicker than plain baking soda. Buy regular charcoal briquettes and use a hammer or brick to crush them into small chunks.

½ cup crushed charcoal

½ cup baking soda

*2 tablespoons
powdered orange or
lemon peel*

*1 tablespoon
ground cloves or cinnamon*

*2 tablespoons
vanilla extract*

*Old, clean nylon stockings, cut
into 2-inch squares*

*½ yard porous fabric (terry
cloth, loose-weave cotton,
muslin, or toweling), cut into
2-inch squares*

*String or ribbon, cut into 8-inch
lengths for tying and hanging*

1. Combine the charcoal, baking soda, citrus peel, and cloves in a medium-size glass or enamel bowl. Sprinkle in the vanilla, stir to mix, and let sit 1 hour.

2. Put 2 tablespoons of the mixture in the center of a nylon stocking square and put this packet in the center of a square of bright fabric. Tie the corners together with the string or ribbon.

3. To use, tie a packet in an inconspicuous spot in the refrigerator or freezer. Or tie onto a shelf inside the door. For longer life, sprinkle with a few drops of vanilla and add 1 teaspoon baking soda after 10 or 12 weeks. Yield: 5 to 7 packets.

Rejuvenating skin cream

For smooth, fresher-looking skin.

*2 capsules (400 IU's each)
vitamin E*

1 tablespoon honey

1 tablespoon coconut oil

1 tablespoon rose water

1 tablespoon olive oil

Remove the vitamin E from the capsules and place with the remaining ingredients in a small bowl; mix well. To use, apply to the skin with cotton balls. Store tightly covered in the refrigerator.

Rose petal lotion

Use this sweet-smelling rinse to remove any traces of soap after washing your face.

*1 tablespoon
dried rosemary or
2 tablespoons fresh rosemary*

*2 tablespoons
dried chamomile flowers*

4 cups water

*2 tablespoons
dried or fresh rose petals*

Combine all the ingredients in a small glass or enameled pan and boil, uncovered, over moderate

heat for 10 minutes. Let cool to room temperature. Strain the liquid, discarding the herbs, and transfer to a bottle with a lid. To use, dab on with cotton balls or transfer to a spray bottle and spritz on the skin. Rinse off. Will keep 2 months tightly covered and refrigerated.

Rose water

Softens dry skin and leaves it smelling sweet and fresh. Use after bathing.

3 tablespoons rose soluble

*2 cups water (use
distilled if your water is hard)*

2 tablespoons glycerin

Place all the ingredients in a small bowl and mix well. Transfer the mixture to a capped or spray bottle (sprayer is best for overall coverage). To use, splash or spray on after showering. Store, tightly covered, in the refrigerator.

Rum balls

A tasty sweet you can make without using the oven. A nice gift.

*1¾ cups
fine vanilla wafer crumbs*

1 cup pecans, finely ground

*1 cup unsifted
confectioners sugar*

¼ cup cocoa

3 tablespoons light corn syrup

*¼ cup light or dark
rum or bourbon*

*⅓ cup
sifted confectioners sugar*

Put all the ingredients except the sifted confectioners sugar in a medium-size bowl and mix well, using your hands if necessary. Roll the mixture into 1-inch balls, then dredge in the sifted sugar. The rum balls will keep 10 days in airtight containers at room temperature. Yield: about 3½ dozen.

Sachet

Tuck in drawers to give your clothes a fresh scent.

10 bay leaves, crumbled

2 tablespoons each dried sage, oregano, basil, thyme, and lavender flowers, crumbled

3 tablespoons dried rosemary, crumbled

¼ cup orrisroot

Combine all the ingredients in a medium-size bowl. Then place 3 tablespoons of the mixture on a 4- x 4-inch piece of cheesecloth. Tie the corners together with a ribbon.

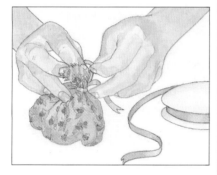

Saddle soap

Softens leather while removing dirt.

7 cups water

1½ cups soap flakes (not detergent)

1 cup melted paraffin or beeswax

½ cup neat's-foot oil

1. Bring the water to a boil in a large saucepan, then reduce to a simmer and gradually stir in the soap flakes.
2. In the top of a double boiler, heat the wax with the neat's-foot oil and stir to combine. Remove from the heat and add to the soap solution. Stir until thick.
3. Transfer to small containers (old shoe polish tins are ideal). Apply to leather with a wet sponge, then buff

until dry with a clean soft cloth.
Caution: Neat's-foot oil and paraffin are both flammable; use with care. Also, the neat's-foot oil might darken some types of leather or make them less receptive to regular shoe polish.

Salt substitute

Adds flavor without adding sodium. Use in place of table salt. Sour salt and powdered citrus peel can be found at most supermarkets.

4½ teaspoons cream of tartar

1 tablespoon each garlic powder, powdered orange peel, arrowroot, and sugar

2 tablespoons each black pepper, celery seed, and onion powder

1½ teaspoons sour salt (powdered citric acid)

1 teaspoon each white pepper, dill weed, and dried thyme, crumbled

½ teaspoon plus a pinch powdered lemon peel

½ teaspoon cayenne pepper

Put all the ingredients in a small electric spice grinder, coffee grinder, or blender. Grind 10 seconds or until the mixture is fine. With a funnel, transfer the salt substitute to a glass saltshaker. Store the excess in a tightly covered container and keep in a cool, dark, dry place. Yield: about 1 cup.

Sausage

Hot and spicy taste with less fat than most commercial sausages and none of the preservatives. For a milder sausage, eliminate the pepper flakes.

1 teaspoon salt

½ teaspoon red pepper flakes, crumbled

¼ teaspoon black pepper

1 teaspoon dried sage, crumbled

½ teaspoon each dried marjoram and summer savory, crumbled

½ teaspoon ground coriander

1 pound ground pork (not too lean)

1. Mix all the herbs and spices in a small bowl. Place the pork in a large bowl, sprinkle the mixture over it, and combine.
2. Shape into a cylinder about 8 inches long. Cover with plastic wrap, then aluminum foil. Refrigerate for several hours to allow the seasonings to blend.
3. Cut the sausage into ½-inch slices, place in an ungreased skillet, and sauté over moderate heat until cooked through and lightly browned—about 10 minutes on each side. Will keep 3 days tightly wrapped in aluminum foil and refrigerated; 2 months at 0°F.

Scouring powder

Cleans kitchen utensils, sinks, pots, and pans—but don't use on items that have a high polish.

¼ cup powdered soap

1 tablespoon powdered borax

1 tablespoon soda ash

7 tablespoons fine pumice

Place all the ingredients in a medium-size bowl and mix well. Strain through a fine (100 mesh) sieve. To use, wet the surface to be cleaned with warm water, sprinkle on the powder, and wash with a wet cloth. Rinse with clear water.

Scratch remover

For use on metal or glass surfaces.

¼ cup glycerin

¼ cup jewelers rouge

¼ cup water

Mix all the ingredients in a medium-size glass or plastic jar until they form a smooth paste. To use, apply to the scratched areas with a clean cloth and rub in. Rinse with clear water. To fill in deeper scratches, repeat the process several times. Store in a tightly covered jar.

Seed-starting soil

A potting mix that's free of soil-borne diseases. Make it in the summer so that it can be sun-dried.

16 quarts garden soil

8 quarts peat moss

8 quarts builders sand

1 tablespoon dolomitic limestone or 3 tablespoons crushed eggshells

3 tablespoons superphosphate

Blend the soil, peat moss, and sand, then pass through a ¼-inch hardware cloth sieve. Add the limestone and superphosphate. To use, pour the mixture into nursery-type black plastic containers. Water until the soil is saturated, then seal in a clear plastic bag and set in a sunny spot for several weeks. If sealed

tightly when stored in the toolshed or garage, the bags of soil should remain disease-free until the following spring.

Self-buffing floor polish

Dries to a shine without polishing and isn't as slippery as wax. For use on resilient floor coverings.

1 quart denatured alcohol

¼ cup gum arabic

¼ cup turpentine

1 cup orange shellac

Place all the ingredients in a bucket and stir until the gum arabic dissolves. To use, wash the floor, then apply with a cloth, sponge, or mop. Let dry for ½ hour. After 2 or 3 applications, strip off with hot water and detergent. Store in a tightly covered jar. Yield: about 5 cups.

Shampoo enhancer

For normal and dry hair. The egg conditions; the lemon juice shines.

1 egg

1 teaspoon lemon juice or cider vinegar

3 tablespoons mild, unscented shampoo

Mix the ingredients in a small bowl. Then shampoo into hair and rinse well with warm water. Store tightly covered in a dry place.

Shellac

It's best to make your own because commercial brands have only a 6-week shelf life and may have deteriorated by the time you buy them.

¾ cup shellac flakes

1 cup ethyl alcohol or denatured alcohol

Place the shellac flakes in a 1-pint jar, then pour in the alcohol. Cover

and let stand 8 hours or overnight, shaking every few hours, until all the flakes have dissolved. Stir well, then apply with a brush. To apply with a rag or spray gun, the mixture will have to be thinned. Add more alcohol until the desired consistency is reached. The shellac will keep 6 weeks stored in a tightly covered container.
Caution: Keep out of the reach of children.

Shrub fertilizer

For acid-loving plants like azaleas, rhododendrons, camellias, and hollies, substitute granite dust for the wood ash.

4 cups coffee grounds

1 cup bonemeal

1 cup wood ash

Place all the ingredients in a bucket and mix well. To use, scatter evenly over the ground shaded by the plant, using 1 pound of fertilizer for each 1 foot of the diameter—a shrub that shades an area 3 feet in diameter should get 3 pounds of fertilizer. (See also *Lawn fertilizer*, p.405; *Lawn fertilizer for fall*, p.406.)

Silver polish

A good all-purpose mix that contains an abrasive for cleaning and a cushioning agent to reduce scratching.

1 cup soap flakes

1 cup whiting

1 tablespoon household ammonia

2 cups boiling water

Combine the soap flakes, whiting, and ammonia in a small glass or enameled pan. Add the boiling water and stir until all the solid particles have dissolved. Let the mixture cool, then transfer to a clean quart glass jar. Label, screw on a tight-fitting lid, and store out of the reach of children. To use, shake well. Wash the silver with soap and warm water, then apply the polish with a soft cloth or sponge. Rub the silver gently, rinse with warm water, and wipe dry.

Skin cleaner

Clears out oil-clogged facial pores.

1 teaspoon milk

1 teaspoon honey

*1 tablespoon
ground almonds*

Combine all the ingredients in a small bowl. Using your hands or a washcloth, apply the mixture to your face and scrub lightly for a minute or two. Rinse. Mix fresh every time. Discontinue use if there is any allergic reaction.

Snow and ice melt

Use on driveways and sidewalks.

4 cups rock salt

4 cups magnesium sulfate

*2 tablespoons
ammonium sulfate*

Mix all the ingredients in a large bucket. To use, sprinkle ½ cup over every 6 square feet of pavement. Store in a tightly covered canister or jar out of the reach of children. Yield: 8 cups.

Soap bubbles

An inexpensive, safe, and fun diversion for children.

½ cup dishwashing detergent

1 cup water

2 drops food coloring

Mix all the ingredients together in a jar and cover. Use a bubble pipe or a store-bought or homemade bubble wand. Store at room temperature in a tightly covered jar. Yield: 1½ cups.

Soda pop

A natural carbonated beverage filled with vitamins and free of refined sugar.

*¼ cup frozen orange, grape,
or apple juice concentrate*

¾ cup club soda

Ice cubes

Pour the frozen juice concentrate into a 12-ounce glass. Add a few tablespoons of the club soda and stir until dissolved. Fill the glass with ice cubes, add the remaining club soda, and mix well. Serve immediately. Yield: 1 serving.

Soilless potting mix

Better for houseplants than garden soil because it's free of soil-borne insects and weed seed.

16 quarts peat moss

16 quarts perlite

*½ cup dolomitic limestone or
1½ cups crushed eggshells*

*1 tablespoon superphosphate
or 2 tablespoons bonemeal*

½ cup 5-10-5 fertilizer

Strain the peat moss and perlite through a sieve into a large bucket. Add the limestone, superphosphate, and fertilizer and mix well. Yield: 1 bushel.

Stainless steel cleaner

Stronger than soap and water. Gives a nice shine to dull flatware.

½ cup soap flakes

¼ cup whiting

*2 tablespoons
household ammonia*

2 tablespoons water

Combine all the ingredients in a medium-size bowl. Transfer to a jar and cap tightly. Label and store out of children's reach. To use, spread

the cleaner on the stainless steel with a clean soft cloth and rub. Then rinse with clear water and buff to dry. Yield: 8 ounces.

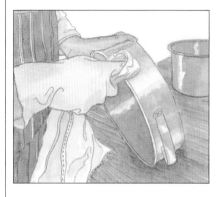

Starch

Cheap and quick. Use 1 tablespoon cornstarch for a light starch; up to 3 tablespoons for a heavier finish.

1 to 3 tablespoons cornstarch

2 cups cold water

Mix the cornstarch and water in a 1-pint spray bottle that gives a fine spray mist. Store out of the reach of children. To use, shake well, spray the area to be starched, then iron immediately.

Strawberry preserves

Not as sweet as commercial brands. For the best flavor, choose firm, ripe strawberries.

½ cup sugar

½ cup fresh orange juice

*2 pounds strawberries,
washed and hulled*

*2 large sweet apples (such as
Cortland or Golden Delicious),
peeled, cored, and
coarsely chopped*

1. Combine the sugar and orange juice in a large glass or enamel bowl. Add the strawberries and toss to coat. Let sit ½ hour at room temperature.

2. Transfer the mixture to a large

nonaluminum saucepan, add the apples, and set over moderately high heat. Cook, uncovered, for 45 minutes or until thick and glossy—220°F on a candy thermometer.

3. Pour the preserves into hot, sterilized preserving jars. Cover, let cool to room temperature, then refrigerate. The strawberry preserves will keep 2 months refrigerated. Yield: 2¾ cups.

Sunburn soother

Takes the bite out of a mild burn.

4 tea bags

2 cups fresh mint leaves
or 1 cup dried mint

4 cups water

Place all the ingredients in a medium-size saucepan and bring to a boil over high heat. Reduce the heat to low and simmer for 5 minutes. Remove from the heat and let steep 15 minutes. To use, strain the liquid into a jar, discarding the tea and mint, and let cool. Dab the mixture on sunburned areas with cotton balls or a washcloth. Or pour the liquid into warm bath water; then remove the tea from the bags and tie it, along with the mint, in a piece of cheesecloth and drop into the bath. Soak in the mixture for 10 to 15 minutes. Repeat as necessary.

Caution: For a second or third degree burn, consult your physician.

Tile and grout cleaner

Eliminate the grimy soap film that forms on and between bathroom tiles.

½ cup baking soda

⅓ cup household ammonia

¼ cup white vinegar

7 cups warm water

Combine the ingredients in a 1-gallon plastic jug, cover, and swish to mix. Label the container and store it out of the reach of children. For small jobs, fill a pump-type container with the solution; spray directly onto the tile surface, then wipe with a damp sponge or cloth. Yield: 2 quarts.

Caution: Do not mix this cleaner with anything containing bleach.

Toilet bowl cleaner

Use regularly to keep your appliance sparkling clean.

1 tablespoon
household ammonia

1 cup hydrogen peroxide

2 quarts water

Mix the ingredients in a bucket, then pour the solution slowly into the toilet. Let stand for 30 minutes, then scrub the inside of the bowl and flush. For stubborn stains, allow the solution to remain in the bowl for several hours. Yield: 2 quarts.

Toothpaste

Leaves a fresh taste in your mouth.

¼ cup each arrowroot,
powdered orrisroot, and water

½ teaspoon each
oil of cinnamon and
oil of cloves

1 teaspoon ground sage

Mix all the ingredients in a small bowl. If the paste is too thick, add

more water until the desired consistency is reached. Use as needed. Store at room temperature in a tightly covered jar. Yield: ½ cup.

Vegetable dip

Superfast and supergood, with a tangy Oriental flavor.

1 cup mayonnaise

¼ teaspoon
Oriental sesame oil

1 teaspoon soy sauce

1 clove garlic, minced

Mix all the ingredients in a small bowl, then transfer to a serving dish. Serve with a plate of cut-up raw vegetables, such as carrots, celery, and zucchini. Yield: 1 cup.

Vegetable fertilizer

Makes garden flowers flourish as well.

1 part dried poultry manure
or 5 parts dried horse manure

1 part bonemeal

1 part wood ash

Mix all the ingredients together. Broadcast over the garden soil at a rate of 5 pounds per 100 square feet or 1 to 2 pounds per 25 feet of row.

Vinyl upholstery cleaner

Never apply leather cleaner to vinyl upholstery; use this gentle solution instead.

¼ cup powdered laundry
detergent

½ cup baking soda

2 cups warm water

Mix the detergent and baking soda together and add to the water. To use, moisten a rough-textured cloth with the solution and rub the vinyl surface with it, concentrating on the arms, seat, and headrest; rinse well and wipe dry. Yield: 2½ cups.

Waffles

You can make these in minutes.

2 large eggs, separated

1¾ cups biscuit mix (p.384)

1 cup water or milk

*3 tablespoons
butter or margarine, melted*

1. Preheat a waffle iron. In a large mixing bowl, lightly beat the egg yolks. Add the biscuit mix, water, and butter and stir just enough to moisten. In a medium-size bowl, beat the egg whites until stiff peaks form. Gently fold into the batter until just blended.
2. Cook according to the waffle iron manufacturer's directions. Serve with butter and syrup if desired. Yield: 5 waffles (8 x 4 inches each).

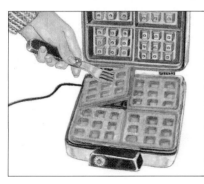

Walnut butter

Serve on crackers or in sandwiches; particularly good with apple butter.

2 cups walnuts

1 teaspoon vegetable oil

½ teaspoon salt

Preheat the oven to 300°F. Spread the walnuts on an ungreased cookie sheet and bake, uncovered, until lightly browned—about 20 minutes; let cool. If a chunky butter is desired, coarsely chop ¼ cup of the nuts and set aside. Transfer the remaining nuts to a blender or food processor. Add the oil and salt and process until creamy, working in batches if necessary, then add the chopped nuts if desired. Will keep 1 month tightly covered and refrigerated. Yield: 1 cup.

Walnut sauce

A superb topping for ice cream.

¾ cup light corn syrup

*½ cup maple
or maple-flavored syrup*

¼ cup water

¼ cup sugar

*1¼ cups
coarsely chopped walnuts*

Place the corn syrup, maple syrup, water, and sugar in a small heavy saucepan and bring to a boil over moderately high heat, stirring constantly. Add the walnuts, turn the heat to low, and simmer, partially covered, 30 minutes. Do not stir. Let cool, then pour into a clean 1-pint jar. Will keep 4 months tightly covered and refrigerated. Yield: 1 pint.

Watercolors

A good make-do substitute for the commercial product.

*1 tablespoon
white or cider vinegar*

2 tablespoons baking soda

1 tablespoon cornstarch

½ teaspoon glycerin

2 drops food coloring

1 teaspoon water

Mix the vinegar and baking soda together in a small bowl; add the cornstarch and glycerin when the soda stops foaming. Stir in the food coloring and add the water if the solution seems too stiff. Store in a tightly covered jar. Yield: ¼ cup.

Wax finish for raw wood

Meant for raw wood, such as exposed beams—not for use over a finish.

1 cup turpentine

1 cup melted beeswax

1 cup boiled linseed oil

Warm the turpentine in the top of a double boiler; stir in the beeswax until it dissolves, then add the oil. Remove from the heat and brush the warm mixture on raw wood. Allow to dry and buff with a clean soft cloth.

Caution: Because this recipe uses flammable materials, take care to see that the mixture does not overheat or spill on a hot surface.

Wax for finished wood

A highly durable finish that repels water and minimizes scratching.

1 cup turpentine

*8 ounces
carnauba wax shavings*

*8 ounces
paraffin shavings*

Warm the turpentine in the top of a double boiler; add the carnauba and paraffin shavings and stir until melted. Remove from the heat, pour into a container, and allow to cool. If the wax becomes too hard to use, soften it in a double boiler and add more turpentine.
Caution: Because this recipe uses flammable materials, take care to see that the mixture does not overheat or spill on a hot surface.

Wheatless brownies

Chocolate treats that are both wheat-and milk-free.

⅓ cup margarine,
at room temperature

1 cup firmly packed
light brown sugar

2 eggs, lightly beaten

2 squares (1 ounce each)
semisweet chocolate, melted

1 teaspoon vanilla extract

⅔ cup unsifted rice flour

½ teaspoon baking powder

¼ teaspoon salt

½ cup coarsely chopped
pecans or walnuts

1. Preheat the oven to 350°F. Cream the margarine and sugar in a large bowl. Add all the remaining ingredients except the nuts and stir until smooth. Stir in the nuts, then pour the batter into a greased 8-inch-square baking pan.
2. Bake uncovered until the edges pull away slightly from the sides of the pan and a toothpick inserted into the center comes out clean— about ½ hour. Cool the brownies upright in the pan on a wire rack, then cut into squares. Will keep 3 days stored in an airtight container. Yield: 16 brownies.

Whipped cream substitute

Much lower in saturated fat than toppings made with heavy cream.

1 can (5 ounces)
evaporated milk

2 tablespoons cold water

1 teaspoon unflavored gelatin

2 tablespoons sugar

3 tablespoons
corn or safflower oil

1. Pour the milk into an empty ice cube tray or a pan and place in the freezer. When crystals form around the edges—about 20 minutes— the milk is cold enough to whip.
2. Meanwhile, place the water in a small heatproof dish and add the gelatin without stirring. Heat 1 inch of water in a small saucepan, remove from the heat, and place the dish of water and gelatin in it. Let stand until the gelatin dissolves —about 5 minutes. Remove the dish from the water, stir the gelatin solution, and let cool.
3. In a medium-size bowl, beat the milk until stiff peaks form. Gradually add the sugar, then the oil, then the gelatin mixture. Continue beating until stiff peaks form again. Cover the bowl with foil and place in the freezer for 10 minutes, then transfer to the refrigerator. The mixture will become stiff; stir to soften it before serving. Will keep 3 days covered with foil and refrigerated. Yield: 4 servings.

White sauce

For a richer sauce, stir in 2 tablespoons butter or margarine during the last minute of cooking.

¼ cup
white sauce mix (below)

1 cup skim or whole milk
or half-and-half

Place the white sauce mix in a medium-size saucepan and gradually whisk in the milk. Set the pan over moderate heat and cook, stirring constantly, for about 2 minutes or until the mixture thickens. Then reduce the heat to low and simmer, stirring constantly, 2 minutes more. This sauce is best made fresh as needed. Yield: 1 cup.
Cheese variation: Add ½ cup or more shredded extra sharp Cheddar cheese, a dash or two of Worcestershire sauce, and a pinch of cayenne pepper in the last 2 minutes of cooking and proceed as directed. Serve on broccoli, cauliflower, potatoes, or other vegetables.

Curry variation: Add 1 teaspoon curry powder to the white sauce mix and proceed as directed. Serve with roast chicken, poached fish fillets, or eggs.
Mushroom variation: At the end of the cooking time, add 1 cup chopped mushrooms that have been sautéed in butter. Serve with chicken or vegetables.
Mustard variation: Stir in 2 tablespoons Dijon or spicy brown mustard along with the milk and proceed as directed. Serve with ham or pork chops.
Paprika variation: Add 1 or more tablespoons paprika to the white sauce mix and proceed as directed. Serve with veal or chicken.
Parsley variation: Add 2 tablespoons minced parsley after adding the milk and proceed as directed. Serve with carrots or fish.

White sauce mix

A low-fat version of the classic recipe in an easy-to-use mix.

1 cup all-purpose flour

1 cup instant nonfat dry milk

1½ teaspoons salt

Combine all the ingredients in a jar, cover, and store at room temperature. Yield: 2 cups dry mix or enough for 8 cups sauce.

Whitewash

A cheap coating that must be reapplied frequently. Excellent for farm buildings because the lime is germicidal. For interior use only.

5 pounds hydrated lime

1 gallon water,
at room temperature

1½ pounds salt

2 quarts warm water

In a large tub, mix the lime with the room-temperature water and let sit overnight. Meanwhile, mix the salt in the warm water and let sit until dissolved. Add the salt water to the lime mixture and stir well. For coloring, add powdered pigment if desired. Store tightly covered. Yield: 2½ gallons.

Windshield cleaner

Especially effective in dealing with dried insects.

½ cup powdered chalk

¼ cup baking soda

1 cup diatomaceous earth

*Enough water to
make a paste*

Combine the ingredients in a small pan or other container and stir slowly until a paste is formed. Apply the mixture directly to the dirty windshield with a sponge, then polish with a dry, lint-free cloth. Yield: 1½ cups

Witch hazel lotion

Use as an astringent or apply in a cold compress to a fevered brow.

¼ cup fresh witch hazel leaves

2 cups water

½ cup rubbing alcohol

Rinse the leaves well, then chop them coarsely. Bring the water to a boil in a glass or enameled saucepan, add the leaves, and simmer for 15 minutes. Let steep until cool,

then strain and stir in the alcohol. Will keep 4 to 5 days tightly covered and refrigerated.

Wood floor cleaner

Gets rid of grime and also preserves the floor.

4½ cups mineral oil

1½ cups oleic acid

¼ cup household ammonia

¾ cup turpentine

Combine the ingredients in a wide-mouth jar. To use, add 1 cup of the cleaner to ½ gallon warm water in a pail. Sponge-mop the floor with the solution; rinsing is optional.
Caution: Store in a safe place, out of the reach of children and away from sources of heat. Yield: 1½ quarts.

Yogurt

For rich yogurt, use a mixture of whole milk and cream. For a healthful substitute for sour cream, use low-fat milk.

1 quart milk

*¼ cup
store-bought plain yogurt*

1. Pour the milk into a small saucepan, prop a candy thermometer inside, and heat to 180°F. Allow the milk to cool to 105°F.
2. Stir in the yogurt and pour the mixture into glass jars. Cap the jars and place in a pan of warm water (105°–112°F) along with the candy thermometer. Allow the yogurt to incubate for 5 to 6 hours, adding hot water as needed to maintain the water temperature. Or set the pan on a stovetop or radiator and check the temperature often. The yogurt is ready when it retains the impression of a spoon pressed into the surface. Remove the jars from the pan and refrigerate for up to 1 week. Yield: 4 containers (8 ounces each).

Zucchini bread

This rich, versatile loaf is good for breakfast, afternoon tea, or dessert.

3 cups sifted all-purpose flour

2 teaspoons baking powder

1 teaspoon salt

½ teaspoon baking soda

1 teaspoon ground cinnamon

½ teaspoon ground allspice

2 eggs

1 cup vegetable oil

¾ cup granulated sugar

*½ cup firmly packed
light brown sugar*

*2 tablespoons
finely grated orange rind*

*2 tablespoons minced
crystallized ginger*

*2 cups packed
shredded unpeeled zucchini
(about 1 pound)*

*1 cup coarsely chopped
walnuts or pecans*

1. Preheat the oven to 350°F. Sift together the flour, baking powder, salt, baking soda, cinnamon, and allspice onto a sheet of wax paper; set aside.
2. In a large bowl, beat the eggs, oil, granulated sugar, brown sugar, orange rind, and ginger until well blended. Stir in the flour mixture, then fold in the zucchini and nuts.
3. Pour the batter into two 8½- x 4½-inch loaf pans that have been greased and dusted with flour. Bake until a toothpick inserted in the center comes out clean—45 to 50 minutes. Cool 15 minutes in the pan on a wire rack, then turn out and let cool to room temperature. Will keep 1 week wrapped in foil and refrigerated or 3 months at 0°F. Yield: 2 loaves.

INDEX

H

Thermometers, 209, 305
oven, 147
Thermostats, 209
Thighs, 41, 42, 74
Thread, 141–142, 314, 318
nail polishing and, 81
for removing blood stains, 23
water soluble, 18
Thrips, 111, 139, 404
Throat, sore, 51, 58, 115, 123, 192–193
Throw rugs. *See* Rugs.
Thumbtacks, 308
Thunderstorms, 50, 209–210
Tie clip, 291, 318
Tie rack, 141
from drying rack, 356
to store electrical cords, 204
Ties, 22, 141, 183
Tiles, 210
cleaning of, 382, 420
trivet from, 347
See also Grout.
Time
personal, 239
telling, 302
Timers, 9, 210, 329
Timesavers, household, 68
Tin cans, 80, 138
Tin snips, 182
Tipping, 31, 73, 281
Tires, 303, 329, 336
Tissue paper, 329
Toasters, 210, 317
Tobacco, 47, 109, 138, 172
Toboggans, 187
Toenails, ingrown, 90
Toggle bolts, 78
Toilet, 211, 314
cleaning of, 48, 228, 420
clogged, 48
water conservation and, 226
Toilet paper tubes
to store electrical cords, 204
to store string, 200
Tomatoes, 95, 139, 211–212, 289
Tomato plants, 318, 319, 329
Tongue, frozen, 92
Tongue depressors, 330
Tonsils, 193
Tool grips, 212
Tools, 267, 287, 303, 307, 308, 310, 322, 327, 333
branding of, 315
cleaning of, 315

Tools *(contd.)*
grease repellent for, 300
rust and, 297, 301, 315
storing of, 50, 212, 289, 290, 296, 301, 305, 311, 322
Toothache, 213
Toothbrush, 43, 53, 213, 330
Tooth brushing, 8, 16, 102, 213
Tooth filling, 213
Toothpaste, 300, 330
as brass cleaner, 25
to defog ski goggles, 187
for crayon marks, 48
formula for, 420
for scuffed heels, 183
as silver cleaner, 186
Toothpicks, 330
cake testing with, 30
as dog brush cleaner, 65
to fix garden hose, 94–95
to fix hinges, 65, 108
nail polishing and, 81
Tornadoes, 213
Towel racks, 213–214, 330
Towels, 328, 330
as draft stoppers, 66
for dusting, 68
as exercise equipment, 74
folding of, 87–88
to renew paint roller, 149
as suede cleaner, 125
wrap from, 340
Towels, paper. *See* Paper towels.
Toys, 214
for babies, 14
batteries for, 18
beach, 309
blocks, 314, 326
centipede, 303
as clutter, 50
play bricks, 324
playground equipment, 158
play logs, 296, 319
shield, 330
storing of, 310, 324, 380
stuffing for, 297, 311, 317, 331
tugboat, 300
water gun, 326
Tracing paper, 306, 329
Tracing wheel, 151
Trampoline, 312
Tranquilizers, 79, 190
Trash compactors, 214
Travel, 280–281
abroad, 91, 215
accommodations and, 110
by air. *See* Air travel.

Travel *(contd.)*
alone, 215–216
on budget, 281
by car, 216, 280
car security and, 39
children and, 215–216
college credit for, 56
customs and, 60
for elderly, 214–215
exchanging currency and, 73–74
exercise and, 85
foreign phrases and, 91
free information and, 91
getting directions and, 97
hotel and. *See* Hotels and motels.
illness and, 9, 114
ironing and, 117
luggage and. *See* Luggage.
packing light, 280
passports and, 151
pets and, 220
photography and, 154, 215
plant care and, 220
prescriptions and, 60
tipping guidelines for, 281
Trays, 288, 314
plastic, 321. *See also* Meat trays, plastic foam.
Treasure chests, 44, 129
Treasury securities, 216–217
Tree blights, 217
Tree branch, post and door handle from, 376
Trees, 307
cooling house and, 58
home security and, 270
keeping pests away from, 21, 62
thinning of, 182
transplant shock in, 214
Trellis, 290, 310, 314, 320, 331, 367
Triplets, 218
Tripod, 217
Trivets, 300, 309, 347
Trowels, 299, 309
T-shirts, 122, 331
Tuition, 53, 56, 109
Tulips, 27, 217
Turkey, 43, 217–218
Tutoring, 52
Tuxedos, 22, 73
Tweezers, 218
Twine, 218
Twins, 218
Twist ties, 320, 331
Typewriters, 296, 330

CREDITS & ACKNOWLEDGMENTS

Bantam Doubleday Dell Publishing Group Inc.
The Doubleday Cookbook by Jean Anderson and Elaine Hanna. Copyright © 1975 by Doubleday, a division of the Bantam Doubleday Dell Publishing Group Inc. Used by permission.

Dover Publications, Inc.
The Standard Book of Quilt Making and Collecting by Marguerite Ickis. Copyright © 1949 by Marguerite Ickis. Reprinted by permission.

E.P. Dutton, A Division of Penguin USA Inc.
Fresh 15-Minute Meals by Emalee Chapman. Copyright © 1986 by Emalee Chapman. Reprinted by permission.

Harmony Books, A Division of Crown Publishers, Inc.
Natural Child Care by Maribeth Riggs. Copyright © 1989 by Maribeth Riggs and Rita Aero. Reprinted by permission.

Harper & Row Publishers, Inc.
Better Than Store-Bought by Helen Witty and Elizabeth Schneider Colchie. Copyright © 1979 by Helen Witty and Elizabeth Schneider Colchie. *Scarne's Encyclopedia of Games* by John Scarne. Copyright © 1973 by John Scarne Games Inc. *Cheaper & Better: Homemade Alternatives to Store-Bought Goods* by Nancy Birnes. Copyright © 1987 by Shadow Lawn Press, Inc. Reprinted by permission.

Little, Brown and Company
The Town & Country Cookbook by James Villas. Copyright © 1985 by James Villas. Reprinted by permission.

Mark Morris Associates, Topeka, Kansas
High Quality Maintenance Diet of Dogs and Cats. Reprinted by permission.

New American Library, A Division of Penguin USA Inc.
Deliciously Simple: Quick and Easy, Low-Sodium, Low-Fat, Low-Cholesterol, Low-Sugar Meals by Harriet Roth. Copyright © 1986 by Harriet Roth. *Deliciously Low: The Gourmet Guide to Low-Sodium, Low-Fat, Low-Cholesterol, Low-Sugar Cooking* by Harriet Roth. Copyright © 1983 by Harriet Roth. Reprinted by permission.

The New York Public Library, Picture Collection

Ten Speed Press
The Moosewood Cookbook by Mollie Katzen. Copyright © 1977. Reprinted by permission.

Times Books, A Division of Quadrangle/ The New York Times Book Co., Inc.
Check Yourself Out, edited by Craig T. Norback. Copyright © 1980 by Craig T. Norback. *The Grass Roots Cookbook* by Jean Anderson. Copyright © 1974 by Jean Anderson. Reprinted by permission.

Zondervan Corporation
Play It! by Wayne Rice and Mike Yaconelli. Copyright © 1986 by Youth Specialties, Inc. Reprinted by permission.

CONSULTANTS

Ron Alford
Jean Anderson
Richard Asa
David A. Barnebl, Sr. V.P., PaineWebber
Jennifer Birckmayer
Walter F. Burghardt, Jr., D.V.M., Ph.D.
John J. Byrne, M.D., F.A.C.S.
Al Carrell
John T. Cavanaugh, M.S., PT/ATC
Russell B. Clanahan
John L. Costa, M.D., F.A.A.P.
Sheila Danko
Seymour Diamond, M.D.
Michael M. Dresdner
Ben T. Etheridge
Michele C. Fisher, Ph.D., R.D.
Todd P. Forte
Michael S. Frank, M.D.
Jim Fremont
Alan French, M.B.A., M.M.
Dora Galitzki

Bernard Gladstone
Leon Grabowski
Ray Greenley
Walter A. Grub, Jr.
Elizabeth Hall
Wade A. Hoyt
Robert E. Hueter, Ph.D.
Marjorie Grossman Jaffe
John Karl
Roberta Ann Kaseman
William J. Keller, Ph.D.
Carolyn Klass
Steven Lamm, M.D.
Frances La Rosa
Walter LeStrange, R.N., M.P.H.
Scott Lewis
Cynthia J. MacKay, M.D.
Jim McCann
Jean McLean
Janet E. Meleney
John Mulligan, Assistant Fire Commissioner, New York Fire Department
Mary E. Purchase, Ph.D.
Ruth Raimon-Wilson
Maureen Reardon

Marilyn S. Rogers
Gertrude Rowland
Lauren B. Scheib
Gerry Schremp
Victor J. Selmanowitz, M.D.
Frances E. Shanahan
Leonard A. Sipes, Jr., M.S.
Stanley H. Smith
Joanne Tunney Stack, J.D.
Eric Stand
Marjabelle Young Stewart
Martha Strohl
Valerie Sutton
John Warde
Paul Weissler, SAE
Stephanie Whalen
Thomas A. Wilson, D.D.S.
Donald E. Witten, National Weather Service

SPECIAL THANKS

American Health and Beauty Aids Institute
American Society of Travel Agents, Inc.
Carole Collins
Consumer Communications Group
Carol Ennis
Gerald Ferguson
Lester Harrison
Melanie Hulse
Det. Bernard Jacobs
Lothian Lynas
National Institute on Aging
Rosemary Nelson
Reynolds Metal Co.
Kelly Riley
Ruth Savolaine
Salt Institute
The Soap and Detergent Association
The Softness Group

Reader's Digest Fund for the Blind is publisher of the Large-Type Edition of *Reader's Digest.* For subscription information about this magazine, please contact Reader's Digest Fund for the Blind, Inc., Dept. 250, Pleasantville, NY 10570.